# ELITE OF THE THIRD REICH

Elite
of the
Third Reich

*The Recipients of the Knight's Cross
of the Iron Cross 1939–45*

WALTHER-PEER FELLGIEBEL

TRANSLATED BY:
C. F. COLTON, MA
AND
DUNCAN ROGERS

This English edition © Helion & Company Limited 2003
26 Willow Road
Solihull
West Midlands
B91 1UE
England
Tel. 0121 705 3393
Fax 0121 711 4075

Email: publishing@helion.co.uk
Website: http://www.helion.co.uk

Originally published as:
Die Träger des Ritterkreuzes des Eisernen Kreuzes 1939–1945. Die Inhaber der höchsten Auszeichnung des Zweiten Weltkrieges aller Wehrmachtteile

German edition © Podzun-Pallas Verlag 2000
Germany 2000
All rights reserved

All rights reserved.
No part of this publication may be reproduced, stored in a retrieval system, or transmitted, in any form, or by any means, electronic, mechanical, photocopying, recording or otherwise, without the express written consent of Helion & Company Limited.

British Library Catalogue-in-Publication Data
A catalogue record for this book is available from the British Library

ISBN 1-874622-46-9

Designed and typeset by Carnegie Publishing Ltd, Lancaster, Lancashire

Printed in the UK by The Cromwell Press, Trowbridge, Wiltshire

Cover photograph shows Oberst Hans-Ulrich Rudel, and is used courtesy of Bildarchiv Preußischer Kulturbesitz.

For details of other military history titles published by Helion & Company Limited contact the above address, or visit our website.

We always welcome receiving book proposals from prospective authors.

With the publication of a new book, *Die Träger des Ritterkreuzes des Eisernen Kreuzes 1939–1945*, a uniquely valuable record was created for the soldiers of the Second World War and for succeeding generations.

For this outstanding achievement on the part of the Chairman of our Awards Commission, Major Walther-Peer Fellgiebel (ret.), I wish to express my great thanks and appreciation, and the thanks of all our comrades in the Ordensgemeinschaft der Ritterkreuzträger.[*]

May this work of contemporary history take its fitting place in the literature of war.

Celle, April 1986

[Horst Niemack, Generalmajor (ret.), President of the Ordensgemeinschaft der Ritterkreuzträger e. V.[†]]

---

[*] Translator's note: Confraternity of Recipients of the Knight's Cross, hereinafter abbreviated as O.d.R.

[†] Translator's note: e. V. indicates official registration as a society

Publishers' Note

The most recent edition in German of this work appeared in 2000. Unlike this German edition, our English translation has absorbed all the corrections directly into the text, rather than presenting them as a series of continuous appendices which make cross-referencing unwieldy. The appearance of more than one introduction as well as a foreword is explained by the fact that a number of editions have appeared in German, each adding a new preliminary section. For ease of reference these have all been grouped together.

The publishers' would like to express their thanks to Richard and Gwyneth Fairbank for their assistance with the preparation of this book.

Contents

Publishers' Note vii
Foreword to the Revised Edition xi
Introduction 1
Introduction to the Supplement Volume 13
Explanatory Notes 17
Abbreviations and Glossary 23

Part

I   Recipient of the Great Cross of the Iron Cross 29

II   Recipient of the Knight's Cross of the Iron Cross
with Golden Oak Leaves, Swords and Diamonds . . . 31

III   Recipients of the Knight's Cross of the Iron Cross
with Oak Leaves, Swords and Diamonds 33

IV   Recipients of the Knight's Cross of the Iron Cross
with Oak Leaves and Swords 35

V   Recipients of the Knight's Cross of the Iron Cross
with Oak Leaves 49

VI   Recipients of the Knight's Cross of the Iron Cross 97

Appendices

I   Ordinance Concerning the Re-formation of the
Order of the Iron Cross, 1 September 1939
with additions 373

II   Guidelines for the award of the Knight's Cross
of the Iron Cross (OKH/PA), 3 June 1941 377

III Promotions and awards made on the autonomous
     authority of Army Groups and Armies 1945 383

IV Copy of the Award sheet OKH/PA/P5,
    Northern zone (Flensburg) 389

V Post-War Name Changes 391

VI Letter From Grand Admiral Dönitz, 20 September 1970 . . 393

VII Comparative Table of Ranks 395

VII Images of the Knight's Cross 397

Foreword to the Revised Edition

I am pleased that a new edition of my work is being published. There is a dictum in specialist circles which says that 'Anyone who is not listed in "Fellgiebel" was certainly never at any time awarded the Knight's Cross of the Iron Cross officially and in proper form!'

Thanks to strenuous efforts on the part of Kapitän-Leutnant Siegfried Wern, it was recently possible to find a contemporary witness who has authentically described how the reputed awards of the Knight's Cross to officers of the Navy after 11 May 1945 came about, although Grossadmiral Dönitz had ordered all decorations and promotions to be suspended from 11 May 1945!

The previously published details relating to the end of May and the beginning of June had been given in *Die deutsche Kriegsmarine 1939–1945* (Lohmann/Hilderbrandt, Podzun-Pallas Verlag), and had always been accepted without question.

The account of the contemporary witness states that some three weeks after the surrender, arriving from Glücksburg, Admiral Friedrich Ruge visited the Second Flotilla in Sieseby (south-west of Kappeln) and took this opportunity to present to Kapitän-Leutnant Hans-Joachim Merks the citation for the Knight's Cross which had been awarded to him. He did not have with him the medal itself, but the contemporary witness, Oberleutnant Dietrich Schneider, made available his own medal for the purpose.

The date of 6 May 1945 was found by Manfred Dörr in his research at WAST Berlin, together with the documentary evidence relating to Kapitän-Leutnant Hans Temming.

During the first days of May Grossadmiral Dönitz had given orders that the achievements of the Navy in the rescue operations in the Baltic were to be honoured. This order led to a 'group of Baltic awards' on 6 May 1945. This group of awards included:

Fregatte-Kapitän Adalbert von Blanc (865) EL 6.5.45
Kapitän-Leutnant (Kpt. Lt) Carl Hoff, 1st Minesweeper Flotilla (Courland)
Kpt. Lt Hans-Joachim Merks, 2nd Minesweeper Flotilla (Courland)
Kpt. Lt. Hans Temming, Commander, T 28 (Hela)
Kpt. Lt. Werner Weinlig, Commander, T 23 (Hela)

Four days earlier, that is, on 2 May 1945, the Knight's Cross was awarded to Kpt. Lt. Ingwer (Jens) Matzen, 6th MTB Flotilla.

Hitherto two other names have been mentioned in this group of awards:

Oberleutnant der Reserve Georg-Wolfgang Feller, 36th Minesweeper Flotilla
Oberleutnant Steuermann Karl Jäckel, helmsman on U–907

There is evidence to verify the fact that Feller improperly received the award of the Knight's Cross on 17.6.1945 from the Oberbefehlshaber der Kriegsmarine (Supreme Commander of the Navy), General-Admiral Warzecha (the successor to General-Admiral von Friedenburg), who was resident in Glücksburg. Jäckel's paybook also confirms his award on 1.6.1945. Thus it is clear that these awards were actually made *de facto*, but cannot be recognized *de jure*.

At this time there was no longer any authority whatever for making awards, even those relating to award recommendations which had already been made.

This finally clarifies the question of the group of awards made to naval personnel after 11.5.1945, which had always given rise to queries. Effectively, there were no official awards, but some medals were presented.

May I take this opportunity to thank my honorary unpaid colleagues who are always prepared to help!

Frankfurt, Autumn 1996
Walther-Peer Fellgiebel

Introduction

The Verification Process

In 1955 *Die Ritterkreuzträger 1939–1945* by Gerhard von Seemen was published. The author had gathered the material with great difficulty from secondary sources because at the time official documents were not available. Secondary sources included press statements, books, personal information etc.

Nobody at that time had any idea that the 30 years later it would be possible to obtain almost complete verification on the basis of the official documents in the Bundesarchiv (German Federal Archives). Some divisional histories or regimental histories which appeared in the post-war period contained incomplete lists of recipients of the Knight's Cross which certainly had been produced conscientiously with the best knowledge available at the time. But since at that time there was still no way of officially confirming details and incorrect reports had also been accepted, both errors and gaps occurred and were shown in the lists, and these errors reappeared time and time again in the relevant literature. The first edition of the previously mentioned book by Gerhard von Seemen in 1955 also contains many errors of this kind.

In other publications which followed other authors perpetuated these errors by referring to von Seemen as a source, or added further errors for the reasons stated above.

On the basis of years of research it is now possible to indicate the various methods by which data has been verified – but also the limitations of these methods.

The details are set out in accordance with the three services of the armed forces at the time – the Army, including the Waffen-SS, the

Luftwaffe and the Navy – since there are different criteria depending upon which service of the armed forces is involved:

A) The least complicated service is the Navy. Relatively early research – using the OKM (Naval High Command) index – limited the field of investigation. There is the additional fact that the number of people is relatively small because there were 'only' 318 recipients of the Knight's Cross in the Navy (cf. Lohmann/Hildebrand *Kriegsmarine 1939–1945* and Clemens Range *Die Ritterkreuzträger der Kriegsmarine*, 1st edition 1974). Despite this, von Seemen's first edition also contained errors with regard to naval personnel.

B) The following applies to the Army, including the Waffen-SS:

The first documentary evidence was included in a list:

For Service Use Only

Army recipients of the Knight's Cross awarded in the period between 30 September 1939 and 19 March 1941 for combat actions in Poland, Norway and France.

This list is in alphabetical order and is not numbered. It contains 261 names, from von Arentschildt to Zürn.

The further lists of awards up to and including 5 April 1945, arranged in numerical order, begin with no. 268 and go up to 4891.

Therefore, in Part 1, 267 names must have been entered instead of 261. The numerical difference relates to the award of the Knight's Cross to six members of the Waffen-SS in 1940 who are not included in the list, but whose awards have been counted in the overall numeration.

From 20 March 1941 the recipients of the Knight's Cross in the Waffen-SS were included in the chronological order of the Army list.

At this point it is interesting to note that there are award numbers. But in addition to these there was also a book of recommendations for all awards with corresponding recommendation numbers which naturally – because many recommendations were not accepted – are higher.

INTRODUCTION

In the entries in the recommendations book a distinction is made between recommendations for the award of the Knight's Cross and recommendations for the award of higher classes of the Knight's Cross. All of them are contained and sequentially numbered in the recommendations entered in the army personnel records.

In addition, the following details were retained: current number, forename and surname, army group, army, service rank, service post, unit, division, campaign, location where the act of gallantry took place, entry, consideration given, decision, date of order, date of award, Iron Cross 1st Class, Iron Cross 2nd Class, German Cross in Gold.

The decision could be: to award, to defer, to refuse, or to award another decoration, e. g. the Ehrenblatt-Spange.

At the end of the war, as a result of the HPA being moved and split, records in this recommendations book were maintained in different locations. Records in the original recommendations book itself were maintained at the HPA Aussenstelle Süd (Area Office South) in Traunstein, and another list was kept at the HPA Aussenstelle Nord (Area Office North) in Mürwick (see appendices).

Most documents continued to be maintained until 16 May 1945. The complete documents are now in the Federal Archives.

In plain language this means that there is no award of the Knight's Cross to members of the Army, including the Waffen-SS, in proper form which cannot – with a few exceptions – be substantiated by the documentation in the Federal Archives.

Thanks to well-known proverbial German thoroughness, even in the critical days as the Second World War drew to an end in April/May 1945, everything was recorded, properly kept, saved from being destroyed, and handed over or left to the victorious powers.

If, after the surrender, in several cases here and there commanders exceeded their authority and assumed powers which did not belong to them, this is indeed typical of the final phase of a war which has been lost, but it is particularly regrettable for the soldiers of all ranks who are affected. Generalleutnant Viktor Linnarz was section head in the Army Personnel Office, the head of Amtsgruppe P 1 and the deputy head of the HPA, with the exception of the months of June, July and

August 1941, from 1 September 1939 continuously until March 1945. If, in his capacity as commander of the 26th Panzer Division, this senior officer, who had particular experience in this field, took it upon himself on his own authority to award the Knight's Cross and the Oak leaves to the Knight's Cross, and even did this in the prisoner of war camp, backdating the dates of award, this could almost be called tragic. It is known from the entries in pay books that Generalleutnant Linnarz was obviously aware that he was not entitled to act in this way, because in these entries he noted 'pending later confirmation by the appropriate authority'.

In practice this means that the soldier in question has been awarded the decoration de facto. De jure, however, he cannot consider himself as a holder of the Knight's Cross of the Iron Cross, because the awarding agency at no time had any authority to make the award.

Apart from awards made by Generalleutnant Linnarz and others, it is known that this kind of unauthorised award on individual initiative was made by Generalfeldmarschall Ferdinand Schörner, Generalleutnant Theodore Tolsdorff, General der Fallschirmtruppen Richard Heidrich, and also by lower ranking commanders, among whom, for example, were also some commanders in the Bavarian forest.

As already mentioned there are no awards in the proper form which cannot be verified in the Bundesarchiv, but there is no rule which is completely without exceptions!

In this instance these exceptions are:

1. Recommendations for awards made specially through party organisations of individual Gauleiters acting outside military channels

2. Awards in the Berlin area between 20 and 30 April 1945 (the date of Hitler's death)

3. Awards on the basis of the orders of 3 May 1945 extending authority to make awards to the commanders of Heeresgruppen and autonomous Armies, paragraph 3, i.e. the for the period from 3 to 11 May 1945

4. Awards on the basis of the Dönitz order issued in the days after the surrender

INTRODUCTION

Re: 1. Not verifiable in the Bundesarchiv, but clearly documented in the press and periodicals are two awards of Knight's Crosses before Cologne Cathedral on 7 February 1945 to the battalion commander of the Cologne Volkssturm, Wilhelm Sitt, and Volksturmmann Jakob Hoffend. These recommendations came through the NSDAP Cologne Gauleitung.

In addition there are further indications of similar recommendations for awards from party Gauleiters, for example Gauleiter Wagner in Baden for the Knight's Cross for Oberst i.G. Brandstätter from 19th Army, Gauleiter Koltermann (Weser-Ems) for the Swords for Oberst Hermann-Heinrich Behrend, commander of the 490th Infantry Division, and also from Gauleiter Hanke in Breslau for the Swords for General der Infanterie Hermann Niehoff, commandant of Fortress Breslau.

In the Bundesarchiv there is a telegram from Reichsleiter Bormann to Gauleiter Wagner giving the news that the award of the Knight's Cross to Oberst i.G. Brandstätter had been refused.

Gauleiter Koltermann's radio message of 6 April 1945 announcing the formation of Kampfgruppe Behrend is also in the Bundesarchiv.

General der Infanterie Niehoff himself stated that Gauleiter Hanke recommended him for the award of the Swords.

For the defence of Nuremburg, the city of the Party rallies, awards of the Oak Leaves, on the recommendation of the Party leadership, are also said to have been made by radio message to Oberst Richard Wolf (nicknamed 'Steppenwolf'), the combat commandant of Nuremburg, and to the commander of SS-Pz. Gren. Rgt 38 'Götz von Berlichingen', SS-Obersturmbannführer Vincenz Kaiser.

Documents relating to these awards have not to date been found.

Re: 2. During the period between 20 and 30 April 1945 direct awards were made in Berlin which were also not registered either by HPA Aussenstelle Nord in Murwick/Flensburg or by HPA Aussenstelle Süd in Traunstein, since during this period both of these offices, in the course of being moved, were still en route. Therefore even in the

ELITE OF THE THIRD REICH

Bundesarchiv today there is no kind of documentation or evidence relating to these awards.

But at least there are some current documents relating to the possession of the awards, and also press reports from the end of April/beginning of May 1945 in the *Flensburger Nachrichten*.

In most instances the soldiers in question have, by means of various forms of evidence (paybook, witnesses, etc), demonstrated to the Awards Commission of the O. d.R. their entitlement to bear the award and have been recognised as having that entitlement.

In this connection, however, instances have become known of several awards which clearly did not take place, although it is not intended here to imply that these instances involved any kind of malicious intent. They are legends which fall under the general rubric: comrade, did you know?

One example of this:

> Erich Bärenfänger, born on 12 January 1915, received the Knight's Cross as an Oberleutnant on 7 August 1942. On 17 May 1943, as a Hauptmann, he received the 243rd award of the Oak Leaves. On 21 January 1944, as a Major, he was decorated with the 45th Swords award and at the same time promoted to Oberstleutnant. On 20 April 1945 he was promoted to Generalmajor, bypassing the rank of Oberst.
>
> There is a legend in circulation which says that Generalmajor Bärenfänger was also decorated with the Diamonds and was killed in action at his command post as commander of Verteidigungs-Abschnitt (Defence Sector) A.

This, too, is a legend.

Erlebtes, the book about the 50th Infanterie-Division, describes on page 139 – in shattering and moving terms – how Bärenfänger died. He committed suicide with his wife when he saw the chaos of the end of the war in Berlin!

Re 3: Commanders of Heeresgruppen and autonomous armies were given authority to award the Knight's Cross (not higher classes of the decoration) for the period from 3 to 11 May 1945.

INTRODUCTION

Special approvals were not given.

There is evidence that all recommendations from the area of Heeresgruppe Mitte went through Aussenstelle Süd of the HPA.

It is known that individual awards of the Knight's Cross – some of these were, however, unfortunately also only alleged – were made by Generalfeldmarschall Ferdinand Schörner before 3 May 1945.

Here, too, there was no clear evidence that Schörner had the authority to make the awards. They were arbitrary decisions on his part.

Heeresgruppe Kurland in May 1945 reported every instance of a Knight's Cross being awarded by an individual commander to Aussenstelle Nord of the HPA. These awards are listed in at the awards gazette.

Re 4: The 'Dönitz order' (see Appendix VI in this book) relates exclusively to recommendations for the award of the Knight's Cross and its higher classes which had arrived at the OKW/HPA before the act of surrender came into force. As a result, these recommendations can, without exception, today be verified in the Bundesarchiv.

But on the other hand this also means that recommendations which were later found among the documents of individual units etc. did not have the necessary recommendations to the Heeresgruppe or autonomous army and did not arrive at the HPA, and therefore cannot be considered as falling under the rubric of the 'Dönitz order'. Therefore they remain simply recommendations and cannot subsequently be recognised and listed as awards.

As already mentioned, awards of the Knight's Cross, among other things, can be verified against the documents in the Bundesarchiv. In order to prevent the documents in the Bundesarchiv being misinterpreted, some additional comments need to be made.

For example, in this book there is a reproduction of a page from the recommendations books. This is one of the documents. It does not fall within the purview of this book to outline all the documents which are available in the Bundesarchiv, but nevertheless it must be said that there are several lists, indexes etc. These are, in part, mutually interdependent – for example, the index relates to the recommendations book – but another index would be kept by another office and another list would similarly be incorporated within the index.

Thus, particularly for the year 1945, there are errors in making entries, typing errors, etc which can only be clarified with reference to all the documents. In cases of doubt, one list on its own is certainly not sufficient to establish the precise facts of any given case.

There follow below some examples which should make this point clearer:

1. RK am 16.11.44
   Gauglitz, Josef Oblt. Fhr, III./Pz. Rgt. 23
   durch 9. Pz.Div./Russland
   [text from the recommendations book]
   Oblt. Fhr. III./Pz. Rgt. 23
   durch 9. Pz.Div./Westen
   [text from List 2]

Here there is an error in transferring information or a typing error, because in the recommendations book the entry reads '9. Pz.Div./Russland'. In actual fact there are, under 'Gauglitz', the names of two soldiers who won the Knight's Cross in Russia. What is actually written in the first entry is 'Russland', but in the case of the latter only one " has been entered, and the same thing has been inadvertently done with the word 'Gauglitz'. Thus, there is clearly one " too many.

At the end of 1944, the 9th Panzer-Division was in action in the West. To it belonged Panzer-Regiment 33. Panzer-Regiment 23 belonged to the 23rd Panzer-Division, which fought in Russia. Therefore, the entry should read: Oblt. Fhr. III./Pz. Rgt. 33

2. RK am 14.4. 45
   according to the recommendations book: 2. Armee recommends
   Siegmund, Bernhard, Oblt., Chef 1./GR 2
   recommended through 542 VGD for action on 17.2.45
   (the recommendation is 1½ months late).

INTRODUCTION

In this example there are three distinctions to be made:
GR (Gebirgsregiment) 2 belonged to 11th Inf.Div., which was in Courland.
2 Armee was at that time in East Prussia.

The 542nd VGD (Volksgrenadier-Division) was merely the Division which sent in the recommendation. Beside it was fighting the 252nd Inf.Div., to which GR 7 belonged.

In this example someone has read the regimental number as '2' instead of '7'. The correct entry should read: Chef 1./GR 7!

3. Here is an example of another error, understandable in the context of the situation at the time, in the partly incorrect entry of data on one of the last pages in the recommendations book: In the original section Vorgelegt* were entered the last details of awards from 30 April 1945, and in the section Verleihung† was entered the date 2 May (in two instances without endorsement), in a recommendation for the award of the Oak Leaves with the endorsement '2.5 refused'. But the index clearly indicates that the other two recommendations were also refused – this is corroborated by the fact that, at Heeres-Personalamt Süd in Traunstein, the 2 May was not a day on which awards were made.

4. Among the awards in January 1945 there suddenly and abruptly appears the award of the Knight's Cross to v. Treskow, Joachim, Gen.Lt. Kdr. 18. Luftw. Feld. -Div., submitted via Heeresgruppe Süd. No date of entry, no date of submission, but only the entry relating to the award. This entry is only to be found on the list, but not in the index. This is clearly an instance of a so-called 'direct' award, something which often happened, especially in the case of higher-ranking officers, and should be borne in mind. It is relatively idle to speculate over the whys and wherefores of this. The name, in conjunction with the date 20.7.44, gives us a good idea why.

---

* Translator's note: 'Date submitted'
† Translator's note: 'Date of award'.

9

5. The award of the Knight's Cross on 9.3.45 to Gen.Maj. Dr. Hübner, Rudolf, Fhr. Grenadier Regiment 529 (location where action took place: Orel) is also a 'direct' award. At this time Dr. Hübner had already been promoted to Generalleutnant, with effect from 1.3.45. But Orel was in 1943! In March 1945 Dr. Hübner was President of the Remagen Court Martial.

There are other clear examples, but these will not be further discussed here. The reason for giving these examples is to illustrate that it was only this book in its present-day form which made it possible to use all the available sources. It is also to show that to use one single document alone is not sufficient, and how this, as can be seen from the examples given, will certainly lead to mistakes being made.

C) In the Luftwaffe, too, there was an awards list for the Knight's Cross, with entries dating from as early as 1939.

This list begins with no. 1, Hermann Göring, and goes up to no. 1567 on 14 January 1945. This original list was subsequently continued and consists of six pages with detailed information. It goes up to 25 February 1945 and ends with award number 1630. Despite the fact that it is in numerical sequence and the pages are numbered, however, in the meantime one error – or, more accurately, a gap – has been noted.

This error relates to the dates 31 October 1944 and 9 November 1944. There exist pictures, press releases, obituaries and similar material relating to some 15 soldiers, which state that the Knight's Cross was awarded to these members of the Luftwaffe, although there is no documentary evidence in the Bundesarchiv.

However, using the official personnel records it was possible to clearly establish 31 October 1944 and 9 November 1944 as dates when the award was made, which are not contained in the award lists. These dates are thus now able to be verified in the Bundesarchiv.

This is a unique exception, and also one which only occurred in the case of the Luftwaffe.

For dates after 25 February 1945, however, there are unfortunately only scattered pieces of documentary evidence in the Bundesarchiv

INTRODUCTION

relating to individual awards of the Knight's Cross to members of the Luftwaffe.

However, on the basis of the detailed records of the Luftwaffe personnel department, it is, fortunately, possible to verify in the Bundesarchiv all awards made on 17 and 28 April 1945.

The recommendations in these records, a small number from 1945, are identified by submission numbers. The exact numbers of all awards can be calculated on the basis of these numbers.

In the Bundesarchiv it is possible to confirm 17 April 1945 as a day on which awards was made, and there are also radio messages and telegrams dated 9 May 1945 which show the backdated award date of 28 April 1945.

Announcements were made of 15 awards on 17 April and 11 awards on 28 April.

It has been possible, on the basis of citations, award photographs, telegrams etc, to establish that further award dates were 12 March, 28 March, 7 April and 20 April.

Luftwaffe historians have also carried out research relating to this documentary evidence. As a result, in this new book some surnames no longer appear which were previously very well known. The reasons for this are the same as the reasons described earlier in the context of awards made by the Army.

D) Higher classes of the Knight's Cross have been deliberately omitted from this introduction, because without exception all names and source documents were set out in Herr Gerhard von Seemen's 1976 book II *Die Ritterkreuztrager 1939–1945*, and appear in the same form in this edition of the book.

Alterations in this edition of information given in von Seemen's book only relate to printing and written errors, and additional information concerning dates of death. However, it was not necessary to make any alterations relating to the documentary evidence.

March 1986
Walther-Peer Fellgiebel

Introduction to the Supplement Volume

Die Träger des Ritterkreuz des Eisernen Kreuzes, which was published by Podzun-Pallas-Verlag at the end of October 1986, struck for me a not wholly unexpected, almost entirely positive resonance. The following should be said about it:

1. Documentation

No changes whatever have been made with regard to the higher classes of the award! But even in the case of the recipients of the Knight's Cross themselves, there were only 15 amendments to be made on the basis of new sources of evidence, but these all had to be provided with numbers, because there were no new items of documentary evidence in the Bundesarchiv.

Unfortunately it became very obvious that many readers of this book had not read, or had not read with sufficient attention, the actual documentation, i. e. page 13 to page 28. Therefore at this point it should be emphasised that there is no scope for interpretation of the 'Dönitz order'! The declaration made by the Grossadmiral is completely unequivocal. Apart from that, the Grossadmiral himself has personally spoken with me about it three times in his house, in the presence of witnesses.

Any person who is not mentioned in his book in an appropriate place, certainly did not, I am convinced, ever receive the Knight's Cross or, for example, the Oak Leaves, legally and in proper form, even if he is mentioned in other publications as having done so.

The error is clearly in the many publications which have appeared from time to time without placing proper value on appropriate specialist documentation. I know that, regrettably, even the OdR – on the initiative of OdR members who do not possess the necessary specialist qualifications – has touted for these 'books' even in the OdR newsletter.

Because I have seen myself how – on about 14 May 1945 – in American internment an active Major awarded five officers the Knight's Cross on his own initiative, and confirmed this in their paybooks (*de facto*, yes – *de jure*, no! See in this regard the introduction), I have always taken great pains to obtain proper substantiating evidence, and it is not least for this reason that since 1955 I have been a member of the OdR Awards Commission, and since 1970 the Chairman of the Awards Commission.

2. Names, dates of death, last rank held, service post

In the official documentary evidence for the early years, for example in the case of higher classes of the award, no forename, and generally only the date of death are indicated. As a result changes are now needed, e. g. in the spelling of proper names: 'ae/ä', 'oe/ö', 'ss/â', 'ue/ü'. Or there are amendments in the case of double Christian names, e. g. instead of 'Josef', 'Josef-Anton', and amendments relating to details of the place of death and the last service post held, that is, information which is not always available in the Bundesarchiv.

In the case of details relating to units I must point out that in some cases these cannot be determined by reference to the books which are now available relating to units, but only by evaluating the documentary evidence in the Bundesarchiv.

Examples:

> 794. Oak Leaves, Kedzia, Ernst-Georg, Major, Kampfkommandant of Fürstenberg an der Oder and Commander of Rgt. 98 (391st Security Div.), 9th Armee.

This cannot now be construed as 'Pz. G.R. 98'/8. Pz.Div. At no time did the 8th Panzer-Division ever fight in this area under the command of the 9th Army. There are also no indications at all of the existence of a Grenadier-Regiment 98, and no indications of the

INTRODUCTION TO THE SUPPLEMENT VOLUME

existence of a Regiment 98. Therefore the entry in the recommendations book is very probably an 'ad hoc' entry.

On the other hand I found that even simple writing errors could mangle unit numbers. There are many examples of this (see introduction). Also, in the recommendations lists there is very rarely any indication whether the man recommended for an award was an active soldier or a reservist, and this is why, on the express wish of many men affected by this, the supplement 'd.R.' has been added.

3. Grammatical, writing and printing errors

Here the necessary amendments have been made. These affect names, units designations, transfers, incomplete information.

4. Unit designations

Under this rubric, too, the necessary amendments have been made, but the following remarks should be taken into account:

The decisive factor is the unit designation which is contained in the recommendation for the award! Until October 1942 there were Infanterie-Regimenter, and only after this were there Grenadier-Regimenter etc. In the case of the Panzer-Grenadier Divisions there is no single date which decided whether they were designated as 'GR mot' or 'Pz. GR'; this can only be discovered from the recommendation and cannot be reconstructed theoretically in retrospect.

The frequently-used designation 'im DAK' is in all instances to be deleted.

Until about the middle of 1944 there were still Sturmgeschütz-Abteilungen, but there were also Sturmgeschütz-Brigaden. In these instances the entry in the recommendations book is taken as being correct. In the case of various new formations, for example the 15th Panzer Grenadier Division in Sicily, initially different designations, such as Regiment 1 or Regiment 2, were used (according to the Bundesarchiv!), than were used a little later when the regular new regimental numbers were introduced and officially confirmed.

The original divisions of the Waffen-SS, because they were constantly being re-formed, bore other unit designations until they were unified at the end of 1943/beginning of 1944. All details have now been adjusted to bring them in line with the corresponding information in the recommendations book.

5. Summary

A total of 1160 alterations have been incorporated. There were some 60 amendments which were absolutely necessary, and in addition to this there were about 300 improvements which in my opinion were desirable. The remaining 800 amendments relate to commas, every bracket, every diagonal slash, in short, to every single error.

As a sober historian, I continue, in the interest of the OdR, but especially in the interest of the historical record, to set great store on the expectation that further documentation, which as yet remains unknown, may be presented at some time in the future.

In summary, I can once again point out that, as a result of these researches, 111 new names have been entered into the records and 109 former soldiers of all ranks can no longer regarded as recipients of the Iron Cross.

Frankfurt am Main, Summer 1988
Walther-Peer Fellgiebel
Member of the Presidium
of the Ordensgemeinschaft der Ritterkreuzträger
and Chairman of the Awards Commission.

Explanatory Notes

From the inception of the Confraternity of Recipients of the Knight's Cross, the executive committee has included the Chairman of the Awards Commission.

The Chairmen were: from September 1955 to October, 1967, Gen.D.Inf. Erich Abraham (ret.), Wiesbaden; from October 1967 to October 1970 Oberst Thiegs von Tycowitz (ret.), Wiesbaden, a member of the Awards Commission from September 1955, and from October 1970 Major Walther-Peer Fellgiebel (ret.), a member of the Awards Commission since September 1955.

The activities of this Awards Commission have proved to be particularly useful, and principally serve the purpose of establishing historical truth. From October 1970 to October 1985, i. e. over a period of 15 years, the Awards Commission dealt with 662 'cases', or an average of 44 'cases' per year.

This work mainly involved checking, researching and, for example, questioning former superior officers who were said to have made awards for which, at least at that particular time, there was no documentary evidence in the Bundesarchiv.

To the best of its knowledge and conscience, the Awards Commission has confirmed and/or recognised awards in various cases, but has also rejected many claims, because it was not considered possible that the award could have been made.

For all the cases of awards which cannot be confirmed by the information in the Bundesarchiv, the following classification system has been set up. It is set out in numerical sequence. This means that an award for which there is no evidence in the Bundesarchiv is designated with a number in brackets. This number relates to the section in question. In each respective case this section outlines the reasons why some documentary evidence or no documentary evidence can be produced.

Information relating to awards which have been considered not to be confirmed, and cases where there is doubt, are not contained in the list.

1. Awards made by the Cologne Gauleitung, 7 February 1945
2. Radio message to AOK East Prussia, 14 May 1945
3. Radio message to Festungs-Div. 'Kreta'
4. Awards made in Ghedi POW camp by Gen.Lt. Linnarz
5. Awards made in Italy by Gen. d. Fallschirmtr. Heidrich
6. Awards of 6th SS Panzerarmee made by SS-Oberstgruppenfhr. Dietrich, 6 May 1945
7. Waffen-SS/Berlin Reichs Chancellery awards made by SS-Brigf. Mohnke
8. Awards made in Berlin between 20 and 30 April 1945
9. As above, as published in the *Flensburger Nachrichten*
10. Awards made in the Halbe pocket by SS-Brig. Fhr. Wagner
11. Awards made by Heeresgruppe Mitte prior to 3 May 1945, by GFM Schörner
12. As above, dates after 3 May 1945
13. Heeresgruppe Süd awards made by Gen. d. Geb.Tr. Konrad
14. 6th Army awards made after 30 June 1945 by Gen.D.Inf. Schubert
15. Awards to SS Kampfgruppe 'Handschar'
16. a) 20th Gebirgs-Armee awards from 3 May 1945; b) Heeresgruppe E awards from 3 May 1945.
17. Luftwaffe – recognition on the basis of evidence not in the Bundesarchiv.
18. Awards of the Knight's Cross recognised by the Bundeswehr.
19. Awards of the Knight's Cross recognized by the OdR (Awards Commission)

Notes

1. Awards made before Cologne Cathedral on 7 February 1945, evidence in the form of published material 1945, pictures, weekly newsreel circulated through the party leadership, thus no evidence in the Bundesarchiv, although there is clear documentary evidence.
2. Radio message of 14 May 1945 from the Dönitz government to AOK East Prussia, award to Generalmajor Macher, Chief of Staff, AOK East Prussia, and three unnamed members of the 7th Inf. Div. who had proved their courage; no indication whether the awards were made or to whom they were made.
3. Fest. Div. 'Kreta' awards are said to have been made on the basis of a radio message. There is no evidence.
4. Awards made, pending authority to make awards subsequently being granted, in the Ghedi prisoner of war camp by Generalleutnant Linnarz, the commander of the 26 Pz.Div., with backdated entries in paybooks – (It is known that one award of the Oak Leaves and two awards of the Knight's Cross were made).
5. Awards as in 4 above by General der Fallschirmtruppe Heidrich. (It is known that 4 awards were made of the Oak Leaves and 5 of the Knight's Cross. Subsequent authority to make awards was not granted either to Linnarz or to Heidrich. No evidence in the Bundesarchiv).
6. Awards made by SS-Oberstgruppenführer Dietrich – see Swords. (It is known that 4 awards were made of the Swords, 4 of the Oak Leaves and at least 8 of the Knight's Cross, but also 15 awards of the German Cross in Gold and 7 awards of the German Cross in Silver. Substantiating evidence from Wilhelm Kment and Hermann Buch; no evidence in the Bundesarchiv).
7. Awards made by SS-Brigadeführer Mohnke in the Reich Chancellery bunker between 20 and 30 April 1945. These awards became known as a result of research carried out by the Awards Commission, and see also Haupt/Kuby/Irving. The number of probable awards varies between 3 and 5 soldiers from the Army and from the Waffen-SS. There is no evidence in the Bundesarchiv.
8. In the period between circa 20 April to 30 April 1945, a few awards were

probably made through General Burgdorf, the Head of the HPA in Berlin, after the HPA was split and moved to Traunstein or Mürwick/Flensburg. In this connection, see also the Oak Leaves list and Swords appendices. There is no evidence in the Bundesarchiv, but individual items of evidence are known of.

9. This group includes these awards which can only be substantiated in an unusual way, because some awards made in the last awards ceremonies were published in April/May 1945 in the newspaper Flensburger Nachrichten.

10. Awards made in the Halbe pocket and after the breakout from it, by SS-Brigadeführer Wagner with approval by SS-Gruppenführer and Generalleutnant der Waffen-SS Kleinheisterkamp (+ 2.5.1945 at Halbe). Three to five members of the Waffen-SS were said to have received the Knight's Cross from Wagner in the form of an Iron Cross Second Class. Some substantiating evidence was provided regarding the recommendations for the awards, but there was no substantiating evidence for the awards themselves. In the Bundesarchiv there is no evidence of any kind.

11. Awards made by the Supreme Commander of Heeresgruppe Mitte, Generalfeldmarschall Schörner, from 3 May 1945 are clearly correct within the terms of the empowering order. Some individual awards, however, were made before this date although there was no authority to make them, but there are also some legends to be found connected with this, all the more so since all recommendations from Heeresgruppe Mitte up to 16 May 1945 verifiably arrived and were processed at the HPA Aussenstelle Traunstein – evidence, among other items, in the recommendations book/Bundesarchiv.

12. Although communications existed between Heeresgruppe Mitte and HPA Aussenstelle Süd, Traunstein, direct awards by Schörner were not reported to Traunstein, but to Heeresgruppe Kurland, which reported all awards to HPA Aussenstelle Nord. Substantiating evidence in the Bundesarchiv is from Aussenstelle Nord.

13. Some awards became known which were made by General der Gebirgs-Truppe Konrad, acting for Heeresgruppe Süd, after 3 May 1945. There is no substantiating evidence.

14. Awards made by AOK 6 (Gen.D.Inf. Schubert) on the basis of earlier

recommendations made on 30 May or 1 June 1945. (5 soldiers of the 1 Geb.Div. are known to have received awards.

According to Keilig, *Heer*, AOK 6 was dissolved on 8.5.1945 in the Mauerkirchen camp.

Under the terms of the empowering order, AOK 6 was not entitled to make awards, and moreover, from 11 May further awards were suspended by the Dönitz government. In addition, according to the Heeresgruppe Mitte order of battle for 1 May 1945, the commander of 6 Armee was General der Panzertruppe Balck.

15. Von Seemen writes – awards under the terms of the empowering order of 3 May 1945 by commander of 6 Armee/Gen. d. Art. de Angelis. According to the Heeresgruppe Mitte order of battle, de Angelis was commander of 2 Pz. Armee, which itself was under the command of Kampfgruppe 'Handschar'. There was no substantiation for the awards.

16. a) 20 Geb. Armee was entitled to make awards under the terms of the empowering order. (It is known that 1 award of the Knight's Cross was made). b) The commander of Heeresgruppe E was entitled to make awards under the terms of the empowering order. (It is known that 1 award of the Knight's Cross was made).

17. A separate group belongs to the Luftwaffe. This is outlined in detail in the introduction. In the endorsement behind the name (17) there is no evidence in the Bundesarchiv. In these cases Herr Ernst Obermaier and the Gemeinschaft der Jagdflieger (Fighter Pilots' Association) provided the evidence. Awards to Luftwaffe personnel after 3 May 1945 were made by OB Süd, General Westphal, and were backdated to 1 May 1945. There is confirmation of these awards provided by General Westphal.

18. There are recipients of the Knight's Cross who have no official evidence in the the Bundesarchiv relating to their awards, but belonged to the Bundeswehr and distinguished themselves as recipients of the Knight's Cross. As is known, these facts, in individual cases, were checked and recognised by the MAD.

19. Here are summarised the cases which have been recognised by the OdR (Awards Commission) and cannot be incorporated in Sections 1 to 17.

Should any particular holder of the Order feel that he has been 'wrongly treated' in this 'sorting-out process', would he kindly hand over to me the proper, legally acceptable evidence for clarification.

Frankfurt, March 1986
Walther-Peer Fellgiebel

Abbreviations and Glossary

*	Geboren am	Date of birth
+	gefallen, verstorben am, vermißt seit	Killed, died, missing from
A.A.	Aufklärungs-Abteilung	Reconnaissance Battalion
Abt.	Abteilung	Battalion/Section/Detachment
Abt.Kdr.	Abteilungskommandeur	Battalion/Section/Detachment CO
Adj.	Adjutant	Adjutant
A.K.	Armeekorps	Army Corps
akt.Offi.	aktiver Offizier	Serving Officer
A.O.K.	Armeeoberkommando	Army
Arko	Artilleriekommando	Corps Artillery Commander
Art.Rgt. (A.R.)	Artillerie-Regiment	Artillery Regiment
Aufkl.	Aufklärung(s)	Reconnaissance
Batt.	Batterie	Battery
bayer.	Bayerische	Bavarian
Befh.	Befehlshaber	Commander
Brig.	Brigade	Brigade
Btl.	Bataillon	Battalion
D., Div.	Division	Division
Div.Kdr.	Divisionskommandeur	Division CO
d.R.	der Reserve	Reserve
Erprob.Gr	Erprobungsgruppe	Experimental unit
Ers.	Ersatz	Replacement
Esk.	Eskadron	Squadron
(F)	Fernaufklärung (Luftwaffe)	Long-range Reconnaissance (Air Force)
Fa.	Feldartillerie	Field Artillery
F.d.S.	Führer der Schnellboote	Commander, Motor Torpedo Boats
	Festung	Fortress
Fhj.	Fahnenjunker	Officer Candidate
FHQ.	Führerhauptquartier	Hitler's Headquarters

23

ELITE OF THE THIRD REICH

Fhr.	Führer	Commander
F.J.R.	Fallschirmjäger-Regiment	Parachute Infantry Regiment
Flg.	Flieger	Aviation; Pilot
Flieg.	Flieger	Aviation; Pilot
Flott.	Flottille	Flotilla
Freg.	Fregatte(n)	Frigate
Fsch.	Fallschirm	Parachute
FschJag.	Fallschirmjäger	Parachute Infantry
Füs.	Füsilier	Fusilier
GD	Großdeutschland	Grossdeutschland
Geb.	Gebirgs-	Mountain
Geb.Jäg.	Gebirgsjäger	Mountain Infantry
gen.	genannt	known as
Gen.d.Inf.	General der Infantry	General of Infantry
Gen.Feld.	Generalfeldmarschall	Field Marshal
Gen.Lt.	Generalleutnant	Lieutenant General
Gen.Maj.	Generalmajor	Major General
Gren.	Grenadier	Grenadier
HG	Heeresgruppe, auch: Hermann Göring	Army Group, also: Hermann Göring
Hptm.	Hauptmann	Captain
i.G.	im Generalstab	in General Staff
Inf.	Infanterie	Infantry
Inf.Div., I.D.	Infanterie-Division	Infantry Division
Inf.Rgt., I.R.	Infanterie-Regiment	Infantry Regiment
Insp.	Inspekteur, Inspektion	Inspector/Inspectorate
Jäg.	Jäger	Light Infantry
	Jagdstaffel	Fighter Squadron
J.G.	Jagdgeschwader	Fighter Wing
J.V.	Jagdverband	Fighter Unit
Kav.	Kavallerie	Cavalry
Kdo.	Kommando	Command
Kdr.	Kommandeur	Commander
Kdt.	Kommandant	Commander
Kfz.	Kraftfahrzeug	Motor Vehicle
K.G.	Kampfgeschwader	Bomber Wing
Kgr.	Kampfgruppe	Battlegroup
Kom.Gen.	Kommandierender General	Commanding General
Komp.	Kompanie	Company
Korv.	Korvette(n)	Corvette
k.u.k.	kaiserlich u. königlich	Imperial and Royal (Austrian army)

ABBREVIATIONS AND GLOSSARY

Landw.	*Landwehr*	Landwehr/Reserves
le.	*leicht(e)*	Light
L.G.	*Lehr-Geschwader*	Training Wing
LSSAH	*Leibstandarte SS "Adolf Hitler"*	Leibstandarte SS "Adolf Hitler"
Lt.	*Leutnant*	Lieutenant
LW	*Luftwaffe*	Air Force
(MA)	*Marineartillerie (mit Dienstgrad)*	Naval Artillery (with rank)
Mar.	*Marine*	Navy
m.F.b.	*mit der Führung beauftragt*	Assigned command of
MG	*Maschinengewehr*	Machine-gun
MOK	*Marineoberkommando*	Naval High Command
(mot.)	*motorisiert (b. Truppenbezeichnung)*	Motorised (troop designation)
MS	*Minensuch-*	Minesweeper
N.J.G.	*Nacht-Jagd-Geschwader*	Night Fighter Wing
N.S.G.	*Nacht-Schlachtgruppe*	Night Ground Attack Wing
OB	*Oberbefehlshaber*	Supreme Commander
	Oberst	Colonel
	Oberfähnrich	Master Sergeant
Oblt.	*Oberleutnant*	Senior Lieutenant
Obstlt.	*Oberstleutnant*	Lieutenant-colonel
Offi.	*Offizier*	Officer
	Offizierstellvertreter	Acting/Provisional Officer
OKH	*Oberkommando des Heeres*	Army High Command
OKL	*Oberkommando der Luftwaffe*	Air Force High Command
OKM	*Oberkommando der Kriegsmarine*	Naval High Command
OKW	*Oberkommando der Wehrmacht*	Armed Forces High Command
Ord.Offz.	*Ordonnanz-Offizier*	Orderly Officer
Pion., Pi.	*Pionier*	Engineer
Pol.	*Polizei*	Police
Pz.	*Panzer*	Tank
Pz.Abw.	*Panzer-Abwehr*	Anti-tank
Pz.Div.	*Panzer-Division*	Armoured Division
Pz.Jäg	*Panzer-Jäger*	Tank Hunter
Pz.K.	*Panzerkorps*	Armoured Corps
Pz.Tr.	*Panzertruppe(n)*	Armoured Troops
RAD	*Reichsarbeitsdienst*	National Labour Service
Reit.	*Reiter*	Cavalry
Res.	*Reserve*	Reserve
Rgt.,R.	*Regiment*	Regiment

ELITE OF THE THIRD REICH

Rittm.	*Rittmeister*	Captain
RLM	*Reichsluftfahrt-Ministerium*	National Air Ministry
S-Boot, S-	*Schnellboot*	Motor Torpedo Boat
Schl.-H.	*Schleswig-Holstein*	Schleswig-Holstein
Schtz.	*Schütze(n)*	Rifle/Private
schw.	*schwer(e), bei Truppenbezeichnung*	Heavy (with troop designation)
S.G.	*Schlachtgeschwader*	Ground Attack Wing
Sich.	*Sicherung(s)*	Security
S.K.G.	*Schnellkampfgeschwader*	Ground Attack/Anti-tank Wing
SS-Gruppenführer	*SS-Gruppenführer*	SS Major-General
SS-Hauptsturmführer	*SS-Hauptsturmführer*	SS Captain
SS-Oberf.	*SS-Oberführer*	SS Brigadier-General
SS-Obersturmbann.	*SS-Obersturmbannführer*	SS Lieutenant-colonel
SS-Obersturmf.	*SS-Obersturmführer*	SS Senior/First Lieutenant
SS-Sturmbann.	*SS-Sturmbannführer*	SS Major
Staffelkpt.	*Staffel-Kapitän*	Squadron Commander
stellv.	*Stellvertretende*	Acting/Provisional
St.G.	*Sturzkampfgeschwader*	Dive Bomber Wing
St.Gesch.	*Sturmgeschütz*	Assault Gun
Stand.	*Standarte*	Standard/SS Regiment
Stuka	*Sturzkampfflugzeug*	Dive Bomber
Tr.	*Truppe(n)*	Unit/Arm/Branch of Service
U.Boot, U.	*Unterseeboot*	Submarine
Uffz.	*Unteroffizier*	NCO/Sergeant
UJ	*Unterseeboot-Jäger*	Anti-submarine/Submarine Hunter
V.G.D.	*Volks-Grenadier-Division*	People's Grenadier Division
	Vizefeldwebel	Vice Sergeant Major
(W)	*Feuerwerker (nach einem Dienstgrad)*	Technical Sergeant (after rank)
WO	*Wachoffizier*	Officer of the Guard
Württb.	*Württembergische*	Württemberg
z.b.V.	*zur besonderen Verwendung*	For Special Purposes
Z.G.	*Zerstörer-Geschwader*	Heavy Fighter Wing
Z.S.	*zur See*	At Sea
Zugfhr.	*Zugführer*	Platoon Leader

Units of the Army, Waffen-SS, Luftwaffe and Kriegsmarine ground troops

Arabic numerals – indicate company, battery (artillery), brigade, regiment, division or army. For example: 12./I.R. 75 (12th Company, 75th Infantry Regt.); 3. Schtz. Brig. (3rd Rifle Brigade); 2./St. Gesch. Brig. 185 (2nd Battery, Sturmgeschütz Brigade 185); 7 P.D. (7th Panzer Division), 8. Armee (8th Army), 1./SS-Pz. Gren. Rgt. 38 (1st Company, SS Panzergrenadier Regt. 38).

Roman numerals – indicate battalion, Abteilung (Panzertruppen), or army corps. For example: II./Gren. Rgt. 332 (II Battalion, 332nd Grenadier Rgt.); III./F.J.R. 1 (III Battalion, 1st Fallschirmjäger Regiment); II./Pz. Rgt. 5 (II Abteilung, 5th Panzer Regiment); XXIV. Pz.K. (XXIV Panzerkorps); XVII. A.K. (XVII Corps).

Aviation units of the Luftwaffe

Arabic numerals – indicate Staffel (Squadron) and/or Geschwader (Wing). For example: 3./J.G. 54 (3rd Staffel, Jagdgeschwader 54); K.G. 76 (Kampfgeschwader 76); N.J.G. 1 (Nachtjagdgeschwader 1).

Roman numerals – indicate Gruppe (Group). For example: II./Z.G. 26 (II Gruppe, Zerstörer-Geschwader 26); III./St.G. 1 (III Gruppe, Sturzkampfgeschwader 1).

I

Recipient of the Great Cross
of the Iron Cross

Göring, Hermann	Gen. Feldm., Reichsminister der Luftfahrt and Oberbefehlshaber der Luftwaffe. Simultaneously promoted to Reichsmarschall des Grossdeutschen Reiches; committed suicide 15.10.1946 in US captivity, Nürnberg	20.7.40

II

Recipient of the Knight's Cross of the Iron Cross with Golden Oak Leaves, Swords and Diamonds

Rudel, Hans-Ulrich	Obstlt., Kdr. S.G. 2 'Immelmann'. Simultaneously promoted to Oberst	29.12.44

III

Recipients of the Knight's Cross of the Iron Cross with Oak Leaves, Swords and Diamonds

1941

1. Mölders, Werner	Oberst, Kmdr. J.G. 51 + 22.11.41 as Oberst and General der Jagdflieger, near Breslau	15.7.41

1942

2. Galland, Adolf	Oberst, Kmdr. J.G. 26 "Schlageter"	28.1.42
3. Gollob, Gordon	Major, Kmdr. J.G. 77	30.8.42
4. Marseille, Hans-Joachim	Oblt., Staffelkpt. 3./J.G. 27 + 30.9.42 as Hptm. u. Staffelkpt. 3./J.G. 27 at El Alamein	3.9.42
5. Graf, Hermann	Oblt. d.R., Staffelkpt. 9./J.G. 52	16.9.42

1943

6. Rommel, Erwin	Gen. Feldm., OB H.Gr. Afrika + 14.10.44 as OB H.Gr.B, forced suicide at Herrlingen (20.7.44)	11.3.43
7. Lüth, Wolfgang	Korv. Kpt., Kdt. "U 181" + 14.5.45 as Kapt. z. See, Stadtkdt. Mürwik/Schl.-H., accidentally	9.8.43
8. Nowotny, Walter	Hptm., Kdr. I./J.G. 54 + 8.11.44 as Major &. Kdr. Erprob.Gr. Nowotny at Achmer-Bramsche	19.10.43
9. Schulz, Adalbert	Oberst, Kdr. Pz. Rgt. 25 + 28.1.44 as Gen. Major & Kdr. 7. Pz.Div. at Shepetowka	14.12.43

1944

10. Rudel, Hans-Ulrich	Major, Kdr. IH./S.G. 2 "Immelmann" Gold Oak leaves 29.12.44	29.3.44

11. Graf Strachwitz v. Gr.Zauche Camminetz, Hyazinth	Oberst d.R., Kdr. Pz. Kampfgr. in H.Gr. Nord. Simultaneously promoted to Gen.Maj. d.R.	15.4.44
12. Gille, Herbert-Otto	SS-Gruppenf & Gen.Lt. d. W-SS, Kdr. 5. SS-Pz.Div. "Wiking"	19.4.44
13. Hube, Hans	Gen. d. Pz.Tr., OB 1. Pz. Armee. Simultaneously promoted to Gen. Oberst. + 21.4.44, shot down over Obersalzberg	20.4.44
14. Kesselring, Albert	Gen. Feldm., OB. Süd (H.Gr.C)	19.7.44
15. Lent, Helmut	Obstlt., Kmdre. N. J.G. 3 Simultaneously promoted to Oberst. + 7.10.44 as a result of wounds received 5.10.44, Paderborn area	31.7.44
16. Dietrich, Josef	SS-Oberstgruppenf. & Gen. Ob. d. W-SS. Kom.Gen. I. SS-Pz.K. "LSSAH"	6.8.44
17. Model, Walter	Gen. Feldm., OB H.Gr. Mitte + 21.4.45, committed suicide as OB H.Gr.B at Ratingen (Ruhr pocket)	17.8.44
18. Hartmann, Erich	Oblt., Staffelkpt. 9./J.G. 52	25.8.44
19. Balck, Hermann	Gen. d. Pz.Tr., m. d. F. b. 4. Pz. Armee	31.8.44
20. Ramcke, Hermann-Bernhard	Gen.Lt., Kdt. Festung Brest. Simultaneously promoted to Gen. d. Fsch. Tr.	19.9.44
21. Schnaufer, Heinz-Wolfgang	Hptm., Kdr. IV./NJ.G. 1	16.10.44
22. Brandi, Albrecht	Korv. Kpt., Kdt. "U 967"	24.11.44

1945

23. Schörner, Ferdinand	Gen. Oberst, OB H.Gr. Nord	1.1.45
24. v. Manteuffel, Hasso	Gen. d. Pz.Tr., OB 5. Pz. -Armee	18.2.45
25. Tolsdorff, Theodor	Gen. Major, Kdr. 340. Volks-Gren. Div. Simultaneously promoted to Gen.Lt.	18.3.45
26. Mauss, Dr. Karl	Gen.Lt., Kdr. 7. Pz.Div.	15.4.45
27. v. Saucken, Dietrich	Gen. d. Pz.Tr., OB AOK Ostpreußen	8.5.45

IV

Recipients of the Knight's Cross of the Iron Cross with Oak Leaves and Swords

1941

1. Galland, Adolf	Obstlt., Kmdr. J.G. 26 "Schlageter" 2nd Diamonds 28.1.42		21.6.41
2. Mölders, Werner	Obstlt., Kmdr. J.G. 51, 1st Diamonds 15.7.41		22.6.41
3. Oesau, Walter	Hptm., Kdr. III./J.G. 3 + 11.5.44 as Oberst & Kmdr. J.G. 1 over the Eifel		15.7.41
4. Lützow, Günther	Major, Kmdr. J.G. 3 + 24.4. 45 missing as Oberst in Jagd-Verb. 44 in the Donauwörth area		11.10.41
5. Kretschmer, Otto	Korv. Kpt., Kdt. "U 99"		26.12.41

1942

6. Rommel, Erwin	Gen. d. Pz.Tr., Befh. Pz. Gr. Afrika 6th Diamonds 11.3.43		20.1.42
7. Bär, Heinrich	Hptm., Staffelkpt. 1./J.G. 51 "Mölders"		16.2.42
8. Philipp, Hans	Hptm., Kdr. 1./J.G. 54 + 8.10.43 as Obstlt. & Kmdr. J.G. 1 over Nordhorn		12.3.42
9. Ihlefeld, Herbert	Hptm., Kdr. I./J.G. 77		24.4. 42
10. Ostermann, Max-Hellmuth	Oblt., Staffelkpt. 7./J.G. 54 + 9.8.42 at Amossowo, south of Lake Ilmen		17.5.42
11. Graf, Hermann	Lt. d.R., Staffelkpt. 9./J.G. 52 5th Diamonds 16.9.42		19.5.42
12. Marseille, Hans-Joachim	Oblt., Staffelkpt. 3./J.G. 27 4th Diamonds 3.9.42		18.6.42
13. Gollob, Gordon	Hptm., Kmdr. J.G. 77 3rd Diamonds 30.8.42		23.6.42
14. Steinbatz, Leopold	Ofw., Flugzeugf. in 9./J.G. 52 + 15.6.42 in the Woltschansk area. Posthumously promoted to Lt.		23.6.42

ELITE OF THE THIRD REICH

15. Kesselring, Albert	Gen. Feldm., OB Süd 14th Diamonds 19.7.44	18.7.42
16. Baumbach, Werner	Hptm., Kdr. 1./K.G. 30	17.8.42
17. Topp, Erich	Kaptlt., Kdt. "U 552"	17.8.42
18. Suhren, Reinhard	Kaptlt., Kdt. "U 564"	l. 9.42
19. Müncheberg, Joachim	Hptm., stellv. Kmdr. J.G. 51 "Mölders" + 23.3.43 as Major & Kmdr. J.G. 77 over Tunisia	9.9.42
20. Helbig, Joachim	Hptm., Kdr. 1./Kampf-Lehr-Geschw. L	28.9.42
21. Eibl, Karl	Gen. Major, Kdr. 385. I.D. + 21.1.43 as Gen.Lt. m.F.b. XXIV. Pz. Korps. Posthumously promoted to Gen.D.Inf.	19.12.42
22. Hube, Hans	Gen.Lt., Kom.Gen. XIV. Pz. Korps 13th Diamonds 20.4.44	21.12.42
23. Wilcke, Wolf-Dietrich	Major, Kmdr. J.G. 3 "Udet" + 23.3.44 as Oberst & Kmdr. J.G. 3 "Udet" over Schöppenstedt	23.12.42

1943

24. Druschel, Alfred	Hptm., stellv. Kdr. 1./Schl. Geschw. I + 1.1.45 as Oberst & Kmdr. S.G. 4 over Belgium	19.2.43
25. Balck, Hermann	Gen.Lt., Kdr. 11. Pz.Div. 19th Diamonds 31.8.44	4.3.43
26. Dietrich, Josef	SS-Obergruppenf. & Gen. d. W-SS, Kdr. SS-Pz. Gren. Div. "LSSAH" 16th Diamonds 6.8.44	14.3.43
27. Graf Strachwitz v. Gr.Zauche u. Camminetz, Hyazinth	Oberst d.R., Kdr. Pz. Rgt. "Großdeutschland" 11th Diamonds 15.4.44	28.3.43
28. Model, Walter	Gen. Oberst, OB 9. Armee 17th Diamonds 17.8.44	2.4.43
29. Lüth, Wolfgang	Kaptlt., Kdt. "U 181" 7th Diamonds 9.8.43	15.4.43
30. Gorn, Walter	Oberst, Kdr. Pz. Gren. Rgt. 10	8.6.43
31. Peltz, Dietrich	Oberst 1. G., Angriffsführer England	23.7.43
32. Lent, Helmut	Major, Kdr. IV./N. J.G. 1 15th Diamonds 31.7.44	2.8.43
33. Schulz, Albert	Obstlt., Kdr. Pz. Rgt. 25 9th Diamonds 14.12.43	6.8.43
34. Rall, Günther	Hptm., Kdr. IR./J.G. 52	12.9.43
35. Hoth, Hermann	Gen. Oberst, OB 4. Pz. Armee	15.9.43
36. Harpe, Josef	Gen. d. Pz.Tr., Kom.Gen. XXXKI. Pz. Korps	15.9.43
37. Nowotny, Walter	Hptm., Kdr. I./J.G. 54 8th Diamonds 19.10.43	22.9.43
38. v. Gazen gen. v. Gaza, Waldemar	Major, Fhr. Pz. Gren. Rgt. 66	3.10.43

39. Dieckmann, August	SS-Obersturmbannf., Kdr. SS-Pz. Gr. Rgt. 10 "Westland" + 10.10.43 at the Dnjepr	10.10.43
40. v. Kluge, Günther	Gen. Feldm., OB H.Gr. Mitte + 19.8.44 (suicide) at Metz; final post O. B. West	29.10.43
41. Graf v. Schwerin, Gerhard	Gen.Lt., Kdr. 16. Pz. Gren. Division	4.11.43
42. Rudel, Hans-Ulrich	Hptm., Kdr. III./Stuka-Geschw. 2 "Immelmann" 10th Diamonds 29.3.44 1st Gold Oak leaves 29.12.44	25.11.43

1944

43. Herrmann, Hajo	Oberst, Inspekteur d. deutschen Luftverteidigung	23.1.44
44. Prinz zu Sayn-Wittgenstein, Heinrich	Major, Kmdr. N. J.G. 2 + 21.1.44 over Schönhausen (Elbe)	23.1.44
45. Bärenfänger, Erich	Major, Kdr. III./G. R. 123. Simultaneously promoted to Obstlt. + 1.5.45 as Gen.Maj. & Kdr. Verteid. Abschnitt A in Berlin, suicide following a failed attempted break-out at the Prenzlauer-Berg subway station	23.1.44
46. v. Saucken, Dietrich	Gen.Lt., Kdr. 4. Pz.Div. 27th Diamonds 8.5.45	31.1.44
47. Gille, Herbert-Otto	SS-Gruppenf & Gen.Lt. d. W-SS, Kdr. SS-Pz. Gren. Div. "Wiking" 12th Diamonds 19.4.44	20.2.44
48. Breith, Hermann	Gen. d. Pz.Tr., Kom.Gen. III. Pz. Korps	21.2.44
49. Bäke, Franz	Obstlt. d.R., Kdr. Pz. Rgt. 11	21.2.44
50. v. Manteuffel, Hasso	Gen.Maj., Kmdr. 7. Pz.Div. 24th Diamonds 18.2.45	22.2.44
51. Mayer, Egon	Obstl., Kmdr. J.G. 2 "Richthofen" + 2.3.44 at Montmedy	2.3.44
52. Barkhorn, Gerhard	Hptm., Kdr. II./J.G. 52	2.3.44
53. Griesbach, Franz	Oberst, Kdr. Gren. Rgt. 399	6.3.44
54. Streib, Werner	Major, Kmdr. N. J.G. 1	11.3.44
55. Heidrich, Richard	Gen.Lt., Kdr. 1. Fsch. Jäg. Div. + 21.12.47 in British captivity, Hamburg-Bergedorf hospital. Final post Gen. d. Fsch. Tr. & K.G. I. Fsch. Korps	25.3.44
56. Schuldt, Hinrich	SS-Oberf., Kdr. 2. lett. SS-Freiw. -Brigade + 15.3.44 at Nevel. Posthumously promoted to SS-Brigadef. & Gen. Major d. W-SS.	25.3.44
57. Postel, Georg-Wilhelm	Gen.Lt., Kdr. 320. I.D. + 20.9.53 in Camp Schachty, Soviet captivity; final post Kom.Gen. XXX. A.K.	26.3.44
58. v. Wietersheim, Wend	Gen. Major, Kdr. 11. Pz.Div.	26.3.44

#	Name	Details	Date
59.	v. Lewinski gen.	Gen. Feldm., OB H.Gr. Süd v. Manstein, Erich	30.3.44
60.	v. Kleist, Ewald	Gen. Feldm., OB H.Gr.A + 16.10.54 in Soviet captivity (Camp Vladimir)	30.3.44
61.	Boerst, Alwin	Major, Kdr. 1./S.G. 2 "Immelmann" + 30.3.44 in the Jassy area of Romania	6.4.44
62.	Dr. Kupfer, Ernst	Oberst, previously Kommodore Stuka-geschw. 2. + 6.11.43 shot down over the Belasia mountains (Greece) as Oberst & Gen. d. Schlachtflieger	11.4.44
63.	Kreysing, Hans	Gen. d. Geb. Tr., Kom.Gen. XVII. A.K.	13.4.44
64.	Jordan, Hans	Gen.D.Inf., Kom.Gen. VI. A.K.	20.4.44
65.	Preiß, Hermann	SS-Brigadef. & Gen.Maj. d. W-SS, Kdr. 3. SS-Pz.Div. "Totenkopf". Simultaneously promoted to to SS-Gruppenf. and Gen.Lt. d. W-SS.	24.4. 44
66.	Brandi, Albrecht	Kaptlt., Kdt. "U 380 22nd Diamonds 24.11.44	9.5.44
67.	Heilmann, Ludwig	Oberst, Kdr. Fsch. Jäg. Rgt. 3	15.5.44
68.	Reinhardt, Georg-Hans	Gen. Oberst, OB 3. Pz. Armee	26.5.44
69.	Niemack, Horst	Oberst, Kdr. Pz. Füs. Rgt. "Großdeutschland"	4.6.44
70.	König, Alfons	Obstl. d.R., Kdr. Gren. Rgt. 199 "List" + 8.7.44 at Bobruisk as Oberst; Posthumously promoted to Oberst d.R.	9.6.44
71.	Wittmann, Michael	SS-Obersturmf., Chef 2./schw. SS-Pz. Abt. 501 + 8.8.44 as SS-Hptsturmf. & Kdr. schw. SS-Pz. Abt. 501 south of Caen, at Gramesnil; Posthumously promoted to SS-Hauptsturmf.	22.6.44
72.	Dietl, Eduard	Gen. Oberst, OB 20. Geb. Armee + 23.6.44 shot down over Hartberg/Steiermark	1.7.44
73.	Priller, Josef	Obstl., Kmdr. J.G. 26 "Schlageter"	2.7.44
74.	Lang, Friedrich	Major, Kdr. III./S.G. 1	2.7.44
75.	Hartmann, Erich	Oblt., Staffelkpt. 9./J.G. 52 18th Diamonds 25.8.44	2.7.44
76.	Frhr. v. Lüttwitz,	Gen.Lt., Kdr. 26. Pz.Div. Smilo	4.7.44
77.	Dorr, Hans	SS-Sturmbannf, Kdr. SS-Pz. Gren. Rgt. 9 "Germania"; badly wounded on 21.1.45 as SS-Obersturmbannf. & Kdr. SS-Pz. Gren. Rgt. 1 "LSSAH" in Hungary; + 17.4.45 in hospital at Judenburg	9.7.44
78.	Hackl, Anton	Major, Kdr. III./J.G. 11	9.7.44
79.	Stahel, Rainer	Gen-Major, Kdt. Fester Platz Wilna Simultaneously promoted to Gen.Lt.; + 30.11.1955 in Soviet captivity at Camp Woikowo	18.7.44

KNIGHT'S CROSS WITH OAK LEAVES AND SWORDS

80. Tolsdorff, Theodor	Obstlt., Kdr. Gren. Rgt. 1067 & Fhr. Kgr. Simultaneously promoted to Oberst 25th Diamonds 18.3.45	18.7.44
81. Bayerlein, Fntz	Gen.Lt., Kdr. Pz. Lehr-Div.	20.7.44
82. Steinhoff, Johannes	Obstlt., Kmdr. J.G. 77	28.7.44
83. Fegelein, Hermann	SS-Gruppenf & Gen.Lt. d. W-SS, Kdr. 8. SS-Freiw. Kav. Div. "Florian Geyer" + 29.4.45 executed in Berlin (Führerbunker); final post Verb. Offz. der W-SS at FHQ	30.7.44
84. Schnaufer, Heinz-Wolfgang	Hptm., Kdr. IV./N. J.G. 1 21st Diamonds 16.10.44	30.7.44
85. v. Scholz, Fritz	SS-Gruppenf & Gen.Lt. d. W-SS, Kdr. 11. SS-Pz. Gren. Div. "Nordland" + 28.7.44 at Narwa , of wounds	8.8.44
86. Steiner, Felix	SS-Obergruppenf & Gen. d. W-SS, Kom.Gen. III. germ. SS-Pz. Korps	10.8.44
87. Fries, Walter	Gen.Lt., Kdr. 29. Pz. Gren. Div.	11.8.44
88. Bühligen, Kurt	Major, Kmdr. J.G. 2 "Richthofen"	14.8.44
89. Mayer, Dr. Dr. Johannes	Gen.Lt., Kdr. 329. I.D.	23.8.44
90. Hausser, Paul	SS-Oberstgruppenf & Gen. Ob. d. W-SS, OB 7. Armee	26.8.44
91. Meyer, Kurt	SS-Standartenf., Kdr. 12. SS-Pz.Div. "Hitlerjugend"; simultaneously promoted to SS-Oberf.	27.8.44
92. Ritter v. Greim, Robert	Gen. Oberst, OB Luftflotte 6 + 24.5.45 suicide in Salzburg; final post Gen. Feldm. & OB d. Luftwaffe	28.8.44
93. Schörner, Ferdinand	Gen. Oberst, OB. H.Gr. Nord 23rd Diamonds 1.1.45	28.8.44
94. Wisch, Theodor	SS-Brigadef. & Gen. Major d. W-SS, Kdr. 1. SS-Pz.Div. "LSSAH"	30.8.44
95. Baum, Otto	SS-Standartenf., Kdr. 2. SS-Pz.Div "Das Reich"; simultaneously promoted to SS-Oberf.	2.9.44
96. Kroh, Hans	Oberst, Fhr. 2. Fsch. Jäg. Div.	12.9.44
97. Wegener, Wilhelm	Gen.D.Inf., Kom.Gen. L. A.K. + 23.9.44 at Wolmar a. d. Düna	17.9.44
98. Nordmann, Theodor	Major, Kdr. H./S.G. 1 + 19.1.45 as Kmdr. S.G. 3 in the Schillen area (East Prussia)	17.9.44
99. Ramcke, Hermann-Bernhard	Gen.Lt., Kdt. Festung Brest 20th Diamonds 19.9.44; simultaneously promoted to Gen. d. Fsch. Tr.	19.9.44
100. v. Knobelsdorff, Otto	Gen. d. Pz.Tr., Kom.Gen. XXXX Pz. Korps	21.9.44
101. Mauss, Dr. Karl	Gen. Major, Kdr. 7. Pz.Div. 26th Diamonds 15.4.45	23.10.44

39

102. Ziegler, Werner	Major, Fhr. Gren. Rgt. 186	23.10.44
103. Feßmann, Fritz	Hptm. d.R., Kdr. Pz. Aufkl. Abt. 5 + 11.10.44 in Pakamonen (East Prussia); posthumously promoted to Major d.R.	23.10.44
104. Recknagel, Hermann	Gen.D.Inf., Kom.Gen. XXXXII. A.K. + 23.1.45 at Petrikau a. d. Weichsel	23.10.44
105. Reichsfrhr. v. Edelsheim,	Gen.Lt., Kdr. 24. Pz.Div. Maximilian	23.10.44
106. Källner, Hans	Gen.Lt., Kdr. 19. Pz.Div. + 18.4.45 m.F.b. XXIV. Pz.K. at Sokolnica in the Olmütz area	23.10.44
107. Mummert, Werner	Oberst d.R., Kdr. Pz. Gren. Rgt. 103 + in January 1950 in Camp Ssuja, in Soviet captivity; final post Gen. Major d.R. & Kdr. Pz.Div. "Müncheberg"	23.10.44
108. Wurmheller, Josef	Hptm., m.F.b. III./J.G. 2 "Richthofen" + 22.6.44 north of Alencon, Normandy as Kdr. III./J.G. 2 "Richtofen"; posthumously promoted to Major	24.10.44
109. Hohn, Dr. Hermann	Gen. Major, Kdr. 72. I.D.	31.10.44
110. v. Obstfelder, Hans	Gen.D.Inf., Kom.Gen. LXXXVI. A.K.	5.11.44
111. Baade, Ernst-Günther	Gen.Lt., Kdr. 90. Pz. Gren. Div. + 5.4.45 badly wounded in Holstein by ground-attack aircraft; 8.5.45 in Bad Segeberg hospital	16.11.44
112. Schulz, Karl-Lothar	Oberst, Fhr. 1. Fschjäg. Div.	18.11.44
113. Kittel, Otto	Oblt., Staffelkpt. 2./J.G. 54 + 14.2.45 as Oblt., m.F.b. 11./J.G. 54 over Libau (Courland)	25.11.44
114. Frhr. v. Boeselager, Georg	Obstlt., Fhr. 3. Kav. Brigade + 27.8.44 at Lomza on the Bug; posthumously promoted to Oberst	28.11.44
115. Weidling, Helmuth	Gen. d. Art., Kom.Gen. XXXXI. Pz.K. 17.11.55 Camp Wladimir, south-east of Moscow, in Soviet captivity; final post Gen. d. Art. & Kom.Gen. LXI. Pz.K. & Kampfkdt. von Berlin	28.11.44
116. Harmel, Heinz	SS-Brigadef & Gen.Maj. d. W-SS, Kdr. 10. SS-Pz.Div. "Frundsberg"	15.12.44
117. Herr, Traugott	Gen. d. Pz.Tr., Kom.Gen. LXXVI. Pz.K.	18.12.44
118. Reinhardt, Alfred-Hermann	Gen.Lt., Kdr. 98. I.D.	24.12.44

1945

119. Peiper, Joachim	SS-Obersturmbannf., Kdr. SS-Pz. Rgt. 1 "LSSAH"	11.1.45	
120. Krüger, Walter	SS-Obergruppenf. & Gen. d. W-SS, Kom.Gen. VI. Waffen-A.K. der SS + 8.5.45 in Courland (suicide)	11.1.45	
121. Kretzschmar, Wolfgang	Oberst, Kdr, Jäg. Rgt. 24 (L) + 27.12.44 at Frauenburg (Courland) as Oberst, Fhr. 12. Feld-Div. (L)	12.1.45	
122. Rendulic, Dr. Lothar	Gen. Oberst, OB 20. Geb. Armee	18.1.45	
123. Wengler, Maximilian	Gen. Major d.R., Kdr. 227. Inf. Div. + 25.4.45 at Pillau-Neutief as Kdr. 83. I.D.	21.1.45	
124. Nehring, Walther	Gen. d. Pz.Tr., Kom.Gen. XXIV. Pz.K.	22.1.45	
125. Hogeback, Hermann	Obstlt., Kmdr. K.G. 6	26.1.45	
126. Rudorffer, Erich	Major, Kdr. II./J.G. 54	26.1.45	
127. Kirchner, Friedrich	Gen. d. Pz.Tr., Kom.Gen. LVII. Pz.K.	26.1.45	
128. Müller, Friedrich-Wilhelm	Gen.D.Inf., Kom.Gen. LXVHI. A.K. + 20.5.47 hanged in Athens; final post OB 4. Armee	27.1.45	
129. Dörner, Helmut	SS-Oberfhr., Fhr. Kampfgr. d. 4. SS-Pol. Pz. Gren. Div. + 11.2.45 during breakout from Budapest, Bolnay-Akademie	1.2.45	
130. Reinert, Ernst Wilhelm	Oblt., Staffelkpt. 14./J.G. 27	1.2.45	
131. Walther, Erich	Oberst, Fhr. Fsch. Pz. Gren. Div. 2 "HG" + 26.12.47 in Soviet captivity at Camp Buchwald; final post GM	1.2.45	
132. Sachsenheimer, Max	Gen. Major, Kdr. 17. Inf. Div.	6.2.45	
133. v. Rundstedt, Gerd	Gen. Feldm., OB West	18.2.45	
134. v. Müller, Dietrich	Gen. Major, Kdr. 16. Pz.Div.	20.2.45	
135. Schulz, Friedrich	Gen.D.Inf., OB 17. Armee	26.2.45	
136. Heinrici, Gotthard	Gen. Oberst, OB 1. Pz. Armee	3.3.45	
137. Lemm, Heinz-Georg	Obstlt., Kdr. Füs. Rgt. 27	15.3.45	
138. Kumm, Otto	SS-Brigadef & Gen.Maj. d. W-SS, Kdr. 7. SS-Freiw. Geb. Div. "Prinz Eugen"	17.3.45	
139. Hartmann, Walter	Gen. d. Art., Kom.Gen. VIII. A.K.	18.3.45	
140. Bochmann, Georg	SS-Standartenf., Fhr. 18. SS-Freiw. - Pz. Gren. Div. "Horst Wessel"	26.3.45	
141. Jüttner, Arthur	Oberst, Kdr. Gren. Rgt. 164	5.4.45	
142. v. Oppeln-Bronikowski, Hermann	Gen. Major, Kdr. 20. Pz.Div.	17.4.45	

143. Mäder, Hellmuth	Gen. Major, Kdr. Führer-Gren. Div.	18.4.45
144. Schroer, Wemer	Major, Kmdr. J.G. 3 "Udet"	19.4.45
145. Batz, Wilhelm	Major, Kdr. II./J.G. 52	21.4.45
146. Blaskowitz, Johannes	Gen. Oberst, OB Niederlande + 5.2.48 suicide at Nürnberg, whilst in American captivity	25.4.45
147. Niehoff, Hermann	Gen. d. Inf, Kdt. Festung Breslau	26.4.45
148. Behrend, Hermann-Heinrich	Gen. Major, Kdr. 490. I.D.	26.4.45
149. Decker, Karl	Gen. d. Pz.Tr., Kom.Gen. XXXIX. Pz. Korps + 21.4.45 suicide in the Großbrunsrode/Brunswick area	26.4.45
150. Weidinger, Otto	SS-Obersturmbannf, Kdr. SS-Pz. Gren. Rgt. 4 "Der Führer"	6.5.45
151. Wisliceny, Günther	SS-Obersturmbannf, Kdr. Pz. Gren. Rgt. 3 "Deutschland"	6.5.45
152. Stadler, Sylvester	SS-Oberführer, Kdr. 9. SS-Pz.Div. "Hohenstaufen"	6.5.45
153. Bittrich, Wilhelm	SS-Obergruppenf. & General d. W-SS, Kom.Gen. II. SS-Pz. Korps	6.5.45
154. Gräser, Fritz-Hubert	Gen. d. Pz.Tr., OB 4. Pz. Armee	8.5.45
155. Meindl, Eugen	Gen. d. Fsch. Tr., Kom.Gen. II. Fsch. Korps	8.5.45
156. Thieme, Carl	Obstlt., Kdr. Pz. Gren. Rgt. 110	9.5.45
157. Frhr. v. Lüttwitz,	Gen. d. Pz.Tr., Kom.Gen. Heinrich XXXXVII. Pz. Korps	9.5.45
158. Hitzfeld, Otto	Gen.D.Inf., Kom.Gen. LXVII. A.K.	9.5.45
159. Bremm, Josef	Obstlt., Kdr. Gren. Rgt. 990	9.5.45

Without a number:

Yamamoto, Isoroku	Admiral, CO Japanese fleet + 18.4.43 over Kahili, Far East; simultaneously awarded Oak leaves; posthumously promoted to Großadmiral	27.5.43

Comments

(144) and (145) Swords

The awards to Majors Schroer and Batz cannot be verified by

evidence in the Bundesarchiv. Confirmation that the awards were made was provided by the Gemeinschaft der Jagdflieger (Fighter Pilots' Association). Major Schroer was wearing the Swords in April 1945 and Major Batz provided the substantiating evidence that the award was made. No exact dates have been established. The dates shown in Ernst Obermaier's book *Die Ritterkreuztrager der Luftwaffe 1939–1945 Band 1: Jagdflieger* are incorrect, as can be seen from the official evidence of award dates and numbers.

(147), (148), (149) Swords

The awards of the decoration to Generals Niehoff, Behrend and Decker cannot be verified in the Bundesarchiv. It must be assumed that the awards were made directly in the period from 20 to 29 April 1945. 26 April 1945 has been assumed to be the date on which the awards were made.

It was possible to ascertain the following facts in support of an award having been made: according to his own statement, the General Niehoff was recommended for the award by Gauleiter Hanke. The fact that the troops in Breslau were holding out and the fact that the Knight's Cross of the Iron Cross was awarded on 30 April 1945 to seven members of the complement of troops in Fortress Breslau suggest that the award was made directly.

According to information provided to the Ordensgemeinschaft der Ritterkreuzträger (OdR) by the former Generalmajor Menneking (Head of Amtsgruppe AG/P 1 at OKH), Generalmajor Behrend, whom the Wehrmacht report of 16 April 1945 shows to have been promoted to Generalmajor, was awarded the Swords in April after he received the promotion which was itself associated with the award. General Behrend himself states that the news of the award was transmitted by radio to the OB Netherlands. His two regimental commanders were similarly decorated with the Oak Leaves to the Knight's Cross of the Iron Cross in April or May 1945.

The award of the Oak Leaves to Oberstleutnant Knaust (843) is supported by evidence that direct awards to related to the achievements of the Division were made. Knaust received the Oak Leaves on 17 April 1945, probably as a direct award, because the recommendation made by Oberst Behrend on 10 April 1945 was supported on 28 April 1945 by Oberst Goecke, head of the HPA/Aussenstelle Nord in the OKH (P 5). Before the award was made it was ascertained that it had already occurred. These events are substantiated by evidence in the Bundesarchiv.

The award to General Decker can similarly not be officially verified. As a Generalleutnant and Commander of the 5th Pz.Div., on 19 November 1944 he was recommended for the award of the Swords, the award was deferred on 8 December 1944 and on 1 January 1945 Decker was promoted to General der Panzertruppe. Decker's Panzer Corps took part in one of the last successful counter-attacks on the Eastern Front at the beginning of March 1945 under the command of General der Panzertruppe Nehring. Then the Corps was transferred to the Western Front and placed under the direct command of OKW. There the XXXXI Panzer Corps, with Pz.Div. Clausewitz, carried out the last counter-attack in the Uelzen-Gifhorn area with some local successes.

There is evidence that three Knight's Crosses were awarded for this action. Shortly afterwards Decker's troops were shattered when the enemy renewed their advance. General Decker chose to commit suicide before he was taken prisoner.

The award of the Swords after a continuous period of outstanding performance in action took place, or is said to have taken place, a little later.

For all three recipients of the Swords it is assumed that the date the awards were made was 26 April 1945.

(150–153) Swords

Awards of the Swords to four members of the Waffen-SS were made, together with awards of the Oak Leaves and the Knight's Cross, by SS-Oberstgruppenführer and Generaloberst der Waffen-SS Sepp Dietrich, commander of the 6th SS-Panzer-Armee.

According to Dietrich's statement, made on oath to the O. d.R., the awards were made for outstanding achievements during the Ardennes offensive (December 1944) and in Hungary (1945). Approval to make the awards, according to Dietrich, was delivered by courier from Berlin.

The date shown is that on which the award was notified or made to the recipient.

(154) Swords

The award of the Swords to General Fritz Hubert Gräser did not take place on 22 April 1945, as had been indicated in 1955. The recommendation only arrived at OKH/PA/P 5 on 29 April 1945 and was supported by the head of the HPA, General Maisel, on 30 April 1945. The recommendation for the award has survived and is in the Bundesarchiv.

Thus the recommendation mainly falls under the rubric of the so-called 'Dönitz order' (the text of which is reproduced in Appendix VI).

(155) Swords

General der Fallschirmtruppe Eugen Meindl was recommended for the award of the Swords. The recommendation was supported

"on 23 March 1945 by Gen. d. Fsch. Tr. Schlemm

"on 28 March 1945 by Generaloberst Blaskowitz, OB Heeresgruppe 'H'

"on 9 April 1945 by Generalfeldmarschall Kesselring, OB West

"on 10 April 1945 by the Supreme Commander of the Luftwaffe, Reichsmarschall Göring.

The award of the Swords was made under the terms of the 'Dönitz order'. Substantiating documentation relating to the recommendation is available in the Bundesarchiv.

(156–159) Swords

The last four awards of the Swords, dated 9 May 1945, can similarly be considered to fall under the rubric of the 'Dönitz order', all the recommendation documentation was confirmed in OKH/PA/P 5, but had not been dealt with. This evidence can be found in the Bundesarchiv.

Oberstleutnant Thieme was recommended for the award on 10 April 1945, with the recommendation itself being supported by Generalfeldmarschall Model, OB Heeresgruppe 'B'.

General von Lüttwitz had already been recommended for the award for his action in the Ardennes, and was recommended a second time for action in the Ruhr pocket. The award is shown in the recommendations book on 28 April 1945 with the remarks 'not dealt with (deferred)'. The recommendation had been supported on 28 March 1945 by Generaloberst Blaskowitz.

General Hitzfeld was recommended for the award in April 1945; the award on 28 April 1945 was deferred.

Oberstleutnant Bremm was recommended for the award on 12 April 1945 by the Commanding General of LXVII Army Corps, General Hitzfeld. The recommendation was supported on 28 April 1945 by OB West, Generalfeldmarschall Kesselring, and on 28 April 1945 was similarly deferred in OKH/PA/P 5. It was said that all that remained to do was to assemble comments from intermediate superior officers, but this was no longer possible in the situation at the time.

The award of the Swords to Oberst Wilhelm von Salisch, commander of Jäger Regiment 49, who was killed in action on 18 March 1945, is said to have been made between 17 and 30 April 1945. Certainly a recommendation was made and submitted by his unit. However, to date no substantiating evidence can be found that this recommendation arrived at OKH/PA/P 5, unlike the recommendations previously mentioned.

There are, however, members of his regiment who speak of a posthumous award. However, it was not possible to produce further information.

According to the Gemeinschaft der Jagdflieger, Major Theodore Weissenberger (+) and Major Ehrler (+ 6 April 1945 near Stendal) were recommended for the award of the Swords. The recommendation made on 19 January 1945 for Major Weissenberger was refused on 20 February 1945. It is not possible to ascertain whether a later recommendation was successful.

Also, according to the Gemeinschaft der Jagdflieger, in the case of Major Ehrler it must be assumed that no award took place. In both cases there is no documentary evidence.

For all other awards there was substantiating evidence in the Bundesarchiv that the awards were made.

V

Recipients of the Knight's Cross of the Iron Cross with Oak Leaves

1940

1. Dietl, Eduard	Gen.Lt., Kom.Gen. Geb. Korps "Norwegen" 72nd Swords 1.7.44 Simultaneously promoted to Gen.D.Inf. later Gen. d. Geb. Tr.	19.7.40
2. Mölders, Wemer	Major, Kmdr. J.G. 51 2nd Swords 22.6.41 1st Diamonds 15.7.41	21.9.40
3. Galland, Adolf	Major, Kmdr. J.G. 26 "Schlageter" 1st Swords 21.6.41 2nd Diamonds 28.1.42	24.9.40
4. Wick, Helmut	Hptm., Kdr. I./J.G. 2 "Richthofen" + 28.11.40 as Major, Kmdr. J.G. 2 "Richthofen" south of the Isle of Wight, the Channel	6.10.40
5. Prien, Günther	Kaptlt., Kdt. "U 47" + 7.3.41 as Korv. Kpt., Kdt. "U 47" west of the Faroe islands	20.10.40
6. Kretschmer, Otto	Kaptlt., Kdt. "U 99" 5th Swords 26.12.41	4.11.40
7. Schepke, Joachim	Kaptlt., Kdt. "U 100" + 17.3.41 south of Ireland	1.12.40

1941

8. Harlinghausen, Martin	Obstlt. i.G., Chef d. St. X. Flg. Korps	30.1.41
9. Oesau, Walter	Hptm., Kdr. III./J.G. 3 3rd Swords 15.7.41	6.2.41
10. Rommel, Erwin	Gen.Lt., Kdr. 7. Pz.Div. 6th Swords 20.1.42 6th Diamonds 11.3.43	20.3.41
11. Joppien, Hermann-Friedrich	Hptm., Kdr. 1./J.G. 51 + 25.8.41 at Briansk	23.4.41
12. Müncheberg, Joachim	Oblt., Staffelkpt. 7./J. G 26 "Schlageter" 19th Swords 9.9.42	7.5.41
13. Liebe, Heinrich	Kaptlt., Kdt. "U 38" Simultaneously promoted to Korv. Kpt.	10.6.41

ELITE OF THE THIRD REICH

14. Endraß, Engelbert	Oblt. z. See, Kdt. "U 46" + 21.12.41 as Kdt. "U 567" north-east of the Azores		10.6.41
15. Schultze, Herbert	Kaptlt., Kdt. "U 48"		12.6.41
16. Ihlefeld, Herbert	Hptm., Kdr. I./J.G. 77 9th Swords 24.4. 42		27.6.41
17. Balthasar, Wilhelm	Hptm., Kmdr. J.G. 2 "Richthofen" + 3.7.41 at Aire, France Posthumously promoted to Major		2.7.41
18. Schnell, Siegfried	Lt., Flugzeugf. in 9./J.G. 2 "Richthofen" + 25.2.44 as Hptm., Kdr. IV./J.G. 54 at Narwa; Posthumously promoted to Major		9.7.41
19. Schmidt, Rudolf	Gen. d. Pz.Tr., Kom.Gen. XXXIX. A.K. (mot.)		10.7.41
20. Baumbach, Werner	Oblt., Staffelkpt. 5./K.G. 30 16th Swords 17.8.42		14.7.41
21. Dinort, Oskar	Obstlt., Kmdr. Stuka-Geschw. 2 "Immelmann"		14.7.41
22. Storp, Walter	Major, Kmdr. S. K.G. 210		14.7.41
23. Schütze, Viktor	Korv. Kpt., Kdt. "U 103"		14.7.41
24. Guderian, Heinz	Gen. Oberst, Befh. Pz. Gruppe 2		17.7.41
25. Hoth, Hermann	Gen. Oberst, Befh. Pz. Gruppe 3 35th Swords 15.9.43		17.7.41
26. Frhr. v. Richthofen, Wolfram	Gen. d. Flg., Kom.Gen. VIII. Flg. Korps + 12.7.45 in American captivity at Bad Ischl; final post Gen. Feldm. & OB. Luftflotte 2 (Italy)		17.7.41
27. Lützow, Günther	Major, Kmdr. J.G. 3 4th Swords 11.10.41		20.7.41
28. Priller, Josef	Oblt., Staffelkpt. 1./J.G. 26 "Schlageter" 73rd Swords 2.7.44		20.7.41
29. Frhr. v. Maltzahn, Günther	Major, Kmdr. J.G. 53		24.7.41
30. Niemack, Horst	Rittm., Kdr. Div. Aufkl. Abt. 5 69th Swords 4.6.44		10.8.41
31. Bär, Heinrich	Lt., Flugzeugfhr. in 1./J.G. 51 7th Swords 16.2.42		14.8.41
32. Hahn, Hans (Assi)	Hptm., Kdr. III./J.G. 2 "Richthofen"		14.8.41
33. Philipp, Hans	Oblt., Staffelkpt. 4./J.G. 54 8th Swords 12.3.42		24.8.41
34. Crüwell, Ludwig	Gen.Lt., Kdr. 11. Pz.Div.		1.9.41
35. Nordmann, Karl-Gottfried	Oblt., Staffelkpt. 12./J.G. 51		16.9.41
36. Hoffmann, Heinrich	Ofw., Flugzeugfhr. 1. d. 12./J.G. 51 + 3.10.41 at Shatalowka in Russia		19.10.41
37. Frhr. v. Lützow, Jürgen	Kurt- Oberst, Kdr. Inf.Rgt. 89		21.10.41
38. Gollob, Gordon	Hptm., Kclr. 11./J.G. 3 13th Swords 23.6.42 3rd Diamonds 30.8.42		26.10.41

KNIGHT'S CROSS WITH OAK LEAVES

39.	Graf v. Kageneck, Erbo	Oblt., Staffelkpt. 9./J.G. 27 + 12.1.42 in Neapel hospital, of wounds as Kdr. III/J.G. 27; Posthumously promoted to Hptm.	26.10.41
40.	Krüder, Ernst-Felix	Kapt. z. See, Kdt. "HSK 5" Hilfskreuzer "Pinguin" (Schiff 33) + 8.5.41 in Indian Ocean	15.11.41
41.	Dietrich, Josef	SS-Obergruppenfhr. & Gen. d. W-SS, Kdr. SS-Div. "LSSAH" (mot.) 26th Swords 14.3.43 16th Diamonds 6.8.44	31.12.41
42.	Eberbach, Heinrich	Oberst. Kdr. 5. Pz. Brigade	31.12.41
43.	Scheidies, Franz	Oberst, Kdr. Inf.Rgt. 22 + 7.4.42 as Fhr. 61. I.D. west of Gluchiza; Posthumously promoted to Gen-Major	31.12.41
44.	Buchterkirch, Ernst-Georg	Oblt., Chef 2./Pz. Rgt. 6	31.12.41
45.	Rogge, Bernhard	Kapt. z. See, Kdt. HSK 2 Hilfskreuzer "Atlantis" (Schiff 16)	31.12.41
46.	Peltz, Dietrich	Hptm., Kdr. II./K.G. 77 31st Swords 23.7.43	31.12.41
47.	Schulz, Adalbert	Hptm., Kdr. I./Pz. Rgt. 25 33rd Swords 6.8.43 9th Diamonds 14.12.43	31.12.41
48.	Eckinger, Dr. Josef-Franz	Major, Kdr. I./Schtz. Rgt. 113 + 17.10.41 at Mednoje a. d. Wolga; Posthumously promoted to Obstlt.	31.12.41
49.	Hoffmann-Schönborn, Günther	Major, Kdr. St. Gesch. Abt. 191	31.12.41
50.	Eibl, Karl	Oberst, Kdr. Inf.Rgt. 132 21st Swords 19.12.42	31.12.41
51.	Lehmann-Willenbrock, Heinrich	Kaptlt., Kdt. "U 96"	31.12.41
52.	Weiß, Otto	Major, Kdr. II. (Schl.)/Lehr- Geschw. 2	31.12.41
53.	Frhr. v. Boeselager, Georg	Rittm., Chef 1./Div. Aufkl. Abt. 6 114th Swords 28.11.44	31.12.41
54.	v. Seydlitz-Kurzbach, Walther	Gen. Major, Kdr. 12. I.D.	31.12.41
55.	Harpe, Josef	Gen. Major, Kdr. 12. Pz.Div. 36th Swords 15.9.43	31.12.41
56.	Suhren, Reinhard	Oblt. z. See, Kdt. "U 564" 18th Swords 1.9.42	31.12.41
57.	Hitschhold, Hubertus	Major, Kdr. 1./Stuka-Geschw. 2 "Immelmann"	31.12.41

1942

58. v. Boddien, Oskar	Obstlt., Kdr. Aufkl. Abt. 22 + 6.1.42 in Eupatoria (Crimea); Posthumously promoted to Oberst	8.1.42
59. Jordan, Hans	Oberst, Kdr. Inf.Rgt. 49 64th Swords 20.4.44	16.1.42
60. Specht, Karl-Wilhelm	Oberst, Kdr. Inf.Rgt. 55 + 3.12.53 in Soviet POW Camp Woikowo near Moscow; final post Gen.D.Inf., Befehlshaber in Wehrkreis XX Danzig-Westpreußen) & Kom.Gen. Korps Hela	16.1.42
61. Frhr. v. Wolff, Hans	Hptm., Kdr. 1./Schtz. Rgt. 28 Simultaneously promoted to Major; + 28.6.44 as Oberst & Kdr. 3. Kav. Brigade in Russia, accidentally, in hospital at Pinsk	16.1.42
62. Hube, Hans	Gen. Major, Kdr. 16. Pz.Div. 22nd Swords 21.12.42 13th Diamonds 20.4.44	16.1.42
63. Noak, Karl-Heinz	Oblt., Chef 1./Pz.Jäg. Abt. 137	16.1.42
64. Helbig, Joachim	Hptm., Kdr. 1./Kampf-Lehr- Geschw. 1 20th Swords 28.9.42	16.1.42
65. Hitzfeld, Otto	Obstlt., Kdr. Inf.Rgt. 213 (158th) Swords 9.5.45	17.1.42
66. Wegener, Wilhelm	Oberst, Kdr. Inf.Rgt. 94 97th Swords 17.9.44	19.1.42
67. Traut, Hans	Oberst, Kdr. Inf.Rgt. 41 & Fhr. 10. I.D. (mot.)	23.1.42
68. Frhr. v. & zu Gilsa, Werner-Albrecht	Gen. Major, Kdr. 216. Inf. Div. + 9.5.45 as Gen.D.Inf. & Fhr. Korps Gilsa in Leitmeritz, Dresden area, suicide	24.1.42
69. Breith, Hermann	Gen. Major, Kdr. 3. Pz.Div. 48th Swords 21.2.44	31.1.42
70. Kaldrack, Rolf	Hptm., Kdr. II./S. K.G. 210 + 3.2.42 shot down at Toropez	9.2.42
71. Borgmann, Heinrich	Hptm., Kdr. III./Inf.Rgt. 46 + 6.4.45 in Magdeburg area by ground-attack aircraft whilst on his way to Div. Scharnhorst as Oberst i.G.	11.2.42
72. v. Kleist, Ewald	Gen. Oberst, Befh. Pz. Gr. 1 60th Swords 30.3.44	17.2.42
73. Reinhardt, Georg-Hans	Gen. d. Pz.Tr., Befh. Pz. Gr. 3 68th Swords 26.5.44	17.2.42
74. Model, Walter	Gen. d. Pz.Tr., Kom.Gen. XXXXI. Pz.K. 28th Swords 2.4.43 17th Diamonds 17.8.44	17.2.42

KNIGHT'S CROSS WITH OAK LEAVES

75. Frhr. v. Langermann & Erlencamp, Willibald	Gen. Major, Kdr. 4. Pz.Div. + 3.10.42 as Gen. d. Pz.Tr., Kom.Gen. XXIV. Pz.K. at Storoshewoje in Russia	17.2.42
76. Wessel, Walter	Oberst, Kdr. Inf.Rgt. 15 (mot.) Simultaneously promoted to Gen.Maj. + 20.7.43 Morano, Italy, accidentally; final post Gen.Lt. b. d. Inspekt. d. Pz.Tr. in OKH	17.2.42
77. Hagen, Walter	Obstlt., Kmdr. Stuka-Geschw. 1	17.2.42
78. Keßelring, Albert	Gen. Feldm., OB Süd 15th Swords 18.7.42 14th Diamonds 19.7.44	25.2.42
79. Köppen, Gerhard	Feldw., Flugzeugfhr. in 8./J.G. 52 + 5.5.42 as Lt. over the Sea of Azov; Posthumously promoted to Lt.	27.2.42
80. Ubben, Kurt	Hptm., Kdr. III./J.G. 77 + 27.4.44 as Major, Kmdr. J.G. 2 "Richthofen" over France	12.3.42
81. Ostermann, Max-Hellmuth	Oblt., Staffelkpt. 7./J.G. 54 10th Swords 17.5.42	12.3.42
82. Eckerle, Franz	Hptm., Kdr. I./J.G. 54 + 14.2.42 at Wellkije Luki	12.3.42
83. Huy, Wolf-Dietrich	Oblt., Staffelkpt. 7./J.G. 77	17.3.42
84. Strelow, Hans	Lt., Staffelkpt. 5./J.G. 51 "Mölders" + 22.5.42 at Nowossil in Russia	24.3.42
85. Spies, Wilhelm	Hptm., Kdr. 1./Z.G. 26 + 27.1.42 at Suchinitischl in Russia; Posthumously promoted to Major	5.4.42
86. Müller, Friedrich-Wilhelm	Oberst, Kdr. Inf.Rgt. 105 128th Swords 27.1.45	8.4.42
87. Topp, Erich	Kaptlt., Kdt. "U 552" 17th Swords 17.8.42	11.4.42
88. Eicke, Theodor	SS-Obergruppenfhr. & Gen. d. W-SS, Kdr. SS "Totenkopf"-Div. + 26.2.43 at Orelka in Russia	20.4.42
89. Hardegen, Reinhard	Kaptlt., Kdt. "U 123"	23.4.42
90. Späte, Wolfgang	Oblt., Staffelkpt. 5./J.G. 54	23.4.42
91. Wünnenberg, Alfred	SS-Brigadefhr. & Gen. Major d. Pol., Kdr. SS-Polizei-Division	23.4.42
92. Scherer, Theodor	Gen. Major, Kdr. 281. Sich. Div. & defender of Cholm	5.5.42
93. Graf, Hermann	Lt. d.R., Staffelfhr. 9./J.G. 52 11th Swords 19.5.42 5th Diamonds 16.9.42	17.5.42
94. Dickfeld, Adolf	Lt., Flugzeugf. 1. d. 7./J.G. 52	19.5.42
95. v. Mackensen, Eberhard	Gen. d. Kav., Kom.Gen. III. Pz. Korps	26.5.42
96. Steinbatz, Leopold	Ofw., Flugzeugfhr. 1. d. 9./J.G. 52 14th Swords 23.6.42	2.6.42

ELITE OF THE THIRD REICH

97. Marseille, Hans-Joachim	Oblt., Flugzeugfhr. in 3./J.G. 27 12th Swords 18.6.42 4th Diamonds 3.9.42	6.6.42
98. Lent, Helmut	Hptm., Kdr. II./N. J.G. 2 32nd Swords 2.8.43 15th Diamonds 31.7.44	6.6.42
99. Frhr. v. Malapert gen. Neufville, Robert-Georg	Hptm., Kdr. H./Stuka-G. 1 + 21.5.42 Sechtschinskaja, Russia	8.6.42
100. Wolff, Ludwig	Gen. Major, Kdr. 22. Inf. Div.	22.6.42
101. Geißhardt, Friedrich	Oblt., Flugzeugfhr. & Adj. in Stab I./J.G. 77 + 6.4.43 as Hptm., Kdr. III./J.G. 26 "Schlageter" at Gent of wounds	23.6.42
102. Setz, Heinrich	Oblt., Staffelkpt. 4./J.G. 77 + 13.3.43 as Hptm., Kdr. 1./J.G. 27 over Abbeville; Posthumously promoted to Major	23.6.42
103. Graf v. Brockdorff- Ahlefeldt, Walter	Gen.D.Inf., Kom.Gen. II. A.K. + 9.5.43 in Potsdam	27.6.42
104. Mützelburg, Rolf	Kaptlt., Kdt. "U 203" + 11.9.42 in Atlantik, accidentally	15.7.42
105. Schnee, Adalbert	Kaptlt., Kdt. "U 201 "	15.7.42
106. Clausen, Erwin	Oblt., Staffelkpt. 6./J.G. 77 + 4.10.43 as Hptm., Kdr. I./J.G. 11 over the North Sea; Posthumously promoted to Major	23.7.42
107. Bauer, Viktor	Oblt., Staffelkpt. 9./J.G. 3 "Udet"	26.7.42
108. Beerenbrock, Franz-Josef	Ofw., Flugzeugfhr. 1. d. 10./J.G. 51 "Mölders"	3.8.42
109. Hackl, Anton	Hptm., Staffelkpt. 5./J.G. 77 78th Swords 9.7.44	9.8.42
110. Herr, Traugott	Gen. Major, Kdr. 13. Pz.Div. 117th Swords 18.12.44	9.8.42
111. Kempf, Werner	Gen. d. Pz.Tr., Kom.Gen. XXXXVIII. Pz.K.	10.8.42
112. Kollewe, Gerhard	Major, Kdr. II./Kampf-Lehr- Geschw. 1 + 17.10.42 over the Mediterranean	12.8.42
113. Gorn, Walter	Obstlt., Kdr., Kradschtz. Btl. 59 30th Swords 8.6.43	17.8.42
114. Brändle, Kurt	Hptm., Kdr. II./J.G. 3 "Udet" + 3.11.43 as Major over the Channel	27.8.42
115. Steinhoff, Johannes	Hptm., Kdr. II./J.G. 52 82nd Swords 28.7.44	2.9.42
116. Sigel, Walter	Obstlt., Kmdr. Stuka-Geschw. 3 + 8.5.44 as Oberst, Schlachtfliegerführer Norwegen, shot down over Trondheim Fjord	2.9.42
117. Zemsky, Johann	Hptm., Kdr. II./Stuka-Geschw. 1 + 28.8.42 at Mal-Rosowka in Russia, by Flak	3.9.42
118. Druschel, Alfred	Hptm., Kdr. I./Schlacht-Geschw. 1 24th Swords 19.2.43	3.9.42

KNIGHT'S CROSS WITH OAK LEAVES

119. Bormann, Dr. Ernst	Oberst, Kmdr. Gefechtsverband Bormann (verstärkt. K.G. 76)	3.9.42
120. Hein, Gerhard	Lt. d.R., Fhr. 5./I.R. 209	6.9.42
121. Ziegler, Werner	Oblt., Fhr. 2./I.R. 186 102nd Swords 23.10.44	8.9.42
122. Wilcke, Wolf-Dietrich	Hptm., Kmdr. J.G. 3 "Udet" 23rd Swords 23.12.42	9.9.42
123. Scholtz, Klaus	Korv. Kpt., Kdt. "U 1083"	10.9.42
124. Schmidt, Heinz	Lt., Flugzeugflir. in 4./J.G. 52 + 5.9.43 as Staffelkpt. 6./J.G. 52 at Markor in Russia; Posthumously promoted to Hptm.	16.9.42
125. Bleichrodt, Heinrich	Kaptlt., Kdt. "U 109"	23.9.42
126. Müller, Friedrich-Karl	Oblt., Staffelkpt. 1./J.G. 3 "Udet" + 29.5.44 as Major & Kmdr. J.G. 3 at Salzwedel; Posthumously promoted to Oberst	23.9.42
127. Crinius, Wilhelm	Feldw., Flugzeugfhr. in 3./J.G. 53	23.9.42
128. Tonne, Wolfgang	Oblt., Staffelkpt. 3./J.G. 53 + 20.4.43 as Hptm. over Tunis	24.9.42
129. Ritter v. Hauenschild, Bruno	Gen. Major, Kdr. 24. Pz.Div.	27.9.42
130. Beißwenger, Hans	Lt., Flugzeugfhr. in 6./J.G. 54 + 6.3.43 as Oblt. & Staffelkpt. in the Cholm area	3.10.42
131. Reinert, Ernst-Wilhelm	Feldw., Flugzeugfhr. in 4./J.G. 77 130th Swords 1.2.45	7.10.42
132. Torley, Karl	Hptm., Kdr. I./Inf.Rgt. 60 (mot.) + 19.7.43 as Major, at Kalinowka; Posthumously promoted to Obstlt.	11.10.42
133. Kümmel, Johannes	Hptm., Kdr. I./Pz. Rgt. 8 + 26.2.44 as Oberst & Kdr. Pz. Rgt. 26 in South Italy, at Cisterna, accidentally; Posthumously promoted to Oberst	11.10.42
134. Rall, Günther	Staffelkpt., Flugzeugfhr. in 8./J.G. 52 34th Swords 12.9.43	26.10.42
135. Kirschner, Ludwig	Obstlt., Kdr. Inf.Rgt. 72 + 11.2.45 as Gen. Major & Kdr. 320 V.G.D. at Saybusch (Galicia)	28.10.42
136. Hupfer, Konrad	Hptm., Kdr. I./Inf.Rgt. 72 + 10.4.44 at Czernowitz as Major, Fhr. Gren. Rgt. 21; Posthumously promoted to Obstlt.	28.10.42
137. Stotz, Max	Ofw., Flugzeugfhr. in 5./JG. 54 + 19.8.43 as Hptm., Staffelkpt. 5./J.G. 54 over Vitebsk	30.10.42

138. Schweickhardt, Heinrich	Hptm., Flugzeugfhr. in 8./K.G. 76 + 9.1.43 as Kdr. I./K.G. 76, missing over the Mediterranean; Posthumously promoted to Major	30.10.42
139. Schenck, Wolfgang	Hptm., Kdr. I./Z.G. 1	30.10.42
140. Seitz, Hermann	Obstlt., Kdr. Pz. Gren. Rgt. 63 + 20.12.42 at Gromoslawka in Stalingrad area; Posthumously promoted to Oberst	31.10.42
141. Zwernemann, Josef	Ofw., Flugzeugfhr. in 7./J.G. 52 + 8.4.44 as Oblt. & Staffelkpt. 1./J.G. 11 at Gardelegen	31.10.42
142. Lüth, Wolfgang	Kaptlt., Kdt. "U 181" 29th Swords 15.4.43 7th Diamonds 9.8.43	13.11.42
143. Töniges, Werner	Kaptlt., Kdt. "S 102" in 1. Schnellbootsflottille	13.11.42
144. Graf Strachwitz v. Gr.Zauche & Camminetz, Hyazinth	Obstlt. d.R., Kdr. I./Pz. Rgt. 2 27th Swords 28.3.43 11th Diamonds 15.4.44	13.11.42
145. Ramcke, Hermann-Bernhard	Gen. Major, Kdr. Fsch. Jäg. Brig. Ramcke 99th Swords 19.9.44 20th Diamonds 19.9.44	13.11.42
146. Wurmheller, Josef	Lt., Flugzeugf. in 7./J.G. 2 "Richthofen" 108th Swords 24.10.44	13.11.42
147. Merten, Karl-Friedrich	Korv. Kpt., Kdt. "U 68"	16.11.42
148. Lang, Friedrich	Hptm., Staffelkpt. 1./Stuka-Geschw. 2 "Immelmann" 74th Swords 2.7.44	21.11.42
149. Boerst, Alwin	Oblt., Staffelkpt. 3./Stuka- Geschw. 2 "Immelmann" 61st Swords 6.4.44	28.11.42
150. Kylling-Schmidt, Ekkehard	Oblt., Chef 4./Füs. Rgt. 26	4.12.42
151. Nobis, Ernst	Obstlt., Kdr. Jäg. Rgt. 204	5.12.42
152. Fischer, Wolfgang	Gen.Lt., Kdr. 10. Pz.Div. + 5.2.43 in Tunisia; Posthumously promoted to Gen. d. PzTr.	9.12.42
153. Allmendinger, Karl	Gen.Lt., Kdr. 5. Jäg. Div.	13.12.42
154. Paepcke, Heinrich	Hptm., Kdr. Hl./K.G. 30 + 17.10.42 over Malta; Posthumously promoted to Major	19.12.42
155. Balck, Hermann	Gen. Major, Kdr. 11. Pz.Div. 25th Swords 4.3.43 19th Diamonds 31.8.44	20.12.42
156. Heitz, Walter	Gen. d. Art., Kom.Gen. VIII. A.K. + 9.2.44 in Soviet captivity in Moscow as Gen. Oberst	21.12.42
157. Fegelein, Hermann	SS-Oberfhr., Kdr. Kampfgruppe 83rd Swords 30.7.44	22.12.42

158. v. Ruckteschell, Hellmuth	Kapt. z. See d.R., Kdt. HSK 9 Hilfskreuzer "Michel" (Schiff 28) + 24.9.48 Hamburg-Fuhlsbüttel, in British captivity	23.12.42
159. Steiner, Felix	SS-Gruppenfhr. & Gen.Lt. d. W-SS, Kdr. SS-Pz. Gren. Div. "Wiking" 86th Swords 10.8.44	23.12.42
160. Lanz, Hubert	Gen.Lt., Kdr. 1. Geb. Div.	23.12.42
161. Schlömer, Helmuth	Gen. Major, Kdr. 3. I.D. (mot.)	23.12.42
162. Reichsfrhr. v. Edelsheim, Maximilian	Oberst, Kdr. Pz. Gren. Rgt. 26 105th Swords 23.10.44	23.12.42
163. v. Ludwiger, Hartwig	Oberst, Kdr. Jäger-Rgt. 83 + 5.5.47 hanged in Yugoslavia; final post Gen.D.Inf., Kom.Gen. XXI. Geb. Korps	23.12.42
164. v. Hirschfeld, Harald	Hptm., Fhr. II./Geb.Jäg. Rgt. 98 + 18.1.45 as Gen. Major, Kdr. 78. Volks- Sturm-Div. at Tarnow, Dunajec; Posthumously promoted to Gen.Lt.	23.12.42
165. Bremm, Josef	Oblt. d.R., Chef 5./Gren. Rgt. 426 (159th) Swords 9.5.45	23.12.42
166. Thumm, Helmuth	Oberst, Kdr. Jäg. Rgt. 56	23.12.42
167. v. Pannwitz, Helmuth	Oberst, Fhr. Kampfgr. "v. Pannwitz" + 16.1.47 hanged in Moscow; final post Gen.Lt. & Kom.Gen. XV. Kos. Kav. Korps d. SS	23.12.42
168. Fiebig, Martin	Gen.Lt., Kom.Gen. VIII. Flg. Korps + 5.5.47 hanged in Yugoslavia; final post Gen. d. Flg., Befh. Luftw. Kdo. Süd	23.12.42

1943

169. Stahel, Rainer	Oberst, Kdr. Luftw. Kampfgruppe 79th Swords 18.7.44	4.1.43
170. Feßmann, Fritz	Oblt. d.R., Chef 1./Kradschtz. Btl. 64 103rd Swords 23.10.44	4.1.43
171. Guggenberger, Friedrich	Kaptlt., Kdt. "U 81"	8.1.43
172. Frank, Heinz	Oblt., Staffelkpt. 3./Schl. Gesch. 1 + 7.10.44 as Major & Kdr. IV./S.G. 151, accidentally	8.1.43
173. Kupfer, Ernst, Dr.	Major, Kdr. II./Stuka-Geschw. 2 "Immelmann" 62nd Swords 11.4.44	8.1.43
174. Dilley, Bruno	Hptm., Kdr. 1./Stuka-Geschw. 2 "Immelmann"	8.1.43
175. Barkhorn, Gerhard	Oblt., Staffelkpt. 4./J.G. 52 52nd Swords 2.3.44	11.1.43
176. v. Wietersheim, Wend	Oberst, Kdr. Pz. Gren. Rgt. 113 58th Swords 26.3.44	12.1.43

#	Name	Details	Date
177.	Mohr, Johann	Kaptlt., Kdt. "U 124" + 3.4.43 as Kdt. "U 124" west of Oporto, North Atlantic; Posthumously promoted to Korv. Kpt.	13.1.43
178.	Paulus, Friedrich	Gen. Ob., OB 6. Armee	15.1.43
179.	Willig, Karl	Major, Kdr. II./Gren. Rgt. 120 (mot.)	18.1.43
180.	Goebel, Günther	Hptm., Fhr. Kampfgruppe	18.1.43
181.	v. Kluge, Günther	Gen. Feldm., OB H.Gr. Mitte 40th Swords 29.10.43	18.1.43
182.	v. Gazen gen. v. Gaza, Waldemar	Hptm., Fhr. Kampfgr. of 13. Pz.Div. (Kdr. I./Pz. G. R. 66) 38th Swords 3.10.43	18.1.43
183.	Kreysing, Hans	Gen.Lt., Kdr. 3. Geb. Div. 63rd Swords 13.4.44	20.1.43
184.	Günzel, Reinhard	Major, Kdr. III./K.G. 27 "Boelcke"	21.1.43
185.	Primozic, Hugo	Oberwachtm., Zugf. in 2./St. Gesch. Abt. 667 Simultaneously promoted to Lt.	25.1.43
186.	Riedel, Willy	Hptm., Kdr. III./Gren. Rgt. 524	25.1.43
187.	Michael, Georg	Oblt. d.R., Fhr. H./Pz. Gren. Rgt. 26 + 19.1.44 as Rittm. of wounds, as Kdr. II./Pz. Gren. Rgt. 26 at Dujeprowka, Nikopol; Posthumously promoted to Major	25.1.43
188.	Pressler, Gustav	Hptm., Kdr. III./Stuka-Geschw. 2 "Immelmann"	26.1.43
189.	Rodenburg, Carl	Gen.Lt., Kdr. 76. I.D.	31.1.43
190.	Knacke, Reinhold	Hptm., Staffelkpt. 3./N. J.G. 1 + 3.2.43 over Holland	7 2.43
191.	Fischer, Erwin	Hptm., Staffelkpt. 1./Fernaufkl. Gr. 121	8.2.43
192.	Hogeback, Hermann	Hptm., Kdr. III./Lehr-Geschw. 1 125th Swords 26.1.45	19.2.43
193.	Bruck, Helmut	Hptm., Kdr. 1./Stuka-Geschw. 77	19.2.43
194.	König, Alfons	Hptm. d.R., Kdr. III./Gren. Rgt. 217 70th Swords 9.6.44	21.2.43
195.	Meyer, Kurt	SS-Ob. Sturmbannf., Kdr. Aufkl. Abt. "LSSAH" 91st Swords 27.8.44	23.2.43
196.	Gildner, Paul	Oblt., Flugzeugf. in 3./N. J.G. 1 + 24.2.43 over Gilze-Rijn (Holland)	26.2.43
197.	Streib, Werner	Major, Kdr. I./N. J.G. 1 54th Swords 11.3.44	26.2.43
198.	Becker, Ludwig	Hptm., Staffelkpt. 12./N. J.G. 1 + 26.2.43 over the German Bucht	26.2.43
199.	Baumgarten-Crusius, Werner	Oblt., Fhr. I./Gren. Rgt. 156 (mot.)	27.2.43
200.	Witt, Fritz	SS-Standartenf., Kdr. SS-Pz. Gren. Rgt. 1 "LSSAH" + 14.6.44 as SS-Brig. Fhr. & Gen. Major d. W-SS & Kdr. 12. SS-Pz.Div. "Hitlerjugend" at Caen	1.3.43
201.	Mikosch, Hans	Oberst, Kdr. Pi. Rgts. Stab z.b.V. 677 & Fhr. Kampfgruppe, Stalingrad	6.3.43

202. Scheunemann, Walter	Hptm., Kdr. I./Gren. Rgt. 272		6.3.43
203. Schmidt, Gustav	Gen.Lt., Kdr. 19. Pz.Div. + 7.8.43 suicide to avoid captivity, Bjelgorod		6.3.43
204. Zahn, Dr. Eberhard	Hptm. d.R., Chef 2./Pz.Jäg. Abt. 33		6.3.43
205. Mickl, Johann	Oberst, Kdr. Pz. Gren. Rgt. 25 + 10.4.45 as Gen.Lt. & Kdr. 392. (kroat.) I.D. in Rijeka hospital, Istria, of wounds		6.3.43
206. v. Malachowski, Wilhelm	Hptm., Kdr. St. Gesch. Abt. 228		6.3.43
207. Kohnz, Bruno	Ofw., Zugf. 1. d. 11./Jäger-Rgt. 207 + 4.4.45 at Leobschütz; final post Hptm. & Kp. Chef		6.3.43
208. Lassen, Georg	Kaptlt., Kdt. "U 160"		7.3.43
209. v. Lewinski, gen. v. Manstein, Erich	Gen. Feldm., OB H.Gr. Süd 59th Swords 30.3.44		14.3.43
210. Rietscher, Georg	Uffz., VB. in 14./Gren. Rgt. 513		14.3.43
211. Langesee, Karl	Major, Kdr. II./Jäger-Rgt. 207		15.3.43
212. Kult, Josef	Oblt. d.R., Chef 3./Jäger-Rgt. 228 + 22.2.43 in Ausheds, south of the Kuban; Posthumously promoted to Hptm. d.R.		15.3.43
213. Hoernlein, Walter	Gen.Lt., Kdr. In£Div. (mot.) "Großdeutschland"		15.3.43
214. Nordmann, Theodor	Oblt., m.F.b. III./Stuka-Geschw. 1 98th Swords 17.9.44		17.3.43
215. Postel, Georg-Wilhelm	Gen. Major, Kdr. 320. I.D. 57th Swords 26.3.44		28.3.43
216. Ritter v. Greim, Robert	Gen. Oberst, Befehlshaber Luftfl. Kdo. Ost (Luftflotte 6) 92nd Swords 28.8.44		2.4.43
217. v. Scheele, Hans-Karl	Gen.Lt., Kom.Gen. "Korps Scheele"		2.4.43
218. Schüler, Heinrich	Hptm. d.R., Kdr. II./Gren. Rgt. 525 + 12.1.45 as Oberst d.R. & Rgt. Kdr. during fighting at the Vistula bend		2.4.43
219. Hudel, Helmut	Hptm., Kdr. 1./Pz. Rgt. 7		2.4.43
220. Schuldt, Hinrich	SS-Standartenf., Kdr. SS-Brig. "Schuldt" 56th Swords 25.3.44		2.4.43
221. Kumm, Otto	SS-Ob. Sturmbannf., Kdr. SS-Pz. Gren. Rgt. "Der Führer"' 138th Swords 17.3.45		6.4.43
222. Schlee, Rudolf	Ofw., Zugf. in 6./Geb.Jäg. Rgt. 13		6.4.43
223. Dönitz, Karl	Großadmiral, Oberbefehlshaber der Kriegsmarine & Befehlshaber der U-Boote		6.4.43
224. Brandi, Albrecht	Kaptlt., Kdt. "U 617" 66th Swords 9.5.44 22nd Diamonds 24.11.44		11.4.43
225. v. Kamptz, Gerhard	Freg. Kpt., Chef 8. Räumbootflottille		14.4. 43

226. Wuppermann, Siegfried	Oblt. z. See, Kdt. "S 56" in 3. Schnellbootflottille	14.4.43
227. Klawe, Erich	Major, Kdr. 1./Gren. Rgt. 23	14.4.43
228. Frantz, Peter	Hptm., Kdr. St. Gesch. Abt. "Großdeutschland"	14.4.43
229. Rudel, Hans-Ulrich	Oblt., Staffelkpt. 1./Stuka-Geschw. 2 "Immelmann" 42nd Swords 25.11.43 10th Diamonds 29.3.44 1st Golden Oak Leaves 29.12.44	14.4.43
230. Hozzel, Paul-Werner	Obstlt., Kmdr. Stuka-Geschw. 2 "Immelmann"	14.4.43
231. Dörffel, Georg	Hptm., m.F.b. I./Schlacht-Geschw. 1 + 26.5.44 as Major & Kmdr. Schl. Geschw. 4 in the Rome area; Posthumously promoted to Obstlt.	14.4.43
232. Mayer, Egon	Hptm., Kdr. III./J.G. 2 "Richthofen" 51st Swords 2.3.44	16.4.43
233. Dieckmann, August	SS-Sturmbannf., Kdr. I./SS-Pz. Gren. Rgt. "Germania" 39th Swords 10.10.43	16.4.43
234. v. Bülow, Otto	Kaptlt., Kdt. "U 404"	26.4.43
235. Borowietz, Willibald	Gen. Major, Kdr. 15. Pz.Div. + 1.7.45 in American captivity, in Clinton/Miss., accidentally; final post Gen.Lt.	10.5.43
236. Stotten, Hans-Günther	Hptm., Kdr. I/Pz. Rgt. 8 + 5.4.45 in Wienerwald area (Lower Danube) as Major i.G. & Ic H.Gr. Süd, shot whilst trying to escape Soviet captivity	10.5.43
237. Laux, Paul	+ 29.8.44 shot down, 2.9. in Riga hospital of his wounds; final post OB 16. Armee	17.5.43
238. Hoehne, Gustav	Gen.Lt., Km. Gen. Korps "Laux" Simultaneously promoted to Gen.D.Inf.	17.5.43
239. Hollidt, Karl-Adolf	Gen.D.Inf., OB 6. Armee	17.5.43
240. Graf von Schwerin, Gerhard	Gen. Major, Kdr. 16. I.D. (mot.) 41st Swords 4.11.43	17.5.43
241. Niggemeyer, Wilhelm	Oblt. d.R., Btl. Adj. Pi. Btl. 26	17.5.43
242. Griesbach, Franz	Oberst, Kdr. Gren. Rgt. 399 53rd Swords 6.3.44	17.5.43
243. Bärenfänger, Erich	Hptm., Kdr. III./Gren. Rgt. 123 45th Swords 23.1.44	17.5.43
244. Grünert, Richard	Major d.R., Kdr. I./Pz. Gren. Rgt. 7 + 13.3.43 south of Isjum; Posthumously promoted to Obstlt.	17.5.43
245. Kruse, Ernst	Ofw., Zugfhr. 7./Pz. Gren. Rgt. 3 + 15.10.44 as Oberfähnr. & Ord. Off. 11./Pz. Gren. Rgt. 3 on Narev at Serock	17.5.43

KNIGHT'S CROSS WITH OAK LEAVES

246. Bochmann, Georg	SS-Sturmbannf., Kdr. II./SS-Kradschtz. Rgt. "Thule" 140th Swords 26.3.45	17.5.43	
247. Löwrick, Karl	Oberst, Kdr. Gren. Rgt. 272 + 8.4.45 as Gen.Lt. & Kdr. 542. V.G.D. at Pillau, accidentally	17.5.43	
248. Grase, Martin	Gen.Lt., Kdr. 1. I.D.	23.5.43	
249. Kemnade, Friedrich	Korv. Kpt., Chef 3. Schnellbootflottille	27.5.43	
250. Gysae, Robert	Kaptlt., Kdt. "U 177"	31.5.43	
251. v. Obstfelder, Hans	Gen.D.Inf. Kom.Gen. XXIX. A.K. 110th Swords 5.11.44	7.6.43	
252. Göbel, Karl	Obstlt., Kdr. Gren. Rgt. 420 + 2.3.45 in Esslingen hospital of severe wounds; final post, Kdr. 299. I.D.; Posthumously promoted to Major	8.6.43	
253. Höhne, Friedrich	Major, Kdr. III./Jäg. Rgt. 204	8.6.43	
254. Klappich, Günter	Oblt., Fhr. III./Gren. Rgt. (mot.) 60 + 22.1.43 at Manytsch; Posthumously promoted to Hptm.	8.6.43	
255. Rödel, Gustav	Major, Kmdr. J.G. 27	20.6.43	
256. Emmermann, Carl	Kaptlt., Kdt. "U 172"	4.7.43	
257. Henke, Werner	Kaptlt. z. V., Kdt. "U 515" + 15.6.44 killed trying to escape American captivity in Camp Fort Meade/Maryland; Posthumously promoted to Korv. Kpt. z. V.	4.7.43	
258. Bayerlein, Fritz	Gen. Major, Deutscher Chef d. Stabes der 1. Italian Army 81st Swords 20.7.44	6.7.43	
259. v. Hünersdorff Walther	Gen. Major, Kdr. 6. Pz.Div. + 17.7.43 in Kursk area, dying of his wounds at a hospital in Kharkov; Posthumously promoted to Gen.Lt.	14.7.43	
260. Sauvant, Bernhard	Major, Kdr. schw. Pz. Abt. 505	28.7.43	
261. Hausser, Paul	SS-Obergruppenf., Gen. d. W-SS, Kom.Gen. SS-Pz. Korps 90th Swords 26.8.44	28.7.43	
262. Bäke, Franz	Major d.R., Kdr. II./Pz. Rgt. 11 49th Swords 21.2.44	1.8.43	
263. Prinz zur Lippe-Weissenfeld, Egmont	Hptm., Kdr. III./N. J.G. 1 + 12.3.44 as Major & Kmdr. N. J.G. 4 over the Ardennes	2.8.43	
264. Meurer, Manfred	Hptm., St. Kpt. 3./N. J.G. 1 + 21.1.44 over Magdeburg as Hptm. & Kdr. 11./N. J.G. 5	2.8.43	
265. Ehrler, Heinrich	Hptm., Kdr. III./J.G. 5 + 6.4.45 over Berlin as Major Geschw. Schwarm J.G. 7	2.8.43	
266. Weissenberger, Theodor	Oblt., Staffelkpt. 7./J.G. 5	2.8.43	

#	Name	Details	Date
267.	Kirschner, Joachim	Oblt., Staffelkpt., 5./J.G. 3 "Udet + 17.12.43 as Hptm. & Kdr. IV./J.G. 27 at Metkovic, Croatia	2.8.43
268.	Schroer, Werner	Hptm., Kdr. II./J.G. 27 (144th) Swords 19.4.45	2.8.43
269.	Herrmann, Hajo	Major, Kmdr. J.G. 300 43rd Swords 23.1.44	2.8.43
270.	Kahl, Bruno	Major, Kdr. III./schw. Heeres- Pz.Jäg. Rgt. 656	8.8.43
271.	Rendulic, Dr. Lothar	Gen.D.Inf., Kom.Gen. XXXV. A.K. 122nd Swords 18.1.45	15.8.43
272.	v. Müller, Dietrich	Oberst, Kdr. Pz. Gren. Rgt. 5 134th Swords 20.2.45	16.8.43
273.	v. Küchler, Georg	Gen. Feldm., OB H.Gr. Nord	21.8.43
274.	Busch, Ernst	Gen. Feldm., OB 16. Armee + 17.7.45 died in Aldershot, England, in British captivity; final post OB Nordwest	21.8.43
275.	Lindemann, Georg	Gen. Oberst, OB 18. Armee	21.8.43
276.	Conrath, Paul	Gen. Major, Kdr. Pz.Div. "HG"	21.8.43
277.	Baum, Otto	SS-Obersturmbannf., Kdr. SS-Pz. Gren. - Rgt. "Totenkopf" 95th Swords 2.9.44	22.8.43
278.	Frhr. v. Funck, Hans	Gen.Lt., Kdr. 7. Pz.Div.	22.8.43
279.	Conrady, Alexander	Oberst, Kdr. Gren. Rgt. 118	22.8.43
280.	Raus, Erhard	Gen. d. Pz.Tr., Kom.Gen. XI. A.K.	22.8.43
281.	v. Saucken, Dietrich	Gen.Lt., Kdr. 4. Pz.Div. 46th Swords 31.1.44 27th Diamonds 8.5.45	22.8.43
282.	Gollnick, Hans	Gen.Lt., Kdr. 36. Pz. Gr. Div.	24.8.43
283.	Eidel, Alfred	Major, Kdr. I./Gren. Rgt. 171 + 23.6.44 as Major, Fhr. Gren. Rgt. 171 at Witebsk	24.8.43
284.	Schultz, Paul	Oberst, Kdr. G. R. 308	26.8.43
285.	v. Cossel, Hans-Detloff	Major, Kdr. I./Pz. Rgt. 35 + 22.7.43 at Orel	29.8.43
286.	Krüger, Walter	SS-Gruppenf. & Gen.Lt. d. W-SS, Kdr. SS-Pz. Gren. Div. "Das Reich" 120. Swords 11.1.45	31.8.43
287.	Rocholl, Rolf	Hptm., Kdr. IR./Gren. Rgt. 569 + 23.8.43 in Russia (Donets)	31.8.43
288.	Grasser, Hartmann	Major, Kdr. H./J.G. 51 "Mölders"	31.8.43
289.	Ettel, Wolf-Udo	Oblt., Staffelkpt. 8./J.G. 27 + 17.7.43 at Catania, Sicily	31.8.43
290.	Prinz zu Sayn-Wittgenstein, Heinrich	Hptm., Kdr. 1./N. J.G. 100 44th Swords 23.1.44	31.8.43
291.	Zorn, Hans	Gen.D.Inf., Kom.Gen. XXXXI. Pz.K. + 2.8.43 at Krassnaya-Roschtocha, south of Orel	3.9.43
292.	Großmann, Horst	Gen.Lt., Kdr. 6. I.D.	4.9.43

KNIGHT'S CROSS WITH OAK LEAVES

293. Nowotny, Walter	Oblt., Staffelkpt. 1./J.G. 54 37th Swords 22.9.43 8th Diamonds 19.10.43		4.9.43
294. Lemelsen, Joachim	Gen. d. Pz.Tr., Kom.Gen. XXXXVII. Pz.K.		7.9.43
295. Jaschke, Erich	Gen.D.Inf., Kom.Gen. LV. A.K.		7.9.43
296. Harmel, Heinz	SS-Standartenf., Kdr. SS-Pz. Gren. Rgt. "Deutschland" 116th Swords 15.12.44		7.9.43
297. Prieß, Hermann	SS-Brigadef. & Gen. Major d. W-SS, Kdr. SS-Pz. Gren. Div. "Totenkopf" 65th Swords 24.4. 44		9.9.43
298. Hoßbach, Friedrich	Gen.Lt., m.F.b. LVI. Pz. Korps		11.9.43
299. Thomaschki, Siegfried	Gen.Lt., Kdr. 11. I.D.		11.9.43
300. Lange, Dr. Walter	Oberst d.R., Kdr. Gren. Rgt. 43		13.9.43
301. Pape, Günther	Oberst, Kdr. Pz. G. R. 394		15.9.43
302. Tolsdorff, Theodor	Major, Kdr. I./Füs. Rgt. 22 80th Swords 18.7.44 25th Diamonds 18.3.45		15.9.43
303. Stadler, Sylvester	SS-Obersturmbannfhr., Kdr. SS-Pz. - Gren. Rgt. "Der Führer" (152nd) Swords 6.5.45		16.9.43
304. Kleemann, Ulrich	Gen.Lt., Kdr. Sturm-Div. Rhodos		16.9.43
305. Student, Kurt	Gen. d. Flg., Kom.Gen. XI. Flg. Korps		27.9.43
306. Reinhardt, Alfred-Hermann	Oberst, Kdr. Gren. Rgt. 421 118th Swords 24.12.44		28.9.43
307. Fritsche, Hans	Major, Kdr. I./Gren. Rgt. 528		2.10.43
308. Spranz, Bodo	Oblt., Chef 1./St. Gesch. Abt. 237 Simultaneously promoted to Hptm .		3.10.43
309. Schreiber, Josef	Ofw., Zugf. in 7./Sturm-Rgt. 14 + 1.2.45 missing as Lt., Zugf. d. Fhjk. -Schule V in Festung Posen		5.10.43
310. Meierdress, Hubert-Erwin	SS-Hauptsturmf., Kdr. I./SS-Pz. Rgt. 3 "Totenkopf' + 4.1.45 as SS-Sturmbannf. & Kdr. 1./SS-Pz. Rgt. 3 in Dunaalmas area, Hungary		5.10.43
311. Pestke, Hans-Gotthard	Hptm., Kdr. 1./Gren. Rgt. 176		14.10.43
312. Ringel, Julius	Gen.Lt., Kdr. 5. Geb. Div.		25.10.43
313. Frhr. v. Roman, Rudolf	Gen. d. Art., Kom.Gen. XX. A.K.		28.10.43
314. Voß, Ernst	Oberst, Kdr. Gren. Rgt. 585 + 11.10.43 at Nowo-Lipiwo; Posthumously promoted to Gen. Major		28.10.43
315. Gille, Herbert-Otto	SS-Brigadef. & Gen. Major d. W-SS, Kdr. SS-Pz. Gren. Div. "Wiking" 47th Swords 20.2.44 12th Diamonds 19.4.44		1.11.43

316. Graf v. d. Goltz, Albert	Obstlt. d.R., Fhr. Geb.Jäg. Rgt. 144 + 16.3.44 as Oberst d.R. & Kdr. Geb.Jäg. Rgt. 138 in Odessa hospital, of wounds		2.11.43
317. Ziemer, Ernst	Hptm., Chef 1./Gren. Rgt. 94		2.11.43
318. König, Eugen	Oberst, Kdr. Gren. Rgt. 451		4.11.43
319. Recknagel, Hermann	Gen.Lt., Kdr. 111. I.D. 104th Swords 23.10.44		6.11.43
320. Grabert, Siegfried	Hptm. d.R., Chef 8./Lehr-Rgt. "Brandenburg" z.b.V. 800 + 25.7.42 Rostov, Bataisk; Posthumously promoted to Major d.R.		6.11.43
321. Kiesling, Heinrich	Major, Fhr. Gren. Rgt. 529 Simultaneously promoted to Obstlt.; + 18.6.44 missing as Oberst & Kdr. G. R. 529, Vitebsk		7.11.43
322. v. Knobelsdorff, Otto	Gen. d. Pz.Tr., Kom.Gen. XXXXVIII. Pz. Korps 100th Swords 21.9.44		12.11.43
323. de Angelis, Maximilian	Gen. d. Art., Kom.Gen. XXXXIV. A.K.		12.11.43
324. Brandenberger, Erich	Gen. d. Pz.Tr., Kom.Gen. XXIX. A.K.		12.11.43
325. Remer, Otto-Ernst	Major, Kdr. I. (gep.)/Gren. Rgt. (mot.) "Großdeutschland"		12.11.43
326. Christiansen, Georg	Korv. Kpt., Chef 1. Schnellbootflottille		13.11.43
327. Dorr, Hans	SS-Hauptsturmf., Kdr. I./SS-Pz. Gren. Rgt. "Germania" 77th Swords 9.7.44		13.11.43
328. Heindl, Josef	Major d.R., Fhr. Gren. Rgt. 199 "List" + 10.9.43 south of Sonmy in Russia; Posthumously promoted to Oberstlt. d.R.		18.11.43
329. Johannmeyer, Willy	Hptm., Kdr. II./Gren. Rgt. 503		18.11.43
330. Dr.Ing. Brill, Karl-Friedrich	Freg. Kpt. d.R., Kdt. MS "Juminda" & Fhr. einer MS-Gruppe; + 22.10.43 on MS "Juminda" west of San Stefano, Italy		18.11.43
331. Block, Johannes	Gen.Lt., Kdr. 294 I.D. + 26.1.45 as Gen.D.Inf. & Kom.Gen. LVI. Pz.K. at Kielce		22.11.43
332. v. Manteuffel, Hasso	Gen. Major, Kdr. 7. Pz.Div. 50th Swords 22.2.44 24th Diamonds 18.2.45		23.11.43
333. Heinrici, Gotthard	Gen. Oberst, OB 4. Armee 136th Swords 3.3.45		24.11.43
334. Schmidt, Hans	Gen.D.Inf. z. V., Kom.Gen. IX. A.K.		24.11.43
335. Dr. Mauss, Karl	Oberst, Kdr. Pz. Gren. Rgt. 33 101st Swords 23.10.44 26th Diamonds 15.4.45		24.11.43
336. Frhr. v. Beust, Hans-Henning	Obstlt., Kmdr. K.G. 27 "Boelcke"		25.11.43
337. Hrabak, Dietrich	Obstlt., Kmdr. J.G. 52		25.11.43

KNIGHT'S CROSS WITH OAK LEAVES

338. Lemke, Wilhelm	Hptm., Kdr. II/J.G. 3 "Udet" + 4.12.43 at Nijmegen	25.11.43
339. Schünemann, Otto	Gen.Lt., Kdr. 337. I.D. + 29.6.44 as Gen.Lt. m.F.b. XXXIX. Pz. Korps at Pagost, on the Beresina	28.11.43
340. Hartmann, Walter	Gen.Lt., Kdr. 87. I.D. 139th Swords 18.3.45	30.11.43
341. Fricke, Ernst-August	Major, Kdr. H./Gren. Rgt. 76 (mot.) + 9.11.43 of wounds received on 13.8.43 ; Posthumously promoted to Oberstlt.	30.11.43
342. Wellmann, Ernst	Obstlt., Kdr. Pz. Gren. Rgt. 3	30.11.43
343. Druffner, Alfred	Oberst, Kdr. Gren. Rgt. 519 + 30.9.43 of wounds in hospital, Orel	30.11.43
344. Grasser, Anton	Gen.Lt., Kdr. 25 Pz. Gren. Div.	5.12.43
345. Walter, Kurt	Obstlt., Kdr. Gren. Rgt. 11 + 27.6.44 missing, as Oberst, Kdr. Gren. Rgt. 11, on the Beresina	5.12.43
346. Weitkunat, Adolf	Major d.R., Kdr. Kampf-Btl. 488	5.12.43
347. Elflein, Walter	Hptm. d.R., Kdr. I./Gren. Rgt. 95 & Fhr. Kampfgr. der 17. I.D.	5.12.43
348. Langkeit, Willy	Obstlt., Kdr. Pz. Rgt. 36	7.12.43
349. Thorey, Andeos	Rittm., Kdr. Aufkl. Abt. 94 + 18.4.44 as Kdr. A.A. 94 on Dnjestr; Posthumously promoted to Major	7.12.43
350. Heinrici, Siegfried	Gen. d. Pz.Tr., Kom.Gen. XXXX. Pz. Korps	9.12.43
351. Voigtsberger, Heinrich	Oberst, Kdr. Gren. Rgt. 60 (mot.)	9.12.43
352. Baacke, Karl	Obstlt., Kdr. Gren. Rgt. 266 + 1.4.44 as Fhr. Kampfgruppe in the Kamenets-Podolski pocket	10.12.43
353. Tychsen, Christian	SS-Sturmbannf., Kdr. H./SS. Pz. Rgt. "Das Reich" + 28.7.44 as SS-Obersturmbannfhr., Fhr. 2. SS Pz.Div. "DR" in Normandy	10.12.43
354. Müller, Alfred	Hptm., Kdr, St. Gesch. Abt. 191	15.12.43
355. Kahler, Hans-Joachim	Obstlt. d.R., Kdr. Pz. Gren. Rgt. 5 Simultaneously promoted to Oberst	17.12.43
356. Kühl, Dr. jur. Ernst	Oberst d.R., Kmdr. K.G. 55 'Greif'	18.12.43
357. v. d. Chevallerie, Kurt	Gen.D.Inf., Kom.Gen. LIX A.K. + 18.4.1945 missing at Kolberg	19.12.43
358. Schmalz, Wilhelm	Oberst, Kdr. Brig. z.b.V. der Pz.Div. "Hermann Gönng"	23.12.43
359. Frey, Albert	SS-Obersturmbannf., Kdr. SS-PZ. Gren. Rgt. 1 "LSSAH" 359th Oak Leaves 20.12.43	29.12.43
360. Ochs, Heinrich	Lt., Zugf. in 1./Pz.Jäg. Abt. 101 + 21.10.43 at Michailowka; Posthumously promoted to Oblt.	30.12.43

1944

361. Klug, Bernd	Korv. Kpt., Chef 5. Schnellbootflottille	1.1.44
362. Feldt, Klaus	Korv. Kpt., Chef 2. Schnellbootflottille	1.1.44
363. Krauß, Walter	Hptm., Kdr. III./Stuka-Geschw. 2 "Immelmann" + 17.7.43 in the Orel area; Posthumously promoted to Major	3.1.44
364. Hannig, Horst	Lt., Staffelfhr. 2./J.G. 2 "Richthofen" + 15.5.43 at Caen; Posthumously promoted to Oblt.	3.1.44
365. Stahlschmidt, Hans-Arnold	Lt., Staffelfhr. 2./J.G. 27 + 7.9.42 missing at El Alamein; Posthumously promoted to Oblt.	3.1.44
366. Kalbitz, Helmut	Hptm., Kdr. Pi. Btl. 31 + 23. - 30.8.44 missing in Rumania, as Major & Kdr. Heeres-Pi. Brig. 127	7.1.44
367. Mulzer, Josef-Georg	Major, Kdr. Pi. Btl. 195	10.1.44
368. Fretter-Pico, Maximilian	Gen. d. Art., Kom.Gen. XXX A.K.	16.1.44
369. Schlemmer, Hans	Gen.Lt., Kdr. 134. I.D.	18.1.44
370. Boigk, Heinrich	Feldw., Zugf. in 2./Jäg. -Rgt. 49	18.1.44
371. Schmidt, August	Gen.Lt., Kdr. 10. Pz. Gren-Div.	23.1.44
372. Wiese, Friedrich	Gen.D.Inf., Kom.Gen. XXXV. A.K.	24.1.44
373. Krüger, Walter	Gen.Lt., Kdr. 1. Pz.Div.	24.1.44
374. Koetz, Karl	Obstlt., Kdr. Gren. Rgt. 185	24.1.44
375. Kraas, Hugo	SS-Obersturmbannf., Kdr. SS-Pz. Gren. Rgt. 2 "LSSAH"	24.1.44
376. Hauser, Eduard	Gen. Major, Kdr. 13. Pz.Div.	26.1.44
377. Peiper, Joachim	SS-Obersturmbannf, Kdr. SS-Pz. Rgt. 1 "LSSAH" 119th Swords 11.1.45	27.1.44
378. Fries, Walter	Gen.Lt., Kdr. 29. Pz. Gren. Div. 87th Swords 11.8.44	29.1.44
379. Sievers, Walther	Obstlt. d.R., Kdr. Gren. Rgt. 415	29.1.44
380. Wittmann, Michael	SS-Untersturmf., Zugf. in 13. (schw.)/SS-Pz. Rgt. 1 "'LSSAH" 71st Swords 22.6.44	30.1.44
381. Flachs, Bernhard	Hptm., Kdr. St. Gesch. Abt. 277 + 8.12.44 as Major & Inspekteur d. St-Gesch. Schule Burg whilst on a tour of the front, Bedburg-Erft area; Posthumously promoted to Obstlt.	31.1.44
382. Heidrich, Richard	Gen.Lt., Kdr. 1. Fsch. Jäg. Div. 55th Swords 25.3.44	5.2.44
383. Nehring, Walther	Gen. d. Pz.Tr., Kom.Gen. XXIV. Pz. Korps 124th Swords 22.1.45	8.2.44

KNIGHT'S CROSS WITH OAK LEAVES

384. Kollberg, Botho	Oberst, Kdr. Gren. Rgt. 23 + 24.1.44 south of Leningrad; Posthumously promoted to Gen. Major	8.2.44
385. Löwe, Erich	Major, Kdr. schw. Pz. Abt. 501 + 24.12.43 at Losovka, Russia; Posthumously promoted to Oberst	8.2.44
386. Hilt, Günther	Hptm. d.R., Kdr. III./Jäg. Rgt. 56 + 21.8.44 as Major & Kdr. III./Jäg. Rgt. 56 on the Bug	8.2.44
387. Breithaupt, Fritz	Korv. Kpt. d.R., Chef 24. Minensuchflottille + 24.12.44 accidentally as Freg. Kpt. d.R.	10.2.44
388. Martinek, Robert	Gen. d. Art., Kom.Gen. XXXIX. Pz. Korps + 28.6.44 accidentally, on the Beresina	10.2.44
389. Schneider, Josef	Lt., Fhr. 13./Jäg. Rgt. 207	10.2.44
390. Möse, Walter	Feldw., Zugf. 1. d. 13./Jäg-Rgt. 49 + 28.11.44 at Goldap, East Prussia; Posthumously promoted to Ofw.	10.2.44
391. Kirchner, Friedrich	Gen. d. Pz.Tr., Kom.Gen. LVII. Pz. Korps 127th Swords 26.1.45	12.2.44
392. Källner, Hans	Gen. Major, Kdr. 19. Pz.Div. 106th Swords 23.10.44	12.2.44
393. Wisch, Theodor	SS-Brigadef. & Gen. Major d. W-SS, Kdr. 1. SS-Pz.Div. "LSSAH" 94th Swords 30.8.44	12.2.44
394. Bronsart v. Schellendorff, Heinrich	Oberst, Kdr. Pz. Gren. Rgt. 13 + 22.9.44 as Oberst & Kdr. 111. Pz. Brig., Geiskirch, Saarland; Posthumously promoted to Gen.Maj.	12.2.44
395. Lorenz, Karl	Oberst , Kdr. Gren. Rgt. "Großdeutschland"	12.2.44
396. v. Lauchert, Meinrad	Oberst, Kdr. Pz. Rgt. 15	12.2.44
397. Karl, Josef	Uffz., Geschützf. in 2./Pz.Jäg. Abt. 49	16.2.44
398. Schörner, Ferdinand	Gen. d. Geb. Tr., Kom.Gen. XXXX. Pz. Korps 93rd Swords 28.8.44 23rd Diamonds 1.1.45	17.2.44
399. Stemmermann, Wilhelm	Gen. d. Art., Kom. Gen XI. A.K. + 18.2.44 whilst attempting to breakout from the Cherkassy pocket	18.2.44
400. Lieb, Theo-Helmut	Gen.Lt., Kom.Gen. XXXXII. A.K.	18.2.44
401. Kästner, Robert	Major, Fhr. Gren. Rgt. 105	21.2.44
402. Baade, Ernst-Günther	Oberst, Fhr. 90. Pz. Gren. Div. Simultaneously promoted to Gen. Major 111th Swords 16.11.44	22.2.44
403. Kolbeck, Rudolf	Obstlt. d.R., Kdr. Gren. Rgt. 316	22.2.44
404. Wengler, Maximilian	Oberst d.R., Kdr. Gren. Rgt. 366 123rd Swords 21.1.45	22.2.44
405. Mix, Walter	Hptm. d.R., Kdr. II./Gren. Rgt. 174	22.2.44
406. Benzin, Otto	Major, Fhr. Gren. Rgt. 89 + 3.7.44 as Major & Fhr. G. R. 531 in Bobruisk area	22.2.44

407. Forst, Werner	Gen.Lt., Kdr. 106. I.D.	22.2.44
408. Weidling, Helmuth	Gen. d. Art., Kom.Gen. XXXXI. Pz. Korps 115th Swords 28.11.44	22.2.44
409. Mieth, Friedrich	Gen.D.Inf., Kom.Gen. IV. A. K + 2.9.44 in Jassy pocket	1.3.44
410. Dr. Hohn, Hermann	Oberst, Fhr. 72. I.D. 109th Swords 31.10.44	1.3.44
411. Walther, Erich	Oberst, Kdr. Fsch. Jäg. Rgt. 4 131st Swords 1.2.45	2.3.44
412. Heilmann, Ludwig	Oberst, Kdr. Fsch. Jäg. Rgt. 3 67th Swords 15.5.44	2.3.44
413. Bühligen, Kurt	Major, Kdr. II./J.G. 2 "Richthofen" 88th Swords 14.8.44	2.3.44
414. Ademeit, Horst	Hptm., Kdr. 1./J.G. 54 + 8.8.44 as Major at Dünaburg	2.3.44
415. Krupinski, Walter	Oblt., Staffelkpt. 7./J.G. 52	2.3.44
416. Geiger, August	Hptm., Kdr. III./N. J.G. 1 + 29.9.43 over the Zuider See	2.3.44
417. Frank, Hans-Dieter	Hptm., Kdr. I./N. J.G. 1 + 27.9.43 over Hannover; Posthumously promoted to Major	2.3.44
418. Wiese, Johannes	Major, Kdr. I./J.G. 52	2.3.44
419. Seder, Reinhard	Major, Kdr. 1./J.G. 54	2.3.44
420. Hartmann, Erich	Lt., Staffelf. 9./J.G. 52 75th Swords 2.7.44 18th Diamonds 25.8.44	2.3.44
421. Behrend, Hermann Heinrich	Oberst, Kdr. Gren. Rgt. 154 (148th) Swords 26.4.45	6.3.44
422. Stühmer, Gustav	Ofw., Zugf. in 11./Gren. Rgt. 399 + 16.2.44 at Narva	6.3.44
423. v. Scholz, Fritz	SS-Brg. Fhr. & Gen. Major d. W-SS, Kdr. 11. SS-Freiw. Pz. Gren. Div. "Nordland" 85th Swords 8.8.44	12.3.44
424. Thulke, Willi	Hptm. d.R., Kdr. I./Gren. Rgt. 501	13.3.44
425. Rettemeier, Josef	Hptm., Kdr. Pz. Abt. 5	13.3.44
426. Frhr. v. Lüttwitz, Smilo	Gen.Lt., Kdr. 26. Pz.Div. 76th Swords 4.7.44	16.3.44
427. Bregenzer, Josef	Obstlt., Kdr. Gren. Rgt. 245 + 15.7.44 at Swinjucki (Poland) of wounds; Posthumously promoted to Oberst	17.3.44
428. Schulz, Friedrich	Gen.Lt., m.F.b. III. Pz. Korps 135th Swords 26.2.45	20.3.44
429. Mummert, Werner	Obstlt. d.R., Kdr. Pz. Gren. Rgt. 103 107th Swords 23.10.44	20.3.44
430. Jabs, Hans-Joachim	Hptm., Kdr. IV./N. J.G. 1	24.3.44
431. Jope, Bernhard	Major, Kmdr. K.G. 100	24.3.44

KNIGHT'S CROSS WITH OAK LEAVES

432. Schmitter, Wilhelm	Major, Staffelkpt. 15./K.G. 2 + 8.11.43 missing over London		24.3.44
433. Dr. Otte, Maximilian	Major, Kdr. II./S.G. 2 "Immelmann" + 20.5.44 in Jassy area		24.3.44
434. Bätcher, Hansgeorg	Major, Kdr. 1./K.G. 4 "General Wever"		24.3.44
435. Koßmala, Georg	Oberst, Kdr. Gren. Rgt. 6 + 5.3.45 missing at Oberglogau as Gen. Major & Kdr. 344. I.D.		26.3.44
436. Grüner, Georg	Hptm., Kdr. 1./Pz. Rgt. 2 + 11.3.44 in Kamenets-Podolski area; Posthumously promoted to Major		26.3.44
437. Tratt, Eduard	Hptm., Kdr. H./Z.G. 26 + 22.2.44 at Nordhausen (Harz); Posthumously promoted to Major		26.3.44
438. Petersen, Fntz	Wachtm., Geschützf. in 6./Flak-Rgt. 4		26.3.44
439. v. Senger & Etterlin, Fridolin	Gen. d. Pz.Tr., Kom.Gen. XIV. Pz. Korps		5.4.44
440. Müller, Ludwig	Gen.Lt., stv. Fhr. XXIX. A.K.		6.4.44
441. Wittchow v. Brese-Winiary, Heinz	Major, Fhr. Pz. Gren. Rgt. 108		6.4.44
442. Schwender, Herbert	Oberst, Kdr. Gren. Rgt. 45 + 22.9.44 at Walk (Baltic)		6.4.44
443. Kroh, Hans	Obstlt., Kdr. Fsch. Jäg. Rgt. 2 Simultaneously promoted to Oberst 96th Swords 12.9.44		6.4.44
444. Radusch, Günther	Obstlt., Kmdr. N. J.G. 5		6.4.44
445. Frießner, Johannes	Gen.D.Inf., Fhr. Armeeabt. Narwa		9.4.44
446. Grislawski, Alfred	Hptm., Staffelkpt. 1./J.G. 1		11.4.44
447. Rudorffer, Erich	Major, Kdr. II./J.G. 54 126th Swords 26.1.45		11.4.44
448. Lang, Emil	Oblt., Staffelkpt. 9./J.G. 54 + 3.9.44 as Hptm. & Kdr. II./J.G. 26 "Schlageter" at St. Trond		11.4.44
449. Kittel, Otto	Lt., Flugzeugfhr. in 1./J.G. 54 113th Swords 25.11.44		11.4.44
450. Schoenert, Rudolf	Major, Kdr. Nachtjagdgruppe 10		11.4.44
451. Herget, Wilhelm	Major, Kdr. I./N. J.G. 4		11.4.44
452. Hafner, Anton	Lt., Flugzeugf. in 6./J.G. 51 "Mölders"' + 17.10.44 as Oblt. & Staffelfhr. 6./J.G. 51 "Mölders" over Königsberg		11.4.44
453. Mayer, Dr. Johannes	Gen.Lt., Kdr. 329. I.D. 89th Swords 23.8.44		13.4.44
454. Hogrebe, Heinz	Hptm., Kdr. II./Gren. Rgt. 422		13.4.44
455. Geißler, Rudolf	Major, Kdr. Pi. Btl. 662 + 13.4.44 in Kowel; Posthumously promoted to Obstlt.		13.4.44

69

456. v. Vietinghoff gen. v. Scheel, Heinrich-Gottfried	Gen. Oberst, OB 10. Armee	16.4.44
457. v. Neindorff, Egon	Gen. Major., Kampfkdt. of Tarnopol + 15.4.44 during breakout from Tarnopol; Posthumously promoted to Gen.Lt.	17.4.44
458. Drewes, Wilhelm	Major, Kdr. 1./Pz. Gren. Rgt. 13	20.4.44
459. Schulz, Karl-Lothar	Oberst, Kdr. Fsch. Jäg. Rgt. 1 112th Swords 18.11.44	20.4.44
460. Schack, Günther	Lt., Staffelkpt. 9./J.G. 51 "Mölders"	20.4.44
461. Pollmann, Otto	Oblt. z. See d.R., Kdt. U-Jäger 2210	25.4.44
462. Stepp, Hans-Karl	Obstlt., Kmdr. S.G. 2 "Immelmann"	27.4.44
463. Möbus, Martin	Major, Kdr. I./S.G. 5 + 2.6.44 at Pori (Finland) accidentally	27.4.44
464. Wolf, Albin	Lt., Flugzeugf. in 6./J.G. 54 + 2.4.44 south-east of Pleskau; Posthumously promoted to Oblt.	27.4.44
465. Vinke, Heinz	Ofw., Flugzeugf. in II./N. J.G. 1 + 26.2.44 over the North Sea	27.4.44
466. Decker, Karl	Gen. Major, Kdr. 5. Pz.Div. (149th) Swords 26.4.45	4.5.44
467. Lorenz, Erich	Obstlt. d.R., Fhr. Gren. Rgt, 287	4.5.44
468. Eggemann, Wilhelm	Obstlt., Kdr. Gren. Rgt. 209	4.5.44
469. v. Lücken, Theodor	Hptm., Kdr. 1./Gren. Rgt. 686	7.5.44
470. Deßloch, Otto	Gen. Oberst, OB Luftflotte 4	10.5.44
471. Münster, Leopold	Lt., Staffelkpt. in 4./J.G. 3 "Udet" + 8.5.44 over Hildesheim	12.5.44
472. Sachsenheimer, Max	Major, Fhr. Jäg. Rgt. 75 132nd Swords 6.2.45	14.5.44
473. Hrustak, Martin	Ofw., Zugf. in 7./Gren. Rgt. 162 + 18.8.44 south-west of Narva, in main dressing station Bärbele, of wounds	14.5.44
474. Schwerdfeger, Johann	Ofw., Zugf. in 1./Jäg. Rgt. 228	14.5.44
475. Vogel, Emil	Gen.Lt., Kdr. 101. Jäger. Div.	14.5.44
476. Frhr. v. Waldenfels, Rudolf	Gen. Major, Kdr. 6. Pz.Div.	14.5.44
477. Müller, Fritz	Oberst, Kdr. Gren. Rgt. 208	14.5.44
478. Weimer, Killan	Major, Kdr. Luftw. Jäg. Rgt. 25	14.5.44
479. Schmidt, Walter	SS-Hptsturmf, Kdr. II./SS-Pz. Gren. – Rgt. 10 "Westland"	14.5.44
480. Ullrich, Karl	SS-Obersturmbannf, Kdr. SS-Pz. Gren. Rgt. 6 "Theodor Eicke"	14.5.44
481. Henze, Karl	Major, Kdr. I./S.G. 77	20.5.44

KNIGHT'S CROSS WITH OAK LEAVES

482. Marienfeld, Willy	Major d.R., Kdr. Gren. Rgt. 123 + 7.6.44 in Konstanza hospital, of wounds; Posthumously promoted to Obstlt. d.R.	25.5.44
483. Wegerer, Ferdinand	Feldw., Zugf. in 1./Pz. Gren. Rgt. 10	4.6.44
484. Hagemann, Wolf	Gen. Major, Kdr. 336. I.D.	4.6.44
485. Strippel, Hans	Ofw., Zugf. in 4./Pz. Rgt. 1	4.6.44
486. Hochbaum, Friedrich	Gen.Lt., Kdr. 34. I.D. + 28.1.55 in Soviet captivity; final post Gen.D.Inf. & Kom.Gen. XVIII. A.K.	4.6.44
487. Hell, Ernst-Eberhard	Gen. d. Art., Kom.Gen. VII. A.K.	4.6.44
488. Hitter, Alfons	Gen.Lt., Kdr. 206. I.D.	4.6.44
489. Pickert, Wolfgang	Gen.Lt., Kom-Gen. III. Flak-Korps	5.6.44
490. Weber, Gottfried	Gen. Major, Kdr. 12. Luftw. Feld-Div.	9.6.44
491. Niederländer, Horst	Obstlt., Kdr. Füs. Btl. 336 + 24.4. 44 in Sevastopol of wounds; Posthumously promoted to Oberst	9.6.44
492. Bonk, Georg	Feldw., Zugf. in 6./Gren. Rgt. 365	9.6.44
493. Pilarski, Hubert	Ofw., Zugf. in 8./Gren. Rgt. 948	9.6.44
494. Hoffmann, Ernst-Wilhelm	Obstlt., Kdr. Pz. Gren. Rgt. 12 Simultaneously promoted to Oberst	9.6.44
495. Zeller, Conrad	Hptm. d.R., Kdr. III./Gren. Rgt. 380 Simultaneously promoted to Major d.R.	9.6.44
496. Domaschk, Joachim	Major, Kdr. 1./Pz. Gren. Rgt. 103	11.6.44
497. Kaminsky, Emil	Ofw., Ord.Offz. 1. d. 1./Gren. Rgt. 446 + 5.7.44 on the Beresina at Bobruisk	12.6.44
498. Stolz, Edwin	Lt. d.R., Fhr. 14./Gren. Rgt. 353 + 17.5.44 in Polozk of wounds; Posthumously promoted to Oblt. d.R.	12.6.44
499. Petersen, Rudolf	Kapt. z. See, Führer der Schnellboote	13.6.44
500. Frhr. v. Mirbach, Götz	Kaptlt., Chef, 9. Schnellbootflottille	14.6.44
501. Diddens, Diddo	Oblt. d.R., Chef 1./St. Gesch. Brig. "Großdeutschland"	15.6.44
502. Sieler, Ernst	Gen.Lt., Kdr. 304. I.D.	24.6.44
503. Marcks, Erich	Gen. d. Art., Kom.Gen. LXXXIV. A.K. + 12.6.44 at St. Lo/Normandie	24.6.44
504. Brux, Albert	Oberst, Kdr. Pz. Gren. Rgt. 40	24.6.44
505. Kaubisch, Horst	Major, Kdr. I./S.G. 1 + 12.2.45 at Lebus	24.6.44
506. Stahl, Hendrik	Oblt., Staffelkpt. 8./S.G. 2 "Immelmann"	24.6.44
507. Schnaufer, Heinz-Wolfgang	Hptm., Kdr. IV./N. J.G. 1 84th Swords 30.7.44 21st Diamonds 16.10.44	24.6.44

508.	Glunz, Adolf	Lt., Flugzeugf. in 6./J.G. 26 "Schlageter"	24.6.44
509.	Skrzipek, Eduard	Hptm., Staffelkpt. 14. (Eis.)/K.G. 27 "Boelcke" + 25.2.45 shot down at Pilsen	24.6.44
510.	Egger, Reinhard	Obstlt., Fhr. Fschjäg. Rgt. 4	24.6.44
511.	Fitz, Josef-August	Major, Kdr. 1./Fsch. Pz. Gren. Rgt. 1 "HG"	24.6.44
512.	Huppertz, Herbert	Hptm., Kdr. III./J.G. 2 "Richthofen" + 8.6.44 over Caen; Posthumously promoted to Major	24.6.44
513.	Graf v. Kageneck, Clemens	Hptm., Kdr. schw. Pz. Abt. 503	26.6.44
514.	Kolb, Werner	Oberst d.R., Kdr. Gren. Rgt. 36	26.6.44
515.	Unrein, Martin	Gen. Major, Kdr. 14. Pz.Div.	26.6.44
516.	Abraham, Erich	Gen.Lt., Kdr. 76. I.D.	26.6.44
517.	Gräser, Fritz-Hubert	Gen.Lt., Kdr. 3. Pz. Gren. Div. (154th) Swords 8.5.45	26.6.44
518.	Dollmann, Friechich	Gen. Oberst, OB 7. Armee + 29.6.44 died in Normandy	1.7.44
519.	v. Rundstedt, Gerd	Gen. Feldm., OB West 133rd Swords 18.2.45	1.7.44
520.	Wulf, Hermann	Major, Kdr. III./Gren. Rgt. 76 (mot.)	3.7.44
521.	Buschenhagen, Erich	Gen.D.Inf., Kom.Gen. LH. A.K.	4.7.44
522.	Fabian, Heinz-Otto	Hptm., Kdr. II./Gren. Rgt. 361 (mot.)	9.7.44
523.	Palmgren, Karl	Korv. Kpt. d.R. z. V., Chef 38. Minensuchflottiffe	11.7.44
524.	Hoffmann, Heinrich	Korv. Kpt., Chef 5. Torpedobootflottille	11.7.44
525.	Lemm, Heinz-Georg	Major, Kdr. I./Füs. Rgt. 27 137th Swords 15.3.45	11.7.44
526.	Batz, Wilhelm	Hptm., Kdr. III./J.G. 52 (145th) Swords 21.4.45	20.7.44
527.	Kientsch, Willy	Oblt., Staffelkpt. 6./J.G. 27 + 29.1.44 at Würen/Belgium	20.7.44
528.	Strüning, Heinz	Hptm. d.R., Staffelkpt. 3./N. J.G. 1 + 24.12.44 as Hptm. & Staffelkpt. 9./N. J.G. 1 over Werl	20.7.44
529.	Weber, Karl-Heinz	Hptm., Staffelkpt. 7./J.G. 51 "Mölders" + 7.6.44 as Kdr. II./J.G. 1 south of Rouen	20.7.44
530.	Weßling, Otto	Obh., Staffelkpt. II./J.G. 3 "Udet" + 19.4.44 over Eschwege	20.7.44
531.	Frank, Rudolf	Ofw., Flugzeugf. in 2./N. J.G. 3 + 26.4.44 over Eindhoven; Posthumously promoted to Lt.	20.7.44
532.	Lamprecht, Herbert	Hptm., Kdr. le. Flak-Abt. 76	25.7.44
533.	v. Salisch, Wilhelm	Major, Fhr. Jäg. Rgt. 49 + 18.3.45 as Oberst & Kdr. Jäg. Rgt. 49, Gut Warnikam (near Balga, East Prussia)	27.7.44

KNIGHT'S CROSS WITH OAK LEAVES

534.	Kruse, Gerhard	Hptm. d.R., Fhr. II./Gren. Rgt. 48 April 45 in Ruhr pocket (badly wounded) missing as Major d.R. & Btl. Kdr.	27.7.44
535.	Carius, Otto	Lt. d.R., Fhr. 2./schw. Pz. Abt. 502	27.7.44
536.	v. Oppeln-Bronikowski, Hermann	Oberst, Kdr. Pz. Rgt. 22 142nd Swords 17.4.45	28.7.44
537.	Demme, Rudolf	Oberst, Kdr. Pz. Gren. Rgt. 59	28.7.44
538.	Schulze, Paul	Major, Kdr. Pz. Abt. 21	28.7.44
539.	v. Tippelskirch, Kurt	Gen.D.Inf., stellv. OB 4. Armee	30.7.44
540.	Mickley, Hovert	Hptm., Kdr. 1./Gren. Rgt. 4 + 30.12.44 as Major & Kdr. II./Pz. Gren. Rgt. "Führer-Begleit-Brigade" at Bastogne; Posthumously promoted to Obstlt.	4.8.44
541.	Wesche, Willy	Oberst, Kdr. Gren. Rgt. 427 + 27.6.44 at Bobruisk	6.8.44
542.	Hilpert, Carl	Gen.D.Inf., Kom.Gen. I. A.K. + 24.12.48 in Soviet captivity near Moscow as Gen. Ob.; final post OB Hrsgr. Kurland	8.8.44
543.	Nickel, Heinrich	Gen. Major, Kdr. 342. I.D.	8.8.44
544.	Schille, Kurt	Major, Kdr. Pi. Btl. 24	8.8.44
545.	Strahammer, Martin	Oberst, Kdr. Gren. Rgt. 146 + 2.5.45 in Italy as Gen. Major & Kdr. 114. Jäg. Div.	11.8.44
546.	Kloskowski, Karl	SS-Obersturmf., Fhr. 7./SS-Pz. Rgt. 2 "Das Reich" + 23.4.45 in the Harz	11.8.44
547.	Simons, Gerhard	Oblt. d.R., Fhr. Stabsbttr./Art.Rgt. 240 & Rgt. Nachr. Offz.	11.8.44
548.	Wünsche, Max	SS-Ob. Sturmbannf., Kdr. SS-Pz. Rgt. 12 "Hitlerjugend"	11.8.44
549.	Kraiß, Dietrich	Gen.Lt., Kdr. 352. I.D. + 2.8.44 at St. Lo in Normandy	11.8.44
550.	Bacherer, Rudolf	Oberst d.R., Kdr. Gren. Rgt. 1049	11.8.44
551.	v. Aulock, Andreas	Oberst, Festungskdt. St Malo	16.8.44
552.	Siggel, Hermann	Obstlt., Kdr. Gren. Rgt. 172	16.8.44
553.	Pick, Gerhard	Major, Kdr. Gren. Rgt. 577 simultaneously promoted to Obstlt.	19.8.44
554.	Macher, Heinz	SS-Oberstumf., Chef 16. (Pi.)/SS-Pz. – Gren. Rgt. 3 "Deutschland"	19.8.44
555.	Warrelmann, Hinrich	Oberst, Kdr. Gren. Rgt. 502	19.8.44
556.	Wulf, Rudolf	Oberst, Kdr. Gren. Rgt. 422	19.8.44
557.	Schulze, Werner	Oberst d.R., Kdr. Gren. Rgt. 551	23.8.44
558.	Melzer, Walter	Gen.Lt., Kdr. 252. I.D.	23.8.44

#	Name	Details	Date
559.	Hinz, Bruno	SS-Obersturmf., Chef 2./SS-Pz. Gren. – Rgt. 38 "Götz v. Berlichingen" & Fhr. of a Kgr. Rgt. 38	23.8.44
560.	Mäder, Hellmuth	Oberst, Fhr. Lehr-Brig. Nord d. H.Gr. Waffenschule Nord & Kampfkdt. v. Schaulen 143rd Swords 18.4.45	27.8.44
561.	Holste, Rudolf	Oberst, Fhr. 4. Kav. Brigade	27.8.44
562.	Pflugbeil, Kurt	Gen. d. Flg., OB Luftflotte 1	27.8.44
563.	Bittrich, Wühelm	SS-Obergruppenf. & Gen. d. W-SS, Kom.Gen. II. SS-Pz. -Korps (153rd) Swords 6.5.45	28.8.44
564.	Meindl, Eugen	Gen. d. Fsch. Tr., Kom.Gen. II. Fsch. Korps (155th) Swords 8.5.45	31.8.44
565.	Flörke, Hermann	Gen.Lt., Kdr. 14. I.D.	2.9.44
566.	Bleber, Martin	Oberst, Fhr. Div. Gruppe 86	2.9.44
567.	Klein, Hermann	Hptm. d.R., Rgt. Adj. Gren. Rgt. 551 + 18.8.44 at Ergli/Courland missing; Posthumously promoted to Major d.R.	2.9.44
568.	Gansmeler, Jakob	Major d.R., Kdr. Div. Füs. Btl. 212 + 8.8.44 at Raseinen (Baltic); Posthumously promoted to Obstlt.	2.9.44
569.	Misera, Walter	Major, Fhr. Div. Gruppe 95	2.9.44
570.	Bock, Friedrich-Wilhelm	SS-Oberf., Kdr. 9. SS-Pz.Div. "Hohenstaufen"	2.9.44
571.	Frhr. v. Lüttwitz, Heinrich	Gen.Lt., Kdr. 2. Pz.Div. (157th) Swords 9.5.45	3.9.44
572.	Greiner, Heinz	Gen.Lt., Kdr. 362. I.D.	5.9.44
573.	Sonntag, Christian	Obstlt., Kdr. Gren. Rgt. 248 + 3.4.45 as Oberst, Kdr. Festung Le Verdon (Gironde-South)	5.9.44
574.	Pfeifer, Hellmuth	Gen.Lt., Kdr. 65. I.D. + 22.4.45 as Gen.Lt. & Kdr. 65. I.D. at Finale (Italy)	5.9.44
575.	Flinzer, Dr. Rudolf	Oberst d.R., Kdr. Gren. Rgt. 317	5.9.44
576.	Neitzel, Walter	Major, Kdr. 1./Gren. Rgt. 409 + 2.9.44 as a result of wounds received on 26.8.44; Posthumously promoted to Obstlt.	5.9.44
577.	Seuss, Richard	Oblt. (MA) d.R., Chef Mar. Küst. Bttr. "Ile de Cezembre" (M. A.A. 608)	2.9.44
578.	Lasch, Otto	Gen.Lt., Kdr. 349. I.D.	10.9.44
579.	Weber, Alois	Oberst, Kdr. Gren. Rgt. 61	10.9.44
580.	Lindemann, Gerhard	Gen. Major, m.F.b. 361. I.D.	10.9.44
581.	Bölter, Johann	Lt., Fhr. 1./schw. Pz. Abt. 502	10.9.44
582.	Reimar, Gustav	Hptm., Kdr. Feldersatz-Btl. 76 + 23.3.45 as Major & Kdr. 11./Pz. G. R. 114 south of Budapest at Kisber (Hungary)	10.9.44

KNIGHT'S CROSS WITH OAK LEAVES

583. Kähler, Otto	Kont. Adm., Seekdt. Festung Brest		15.9.44
584. Pietzonka, Erich	Oberst, Kdr. Fsch. Jäg. Rgt. 7		16.9.44
585. Gericke, Walter	Major, Kdr. Fsch. Jäg. Rgt. 11		17.9.44
586. Trettner, Heinrich	Gen Major, Kdr. 4. Fschjg. Div.		17.9.44
587. Thurner, Hans	Hptm., Kdr. I./K.G. 6 + 11.6.44 over England		17.9.44
588. Zorner, Paul	Hptm., Kdr. III./N. J.G. 5		17.9.44
589. v. d. Mosel, Hans	Gen. Major, Chef d. Stabes Festg. Brest		18.9.44
590. Haen, Rudolf	Major, Kdr. Pz. Abt. 103 + 9.5.45 shot in American captivity as Obstlt. i.G. Ia 14. Armee		21.9.44
591. Scholz, Helmut	SS-Obersturmf, Fhr. II./SS-Freiw. – Pz. Gren. Rgt. 49 "De Ruyter"		21.9.44
592. Schury, Otto	Oberst, Kdr. Jäg. Rgt. 229		21.9.44
593. Marcks, Werner	Gen. Major, Kdr. 1. Pz.Div.		21.9.44
594. Boege, Ehrenfried-Oskar	Gen.D.Inf., Kom.Gen. XXXXIII. A.K.		21.9.44
595. Becker, Hellmuth	SS-Oberf., Kdr. 3. SS-Pz.Div. "Totenkopf' + 9.5.45 shot in Soviet captivity at Swerdlowsk, final post SS-Brigadef. & Gen. Major d. W-SS		21.9.44
596. Mühlenkamp, Johannes-Rudolf	SS-Standartenf., Fhr. 5. SS-Pz.Div. "Wiking"		21.9.44
597. Schack, Friedrich	Gen.Lt., Kdr. 272. I.D. August		21.9.44
598. König, Ernst	Oberst, Kdr. Gren. Rgt. 12		21.9.44
599. Philipp, Ernst	Major, Pz. Offz. in Stab AOK 8		30.9.44
600. Kretzschmar, Wolfgang	Obstlt., Kdr. Jäg. Rgt. 24 (L) 121st Swords 12.1.45		30.9.44
601. Meyer, Otto	SS-Ob. Sturmbannf, Kdr. SS-Pz. Rgt. 9 "Hohenstaufen", + 24.8.44 at the Seine crossing at Duclair		30.9.44
602. Scharnagel, Hermann	Major, Kdr. Pi. Btl. 173 + 8.5.44 at Sevastopol; Posthumously promoted to Obstlt.		30.9.44
603. Sauer, Konrad	Lt. d.R., Fhr. 1./St. Gesch. Brig. 393		30.9.44
604. Burg, Jörg	Oblt. d.R., Chef 7./Pz. Rgt. "Großdeutschland" + 21.8.44 at a field dressing station, Schaulen, of wounds; Posthumously promoted to Hptm. d.R.		4.10.44
605. Behnke, Gerhard	Major, Kdr. St. Gesch. Brig. 322		4.10.44
606. Kunert, Gerhard	Uffz., Gruppenf. in 6./Pz. Gren. Rgt. 33 + 31.8.44 Mitau		4.10.44
607. Kohler, Wilhelm	Hptm., Ord.Offz. d. Kampfgr. 9. Pz.Div.		4.10.44
608. Reinefarth, Heinz	SS-Gruppenf. & Gen.Lt. d. Polizei, Kdr. Kampfgr. in Korpsgr. v. d. Bach		30.9.44
609. Straube, Erich	Gen.D.Inf., Kom.Gen. LXXIV. A.K.		30.9.44
610. Graf v. Rittberg, Georg	Gen. Major, Kdr. 88. I.D. simultaneously promoted to Gen.Lt.		10.10.44

611. v. Kessel, Mortimer	Gen.Lt., Kdr. 20. Pz.Div.	16.10.44
612. Koch, Willi	Ofw., Fhr. 6./Gren. Rgt. 32 + 29.4.45 as Fhr. 3./Alarm-Btl. 102 in Berlin, near Ferch-Leunen railway station	16.10.44
613. Strohm, Friedrich	Obstlt., Kdr. G. R. 470 + 24.9.44 at Lyck (East Prussia) (Rückkämpfer) died of wounds; Posthumously promoted to Oberst	18.10.44
614. Krancke, Theodor	Admiral, OB Marine-Gruppenkdo. West	18.10.44
615. Jakob, Georg	Major, Kmdr. S.G. 10	30.9.44
616. Schuck, Walter	Lt., Flugzeugf. in 9./J.G. 5	30.9.44
617. Frhr. v. d. Heydte, Dr. Friedrich August	Obstlt., Kdr. Fsch. Jäg. Rgt. 6	30.9.44
618. Bauer, Herbert	Hptm., Kdr. I./S.G. 2 "Immelmann"	30.9.44
619. Kieslich, Franz	Hptm., Kdr. III./S.G. 77	10.10.44
620. Lukesch, Dieter	Hptm., Staffelkpt. 9./K.G. 76	10.10.44
621. Bleckwenn, Wilhelm	Oberst, Kdr. Gren. Rgt, 487	18.10.44
622. Jüttner, Arthur	Oberst, Kdr. Gren. Rgt. 532 141st' Swords 5.4.45	18.10.44
623. Richert, Johann-Georg	Gen.Lt., Kdr. 35. I.D. + 30.1.46 hanged in Minsk	18.10.44
624. Gust, Werner	Major, Fhr. Gren. Rgt. 405	18.10.44
625. Kreuzinger, Othmar	Oblt. d.R., Chef 4./Pz. Aufkl. Abt. 19 + 13.9.44 in the area of Warsaw; Posthumously promoted to Hptm. d.R.	18.10.44
626. Weller, Franz	Oberst, Kdr. Jäg. Rgt. 54	23.10.44
627. Thieme, Carl	Major, Fhr. Pz. Gren. Rgt. 111 (156th) Swords 9.5.45	23.10.44
628. Stock, Hans-Christian	Hptm., Chef 2./Pz.Jäg. Abt. 152 + 12.1.45 as Hptm. & Kdr. Pz.Jäg. Abt. 152 at Makranz, south of Kaschau, southern Slovakia; Posthumously promoted to Major	23.10.44
629. Schubert, Gustav	Oblt., Flugzeugf. in 9./S.G. 1 + 20.1.45 east of Hohensalza	24.10.44
630. Schalanda, Hans	Oblt., Staffelkpt. 3./S.G. 1 + 26.3.45 south-west of Küstrin as Hptm.	24.10.44
631. Leicht, Helmut	Major, Kdr. ILI./S.G. 10 + 26.6.44 Vitebsk	24.10.44
632. Tonne, Günther	Major, Kmdr. S. K.G. 10 + 15.7.43 shot down over Reggio (Italy)	24.10.44
633. Reuter, Benno	Stabsfeldw., Fhr. 6./Jäg. Rgt. 49	28.10.44
634. Ecker, Paul	Major, Kdr. 1./Pz. Gren. Rgt. 9	28.10.44
635. Frhr. v. Hauser. Paul	Obstlt., Kdr. Pz. Gren. Lehr-Rgt. 901	28.10.44

636. Schultz, Fritz-Rudolf	Major d.R., Fhr. Pz. Rgt. 35	28.10.44
637. Busse, Heinrich	Obstlt., Kdr. Gren. Rgt. 203	28.10.44
638. Brunner, Eduard	Hptm., Kdr. 1./Gren. Rgt. 62	28.10.44
639. Simon, Max	SS-Gruppenf & Gen.Lt. d. W-SS, Kdr. 16. SS-Pz. Gren. Div. "RFSS"	28.10.44
640. Blaskowitz, Johannes	Gen. Oberst, OB H.Gr.G (146th) Swords 25.4.45	29.10.44
641. Hilgemann, Klaus	Major, Kdr. II./Gren. Rgt. 426	29.10.44
642. Friedrich, Gerhard	Obstlt., Kdr. Pz. Gren. Rgt. 13	3.11.44
643. Felzmann, Maximilian	Gen.Lt., Kdr. Korpsabteilung E	3.11.44
644. Eckhardt, Johann-Heinrich	Gen.Lt., Kdr. 211. I.D. + 15.5.45 died of wounds in in Soviet captivity	3.11.44
645. Hartmann, Werner	Kapt. z. See, Fhr. d. U-Boote Mittelmeer, vorher Kdt. "U 198"	5.11.44
646. Weiß, Walter	Gen. Oberst, OB 2. Armee	5.11.44
647. v. Zangen, Gustav-Adolf	Gen.D.Inf., m.F.b. 15. Armee	5.11.44
648. Ruge, Gerd	Major, Fhr. Pz. Gren. Rgt. 128	16.11.44
649. Weidenbrück, Wilhelm	Major, Kdr. Pz. Abt. d. Pz. Brig. 104	16.11.44
650. Dörner, Helmut	SS-Standartenf., Kdr. SS-Pz. Gren. Rgt. 8 129th Swords 1.2.45	16.11.44
651. Krügel, Albrecht	SS-Obersturmbannf., Kdr. SS-Freiw. – Pz. Gren. Rgt. 24 "Danmark" + 16.3.45 at Altdamm railway station, Stettin	16.11.44
652. Badorrek, Emil	Major, Staffelkpt. 4./Fernaufkl. Gr. II + 26.12.44 as Major, Kdr. Fernaufkl. Gr. 3 over Cracow	18.11.44
653. Mietusch, Klaus	Major, Kdr. III./J.G. 26 "Schlageter" + 17.9.44 over Rath (Belgium)	18.11.44
654. Meyer, Heinz	Hptm. d.R., Fhr. III./Fsch. Jäg. Rgt. 15	18.11.44
655. Antrup, Wilhelm	Obstlt., Kmdr. K.G. 55	18.11.44
656. Höfer, Heinrich	Major, Kdr. II./K.G. 55	18.11.44
657. Schirmer, Gerhart	Obstlt., Kdr. Fsch. Jäg. Rgt. 16 (Ost)	18.11.44
658. Seidemann, Hans	Gen.Lt., Kom.Gen. VIII. Flg. Korps	18.11.44
659. Hoßfeld, Hans	Korv. Kpt. (MA), Kdr. Mar. Art. Abt. 531 + 19.11.44 at Sworbe, Riga Bucht	25.11.44
660. Dörnbrack, Werner	Major, Kdr. I./S.G. 4	25.11.44
661. Pölz, Hubert	Hptm., m.F.b. I./S.G. 151	25.11.44
662. Witzig, Rudolf	Major, Kdr. 1./Fsch. Pi. Rgt. 21	25.11.44
663. Eder, Georg-Peter	Hptm., Staffelkpt. 6./J.G. 1	25.11.44
664. Rennecke, Rudolf	Major, Fhr. Fschjäg. Rgt. 1	25.11.44

#	Name	Details	Date
665.	Dommeratzky, Otto	Lt., Staffelfhr. in 6./S.G. 2 "Immelmann" + 13.10.44 at Mährisch-Weißkirchen	25.11.44
666.	Kennel, Karl	Hptm., Kdr. II./S.G. 2 "'Immelmann"	25.11.44
667.	Michalski, Gerhard	Major, Kmdr. J.G. 4	25.11.44
668.	Bremer, Gerhard	SS-Sturmbannf., Kdr. SS-Pz. Aufkl. - Abt. 12 "Hitlerjugend"	26.11.44
669.	v. Bismarck, Klaus	Major, Kdr. Gren. Rgt. 4	26.11.44
670.	Phleps, Arthur	SS-Obergruppenf. & Gen. d. W-SS, Kom.Gen. V. SS-Geb. Korps & Höh. SS- & Pol. Fhr. as well as Dt. Befehlsh. in Siebenbürgen + 21.9.44 in Siebenbürgen	24.11.44
671.	Wöhler, Otto	Gen.D.Inf., OB. 8. Armee	28.11.44
672.	Reymann, Hellmuth	Gen.Lt., Kdr. 11. I.D.	28.11.44
673.	Ehle, Curt	Major, Fhr. Pz. Brig. 102	29.11.44
674.	Maier, Kurt	Hptm., Staffelkpt. 9./K.G. 1 "Hindenburg"	6.12.44
675.	Sattler, Georg	Obh., Staffelkpt. 1./Lehr-Geschw. 1 + 30.8.44 shot down	6.12.44
676.	Hahm, Walther	Gen.Lt., Kdr. 389. I.D.	9.12.44
677.	Braun, Christian	Ofw., MG-Zugf. in 8./Gren. Rgt. 308	9.12.44
678.	Arndt, Fritz	Feldw., Zugf. in 1./Pz. Pi. Btl. 32	9.12.44
679.	Engel, Gerhard	Gen. Major, Kdr. 12. Volks-Gren. Div.	11.12.44
680.	Wagner, Jürgen	SS-Brigadef. & Gen. Major d. W-SS, Kdr. 4. SS-Freiw. Pz. Gren. Brig. "Nederland" + 5.4.47 hanged in Belgrade	11.12.44
681.	Jakob, Friedrich	Major, Fhr. Gren. Rgt. 1149	18.12.44
682.	Hoppe, Harry	Gen.Lt., Kdr. 278. I.D.	18.12.44
683.	Crasemann, Eduard	Gen,. Major, Kdr. 26. Pz.Div. + 29.4.50 in British captivity at Werl; final post Gen.Lt. m.F.b. XII. SS-K.	18.12.44
684.	Kuffner, Andreas	Hptm., Staffelkpt. 10. (Pz.)/S.G. 3 + 30.4.45 over Sulte airfield, Schwerin, as Kdr. I(Pz.)/S.G. 9	20.12.44
685.	Biermeier, Fritz	SS-Sturmbannf., Kdr. 11./SS-Pz. Rgt. 3 "Totenkopf" + 11.10.44 in Modlin	26.12.44
686.	Klatt, Paul	Gen.Lt., Kdr. 3. Geb. Div.	26.12.44
687.	Wisliceny, Günther	SS-Obersturmbannf., Kdr. SS-Pz. Gren. - Rgt. 3 "Deutschland" (151st) Swords 6.5.45	26.12.44
688.	Weidinger, Otto	SS-Obersturmbannf., Kdr. SS-Pz. Gren. -Rgt. 4 "Der Führer" (150th) Swords 6.5.45	26.12.44

1945

689. Baron v. Behr, Heinrich	Oberst, Kdr. Pz. Gren. Rgt. 200	9.1.45
690. Frhr. v. Mühlen, Kurt-Hermann	Gen. Major, Kdr. 559. Volks-Gren. Div.	9.1.45
691. Lucht, Walther	Gen. d. Art., Kom.Gen. LXVI. A.K.	9.1.45
692. Frhr. v. Gravenreuth, Sigmund-Ulrich	Obstlt., Kmdr. K.G. 30 + 16.10.44 shot down over Breslau	9.1.45
693. Gröschke, Kurt	Obstlt., Kdr. Fsch. Jäg. Rgt. 15	9.1.45
694. Herzog, Kurt	Gen. d. Art., Kom.Gen. XXXVIII. A.K. + 1948 in Soviet captivity	12.1.45
695. Eisele, Alois	Major, Kdr. III./Gren. Rgt. 61	12.1.45
696. Riedesel Frhr. zu Eisenbach, Volprecht	Obstlt., Kmdr. K.G. 54 + 9.2.45 over Idstein, Hesse; Posthumously promoted to Oberst	14.1.45
697. Brendel, Joachim	Hptm., Kdr. III./J.G. 51 "Mölders"	14.1.45
698. Hasse, Wilhelm	Gen.D.Inf., Kom.Gen. II. A.K. + 9.5.45 in Camp Pisek, in Soviet captivity; final post OB 17. Armee	14.1.45
699. Gollert-Hansen, Detlef	Rittm., Kdr. 11./Reiter-Rgt. 31 + 6.3.45 in Plattensee area	14.1.45
700. Breger, Claus	Hptm., Kdr. 1./Füs. Rgt. 27 + 17.12.44 died of wounds in Aachen area	14.1.45
701. Streckenbach, Bruno	SS-Gruppenf. & Gen.Lt. d. W-SS, Kdr. 19. Waffen-Gren. Div. der SS (lett. Nr. 2)	16.1.45
702. Reinwald, Max	Oberst d.R., Kdr. Gren. Rgt. 19 "List"	18.1.45
703. Henze, Richard	Obstlt. d.R., Kdr. Gren. Rgt. 489	18.1.45
704. Risse, Walther	Gen.Lt., Kdr. 225. I.D.	18.1.45
705. Löhr, Alexander	Gen. Oberst, OB H.Gr.E + 26.2.47 shot in Belgrade	20.1.45
706. Schmidhuber, Gerhard	Gen. Major, Kdr. 13. Pz.Div. + 11.2.45 during attempted breakout from Budapest	21.1.45
707. Schöning, Wilhelm	Major d.R., Fhr. Pz. Gren. Rgt. 66	21.1.45
708. Kündiger, Herbert	Obstlt., Fhr. of a Kgr. d. 271. I.D. in Festung Budapest	21.1.45
709. Henze, Albert	Gen. Major, Kdr. Gruppe Henze (Feld-Div. 21 (L)	21.1.45
710. Reuter, Erich	Gen. Major, Kdr. 46. I.D.	21.1.45
711. Dahlmann, Kurt	Major, Kdr. N.S.G. 20	24.1.45
712. Plenzat, Kurt	Lt., Flugzeugf. in 2./S.G. 2 "Immelmann"	24.1.45
713. Rollwage, Herbert	Lt., Staffelkpt. 5./J.G. 53	24.1.45
714. Schäfer, Max	SS-Standartenf., Korps-Pi. Fhr. III. (germ.) SS-Pz. Korps	25.1.45

ELITE OF THE THIRD REICH

715. Pröll, Karl	Obstlt., Kdr. Pz. Gren. Rgt. 35	25.1.45
716. Böhlke, Hellmuth	Gen.Lt., Kdr. 334. I.D.	25.1.45
717. Süß, Walter	Ofw., Zugf. in Stabskp./Gren. Rgt. 273 + missing in Courland, early March 1945	25.1.45
718. Spindler, Wilhelm	Major, Fhr. Geb.Jäg. Rgt. 99 Simultaneously promoted to Obstlt.	31.1.45
719. Arndt, Karl	Gen.Lt., Kdr. 359. I.D.	1.2.45
720. Wahl, Kurt	SS-Sturmbannf., Kdr. SS-Pz. Auflkl. - Abt. 17 "Götz v. Berlichingen"	1.2.45
721. Rumohr, Joachim	SS-Brigadef. & Gen. Major d. W-SS, Kdr. 8. SS-Kav. Div. "Florian Geyer" + 11.2.45 in Budapest	1.2.45
722. Zehender, August	SS-Brigadef. & Gen. Major d. W-SS, Kdr. 22. SS-Freiw. Kav. Div. + 11.2.45 in Budapest	1.2.45
723. Pfeffer-Wildenbruch, Karl	SS-Obergruppenf. & Gen. d. W-SS, Kom.Gen. IX. Waffen-Geb. Korps d. SS	1.2.45
724, Dahl, Walther	Major, Kmdr. J.G. 300 Simultaneously promoted to Obstlt.	1.2.45
725. Roßmann, Karl	Major, Kdr. Fsch. Pz. Rgt. 1 "Hermann Göring"	1.2.45
726. Jansa, Ernst	Oberst, Kdr. Flak-Sturm-Rgt. 12	1.2.45
727. Harder, Jürgen	Major, Kmdr. J.G. 11 + 17.2.45 over Berlin-Straugberg	1.2.45
728. Vincon, Otto	Major d.R., Kdr. I./Gren. Rgt. 460 + 13.4.45 as Mjor & Kdr. Gren. Rgt. 466 missing at Wildbach, Black Forest	5.2.45
729. Sander, Joachim	Oberst, Kdr. Pz. Rgt. 31 + 3.11.44 in Goldap	5.2 . 45
730. Graf v. Plettenberg, Georg	Rittm., Kdr. schw. Kav. Abt. 4	5.2.45
731. Frhr. v. Weichs, Maximilian	Gen. Feldm., OB Südost (H.Gr.F)	5.2.45
732. Osterhold, Wilhelm	Obstlt., Kdr. Gren. Rgt. 48	10.2.45
733. Jauer, Georg	Gen.Lt., Kdr. 20. Pz. Gren. Div.	10.2.45
734. Oesterwitz, Karl-Heinz	Obstk., Kdr. Jäger-Rgt. 2 "Brandenburg"	10.2.45
735. Wittmann, Herbert	Major, Kdr. II./K.G. 53 "Legion Condor"	11.2.45
736. Schramm, Herbert	Oblt., Staffelkpt. 5./J.G. 27 + 1.12.43 over Eupen; Posthumously promoted to Hptm.	11.2.45
737. France, Anton-Otto	Hptm., Kdr. Heeres-Pz.Jäg. Abt. 743 + 8.3.45 in Silesia	7.2.45
738. Müller, Anton	Hptm., Kdr. II./Gren. Rgt. 503	14.2.45
739. Zorn, Eduard	Oberst i.G., Fhr. 189. I.D. + 4.2.45 at Colmar in Alsace; Posthumously promoted to Gen. Major	16.2.45

KNIGHT'S CROSS WITH OAK LEAVES

740. Schülke, Willi	Hptm., Kdr. III./Ski-Jäger-Rgt. 1 + 10.3.45 at Großneukirch, Upper Silesia; Posthumously promoted to Major	16.2.45
741. Blumentritt, Günther	Gen. d. Inf, m.F.b. 25. Armee	18.2.45
742. Heichele, Josef	Major, Kdr. Füs. Btl. 129	17.2.45
743. Gebhardt, Georg	Obstlt. d.R., Kdr. Sturm-Rgt. 195	19.2.45
744. Knebel, Ernst	Oberst, Kdr. Armee-Waffenschule Pz. AOK 3 + 24.1.45 badly wounded in East Prussia, 13.3.45 died in hospital; posthumously promoted to Gen.Maj.	19.2.45
745. Klasing, Fritz	Oberst d.R., Kdr. Gren. Rgt. 232	19.2.45
746. Blaurock, Edmund	Gen. Major, Kdr. 56 I.D.	19.2.45
747. Schulz, Ludwig	Gen. Major, Kdr. d. Kampfgr. d. Luftkriegsschule 5	19.2.45
748. Hermichen, Rolf	Major, Kdr. I./J.G. 11	19.2.45
749. Krebs, Hans	Gen.D.Inf., Chef d. Gen. St. H. GR. B + 2./3.5.45 suicide in Berlin; final post Chef des Gen. Stabes des Heeres	20.2.45
750. Ewert, Heinz-Martin	Major, Abschnittskdt. in Festung Posen	22.2.45
751. v. Rappard, Fritz-Georg	Gen.Lt., Kdr. 7. I.D. + 29.1.46 hanged in Welikije-Luki	24.2.45
752. Jakwert, Josef	Lt., Zugf. in 2./Pz.Jäg. Abt. 1562	24.2.45
753. Warschnauer, Horst	Hptm. d.R., Kdr. Pz. Pi. Btl. "Großdeutschland"	24.2.45
754. v. Rohr, Hans-Babo	Lt. 5 Fhr. 2./Pz. Rgt. 25 + 14.2.45 at Konitz, West Prussia Posthumously promoted to Oblt.	24.2.45
755. Krag, Ernst-August	SS-Sturmbannf., Kdr. SS-Pz. Aufkl. Abt. 2 "Das Reich"	28.2.45
756. Schmelzer, Heinrich	SS-Hptsturmf. d.R., Chef 1./SS Pz. Pi. Btl. 2 "Das Reich"	28.2.45
757. Kempas, Traugott	Hptm., Kdr. 1./Gren. Rgt. 176 + 13.3.45 as Major, Kdr. 1./Gren. Rgt. 176 in East Prussia at Königsberg	28.2.45
758. Kullmer, Arthur	Gen.Lt., Kdr. 558. Volks-Gren. Div. + 28.3.53 in Soviet captivity	28.2.45
759. Pössinger, Michael	Major, Kdr. 1./Gren. Rgt. 1123	28.2.45
760. Pollmann, Othmar	Major, Div. Adj. 95. I.D.	28.2.45
761. v. Baer, Bern	Obstlt. i.G., Chef d. Stabes Fsch. Pz. Korps "HG"	28.2.45
762. Reichardt, Hans	Oberst, Kdr. Kampfgruppe Steinau d. 408. I.D. + 2.2.45 at Steinau, Oder	5.3.45
763. Ebeling, Werner	Obstlt., Kclr. Gren. Rgt. 154	5.3.45
764. Niehoff, Hermann	Gen.Lt., Kdr. 371. I.D. (147th) Swords 26.4.45	5.3.45

765. Götz, Heinrich	Gen. Major, Kdr. 21. I.D.		5.3.45
766. v. Bünau, Rudolf	Gen.D.Inf., Kom.Gen. XI. A.K.		5.3.45
767. Karczewski, Bruno	Major, Fhr. Gren. Rgt. 176 Simultaneously promoted to Obstlt.		5.3.45
768. Schneider, Dipl.-Ing. Erich	Gen.Lt., Kdr. 14. I.D.		6.3.45
769. Welter, Kurt	Oblt., Staffelkpt. 10./N. J.G. 11		11.3.45
770. Renschler, Helmut	Hptm. d.R., Chef 1./Art.Rgt. 5		11.3.45
771. Dr. Rust, Wolfgang	Hptm., Kdr. II./Gren. Rgt. 11		11.3.45
772. Sixt, Friedrich	Gen.Lt., Kdr. 5. Jäg. Div.		11.3.45
773. Witschel, Kurt	Oblt., Fhr. 9./Jäg. Rgt. 28		11.3.45
774. Betzel, Clemens	Gen.Lt., Kdr. 4. Pz Div. + 27.3.45 in Danzig		11.3.45
775. Rogalski, Franz	Lt. d.R., Adj. II./Gren. Rgt. 45		11.3.45
776. Grimminger, Johannes	Hptm. d.R., Kdr. 11./Pz. Gren. Rgt. 192 + 16.4.45 at Forst, Lausitz, as Major d.R. & Kdr., Fhr. Pz. Gren. Rgt. 192		11.3.45
777. Kutschkau, Ernst	Ofw., Fhr. 6./Gren. Rgt. 3 + 4.2.47 in Belgian captivity, camp Châtelinieau		11.3.45
778. Aghta, Egon	Hptm. (W.), Fhr. eines Sprengkdos. in Berlin area (Luftgaukdo. IH) + 2.5.45 in attempted breakout from Berlin-Spandau		12.3.45
779. Schröder, Wilhelm	Oberst, Kdr. Kampfgr. Schröder in 408. I.D.		13.3.45
780. Becker, Karl-Heinz	Obstlt., Kdr. Fsch. Jäg. Rgt. 5 Simultaneously promoted to Oberst		12.3.45
781. Rökker, Heinz	Hptm., Staffelkpt. 2./N. J.G. 2		12.3.45
782. Weiß, Robert	Hptm., Kdr. III./J.G. 54 + 29.12.44 shot down over Lingen a. d. Ems		12.3.45
783. Pötschke, Werner	SS-Sturmbannf., Kdr. 1./SS. -Pz. Rgt. 1 "LSSAH" + 21.3.45 at Veszprem, Hungary		15.3.45
784. Matern, Alfred	Ofw., Zugf. in 5./Füs. Rgt. 22 + March 45 in East Prussia		16.3.45
785. Vogt, Fritz	SS-Hauptsturmf., Kdr. I./SS-Gren. Rgt. 23 "Norge"' + 3.4.45 as SS-Sturmbannf., Kdr. SS-Pz-Aufkl. Abt. 5 "Wiking" in Graz, of wounds		16.3.45
786. Jaeger, Karl-Heinz	Hptm. d.R., Fhr. Gren. Rgt. 448		16.3.45
787. Wandrey, Max	Major d.R., Kdr. II./Jäg. Rgt. 1 "Brandenburg" + 21.2.45 of wounds, Kruschwitz, Saxony		16.3.45
788. Engelien, Hans	Obstlt., Kdr. Pz. Gren. Rgt. 25 + (9.5.45) missing in Courland following the surrender		16.3.45
789. Ruhl, Heinrich	Major, Kdr. Füs. Btl. 122		16.3.45
790. Frankewitz, Bruno	Gen.Lt., Kdr. 215. I.D.		16.3.45

KNIGHT'S CROSS WITH OAK LEAVES

791.	Scheuerpflug, Paul	Gen.Lt., Kdr. 68. I.D. + 8.8.45 in Soviet captivity at hospital in Auschwitz, Soviet captivity	16.3.45
792.	Becker, Martin	Hptm., Kdr. IV./N. J.G. 6	20.3.45
793.	Werner, Gerhard	Major, Kdr. I./Jag. Rgt. 734 + 8.9.44 in SE Banat, Romania; Posthumously promoted to Obstlt. befördert	23.3.45
794.	Kedzia, Ernst-Georg	Major, Kampfkdt. von Fürstenberg a. d. Oder & Kdr. Rgt. 98 (391. Sich. Div.)	23.3.45
795.	v. Meyer, Kuno	Obstlt., Kdr. Pz. Rgt. "Coburg" in Pz. Brig. 103	23.3.45
796.	Prüß, Walter	Oblt., Chef 8./Pz. Gren. Rgt. 76	23.3.45
797.	Konopacki, Günther	Rittm., Kdr. I./Radf. Jäg. Brig. 10	23.3.45
798.	Herzog, Hans-Georg	Obstl., Kdr. Pz. Gren. Rgt. 14	23.3.45
799.	Trittel, Rudolf	Obstlt. d.R., Kdr. Gren. Rgt. 9 + 26.3.45 badly wounded in Allenstein area, 1.4. died of wounds in Danzig	23.3.45
800.	Wanka, Karl	Major d.R., Kdr. I./Gren. Rgt. 53	23.3.45
801.	Frhr. v. Elverfeldt, Harald	Gen. Major, Kdr. 9. Pz.Div. + 6.3.45 in Cologne; posthumously promoted to Gen.Lt. bef.	23.3.45
802.	Jeckeln, Friedrich	SS-Obergruppenf & Gen. d. W-SS, Kom.Gen. V. SS-Korps + 3.2.46 hanged in Riga	8.3.45
803.	Fullriede, Fritz	Oberst, Festungskdt. Kolberg	23.3.45
804.	Spielmann, Johann	Major, Kdr. St. Gesch. Brig. 202	28.3.45
805.	Keese, Heinrich	Major d.R., Kdr. Pi. Btl. 20 (mot.)	28.3.45
806.	Berger, Lothar	Oberst, Kdr. Brigade z.b.V. 100	28.3.45
807.	Hufenbach, Helmuth	Oberst, Fhr. 562. Volks-Gren. Div. + 27.3.45 at Balga (Frisches Haff); Posthumously promoted to Gen. Major	28.3.45
808.	Schroedter, Erich	Rittm., Kdr. Pz. Aufkl. Abt. "Großdeutschland"	28.3.45
809.	v. Usedom, Horst	Oberst, Fhr. Pz. Brig. "Courland"	28.3.45
810.	Josten, Günther	Oblt., Staffelkpt. 3./J.G. 51 "Mölders"	28.3.45
811.	Gläser, Alexander	Hptm., Kdr. II./S.G. 77	28.3.45
812.	Stähler, Wilhelm	Oblt., Staffelkpt. 7./S.G. 2 "Immelmann"	28.3.45
813.	Stüdemann, Gerhard	Hptm., Kdr. III./S.G. 77	28.3.45
814.	Girg, Walter	SS-Hptsturmf., Führer eines Sonder- kommandos in SSJagdverb. Mitte	1.4.45
815.	v. Mellenthin, Horst	Gen.Lt., Kdr. 205. I.D.	4.4. 45
816.	Steglich, Martin	Major, Fhr. Gren. Rgt. 1221	5.4.45

817. Neubert, Rudolf	Obstlt., Kdr. Gren. Rgt. 31	5.4.45
818. Richter, Friedrich	Obstlt., Kdr. Gren. Rgt. 1222	5.4.45
819. Kuppinger, Ernst	Hptm., Kdr. Füs. Btl. 246	5.4.45
820. Paetsch, Otto	SS-Obersturmbannf., Kdr. SS-Pz. Rgt. 10 "Frundsberg" + 16.3.45 at Altdamm, Stettin; Posthumously promoted to SS-Standartenfhr.	5.4.45
821. v. Tettau, Hans	Gen.Lt., Fhr. Korpsgruppe "v. Tettau"	5.4.45
822. Thyben, Gerhard	Oblt., Staffelkpt. 7./J.G. 54	8.4.45
823. Burchardi, Theodor	Admiral, Kom. Adm. eastern Baltic	8.4.45
824. Thiele, August	Vizeadm., Befehlsh. Kampfgr. Thiele	8.4.45
825. Richter, Bruno	Rittm., Kdr. Füs. Btl. 24	8.4.45
826. Skorzeny, Dipl.-Ing. Otto	SS-Obersturmbannf. d.R., Kdr. der SS-Jagdverbände & Kampfkdt. Schwedt, Oder	9.4.45
827. v. Krosigk, Ernst-Anton	Gen.D.Inf., Kom.Gen. XVI A.K.+ 16.3.45 as OB 16. Armee at Kanden, Courland	12.4.45
828. Borchardt, Helmut	Ofw., Fhr. Kp. "Borchardt" in Rgt. "Kohlmann" in 402. I.D.	14.4. 45
829. Becker, Carl	Gen.Lt., Kdr. 253. I.D.	14.4. 45
830. Röpke, Kurt	Gen. d. Inf, Kom.Gen. XXIX. A.K.	14.4. 45
831. Rögelein, Friedrich	Oberst, Kdr. Gren. Rgt. 109	14.4. 45
832. Simm, Alfred	Hptm., Fhr. II./Gren. Rgt. 31	14.4. 45
833. Raht, Gerhard	Hptm., Kdr. I./NJ.G. 2	15.4.45
834. Ostermeier, Hans-Arno	Major, Fhr. Fsch. Pz. Gren. Rgt. 3 "HG"	15.4.45
835. Hansen, Max	SS-Standartenf., Kdr. SS-Pz. Gren. Rgt. 1 "LSSAH"	17 4.45
836. Lütje, Herbert	Major, Kmdr. N. J.G. 6	17.4.45
837. Lipfert, Helmut	Hptm. d.R., Kdr. I./J.G. 53	17.4.45
838. Kraft, Josef	Hptm., Staffelkpt. 12./NJ. G 1	17.4.45
839. Drewes, Martin	Major, Kdr. III./N. J.G. 1	17.4.45
840. Greiner, Hermann	Hptm., Kdr. IV./NJ.G. 1	17.4.45
841. Semrau, Paul	Major, Kdr. I./NJ.G. 2 + 8.2.45 over Twente, Holland as Kmdre. N. J.G. 2 shot down whilst landing	17.4.45
842. Raegener, Adolf	Gen.Lt., Kdt. Veiteidigungsbereich Magdeburg	17.4.45
843. Knaust, Hans-Peter	Obstlt., Kdr. Rgt. "Knaust"/490. I.D. (Above last officially assigned number)	17.4.45
(844.) Hack, Franz	SS-Obersturmbannf, Kdr. SS-PZ. Gren. Rgt. 10 "Westland"	18.4.45
(845.) Kausch, Paul-Albert	SS-Obersturmbannf., Kdr. SS-Pz. Rgt. 11	23.4.45
(846.) Brandner, Josef	Major, Kdr. St. Gesch. Brig. 912	26.4.45
(847.) Rodt, Eberhard	Gen.Lt., Kdr. 15. Pz. Gren. Div.	28.4.45

KNIGHT'S CROSS WITH OAK LEAVES

(848.) Ziegler, Joachim	SS-Brigadef. & Gen. Major d. W-SS, Kdr. 11. SS-Freiw. Pz. Gren. Div. "Nordland" + 30.4./1.5.45 in Berlin	28.4.45
(849.) Kappis, Hans-Joachim	Oblt. d.R., Fhr. 19./Gren. Rgt. 45	28.4.45
(850.) Schrepfer, Karl	Major, Kdr. III./S.G. 1	28.4.45
(851.) Prentl, Josef	Major, Kdr. Flak-Rgt. 116	28.4.45
(852.) Thomsen, Rolf	Kaptlt., Kdt. "U 1202"	29.4.45
(853.) Lange, Hans-Günther	Kaptlt., Kdt. "U 711"	29.4.45
(854.) Laebe, Heinz-Oskar	Oberst, Kdr. Gren. Rgt. 44	29.4.45
(855.) Hax, Heinrich	Gen. Major, Kdr. 8. Pz.Div.	30.4.45
(856.) Laengenfelder, Hanns	Gen. Major, Kdr. 15. I.D.	30.4.45
(857.) Daniel, Richard	Gen. Major, Kdr. 45. Volks-Gren. -Div.	30.4.45
(858.) v. Obstfelder, Wolfgang	Major, Kdr. Pz.Jäg. Abt. 346	30.4.45
(859.) v. Bostell, Wolfgang	Lt., Zugf. in Pz.Jäg. Abt. 205	30.4.45
(860.) Mokros, Gerhard	Oberst, Kdr. Gren. Rgt. 423	5.5.45
(861.) Ostendorf, Werner	SS-Gruppenf. & Gen.Lt. d. W-SS, Kdr. 2. SS-Pz.Div. "Das Reich" + 5.5.45 in Bad Aussee of wounds	6.5.45
(862.) Lehmann, Rudolf	SS-Standartenf, Fhr. 2. SS-Pz.Div. "Das Reich"	6.5.45
(863.) Kreutz, Karl	SS-Standartenf., Kdr. SS-Pz. An. Rgt. 2 "Das Reich"	6.5.45
(864.) Werner, Heinz	SS-Sturmbannf, Kdr. III./SS-Pz. Gren. - Rgt. 4 "Der Führer"	6.5.45
(865.) Jodl, Alfred	Gen. Oberst, Chef Wehrmachtsführungs- stab in OKW & stellv. Chef OKW + 16.10.46 hanged in Nürnberg	10.5.45
(866.) v. Blanc, Adalbert	Freg. Kpt., Fhr. 9. Marine-Sich. Div.	6.5.45
(867.) Plocher, Hermann	Gen.Lt., Kdr. 6. Fsch. Jäg. Div.	8.5.45
(868.) Graßmel, Franz	Major, Kdr. Fsch. Jäg. Rgt. 20	8.5.45
(869.) Lier, Friedrich	Obstlt., Kdr. Kampfgr. in 490. I.D.	8.5.45
(870.) Dennhardt, Oskar-Hubert	Major, Fhr. Gren. Rgt. 1143	9.5.45
(871.) Kleinheisterkamp, Matthias	SS-Obergruppenf. & Gen. d. W-SS, Kom-Gen. XI. SS-Pz. Korps + 2.5.45 in Halbe pocket	9.5.45
(872.) Lohmann, Hanns-Heinrich	SS-Obersturmbannf, Fhr. SS-Freiw. Pz. Gren. Rgt. 49 "De Ruyter"	9.5.45
(873.) Montag, Alfred	Hptm. d.R., Fhr. St. Gesch. Brig. 341	9.5.45

(874.) Meier, Hans	Hptm., Kdr. 1./Pz. Gren. Rgt. 74	9.5.45
(875.) Rebane, Alfons	Waffen-Obersturmbannf., Kdr. Waffen-Gren. Rgt. d. SS 46	9.5.45
(876.) Schlags-Koch, Walter	Obstlt. d.R., Kdr. Sturm-Rgt. AOK 2	9.5.45
(877.) Schmidt, Erich	Major, Fhr. Pz. Rgt. d. Führer-Gren. Div.	9.5.45
(878.) v. Siegroth, Joachim	Gen. Major, Kdr. 712. I.D. + 2.5.45 in Halbe pocket	9.5.45
(879.) Stahl, Dr. Paul	Obstlt. d.R., Kdr. Pz. G. R. 114	9.5.45
(880.) Störck, Georg	Hptm. d.R., Kdr. 1./Pz. Gren. Rgt. d. Führer-Begleit-Div.	9.5.45
(881.) Sensfuß, Franz	Gen.Lt., Kdr. 212. I.D.	9.5.45
(882.) v. Radowitz, Joseph	Gen.Lt., Kdr. 23. Pz.Div.	9.5.45

Notes regarding the award of the Oak Leaves to the Knight's Cross of the Iron Cross

72nd–76th Oak Leaves

These were the awards which had originally been deferred during the winter crisis of 1941/42. Recommendations had already been submitted in the period between August and October 1941. At the time of the award, all recipients occupied a higher rank.

(810th) Oak Leaves

Confirmation that Oberleutnant Josten was decorated with the Oak Leaves is to be found in the Bundesarchiv. He was decorated with the award on 2 April 1945 by General Uebe, who at the same time decorated Oberfeldwebel Schönfelder with the Knight's Cross of the Iron Cross.

(811th)–(812th)–(813th.) Oak Leaves

There are various forms of documentary evidence substantiating these awards; for example, a congratulatory telegram on the occasion of the award dated 7 April 1945 from General der Flieger Seidemann. The three officers (Stüdemann, Gläser, Stähler, and an unknown woman to whom the Iron Cross was said to have been awarded) travelled at the beginning of April 1945 to 'Karinhall', where

Reichsmarschall Göring decorated them shortly before he evacuated his country seat.

(833th) Oak Leaves

Raht – who in previous years had been designated as the 811th holder of the Oak Leaves – had, according to information ascertained to date, chalked up his 55th victory as a nightfighter pilot with 5 aircraft he had shot down on 15 March 1945. He was recommended for the Oak Leaves between his 50th and 55th victory. Thus, if the recommendation was submitted in mid-March, the decoration, taking into account the usual time it took the Luftwaffe to process recommendations, could not have been awarded before mid-April 1945.

(834th) Oak Leaves

Similarly, the award to Major Ostermaier was first shown in the book *Fallschirmjäger* as having been made on 30 April 1945. Ostermaier himself gave 20 April 1945 as the date he was awarded the decoration, or notified of the award. In a similar way to the case of Raht above, assuming that it took five to seven days before the announcement of the award was made, both awards of the Oak Leaves must correspond with the only available numbers 833/34, since these numbers were verifiably not assigned to the Army or to the Navy.

(844th) Oak Leaves

The award of the Oak Leaves to SS-Obersturmbannführer Hack was, according to his own statement, made at the end of April 1945 by SS-Obergruppenführer and General der Waffen-SS Gille, the Commanding General of the 4th SS Panzer-Korps, and by the Divisional commander SS-Oberführer Ulrich before his regiment in Hungary.

Confirmed by an entry around 15 to 20 April 1945, undated, in the recommendations book of OKH/PA/P 5.

(845th) Oak Leaves

SS-Obersturmbannführer Kausch – lying wounded in the Reich Chancellery bunker – learned from SS-Brigadeführer and Generalmajor der Waffen-SS Joachim Ziegler (himself awarded the Oak Leaves on 28 April 1945) that, in accordance with a radio message to Pz. AOK 11, he had been awarded the Oak Leaves on 23 April 1945.

(846th) Oak Leaves

According to his own statement, Hauptmann Brandner received the Oak Leaves from the Commanding General of XXXVIII AK, General d. Art. Herzog. There still exist photographs which show him with the Oak Leaves. He did not receive the Knight's Cross on 17 January 1945 – as is stated in other publications – , but only on 17 March 1945 (according to the OKH/PA/P 5 recommendations book). The extraordinary achievements of Sturmgeschütz-Brigade 912 in Courland in April 1945 suggest a direct award from Berlin. The date of the award is assumed to be 26 April 1945.

(861st)–(864th) Oak Leaves

The awards of Oak Leaves Nos 861–864 were made by SS-Oberstgruppenführer and Generaloberst der Waffen-SS, Sepp Dietrich, OB 6th SS-Pz. Armee (see also section 'Swords'). It is not possible to verify this in the Bundesarchiv.

(867th)–(869th) Oak Leaves

These are awards made by the Dönitz government. The recommendations for Generalleutnant Plocher, Major Grassmel and Oberstleutnant Lier were supported by all their superior officers and the awards were made by Grossadmiral Dönitz without the recommendation receiving the last signature, as a result of the situation at that time.

(870th)–(881st) Oak Leaves

Dennhardt (870th) – Recommendation for award of Oak Leaves made

KNIGHT'S CROSS WITH OAK LEAVES

on 11 April 1945 – arrived at OKH/PA/P 5 19 April 1945, but not processed there.

Kleinheisterkamp (871st) – Recommendation sent by telegram on 19 April 1945 through OB 9 Armee, General d. Inf. Busse. Arrived at OKH/PA/P 5 on 21 April 1945; Remarks: Await recommendation with regard to immediate award being made through normal official channels.

Lohmann (872nd) – Recommendation for award of Oak Leaves made on 26 February 1945 – arrived at OKH/PA/P 5 on 23 April 1945, supported by Gen.Lt. Unrein, Commanding General, III. (germ.) SS-Pz. Korps on 19 March 1945.

Montag (873rd) – Recommendation for award of Oak Leaves made on 11 March 1945 – arrived at OKH/PA/P 5 on 30 April 1945, supported by OB West, Gen. Feldm. Kesselring on 23 April 1945.

Maier (874th) – Recommendation for award of Oak Leaves made on 17 March 1945, arrived at OKH/PA/P 5 on 12 April 1945, supported by OB 3 Pz. Armee, Gen. d. Pz.Tr. Gräser on 2 April 1945 and by OB H.Gr. Mitte, Gen. Feldm. Schörner, on 8 April 1945.

Rebane (875th) – Recommendation for award of Oak Leaves made on 3 April 1945, arrived at OKH/PA/P 5 on 12 April 1945, supported by Gen. d. Kav. Koch-Erpach, Commanding General of LVI Pz. Korps, and Reichsführer-SS.

Schlags-Koch (876th) – Recommendation for award of Oak Leaves made on 24 March 1945 – arrived at OKH/PA/P 5 on 6 April 1945. Remarks: Resubmitted 5 May 1945.

Schmidt (877th) – Arrived at OKH/PA/P 5 on 24 March 1945, submitted 29 March 1945. According to statements by the Divisional Commander and Divisional Adjutant, the award was made.

von Siegroth (878th) – Recommendation sent by telegram on 19 April 1945 through OB 9 Armee, General d. Inf. Busse, arrived at OKH/PA/P 5 on 21 April 1945; Remarks: Await recommendation with regard to immediate award being made through normal official channels.

Stahl (879th) – Arrived at OKH/PA/P 5 on 15 April 1945 – supported by SS-Obergruppenf. und Gen. der W-SS Bittrich,

Commanding General of the II SS-Pz. Korps, and OB H.Gr. Süd, Generaloberst Dr. Rendulic.

Störck (880th) – Recommendation for award of Oak Leaves made on 2 March 1945 through Gen. Major Remer, Commander, Führer-Begleit-Division. Arrived at OKH/PA/P 5 on 9 March 1945; remarks on processing: 'Ja Domaschk 10.3.45 – severely wounded while carrying out the action for which Oak Leaves recommended'.

Sensfuss (881st) – Recommendation for award of Oak Leaves supported by Reichsführer-SS on 10 March 1945, OB H.Gr. 'B', Gen. Feldm. Model, on 14 March 1945, and OB West, Gen. Feldm. Kesselring, on 21 March 1945.

von Radowitz (882nd) – Recommendation for award of Oak Leaves arrived at OKH/PA/P 5 on 30 April 1945, not processed, supported on 11 April 1945 by OB 2 Pz. Armee, Gen. d. Art. de Angelis.

After the express order to suspend awards was issued by Grossadmiral Dönitz on 11 May 1945, the following recommendations arrived at OKH/PA/P 5, and thus do not fall under the rubric of the 'Dönitz order':

Fretter-Pico, Otto, Gen.Lt., Commander 148 I.D.:

Recommendation for award of Oak Leaves made on 12 May 1945 by OB 14th Armee, Gen. d. Pz.Tr. Lemelsen, arrived at OKH/PA/P 5 on 13 May 1945 – Telegram of 16 May 1945 asking for comments from H.Gr.'C' not processed.

Eggermann, Walter, Major in Special Staff v. Gottberg of OB North-West: Recommendation for award of Oak Leaves made on 5 May 1945, arrived at OKH/PA/P 5 on 13 May 1945. Remained unprocessed.

There is also the unverifiable assumption that during the period 20 to 30 April 1945 (2 May 1945) in Berlin (Oberst von Below), awards could have been made to members of the Luftwaffe, in particular, posthumous awards to:

Hrdlicka, Franz – Hauptmann, Commander I./Jagdgeschwader (JG) 2 'Richtofen'(+ 25 March 1945 in Betzdorf/Hessen, killed after being shot down).

Waldmann, Hans – Oblt., Staffelführer 8./J.G. 3 'Udet'(+ 28

March 1945 as Oblt. and Flight Leader 3./J.G. 7 'Hindenburg' in the Kaltenkirchen area in Holstein).

According to Ernst Obermaier's book *Die Ritterkreuzträger der Luftwaffe – Band 1 – Jagdflieger*, there are another 22 soldiers of the Luftwaffe who were recommended for the award of the Oak Leaves. Eleven of these were killed in action in 1944/45. However, in the Bundesarchiv there is no documentation relating to recommendations or to awards which took place. The alleged award of the Oak Leaves to Oberleutnant Karl-Heinz Stahnke (awarded the Knight's Cross on 24 October 1944) on 27 March 1945, which continues to be mentioned, has to date not been able to be substantiated, even with the documents which were submitted.

A further group is the 'Italy group'. After communications with Führer Headquarters were cut off, the Oak Leaves and the Knight's Cross of the Iron Cross were awarded to the senior commanders etc, some of them pending later confirmation by the appropriate authority. Of these, the following awards are known:

30.4.45 Dr. Polack, Fritz, Gen.Lt. and commander, 29 Pz. Gren. Div. Award announced and confirmed by OB 10th Armee, Gen. d. Pz.Tr. Traugott Herr, who stated that he received approval to make the award after a telephone enquiry to HPA Traunstein.

30.4.45 Veth, Kurt, Major and commander, II./Fallschirmjäger-Rgt. 3

30.4.45 Görtz, Helmut (5), Oblt., 1 Fsch. Jäg. Div. Award was made by Gen. d. Fsch. Tr. Heidrich after communications were severed.

12.4.45 (3.6.45) Stracke, Walter (4), Hauptmann der Reserve and commander, Pz. Aufkl. Abt. 26 Award was made by Gen.Lt. Linnarz, commander, 26th Pz.Div., while a prisoner in the Ghedi prisoner-of-war camp, with backdated date of award.

Awards not yet clarified

20.4.45 Reimann, Richard, Gen. d. Flakart. and Commanding General, I. Flakkorps. The information appears in the book *Flakartillerie*, 2nd edition, by Hans-Adalbert Koch. According to the author, there is no official substantiating evidence. Above all, General Reimann knows nothing about his having been awarded the Oak Leaves and does not claim to have been awarded it. Possibly, General Reimann was in fact recommended for the award of the Oak Leaves, but the recommendation did not reach the authorities responsible for the decision to make the award.

21.4.45 Lobmeyer, Jakob, SS-Hauptsturmführer and commander of SS-Jagdpanzer Abteilung 561. Information relating to this award appeared for the first time in the first and second editions of the book *Die Ritterkreuzträger der Waffen-SS* by E G Krätschmer. The Knight's Cross of the Iron Cross was possibly awarded to Lohmeyer on 28 April 1945. SS-Jagd-Pz. Abt 561 was deployed in action within the framework of V SS Korps, in the area of which direct awards of the Knight's Cross were made from Berlin at the end of April. Only one award can have been made at this late point in time, because otherwise, in the case of an award which went through the normal channels, some evidence would have to be available. There is no evidence available concerning this award in the Bundesarchiv. The Knight's Cross is said to have been awarded by the Commanding General, SS-Obergruppenführer der W-SS Jeckeln, confirmation being for the period at the end of April. It is possible that a recommendation was made for the award of the Oak Leaves which did not reach its destination. An award was not made.

22.4.45 Tittel, Rolf, Feldwebel, acting platoon commander, 11./G. R. 31

Krüger, Rudolf, Hauptmann, commander, 5./G. R. 32

According to the first edition of von Seemen's *Die Ritterkreuzträger 1939/45*, Oak Leaves awards Nos 833 and 834 according to information given by Generals Versock and von Tettau in the *Geschichte der 24. I.D.* There is no substantiating evidence in the Bundesarchiv of any awards or recommendations for awards.

Further information came to light concerning awards of the Oak Leaves to members of the Army (and the Waffen-SS), for which no substantiating evidence can be produced. Moreover, even in the empowering order of 3 May 1945 (until 11 May 1945) expanding the authority for giving awards, authority was not extended to awarding the Oak Leaves. The source of the information — as far as is known — has been indicated. It is possible that some awards (announced by radio) for exceptional achievements (e. g. the awards announced by radio after Nuremberg) were made directly from the Reich Chancellery through the Party leadership (the Commissioner for Reich Defence). Certainly, recommendations were also made by units which were lost en route and therefore did not reach OKH/PA/P 5.

19.4.45 Wolf, Richard, Oberst and Kampfkommandant of Nuremberg

Kaiser, Vincenz, SS-Obersturmbannführer, Commander, SS-Pz. Gren. Rgt. 38 'Götz von Berlichingen' (+ 20.4.45 in the Nuremberg area)

For his part, Oberst Wolf has stated that he heard over the radio that he had been awarded the Oak Leaves for the defence of Nuremberg. By contrast, the award of the decoration to Kaiser was first mentioned in the book *Die Ritterkreuzträger der Waffen-SS* by E. G. Krätschmer. The history of the 17th SS-Panzer Grenadier Division states: "At the end of April news reaches the Division of the award of the Oak Leaves to Obersturmbannführer Kaiser, who was killed in action, with the note that he is the 787th recipient of the Oak Leaves." Because this award number, like all the other Oak Leaves award numbers, has in the meanwhile been able to be verified in the Bundesarchiv, there is nevertheless the possibility that SS-Obersturmbannführer Kaiser was also decorated for the defence of Nuremberg. Certainly, substantiating evidence for both the above mentioned awards could not be produced.

1.5.45 Huppert, Helmut, Oberst, Commander, Pz. Gren. Rgt. 1. This information comes from the Divisional History of the 1st Pz.Div. The award is said to have been made at the end of April/beginning of May. Confirmed by the OB 6 Armee, Gen. d. Pz.Tr. Balck, and the Commander, 1 Pz.Div., Gen. Major Thunert. There is no substantiating documentary evidence.

4.45 Kerscher, Albert, Oberfeldwebel, acting commander, 2./s. Pz.

Abt. 502. Not possible to verify the award. Action in the area of AOK East Prussia. Recommendation did not reach OKH/PA/P 5.

25.4.45 Meissner, Siegfried, Oberstleutnant, Commander, Gren. Rgt. 685 (+ 23.4.45 at Nieheim/Höxter)

4.45 Müller, Albrecht, Hptm. der Reserve, battalion commander in Gren. Rgt. 446

4.45 Austermann, Johannes, Oberstlt., Commander, Gren. Rgt. 1146 and commander of a Kampfgruppe in the south-eastern Prussian pocket. The information comes from the commanders of the 134th and 340th I.D. s. Substantiating documentary evidence for the award could not, however, be produced or was not available. In all likelihood, this is once again a case of recommendations made by the unit.

4.45 Denk, Wilhelm, Hptm. and Kampfkommandant of Fürstenfeld (Styria). The award is said to have been made by the Reich Defence Commissioner, Steiermark. Whether it was made or not could not be clarified, particularly since there was no substantiation for the award.

For all other awards of the Oak Leaves there is documentary evidence in the Bundesarchiv.

Award of the Oak Leaves to members of foreign armed forces

(Listed in order of date of award; award numbers were not issued)

1. Lascar, Mihail Gen.Lt., Kdr. Romanian 6th Army 22.11.42
2. Munos-Grande, Augustin Gen.Lt., Kdr. Spanish "Blue Division" (250th I.D.) 13.12.42
3. Yamamoto, Isoroku Großadm., Japanese Fleet CO 27.5.43 (simultaneously awarded the Swords)
4. Teodorini, Corneliu Gen.Maj., Kdr. Romanian 6th Cavalry Div 8.12.43.
5. Dumitrescu, Petre Gen. Oberst, OB 3rd Romanian Army 4.4.44
6. Koga, Yneichi Großadm., Japanese Fleet CO 12.5.44 + 31.3.44 shot down en-route to Mindanao

7. Frhr. Mannerheim, Carl Marshal of Finland, State President, Gustaf Emil CO Finnish army 5.8.44
8. Degrelle, Léon SS-Sturmbannf., Kdr. 5. SS-Freiw. – Sturm. -Brig. "Wallonien" 27.8.44

VI

Recipients of the Knight's Cross of the Iron Cross

A

Abel, Adolf	Major, Kdr. 1./G. R. 364 24.8.44 missing as Oberstlt. & Kdr. G. R. 570 + 26.8.44 at Gura Galbena (Russia) as Oberstlt. & Kdr. G. R. 570	23.9.43
Abel, Josef	Ofw., Zugf. in 7./I.R. 217	23.11.41
Abele, Arnulf	Hptm., Kdr. 1./Reichsgren. Rgt. "Hoch- & Deutschmeister"	12.2.44
Abraham, Erich	Oberst, Kdr. Inf.Rgt. 230 516th Oak Leaves 26.6.44	13.11.42
Abraham, Erich	Lt. d.R., Fhr. 2./Pz. G. R. 13 + 8.12.43 Wjassaowice (Russia); posthumously promoted to Oblt.	20.1.44
Abrahamczik, Rudolf	Oblt., Staffelfhr. 14./K.G. 2	29.2.44
Abratis, Herbert	Hptm., Fhr. II./Fsch. Jäg. Rgt. 1 + 28./29.3.45 Oderbruch, south of Stettin as Major, Kdr. Fschjäg. Rgt. 27	24.10.44
Achilles, Albrecht	Kaptlt., Kdt. "U 161" +27.9.43 off Brazil; posthumously promoted to Korv. Kapt.	16.1.43
Ackermann, Georg	Lt., Staffelkpt. & Techn. Offz. in 5./K.G. 53 "Legion Condor"	28.2.45
Adam, Helmut	Oblt., Chef 3./St. Gesch. Abt. 192 + 1.12.42 north-east of Beloje (Russia) as Hptm. & Fhr. St. Gesch. Abt. "GD"; posthumously promoted to Major	21.11.41
Adam, Paul	Major d.R., Fhr. G. R. 158	18.4.43
Adam, Wilhelm	Oberst, Adj. AOK 6	17.12.42
Adamowitsch, Felix	Hptm., Chef 3./St. Gesch. Brig. 904	20.10.44
Adamsons, Miervaldis	Waffen-Untersturmfhr., Chef 6./Waffen-Gren. Rgt. 44 (lett. Nr. 6) d. SS + 1946 at Murmansk, as Hpt. St. Fhr., in Soviet captivity	25.1.45
Ademeit, Horst	Lt. Flugzeugfhr. in I./J.G. 54 414th Oak Leaves 2.3.44	16.4.43

97

Name	Details	Date
Adolff, Paul	Hptm. d.R., Fhr., Fsch. Pi. Btl. 1 + 17.7.43 at Reitano (Sicily); posthumously promoted to Major d.R.	26.3.44
Adolph, Walter	Hptm., Kdr. II./J.G. 26 "Schlageter" + 18.9.41 at Ostend (Belgium)	13.11.40
Adrario, Friedrich	Hptm., Fhr. Pzjäg. Abt 272	26.12.44
Adrian, Josef-Hubert	Ofw., Fhr. 6./G. R. 24 Missing (declared dead 18.6.60)	28.3.45
Aechtner, Fritz	Ofw., Flugzeugfhr. & Beob. in I./NAG 5	20.12.44
Afheldt, Eckard	Oblt., Fhr. II./Jäger-Rgt 2 "Brandenburg"	17.3.45
Aghta, Egon	Oblt. (W) d.R., Fhr. Sprengkdo. Luftgaukdo Berlin 778th Oak Leaves 12.3.45	3.2.45
Ahnert, Heinrich-Wilhelm	Ofw., Flugzeugfhr. in I./J.G. 52 + 23.8.42 at Koptewo (Russia)	23.8.42
Ahrens, Albert	Ofw., Zugf. in 3./Pzjäg. Abt. 31	25.7.43
Ahrens, Hinrich	Uffz., Geschützfhr. in 13./G. R. 1141	9.1.45
Ahrens, Wilhelm	Hptm., Kdr. III. (Jäger)/G. R. 17	4.5.44
Aigen, Reinhard	Ofw., Bordmechaniker in 7./K.G. 4 + 19.9.43 at Orscha (Russia)	9.6.44
Alber, Hermann	SS-Sturmmann, Kp. Truppmelder in 9./SS-Pz. G. R,. 20 "Hohenstaufen" + 2.8.44 in Normandy, Hill 176 west of MontChauvet (France)	26.12.44
Alber, Robert	Hptm. d.R., Fhr. I./Pz. Rgt. 201	7.9.43
Albers, Hans-Wilhelm	Hptm., Kdr. I./A.R. 1 "Afrika" + 4.6.44 as Major in a field hospital in Italy of wounds	10.5.43
Albert, Wilhelm	Hptm. d.R., Kp. Chef in Pzjäg. Abt. 35	14.2.45
Alberts, Otto	Oberst d.R., Kdr. G. R. 501 + 10.12.43 on Dolyskoje-See (Russia), of wounds	10.12.43
Albrecht, Egon	Oblt., Staffelfhr. 9./Z.G. 76 (later 6./SKG 210) + 25.8.44 in France as Hptm. & Kdr. III./Z.G. 76	22.5.43
Albrecht, Fritz	Oberst, Fhr. Kampfgr. in Magdeburg area	19.4.45
Albrecht, Kurt	Oberst, Kdr. A.R. 172	3.11.44
Albrecht, Kurt	Oberst d.R., Kdr. G. R. 948	28.2.45
Albrecht, Oskar	Uffz., Geschützfhr. 14. (Jäg.)/I.R. 15	24.7.41
Albrecht, Willy	Hptm. d.R., Kdr. I./Jäg. Rgt. 734	9.5.45
Albust, Rudolf	Obgefr., Richtsch. in 2./Pz.Jäg. Abt. 129	19.12.43
Alex, Ernst	Owm., Zugf. in 1./St. Gesch. Abt. 243	1.8.41
Allersmeler, Heinz	Major d.R., Fhr. F. E. B. 181	9.12.44
Allmacher, Friedrich	Hptm. d.R., Kdr. III./G. R. 366 + 26.12.44 Berzi (south of Frauenburg/Kurland) as Major d.R. & Kdr. Füs. Btl. 227	7.3.44

KNIGHT'S CROSS OF THE IRON CROSS

Allmendinger, Karl	Gen. Major, Kdr. 5. Inf. Div. 153rd Oak Leaves 13.12.42	17.7.41
Alm, Karl	Hptm., Fhr. II./G. R. 353 + 23.11.44 Frauenburg (East Prussia) as Fhr. 1./G. R. 353; posthumously promoted to Major	12.8.4-4
Alpers, Friedrich	Major, Kdr. Fernaufkl. Gruppe 4 + 3.9.44 suicide at Mons (Belgium) following severe wounds as Fhr. Fsch. Jäg. Rgt. 9	14.10.42
Altacher, Eduard	Hptm., Fhr. II./Geb.Jäg. Rgt. 143	18.11.44
Altermann, Karl-Heinz	Oblt., Chef 1./Pz. G. R. 25	4.10.44
Altmann, Gustav	Oblt., in Fsch. Jäg. Sturmabt. "Koch" Fhr. d. Sturmgruppe "Stahl" when capturing the Veldwezelt bridges (Belgium); simultaneously promoted to Hptm.;	12.5.40
Altstadt, Rudolf	Hptm. d.R., Kdr. 1./G. R. 380	14.5.44
Alvermann, Gustav	Hptm. d.R., Chef 10./I.R. 47 + 7.6.42 at Sevastopol (Russia) as Major d.R. & Btl. Kdr. posthumously promoted to Oberstlt. d.R.	26.5.40
Amarin, Herbert	Oblt., Chef 1./St. Gesch. Abt. 905 + 12.1.44 at Kirowograd (Russia) of wounds; posthumously promoted to Hptm.	10.2.44
Amann, Paul	Ofw., Beobachter in 3./K.G. 4 "General Wever"	12.3.45
Ambrosius, Dr. Lothar	Oberst, Fhr. Div. Kampfgr. 268	24.1.44
Ameiser, Anton	SS-Sturmbannfhr. d.R., Fhr. SS-Freiw. Kav. Rgt. 52 "Hungary"	1.11.44
Amelung, Günter	Lt. d.R., Fhr. 5./Schnefle Abt. 123 + 29.3.44 as Chef 1./A.A. 55 at Oborova (Croatia); posthumously promoted to Rittm. d.R.	15.1.43
Amelung, Heinz-Günter	Hptm., Staffelkpt. 5./Stuka-Geschw. 77	15.7.42
Amerkamp, Siegfried	Obgefr., MG-Schütze & stellv. Gruppenfhr. in Sturmkp./G. R. 459	22.11.43
Amling, Fritz	Wachtm., Zugf. in 3./St. Gesch. Abt. 202	11.12.42
Ammann, Franz	Lt., Fhr. 5./G. R. 256 + 18.8.43 at Boromlja (Russia); posthumously promoted to Oblt. d.R.	23.8.43
Ammer, Hermann	Oblt. d.R., Fhr. II./G. R. 62	12.10.43
v. Amsberg, Joachim	Oberst, Kdr. Gren-Rgt. 502	9.5.45
Ancans, Robert	Waffen-Ustuf., Fhr. of the close combat training/Waffen-Felders. Btl. SS Nr. 19	25.1.45
Anders, Carl	Oberst, Kdr. G. R. 484	4.5.44
Anders, Friedrich	Ofw., Zugf. 3./Pz. Aufkl. Abt. 2	14.8.43
Anders, Richard	Oblt., Flugzeugf. in II. (H)/Nahaufkl. Gr. 12	27.7.44
Andersen, Kurt	Oberst, Kdr. Flak-Rgt. 153	23.12.42
Anding, Friedrich	Lt. d.R., Adj. Pzjäg. -Abt. "GD"	8.5.45

Andorfer, Anton	Oblt., Staffelf. 2./Stuka-G. 77 + 11.4.45 at Cottbus as Hptm. & Staffelkpt. 2./S.G. 77	26.3.44
Andreae, Wolf	Oberst, Kdr. Werfer-Rgt. 71	24.6.44
Andree, Harry	Major, Kdr. 1./Gren. Rgt. 504 + 15.8.44 at main dressing station, San. Kp. 1/172, Borcezin, on the Vistula (Russia), of wounds, as Fhr. G. R. 504; posthumously promoted to Obstlt.	4.5.44
Andres, Ernst	Oblt., Flugzeugfhr. in Stabsstaffel/K.G. 2 + 11.2.45 at Ocide (Westphalia) as Hptm. & Staffelkpt. 5./N. J.G. 4	20.4.44
Andres, Hans	Obgefr., MG-Schütze in 2./Pz. G. R. 128; + 25.3.44 at base hospital, Troppau (Upper Silesia) of wounds posthumously promoted to Feldw. d.R.	4.5.44
Angel, Otto	Uffz. d.R., Zugf. in Pzjagd-Abt. 6	15.3.45
de Angelis, Maximilian	Gen.Lt., Kdr. 76 I.D. 323rd Oak Leaves 12.11.43	9.2.42
Angelmaier, Heinz	Hptm. d.R., Fhr. St. Gesch. Bng 279	18.2.45
Angern, Günther	Oberst, Kdr. 11. Schtz. Brigade + 2.2.43 suicide at Stalingrad (Russia) as Gen.Lt. & Kdr. 16. Pz.Div.	5.8.40
Angerstein, Karl	Oberst, Kommodore K.G. "Hindenburg"	2.11.40
Anhalt, Günther	SS-Standartenfhr. & Oberst der Schutzpolizei, Kdr. SS-Pol. Rgt. 2 + 27.4.45 in Berlin	12.8.44
Anhalt, Wilhelm	Kaptlt., Chef 4. Räumbootsflottille	3.7.44
Anneken, Udo	Lt. d.R., Fhr. 1./Füs. Btl. 83	9.6.44
Ansons, Zanis	Waffen-Hptscharfhr., Zugfhr. in 3./Waffen-Gren. Rgt. 44 d. SS killed in Soviet captivity	16.1.45
Anton, Werner	Gen. Major, Kdr. 6. Flak-Div. (mot.)	11.6.44
Antrup, Wilhelm	Hptm., Staffelkpt. 5./K.G. 55 655th Oak Leaves 18.11.44	13.11.42
v. Apell, Wilhelm	Gen.Maj., Kdr. 9. Schtz. Brigade	14.5.41
Apelt, Fedor	Oberst, Kdr. G. R. 102	8.2.44
Aperats, Karlis	Waffen-Obstubafhr., Kdr. Waffen-G. R. 32 (Lett. Nr. 1) of the Waffen-SS + 16.7.44 at Mosuli, Lake Peipus (Russia); posthumously promoted to Waffen-Standartenfhr.	21.9.44
Apitz, Willy	Obgefr., Funker in 10./A.R. 81	1.1.44
Apitzsch, Karl-Arthur	Oblt., VB in 4./A.R. 3 (mot.) missing	4.11.43
Arendt, Kurt	Hptm., Kdr. Pz. Abt. 5 + 9.1.45	24.2.45
Arendt, Velten	Hptm., Fhr. I./Pz. Rgt. 36 + in March 1945 in Kurland	28.3.45

v. Arentschildt, Alexander	Hptm., Chef 2./Pz. Abt. 67	5.8.40
Armberger, Josef	SS-Obersturmfhr., Chef 8./SS-Pz. Rgt. 1 "LSSAH" + 20.8.44 in France	31.10.44
Arndt, Fritz	Obgefr., MG-Schütze in Stabskp./Pz. Pi. Btl. 32 678th Oak Leaves 9.12.44	31.3.43
Arndt, Johannes	Obstl., Kdr. G. R. 391 + 6.7.44 at Molidesno (Russia) as Oberst	23.2.44
Arndt, Karl	Oberst, Kdr. I.R. 511 719th Oak Leaves 1.2.45	23.1.42
v. Arnim, Hans-Jürgen	Gen.Lt., Kdr. 17. Pz.Div.	4.9.41
Arning, Karl	Oberst, Kdr. G. R. 24	11.10.43
Arnold, Friedrich	Oblt. d.R., Zugf. in 2./St. Gesch. Abt. 237	16.11.43
Arpke, Helmut	Feldw., in Fschjäg. Sturmabt. "Koch" + 16.1.42 at Schaikowka (Russia) of wounds as Lt., Fhr. 3./Fschjäg. Sturm-Rgt. 1	13.5.40
Ascher, Dietrich	Lt. d.R., Zugf. in 2./St. Gesch. Brig. 259	28.2.45
Ascherfeld, Willi	Hptm. d.R., Kdr. II./G. R. 926 + 13.4.45 at Neukkuhren (East Prussia)	14.2.45
Assmann, Alois	Obgefr., Richtsch. in 1./Pzjäg. Abt. 61 (11. Pz.Div.)	18.9.42
Assmann, Dr. med. dent. Walter	Gen.Maj., Kdr. 101. Jäg. Div.	10.2.45
Attenberger, Franz-Xaver	Stgefr., Kraftf. in 3./A.R. 114	21.1.45
Audenrieth, Georg	Stgefr., Grupppenfhr. in 3./Gebjäg. Rgt. 99	10.2.45
Audorff, Paul	Obstit., Kdr. G. R. 754	13.5.43
Auer, Karl	SS-Hptsturmfhr., Fhr. 1./SS-Pol. Pz. G. R. 8	31.10.44
Auert, Heinz	Lt., Fhr. 2./Pz. Aufkl. Abt. 116	28.2.45
Augenstein, Hans-Heinz	Oblt., Staffelfhr. 7./N. J. G 1 + 6.12.44 at Münster-Handorf (Westphalia) as Hptm. & Staffelkpt. 12./N. J.G. 1	9.6.44
Augsberger, Franz	SS-Brigadefhr. & Gen.Maj. d. Waffen-SS, Kdr. 20. Waffen-Grenadier-Div. d. SS (estnische Nr. 1) + 19.3.45 at Neustadt (Upper Silesia)	8.3.45
v. Aulock, Andreas	Oberst, Kdr. G. R. 226 551st Oak Leaves 16.8.44	6.11.43
Austen, Hans	Hptm., Kdr. II./G. R. 487	5.12.43
Austermann, Johannes	Major, Kdr. II./G. R. 1146	10.2.45
Ax, Adolf	SS-Oberfhr., Führungsstab Ostküste, Fhr. 15. Waffen-Gren. Div. der SS	9.5.45
Axthammer, Erich	Feldw., Flugzeugfhr. i. Stab/S.G. 10	28.4.45
v. Axthelm, Walther	Gen.Maj., Kom.Gen. I. Flak-Korps	4.9.41

Axtmann, Fritz	Ofw., Kp. Truppfhr. in 7./I.R. 20 (mot.) + 13.9.43 of wounds in hospital at Kiev (Russia) as Lt. & Kpfhhr.; posthumously promoted to Oblt.	25.8.41

B

Baacke, Karl	Hptm., Chef 2./Grenz-Inf.Rgt. 124 352nd Oak Leaves 10.12.43	30.6.41
Baade, Ernst-Günther	Oberst, Kdr. Schtz. Rgt. 115 402nd Oak Leaves 22.2.44 111th Swords 16.11.44	27.6.42
Baader, Heinz (17)	Hptm. Nahaufkl. -Gruppe 5	26 4.45
Baagoe, Sophus	Oblt., Flugzeugfhr. in 5./Z.G. 26 "Horst Wessel" + 14.5.41 over Crete	14.6.41
Baake, Werner	Oblt., Staffelkpt. 3./N. J.G. 1	27.7.44
Baasch, Johannes	Oblt. d. R, Kdr. III./G. R. 410 + 10.8.44 in Russia as Hptm., Kdr. III./I.R. 410	3.5.42
Baasner, Hans	Oblt., Flugzeugfhr. & Beob. in 3./Fernaufkl. Gr. 121	11.3.43
Bach, Wilhelm	Hptm. d.R., Kdr. I./Schtz. Rgt. 104 + 22.12.42 as Major d.R. in Toronto (Canada); posthumously promoted to Oberstlt. d.R.	9.7.41
von dem Bach-Zelewski, Erich	SS-Obergruppenfhr. & Gen. d. Pol., Kom.Gen. der Korpsgruppe "von dem Bach" in Warsaw	30.9.44
Bachem, Erich	Lt., V. B. in IV./A.R. 262	6.1.42
Bacherer, Rudolf	Oberst d.R., Kdr. G. R. 234 550th Oak Leaves 11.8.44	30.10.43
Bachmaier, Ludwig	Hptm. d.R., Fhr. I/I.R. 179	26.12.41
Bachmann, Christian	SS-Hptsturmfhr., Fhr. 11./SS-Pz. G. R. 5 "Totenkopf" + 13.3.45 at Stuhlweißenburg (Hungary) as SS Sturmbannfhr and Btl. Kdr.	28.2.45
Bachmann, Erwin	SS-Obersturmfhr., Adj. 1./SS-Pz. Rgt. 10 "Frundsberg"	10.2.45
Bachmann, Fritz	Obgefr. in 1./Pz. G. R. 7	5.4.45
Bachmeier, Josef	SS-Hptsturmfhr., Fhr. 11./Freiw. -SS-Pz. G. R. 23 "Norge"	23.8.44
Bachnick, Herbert	Fhj. -Feldw., Flugmugfhr. in 9./J.G. 52 + 7.8.44 at Myslowitz (Upper Silesia) as Lt.	27.7.44
Bachor, Willy (19)	Owm., Zugf. in 12./Pz. Rgt. 24	11.5.45
Back, Hans-Ulrich	Obstlt., Kdr. 1./Schtz. Rgt. 2	5.8.40
Backhauss, Fritz	Hptm., Kdr. III./Gebjäg. Rgt. 13	8.2.44
Bade, Kurt	Uffz., Zugf. in 4./Pz. Aufkl. Abt. 23	26.8.43
Bader, Edwin	Oblt., Beob. in 2./Nahauflkl. Gr. 16 + 12.7.44 suicide in Germany	26.3.44

KNIGHT'S CROSS OF THE IRON CROSS

Bader, Friedrich	Major, Kdr. Hochgebirgs-Jäg. Btl. 3	12.8.44
Bader, Josef	Hptm., Kdr. II./Gren. Rgt. 95	23.8.43
Badinski, Curt	Oberst, Kdr. I.R. 489	11.10.41
Badorrek, Emil	Hptm., Staffelkpt. 4./Fernaufkl. Gruppe 11 652nd Oak Leaves 18.11.44	22.11.43
Badum, Johann	Lt., Flugzeugfhr. in 6./J.G. 77 + 12.1.43 at Tripoli (North Africa)	15.10.42
Badzong, Alfred	Gefr., M. G-Schütze in 1./G. R. 273	5.2.45
Bäcker, Rudolf	San. -Feldw., Stab. II./G. R. 36	18.9.43
Bäder, Wilhelm	Oblt., d.R., Chef. 8./G. R. 958 + 22.3.45 in Hofen/Berg. Kreis	14.4. 45
Bäke, Dr. med. dent. Franz	Major d.R., Kdr. II./Pz. Rgt. 11 262nd Oak Leaves 1.8.43 49th Swords 21.2.44	11.1.43
v. Baer, Bern	Obstlt. i.G., Ia 16. Pz.Div. 761st Oak Leaves 28.2.45	13.1.44
Bär, Heinrich (Heinz)	Lt., Flugzeugfhr. in 1./J.G. 51 31st Oak Leaves 14.8.41 7th Swords 16.2.42	2.7.41
Bärenfänger, Erich	Oblt., Fhr. III./I.R. 123 243rd Oak Leaves 17.5,43 45th Swords 23.1.44	7.8.42
Bätcher, Hansgeorg	Hptm., Staffelkpt. 1./K.G. 100 434th Oak Leaves 24.3.44	21.12.42
Bätge, Niels	Kaptlt., Chef 4. Schnellbootsflottille + 12.12.44 on Finnish lakes as Korv. Kpt. & Kdt. Zerstörer "Z 35"	4.1.42
Bäuchl, Johann	Ofw., Zugf. in 5./Pz. G. R. 33	23.10.44
Bäuerle, Emil	Oblt. d.R., Chef 8./Jäger-Rgt. 56	4.5.44
Bäumler, Gottfried	Uffz., Zugf. in 11./Gren. R. 41 (mot.) + 26.1.45 at Owczegtowy near Kattowitz	14.5.44
Bäumler, Heinz	Oblt., Fhr. 6./A.R. 17 + 12.1.45 as Hptm.	11.6.44
Bahns, Kurt	Oblt., Chef 6./I.R. 216 + 18.2.45	13.11.42
Bahr, Artur	Oblt., Chef 7./G. R. 44 + 27.11.44 at main dressing station Eglieni (Russia) of wounds; posthumously promoted to Hptm.	3.12.44
Bahr, Günther	Ofw., Flugzeugfhr. in 1./NJ.G. 6	28.3.45
Baler, Joseph	Obstlt., Kdr. G. R. 36	9.5.45
Baier, Karl	Hptm. d.R., Kdr. II./G. R. 1036	16.10.44
Baindner, Hans	Gefr., MG-Schütze in 11./Jäger-Rgt. 228	24.6.44
Bajorat, Kurt	Obgefr., Gruppenfhr. in 3./Pz. G. R. 13 + 15.1.45 at Katenau (East Prussia)	15.5.44
Balck, Hermann	Obstlt., Kdr. Schützen-Rgt. I 155th Oak Leaves 20.12.42 25th Swords 4.3.43 19th Diamonds 31.8.44	3.6.40
Baldauf, Horst	Lt., Beobachter in 2./Fernaufkl. Gruppe 22 + 10.6.44 at Winniza (Russia)	8.8.44

ELITE OF THE THIRD REICH

Baldauf, Johann	Feldw., Zugf. in 3./Geb. Pi. Btl. 91	18.11.44
Baldes, Josef (17)	Fhj. -Ofw., Flugzeugfhr. 1. (F)/Aufkl. Gr. 124	9.5.45
Ball, Gerhard	Hptm., Fhr. Aufkl. Abt. 53 (mot.) + 9.10.41	23.11.41
Edler v. Ballasko, Otto	Oblt., Staffelkpt. 9./K.G. 1 "Hindenburg"	13.8.42
Balthasar, Wilhelm	Hptm., Staffelkpt. 7./J.G. 27 17th Oak Leaves 2.7.41	14.6.40
Balzer, Udo	Major, Kdr. Füs. Btl. "Deba" + 14.4. 44 in Tarnopol (Russia) as Obstlt.	9.4.44
Banach, Friedrich	Feldw., Zugf. in 4./Pz. Rgt. 36 + 13.3.43 in Russia as Ofw.	30.11.42
Banaski, Helmut	Lt. d.R., Zugf. in Stabskp./G. R. 1077	18.2.45
Banholzer, Alfred	Hptm., Staffelkpt. 1./K.G. 55	14.1.45
Bansen, Erich	Ofw., Zugf. in 1./s. Pzjäg. Abt. 519	15.3.44
Banze, Karl-Heinrich	Owm., Zugf. in 1./St. Gesch. Abt. 244 + January 1943	27.5.42
Barall, Benno	Hptm. d.R., Kdr. Pz.Jäg. Abt. 227	21.9.44
Baranek, Ewald	Oblt., Fhr. Pz. Pi. Btl. 58 + 1.2.44 in Italy; posthumously promoted to Major	12.2.43
v. Barby, Hans-Levin	Obstlt., Kdr. Schütz. -Rgt. 361 and Fhr. of a Kampfgr. + 27.5.42 in hospital in Derna (North Africa) of wounds as Oberst	13.12.41
Barde, Konrad	Oberst, Kdr. A.R. 104 + 4.5.45 suicide in Traunstein as Gen. Malor & Kdr. 198. Inf. Div.	5.1.43
Barge, Johannes (3)	Oberst, Kdr. Festg. G. R. "Kreta"	10.5.45
v. Bargen, Hans	Oblt., Adj. & Tech. Offz. 1./Stuka-Gechw. 3 + 6.7.44 in Finland as Hptm. & Grukdr.	19.9.42
Bargsten, Klaus	Kaptlt., Kdt. "U 521"	30.4.43
Barkhorn, Gerhard	Oblt., Staffelkpt. 4./J.G. 52 175th Oak Leaves 11.1.43 52nd Swords 2.3.44	23.8.42
Barkmann, Ernst	SS-Unterscharfhr., Pz. Kdt. in 4./SS-Pz. Rgt. 2 "Das Reich"	27.8.44
Barmetler, Josef	Oblt. d.R., Fhr. 7./Fsch. Jäger-Sturm-Rgt. + 20.2.45 in Kempten (Allgäu) of wounds as Major d.R.	9.7.41
Barnbeck, Hermann	Oberst, Kdr. Inf.Rgt. 211 + 25.10.44 of wounds, at hospital in Minden (Westphalia)	29.10.42
Bartel, Ewald	Hptm. d.R., Kdr. Pz. Gren. Btl. 106 "Feldherrnhalle"	31.12.44
Bartels, Hans	Kaptlt., Kdt. "M 1" + 31.7.45 as Korv. Kapt.	16.5.40
Bartels, Hans-Werner	Hptm. d.R., Fhr. 1./G. R. 399	26.1.44
Bartels, Heinrich	Uffz., Flugzeugfhr. in 8./J.G. 5 + 23.12.44 over Bonn as Ofw. & Flugzeugfhr. in 15./J.G. 27	13.11.42
Bartels, Herbert	Oblt., Fhr. 3./Flak-Rgt. 293 (rnot.)	22.11.43

Barten, Franz	Oblt., Staffelkpt. 9./J.G. 53 + 4.8.44 over Reinsehlen at Soltau; posthumously promoted to Hptm.	29.10.44
Barth, Eitel-Albert	Oblt., Staffelfhr. 4./K.G. 55	24.3.43
Barth, Joachim	Hptm., Kdr. Pzjäg. Abt. 13	17.12.42
Barth, Karl	Oblt., Flugzeugfhr. in 3./Küstenflieger-Gr. 506 + 9.11.42 in Mediterranean as Hptm. & Staffelkpt. 6./K.G. 26	14.12.40
Barth, Ludwig	Stabsfeldw., Zugf. in 14. (PzJäg.)/Inf.Rgt. 14 + 25.11.42 in Chpepen- Prudy (Russia)	20.8.42
Barth, Otto	Oberst, Kdr. A.R. 117	8.5.43
Barth, Otto	Major, Kdr. II./G. R. 688 + 20.2.45 in Lichtenthal at Pr. Stargard (Pomerania)	9.2.45
Barth, Siegfried	Hptm., Staffelkpt. 4./K.G. 51	2.10.42
Barthle, Hans	Oblt. d.R., Chef 7./G. R. 119 (mot.)	19.12.43
Barths, Karl-Ludwig	Hptm., Fhr. He. St. Gesch. Brig. 393	14.1.45
Bartkowiak, Hans	Lt., Pi. Zugf. in Stabskp./G. R. 30 (mot.)	25.10.43
Bartl, Leopold	Major, Kdr. Pi. Btl. 335	6.11.43
Bartsch, Günter	Uffz., Gruppenfhr. in 2./Pz. G. R. 110	12.11.43
Barz, Herbert	Uffz., Richtschtz. in 3./s. Pzjäg. Abt. 519	18.7.44
v. Basse, Hans-Dieter	Major, Kdr. I./Pz. Füs. Rgt. "GD" + 16.4.45 at Godnicken (East Prussia) as Rgt. Fhr.; posthumously promoted to Oberstlt.	10.9.44
Graf v. Bassewitz-Levetzow,	Oberst d.R., Kdr. G. R. 96 Werner	17.9.44
Bastian, Heinrich (6)	SS-Obersturmfhr., Fhr. II./SS-Pz. G. R. 3 "Deutschland"	6.5.45
Bastian, Helmut	Kaptlt., Fhr. Sprengbootflottille (Kleinkampfverband)	3.11.44
Bastian, Karl	SS-Hptsturmfhr., Fhr. II./SS-Pz. G. R. 21 "Frundsberg" + 11.8.44 died of his wounds at Cui (France)	23.8.44
Batz, Wilhelm	Oblt., Staffelkpt., 5./J.G. 52 526th Oak Leaves 20.7.44 145th Swords 21.4.45	26.3.44
Bauer, Erhard	Gefr., Tr. Fhr. in 1./Pi. Btl. 102	4.10.44
Bauer, Ernst	Kptlt., Kdt. "U 126"	16.3.42
Bauer, Friedrich	Hptm., Fhr. I./Pz. Rgt. 33 + 10.9.43 in Russia of wounds	13.9.43
Bauer, Gerhard	Ofw., Flugzeugfhr. in 8./Stuka-Geschw. 77 + 17.4.45 at Kamenz as Lt. & Staffeloffz.	29.2.44
Bauer, Hans	SS-Obersturmfhr., Fhr. 3./SS-Pz. Gren. Btl. 506	5.4.45
Bauer, Dr. jur. Heinz	Oblt. d.R., Rgt. Adj. G. R. 585 + in Soviet captivity	12.6.44

Name	Details	Date
Bauer, Helmut	SS-Oberscharfhr., Zugf. in 3./SS-Pz. Rgt. 5 "Wiking"	12.9.43
Bauer, Herbert	Oblt., Staffelkpt. 3./Stuka-Geschw. 2 "Immelmann" 618th Oak Leaves 30.9.44	31.12.43
Bauer, Hermann	Hptm., Kdr. Gren. Btl. Belgard in Festung Schneidemühl + 1945	14.2.45
Bauer, Joachim	Oberst i.G., Fliegerfhr. in Luftfl. Kdo. 4	14.5.44
Bauer, Johann	Oberjäger, Gruppenfhr. in 6./Geb.Jäg. Rgt. 99	27.6.42
Bauer, Konrad (17)	Feldw., Flugzeugf. in 5./J.G. 300	31.10.44
Bauer, Ludwig	Uffz., Gruppenfhr. in 5./Gren. Rgt. 117 + 26.10.44 in a dressing station, Rimini (Italy)	23.10.44
Bauer, Ludwig (18)	Lt., Fhr. 1./Pz. Rgt. 33	29.4.45
Bauer, Michael	Major, Kdr. I./I.R. 499 + 15.2.43 in a field hospital at Sclobodka (Russia) as Oberst & Kdr. G. R. 488	2.2.42
Bauer, Oskar	Major, Kdr. II./Flak-Rgt. 4	22.10.41
Bauer, Robert	Major, Fhr. Kampfgr. der 15. I.D.	11.3.45
Bauer, Viktor	Oblt., Staffelkpt. 9./J.G. 3 107th Oak Leaves 26.7.42	30.7.41
Bauhaus, Gerhard	Hptm. d.R., Staffelkpt. 8./Stuka-Gechw. 77 + 2.9.42 in hospital at Greifswald of wounds	25.5.42
Baum, Adolf	Oblt., Bttr. Fhr. in Flak-Rgt. 37 (mot.) + 4.12.42 in Russia	21.12.42
Baum, Adolf	Ofw., Zugf. in 1./Div. Füs. Btl. 197	26.3.44
Baum, Otto	SS-Sturmbannfhr., Kdr. II./SS-Totenkopf-Inf.Rgt. 3 277th Oak Leaves 22.8.43 95th Swords 2.9.44	8.5.42
Baumann, Paul	Ofw., Zugf. in Radf. Kp./G. R. 422 + 6.2.44 in a dressing station at Luga (Russia)	1.9.43
Baumann, Willi	SS-Sturmbannfhr., Quartiermeister XI. SS-A.K. & Fhr. of a Kampfgruppe	27.1.45
Baumbach, Werner	Lt., Flugzeugfhr. in 5./K.G. 30 20th Oak Leaves 14.7.41 16th Swords 17.8.42	8.5.40
Baumgarten-Crusius, Werner	Oblt., Chef 5./I.R. 156 (mot.) 199th Oak Leaves 27.2.43	99.2.42
Baumgartl, Erich	Oblt., Staffelkpt. 3./K.G. 55 + 12.7.44 in NW Europe as Hptm. & Kdr. 1./K.G. 30	31.7.43
Baunach, Gregor	Major, Kdr. I./G. R. 173	5.9.44
Baur, Eugen	Major, Fhr. Inf.Rgt. 470	2.2.42
Baurmann, Heinz (12)	Hptm., Kdr. St. Gesch. Brig. 300 (Feld)	4.5.45
Bausch, Dr. jur. Albert	Hptm. d.R., Kdr. St. Gesch. Abt. 286 + 29.8.44 at Piatra-Neamt (Rumania) as Major d.R.	10.2.44
Bausch, Friedrich	Lt., Kpfhr. 3./Fsch. Pi. Btl. 5	12.3.45

Name	Rank/Unit	Date
Bausch, Richard	Hptm. d.R., Fhr. II./G. R. 57	9.6.44
Baxmann, Karl	Oblt., Fhr. II./Pz. G. R. 73	14.5.44
Bayer, Anton	Ofw., Zugf. in 14. (Pz.Jäg.)/G. R. 19	5.10.43
Bayer, Franz	Hptm., Kdr. I./Pz. Rgt. 26	9.5.45
Bayer, Hans (17)	Hptm., Staffelkpt. 3. (F)/Aufkl. Gr. 33	1.5.45
Bayer, Heinz	Obstlt., Kdr. Kradschützen-Btl. 22	17.7.41
Bayer, Rudolf	Ofw., Zugf. in 14. (Pz.Jäg.)/G. R. 112 + 14.7.44 of wounds, in field hospital at Sokal (Russia); posthumously promoted to Oblt. d.R.	21.2.44
Bayerlein, Fritz	Obstlt. i.G., Chef d. Gen. St. DAK 258th Oak Leaves 6.7.43 81st Swords 20.7.44	26.12.41
Frhr. v. Beaulieu-Marconnay, Sigurt-Horstmar	Oberst, Kdr. G. R. 29 (mot.) + 8.10.53 in Camp Krasnopolje in Soviet captivity	20.1.43
Bebel, Hermann	Obgefr., in 1./Div. Füs. Btl. 88	18.2.44
Becher, Karl	Owm., Bttr. Offz. in 8./A.R. 125	25.10.43
Bechler, Helmut	Oberst, Kdr. G. R. 504	26.3.44
Beck, Josef	Feldw., Zugf. in 7./G. R. 320	11.3.45
Beck, Karl	Major, Kdr. I./G. R. 290 + 17.1.45 at Radom (Poland) as Oberst & Rgt. Kdr.	2.4.43
Beck, Wilhelm	SS-Obersturmfhr., Fhr. 2./SS-Pz. Rgt. 1 "LSSAH" + 10.6.44 at La Cain (France) as SS-Hauptsturmfhr.	28.3.43
Beck-Broichsitter, Helmut	Oblt., Chef 14. (Pzjäg.)/I.R. "GD"	4.9.40
Becker, Anton	Hptm., Rgt. Adj. G. R. 77	5.4.45
Becker, Arthur	Uffz., Gruppenfhr. in 7./Schützen-Rgt. 394	25.8.41
Becker, Carl	Oberst, Kdr. I.R. 18 829th Oak Leaves 14.4.45	29.10.42
Becker, Erich	Major, Kdr. Gren. Rgt. Gruppe 425	21.9.44
Becker, Felix	Oberst, Kdr. G. R. 418	25.1.43
Becker, Fritz	Gen. Major, Kdr. 370. I.D.	6.4.43
Becker, Günther	Ofw., Flugzeugfhr. in 3./Fernaufkl. Gr. 122	28.2.45
Becker, Hanns	Major d.R., Kdr. Ost-Btl. 439	23.8.44
Becker, Hans	SS-Hptsturmfhr., Chef 2./2. Pz. Gren. Rgt./Pz. Gren. Div "LSSAH" + 20.8.44 at St. Lambert in France (Normandy) as SS-Strmbannfhr. & Kdr. I./SS-Pz. G. R. 2	28.3.43
Becker, Hans	Lt., d.R., Fhr. 2./I.R. 116	28.11.40
Becker, Heinrich	Ofw., Zugf. in 8./Pz. Rgt. 31	15.3.43
Becker, Heinrich	Uffz., Gruppenfhr. in 8./G. R. 529	6.4.44
Becker, Hellmuth	SS-Standartenfhr., Kdr. SS-Pz. G. R. 6 "Theodor Eicke" 595th Oak Leaves 21.9.44	7.9.43

Name	Details	Date
Becker, Karl-Heinz	Oblt., Chef II./Fschjäger-Rgt. 1 780th Oak Leaves 12.3.45	9.7.41
Becker, Karl-Heinz	Oblt., Fhr. I./I.R. 503 + 8.2.42 at Pustynka (Russia)	27.1.42
Becker, Karl-Heinz	Lt. d.R., Fhr. 1./Jäger-Rgt. 503 + 8.2.42 at Pustynka east of Pola (Russia); posthumously promoted to Hauptmann	27.1.42
Becker, Ludwig	Oblt., Staffelkpt. 12./N. J.G. 1 198th Oak Leaves 26.2.43	1.7.42
Becker, Martin	Oblt., Flugzeugfhr. in IV./N. J.G. 6 792nd Oak Leaves 20.3.45	1.4.44
Becker, Paul	Obgefr., Richtkan. in 10./A.R. 3 (mot.) simultaneously promoted to Uffz.	25.10.42
Becker, Rudolf	Oblt., Chef I./Pz. G. R. 66 + 13.10.44 north of Püspök-Ladany (Hungary); posthumously promoted to Hauptmann	23.2.44
Becker, Wilhelm	Uffz., Geschützfhr. in II./Flak-Rgt. 43	4.5.44
Becker, Wilhelm	Ofw., Zugfhr. in Pzjäger-Kp. 1299	18.2.45
Beckh, Friedrich	Major, Kommodore J.G. 51 + 21.6.42 east of Kharkov (Russia) as Kmdr. J.G. 52; posthumously promoted to Oberstlt.	18.9.41
Beckmann, Josef	Obgefr., in Stab IR./Füs. Rgt. 39	7.9.43
Beckmann, Dr. jur. Julius	Obstlt., Kdr. G. R. 457 + 28.8.44 in Raum Jassy-Tighina (Rumania) as Oberst	9.6.44
Beckmann, Ludwig	Obstlt., Kdr. Kampfgruppe z.b.V. 500 (Transport)	14.3.43
Beckmann, Ludwig	Owm., V. B. in 2./Pz. A.R. 27	26.10.43
Beckmann, Theodor	Oberst, Kdr. IV./K.G. z. bV. 1	23.12.42
Beeger, Horst	Oblt., Staffelkpt. 3. (K)/Lehr-Geschw. 1	23.11.41
Beerenbrock, Franz Josef	Uffz., Flugzeugfhr. in 10./J.G. 51 108th Oak Leaves 3.8.42	6.10.41
Begemann, Franz	Lt. d.R., Fhr. I./Pz. Rgt. 21	19.12.43
Begemann, Hermann	Obstlt., Kdr. I.R. 132 simultaneously promoted to Oberst	18.12.42
Beginen, Josef	Ofw., Zugf. in 4./Pz. Rgt. 35	23.2.44
Behlendorff, Hans	Gen.Lt., Kdr. 34. I.D.	11.10.41
Behler, Klemens	SS-Obersturmfhr., Chef 3./SS-Art.Rgt. 54 "Nederland"	17.3.45
Behm, Herbert (17)	Oblt., Chef 4./Flak-Rgt. 33	1.4.45
Behne, Friedrich	Major d.R., Kdr. Sicherungs-Btl. 738 + 7.6.44 in Russia of wounds	26.3.44
Behnke, Gerhard	Hptm., Fhr. St. Geschütz-Abt. 203 605th Oak Leaves 4.10.44	8.2.43

Behnke, Heinz	Lt. d.R., Zugf. in 14. (Pz.Jäg.)/G. R. 668	20.1.44
Behnken, Hans	Hptm. z. V., Kdr. I./G. R. 161 + 5.10.44 of his wounds at Thorn base hospital as Oberstlt. and Kdr. Gr. Rgt. 696	19.12.42
Baron v. Behr, Heinrich	Oberst, Kdr. G. R. 200 (mot.) 689th Oak Leaves 9.1.45	23.2.44
Behr, Paul	Hptm. d.R., Chef 13./Füs. Rgt. 39	28.3.45
Behr, Rudolf	Hptm., Kdr. III./Pz. Gren. Rgt. 201 + 23.7.43 in Russia as Abt.Kdr. Pz. Rgt. 4; posthumously promoted to Major	25.1.43
Behr, Winrich	Oblt., Chef 3./Au&I. Abt. 3 in DAK	15.5.41
Behre, Friedrich	Lt., Kp. Fhr. in I./Fsch. Pz. G. R. 1 "HG"	9.5.45
Behrend, Hermann-Heinrich	Major, Kdr. I./I.R. 489 421st Oak Leaves 6.3.44 148th Swords 26.4.45	15.7.41
Behrends, Heinrich	Uffz., Gruppenfhr. in 6./Pz. G. R. 5	24.12.44
Behrens, Heinz-Georg	Lt. d.R., stellv. Fhr. 3./Pz. Abt. 5 + 16.6.44	12.3.44
Behrens, Wilhelm	Oberst, Kdr. I.R. 106 simultaneously promoted to Gen. Major	27.3.42
Beier, Gerhard	Lt. d.R., Fhr. Pz.Jäg. Kp. 1193	17.3.45
Beier, Karl	Oblt., Flugzeugfhr., Beobachter & Verb-Offz. to 5. Rumanian Kampfgr.	6.12.44
Beier, Wilhelm	Ofw., Flugzeugfhr. in 3./N. J.G. 2	10.10.41
Beigel, Fritz	Major, Kdr. Pz. Pi. Btl. 39	9.7.41
Beilhack, Xaver	Lt. d.R., Fhr. 9./G. R. 19 "List" + 24.1.45 at Friedeberg (Pomerania) as Oblt. d.R.	5.11.44
Beine, Erich	Hptm., Fhr. 1./Fsch. Jäg-Rgt. 12	5.9.44
Beißwenger, Hans	Lt., Flugzeugfhr. in 6./J.G. 54 130th Oak Leaves 3.10.42	9.5.42
Graf v. Bellegarde, Franz	Hptm., Chef 3./Pz. Aufkl. Abt. 25 + 19.12.41 of his wounds in a field hospital in Armenskaja (Russia) as Kdr. Pz. Aufkl. Abt. 25	28.11.40
Bellinger, Hans-Joachim	Hptm., Chef 9./Fsch. Pz. Rgt. "HG"	30.9.44
Bellof, Ludwig	Ofw., Flugzeugfhr. in 1./Nacht-Schlacht-Gruppe 3	28.1.45
Below, Dr.-Ing. Fritz	Obstl., Kdr. G. R. 669	21.9.44
v. Below, Gerd-Paul	Oberst d.R., Kdr. Div. Stab z.b.V. 615 + 8.12.53 in Soviet captivity in Camp Wolkowo in Moscow, final post Generalmajor d.R. & Kdr. Of the 207. Sich. Div.	28.2.43
Belser, Helmut	Hptm., Staffelkpt. in 3./J.G. 53 + 19.6.42 in Castel Benito, Tripoli (North Africa)	6.9.42
Belz, Kurt	Oblt., Chef 3./Pz. G. R. 25	30.4.45
Belz, Josef	Oblt., Flugzeugfhr. in K.G. z.b.V. 500 + 2.11.44 as Major & Gr. Kdr. in T. Geschw. 1	23.12.42

Belzer, Hans	Major d.R., Kdr. IV./A.R. 227	4.10.44
Benack, Gerhard	Oblt., Chef 1./Kradschtz. Btl. 38	13.8.41
Bender, Hans-Wilhelm	Ofw., Flugzeugfhr. in 5./K.G. 3	8.9.41
Bendert, Karl-Heinz	Ofw., Flugzeugfhr. in 5./J.G. 27	30.12.42
Benedikt, Johann	Obgefr., Kp. Trupp-Melder in 6./Geb.Jäg. Rgt. 138	11.12.43
Benekamp, Peter	Feldw., Kp. Tr. Fhr. in 2./G. R. 546	28.10.44
Benkendorff, Helmut	Ofw., Flugzeugfhr. in II./Stuka-Geschw. 1	26.3.44
Bennemann, Hans	Oblt., Flugzeugfhr. in 7./K.G. 55	26.3.44
Bennernann, Dr. med. dent., Helmut	Hptm., Kdr. I./J.G. 52	2.10.42
Benner, Heinrich	Hptm. d.R., Kdr. II./Pz. A.R. 102	27.10.44
Benning, Anton	Lt., Staffelkpt. I./J.G. 301	13.4.45
Benthack, Hans-Georg (3)	Gen. Major, Kdr. Festungs-Div. Crete	10.5.45
Bentin, Kurt	Oblt., Fhr. Gren. Btl. 8/9 "FHH" (Alarm unit in Festung Schneidemühl)	12.2.45
Benz, Kurt	Hptm., Staffelfhr. in Kampfgr. z.b.V. 500	24.3.43
Benzin, Otto	Oblt., d.R., Chef 9./I.R. 89 406th Oak Leaves 22.2.44	31.12.41
v. Bercken, Werner	Gen.Lt., Kdr. 102. I.D.	23.10.44
Berg, Anton	Major, Kdr. I./G. R. 358	16.10.44
Berg, Karl-Erich	Oblt., Chef 2./St. Gesch. Abt. 191	6.4.44
Berg, Martin	Oberst, Kdr. G. R. 166	30.12.43
Berg, Wilhelm	Owm., V. B. in II./A.R. 361	9.6.44
Bergelt, Karl	Korv. Kpt., Chef 1. Minensuchflottille	3.8.42
Bergen, Hans	Oberst, Kdr. I.R. 187	9.7.41
Berger, Franz	Feldw., Stoßtruppfhr. in II./I.R. 130 + 29.12.42 at Stalingrad (Russia) as Fhr. 10./Pz. Gr. Rgt. 79 of wounds; posthumously promoted Hauptm. d.R.	19.7.40
Berger, Fritz	Freg. Kpt., Chef 1. Zerstörer-Flottille	4.8.40
Berger, Heinz	Gefr., Richtschütze in 14. (PzJag.)/I.R. 187	17.9.41
Berger, Heinz	Oblt., Bttr. Fhr. in II./Flak-Rgt. 411 in Flak-Rgt. 151 (mot.)	3.4.43
Berger, Herbert	Ofw., Zugf. in 10./G. R. (mot.) "Feldherrnhalle"	12.3.44
Berger, Karl	Lt. d.R., Kp. Fhr. 10./Fsch. Jäg. Rgt. 15	7.2.45
Berger, Lothar	Major, Kdr. III./I.R. 84 806th Oak Leaves 28.3.45	5.8.40
Berger, Robert	Major, Kdr. I./G. R. 2	7.3.44
Berger, Rudolf	Feldw., Zugf. in 1./Pi. Btl. 296	14.4. 43

Bergerhoff, Dr. jur. Günther	Oblt. d.R., Adj. 1./G. R. 162	15.4.44
Bergerhoff, Kurt	Oblt., Chef 3./Pz. Aufkl. Abt. 23 + 10.8.44 posthumously promoted to Hptm.	27.8.44
Bergmann, Gustav	Obgefr., Gruppenf. in 9./G. R. 696 + 26.8.45 missing on the Eastern Front as Uffz. d. R in 7./Gr. Rgt. Ostpreußen (4/1145)	4.10.42
Bergmann, Heinz	Ofw., Zugf. in 4./Pz. Rgt. 26	26.11.44
Bergmann, Helmut	Hptm., Staffelkpt. 8./N. J.G. 4 + 6.8.44 at Avranches (France)	9.6.44
Bering, Rolf	Major, Fhr. Fähnrichs-Rgt. 1 der Div. "Märk. Friedland"	11.3.45
Berkenbusch, Wilhelm	Ofw., Zugf. in I./G. R. 914	15.1.45
Berlin, Wilhelm	Gen.Lt., Kdr. 227. I.D.	6.3.44
Bermadinger, Matthias	Oblt., Staffelkpt. 14./K.G. 55 + 18.2.44 at Pleskau (Russia); posthumously promoted to Hptm.	5.4.44
Berndl, Alois	Ofw., Bordschütze in III./Schlacht-Geschw. 1	16.6.44
Berneike, Rudolf	Major, Fhr. Fsch. Jäger-Rgt. 15	15.3.45
Berner, Emil	Gefr., Richtkan. in 3./Flak-Rgt. 18	3.11.42
Berner, Erhard	Oberst, Kdr. Jäger-Rgt. 28	18.1.45
Bernhard, Alfred	Hptm., Insp. Chef in Heeres-Uffz. -Schule Jauer	14.2.45
Bernhard, Hans	Hptm. d.R., Kdr. II./G. R. 165	9.1.45
v. Bernuth, Julius	Obstlt. iG., Chef d. Gen. St. XV. A.K. + 12.7.42 at Sokranaja (Russia) as Gen. Major & Chef d. Gen. St. Pz. AOK 4 (shot down)	5.8.40
Berrer, Herbert	Ob. Fernschreibmeister. Matrose, in K. d. K. -Verband	5.8.44
Berres, Heinz-Edgar	Oblt., Staffelkpt. 1./J.G. 77 + 25.7.43 over the straights of Messina, (1.3.44. Hptm.)	19.9.43
Berthold, Gerhard	Gen. Major, Kdr. 31. I.D. + 14.4. 42 at Juchnow (Russia); posthumously promoted to Gen.Lt.	4.12.41
Bertram, Hans-Wilhelm	Hptm., Staffelkpt. 3./K.G. 6	14.1.45
Bertram, Karl Eric (17)	Oberst, Kdr. Fsch. Pz. G. R. 1 "HG" + on date of his award, at Neisse, Upper Silesia	26.3.45
Bertram, Ludwig	Oblt., Chef 1./St. Gesch. Brig. 237	12.8.44
Bertram, Otto	Hptm., Kdr. III./J.G. 2 "Richthofen"	28.10.40
Beschle, Karl	Lt., Fhr. 4./A.R. 114	3.11.44
Beschnidt, Werner	Oblt., Fhr. 2./Pz. Abt. 103	4.10.44
Frhr. v. Beschwitz, Werner	Major, Kdr. s. Pz. Abt. 505	27.7.44
Besler, Erwin	Rittm., Kdr. Schnelle Abt. 123	29.12.42

Beßlein, Georg-Robert	SS-Obersturmbannfhr., Kdr. SS-Festg. Rgt. 1 "Beßlein" in Festg. Breslau	30.4.45
Bestmann, Walter	SS-Sturmbannfhr., Kdr. Aufkl. Abt. "Totenkopf'	28.9.41
Bethke, Hans-Günther	Oblt., Fhr. 5./Pz. Rgt. 11 + 14.9.42 at Mga (Russia) as Hptm. & Chef 1./Pz. Abt. z.b.V. 66 s. Verw. erlegen	4.9.40
Betke, Siegfried	Oblt., Staffelkpt. 9./K.G. 26	8.8.44
Betz, Franz-Eugen	Uffz., Gruppenfhr. in 7./I.R. 41 (mot.) + 22.8.42 at Rshew (Russia); posthumously promoted to Feldw.	30.8.42
Betz, Karl	Hptm., Fhr. II./Schtz. Rgt. 2 + 2.7.42 at Parnewo (Russia) as Major and Kdr. I./Schützen Rgt. 2	6.3.42
Betz, Paul	Oberst, Fhr. 50. I.D. + 9.5.44 at Sevastopol (Russia); posthumously promoted to Gen. Major	16.6.44
Betzel, Clemens	Gen. Major, Kdr. 4. Pz.Div. 774th Oak Leaves 11.3.45	5.9.44
Beukemann, Helmuth	Oberst, Kdr. I.R. 382	14.5.41
Beukemann, Lothar	Major, Kdr. Pz. Pi. Btl. 79	25.1.45
Frhr. v. Beust, Hans-Henning	Hptm., Kdr. III./K.G. 27 "Boelcke" 336th Oak Leaves 25.11.43	17.9.41
Beutelspacher, Ernst	Oblt., Staffelfhr. 6./Schlacht-Geschw. 2 "Immelmann" + 22.7.44 at Focsani (Rumania) as Staffelkpt.	4.5.44
Beutler, Heinz	Oblt., Chef 3./Pz. Rgt. 2	14.2.45
Beutler, Walter	Owm., St. Geschützfhr. in 3./St. Gesch. Abt. 245	13.8.43
Beutner, Manfred	Major, Div. Adj. 329 in & Kdr. Schnelle Abt. 329	30.9.44
Beuttel, Wilhelm	Major d.R., Kdr. II./G. R. 45 + 24.3.45 at Lütkenfürst/East Prussia as Fhr. G. R. 3	5.3.45
Bevernis, Heinz	Ofw., Bordschütze in 7./Stuka-Geschw. 1 + 19.7.42 at Staraja Russa (Russia)	19.9.42
Bey, Erich	Kapt. z. See, Chef 4. Zerstörer-Flottille + 26.12.43 in the North Sea, aboard the "Scharnhorst" as Konteradm., Führer der Zerstörer & Befehls. of Kampfgruppe North Norway	9.5.40
Beyer, Franz	Oblt., Staffelkpt. 8./J.G. 3 + 11.2.44 at Venlo (Holland) as Major & Kdr. IV./J.G. 3 "Udet"	30.8.41
Beyer, Dr. jur. Franz	Oberst, Kdr. I.R. 131	12.9.41
Beyer, Herbert	Hptm., Kdr. I./Fschjäger-Rgt. 4	9.6.44

Beyer, Reinhard	Oblt. d.R., Chef 2./I.R. 694 + 1.11.43 at Jassnogorodka (Russia) as Fhr. Gr. Rgt. 696; posthumously promoted to Major	17.10.42
Bialetzki, Alfons	Lt. d.R., Fhr. 1./G. R. 333	17.9.44
Frhr. v. Bibra, Ernst	Major, Kdr. III./K.G. 51 + 15.2.43 in the Donets area (Russia)	23.12.42
Bickel, Rolf-Günther	Oberst, Art. -Kdr. 35	8.8.44
Bieber, Martin	Oberst, Kdr. G. R. 184 566th Oak Leaves 2.9.44	28.7.43
Biecker, Albert	Hptm. d. Landwehr, Chef 9./I.R. 386 + 1.5.42 at Cholm (Russia)	18.3.42
Bieg, Karl	Hptm., Fhr. II./G. R. 868	17.9.43
Frhr. v. Biegeleben, Arnold	Gen.Lt., Kdr. 6. I.D. + 11.10.40 at Jullonville (France)	5.8.40
Biegi, Fritz	SS-Oberscharfhr., Zugfhr. in 5./SS-Pz. G. R. 9 "Germania" + 16.3.45 north of Leobschütz (Upper Silesia) as SS-StandartenOberjunker	16.6.44
Bichl, Johann	Feldw., Zugl. in 2./I.R. 124	30.7.42
Biehler, Ernst	Gen. Major, Festg. Kdt. Frankfurt/Oder	9.5.45
Bieler, Bruno	Gen.Lt., Kdr. 73. I.D.	26.10.41
Bielig, Gerhard	Kaptlt. (Ing.). Leit. Ing. auf "U 177"	10.2.43
Bielig, Martin	Ofw., Zugf. in 13./Pz. Gr. Rgt. "GD"	7.10.44
Bienck, Fritz	Oblt., Chef 5./G. R. 281	14.4. 45
Bierbrauer, Günther	Feldw., Flugzeugfhr. in 14./K.G. 27 "Boelcke"	17.4.45
Bierlin, Otto	Rittm., Kdr. Div. Füs. Btl. 35	26.11.44
Biermann, Fritz	Oblt., Fhr. 3./Pz. Aufkl. Abt. 6 + 30.3.45 at Raab (Hungary)	31.8.43
Biermeler, Fritz	SS-Hptsturmfhr., Fhr. II./SS-Pz. Rgt. 3 "Totenkopf" 685th Oak Leaves 26.12.44	10.12.43
Biesenbach, Willi	Ofw., Zugfhr. in 2./Heeres-Uff-z. -Schule Jülich + 16.11.44	11.12.44
Bigalk, Gerhard	Kaptlt., Kdt. "U 751" + 18.7.42 in north Atlantic	26.12.41
Biggemann, Werner	Lt. d.R., Fhr. 3./Landungs-Pi. Btl. 86 + 4.4. 45 at Borgeln in Soest (Westphalia)	26.11.44
Bingemer, Dr. Fritz	Oberst, Kdr. I.R. 442	9.4.43
Binnig, Otto	Obergefr., Melder in 7./G. R. 463	5.10.44
v. Birckhahn, Eberhard	Rittm., Kdr. Aufkl. Abt. 321 + 5.4.44	10.2.45
Birk, Walter	Oblt., Chef 2./Div. Aufkl. Abt. 44	2.11.41
Birkner, Hans-Joachim	Fhj. -Feldw., Flugzeugfhr. in 9./J.G. 52 + 14.12.44 in Cracow (Poland) as Lt. & Staffelfhr.	27.7.44
Birnbacher, Heinz	Kaptlt., Chef 1. Schnellbootsflottille	17.6.40
Birnbaum, Fritz	Ob. Fähnr., Zugf. in 8./Fsch. Pz. Rgt. "HG"	19.10.44

Birnkraut, Paul	Oblt., Flugzeuf. in 1./Fern. Aufkl. Gruppe 121	10.5.43
Bischof, Kurt	Obgefr. in 5./G. R. 337	14.4. 45
Bischoff, Adolf	Obgefr., Gr. Fhr. in 1./Pz. G. R. 112	12.3.44
Bischoff, Hans	Major, Fhr. Pz. G. R. 5	9.12.44
Bischoff, Leonhard	Lt., Zufhr. in 1./Pz. G. R. 115	30.4.45
Bischoff, Otto	Oblt., Staffelkpt. 4./K.G. 77+ 2.4.42 over Malta	3.5.42
v. Bischoffshausen, Lothar	Oberst, Kdr. Pz. G. R. 2	4.10.42
v. Bismarck, Georg	Oberst, Kdr. Schtz. Rgt. 7 + 31.8.42 at El Alamein (North Africa) as Gen. Major & Kdr. 21. Pz.Div. posthumously promoted to Gen.Lt.	29.9.40
v. Bismarck, Klaus	Oblt., Fhr. II./I.R. 4 669th Oak Leaves 26.11.44	31.12.41
Bisping, Joseph	Oblt., Beobachter in 4. (F)/Aufkl. Gr. des OB der Luftwaffe + 13.2.45 in Berlin as Hptm. & Fhr. Nachtjagdversuchsverband des OKL	22.10.41
Bitsch, Emil	Oblt., Staffelkpt. 8./J.G. 3 "Udet" + 15.3.44 at Volkel (Holland) as Hptm.	29.8.43
Bittl, Xaver	Ofw., Zugf. in 3./G. R. 423 + 26.5.44 in Russia, of wounds	4.11.43
Bittlingmaier, Georg	Oblt. d.R., Fhr. I./I.R. 391 + 30.6,42 at Sevastopol (Russia), of wounds	25.7.42
Bittner, Herwig	Lt., Zugf. in 1./St. Gesch. Abt. 270 + 22.8.44 in Russia	18.1.44
Bittner, Rudolf	Gefr., Richtkan. in 2./Pz.Jäg. Abt. 561 + 21.1.45 missing	28.11.42
Bittorf, Otto	Lt., Fhr. 5./Pz. G. R. 4	18.11.44
Bittrich, Wilhelm	SS-Oberfhr., Kdr. SS-I.R. "Deutschland" 563rd Oak Leaves 28.8.44 153rd Swords 6.5.45	14.12.41
Bix, Hermann	Ofw., Zugf. in 3./Pz. Rgt. 35	22.3.45
Bladt, Wilhelm	Oblt. d.R., Chef 6./A.R. 30 + 10.8.44 in Estonia as Hptm. d.R.	22.12.42
Blaich, Albert	Ofw., Zugf. in 12./Pz. Rgt. 6 + 15.3.45 at Orgekeghi (Hungary) as Oblt. & Fhr. 2./Pz. Rgt. 6	24.7.41
v. Blanc, Adalbert	Freg. Kpt., Fhr. d. 9. Sicherungs-Div. 866th Oak Leaves 10.5.45	27.11.44
Blanchois, Gustav-Adolf	Hptm., Kdr. I. (gep.)/Pz. G. R. 25	20.7.44
Blasberg, Kurt	Oblt. z. See d.R., Gruppenf. in 36. Minensuchflottille	7.9.44
Blasig, Arnulf	Hptm., Kdr. IV. (Stuka)/Lehr-Geschw. 1	4.9.41
Blaskowitz, Johannes	Gen.D.Inf., O. B. 8. Armee 640th Oak Leaves 29.10.44 146th Swords 25.4.45	30.9.39
Blauensteiner, Ernst	Obstlt. i.G., Chef d. Gen. St. 11. Fallsch. Korps	29.10.44

Name	Details	Date
Blaurock, Edmund	Oberst i.G., Kdr. G. R. 320 746th Oak Leaves 19.2.45	27.7.44
Blechschmidt, Joachim	Major, Kdr. 1./Z.G. 1 + 2.7.43 missing at Orel; posthumously promoted to Oberstlt.	17.3.43
Bleckl, Karl	Oblt., Staffelfhr. 7./Stuka-Geschw. 1	3.11.42
Bleckmann, Günther	Hptm. d.R., Staffelkpt. 6. & Fhr. II./Schlacht-Geschw. 2 "Immelmann" + 4.6.44 at Stanitza (Rumania); posthumously promoted to Major d.R.	9.6.44
Bleckwenn, Wilhelm	Oberst, Kdr. G. R. 487 621st Oak Leaves 18.10.44	6.4.44
Bleher, Georg	Oblt. d.R., Adj. Stab 1./G. R. 358	6.5.45
Bleiehrodt, Heinrich	Kaptlt., Kdt. "U 48" 125th Oak Leaves 23.9.42	24.10.40
Bleyer, Eugen-Heinrich	Obstlt., Kdr. I.R. 379	14.12.41
Bleyer, Werner	Feldw., Zugf. in 4./s. II. Pzjäg. Abt. 563 + 28.2.45	24.2.45
Bliesener, Fritz	Lt., Flugzeugfhr. in 5./K.G. 55 + 25.11.42 in Russia as Oblt. & Geschw. Adj. K.G. 55	20.12.41
Bloch, Johann	Ofw., Kp. Truppfhr. in I./G. R. 44	14.4. 45
Bloch, Johannes	Oberst, Kdr. I.R. 202 331st Oak Leaves 22.11.43	22.12.41
Block, Josef	Uffz., Gruppenfhr. in 5./G. R. 2	6.6.43
Bloedorn, Erich	Major, Kdr. III./K.G. 4 "General Wever"	13.10.40
Blond, Friedrich (10)	SS-Untersturmfilhrer, Fhr. 12./SS-Pz. Gren. A. & E. Btl. 1 "LSSAH"	28.4.45
Bloos, Ludwig	Ofw., Zugf. in 8./Pz. Rgt. 11	6.4.44
Graf v. Blücher(-Fincken), Wolfgang	Lt. d.R., Zugf. in 2./Fschjäg. Rgt. 1 + 20.5.41 at Heraklion, Crete, as Oblt. & Zgfhr.	24.5.40
Blümel, Josef	Feldw., Flugzeugfhr. in 10. (Pz.)/Schl. Geschw. 3 + 19.9.44 south of Riga (Latvia) murdered	28.1.45
Blümke, Friedrich	Oberst, Kdr. G. R. 347 + 2.9.44 on the Dnjestr (Russia) as Gen. Major & Kdr. 257. I.D.	6.11.43
Blümm, Oskar	Gen.Lt., Kdr. 57. I.D.	23.11.41
Blume, Hermann	Rittm., Kdr. Pz. AufklAbt. 24	11.3.45
Blume, Werner	Lt., Flugzeugf. in 1./FernauflA. Gruppe 122 + 3.7.42 in North Africa; posthumously promoted to Oblt.	1.7.42
Blumenroth, Willi	Uffz., Gruppenfhr. in 3./I.R. 124 + 17.6.42 Sevastopol (Russia) as Feldw. & Zugf.	23.10.41
Blumenthal, Carl-Ludwig	Oblt. d.R., Chef 7./I.R. "GD"	18.9.42

ELITE OF THE THIRD REICH

Blumentritt, Günther	Gen.D.Inf., Chef d. Gen. St. H.Gr.D 741st Oak Leaves 18.2.45	13.9.44
Bob, Hans-Ekkehard	Oblt., Staffelkpt. 9./J.G. 54	7.3.41
Bobbe, Reinhold	Hptm., Kdr. I./G. R. 870	23.3.45
Bochentin, Richard	Major, Kdr. II./G. R. 405 + 23.2.45 as Obstlt., Kdr. G. R. 408 in Kurland	12.2.44
Bochmann, Georg	SS-Hauptsturmfhr., Kdr. SS-Pz.Jäg. Abt. "Totenkopf" 246th Oak Leaves 17.5.43 140th Swords 26.3.45	3.5.42
Bochnig, Helmut	Major, Kdr. Pzjäg. Abt. 228	9.6.44
Bock, Albert	Stabsfeldw., Beob. in Stab/Stuka-Geschw. 2 "Immelmann"	4.9.41
v. Bock, Fedor	Gen. Oberst, O. B. Heeresgruppe Nord + 3.5.45 at Lensahn (Holstein) as Gen. Feldm. by ground-attack aircraft	30.9.39
Bock, Friedrich-Wilhelm	SS-Obersturmbannf. & Obstlt. d. Schupo, Kdr. II./SS-Pol. Art.Rgt. 4 570th Oak Leaves 2.9.44	28.3.43
Bock, Hans	Hpt., Kdr. schw. Pz. Abt. "GD"	5.2.45
Bock, Karl	Hptm. d.R., Kdr. III./I.R. 97 + 20.1.43 in western Caucasus (Russia)	3.5.42
Bockhoff, Engelbert	Hptm., Kdr. Pz. Aufkl. Abt. 9	18.11.43
v. Boddien, Oskar	Obstlt., Kdr. Div. AufkLAbt. 22 58th Oak Leaves 8.1.42	2.10.41
Bode, Helmut	Hptm., Kdr. III./Stuka-Geschw. 77	10.10.41
Bodendörfer, Kurt	Major, Fhr. G. R. 689	14.2.45
Frhr. v. Bodenhausen, Erpo	Gen. Major, Kdr. 12. Pz.Div. + 9.5.45 in Kurland as Gen.Lt. & m. d. F. b. L A.K. (suicide)	17.12.43
Böbel, Hermann	Obgefr. Of 1./Div. Füs. Btl. 88	18.2.44
Böck, Wilhelm	Oberst, Kdr. Art. Rgt 176 + January 43 in Stalingrad (Russia)	20.1.43
Böckel, Dr. jur. Hermann	Oberst d.R., Kdr. G. R. 688	12.8.44
Boecker, Heinrich	Hptm., Staffelkpt. 12. (K)/Lehr-Geschw. 1	29.2.44
Boeckh-Behrens, Hans	Gen.Lt., Kdr. 32. I.D. + 13.2.1955 in Soviet captivity in Russia	9.12.44
v. Böckmann, Herbert	Gen.Lt., Kdr. 11. I.D.	4.12.41
Boeckmann, Dr. rer. pol., Rudolf	Major d.R., Kdr. schw. Art. Abt. 408 + 19.9.44 at Slimisti/Estonia as Oberst d. R & Kdr. A.R. 187	23.7.42
Bödicker, Heinz	Hptm. d.R., Fhr. Pz. Pi. Btl. 209 + 9.3.45 in Rheinbreitbach as Major & Kdr. Pz. Pl. Btl. 209	9.1.44
Boege, Ehrenfried-Oskar	Oberst, Kdr. I.R. 7 594th Oak Leaves 21.9.44	22.12.41

KNIGHT'S CROSS OF THE IRON CROSS

Bögel, Hermann	Lt. z. See d.R., Kdt. "M 4040"	13.10.42
Boehlein, Rudolf	Oblt., Chef 2./Fschjäger-Rgt. 4	30.11.44
Böhlke, Hellmuth	Oberst, Kdr. I.R. 430 716th Oak Leaves 25.1.45	24.9.42
Böhm, Ernst	Hptm., Chef 2./Flak-Rgt. 241 (mot.)	20.6.43
Böhm, Fritz	Ofw., Zugf. in 6./Pz. Rgt. 26	23.8.44
Böhm, Walter	Ofw., Pz. Spähtruppfhr. in 1./Pz. Au&I. Abt. 8	17.3.45
Böhme, Franz	Gen.Lt., Kdr. 32. I.D. + 29.5.47 suicide in Nürnberg as Gen. d. Geb. Tr. & O. B. 20. Geb. Armee (in American captivity)	29.6.40
Böhme, Friedrich	Kapt. z. See, Einsatzleiter der Kriegsmarine-Kleinkampfmittel in France	26.8.44
Böhme, Herbert	Major, Kdr. III./I.R. 28 + 27.12.43 in Russia as Oberst & Kdr. G. R. (mot.) "FHH"	19.7.40
Boehmer, Hans	Rittm., Kdr. Aufkl. Abt. 238	10.9.43
Böhmer, Kurt	Kapt. z. See, Chef d. St. d. Befehlshaber der Sicherung Nordsee + 1.10.44 at Windau (Lithuania) as Konteradm. & Fhr. 9. Sich. Div.	6.10.40
Böhmer, Leopold	Major, Kdr. IR./I.R. 270 + Killed as Oberst	13.7.40
Böhmke, Reinhold	Ofw., Zugf. in 13. (l. G.)/G. R. 162	6.4.44
Böhmler, Rudolf	Major, Kdr. 1./Fsch. Jäger-Rgt. 3	26.3.44
Böhrendt, Max	Oblt., Fla-Zugf. in Stabskp./Gren. Rgt. "GD"	8.2.43
Boelsen, Dr. jur. Dr. rer. pol. Hans	Oberst, Kdr. Pz. Gren. Rgt. 111	17.9.43
Bölter, Johannes	Lt., zugf. in 1./schw. Pz. Abt. 502 581st Oak Leaves 10.9.44	16.4.44
Böhnk, Georg	Oblt., Fhr. II./Pz. Füs. Rgt. "GD"	18.2.45
Boenicke, Walter	Gen.Lt., Kdr. 3. Flieger-Div. + 21.4.47 in Munsterlager as Gen. d. Flieger in British captivity (suicide)	14.5.44
Böning, Georg	Fhj. -Ofw., Zugf. in 13. (l. G.)/G. R. 412 + 23.2.45	27.8.44
de Boer, Johannes	Obstlt., Kdr. Art.Rgt. 22	19.6.40
Börngen, Ernst	Hptm., Staffelkpt. 5./J.G. 27	3.8.44
Boerst, Alwin	Oblt., Flugzeugf. in 3./Stuka-Geschw. 2 "Immelmann" 149th Oak Leaves 28.11.42 61st Swords 6.4.44	5.10.41
Bösel, Otto	Wachtm., Geschützfhr. in 1./Flak-Rgt. 43 (mot.) "Afrika"	11.6.44
Frhr. v. Boeselager, Georg	Oblt., Chef 1. (reit.)/Div. Aufkl. Abt. 6 53rd Oak Leaves 31.12.41 114th Swords 28.11.44	18.1.41
Frhr. v. Boeselager, Philipp	Major, Kdr. I./Kav. Rgt. Mitte	20.7.44
Böttcher, Karl	Gen. Major, Kdr. 21. Pz.Div.	13.12.41

ELITE OF THE THIRD REICH

Boettcher, Kurt	Major, Kdr. I./A.R. 27 (mot.) + 2.9.41 at Berlje-Berjoski (Russia)	4.9.41
Boettcher, Kurt	Major, Kdr. Pi. Btl. 44 + 27.6.44 at Narva (Russia) as Obstlt.; posthumously promoted to Oberst	21.2.43
Böttcher, Paul	Owm., Schwadr. Fhr. 2. Marschkp./Feldersatz-Btl. 89	30.9.44
Böttcher, Walther-Hans	Oblt., Fhr. 1./G. R. 216 + 6.6.43 at Archangelskoje (Russia) as Hptm. & Kdr. Sturm-Btl./Gr. Rgt. 186	8.2.43
Böwe, Johannes	Hptm. d.R., Chef 14. (Pzjäg.)/G. R. 397	11.12.43
Böwing-Treuding, Wolfgang	Oblt., Staffelfhr. 10./J.G. 51 "Mölders" + 11.2.43 at Welikje-Luki (Russia)	24.3.43
Boffer, Wilhelm	Major d.R., Fhr. Gren. Rgt. 1039	16.10.44
Bogatsch, Rudolf	Gen. d. Flg., General d. Luftw. in the Oberbe-fehlshaber des Heeres	20.3.42
Bogert, Bruno	Hptm. d.R., Kdr. Sich. Btl. 670	21.4.44
Bohlens, Helmut	Oblt., Flugzeugfhr. in 5./Fernaufkl. Gruppe 122 + 19.4.43 in Mediterranean area	21.6.43
Bohlken, Erwin	Feldw., Zugf. in 1./Pz. Rgt. 1	17.3.45
Bohlmann-Combrinck, Theodor	Oberst, Kdr. Schtz. Rgt. 111	8.8.41
Bohn, Wolfgang	Hptm., Kdr. III./Pz-Gren. Rgt. 8 + in April 1945 at Raum Brünn (Böhmen-Mähren) as Kdr. I./Pz. Gren. Rgt. 98	9.12.44
Bohnenkamp, Hans	Major d.R., Kdr. III./Art.Rgt. 295	22.1.43
Bohnstedt, Wilhelm	Gen. Major, Kdr. 32. I.D.	13.10.41
Bolgk, Heinrich	Oberjäger, Gruppenfhr. in 2./Jäger-Rgt. 49 370th Oak Leaves 18.1.44	5.5.43
Reichfrhr. v. Boineburg-Lengsfeld, Hans	Oberst, Kdr. 4. Schtz. Brig.	19.7.40
Boje, Arthur	Oberst, Kdr. I.R. 134	5.2.42
Boje, Johannes	Oberst, Kdr. G. R. 37 + 26.6.44 at Kabanowka (Russia)	11.1.44
Bolbrinker, Ernst, Dipl.Ing.	Major, Kdr. I./Pz. Rgt. 5	15.5.41
Boldt, Gerhard	Oblt. d.R., Fhr. 3./Div. Aufkl. Abt. 158	18.4.43
Bollmann, Burghardt	Hptm. d.R., Kdr. I./G. R. 1038 + 21.10.44	5.11.44
Bollmann, Fred	Major d.R., Kdr. III./K.G. 55	29.10.44
Bolm, Hermann-Ernst	Hptm. d.R., Fhr. II./G. R. 434 + 20.10.44 at Ebenroda (Saxony) as Btl. -Kdr.	20.4.44

KNIGHT'S CROSS OF THE IRON CROSS

v. Boltenstern, Walter	Gen. Major, Kdr. 29. I.D. (mot.) + 1952 as Gen.Lt. in Soviet captivity; last post Kdr. Pz.Div. 179; militarily unemployed from 30.1.45	13.8.41
Bonath, Hans	Oblt., Staffelkpt. Wettererkundungsstaffel 27	26.3.44
Bonertz, Hans	Hptm., Fhr. III./I.R. 46	27.3.42
v. Bonin, Dietrich-Siegwart	Rittm. d.R., Kdr. I./Pz. G. R. 21	18.2.45
v. Bonin, Eckart-Wilhelm	Hptm., Kdr. II./NJ.G. 1	5.2.44
v. Bonin, Hubertus	Major, Kdr. III./J.G. 52 + 15.12.43 at Vitebsk (Russia) as Kmdr. J.G. 54; posthumously promoted to Obstlt.	21.12.42
Bonk, Georg	Obgefr., MG-Schtz. in 6./G. R. 365 492nd Oak Leaves 9.6.44	17.8.43
Bonnke, Friedrich	Oblt., Chef 3./Flak-Rgt. 42 (mot.)	6.12.44
Bonte, Friedrich	Kapt. z. See & Kommodore, Führer d. Zerstörer & d. Kampfgr. Narvik + 10.4.40 Narvik (north Norway)	17.10.40
Book, Wilhelm	Oblt., Fhr. 10./I.R. 6 + 21.12.41 south of Lake Ilmen (Russia)	26.11.41
Boos, Johann	Ofw., Flugzeugfhr. in 9./K.G. 55	9.10.43
Boosfeld, Joachim	SS-Obsturmfhr., Chef 4./SS-Kav. Rgt. 16 'Florian Geyer"	21.2.45
Bopp, Alfred	Oblt., Chef 9./I.R. 216	21.12.40
Frhr. v. d. Borch, Alhard	Rittm., Kdr. Pz. Aufkl. Abt. 115	19.8.44
Borchardt, Erich	Ofw., Fhr. i./G. R. 122 + 9.4.44 of wounds	17.3.44
Borchardt, Helmut	Uffz., Gruppenfhr. in 2./G. R. 409 828th Oak Leaves 14.4. 45	30.4.43
Borchardt, Herbert	Lt. d.R., Stoßtr. Fhr. in 7./G. R. 189	20.3.44
Borchardt, Robert	Hptm., Chef Pz. Späh-Kp./Aufkl. Abt. (mot.) 341	23.8.41
Borchers, Adolf	Hptm., Staffelkpt. II./J.G. 51 "Mölders"	22.11.43
Borchers, Hermann	SS-Hptstrmfhr., Fhr. I./SS-Pz. G. R. 19 "Hohenstaufen"	16.10.44
Borchers, Walter	Major, Kmdr. N. J.G. 5 + 5.3.45 over Altenburg (Thuringia) as Obstlt.	27.7.44
Borchert, Ernst	Oblt., Chef I./I.R. 29 (mot.)	29.9.41
Borchert, Wilhelm	Hptm. d.R., Fhr. III./G. R. 121	11.3.43
Borck, Hans-Georg	Oblt. d.R., Chef 3./Pz. Pi. Btl. 209	23.12.43
Bordellé, Walter	Oblt., Flugzeugfhr. in 5./Transport-Geschw. 2	26.3.44
v. Boremski, Eberhard	Ofw., Flugzeugfhr. in 7./J.G. 3 "Udet"	3.5.42
Borgmann, Heinrich	Oblt., Chef 9./I.R. 46 71st Oak Leaves 11.2.42	19.7.40
Bork, Max (19)	Gen.Lt., Kom.Gen. "Korps Bork"	11.5.45

119

ELITE OF THE THIRD REICH

Bormann, Dr.Ing. Ernst	Obstlt., Kommodore K.G. 76 119th Oak Leaves 3.9.42	5.10.41
Born, Ernst	Feldw., Zugf. in 7./G. R. 2 + 27.3.44 on Lake Peipus, Russia	21.4.44
Born, Heinrich	Oblt., Fhr. 4./Pz. Gren. Rgt. 104	14.4. 45
v. Born-Fallois, Gerd	Major, Kdr. Pz. Aufkl. Lehr-Abt. 130	2.1.45
Bornemann, Ralf	Lt., in Stab I./Flaksturm-Rgt. 5 (mot.)	17.4.45
Bornhof, Rudolf	Lt. d.R., Fhr. I./Jäger-Rgt. 38 + 26.1.44 in Russia as Hptm. d.R. & Kp. Chef	3.5.42
Bornschein, Walter	Oblt., Flugzeuf. in II./K.G. 2 + 27.4.44 over Schweinfurt as Hptm. & Staffelkpt.	24.9.42
Borowietz, Willibald	Obstlt., Kdr. Schtz. Rgt. 10 235rd Oak Leaves 10.5.43	24, 7.41
Borries, Hermann	Obstlt., Fhr. I.R. 46 + 16.2.43 in Russia, of wounds as Oberst and Kdr. I.R. 377	3.5.42
Borris, Carl	Major, Kdr. I./J.G. 26 "Schlageter"	25.11.44
Borrmann, Joachim	Hptm., Kdr. III./G. R. 427	13.10.43
Bose, Georg	Lt., Zugf. in 1./St. Gesch. Abt. 177	21.9.44
v. Bose, Jobst-Hilmar	Obstlt., Kdr. I./I.R. 289	4.12.41
Boska, Karl-Heinz	SS-Obstrmfhr., Adj. 111/SS-Pz. Rgt. 2 "Das Reich"	16.12.43
v. Bostell, Wolfgang	Lt., Zugf in PzJäger-Sturmgeschütz-Kp. 1023 859th Oak Leaves 30.4.45	2.9.44
v. Both, Kuno-Hans	Gen. d. Inf, Kom.Gen. I. A.K.	9.7.41
Both, Paul	Feldw., Zugf in 3./G. R. 411 + 12.8.44 in Metz (Lorraine); posthumously promoted to Lt. d.R.	23.12.42
Botsch, Walter	Gen.Lt. m.F.b. LVIII. Pz. Korps	9.5.45
Bottler, Alfred	Major, Kdr. I./Gren. Rgt. 200 (mot.)	3.11.44
v. Boxberg, Albrecht	Major, Kdr. II./Pz. Rgt. 3	7.2.44
Braake, Günter	Oblt., stellv. Fhr. I./Gren. Rgt. 422	27.8.44
Brachat, Albert	Feldw., Zugf. in I./Inf.Rgt. 14 + 14.8.43 as Kp. Chef, at a field dressing station in Karatschev (Russia), of wounds; posthumously promoted to Hptm.	4.7.40
Bracher, Dr. agrar. Hermann	Oberst, Kdr. Gren. Rgt. 460	23.8.43
Frhr. v. Brackel, Dr. jur. Bruno	Oblt., Fhr. 3./Pz. Rgt. 15 + 13.8.41 in the Ukraine (Russia); posthumously promoted to Hptm.	23.8.41
Bradel, Emst-Joachim	Obstlt., Kdr. Pz. Gren. Rgt. 113	15.12.43
Bradel, Walter	Hptm., Staffelkpt. 9./K.G. 2 + 5.5.43 over England as Major & Kmdr. K.G. 27	17.9.41

Name	Details	Date
Brändle, Kurt	Hptm., Kdr. II./J.G. 3 "Udet" 114th Oak Leaves on 27.8.42	1.7.42
Bräuer, Bruno	Oberst, Kdr. Fschjäger-Rgt. 1 + 20.5.47 shot at Xaidari, Athens (Greece); final post Gen. d. Fsch. Tr. & K.G. d. Luftw. on Crete	24.5.40
Bräundle-Schmidt, Kai	Hptm. d.R., Rgt. Adj. Gren. Regt. 501	26.3.44
Brakat, Otto	Uffz., Gruppenfhr. in 2./Radf. Abt. I	27.7.41
Brambrink, Bernhard	Oblt., Fhr. 2./Pi. Btl. 97	1.9.43
Bramesfeld, Heinrich	Kapt. z. See, Fhr. 2. Sich. Div.	21.1.43
Brand, Hans-Joachim	Oblt., Staffelkpt. 1./Stuka-Gechw. 77 + 18.4.45 at Cottbus as Hptm. & Kdr. 1./S.G. 77	5.12.43
Brandenberger, Erich	Gen. Major, Kdr. 8. Pz.Div. 324th Oak Leaves 12.11.43	15.7.41
Brandenburg, Johannes	Oblt., Staffelfhr. 2./Stuka-Geschw. 2 "Immelmann" + 28.2.42 at Cholm (Russia) as Hptm. & Staffelkpt. 4./K.G. 1 "Hindenburg"	18.9.40
Brandenburg, Max	Feldw., Flugzeuf. in 5./K.G. 101	11.6.44
Brandes, Ernst	Lt. d.R., Fhr. 6./Gren. Rgt. 9	5.3.45
Brandes, Walter	Hptm., Kdr. II./Pz. Rgt. 25 + 14.2.45 Konitz (West Prussia) as Major	28.10.44
Brandi, Albrecht	Kaptlt., Kdt. "U 617" 224th Oak Leaves 11.4.4 66th Swords 9.5.44 22nd Diamonds 24.11.44	21.1.43
Brandner, Josef	Hptm., Kdr. Sturmgeschütz Brig. 912 846th Oak Leaves 26.4.45	17.3.45
Brandner, Kaspar	Oberjäger, Gruppenfhr. in 8./Gebjäg. Rgt. 91	28.10.44
Brandt, Franz	Ofw., Stoßtruppfhr. in II./Gr. Rgt. 953	30.9.44
Brandt. Friedrich	Oblt., Chef 3./Pz. Pi. Btl. 39	20.8.42
Brandt, Gerhard	Oblt., Chef 1./Sturmgeschiltz-Brig. 202	12.12.44
Brandt, Dr. med. Günther	Korv. Kpt. d.R., Chef 21. U-Jagdflottille	23.12.43
Brandt, Hans-Georg	Obstlt., Fhr. Inf.Rgt. 577 + 4.1.43 in Stalingrad (Russia); posthumously promoted to Oberst	22.1.43
Brandt, Hans-Otto	Lt., zugf. in 10./I.R. 67 + 22.7.43 at Mga (Russia) as Hptm. & Kdr. I./G. R. 67	21.8.41
Brandt, Heinz	Stabsfeldw., Zugf. in 4./G. R. 1124	5.3.45
Brandt, Heinz	Lt. d.R., Kp. Fhr. in Pz. G. R. 103	6.5.45
Brandt, Paul	Ofw., Flugzeugfhr. in J.G. 54 + 24.12.44 over Münster as Lt. & Staffelfhr. 16./J.G. 54	5.9.44
Brandt, Walter	Ofw., Flugzeugfhr. in 1./J.G. 77	24.3.43
Brandt, Walter	Major, Kdr. Pz. Pi. Btl. 130	18.7.44
Bransch, Günther	Hptm. d.R., Kdr. Div. Aufkl. Abt. 392 (kroat.)	9.12.44
Brasack, Paul	Kpdt., Kdt. "U 737"	30.10.44

Name	Details	Date
Brasche, Rudi	Obgefr., Gruppenfhr. in 4./Pz. Gren. Rgt. 93	9.11.42
Brassert, Karl	Oberst, Kampfgr. Kampfkommandant Marienburg (West Prussia)	10.2.45
v. Brauchitsch, Walther	Gen. Oberst, Oberbefehlshaber d. Heeres + 18.10.48 in Hamburg as Gen. Feldm., in British captivity	30.9.39
Brauer, Walter	Oblt. d.R., Chef 14. (Pzjäg.)/G. R. 507	10.9.44
Braun, Alfred	Ofw., Zugf. in 3./G. R. 544 + 15.7.44	12.8.44
Braun, Christian	Ofw., Zugf. in 8. (M. G.)/G. R. 308 677th Oak Leaves 9.12.44	15.7.44
Braun, Rudolf	Lt., Staffelfhr. 1./Stuka-Geschw. 3	14.6.41
Braun, Wilhelm	Major, Kdr. II./Inf.Rgt. 576 + 1943 in Stalingrad; posthumously promoted to Obstlt.	20.1.43
Braun, Willi	Fhj. -Feldw., Beobachter in 4./K.G. 55	9.6.44
Braun v. Stumm, Hans-Günther	Rittm., Fhr. Div. Aufkl. Abt. 100 + 15.9.41 in the Ukraine (Russia), of wounds	20.7.42
Braunegg, Herward	Oblt., Flugzeugf. & Beob. in Nahaufkl. Gruppe 9	28.3.44
Braunels, Erich	Freg. Kpt., Chef 24. Landungsflottille	28.12.44
Brecht, Eugen	Major i.G., Ib 131. I.D. 27.6.44 missing; posthumously promoted to Oberstlt. i.G.	3.10.43
Bredemeier, Wilhelm	Feldw., Zugf. in 12. (M. G.)/Gebjäg. Rgt. 91	9.11.42
Bredemeyer, Franz	Feldw., Zugf. in 2./Inf.Rgt. 156 (mot.)	23.8.43
Breer, Hermann	Uffz., Zugf. in 6./G. R. 78 + 19.7.44 in Russia	8.8.44
Breese, Werner	Hptm., Flugzeugfhr. in 5. (F)/Aufkl. Gruppe 122	29.2.44
Bregenzer, Josef	Hptm., Kdr. I./G. R. 245 427th Oak Leaves 17.3.44	20.4.43
Breger, Claus	Stabsfeldw., Zugf. in 1./I.R. 27 700th Oak Leaves 14.1.45	4.9.42
Brehme, Gerhard	Ofw., Zugf. in I./Pz. Abt. 52 + 27.7.43 in Russia, of wounds	23.8.43
Brehmer, Gustav	Major d.R., Kdr. Pi. Btl. 271	9.12.44
Brehmer, Rudolf	Oberstlt., Kdr. Inf.Rgt. 347	22.2.42
Breidenbach, Friedr. -Wilhelm	Major, Fhr. Pz. Brigade 101	30.9.44
Breith, Hermann	Oberst, Kdr. 5. Pz. -Brigade 69th Oak Leaves 31.1.42 48th Swords 21.2.44	3.6.40
Breithaupt, Fritz	Korv. Kpt. d.R., Chef 12. Minensuchflottille 387th Oak Leaves 10.2.44	3.8.41
Bremer, Gerhard	SS-Obsturmfhr., Fhr. 1. (Kradschütz)/Aufkl. -Abt. "LSSAH" 668th Oak Leaves 26.11.44	30.10.41
Bremermann, Oskar	Feldw., Zugf. in 6./G. R. 209	9.5.45

KNIGHT'S CROSS OF THE IRON CROSS

Name	Details	Date
Bremm, Josef	Lt. d.R., Chef 5./I.R. 426 165th Oak Leaves 23.12.42 159th Swords 9.5.45	18.2.42
Brendel, Albert	Oberst, Kdr. Inf.Rgt. 274 + in captivity, Stalingrad	20.1.43
Brendel, Hans	Oberst, Kdr. Inf.Rgt. 689 + 3.5.45 suicide	7.12.42
Brendel, Joachim	Oblt., Staffelkpt. I./J.G. 51 "Mölders" 697th Oak Leaves 14.1.45	22.11.43
Brenig, Peter	Uffz., Fhr. Rgts. Pi. Zug/G. R. 669 + 23.3.44	15.6.44
Brennecke, Kurt	Gen.D.Inf., Kom.Gen. XXXIII. A.K.	12.7.42
Brennecke, Wilhelm	Ofw., Flugzeugfhr. in Stab II./K.G. 55	26.3.44
Brenner, Gerhard	Lt. d.R., Flugzeugfhr. in 2./(K)Lehr-Geschw. 1 + 14.6.42 south of Gardos (Aegean)	5.7.41
Brenner, Harro	Lt. d.R., Fhr. d. Inf. Kp. de Kasta	16.4.43
Brenner, Karl-Heinrich	SS-Gruppenfhr. & Gen.Lt. der Waffen-SS, Kdr. 6. SS-Geb. Div. "Nord"	27.12.44
Brentführer, Gerhard	Oblt., Chef 4. (M. G.)/Gren. Rgt. 9 + 22.11.44 in Sworbe, Oesel (Baltic)	4.10.44
Bretnütz, Heinz	Hptm., Kdr. II./J.G. 53 + 27.6.41, field dressing station, Jubarkas (Russia)	21.10.40
Bretschneider, Heinz	Owm., Bttr. Offz. in 1./Flak-Rgt. 13 (mot.) simultaneously promoted to Lt.	3.2.43
Brettschneider, Klaus	Lt., Flugzeugfhr. in 5./J.G. 300 + 24.12.44 near Kassel as Oblt. u- Staffelkapt. 8./J.G. 300	18.11.44
Brettschneider, Konrad	Oblt., Fhr. 1./Sturrngeschütz-Brig. 904	1.2.45
Bretz, Hans (12)	Obfähnr., Zugf. in Pz. Vernichtg. Brig. Oberschlesien	6.5.45
Breu, Peter Paul	Hptm., Kdr. II./K.G. 3 "Lützow"	2.10.42
Breuker, Helmuth	Hptm., Kdr. I./Geb.Jäg. Rgt. 141	26.11.44
Briegel, Hans	Major, Fhr. Fsch. Pz. Gren. Rgt. 2 "HG"	14.1.45
Briel, Georg	Major, Kdr. Heeres-Fla-Btl. 606	23.7.42
v. Briesen, Kurt	Gen.Lt., Kdr. 30. I.D. + 20.11.41 at Poltava (Russia) as Gen.D.Inf. & Kom.Gen. LII. A.K.	27.10.39
Brill, Dr.-Ing. Karl-Friedrich	Korv. Kpt. d.R., Kdt. Minenschiff "Cobra" & Fhr. einer Minenschiffgruppe 330th Oak Leaves 18.11.43	27.12.41
Brill, Kurt	Major, stellv. Fhr. G. R. 956	4.7.44
Brinckmann, Friedrich	Oblt., Flugzeugfhr. in 6. (F)/Aufkl. Gruppe 122	30.12.43
Brinkforth, Hubert	Gefr., Richtschtz. in 14. (Pzjäg.)/Inf. Rgt. 25 + 5.6.42 south of Pogostje, Volkhov (Russia) as Uffz.	7.3.41
Brinkmann, Helmuth	Vizeadm., Kom. Adm. Black Sea	17.5.44
Britzelmayr, Karl	Obstlt., Kdr. Inf.Rgt. 217	2.2.42
v. Britzke, Achim	Hptm., Chef Pzjäger-Sturmgeschütz-Kp. 1299 + 27.3.45 Ittenbach (Rhineland)	23.10.44

ELITE OF THE THIRD REICH

Broch, Hugo	Feldw., Flugzeugfhr. in 8./J.G. 54	12.3.45
Baron v. Brockdorff, Cay-Lorenz	Oblt., Rgt. Adj. Pz. Rgt. 15	14.4. 45
Graf v. Brockdorff-Ahlefeldt, Ernst-Albrecht	Rittm., Kdr. Kradschtz. Btl. 22 + 14.2.43 in Berlin, of wounds, as Major	26.12.42
Graf. v. Brockdorff-Ahlefeldt, Walter	Gen.D.Inf., Kom.Gen. II. A-K. 103rd Oak Leaves 27.6.42	15.7.41
Brocke, Jürgen	Lt., Flugzeugfhr. in 4./J.G. 77 + 15.9.42 at Voronezh (Russia)	9.12.42
Brocks, Dr. Karl,	Hptm. d.R., Rgt. Adj. Gren. Rgt. 123	30.9.44
Brocks, Roland	Hptm., Kdr. III./G. R. 467 + 5.1.44 in Russia, of wounds	23.2.44
Brodowski, Heinrich	Obgefr., MG-Schtz. in 8. (M. G.)/G. R. 386	18.12.44
Bröckerhoff, Wilhelm (19)	Major, Fhr. Pz. A.R. "Brandenburg"	8.5.45
Broeffel, Wilhelm	Hptm., Kdr. II./Gren. Rgt. 502 +24.6.44 at Fedkowo (Russia) as Major	14.11.43
Brökelmann, Jost	Korv. Kpt., Chef 2. Areabootsflottille	14.6.42
Broennle, Herbert	Ofw., Flugzeugfhr. in 4./J.G. 54 + 4.7.43 over Platz Catanla (Sicily) as Lt. in 2./J.G. 53	14.3.43
Brösamle, Karl	Uffz., Gewehrfahrer in 4. (M. G.)/G. R. 330	26.6.44
Brogsitter, Eduard	Oblt., Staffelfhr. in II./K.G. 76	24.3.43
Frhr. v. Broich, Friedrich	Oberst, Kdr. 24. Pz. Gren. Brig.	29.8.42
Broich, Peter	Ofw., Flugzeugfhr. in 2./K.G. 2	24.9.42
Bromen, Wilhelm	Lt. d.R., Flugzeugfhr. & z.b.V. Offz. in 4./Stuka-Geschw. 2 "Immelmann"	16.4.43
Brommann, Karl (19)	SS-Untersturmf., Fhr. 1./s. SS-Pz. Abt. 503	29.4.45
Bronsart v. Schellendorff, Heinrich-Walter	Oberst, Kdr. Pz. G. R. 13 394th Oak Leaves 12.2.44	10.9.43 13.11.43
Brosow, Siegfried	SS-Hptsturmfhr., Chef 1./SS-Pz. Pi. Btl. "Das Reich"	
Brucher, Paul	Lt., Zugf. in 3./Inf.Rgt. 447	23.10.41
Bruchmann, Gerhard	Uffz., Gruppenfhr. in 3./G. R. 12	6.8.43
Bruck, Helmut	Hptm., Staffelkpt. i./Stuka-Geschw. 77 193rd Oak Leaves 19.2.43	4.9.41
Bruck, Viktor	Hptm. d.R., Kdr. I./G. R. 376	20.10.44
Brucker, Johann	Obstl., Kdr. G. R. 959	5.4.45
Brucker, Walter	Hptm., Fhr. III./Jäger-Rgt. 56	16.4.43
Brücker, Heinrich	Hptm., Kdr. III./Stuka-G. 2 "Immelmann"	22.6.41
Brücker, Otto-Hermann	Gen. Major, Kdr. 6. Volks-Gren. Div.	14.4. 45

Name	Details	Date
v. Brückner, Erich	Oberst, Kdr. Jager-Rgt. 1 "Brandenburg"	11.3.45
Brückner, Wilhelm	Uffz., Geschützf. in 14. (Pzjäg.)/I.R. 253 + 15.11.41 Moscow (Russia)	5.10.41
Brückner, Wolfgang	Oblt., Staffelkpt. 3./K.G. 1 "Hindenburg" + 14.7.43; posthumously promoted to Hptm.	5.12.43
Brüggemann, Heinrich	Feldw., Kp. Tr. Fhr. in 3./G. R. 178	5.4.45
Brüggemann, Karl	Uffz., Gruppenfhr. in Stabskp./I.R. 5	28.11.40
Graf v. Brühl, Friedrich-August	Hptm. d.R., Chef 8./Pz. Rgt. 2	3.11.42
Brüning, Walter	Lt., Kp. Chef in III./I.R. 508	12.1.42
Bruer, Alfred	Oberst, Kdr. Pz. Art.Rgt. 155	30.7.42
Bruetsch, Josef	Uffz., Gr. Fhr. in I./Div. Füs. Btl. 305	17.3.45
Bruhn, Hans	Oblt., Chef 3./G. R. 90	29.12.42
Bruhn, Johannes	Oberst, A-rt. Kdr. 149	20.12.43
Bruins, Derk-Elsko	SS-Rottenfhr., Gesch. Fhr. in I./SS-Pzjg. Abt. 54 "Nederland"	23.8.44
Brunk, Edgar	Oblt., Chef 2./Füs. Rgt. 202	3.7.44
Brunner, Albert	Ofw., Flugzeugf. in 6./J.G. 5 + 7.5.43 Arctic	3.7.43
Brunner, Eduard	Hptm., Fhr. I./G. R. 62 638th Oak Leaves 28.10.44	27.2.44
Bruns, Arthur	Major, Fhr. G. R. 245 + 4.2.43	3.4.43
Bruns, Dr. jur. Axel	Oblt. d.R., Fhr. 7./A.R. 241	29.8.43
Bruns, Diedrich	Major d.R., Kdr. II./I.R. 16	9.8.42
Bruns, Gustav-Adolf	Obstlt., Kdr. Pz. Gren. Rgt. 74 + 4.11.44 as Oberst	15.10.42
Brunsiek, Karl-Heinz	Lt., Fhr. 4./G. R. 43	5.4.45
Brutscher, Fritz	Lt. d.R., Fhr. 3./Pz. Pi. Btl. 92 + 15.2.43 north-east of Kursk (Russia)	22.1.43
Brux, Albert	Hptm., Kdr. I./Schtz. Rgt. 66 504th Oak Leaves 24.6.44	12.9.41
Buchenau, Fritz	Major, Kdr. Fahnenjunker-Rgt. 4 der Art. Schule 11 Groß-Born	28.3.45
Buchholz, Hans	Oblt. d.R., Flugzeugfhr. I./K.G. 40 + 19.5.41 as Hptm. d.R.	24.3.41
Buchler, Helmut-Wolfgang	Hptm., Kdr. I./I.R. 204 + 10.12.41	6.1.42
Buchner, Franz	Oblt., Chef 5./I.R. 30 (mot.) + 27.11.41	2.10.41
Buchner, Hermann	SS-Hptsturmfhr., Kdr. III./SS-Pz. G. R. 5 "Totenkopf" + 17.11.44 east of Warsaw (Poland) as SS-Sturmbannfhr.	16.6.44
Buchner, Hermann	Ofw., Flugzeugfhr. in 6./Schlacht-Geschw. 2 "Immelmann"	20.7.44
Bucholz, Max	Oblt., Staffelkpt. in I./J.G. 3	12.8.41

Buchterkirch, Ernst-Georg	Oblt., Zugf. in 2./Pz. Rgt. 6 44th Oak Leaves 31.12.41	29.6.40
Buck, Albert	Oberst, Kdr. I.R. 305 + 6.9.42 at Noworossijsk (Russia) as Gen. Maj & Kdr. 198. I.D.	17.7.41
Buck, Friedrich	SS-Oberscharfhr., Fhr. 5./SS-Kav. Rgt. 15 "Florian Geyer"	27.1.45
Buck, Wilhelm	Obstlt., Kdr. Pz. Gren. Rgt. 2 + 24.9.43 at Tschernobyl in Russia	31.7.43
Buckel, Karl	Oblt. d.R., Chef 3./Sturmgeschütz-Brig. 277	15.7.44
Budäus, Kurt	Oblt., MG-Zugf. in 1./I.R. 307	21.12.40
Budahl, Georg	Lt., Zugfhr. in 1./Pz.Jäg. Abt. 121	21.9.44
Budka, Franz	SS-Untersturmfhr., Fhr. 1./SS-Festg. Rgt. 1 "Besslein" + 6.5.45 in Breslau as SS-Obersturmfhr.	19.4.45
Büchau, Bruno	Hptm. d.R., Fhr. 11./G. R. 159	19.8.44
Büchting, Hermann	Kaptlt., Kdt. "S 27" in 1. Schnellbootsflottille	22.4.43
Bühlbecker, Hermann	Hptm., Kdr. 11./G. R. 436	23.8.44
Bühler, Karlheinz (6)	SS-Obersturmbannf., Kdr. SS-Pz. G. R. 9 "Germania"	6.5.45
Bühligen, Kurt	Ofw., Flugzeugfhr. in II./J.G. 2 "Richthofen" 413th Oak Leaves 2.3.44 88th Swords 14.8.44	4.9.41
Frhr. v. Bülow, Karl-August	Oberst, Kdr. Pz. Rgt. 24	12.12.44
v. Bülow, Otto	Kaptlt., Kdt. "U 404" 234th Oak Leaves 26.4.43	20.10.42
v. Bülow-Bothkamp, Harry	Obstlt. d.R., Kmdr. J.G. 2 "Richthofen"	22.8.40
Bülowius, Alfred	Oberst, Kmdr. (K.)Lehr-Geschw. 1	4.7.40
v. Bünau, Rudolf	Oberst, Kdr. I.R. 133 766th Oak Leaves 5.3.45	15.8.40
v. Bünau, Rudolf	Hptm., Kdr. Pz. Aufkl. Abt. 9 + 15.8.43 southern Roslawl (Russia); posthumously promoted to Major	8.8.43
Büntemeyer, Hans	Hptm. d.R., Kdr. 11./G. R. 399 + 17.3.45 in East Prussia; posthumously promoted to Major d.R.	18.2.45
Bürgel, Wilhelm	Owm., Bttr. Offz. in 5./Geb. Art.Rgt. 8	29.2.44
Bürger, Albert	Oblt., Stab 4. Flak-Div.	17.4.45
Bürger, Otto	Oblt., Chef 1./Pz. Gren. Rgt. 3	14.4. 45
Bürger, Thomas	Hptm., Kdr. III./I.R. 528	4.3.42
Bürgerhoff, Wilhelm	Ofw., Zugf. in 7./G. R. 166	5.5.43
Bürker, Ulrich	Obstlt. i.G., Ia 10. Pz.Div.	19.1.43
Büsen, Dr. Nikolaus	Hptm., Staffelfhr. 1./Fernaufkl. Gruppe 122 + 14.6.42 in North Africa of wounds	4.9.42

Name	Details	Date
Büsing, Otto	Obstlt., Kdr. Pz. Rgt. 39 + 8.3.44 in main dressing station, Rownoje (Russia) as Oberst & Kdr. Pz. -Rgt. "GD" of wounds; posthumously promoted to Gen. Major	21.11.42
Büsing, Wilhelm	Hptm. d.R., Fhr. 1./G. R. 280 + 16.4.45 at Tiberg (Samland)	28.2.45
Büssecke, Arthur	Uffz., Geschützfhr. in 2./Flak-Rgt. 49 (mot.)	23.12.42
Bütow, Hans	Kapt. z. See, Führer der Torpedoboote (F. d. T.)	12.3.41
Büttner, Franz	Obgefr., Gruppenfhr. in 7./G. R. 67 + 28.2.45	18.12.44
Büttner, Manfred (18)	Fhj. -Feldw. Führer 2./Fsch. Jäg. Rgt. 26	29.4.45
Buffa, Ernst	Gen.Lt., Kdr. 12. Flak-Div. (mot.)	5.9.44
Buhr, Martin	Major, Kdr. Sturmgeschütz-Abt. 202	11.9.43
de Buhr, Rudolf	Uffz., Gruppenfhr. in 5./I.R. 76 (mot.)	2.10.43
Buhse, Rudolf	Obstlt., Kdr. I.R. 47	17.8.42
Bujak, Hans	Feldw., Zugf. in 10./G. R. 7	27.8.44
Bukatschek, Otto	Uffz., Gruppenfhr. in 10./Schtz. Rgt. 52	24.7.41
Bulla, Ludwig	Obstlt., Kdr. Flak-Rgt. 164 (mot.)	11.6.44
Bullinger, Herbert	Rittm., Kdr. II./Kav. Rgt. 5 "Feldmarschall v. Mackensen"	1.2.45
Bulmahn, Karl	Hptm., Kdr. II./G. R. 1126	31.1.45
Bumen, Robert	Feldw., Flugzeugfhr. in 1./Stuka-Geschw. 77 + 25.7.44 missing at Przemysl (Poland)	29.10.44
Bund, Walter	Uffz., Gruppenfhr. in 1./G. R. 669	20.10.44
Bundesmann, Heinz	Lt., Fhr. 3./G. R. 88	14.1.45
Bundrock, Kurt	Ofw., Bordfunker in Stab Nacht-Jagd-Geschw. 1	30.6.44
Bunge, Ernst	Hptm. d.R., Kdr. II./G. R. 121 + 12.5.44 at Chersones (Crimea/Russia) as Major d.R.	16.11.43
Bunge, Hellmut	Hptm., Fhr. II./PGR. "FHH"	1.2.45
Bunse, Fritz	SS-Sturmbannfhr., Kdr. SS-Freiw. -Pi. Btl. 11 "Nordland"	30.1.44
Bunzek, Johannes	Lt., Flugzeugfhr. in 7./J.G. 52 + 11.12.43 over Nikopol bridgehead (Russia)	6.4.44
Bunzel, Hans	Ofw., Zugf. in 3./Pz. Abt. 116	10.2.43
Bunzel, Willi	Major, Kdr. III./I.R. 426 + 25.10.41 in field hospital at Porchow, near Pleskau (Russia) of wounds	11.10.41
Burbach, Hans	Uffz., Geschützfhr. in 2./Pz.Jäg. Abt. 41	18.11.43
Burchard, Dipl.-Ing, Heinrich (17)	Gen.Lt., Kdr. 7. Flak-Div. + 11.4.45 as Gen. d. Flakart. z.b.V. (suicide)	31.10.44
Burchardi, Theodor	Vizeadm., Kom. Adm. Ostland 823rd Oak Leaves 8.4.45	29.9.44

Name	Rank/Unit	Date
Burckhardt, Lutz-Wilhelm	Lt., Flugzeugfhr. in 4./J.G. 77	15.10.42
Burdach, Karl	Gen.Lt., Kdr. 11. Inf. Div.	23.2.44
Burg, Jörg	Lt. d.R., Zugf. in 2./Pz. Abt. 18 604th Oak Leaves 4.10.44	3.3.43
Burgdorf, Wilhelm	Oberst, Kdr. Inf.Rgt. 529 + 2.5.45 suicide in the Reichs Chancellery bunker Berlin as Gen.D.Inf., final post Chefadj. Der Wehrmacht, Führer & Chef des Heerespersonalamtes in OKH Oberst, Kdr. Gren. Rgt. 524	29.9.41
Burgemeister, Alfred		2.5.45
Burgfeld, Georg	Hptm., Chef 14. (Pz.Jäg.)/Div. Gr. 112	21.2.44
Burghartswieser, Max	Ofw., Stoßtruppfhr. in 7./Geb.Jäg. Rgt. 100 + 22.8.42 at Neva bend (Russia) as Zugfhr.	9.7.41
Burgholte, August	Ofw., Zugf. in 3./Pz. Abt. 102	9.12.44
Burgmann, Gert	Hptm., Chef 1./Sturmbtl. A.O.K. 4 + 26.10.44 at Goldap (East Prussia)	18.12.44
v. Burgsdorff, Dr. jur. Curt	Major d.R., Fhr. G. R. 580	2.4.43
Burian, Ewald	Oberst, Kdr. G. R. 980	4.10.44
Burkhardt, Fritz	Oblt., Chef 8./Gren. Rgt. 417	17.4.45
Burmeister, Arnold	Gen. Major, Fhr. 25. Pz. Gren. Div.	14.1.45
Burmester, Hans-Jürgen	Hptm., Kdr. schw. Pz. Abt. 509	2.9.44
Burr, Leonhard	Ofw., Bordfunker in 7./Stuka-Geschw. 77	30.11.44
Bursche, Gustav-Adolf	Lt., Fhr. 6./Inf.Rgt. 90	13.10.41
Burst, Reinhard	Major, Fhr. Gren. Rgt. 111	12.8.44
Busch, Ernst	Gen.D.Inf., OB 16. Armee 274th Oak Leaves 21.8.43	26.5.40
Busch, Hans	Major, Kdr. II./G. R. 4	10.9.44
Busch, Rudolf	Ofw., Flugzeugfhr. in I./FernAufkl. Gruppe 121	9.6.44
Busch, Walter	Lt. d.R., Fhr. I./Inf. Btl. z.b.V. 561	14.10.43
Busch, Walter	Hptm., Chef I./Flak-Rgt. 2 (mot.) + 7.4.45	9.6.44
Busche, Karl	Oberst, Kdr. Jäger-Rgt. 228 + 28.5.43 in Russia of wounds	28.2.43
Buschenhagen, Erich	Gen.Lt., Kdr. 15. I.D. 521st Oak Leaves 4.7.44	5.12.43
Buschhausen, Friedrich-Wilhelm	Major, Kdr. I./Pz. Gren. Rgt. 69	9.5.43
Buss, Wilhelm	Ofw., Pz. Kdt. in I./Pz. Rgt. 31	9.12.44
Frhr. v. dem Bussche-Streithorst, Axel	Hptm., Kdr. I./G. R. 9	7.3.44
Busse, Heinrich	Major, Kdr. Div. Füs. Btl. 328 637th Oak Leaves 28.10.44	26.3.44

Busse, Theodor	Gen.Lt., Chef d. Gen. Stab. H.Gr. Süd	30.1.44
Busse, Wilhelm	Major, Fhr. G. R. 82 + 28.6.44 as Obstlt, at Mogilew (Russia)	12.3.44
Butkus, Zanis	Waffen-Hptsturmfhr., Fhr. 10./SS-Feld-Ers. Btl. 19	21.9.44
Butz, Plus	Oberjäger, Geschützfhr. in 16. (I. G.)/Jäg-Rgt. 228 + 16.4.44 at Piotrow/Dnjestr (Russia) as Feldw. & Zugf.	6.3.44
Buxa, Werner	Hptm., Kdr. I./Gren. Rgt. 44	23.3.45

C

Canders, Werner	Major, Kdr. III./G. R. 408	6.4.44
Frhr. v. Canstein, Ulrich	Obstlt., Kdr. G. R. 220	12.2.44
Capesius, Kurt	Hptm., m.F.b. III./K.G. 66	30.11.44
Cappel, Wilhelm	Obstlt., Kdr. G. R. 424 + 18.7.44 at Lundsen (Baltic) as Oberst	23.2.44
Carganico, Horst	Oblt., Staffelkpt. 6./J.G. 5 + 27.5.44 in Alsace (France) as Major & Kdr. II./J.G. 5	25.9.41
Carius, Otto	Lt. d.R., Zugf. in 2./schw. Pz. Abt. 502 535th Oak Leaves 27.7.44	4.5.44
Carl, Friedrich	Oblt., Fhr. 11./A.R. 269	9.5.42
Carls, Rolf	Admiral, Marinegruppenbefehlsh. Ost + 15.4.45 at Bad Oldesloe (Holstein) during ground attack as Gen. Adm., final post Marinegruppenbefehlshaber Nord	14.6.40
Carpaneto, Alfredo	Uffz., Pz. Kdt. in 2./schw. Pz. Abt. 502 + 26.1.45 at Neuhausen (East Prussia)	28.3.45
Casper, Carl	Oberst, Kdr. Inf.Rgt. 118 (mot.)	22.9.41
Graf zu Castell-Castell, Prosper	Lt. d.R., Fhr. 9./Pz. G. R. 14	23.2.44
Castka, Horst	Owm., VB in 11./A.R. 1562	11.3.45
Celerin, Albert	Oblt., Flugzeufhr. & Beob. in Fernaufkl. Gruppe 4	10.10.44
v. Chamier-Glisczinski, Wolfgang	Oberst, Kmdr. K.G. 3 + 12.8.43 at Agram (Croatia) as Gen.Maj. & Flieger- führer Croatia, murdered by Partisans; posthumously promoted to Gen.Lt.	6.10.40
v. Chappuis, Friedrich-Wilhelm	Gen.Lt., Kdr. 15. I.D. + 27.8.42 in Magdeburg as Gen.D.Inf. & Kom.Gen. XXXVIII. A.K. (suicide)	15.8.40
v. Charpentier, Hans-Georg	SS-Hauptsturmfhr., Chef 3./SS-Reiter-Rgt. I + 11.2.45 at Budapest (Hungary) as SS-Sturmbannfhr. & Kdr. SS-Kav. Rgt. 18	29.12.42

v. der Chevallerie, Hellmut	Gen.Maj., Kdr. 13. Pz.Div.	30.4.43
v. der Chevallerie, Kurt	Gen.Lt., Kdr. 99 la Div. 357th Oak Leaves 19.12.43	23.10.41
v. La Chevallerie, Botho	Major, Kdr. I./I.R. 408 + 16.11.43 at Krementschug (Russia) as Rgt. Kdr.; posthumously promoted to Oberst	24.7.41
Chill, Kurt	Gen.Lt., Kdr. 122. I.D.	25.10.43
Chmel, Max	Obgefr., Gruppenfhr. in 8./Gr. R. 200 (mot.)	18.11.44
v. Choltitz, Dietrich	Obstlt., Kdr. III./I.R. 16 (LL)	18.5.40
Chowanetz, Otto	Feldw., Zugf. in 1./G. R. 17 + 17.3.43 at Orel (Russia)	8.8.43
Christ, Torsten	Obstlt. i.G., Chef d. Gen. St. VIII. Fliegerkorps	21.10.42
Christel, Kurt	Hptm., Kp. Chef in Bau-Btl. 132 + 3.3.42 at Zemena (Russia)	4.3.42
Christen, Fritz	SS-Sturmmann, Richtschz. in 2./SS-Pz. jäg. Abt. 3 "Totenkopf"	20.10.41
Christern, Hans	Major, Kdr. II./Pz. Rgt. 31	31.1.41
Christiansen, Georg	Oblt. z. See, Kdt. "S 101" in 1. Schnellbootsflottille 326th Oak Leaves 13.11.43	8.5.41
Christl, Georg	Hptm., Kdr. III./Zerstörer-Geschw. 26 "Horst Wessel"	18.3.42
Christmann, Karl	Ofw., Beob. in 6./K.G. 53 "Legion Condor" + 5.11.44 over the North Sea	5.4.44
Christofzik, Kurt	Oblt. d.R., Chef 6./G. R. 530	22.8.43
Christopherson, Egon	SS-Unterscharfhr., Gruppenfhr. in 7./SS-Freiw. Pz. G. R. 24 "Danmark"	11.7.44
Chrobek, Bruno	Major, Kdr. 1./I.R. 54 + 8.12.42 at Dimitrajewska/Stalingrad as Oberst & Kdr. G. R. 672; posthumously promoted to Gen. Major	4.7.40
Chrzonsz, Günter	Owm., Zugfhr. in 2./Sturmgeschütz-Abt. 277	12.11.43
Cierpka, Walter	Major, Kdr. Heeres-Art. Abt. 774	5.4.45
Ciliax, Otto	Vizeadm., Befehlshaber der Schlachtschiffe	21.3.42
Cipa, Oskar	Uffz., Gruppenfhr. in 1./I.R. 305	13.11.42
Cirener, Wilhelm	Oblt., Chef 3./Pi. Btl. 33 + 1.5.41 near Tobruk (North Africa)	13.7.40
Claas, Paul	Major, Kdr. I./K.G. 100 + December 1942 over the Sea of Azov (Russia)	14.3.43
Claassen, Richard	Obstlt., Kdr. I.R. 517 + 1943 Stalingrad (Russia)	29.1.43
Claassen, Theo	Lt., Zugfhr. in 14. (Pz.Jäg.)/G. R. 899	27.8.44
Clausen, Erwin	Oblt., Staffelkpt. 6./J.G. 77 106th Oak Leaves 23.7.42	19.5.42

KNIGHT'S CROSS OF THE IRON CROSS

Clausen, Karl-Ulrich	Hptm., Chef 2./A.R. 30 + 5.1.45 at main dressing station Skuodar (Kurland) as Major & Kdr. III./A.R. 30 of wounds	16.4.44
Clausen, Nicolai	Kaptlt., Kdt. "U 129" + 15.5.43 in South Atlantic as Kdt. "U 182"; posthumously promoted to Korv. Kapt.	13.3.42
Clembotzki, Walter	Lt. d.R., Fhr. 3./(schw.)Flak-Abt. 442 (mot.)	11.2.45
Clemente, Ernst	Obgefr., Pakschtz. 1 in 16./Geb.Jäg. Rgt. 13	30.9.44
Clemm v. Hohenberg, Dieter-Hans	Hptm., Kdr. II. (K)/Lehr-Geschw. 1 + 30.6.44 at Wiesbaden; posthumously promoted to Major	18.11.44
Cleve, Rudolf	Hptm., Chef 3./Flak-Rgt. 4 (mot.)	4.5.44
Clößner, Erich	Gen.Lt., Kdr. 25. I.D.	29.9.40
Clüver, Hans	Major d.R., Kdr. II./G. R. 266	22.1.44
Coeler, Joachim	Gen. Major, Kdr. 9. Flieger-Div.	12.7.40
Cohrs, Erwin	Major, Kdr. II./Pz. G. R. 67	9.12.44
Collani, Hans	SS-Obsturmbannfhr., Kdr. niederl. SS-Freiw. Pz. G. R. 49 "De Ruyter" + 29.7.44 at Narva (Russia) of wounds; posthumously promoted to SS-Standartenfhr.	19.8.44
Colli, Robert	Oberst, Kdr. G. R. 547	19.2.44
Condné, Johann	Hptm., Fhr. II./Pz. G. R. 6	5.4.45
Conrad, Dipl.-Ing. Gerhard	Oberst, Kmdre. K.G. z.b.V. 2	24.5.40
Conrad, Hermann	Ofw., Stoßtruppfhr. in 7./I.R. 330 + 6.10.42 in Russia of wounds; posthumously promoted to Oblt.	9.7.41
Conrady, Alexander	Obstlt., Kdr. 1./I.R. 118 (mot.) 279th Oak Leaves 22.8.43	17.10.42
Conrath, Paul	Oberst, Kdr. Flak-Rgt. (mot.) "General Göring" 276th Oak Leaves 21.8.43	4.9.41
Coracino, Klaus	Oblt. d.R., Chef St. Geschütz-Begleitkp. 254 in 1./Gren. Rgt. 431	2.9.44
Cordes, Udo	Lt., Flugzeugfhr. in 9. (Eis.)/K.G. 3 "Lützow"	12.6.43
Corßen, Günter	Hptm., Abt. Fhr. in Pz. Rgt. 39	8.2.43
Corts, Helmut	Oblt., Zugf. in 2./Flak-Rgt. 64 (mot.)	20.6.40
v. Cossel, Hans-Detloff	Oblt., Fhr. 1./Pz. Rgt. 35 285th Oak Leaves 29.8.43	8.9.41
le Coutre, Georg	Lt., Fhr. 10./Fsch. Jäger-Rgt. 6	7.2.45
Cramer, Hans	Obstlt., Kdr. Pz. Rgt. 8 in DAK	27.6.41
Cramer, Heinz	Major, Kdr. II. (K)/Lehr-Geschw. 1	18.9.40
Frhr. v. Cramm, Wilhelm-Ernst	Major, Kdr. Div. Füsilier-Btl. 58	11.4.44

Name	Details	Date
Crantz, Friedrich	Oblt. d.R., Chef 10./G. R. 416 22.8.44 posted missing	3.3.43
Cranz, Friedrich-Karl	Gen.Lt., Kdr. 18. I.D. + 24.3.41 accidentally at Neuhammer troop training grounds	29.6.40
Crasemann, Eduard	Obstlt., Kdr. A.R. 33 (mot.) 683rd Oak Leaves 18.12.44	26.12.41
Cremer, Erich	Kaptlt., Kdt. "U 333"	5.6.42
Crinius, Wilhelm	Feldw., Flugzeugfhr. in 3./J.G. 53 127th Oak Leaves 23.9.42	23.9.42
Crisolli, Wilhelm	Obstlt., Kdr. Schtz. Rgt. 8 + 12.9.44 murdered in Italy as Gen.Maj. & Kdr. 20. Lw.-Feld-Div.	15.7.41
Crüger, Arved	Hptm., Staffelkpt. 5./K.G. 30 + 22.3.42 over Malta as Major & Kmdr. K.G. 77	14.6.40
Crüwell, Ludwig	Gen. Major, Kdr. 11. Pz.Div. 34th Oak Leaves 1.9.41	14.5.41
Crusius, Heinz	Oblt., Chef 4./Inf.Rgt. 453 + 31.3.42 in Russia of wounds	3.5.42
Cullmann, Kurt	Obfähnr., stellv. Fhr. 2./Div. Füs. Btl. 260 + 29.3.44 at Tschaussy (Russia)	9.6.44
Cuno, Kurt	Oberst, Kdr. Pz. Rgt. 39	18.1.42
Cygan, Leo	Lt. d.R., Zugf. in 1./Pi. Btl. 102	5.1.44
Czekay, Richard	Hptm., Staffelkpt. 3./Stuka-Geschw. 2 "Immelmann" & Adj. I./S.G. 2	30.12.42
Czernik, Gerhard	Oblt., Staffelkpt. 6./K.G. 2 + 20.10.41 over England as Hauptmann	16.5.41
Czorny, Wilhelm	Gefr., MG-Fhr. in 2./Pz. Gren. Rgt. "GD"	4.10.44

D

Name	Details	Date
Dähne, Paul-Heinrich	Oblt., Staffelkpt. 12./J.G. 11 (previously 2./J.G. 52) + 24.4. 45 over Warnemünde as Kdr. 11./J.G. 1; posthumously promoted to Hptm.	6.4.44
Dahl, Walther	Major, Kdr. III./J.G. 3 "Udet" 724th Oak Leaves 1.2.45	11.3.44
Dahlke, Hermann	SS-Oberscharfhr., Kp. Truppfhr. in 3./1. Pz. Gr. Rgt. + 2.7.43 at Bjelgorod (Russia) as SS-Untersturmfhr. & Kp. Fhr.	3.3.43
Dahlmann, Kurt	Major, Kdr. I./Schnell-K.G. 10 711th Oak Leaves 24.1.45	11.6.44
Dahmer, Hugo	Ofw., Flugzeugfhr. in 6./J.G. 5	1.8.41
Dahms, Paul	Hptm., Fhr. St. Geschütz-Brig. 286	3.11.44

KNIGHT'S CROSS OF THE IRON CROSS

Name	Details	Date
Dallmann, Werner	SS-Untersturmfhr., Rgt. Adj. SS-Kav. Rgt. 53 "Florian Geyer" + Febr. 1945 in Budapest (Hungary) as SS-Obersturmfhr., of wounds	17.1.45
Dallmeier, Josef	Lt., Fhr. Pz.Jäger-Kp. 1183	28.3.45
Dally, Hans	Hptm., stv. Kdr. gem. Flak-Abt. 5 (L) (mot.)	11.6.44
Frhr. v. Dalwigk zu Lichtenfels, Friedrich-Karl	Hptm., Kdr. 1./Stuka-Geschw. 77 + 9.7.40 over the English Channel; posthumously promoted to Major	21.7.40
Damerius, Dieter	Lt. d.R., Fhr. 5./G. R. 273	24.2.45
Damm, Otto	Ofw., Zugf. in 10./G. R. 216 + 16.7.43 in Russia	4.8.43
Dammeier, Heinrich	Stabsobermaschinist, Obermaschinist auf "U 270"	12.8.44
Dammers, Hans	Feldw., Flugzeugfhr. in 9./J.G. 52 + 17.3.44 in Russia of wounds; posthumously promoted to Lt.	23.8.42
Damsch, Werner	SS-Hptsturmfhr., Kdr. 1./SS-Pz. Gren. Rgt. 25 "Hitlerjugend"	17.4.45
Danhauser, Paul	Oberst, Kdr. Inf.Rgt. 427	10.2.42
Daniel, Richard	Obstlt., Kdr. 1. -R. 391 857th Oak Leaves 30.4.45	25.7.42
Edler v. Daniels, Alexander	Gen. Major, Kdr. 376. I.D.	18.12.42
Dannebaum, Alfred	Rittm., Fhr. Pz. Aufkl. Abt. 24	17.9.44
Danowski, Franz	Oblt., Fhr. 10./Pz. G. R. 111 + 10.10.44 in the West; posthumously promoted to z. Hptm.	18.10.44
Danzer, Hermann	Lt., Zugf. in 2./Pz. Pi. Btl. 57 + 20.6.40 at Epinal (France)	21.12.40
Darges, Fritz	SS-Obersturmbannfhr., Fhr. SS-Pz. Rgt. 5 "Wiking"	5.4.45
Dargies, Walter	Hptm. d.R., Btl. Fhr. in G. R. 418	11.1.43
Darius, Wolfgang	Hptm., Kdr. Pz. Abt. 21	22.8.43
Darjes, Paul-Friedrich	Major, Kdr. II./Schlacht-Geschw. 1	14.10.42
Darnedde, Erich	Hptm. d.R., Fhr. 1./G. R. 277	8.2.43
Daser, Edmund	Hptm., Staffelkpt. 1./K.G. 40	21.2.41
Daske, Karl	Hptm., Kdr. Div. Füs. Btl. 12	14.4. 45
Dassow, Rudi	Lt., Flugzeugfhr. in U./Zerst. Gechw. 26 "Horst Wessel" + 25.8.44 at Laon (France)	5.9.44
Dath, Friedrich	Owm., Zugf. in 3./St. Geschütz-Brig. 286	9.12.44
Daubert, Dr. jur. Henning	Oberst, Kdr. G. R. 426	5.3.45
Daumiller, Hans	Oblt., Chef 11./Geb.Jäger-Rgt. 98 + 12.1.42 accidentally in Russia as Hptm.	29.9.40

Dauner, Klaus	Oberst, Kdr. Jäger-Rgt. 737	16.11.44
Dauser, Hans	SS-Oberscharfhr., Zugf. in 2./SS-Pz. Rgt. 1 "LSSAH"	4.6.44
David, Ernst	Obgefr., MG-Schtz. in 3./G. R. 118 + 11.8.43 in Russia	16.8.43
Dawedeit, Herbert	Ofw., Flugzeugfhr. in 8./Stuka-Geschw. 77	29.2.44
Debiel, Leo Otto	Obwachtm., Bttr. Offz. in 2./A.R. 253 + 9.10.44 in Russia	19.11.44
Deboi, Heinrich-Anton	Gen. Major, Kdr. 44. I.D.	10.9.42
Debus, Heinrich	SS-Obsturmfhr., stv. Fhr. SS-Pz. Aufkl. Abt. 5 "Wiking"	4.5.44
Debus, Otto	Oblt., Beob. in 1. (H)/Nahaufkl. Gruppe 12	5.4.44
Decker, Karl	Obstlt., Kdr. 1./Pz. Rgt. 3 466th Oak Leaves 4.5.44 149th Swords 26.4.45	13.6.41
Dederichs, Bruno	Major, Fhr. G. R. 409 + in Soviet captivity	14.4. 45
Deegener, Johannes	Obstlt. i.G., Fhr. Jäger-Rgt. 49 + 31.7.43 at Lake Ladoga (Russia); posthumously promoted to Oberst 1. G.	22.8.43
Degen, Günther	SS-Hptsturmfhr., Fhr. 1./SS-Geb.Jäger-Rgt. 11 "Reinhard Heydrich" + 13.3.45 in Pfaffenheck/Hunsrück	7.10.44
Degen, Hans	Gen.Lt., Kdr. 2. Geb. Div.	11.3.45
Degl, Franz	Uffz., Gruppenfhr. in 8./G. R. 62	23.10.44
Degrelle, Léon	SS-Hptsturmfhr., Fhr. SS-Freiw. Brig. "Wallonie" (without number) Oak Leaves 27.8.44	20.2.44
Dehmel, Ernst	SS-Hptsturmfhr., stv. Fhr. SS-St. Gesch. Abt. 3 "Totenkopf" + 7.8.45 at Remscheid, in French captivity, as SS-Sturmbannfhr.	15.8.43
Dehner, Ernst	Gen. Major, Kdr. 106. I.D.	18.10.41
Deichen, Kurt	Hptm. d.R., Kdr. Pz. Aufkl. Abt. 3	10.9.43
Deichmann, Paul	Gen.Lt., Kom.Gen. II. Fliegerkorps	26.3.44
Deisenberger, Hermann	Major, Kdr. 11./Pz. A.R. 16	20.10.44
Deisenhofer, Dr. jur. Eduard	SS-Sturmbannfhr., Kdr. of a Kampfgr. in 3. SS-Totenkopf-Division + 31.1.45 at Arnswalde (Pomerania) as SS-Oberfhr.	8.5.42
Delica, Egon	Lt., stv. Fhr. Sturmgr. "Granit" in Fsch. Jäger-Sturm-Abt. "Koch" simultaneously promoted to Oblt.	12.5.40
Delius, Paul	Major, Ia b. Festg. Kdr. Abschnitt 44 Gen. Matterstock	11.3.45
Demand, Waldemar	Lt., Fhr. 1./Füs. Rg. 22 + 21.2.45 in East Prussia	17.3.45
Demke, August	Ofw., Meldestaffelfhr. in 2./G. R. 24	17.3.45

KNIGHT'S CROSS OF THE IRON CROSS

Demme, Rudolf	Oberst, Kdr. Pz. G. R. 59 537th Oak Leaves 28.7.44	14.8.43
v. Demming, Diethelm	Major, Kdr. II./Pz. Gren. Rgt. 9 + 29.4.45 on the Prenta (Italy)	30.4.45
Deneke, Siegfried	Uffz., Gruppenfhr. in 6./G. R. 166 + 16.3.44 south of Vinnitsa (Russia)	9.6.44
Denk, Gustav	Oblt., Flugzeugfhr. in II./J.G. 52 + 13.2.43 at Krasnodar (Caucasus/Russia)	14.3.43
Denk, Wilhelm	Lt. d.R., Fhr. 1./Pz. G. R. 74	14.5.44
Denkert, Walter	Oberst, stv. Fhr. 19. Pz.Div.	14.5.44
Dennhardt, Oskar-Hubert	Major, Kdr. II./G. R. 11 & Rgt. Fhr. 870th Oak Leaves 9.5.45	17.3.44
Denninger, Rudolf	Oblt. d.R., Chef 1./G. R. 439	1.9.43
Denzinger, Franz, Dipl.-Ing.	Oberst, Kdr. Rgt. Stab A.R. 553 z.b.V.	5.9.44
Deppe, Hans-Werner	Oblt., Chef 3./G. R. 58	14.8.43
Deßloch, Otto	Gen. Major, Kom.Gen. II. Flak-Korps 470th Oak Leaves 10.5.44	24.6.40
Dethleffsen, Erich	Oberst. i.G., Chef d. Gen. St. XXXIX. Pz. Korps	23.12.43
Detmers, Theodor	Freg. Kpt., Kdt. Hilfskreuzer "Kormoran" (HSK 8)	4.12.41
Dettenberg, Werner	Oblt. d.R., Chef 6./G. R. 852 + 12.9.44 at Brest (France) of wounds	18.9.44
Dettke, Oskar	Hptm., Staffelkpt. 9./K.G. 55	7.4.45
Deutsch, Ferdinand (12)	Oblt. d.R., Fhr. of a Kampfgr.	6.5.45
Deutsch, Heinz	Lt. d.R., Fhr. 3./Fsch. Sturmgeschütz-Brig. 12	28.4.45
Deutschländer, Erich	Hptm., Kdr. II./G. R. 328	26.3.44
Deutschmann, Siegfried	Ofw., Fhr. 8./G. R. 463	11.12.44
Deventer, Hugo	Uffz., Gruppenfhr. in 3./Pi. Btl. 31	30.7.43
Devers, Hans-Werner	Oblt. d.R., Chef 3./Aufkl. Abt. 101	2.6.43
v. Dewitz, Eckhardt	Lt. d.R., AdJ. II./Geb.Jäger-Rgt. 143 + 5.7.43 at Bielgorod (Russia) as Oblt. d.R. & Btl. fhr. in Pz. Füs. Rgt. "GD"	17.8.42
Dicke, Anton	Obgefr., Gruppenfh. in 5./G. R. 3	21.2.43
Dickfeld, Adolf	Lt., Flugzeugfhr. in 7./J.G. 52 94th Oak Leaves 19.5.42	19.3.42
Diddens, Diddo	Lt. d.R., Zugf. in 2./St. Gesch. Abt. 185 501st Oak Leaves 15.6.44	18.3.42
Dieckmann, August	SS-Sturmbannfhr., Kdr. I./SS-Rgt. "Germania" 233rd Oak Leaves 16.4.43 39th Swords 10.10.43	23.4.42
Diefenthal, Josef	SS-Hptsturmfhr., Kdr. III. (gep.)/SS-Pz. G. R. 2 "LSSAH"	5.2.45
Diekwisch, Erwin	Lt., Flugzeugfhr. in 9./Stuka-Geschw. 1	15.10.42

Name	Details	Date
Dieling, Horst	Lt., Fhr. 7./G. R. 434 + 5.1.44 east of Mogilew (Russia)	18.1.44
Diem, Otto	Wachtm., Geschützfhr. in 3. (schw.)/Aufkl. Abt. 9 + 8.8.43 at Kuban bridgehead (Russia)	23.9.43
Dienenthal, Erich	Oblt., Fhr. 2. (Radf.)/Div. Aufkl. Abt. 45	14.12.41
Dienhold, Johannes	Oblt. d.R., Chef 3./Flak-Rgt. 23 (mot.)	14.6.41
Diepold, Max	Oblt., Staffelkpt. 10. (Pz.)/S.G. 77	28.3.45
Diergarten, Hans	SS-Sturmbannfhr., Ia d. 8. SS-Kav. Div. "Florian Geyer" + 21.8.44 as Obersturmbannfhr. at Petrikau (Poland)	16.1.44
Dierks, Karl-Heinz	Hptm., Fhr. II/G. R. 42	13.1.45
Diesener, Joachim	Hptm., Kdr. I./Pz. G. R. 33	9.6.44
Diesing, Ulrich	Major, Kmdre. Zerst. Geschw. 1 + 17.4.45 accidentally at Boizenburg (Elbe) as Gen. Major & Chef Techn. Luftrüst. in RLM	6.9.42
Diestel, Erich	Gen.Lt., Kdr. 346. I.D.	8.10.44
Dietl, Eduard	Gen.Lt., Kdr. 3. Geb. Div. 1st Oak Leaves 19.7.40 72nd Swords 1.7.44	9.5.40
Dietlen, Walter	Obstlt., Kdr. Kradschtz. Btl. 54	4.12.41
Dietrich, Gerhard	Fhj. -Fw., Flugzeugfhr. in Stab/K.G. 55	9.6.44
Dietrich, Johann	Hptm., Chef 2./Flak-Rgt. 49 (mot.) + January 43 in Soviet captivity of spotted fever	23.12.42
Dietrich, Josef	SS-Obergruppenfhr. & General d. Waffen-SS, Kdr. SS-InfRgt. (mot.) "LSSAH" 41st Oak Leaves 31.12.41 26th Swords 14.3.43 16th Diamonds 6.8.44	4.7.40
Dietrich, Karl-Heinz	Hptm. d.R., Kdr. 11./Pz. G. R. 3	26.6.44
Dietrich, Wilhelm	SS-Hptsturmfhr. & Hptm. d. Schupo, Fhr. III./SS-Pol. Schütz. -Rgt. 1 + 12.3.44 in hospital at Dorpat (Estonia) as SS-Obsturmbannfhr. & Obstlt. d. Schupo & Rgt. Kdr. of wounds	15.10.42
Dietsche, Bernhard	SS-Sturmbannfhr., Kdr. II./SS-Geb.Jäg. Rgt. 2	17.7.43
Dietz, Edwin-Oskar-Heinrich	Lt., Zugf. in 1./Schtz. Rgt. 11 + 16.7.41 as Oblt. & Kp. Chef of wounds	15.8.40
Dietz, Valentin	Hptm., Kdr. 1./Jäger-Rgt. 204	30.12.43
Baron Digeon v. Monteton, Constantin	Gen. Major. Kdr. Armeewaffenschule Pz. AOK 3 + 27.6.44 at Gorodez (Russia); posthumously promoted to Gen. Major	14.8.4–4
Dilley, Bruno	Hptm., Kdr. 1./Stuka-Geschw. 2 "Immelmann" 174th Oak Leaves 8.1.43	4.6.42
Dilz, Fritz	Ofw., Zugf. in 7./Pz. G. & 5	18.1.45
Dimmig, Joseph	Uffz., Gruppenfhr. In 14. (Pz.Jäg.)/Div. Gruppe 112	21.2.44

Dinger, Fritz	Lt., Staffelfhr. 4./J.G. 53 + 27.7.43 in south Italy as Oblt. & Staffelkpt.	23.12.42
Dinkelaker, Ulrich	Oberst, Kdr. A.R. 36 (mot.)	9.12.43
Dinort, Oskar	Major, Kmdr. Stuka-Geschw. 2 "Immelmann" 21st Oak Leaves 14.7.41	20.6.40
Dipberger, Wilhelm	Fhj. -Ofw., Beob. i. Stab/K.G. 6	9.1.45
Dirkmorfeld, Josef	Obgefr., Gruppenfhr. i. d. 2./Pi. Btl. 208	12.3.43
Dirlewanger, Dr. Oskar	SS-Oberfhr. d.R., Kdr. SS-Brigade "Dirlewanger" + 7.6.45 in Altshausen (Kr. Saulgau)	30.9.44
Ditter, Hans	Ofw., Kp. Truppfhr. in 1./Pz. G. R. 7	11.12.44
Dittfeld, Johannes	Major, Kdr. 1./G. R. 466 posted missing as Rgt. Fhr.	11.7.44
Dittlof, Heinrich	Oblt., Chef 9./G. R. 422 + 20.2.45 at Libau (Kurland) as Fhr. II./Gr. Rgt. 422	10.9.44
Dittmer, Joachim	Hptm., Kdr. 1./Pz. G. R. 3 + 3.11.43 east of Jekaterinowka (Russia) as Major & Rgt. Fhr.	3.4.43
Dittrich, Dr. jur. Stefan	Oblt. d.R., Chef 4./1a A.R. 46	4.6.44
Dix, Kurt	Feldw., Kp. Truppfhr. in 3./G. R. 510	31.3.43
Dixius, Karl	Hptm., Kdr. I./Jäg. Rgt. 229	26.11.44
Dobberkau, Hans	Lt. d.R., Fhr. 7./G. R. 284	21.9.44
Dobberstein, Werner	Kaptlt., Chef 5. Räumbootsflottille	4.9.41
Dobratz, Kurt	Kapt. z. See, Kdt. "U 1232"	23.1.45
Döbele, Anton	Ofw., Flugzeugfhr. in 3./J.G. 54 + 11.11.43 on the Witebsk-Smolensk highway; posthumously promoted to z. Lt.	26.3.44
Döbrich, Hans	Feldw., Flugzeugfhr. in 6./J.G. 5	19.9.43
Doench, Fritz	Major, Kdr. I./K.G. 30 + 14.6.42 accidentally at Foggia (Italy) as Oberst i.G. & Abt. Chef in R. L. M.	14.6.40
Doenicke, Hans-Günther	Hptm., Kdr. 1./G. R. 71 (mot.) + 1.7.44 north of Segni (Italy); posthumously promoted to Major	27.7.44
Dönitz, Karl	Konteradmiral, Befehlshaber der U-Boote (B. d. U.) 223rd Oak Leaves 6.4.43	21.4.40
Dörfel, Josef	Ofw., Zugf. in 6./I.R. 439	4.3.42
Dörffel, Georg	Oblt., Staffelkpt. i. 5./(S)Lehr-Geschw. 2 231st Oak Leaves 14.4. 43	21.8.41
Dörflinger, Walter	Oblt. d.R., stv. Fhr. 11./G. R. 332 + 25.9.44	7.4.44
Doergens, Hans-Joachim	Hptm. d.R., Fhr. Pi. Btl. 225	26.6.44
Doering, Alfred	Ofw., Fhr. 11./G. R. 6 + 22.9.44 at main dressing station Kalu-Salas (Latvia) of wounds	2.2.44
Döring, Arnold	Lt., Flugzeugfhr. in 10./N. J.G. 3	17.4.45

v. Doering, Bernd	Major, Kdr. II./Schtz. Rgt. 79 + 7.7.44 2 km south of Florenz as Adj. in Stab der H.Gr.C; posthumously promoted to as Gen. Major	30.11.40
Doering, Ernst	Rittm., Kdr. Div. Füs. Btl. (A.A.) 329 + End of 1944 at Westen as Major	16.3.44
Döring, Johann	Ofw., Nachr. -Staffel-Fhr. in 1./G. R. 958	5.4.45
Döring, Wilhelm	Lt. Beob. in 2./K.G. 53 "Legion Condor"	19.2.43
Doering-Manteuffel, Hans-Wilhelm	Oberst, Kdr. Flak-Rgt. 101 (mot.)	10.9.44
Dörmann, Friedrich	Hptm. z. V., Kdr. 11./G. R. 528	18.1.44
Dörmann, Karl	Lt., Fhr. 9./A.R. 1542 + 4.5.45 at Danzig	9.2.45
Dörnbrack, Werner	Oblt., Staffelkpt. 4./(S.) Lehr-Geschw. 2 660th Oak Leaves 25.11.44	21.8.41
Dörnemann, Heinrich	Major, Kdr. Pz. Aufkl. Abt. 16	28.11.43
Dörner, Helmut	SS-Sturmbannfhr. & Major der Schupo, Kdr. II./SS-Pol. Schtz. Rgt. 2 650th Oak Leaves 16.11.44 129th Swords 1.2.45	15.5.42
Dörr, Franz	Hptm., Kdr. III./J.G. 5	19.8.44
Dörries, Helmut	Fhj. -Ofw., Beob. in 2. (F.)/Aufkl. Gruppe 123	27.7.44
Dörries, Josef	Uffz., Gr. Fhr. in 6./G. R. 87	5.4.44
Doff, Franz	Gefr., Gruppenfhr. in 10./Geb.Jäg. Rgt. 98	20.7.42
Dohle, Herbert	Hptm., Fhr. II./G. R. 317	28.11.43
Dollmann, Friedrich	Gen. d. Art., OB 7. Armee 518th Oak Leaves 1.7.44	24.6.40
Dollwet, René	Lt. d.R., Fhr. 2./G. R. 485	29.2.44
Domaschk, Erich	Hptm., Fhr. II./Pz. Gren. Rgt. 103	3.11.42
Domaschk, Joachim	Oblt., Fhr. I./Pz. G. R. 108 496th Oak Leaves 11.6.44	12.10.43
Dombacher, Kurt	Lt., Flugzeugfhr. in 1./J.G. 51 "Mölders"	8.4.45
Dombrowski, Kurt	Major, Kdr. II./Sich. Rgt. 360	17.12.44
Dominik, Hans	Freg. Kpt., Chef der 9. Torpedobootsflottille	28.12.44
Dommeratzky, Otto	Ofw., Flugzeugfhr. in 8./Schl. Geschw. 1 665th Oak Leaves 25.11.44	5.1.43
Dommes, Wilhelm	Kaptlt., Kdt. "U 431"	2.12.42
Domrich, Otto	Hptm., Kdr. 1./Pz. G. R. 2 + 11.8.43; posthumously promoted to Major	8.8.43
Donat, Gottfried	Oblt. d.R., Chef 5./G. R. 519 + 24.6.44 in Russia as Hptm. d.R. & Btl. Kdr.	24.4. 43
Donhauser, Georg	Ofw., Zugl. in 1./I.R. 501	26.9.41
Donnhauser, Anton	Hptm., Kdr. II./Pz. G. R. 111	18.7.43
Donth, Rudolf	Feldw., Fhr. 6./Fsch. Jäg. Rgt. 4	14.1.45
Dorenbeck, Paul	Oberst, Kdr. G. R. 170	4.6.44
Dorfmeister, Hans	Oblt. d.R., Chef 1./G. R. 355	16.10.44

KNIGHT'S CROSS OF THE IRON CROSS

Dormann, Hermann	Hptm., Kdr. II./Pz. G. R. 64 + January 1943 in Stalingrad (Russia) as Major	4.1.43
Dorn, Heinrich	Oberst, Kdr. G. R. 7	16.11.44
Dorow, Otto	Obstlt., Kdr. I.R. 514	3.4.42
Dorr, Hans	SS-Hptsturmfhr., Chef 4./SS-Inf.Rgt. "Germania" 327th Oak Leaves 13.11.43 77th Swords 9.7.44	27.9.42
Dorsch, Walter	Feldw., Kp. Tr. Fhr. in 14./G. R. 544	14.4. 45
Dortenmann, Hans	Oblt., Staffelkpt. 3./J.G. 26 "Schlageter"	20.4.45
Dose, Paul	Oblt., Staffelkpt. 9./Stuka-Geschw. 2 "Immelmann"	4.5.44
Doser, Otto	Oberjäger, Zugf. in 7./Jäger-Rgt. 75	14.3.43
Dous, Willi	Oblt., Flugzeugfhr. in 8./K.G. 3 "Lützow" + 17.8.41 in Russia; posthumously promoted to Hptm.	5.7.41
Dowerk, Paul	Oblt., Chef 5./I.R. 215 + 23.6.44 in Orscha (Russia) as Btl. Kdr.; posthumously promoted to Major	15.1.42
Drange, Günther	Oberst, Kdr. G. R. 428	16.10.44
Dratwa, Johannes	Hptm. d.R., Chef 2./st. Gesch. Brig. 184	5.3.45
Draxenberger, Sepp	SS-Hptscharfhr., Zugf. in Stabskp./SS-Pz. Rgt. 5 "Wiking" + 23.3.45 at Stuhlweißenburg (Hungary)	17.4.45
v. Drebber, Moritz	Oberst, Kdr. I.R. 523	30.6.42
Drechsler, Gerhard	Feldw., Zugf. in 3./Div. Füs. Btl. 14	11.4.44
Drees, Karl-Heinz	Gefr., Richtschtz. in 14. (Pz.Jäg.)/G. R. 552	8.2.44
Dreher, Johann	Oblt., Flugzeugfhr. in 5./K.G. 53 "Legion Condor" + 4.3.45 over England as Hptm. & Staffelkpt. in IV./N. J.G. 3	5.4.44
Dreike, Franz-Josef (6)	SS-Hptsturmfhr. d.R., Kdr. SS-Flak-Abt. 2 "Das Reich"	6.5.45
Drekmann, Dipl.-Ing. Paul	Gen.Lt., Kdr. 252. I.D.	28.3.45
Drescher, Georg-Wilhelm	Oblt. d.R., Chef Stabskp./Jäger-Rgt. 24 (L)	1.2.45
Drescher, Otto	Gen.Lt., Kdr. 267. I.D. + 13.8.44 at Memel (Baltic)	6.4.44
Dresel, Bernhard	Hptm. d.R., Kdr. I./G. R. 326	3.11.44
Dressel, Albert	Feldw., Zugf. in 3./Pz. Abt. 160 + 8.9.44 in NW Europe as Ofw.	13.10.42
Drewes, Dr. jur. Heinrich	Major d.R., Kdr. Kradschtz. Btl. 10	24.4. 43
Drewes, Martin	Hptm., Kdr. III./Nacht-J.G. 1 839th Oak Leaves 17.4.45	27.7.44

ELITE OF THE THIRD REICH

Drewes, Wilhelm	Hptm., Fhr. I./Pz. G. R. 13 458th Oak Leaves 20.4.44	27.10.43
Drexel, Hans	SS-Obsturmfhr., stv. Fhr. II./SS-Pz. G. R. "Westland"	14.10.43
Drexel, Johann	Uffz., Gesch. Fhr. in 14. (Pz.Jäg.)/G. R. 408	23.8.43
Drexel, Josef	Oberst d.R., Kdr. G. R. 436	27.8.44
Drexler, Hans	Major, Kdr. III./G. R. 232	14.8.43
Drexler, Hans	Hptm., Chef 4./Pz. Aufkl. Abt. 129	12.1.45
Drexler, Oskar	SS-Obersturmbannfhr., Kdr. SS-Pz. A.R. 12 "Hitlerjugend"	6.5.45
Drexler, Walter	SS-Sturmbannfhr., Kdr. SS-Aufkl. Abt. 8 "Florian Geyer" + February 1945 in Budapest (Hungary)	11.12.44
Dreyer, Georg	Obstlt., Kdr. G. R. 1053	5.11.44
Drössiger, Kurt	Gefr., MG-Schütze in 4./I.R. 415	10.2.42
Droitsch, Herbert	Oblt. d.R., Chef 1./G. R. 187	25.1.45
Drolshage, Hubertus	Lt. d.R., Zugf. in Pz.Jäg. Abt. 41 (sf.) + 12.10.44	6.4.44
Drolshagen, Franz	Uffz., Gruppenfhr. in 5./G. R. 698	16.10.44
Dropmann, Hermann	Obstlt., Fhr. G. R. 1050	12.7.44
Drossel, Leo	Hptm., Kdr. III./I.R. 102	19.7.40
Droste, Hans	Lt., Stoßtruppfhr. in 7./I.R. 124	13.6.41
Drude, Hans	Ofw., Zugfhr. in 1./Pz. Gren. Rgt. 14	10.2.45
Drüke, Wilhelm	Obstlt., Kdr. G. R. 294	30.12.44
Drünkler, Ernst-Georg	Hptm., Staffelkpt. 1./N. J.G. 5	20.3.45
Druffner, Alfred	Obstlt., Kdr. G. R. 519 343rd Oak Leaves 30.11.43	6.4.43
Druschel, Alfred	Oblt., Staffelkpt. 2./(S.)Lehr-Geschw. 2 118th Oak Leaves 3.9.42 24th Swords 19.2.43	21.8.41
Dubicki, Albert	Uffz., VB in 1./Werfer-Rgt. 14	12.8.44
Dubigk, Karl	Hptm. d.R., Fhr. Div. Füs. Btl. 131	18.11.44
Dudeck, Gerhard	Hptm., Kdr. III./Transportflieger-Geschw. 2	9.6.44
v. Dücker Graf v. Plettenberg, Georg	Rittm., Kdr. schw. Kav. Abt. 4 (mot.) 730th Oak Leaves 5.2.45	12.8.44
Düe, Rolf	Hptm. d.R., Chef 1./Pz.Jäg. Abt. 19	23.3.45
Düllberg, Ernst	Major, Kdr. III./J.G. 27	20.7.44
Dünkel, Friedrich	Hptm., Flugzeugfhr. in 2./Nahaufkl. -Gruppe "Tannenberg"	28.4.45
Dünker, Edgar	Hptm., Kdr. I./I.R. 336 + 29.12.41 of wounds	31.12.41
Dünkler, Joachim	Major, Kdr. I./Pz. G. R. 7 + 19.4.45 in hospital at Haldensleben	18.2.45

KNIGHT'S CROSS OF THE IRON CROSS

Dünser, Lothar	Oblt., Chef 8./Flak-Rgt. 38 (mot.) + 14.8.43 at Charkow (Russia) of wounds	26.8.43
Düppenbecker, Herbert	Hptm., Kdr. 1./Pz. Gr. Rgt. 79	4.10.44
Dürbeck, Wilhelm	Hptm., Staffelkpt. 8./(K.) Lehr-Geschw. I + 19.1.41 missing over Malta	3.12.40
Dürr, Emil	SS-Unterscharfhr., Geschützf. in 4. (schw.)/SS-Pz. G. R. 26 "Hitlerjugend" +27.6.44 at St. Mauvieu (Area Caen/France)	23.8.44
Dürrwanger, Alfred	Hptm., Chef 10. (schw.)/Jäg. Rgt. 83	10.7.42
Düskow, Alwin	Hptm., Kdr. II./A.R. 295	21.3.42
Düttmann, Peter	Lt., Flugzeugfhr. in 5./J.G. 52	9.6.44
Düvert, Walter	Gen.Maj., Kdr. 13. Pz.Div.	30.7.41
Düwell, Klaus	Oblt., Chef 12./Geb.Jäg. Rgt. 137	19.11.41
Dumke, Günther	Hptm. d.R., Kdr. II./G. R. 283 + 28.1.44 at Schepetowka (Russia)	6.3.44
Dumßner, Andreas	Uffz., Gruppenfhr. in 3./G. R. 423	16.1.45
Duncker, Christoph	Lt. d.R., Fhr. 2./Pi. Btl. 158	21.11–42
Dunkel, Konrad	Major, Kdr. Pz.Jäg. Abt. 1542 + 20.2.45	28.2.45
Durchdenwald, Wilhelm	Oblt., Fhr. II./I.R. 544 + 17.8.42 am Don (Russia)	13.11.42
Dutter, Franz	Major, Kdr. II./G. R. 2	20.3.44
Duve, Werner	Major, Fhr. G. R. 183 + 3.3.45 at Euskirchen	2.2.45
Dyroff, Adam	Major, Kdr. III./Pz. G. R. 115	11.12.44

E

Ebel, Paul	Uffz., Gruppenfhr. in Stabskp. (Pi. -Zug)/G. R. 50	17.2.43
Ebeling, Dr. med. Ernst	Hptm., Staffelkpt. 3./K.G. 53 "Legion Condor"	20.3.45
Ebeling, Heinz	Lt., Staffelkpt. 9./J.G. 26 "Schlageter"	5.11.40
Ebeling, Werner	Major, Kdr. II./G. R. 220 763rd Oak Leaves 5.3.45	9.4.44
Ebener, Kurt	Feldw., Flugzeugfhr. in 4./J.G. 3 "Udet"	7.4.43
Eberbach, Heinrich	Obstlt., Kdr. Pz. Rgt. 35 42nd Oak Leaves 31.12.41	4.7.40
Eberhardt, Erich	SS-Obstrmbannfhr., Ia 3. SS-Pz.Div. "Totenkopf"	23.8.44
Eberhardt, Friedrich-Georg	Gen.Lt., Kdr. 60. I.D. (mot.)	31.12.41
Eberhardt, Georg	SS-Sturmbannfhr., Kdr. estn. Freiw. -SS-Pz. Gren. Btl. "Narwa" + end July 1943 at Sawodskoje. Donets (Russia)	4.8.43
Ebersbach, Hans	Oblt., Staffelkpt. 6./K.G. 76 + 31.5.44	8.8.44

Eberspächer, Dipl.-Ing. Helmut	Hptm., Staffelkpt. 3./Nachtschlacht-Gruppe 20	26.1.45
Ebert, Franz	Oblt., Chef 10./Flak-Rgt. 23 (mot.)	14.4. 45
Ebinger, Edwin	Ofw., Kp. Truppf. in 12./Geb.Jäg. Rgt. 13 + 4.3.44 in Russia of wounds	4.11.43
Ebke, August-Friedrich	Obstlt. d.R., Kdr. G. R. 464	14.4. 45
Ebner, Adam	Ofw., Zugf. in 3./Geb.Jäg. Rgt. 137	19.11.41
Ebner, Fridolin	Ofw., Zugf. in 9./G. R. 7	28.10.44
Eck, Josef	Hptm., Fhr. 4./Pz. Rgt. 4	15.7.44
Eckardt, Reinhold	Oblt., Adj. II./N. J.G. 1 + 30.7.42 at Brussels (Belgium)	30.8.41
Eckardt, Willi	Major, Kdr. IR./G. R. 521	7.12.43
Eckebrecht, Fritz (17)	Oblt., Beob. in 4. (H)/Aufkl. Gruppe 31	9.11.44
Ecker, Paul	Major, Kdr. I./Pz. G. R. 9 634th Oak Leaves 28.10.44	16.3.44
Eckerle, Franz	Hptm., Staffelkpt. I./J.G. 54 82nd Oak Leaves 12.3.42	18.9.41
Eckert, Alois	Feldw., Zugf. in 9./Pz. Rgt. 33 + 12.10.43 in Russia as Ofw. of wounds	3.8.42
Eckert, Ernst	Oblt. d.R., Fhr. 11./Jäg. Rgt. 229 + 27.7.44 south of Kopiatyn (Russia); posthumously promoted to Hptm. d.R.	9.6.44
Eckert, Hans	SS-Obsturmfhr. d.R., Fhr. II./SS-Pz. G. R. 3 "Deutschland" SS-Pz. Kampfgr. "Das Reich"	4.5.44
Eckhardt, Alfons	Major, Kdr. III./I.R. 11 (mot.) + 11.8.42 at Rshew (Russia)	6.10.42
Eckhardt, Hermann	Feldw., Zugf. in I./Pz. Abt. 8	28.3.45
Eckhardt, Johann-Heinrich	Oberst, Kdr. Jäger-Rgt. 38 644th Oak Leaves 3.11.44	20.5.42
Eckhardt, Wilhelm	Hptm. d.R., Kdr. II./G. R. 503	17.9.44
Eckholt, Oskar	Oberst, Kdr. A.R. 178	9.4.43
Eckinger, Dr. Josef-Franz	Hptm., Fhr. II./Schtz. Rgt. 1 48th Oak Leaves 31.12.41	17.3.41
Eckstein, Fritz	SS-Rottenfhr., Richtschtz. in I./SS-Pz.Jäger-Abt. 12 "Hitlerjugend"	18.11.44
Reichsfreiherr v. Edelsheim, Maximilian	Obstlt., Kdr. Radf. Abt. 1 162nd Oak Leaves 23.12.42 105th Swords 23.10.44	30.7.41
Eder, Anton (8)	Oberst, Abschnittskdt. eines Verteidigungs- bereiches in Berlin	26.4.45
Eder, Georg-Peter	Oblt., Staffelkpt. 6./J.G. 1 663rd Oak Leaves 25.11.44	24.6.44
Eder, Martin	Hptm., Fhr. I./I.R. 481	28.11.40

KNIGHT'S CROSS OF THE IRON CROSS

Edhofer, Heinz	Ofw., Flugzeugfhr. in 7./Schlacht-Geschw. 2 "Immelmann"	30.11.44
Eding, Alois	Oblt. d.R., Fhr. I./G. R. 19	12.10.43
Edse, Heinrich	Oblt. d.R., Fhr. I./G. R. 407	15.4.44
Edtbauer, Franz	Lt. d.R., Fhr. I./Pz. G. R. 11 + 13.4.44 in Russia of wounds; posthumously promoted to z. Oblt. d.R.	4.6.44
Eggemann, Walter	Lt. d.R., Ord.Offz. i. Stab/G. R. 680	18.4.43
Eggemann, Wilhelm	Major, Kdr. II./G. R. 94 468th Oak Leaves 4.5.44	20.4.43
Egger, Paul	SS-Obsturmfhr., Zugf. in I./schw. SS-Pz. Abt. 502	28.4.45
Egger, Reinhard	Oblt., Fhr. 10./Fsch. Jäger-Rgt. 1 510th Oak Leaves 24.6.44	9.7.41
Eggers, Hermann	Hptm., Chef 3./Flak-Rgt. 64	21.8.42
Eggers, Johann	Uffz., Richtschtz. in 7./Pz. Rgt. 6	14.12.43
Eggers, Walter	Oblt., Chef 7./G. R. 116	29.8.43
Eggers, Wilhelm	Oblt., Chef 13. (1. G.)/I.R. 490	16.3.42
Egghardt, Alfred	Lt. d.R., Chef 2./Sturmgeschütz-Brig. 912	20.4.45
Egle, Kurt	Oblt., Fhr. 8./Luftnachr. Rgt. 53	5.7.44
Eglseer, Karl	Gen. Major, Kdr. 4. Geb. Div. + 23.6.44 accidentally at Hartberg (Steiermark) as Gen. d. Geb. Tr. & K,om. Gen. XVÜII. Geb. K.	23.10.41
Ehinger, Josef	Objäger, Gruppenfhr. in 6./Geb.Jäg. Rgt. 100	22.8.43
Ehle, Curt	Hptm. d.R., Fhr. 1./Kradschtz. Btl. 15 673rd Oak Leaves 29.11.44	27.7.41
Ehle, Walter	Major, Kdr. II./N. J.G. 1 + 17.11.43 at St. Trond (France)	29.8.43
Ehlers, Hans	Oblt., Staffelkpt. 3./J.G. 1 "Oesau" + 27.12.44 over the Eifel as Major & Kdr. 1./J.G. 1 "Oesau"	9.6.44
Ehm, Bruno	Ofw., Zugf. in 8./G. R. 162	1.2.45
Ehrath, Fritz	SS-Obsturmbannfhr., Kdr. SS-Pz. G. R. 9 "Germania"	23.2.44
Ehrenberger, Rudolf	Ofw., Flugzeugfhr. in 6./J.G. 53 + 8.3.44 at Jüterbog	6.4.44
Ehrhardt, Ernst	Uffz., Gruppenfhr. in G. R. 481	23.3.45
Ehrig, Werner	Obstlt. i.G., Ia 22. I.D. (LL)	26.5.40
Ehrler, Heinrich	Lt., Flugzeugfhr. in 6./J.G. 5 265th Oak Leaves 2.8.43	4.9.42
Ehrt, Günther	Hptm., Fhr. 1./I.R. 41 (mot.) + 20.11.44	3.5.42
Eibl, Karl	Obstlt., Kdr. III./I.R. 131 50th Oak Leaves 31.12.41 21st Swords 19.12.42	15.8.40

143

Eich, Karl	Ofw., Zugf. in 6./G. R. 282 + 20.11.43 north of Kertsch (Russia)	20.1.44
v. Eichel-Streiber, Diethelm	Hptm., Staffelkpt. Stab/J.G. 51 "Mölders"	5.4.44
Eichert, Hans-Henning	Oblt., Chef 6./Schtz. Rgt. 11 + 9.7.43 at Nowo Chuto, Orel (Russia) as Hptm. in Div. Stab; posthumously promoted to z. Major	14.3.42
Eichert, Robert	Ofw., Zugf. in 8./PZ. Rgt. 36 + 23.9.44 in Russia as Lt. & Fhr. 4./Pz. Rgt. 36	20.4.43
Eichhorn, Hugo	SS-Hptsturmfhr. d.R., in Stab SS-Pi. Btl. 5 "Wiking"	15.1.43
Eichler, Erich	Hptm., stellv. Fhr. II./A.R. 20 (mot.)	21.9.44
Eichler, Hilmar	Oberst d.R., Kdr. G. R. 306	16.11.44
Eichler, Kurt	Hptm., Fhr. II./G. R. 189	12.8.44
Eichler, Richard	Obstlt., Kdr. G. R. 212	29.1.43
Eichler, Wolfgang	Lt. d.R., Fhr. 6./Pz. Rgt. 29 + 4.7.44 in Russia as Fhr. 6./Pz. Rgt. 29; posthumously promoted to z. Oblt. d.R.	20.12.43
Eichloff, Otto	Feldw., Flugzeugfhr. in 4./K.G. 30	16.8.40
Eichmeier, Hans	Major d.R., Kdr. Le. Flak-Abt. 854 (mot.)	11.6.44
v. Eichstedt, Werner	Oberst, Kdr. Inf.Rgt. 436 + 26.8.44 at Kishinew (Russia) as Gen. Major & Kdr. 294. I.D.	18.8.42
Eick, Alfred	Oblt. z. See, Kdt. "U 510"	31.3.44
Eicke, Theodor	SS-Gruppenfhr. & Gen.Lt. d. Waffen-SS, Kdr. SS-Div. "Totenkopf' 88th Oak Leaves 20.4.42	26.12.41
Eidel, Alfred	Hptm., Fhr. I./I.R. 171 283rd Oak Leaves 24.8.43	24.9.42
Eiden, Karl	Ofw., Zugf. in 8. (MG.)/G. R. 97	5.3.43
Eikmeier, Hans	Rittm., Fhr. II./Reiter-Rgt. 32	30.9.44
Eil, Peter	Feldw., Zugf. in I./G. R. 105	11.1.44
Eilers, Adolf	Major, Kdr. Gren. Rgt. Gruppe 184	10.9.44
v. Einem gen. v. Rothmaler, Friedrich-Wilhelm	Lt. d.R., V. B. in I./A.R. 230	4.12.42
v. Einem, Hans-Egon (19)	Oberst, Kdr. Pz. G. R. 21	11.5.45
Einfalt, Johann	Obetgefr. in III./Jg. Rgt. 38	28.2.45
Einhoff, Georg	Oblt. d.R., Chef 8. (MG.)/G. R. 366 + 18.2.45 as Major d.R.	6.6.43
Eisele, Alois	Hptm., Kdr. III./G. R. 61 695th Oak Leaves 12.1.45	15.12.43
Eisenach, Franz	Hptm., Staffelkpt. 3./J.G. 54	10.10.44
Eisenblätter, Erich	Ofw., Zugf. in Stabskp./G. R. 176	5.4.44

Name	Details	Date
Eisermann, Erich	Feldw., Spähtruppfhr. in 1./(Pz. Späh)/Pz. Aufkl. Abt. 23	9.12.44
Eisermann, Johannes	Oberst. Kdr. I.R. 156 (mot.)	25.8.42
Eisgruber, Johann	Feldw., Pi. Zugf. in Stabskp./G. R. 62	31.8.43
Eisgruber, Karl (14)	Obstlt., Kdr. Geb.Jäg. Rgt. 98	1.6.45
Eisl, Alois	Major, Fhr. Geb.Jäg. Rgt. 98	9.12.44
Eitel, Emil	Hptm., Kdr. III./Luftw. Jäger-Rgt. 30 + 14.9.44 in Russia	8.8.44
Eitner, Dr. med. Volkhard	Hptm., Kdr. I./G. R. 212	10.6.43
v. Ekesparre, Arthur	Obstlt. i.G., Ia 13. Pz.Div, + 12.2.45 posted missing, Budapest (Hungary)	15.1.45
Elbl, Josef	Oberst, Kdr. G. R. 330 + 10.11.43 in Russia	22.8.43
Elflein, Walter	Oblt. d.R., Fhr. 2./G. R. 95 347th Oak Leaves 5.12.43	8.10.43
Ellmer, Konrad	Ofw., Beob. in 14. (Eis.)/K.G. 27 "Boelcke" + 9.12.44 in France	9.6.44
Ellmers, Gustav	Oblt., Chef 2./Pz. G. R. 14	28.2.45
Eltrich, Herbert	Hptm., Kdr. Heeres-Pi. Btl. 52 (mot.)	9.12.43
Frhr. v. Elverfeldt, Harald	Gen. Major, Fhr. 9. Pz.Div. 801st Oak Leaves 23.3.45	9.12.44
Emig, Hans	Obstlt., Kdr. Kampfgr. 806 + 28.6.41 Stalinkanal (Russia)	21.8.41
Emmerling, Heinz	Hptm. d.R., Kdr. II./G. R. 464	23.2.44
Emmermann, Carl	Kaptlt., Kdt. "U 172" 256th Oak Leaves 4.7.43	27.11.42
Emmert, Dr. jur. Ernst	Oblt. d.R., Fhr. I./I.R. 282 + 22.1.45 Glogau (Silesia) as Obstlt. d.R. & Kdr. G. R. 282 of wounds	31.12.41
Endell, Werner	Kapt. z. See, Hafenkdt. St. Malo	18.8.44
Ender, Eduard	Ofw., Zugf. in 1./Pz.Jäger-Abt. 49	23.2.44
Ender, Hans	Hptm., Kdr. II./G. R. 545	5.4.45
Endraß, Engelbert	Oblt. z. See, Kdt. "U 46" 14th Oak Leaves 10.6.41	5.9.40
Endres, Hans	Hptm., Fhr. I./Pz. A.R. 74	14.8.43
Endres, Theodor	Gen.Lt. z. V., Kdr. 212. I.D.	13.7.40
Endreß, Hans	SS-Hptsturmfhr. d.R., Fhr. II./SS-Pz. G. R. 6 "Theodor Eicke"	23.3.45
Endriß, August	Hptm. d.R., Chef 4./A.R. 219	14.8.43
Engbrecht, Herbert	Hptm., Kdr. III./I.R. 3 + 7.8.42 at Kirischi (Wolchow/Russia)	23.11.41
Engel, Gerhard	Obstlt., Kdr. Füs. Rgt. 27 679th Oak Leaves 11.12.44	4.7.44
Engel, Heinrich	Uffz. d.R., Geschützfhr. in 2./Sturmgeschütz-Abt. 259	2.11.43

Engel, Hermann	Hptm., Kdr. I./G. R. 1122	17.3.45
Engel, Otto	Lt. d.R., Flugzeugfhr. in 5./K.G. 53 "Legion Condor"	28.2.45
Engel, Walter	Hptm., Staffelkpt. 3./NJ.G. 5 + May 1945 apparently accidentally	28.2.45
Engelbrecht, Erwin	Gen. Major, Kdr. 163. I.D.	9.5.40
Engelbrecht, Karl	Wachtm., Zugf. in 1./Div. Füs. Btl. 98	20.1.44
Engelbrecht, Wilhelm	SS-Hptsturmfhr. & Hptm. d. Schupo, Fhr. II./SS-Polizei-Schützen-Rgt. 19	11.12.44
Engelhardt, Günter	Oberst, Kdr. G. R. 30 (mot.)	9.4.43
Engelhardt, Johann	Oblt., Chef 8./Fsch. Jäger-Rgt. 6	29.2.44
Engelhardt, Kurt	Owm. d.R., Zugf. in 2./Heeres-St. Gesch. Brig. 232	28.2.45
Engelien, Fritz	Major, Fhr. Div. Füs. Btl. 15	18.12.44
Engelien, Hans	Major, Fhr. Pz. Aufkl. Abt. 12 788th Oak Leaves 16.3.45	12.8.44
Engelmann, Richard	Hptm., Chef I./St. Gesch. Brig. 912 + 19.10.44 main dressing station, Jampils (Russia) of wounds	27.7.44
Engfer, Alfred	Hptm., Kdr. III./I.R. 523 + 1.9.42 at Stalingrad (Russia) of wounds	13.9.42
Engfer, Siegfried	Feldw., Flugzeugfhr. in III./J.G. 3 "Udet" + April 45 accidentally as Oblt.	2.10.42
Engler, Alfred	Major, Fhr. G. R. 97	18.11.44
Enneccerus, Walter	Hptm., Kdr. II./Stuka-Geschw. 2 "Immelmann"	21.7.40
Ens, Karl	Major, Kdr. II./I.R. 125 (mot.)	14.5.41
Enseling, Rudolf	SS-Sturmbannfhr., Kdr. 1./SS-Pz. Rgt. 2 "Das Reich"	23.8.44
Ensle, Wolfgang	Fhj. -Feldw., Flugzeugfhr. I.D. 3./Schlacht-Geschw. 2 "Immelmann"	8.8.44
Enßle, Alfred	Hptm., Staffelkpt. 2./K.G. 76	31.12.43
Enzensberger, Josef	Ofw., Flugzeugfhr. in 1./S.G. 10	28.2.45
Eppen, Heinrich	Oblt., Staffelkpt. 1./Stuka-Geschw. 3 + 4.6.42 at Tobruk (North Africa) as Hptm. & Kdr. I./Stuka-Geschw. 3	5.7.41
Erasmus, Dr. jur. Johannes	Major i.G., Ia XXXXVI. Pz. Korps	13.4.44
Erath, Ludwig	Uffz., Tr. Fhr. in 8./G. R. 351	24.12.44
Erdmann, Albrecht	Obstlt., Kdr. Kradschtz. Btl. 53 + 15.4.42 south of Wjasma (Russia) as Kdr. Schtz. Rgt. 14; posthumously promoted to z. Oberst	12.9.41
Erdmann, Armin	Oblt., Fhr. 6./Pz. G. R. 79	3.1.43
Erdmann, Hans	Hptm., Kdr. 1./Pz. G. R. 3 + 7.12.42 north of Terek (Russia)	10.12.42

Name	Details	Date
Erdmann, Otto	Lt., Fhr. 2./Pz. G. R. 66	9.12.44
Erdmann, Rudolph	Oberst, Kdr. Flak-Rgt. 153 (mot.)	13.2.45
Erdmann, Dipl.-Ing. Wolfgang	Gen.Lt., Kdr. 7. Fsch. Jäg. Div. + 5.9.46 in British captivity, Munsterlager (Suicide)	8.2.45
v. Erdmannsdorff, Gottfried	Oberst, Kdr. I.R. 171 + 30.1.46 in Minsk (Russia) hanged as Gen.Maj. & Kdt. v. Mogilew & Kdr. Div. Nr. 465	20.3.42
v. Erdmannsdorff, Werner	Oberst, Kdr. I.R. 30 (mot.) + 5.6.45 murdered by partisans at Laibach (Yugoslavia) as Gen.D.Inf. & Kom.Gen. LXXXXI. A.K.	27.2.42
Erdmenger, Hans	Korv. Kpt., Kdt. Zerstörer "Wilhelm Heidkamp" + 27.12.43 in the Bay of Biscay as Kapt. z. See & Chef 8. Zerstörerflottille	3.11.40
Erler, Rudolf	Oberst d.R., Kdr. G. R. 538	15.3.43
Ermoneit, Helmut	Oblt., Adj. II./K.G. 4 "General Wever"	8.8.44
Ernst, Albert	Lt., Zugf. in 1./schw. Pz.Jäger-Abt. 519	22.1.44
Ernst, Heinrich	Ofw., stv. Fhr. 2./Pz. Aufkl. Abt. 9	23.3.45
Ernst, Otto	Hptm., Kdr. 11./G. R. 725	6.10.44
Ernst, Richard	Obstlt., Kdr. Geb.Jäg. Rgt. 100	20.10.44
Ertel, Karl-Heinz	SS-Hptsturmfhr. d.R., Rgt. -Adj. niederl. SS-Freiw. -Pz. G. R. 49 "De Ruyter"	23.8.44
Ertel, Reinhold	Oblt., Fhr. 1./St. Gesch. Abt. 276 + 22.1.45 near Jülich as Hptm. & Fhr. St. Gesch. Brig. 341	31.1.44
Ertolitsch, Franz	Obgefr., MG-Schtz. in 6./Pz. G. R. 12	9.1.45
Esch, Albin	Major, Kdr. III./Geb.Jäg. Rgt. 85	13.6.41
Eschenbacher, Georg	Ofw., Zugf. in 4. (M. G.)/G. R. 451 + 9.1.44 in Russia	24.9.43
Eschmann, Fritz	Oblt., Fhr. 4./Feldersatz-Btl. 116	12.8.44
Frhr. v. Esebeck, Hans-Karl	Oberst, Kdr. 6. Schtz. Brigade	4.7.40
Eske, Otto	Feldw., Zugf. in 5./I.R. 4 + 8.11.41 south of Lake Ilmen (Russia)	27.7.41
Eßbach, Gotthard	Oblt., Chef 9./I.R. 31	22.9.41
Essig, Richard	Hptm. d.R., Fhr. 1./G. R. 273	2.9.44
Eßlinger, Willi	SS-Hptscharfhr., Zugf. in 3./SS-Pz.Jäg. Abt. 5 "Wiking" + 25.8.44 at Radzymin (Poland)	19.6.43
Ettel, Wolf-Udo	Lt., Staffelfhr. 4./J.G. 3 "Udet" 289th Oak Leaves 31.8.43	1.6.43
Etthöfer, Alois	SS-Sturmbannfhr. & Major der Schutzpolizei, Kdr. SS-Pol. Pz. Abt. 4 + 20.11.44 at Hatvan (Hungary)	17.3.45
Etzold, Gerhard	Oblt., Zugfhr. 2./Kradschtz. Btl. 8 + 6.5.41 in Schrnölln (Thür.) as Komp. Chef of wounds	3.6.40

Graf zu Eulenburg, Jonas	Oberst. Kdt. Festung Glogau + 8.4.45 during breakout attempt, Bunzlau Forest (Silesia)	22.3.45
Euling, Karl-Heinz	SS-Hptsturmfhr., Kdr. 1./SS-Pz. Gr. Rgt. 22 "Frundsberg"	15.10.44
Everling, Dr. rer. pol. Wolfgang	Hptm., Chef 3./Pz. Rgt. 36	10.2.45
Evers, Franz	Lt., Flugzeugfhr. in 3./Fernaufkl. Gruppe 121	17.10.41
Evers, Walter	Lt. d.R., Fhr. 11./I.R. 271 + 28.12.43 in Russia as Hptm. d.R. & Kdr. III./G. R. 106	4.12.41
Everth, Wolfgang	Hptm., Fhr. Pz. Aufkl. Abt. 3	6.7.42
Ewald, Edwin	Lt. d.R., Zugf. in 2./Pi. Btl. 298	21.8.41
Ewald, Heinz	Lt., Flugzeugfhr. in 5./J.G. 52	20.4.45
Ewald, Werner	Major, Kdr. II./Fsch. Jäg. Rgt. 2	12.9.44
Ewald, Wolfgang	Major, Kdr. III./J.G. 3 "Udet"	9.12.42
Ewert, Heinz-Martin	Hptm., Kdr. II./I.R. 2 750th Oak Leaves 22.2.45	23.11.41
Ewert, Herbert	Oberst, Kdr. Pz. Gren. Rgt. 104	18.8.42
Ewert, Wolf	Obstlt., Kdr. Gren. Rgt. 274	18.7.44
Eymer, Herbert	Oblt. d.R., Kdr. II. (gep.)/Pz. G. R. 129 + 20.2.43 at Uspenka (Russia)	18.4.43
Eyssen, Robert	Konteradm., Kdt. Hilfskreuzer "Komet" (HSK 7)	29.11.41
Eysser, Oskar	Hptm., Chef. 3./Pz. Rgt. 31	3.11.44

F

Faasch, Hans	Obstlt., Kdr. II./I.R. 164	18.11.41
Fabian, Heinz-Otto	Oblt., Fhr. III./G. R. 534 522nd Oak Leaves 9.7.44	15.3.43
Fabich, Maximilian	Obstlt., Kdr. Pz. Füs. Rgt. "GD"	9.5.45
Fabritius, Albert	Wachtm., Kp. Tr. Fhr. in 8./G. R. 404	9.2.45
Fach, Ernst	Hptm., Staffelkpt. 9. (Eis.)/K.G. 3 "Lützow" + 15.5.43 shot down over Poltawa (Russia)	3.9.43
Fackler, Siegfried	Hptm. d.R., Chef 14. (Pz.Jäg.)/G. R. 521 + 27.6.44 in Russia	2.11.43
Fahlbusch, Wilhelm	Oblt., Chef 8./Flak-Rgt. 11 (mot.)	31.12.41
Fahrenberg, Wolfgang	Hptm. d.R., Fhr. I./G. R. 426	17.9.44
Fahrenholz, Alfred	Owm., Zugf. in 5./A.R. 240	5.5.43
Fahrmbacher, Wilhelm	Gen.Lt., Kdr. 5. I.D.	24.6.40
Falck, Wolfgang	Major, Kmdre. N. J.G. 1	1.10.40
Falk, Ernst	Obgefr., Melder in 10./G. R. 61	30.9.44
v. Falkenhayn, Günter	Lt., Fhr. 7./Jäger-Rgt. 75 + 3.1.44 at Witebsk (Russia) as Hptm. & Kp. Chef	25.11.42

v. Falkenhorst, Nikolaus	Gen.D.Inf., Befehlshaber Gruppe XXI (Norwegen)	30.4.40
Falley, Wilhelm	Obstlt., Kdr. I.R. 4 + 6.6.44 at Schloß Château Haut (Normandie/Frankr.) as Gen.Lt. & Kdr. 91. I.D. (LL)	26.11.41
Famula, Günther	Lt. d.R., Zugfhr. in V./G. R. "GD" (Pz. Kgr. Graf Strachwitz) + 22.4.44 at Narwa (Russia) of wounds; posthumously promoted to z. Oblt. d.R.	4.5.44
Fanderl, Georg	Feldw., Flugzeugfhr. in 1./K.G. 51	24.1.42
Fangohr, Friedrich	Gen.Lt., Chef d. Gen. St. Pz. A.O.K. 4	9.6.44
Fasel, Walter	Feldw., Zugf. in 14. (Pz.Jäg.)/Füs. Rgt. 26	31.8.43
v. Fassong, Horst-Günther	Hptm., Kdr. III./J.G. 11 + 1.1.45 in Belgium	27.7.44
Fath, Fridolin	Major, stv. Kdr. IV./K.G. z.b.V. 1	23.12.42
Faulhaber, Karl	Oberst, Kdr. G. R. 282	19.12.43
Faulhaber, Markus	SS-Obsturmfhr., Chef 3./SS-Inf.Rgt. "Germania" + 11.5.45 drowned at Unterwasser-Weiding, Salzach as SS-Sturmbannfhr. & Btl. Kdr. in 38. SS-Pz. Gr. Div. "Nibelungen"	25.12.42
Faulmüller, Dr. Klaus	Oblt. d.R., Fhr. 7./Geb.Jäg. Rgt. 13 + 25.10.43 in Russia	25.6.43
Faust, Fritz	Obgefr. in 3./Füs. Rgt. 26	20.8.42
Fechner, Fritz	Major, Kdr. III./Pz. Rgt. 23	6.10.43
Fechner, Konrad	Feldw., Flugzeugfhr. in 6./Stuka-Geschw. 77	4.5.44
v. d. Fecht, Karl-August	Hptm., Staffelkpt. 2./K.G. 3. "Lützow"	30.12.42
Fegelein, Hermann	SS-Standartenfhr., Kdr. SS-Kav. Brig. 157th Oak Leaves 22.12.42 83rd Swords 30.7.44	2.3.42
Fegelein, Waldemar	SS-Sturmbannfhr., Fhr. SS-Reiter-Rgt. 2	16.12.43
Fehn, Gustav	Oberst, Kdr. Schtz. Rgt. 33 + 5.6.45 in Yugoslavia murdered by partisans; final post Gen. d. Pz.Tr. & Kom.Gen. XV. Gebirgskorps	5.8.40
Fehr, Erich	Hptm., Fhr. I./G. R. 504 + 13.7.44 in Russia as Btl. Kdr.; posthumously promoted to Obstlt.	26.1.44
Fehre, Siegfried	Lt., V. B. in 10./A.R. 126 + 23.1.44 at Tuganitzl (Russia) as Oblt. & Chef 12./A.R. 126	13.12.42
Feiertag, Paul	Uffz., Gruppenfhr. in 3./Div. Füs. Btl. 96	30.9.44
Feig, Georg	Oblt. d.R., Chef 3./Schtz. Rgt. 113	4.12.41
Felber, Hans-Gustav	Gen. d. Inf, Kom.Gen. XIII. A.K.	17.9.41
Felder, Paul	Oblt., Flugzeugfhr. in 1. (F)/Aufkl. Gr. 121	29.2.44
Felder, Wendelin	Oblt., Bttr. Chef in IV./A.R. 85 + 23.10.43 missing at Wassiljewka (Russia)	23.2.44
Feldkamp, Heinrich	Owm., Zugf. in 2./Heeres-St. Gesch. Brig. 341	14.4. 45

Feldmann, Alfred	Hptm., Fhr. I./I.R. 454 + 14.1.43 Lake Ilmen (Russia) as Btl. Kdr.	20.8.42
Feldt, Klaus	Oblt. z. See, Kdt. "S 30" in 2. Schnellbootsfl. 362nd Oak Leaves 1.1.44	25.4.41
Feldt, Kurt	Gen. Major, Kdr. 1. Kav. Div.	23.8.41
Felgenhauer, Rudolf	Fhj. -Feldw., Zugf. in 3./Gren. Rgt. Gruppe 385	9.6.44
Felgenhauer, Waldemar	Oblt., Flugzeugfhr. in 2. (F)/Aufkl. Gruppe 123	14.1.42
Feller, Fritz	Lt. d.R., Fhr. 1./Pz. G. R. 5 + 5.1.45 as Oblt. d.R.	23.2.44
Fellerer, Leopold	Hptm., Kdr. II./N. J.G. 5	8.4.44
Fellgiebel, Walther-Peer	Oblt., Chef 2./le. Heeres-Art. Abt. 935 (mot.)	7.9.43
Fellmann, Erich	Hptm., Kdr. II./G. R. 409	6.4.43
Fels, Konrad	Obgefr., Gruppenfhr. in 7./G. R. 23	23.10.44
Felten, Peter	Obgefr., Melder in I./G. R. 377	12.8.44
Felzmann, Maximilian	Gen. Major, Kdr. 251. I.D. 643rd Oak Leaves 3.11.44	28.11.43
Fenet, Henri-Joseph (7)	Waffen-Hauptsturmfhr., Kdr. Sturmbtl. 33. SS-Freiw. -Gren. Div. "Charlemagne"	29.4.45
Fenn, Dr. rer. pol. Paul	Kapt. z. See (MA), Kdr. Marine-Flak-Rgt. 9	25.3.45
Fenski, Günther	Major, Kdr. I./Pz. Rgt. 8 + 23.11.41 El Agheila (North Africa) of wounds	31.12.41
Fenski, Horst-Arno	Oblt. z. See, Kdt. "U 410"	26.11.43
Fernau, Dr. Hans (13)	Hptm. d.R., Kdr. I./G. R. (mot.) "Feldherrnhalle"	4.5.45
Feßmann, Fritz	Lt. d.R., Zugf. in 1./Pz. Aufkl. Abt. 7 170th Oak Leaves 4.1.43 103rd Swords 23.10.44	27.10.41
Feuchtinger, Edgar	Gen. Major, Kdr. 21. Pz.Div.	6.8.44
Feuerer, Alois	Oblt., Fhr. 2./I.R. 351 + 5.7.44 in France as Kdr. Feld-Ers. Btl. 271; posthumously promoted to Obstlt.	27.1.42
Feuker, Gerhard	Major, Kdr. I./G. R. 53 (mot.) + 30.11.42 in Area Rshew (Russia)	23.12.42
Feurstein, Valentin	Gen. d. Geb. Tr., Kom.Gen. Ll. Geb. A.K.	12.8.44
Fey, Willi (18)	SS-Oberscharfhr., Pz. Kdt. in schw. SS-Pz. Abt. 502	29.4.45
Feyerabend, Gerhard	Gen.Lt., Kdr. II. I.D.	5.4.45
Fick, Ernst	Hptm., Staffelkpt. 6./Stuka-Gechw. 2 "Immelmann" + 27.7.42 north-west of Kalatsch (Russia)	19.9.42
Fick, Jakob	SS-Sturmbannfhr., Kdr. I./SS-Kradschtz. Rgt. "Langemarck"	23.4.43
Fickel, Helmut	Lt., Staffelfhr. Stabsst. III./Schl. Geschw. 2 "Immelmann"	9.6.44

Name	Details	Date
Fiebig, Heinz	Gen. Major, Kdr. 84. I.D.	8.5.45
Fiebig, Martin	Oberst, Kommodore K.G. 4 "General Wever" 168th Oak Leaves 23.12.42	8.5.40
Fiederer, Wilhelm	Lt. d.R., Chef 5./I.R. 164 + 16.9.42 at Woronesh (Russia)	14.9.42
Fiedler, Alex	Lt. d.R., Zugf. in 3./G. R. (mot.) 200	16.10.44
Fiedler, Hans	Rittm., Fhr. Aufkl. Abt. 118	26.12.44
Fiedler, Hans	Ofw., Kp. Truppfhr. in 9./G. R. 309	18.2.45
Fiedler, Johann	SS-Unterscharfhr., Zugf. in 5./SS-Pz. G. R. 6 "Theodor Eicke"	16.6.44
Fiedler, Walter	Gefr., Fernsprecher in Stabsbattr. II./Art.Rgt. 219	28.12.44
Filius, Ernst	Ofw., Bordfunker in I./Schl. Geschw. 2 "Immelmann" + 30.3.44 at Jassy (Rumania)	4.5.44
Filinger, Friedrich	Major, Kdr. III./A.R. 8	5.6.40
Fimmen, Kurt	Oblt. z. See, Kdt. "S 26" in 1. Schnellbootsflottille	14.8.40
Findeisen, Herbert	Hptm., Flugzeugfhr. & Beob. in 2. (H)/Nahaufk. 1. Gr. 4	29.2.44
Finger, Arthur	Oberst, Kdr. Art.Rgt. 306 + 17.1.45 at Tschenstochau (Poland) as Gen.Maj. & Kdr. 291. I.D.	16.11.43
Fink, Günter	Oblt., Flugzeugfhr. in 8./J.G. 54 + 15.5.43 missing south of Helgoland as Hptm. & Staffelkpt.	14.3.43
Fink, Dipl.-Ing. Johannes	Oberst, Kommodore K.G. 2	20.6.40
Fink, Josef	Gefr., Gruppenfhr. in Gren. Btl. 106 "Feldherrnhalle"	9.12.44
Fink, Karl-Heinrich	Lt., Adj. II./Pz. G. R. 113	20.2.43
Finkbeiner, Wilhelm	Oblt. d.R., Fhr. 14./G. R. 147	20.7.44
Finke, Andreas	Lt., Flugzeugfhr. in 6. (F)/Aufkl. Gruppe 122 + 2.9.44 at Brescia (Italy)	6.12.44
Finke, Heinz	Hptm., Kdr. I./G. R. 51 (mot.)	4.5.44
Fischbach, Adolf	Oblt., Staffelkpt. 4./K.G. 27 "Boelcke"	29.2.44
Fischer, Adolf	Oberst, Kdr. G. R. 459 + Oktober 1947 hanged in Belgrade; final post Gen. Major & Kdr. der Kampfgr. Südost	4.5.44
Fischer, Alfred (19)	SS-Sturmbannfhr., Kdr. II./SS-Pz. A-rt. Rgt. 11 "Nordland" + 28.7.45 Landsberg (Warthe) in Soviet captivity of wounds	11.5.45
Fischer, Erich	Lt., Fhr. 1./Sturm-Rgt. 14	31.3.43
Fischer, Erwin	Oblt., Flugzeugfhr. in 1. (F)/Aufkl. Gr. 121 191st Oak Leaves 8.2.43	21.4.41

Fischer, Franz	Feldw., Zugfhr. in 2./Führer-Pz. Rgt. 1 Führer-Begl. Div.	30.4.45
Fischer, Friedrich	Lt., Fhr. 6./G. R. 278	7.4.44
Fischer, Gerhard	Oblt., Chef 8./Pz. Rgt. 23	28.12.43
Fischer, Gerhard	SS-Unterscharfhr., stellv. Zugf. in 3./SS-Pz.Jäg. Abt. 5 "Wiking"	4.5.44
Fischer, Gotthard	Oberst, Fhr. 126. I.D.	7.2.44
Fischer, Hans	Obgefr., Gruppenfhr. in 6./Geb.Jäg. Rgt. 143	9.12.44
Fischer, Hans-Ulrich	Lt. d.R., Fhr. 11./I.R. 431 + 14.11.41	23.10.41
Fischer, Heinz	Hptm., Staffelkpt. 9./Stuka-Geschw. 1 + 26.10.42 at Sterizi on Wolchow (Russia)	25.11.42
Fischer, Hermann	Oberst, Kdr. I.R. 340	9.5.40
Fischer, Hermann-Georg	Hptm., Kdr. I./G. R. 1082	10.2.45
Fischer, Josef	Major, Kdr. II./G. R. 507	6.8.43
Fischer, Karl-Heinz	Steuermannsmaat, Steuermann auf "Vp. 711" in 7. Vorpostenflottille	3.5.43
Fischer, Michael	Oblt., Bttr. Chef in 1./Flak-Rgt. 14 (mot.)	8.4.43
Fischer, Otto	Obstlt., Kdr. G. R. 156 (mot.)	27.8.43
Fischer, Robert	Feldw., Zugf. in Jagdpz. Kp. 1257	29.4.45
Fischer, Siegfried	Ofw., Flugzeugfhr. in 8./Schl. Geschw. 1	28.2.45
Fischer, Dr. phil. Walther	Korv. Kpt. d.R., Chef 13. Vorpostenflottille	8.5.43
Fischer, Wilhelm	Lt., Fhr. 3./G. R. 24	28.3.45
Fischer, Wolfgang	Oberst, Kdr. 10. Schtz. Brig. 152nd Oak Leaves 9.12.42	3.6.40
Fischer v. Weikersthal, Walther	Gen.Lt., Kdr. 35. I.D.	6.8 . 41
Fitz, Josef-August	Hptm., Kdr. I./Pz. Gren. Rgt. 74 511th Oak Leaves 24.6.44	11.12.42
Fitzek, Josef	Feldw., Zugf. in 5./G. R. 482	16.6.43
Fitzner, Karl	Lt., Staffelfhr. 1./Stuka-Geschw. 77 + 8.7.43 at Bjelgorod (Russia) as Hptm. & Staffelkpt.	27.11.42
Flachs, Bernhard	Hptm., Ia in HQ Art. Kdr. 149 381st Oak Leaves 31.1.44	30.10.42
Flack, Werner	Oblt. d.R., Chef 12./Jäg. Rgt. 49 + 16.12.43 in Russia as Hptm. d.R.	22.8.43
Flad, Eugen	Gefr., MG. -Schtz. in 2. (Radf.)/Div. Füs. Btl. 252	20.7.44
Flad, Kurt	Oblt. d.R., Chef 6./A.R. 219	20.12.43
Flebbe, Rudolf	Oblt., Chef 9./A.R. 218	29.11.44
Flechner, Willi	Hptm., Staffelkpt. 5./K.G. 30 + 28.8.42 over Archangelsk (Russia)	13.8.42
Flechsig, Gerhard	Feldw., Zugf. in Stabskp./Pz. G. R. 12	18.11.44

Fleck, Hermann	Feldw., Zugf. in 2./G. R. 270	9.1.45
Fleckenstein, Hubert	Feldw., Zugf. in Stabskp./G. R. 106	31.1.44
Fleig, Erwin	Lt., Flugzeugf. in 2./J.G. 51	12.8.41
Fleige, Karl	Oblt. z. See, Kdr. "U18"	18.7.44
Fleischer, Hermann	Ofw., Zugf. in 2./I.R. 517 + 22.12.44 Senio bridgehead (Italy) as Lt. & Fhr. 1./G. R. 992	29.10.42
Fleischer, Rudolf	Major, Kdr. Heeres-Fla-Abt. 314	9.5.45
Fleischmann, Josef	Major, Kdr. I./Geb.Jäg. Rgt. 99 + 3.3.42 on the Donets (Russia) of wounds	31.3.42
Fleischmann, Ludwig	Ofw., Zugf. in 6./Jäg. Rgt. 207	17.12.43
Flex, Hermann	Uffz., Gruppenfhr. in 7./G. R. 337 + 9.3.43	12.3.43
Fliegel, Fritz	Hptm., Kdr. I./K.G. 40 + 1942 over the Atlantic	25.3.41
Fließbach, Peter	Oblt., Fhr. 4./A.R. 23 + 21.3.44 as Major & Kdr. III./A.R. 367	20.12.41
Flinzer, Dr.-Ing. Rudolf	Obstlt. d.R., Kdr. G. R. 317 575th Oak Leaves 5.9.44	6.4.43
Flocke, Paul	Lt., Fhr. 5./G. R. 915	30.4.45
Flögel, Josef	Ofw., Flugzeugfhr. in 3./Nacht-Schlacht-Gruppe 5	19.2.45
Floer, Hans-Joachim	Oblt. d.R., Chef 1. (gep.)/Pz. G. R. 25	5.3.45
Flörke, Hermann	Gen. Major, Kdr. 14. I.D. 565th Oak Leaves 2.9.44	15.12.43
Florin, Gerhard	Hptm. d.R., Kdr. II./Schtz. Rgt. 111 + 20.7.42 in Russia as Major d.R. of wounds	2.2.42
Florschütz, Wilhelm	Hptm., Kdr. Volks-Pi. Brig. 47 (mot.)	9.5.45
v. Flotow, Jürgen	Oblt., Fhr. 1./Schtz. Rgt. 8 + 20.8.41 at Leningrad (Russia)	25.8.41
Flügel, Hans	SS-Hptsturmfhr. d.R., Fhr. II./SS-Pz. Rgt. 5 "Wiking"	16.10.44
Flügel, Otto	Steuermannsmaat d.R., Steuermann auf "VP 1525" 15. Vorpostenflottille	3.5.43
Fluhs, Friedrich	Ofw., Zugf. in 5./G. R. 255	4.11.43
Focke, Fritz, Dr. phil.	Major d.R., Kdr. I./G. R. 368	28.3.45
Baron v. Foelkersam, Adrian	Lt. d.R., Adjutant in Stabc I./Lehr-Rgt. z.b.V. 800 "Brandenburg" + 21.1.45 in Hohensalza as Chef d. Stabes d. SS-Jagdverbände; posthumously promoted to SS-Sturmbannfhr.	14.9.42
Fönnekold, Otto	Fahnenj. -Fw., Flugzeugfhr. in II./J.G. 52 + 31.8.44 Budack (Siebenbürgen) as Oblt. & Staffelfhr. 5./J.G. 52	26.3.44
Förderer, Ernst	Hptm., Kdr. II./G. R. 1082 + 1945	11.3.45
Förster, Friedrich	Hptm., Fhr. Kampfgr. "Derrer"	24.12.44
Förster, Hans-Joachim	Oblt. z. See, Kdt. "U 480" + 24.2.45 in Kanal	18.10.44

Förster, Helmuth	Gen. d. Flg., Kom.Gen. I. Flg. Korps	22.2.42
Förster, Otto-Hermann	Gen. d. Pi., Kom.Gen. VI. A.K.	23.8.41
Förster, Otto-Lutz	Oberst, Lufttransportführer Luftflotte 4	23.12.42
Foertsch, Friedrich	Gen. Major, Chef d. Gen. St. 18. Armee	5.9.44
Foertsch, Hermann	Gen.Lt., Kdr. 21. I.D.	27.8.44
Főző, Josef	Hptm., Kdr. II./J.G. 51	2.7.41
Foldenauer, Richard	Obgefr., Kp. Melder in 2./G. R. 460 missing	12.11.43
Folkers, Ulrich	Kaptlt., Kdt. "U 125" + 6.5.43 in North Atlantic	27.3.43
Foltin, Ferdinand	Hptm., Kdr. II./Fsch. Jäg. Rgt. 3	9.6.44
Fondermann, Otto	Hptm., Kdr. II./Schtz. Rgt. 79	13.10.41
Forgatsch, Heinz	Oblt., Flugzeugfhr. in Kampfgr. 806 + 23.9.41 at Rechlin as Oblt. & Fhr. d. Erprob. Staffel Me 210	14.6.41
Forst, Werner	Gen.Lt., Kdr. 106. I.D. 407th Oak Leaves 22.2.44	29.8.43
Forstmann, Gustav	Korv. Kpt., Chef 1. Räumbootsflottille	28.7.41
Forstner, Rupert	Feldw., Zugf. in 2./G. R. 19 "List"	3.11.44
Frhr. v. Forstner, Siegfried	Kaptlt., Kdt. "U 402" + 22.10.43 in Atlantic as Korv. Kapitän; posthumously promoted to Freg. Kapt.	9.2.43
Fortun, Horst	Hptm., Kdr. I./Pz. Rgt. 25 + 6.7.43 south of Bjelgorod (Russia)	7.8.43
Forwerk, Hans-Werner	Hptm. d.R., Fhr. I./G. R. 187	14.4. 45
Frach, Hans	Ofw., Flugzeugf. in 6./K.G. 51	29.10.44
Francois, Edmund	Hptm., Kdr. Pz. Gr. Brig. "v. Werthern" in Fsch. Pz.Div. "HG" + 6.3.45 Graudenz (West Prussia) as Major & Abt.Kdr.	20.10.44
Francsi, Gustav	Lt., Flugzeugf. in I./NJ.G. 100	29.10.44
Franek, Dr. rer. pol. Friedrich	Oberst, Kdr. I.R. 405	4.11.41
Frank, Anton-Otto	Hptm., Chef I./Pz.Jäg. Abt. (SF) 15 737th Oak Leaves 7.2.45	26.6.44
Frank, Erich	Hptm. d.R., Kdr. III./G. R. 116	24.6.44
Frank, Hans-Dieter	Hptm., Staffelkpt. 2./N. J.G. 1 417th Oak Leaves 2.3.44	20.6.43
Frank, Heinz	Oblt., Staffelkpt. 3./SG 1 172nd Oak Leaves 8.1.43	3.9.42
Frank, Otto	Major, Kdr. I./G. R. 278	18.10.43
Frank, Robert	SS-Sturmbannfhr., Kdr. II./SS-Pz. G. R. 20 "Hohenstaufen" + 13.4.44 Tarnopol (Russia)	4.6.44
Frank, Rudolf	Feldw., Flugzeugf. in 2./N. J.G. 3 531st Oak Leaves 20.7.44	6.4.44

KNIGHT'S CROSS OF THE IRON CROSS

Frank, Walter	Ofw., Zugf. in 2./schw. Pz.Jäger-Abt. 666 + 18.2.45 Berzini (Kurland)	7.2.44
Franke, Adolf	Uffz,., in Wach-Rgt. "GD" in Festg. Berlin	26.4.45
Franke, Alfred	Ofw., Flugzeugf. in 2./J.G. 53 + 9.9.42 north of Stalingrad (Russia); posthumously promoted to z. Lt.	29.10.42
Franke, Heinz	Kaptlt., Kdt. "U 262"	30.11.43
Franke, Herbert	Hptm., Kdr. I./A.R. 162	5.10.43
Franke, Kurt	SS-Hptscharfhr., Stoßtruppfhr. in 11./SS-Pz. G. R. 6 "Theodor Eicke" + 19.1.45 in field hospital, Veszprém (Hungary) as SS-Obersturmfhr. & Kp. Chef	3.10.43
Franken, Werner	Oblt., Flugzeugfhr. in I./K.G. 26 + 24.2.43 in Mediterranean	24.3.43
Franken, Wilhelm	Kaptlt., Kdt. "U 565" + 13.1.45 accidentally as Korv. Kpt., final post Referent in Stab Kom. Admiral der U-Boote	30.4.43
Frankenfeld, Erwin	Lt., Fhr. I./Jäger-Rgt. 49	23.3.45
Frankewitz, Bruno	Gen.Lt., Kdr. 215. I.D. 790th Oak Leaves 16.3.45	29.2.44
Frantz, Gotthard	Gen.Lt., Kdr. 19. Flak-Div. (mot. trop.) "Afrika"	18.5.43
Frantz, Peter	Oblt., Sturmgeschützfhr. in 16./I.R. "GD" (mot.) 228th Oak Leaves 14.4. 43	4.6.42
v. Frantzius, Botho	Obstlt., Kdr. Aufkl. Abt. 161 + 10.12.42 at Toropez-Newel (Russia) as Oberst & Kdr. G. R. 504; posthumously promoted to Gen. Major	4.11.41
Franz, Egon	SS-Unterscharfhr., Zugf. in 3./SS-Pz. G. R. 9 "Germania" + July 1945 in Czech captivity	16.10.44
Franz, Gerhard	Obstlt. i.G., Ia der 29. I.D. (mot.)	24.7.41
Franz, Ludwig	Hptm. d.R., Fhr. I./G. R. 35 + 5.7.44 Beleja-Luscha (Russia) as Btl. Kdr.; posthumously promoted to Obstlt. d.R.	8.10.43
Franzisket, Ludwig	Oblt., Adj. I./J.G. 27	20.7.41
Fraps, Ernst	Obgefr., Richtschtz. in 2./Pz.Jäg. Abt. 28 + 26.1.43 Lake Ladoga (Russia) as Uffz. & Geschützfhr.	18.5.42
Frauenheim, Fritz	Kaptlt., Kdt. "U 101"	29.8.40
Frauscher, Franz	SS-Hptscharfhr., Zugf. in 4./SS-Pz. Rgt. 2 "Das Reich"	31.12.44
Frech, Ferdinand	Oblt., Chef I./Jäger-Btl. 2 + November 1944 south of Preuß. Stargard (Pomerania) as Hptm.	5.12.43
Fredebold, Dipl.-Ing. Reinhard	Major d.R., Kdr. III./I. R 191	30.8.42

Freimanis, Andrejs	Waffen-Obersturmfhr., Fhr. 13./Waffen-Gren. Rgt. d. SS 44 (lett. Nr. 6)	5.5.45
Freitag, Bruno	Oblt., Staffelkpt. 3./Stuka-Geschw. 2 "Immelmann"	5.10.41
Freitag, Fritz	SS-Brigadef. & Gen. Major d. Waffen-SS, Kdr. 14. Waffen-Gren. Div. der SS + 20.5.45 at Salzburg in US captivity (suicide)	30.9.44
Fremerey, Max	Gen. Major, Kdr. 29. I.D. (mot.)	28.7.42
Frenzel, Günther	Feldw., Flugzeugf. in 11./K.G. z.b.V. 1	23.12.42
Frese, Ernst	Lt. d.R., Fhr. 6./G. R. 869	27.8.44
Fretter-Pico, Maximilian	Gen. Major, Kdr. 97. Jäger-Div. 368th Oak Leaves 16.1.44	26.12.41
Fretter-Pico, Otto	Gen.Lt., Kdr. 97. Inf. Div.	12.12.44
Freutsmiedl, Simon	Feldw., Zugf. in 9./Jäger-Rgt. 204	26.8.43
Freuwörth, Wilhelm	Feldw., Flugzeugfhr. in 2./J.G. 52	5.1.43
Frewer, Karl	Major, Kdr. I./G. R. 167 + 6.3.45 of wounds as Obstlt. & Fhr. Div. Gr. 86	12.11.43
Frey, Albert	SS-Sturmbannfhr., Kdr. I./SS-Pz. G. R. "LSSAH" 359th Oak Leaves 20.12.43	3.3.43
Frey, Emil	Hptm. d.R., Kdr. I./G. R. 220	5.9.44
Frey, Harry	Lt., Staffelfhr. 7./K.G. 6 + 11.7.43 in Russia	5.12.43
Frey, Hugo	Hptm., Staffelkpt. 7./J.G. 11 + 6.3.44 at Sleen (Holland)	4.5.44
Freyer, Siegfried	Wachtm., Zugf. in 4./Pz. Rgt. 24	23.7.42
Freytag, Siegfried	Oblt., Flugzeugfhr. in I./J.G. 77	3.7.42
Fricke, Ernst-August	Oblt., Chef 7./I.R. 76 (mot.) 341st Oak Leaves 30.11.43	17.1.42
Fricke, Kurt	Admiral, Chef des Stabes der Seekriegsleitung in OKM + 2.5.45 in Berlin	1.10.42
Frieb, Erwin	Lt., Zugf. & V. B. in 1./A.R. 1558	19.2.45
Friebe, Helmut	Oberst, Kdr. I.R. 164	13.8.41
Friebe, Werner	Oberst, Fhr. des gep. Verbandes der 8. Pz.Div.	21.4.44
Friebel, Herbert	Ofw., Flugzeugfhr. in 12./J.G. 51 "Mölders" + 15.5.44 west of Tarnopol (Russia) as Lt. & Staffelfhr. 10./J.G. 51 "Mölders"	24.1.43
Friedel, Herbert	Wachtm., Zugf. in 2./St. Gesch. Brig. 232	23.8.44
Friedmann, Friedrich	Oberst, Kdr. Geb.Jäg. Rgt. 144 + 21.8.43 at Kuibyschewo (Russia) of wounds	12.2.43
Friedmann, Theodor	Hptm., Kdr. I./A.R. 156 + 10.1.42 in Russia of wounds; posthumously promoted to Major	15.8.40
Friedrich, Erich	Ofw., Kp. Truppf in 1./Pz. G. R. 33	2.9.44
Friedrich, Gerhard	Hptm., Kdr. I./Pz. G. R. 13 642nd Oak Leaves 3.11.44	6.4.43

KNIGHT'S CROSS OF THE IRON CROSS

Friedrich, Gerhard	Major, Kdr. I./N. J.G. 6 + 16.3.45 shot down at Böblingen	15.3.45
Friedrich, Gustav	Rittm., Chef 6./Reiter-Rgt. 31	3.11.44
Friedrich, Kurt	Hptm., Fhr. III./G. R. 525	13.9.43
Friedrich, Max	Obgefr., stv. Gruppenfhr. in 3./G. R. 558	15.3.44
Friedrich, Max	Oblt., Chef d. Pi. Kp. der Div. Nr. 408 in Kampfgr. Jollasse	23.3.45
Friedrich, Rudolf	Obgefr., stv. Gruppenfhr. in 9./G. R. 361 (mot.)	6.10.44
Friedrich, Werner	Major, Fhr. G. R. 503 + 23.12.43 on Jasno-See at Newel (Russia)	26.12.43
Frielinghaus, Gustav	Hptm., Kdr. IV./J.G. 3 "Udet"	5.2.44
Fries, Anton	Ofw. d.R., Fhr. 1./G. R. 1123 + 6.2.45	28.2.45
Fries, Herbert	Gefr., Geschützfhr. in 2./Fsch. Pz.Jäg. Abt. 1	5.9.44
Fries, Leonhard	Ofw., Zugf. in II./G. R. 1084	14.2.45
Fries, Walter	Oberst, Kdr. I.R. 87 (mot.) 378th Oak Leaves 29.1.44 87th Swords 11.8.44	14.12.41
Frießner, Johannes	Gen. d. Inf, Kom.Gen. XXIII. AK. 445th Oak Leaves 9.4.44	23.7.43
Friker, Dr. med. August	Oberst, Kdr. G. R. 480	4.9.43
Frink, Helmut	Hptm., Chef 9./A.R. 251 + 28.8.43 in Russia; posthumously promoted to Major	21.10.43
Fritsch, Heinz	Uffz., in 2./Pz. Pi. Btl. 37	18.10.41
Fritsche, Hans	Hptm., Kdr. II./G. R. 528 307th Oak Leaves 2.10.43	10.3.43
Fritz, Dr. Herbert	Hptm., Chef 16./Geb.Jäg. Rgt. 13	17.3.44
Fritzler, Heinz	Lt. d.R., Fhr. 1./Div. Füs. Btl. 110	5.12.43
Fritzsche, Immo	Oblt., Staffelkpt. 8./Stuka-Geschw. 2 "Immelmann" + 13.12.43 at Schiroskaja (Russia) of wounds; posthumously promoted to Hptm.	16.4.43
Fröhlich, Bruno	Fw., Zugf. in 7./G. R. 430 + 16.12.42 Rshew (Russia) of wounds	22.1.43
Fröhlich, Karl	Oblt., Chef 2./Pz. Abt. 18	28.9.43
Fröhlich, Kurt (6)	SS-Hptsturmf, Fhr. II./SS-Pz. Rgt. 9 "Hohenstaufen"	6.5.45
Fröhlich, Stefan	Gen. Major, Kmdre. K.G. 76	4.7.40
Fröhlich, Gottfried	Oberst, Fhr. 8. Pz.Div.	20.12.43
Frömming, Ernst	Major, Kdr. Fsch. Pi. Btl. 1	18.11.44
Fromm, Friedrich	Gen. d. Art., Chef der Heeresrüstung & Befehlshaber des Ersatzheeres + executed 19.3.45, Zuchthaus Brandenburg a. d. Havel in connection with 20.7.44; final post Gen. Oberst	6.7.40

ELITE OF THE THIRD REICH

Fromm, Walter	Hptm., Kdr. I./Flak-Rgt. 33 (mot.) in DAK	9.7.41
Fromme, Rolf	Lt., Fhr. 3./Pz. Rgt. 1	29.9.41
Fronhöfer, Erich	Obstlt., Kdr. Pz. Rgt. 10	24.7.41
Frost, Rupert	Major, Kdr. Nacht-Schlacht-Gr. 9	25.11.44
Frost, Willi	Ofw., Zugf. in 4./Pz. Rgt. 15 + 24.1.45	24.9.43
Frotscher, Werner	Oberst, Kdr. G. R. 422	11.3.45
Frühauf, Carl-Heinz	SS-Hptsturmfhr. d.R., Fhr. II./niederl. SS-Freiw. Pz. G. R. 49 "De Ruyter"	4.6.44
Fuchs, August	Hptm., Fhr. a Kampfgr. Feld-Ers. -Btl. 299	18.2.45
Fuchs, Jakob	Uffz., Zugfhr. in 3./G. R. 124	23.10.44
Fuchs, Dipl.-Ing. Robert	Oberst, Kmdre. K.G. 26	6.4.40
Fuchs, Rudolf	Ofw., Zugf. in 2./G. R. 42	26.8.43
Fuchs, Siegfried	Feldw., Zugf. in 12./Jäger-Rgt. 75 + 11.4.44 in a field hospital, Russia, of wounds	15.5.44
Füllgrabe, Heinrich	Ofw., Flugzeugfhr. in 9./J.G. 52 + 30.1.45 at Brieg (Silesia) as Oblt.	2.10.42
Fürguth, Benedikt	Wachtm., Bttr. Offz. & V. B. in 3./A.R. 7 + 23.10.43 in Russia	23.9.43
Fürguth, Helmut	Oberst, Kdr. A.R. 211	28.7.42
Fütterer, Bernhard	Lt., stv. Fhr. e. Kampfgr. des Inf. Btl. z.b.V. 560	26.12.44
Fuhrhop, Helmut	Major, Kdr. I./K.G. 6 + 29.2.44 over England	22.11.43
Fuhrmann, Georg	Hptm., Kdr. II./G. R. 501	13.7.43
Fulda, Wilhelm	Lt., Zugf. in 6./Fsch. Jäg. Rgt. 2	14.6.41
Fullriede, Fritz	Obstlt., Kdr. Kampfgr. Fullriede in Pz. AOK. 5 803rd Oak Leaves 23.3.45	11.4.43
Frhr. v. Funck, Hans	Gen. Major, Kdr. 7. Pz.Div. 278th Oak Leaves 22.8.43	15.7.41
Funk, Alois	Uffz., Gruppenfhr. in 5./G. R. 316	15.4.44
Funk, Heinrich	Major, Fhr. of a Kampfgr. in Berlin	28.4.45
Furbach, Heinz (19)	Oberst, Kdr. I.R. 58	4.10.42
Fuß, Hans	Lt., Flugzeugfhr. in II./J.G. 3 "Udet" + 10.11.42 in Berlin (Luftwaffe hospital) of wounds as Staffelfhr. in J.G. 51 "Mölders"	23.8.42

G

Frhr. v. Gablenz, Eccard	Gen.Lt., Kdr. 7. I.D.	15.8.40
Gabriel, Erdmann	Ofw., Zugf. in II./Pz. Rgt. 35	30.8.41
Gadermann, Dr. med. Ernst	Stabsarzt, Gruppenarzt III./Stuka-Geschw. 2 "Immelmann"	19.8.44
Gaeb, Friedrich	Uffz., Zugf. in 1. (reit.)/Div. Aufkl. Abt. 97	19.12.43
Gaedcke, Heinrich	Oberst i.G., Chef d. Gen. St. XI. A.K.	7.4.44

KNIGHT'S CROSS OF THE IRON CROSS

Gaedckens, Ernst	Ofw., Zug- & Stoßtruppfhr. in 2./G. R. 46	2.4.43
Gänsler, Wilhelm	Ofw., Bordschütze in Stabsstaffel d. IV./N. J.G. 1	27.7.44
Gärtner, Georg	Hptm., Kdr. I./Sturm-Rgt. 195	21.9.44
Gaigals, Roberts	Waffen-Obersturmfhr., Fhr. 6./Waffen-Gren. Rgt. 42 of the SS "Voldemars Veiss"	5.5.45
Gaillinger, Otto	Oblt., Fhr. 1./Inf. Btl. z.b.V. 500 + 29.9.43 at Oktoberfeld	8.10.43
Gaiser, Otto	Ofw., Flugzeugfhr. in 10./J.G. 51 "Mölders" + 22.1.44 at Ljuban (Russia); posthumously promoted to z. Lt.	9.6.44
Gaißer, Wilhelm	Lt. d.R., Fhr. 1./G. R. 3	17.3.45
Galdins, Nikolajs	Waffen-Obersturmbannfhr., Kdr. Waffen-Gren. Rgt. der SS Nr. 42 "Voldemars Veiss" + 1945 hanged in Leningrad (Russia) in Soviet captivity	25.1.45
Gall, Eugen	Lt., Fhr. 6./G. R. 335	17.3.45
Gall, Franz	Gen. Major, defender of Elba + 27.12.44 in Italy as Gen.Lt. & Kdt. Verteidigungsbereich Venedig	19.6.44
Galland, Adolf	Major, Kdr. III./J.G. 26 "Schlageter" 3rd Oak Leaves 24.9.40 1st Swords 21.6.41 2nd Diamonds 28.1.42	29.7.40
Galland, Wilhelm-Ferdinand	Hptm., Kdr. II./J.G. 26 "Schlageter" + 17.8.43 at Lüttich (Belgium) as Major	18.5.43
Galle, Josef	Wachtm., Zugf. in 3./St. Gesch. Abt. 244 + 28.1.43 in Stalingrad (Russia), posthumously promoted to Owm.	25.1.43
Gallenkamp, Curt	Gen.Lt., Kdr. 78. I.D.	19.11.41
Gallowitsch, Bernd	Lt., Flugzeugfhr. in 12./J.G. 51 "Mölders"	24.1.42
Galow, Friedrich	Wachtm., V. B. in 8./A.R. 389 + 21.7.44 in Russia	10.9.44
Gambietz, Richard	Obgefr., in Stabskp./Schtz. Rgt. 93 + 25.4.44 6 km west of Delachen (Dnjestr/Russia) as Uffz.	27.5.42
Gamer, Berthold	Hptm., Kdr. II./A.R. 178 (mot.)	25.1.43
Gansmeier, Jakob	Hptm. d.R., Kdr. Div. Füs. Btl. (A.A.) 212 568th Oak Leaves 2.9.44	29.2.44
Ganssen, Franz-Josef	Uffz., Kp. Truppfhr. in 9./G. R. 159	29.2.44
Gapp, Franz	Ofw., Flugzeugfhr. in 8./K.G. 6	18.9.43
Garbers, Heinrich	Lt. z. See d.R., Kdt. Hilfskriegsschiff "Passim" & Fhr. v. Sonderunternehmungen	1.11.44
Gareis, Martin	Gen.Lt., Kdr. 98. I.D.	29.11.43
Garels, Wilhelm	Oberst d.R., Kdr. A.R. 3 (L) + 18.12.43 in Russia	5.2.44

v. Garn, Arnulf	Major, Kdr. Div. Füs. Btl. 252	2.9.44
Graf v. Garnier-Turawa, Detlev	Oblt. d.R., Kdr. 1./G. R. 439 + 27.6.44 west of Babins (Russia) as Hptm. d.R.	18.1.44
Garski, Eugen	Obstlt., Kdr. III./I.R. "GD" (mot.) + 30.9.42 Rshew (Russia) as Oberst & Kdr. Füs. Rgt. "GD"; posthumously promoted to z. Gen. Major	19.7.40
Gartenfeld, Karl-Edmund	Hptm., Staffelfhr. in (F.) Aufkl. Gr. d. OB d. L.	3.2.43
v. Gartzen, Wirich	Korv. Kpt., Chef 10. Torpedobootsflottille	24.6.44
Garz, Walter	Feldw., Zugf. in 3./Pz. G. R. 74	16.12.42
Gaßmann, Peter	Hptm., Kdr. III./Stuka-Geschw. 1	25.5.42
Gast, Robert	Lt., Führer 9./Fsch. Jäg. Rgt. 7	6.10.44
Gast, Wolfgang	SS-Obersturmfhr., Fhr. 1./SS-Pz. A.R. 2 "Das Reich"	4.6.44
Gath, Heinrich	Stabsfeldw., Zugf. in 2./Pz. Aufkl. Abt. 2	11.10.43
Gathmann, Wilhelm	Major, Kdr. 11./A.R. 14	28.3.45
Gattermann, Helmut	Hptm. d.R., Chef 1./St. Gesch. Brig. 209	12.8.44
v. Gaudecker-Zuch, Gerlach	Obstlt., Kdr. Pz. G. R. 33	8.8.44
Gauglitz, Josef	Oblt., Fhr. III./Pz. Rgt. 33	16.11.44
Gaum, Albert	Hptm., Chef 11./Geb.Jäg. Rgt. 100	13.6.41
Reichsfrhr. v. Gaupp-Berghausen, Georg	Hptm., Kdr. 11./Pz. G. R. 12	30.9.44
Gause, Alfred	Gen. Major, Chef d. Gen. St. Pz. Gr. "Afrika"	13.12.41
Gauß, Jürgen	Hptm., Fhr. e. Kampfgr. of the 12./Pz.Div.	28.3.45
v. Gazen gen. v. Gaza, Waldemar	Oblt., Chef 2./Pz. G. R. 66 182nd Oak Leaves 18.1.43 38th Swords 3.10.43	18.9.42
Gebauer, Fritz	Ofw., Stoßtruppfhr. in 3./Grenz-Pi. Btl. 74	13.7.40
Gebhard, Georg	Major, Kdr. III./Gren. Brigade 503	23.10.44
Gebhard (6)	SS-Oberscharfhr., Zugf. in 2./SS-Pz. Pi. Btl. 2 "Das Reich"	6.5.45
Gebhardt, Georg	Hptm. d.R., Kdr. III./Jäger-Rgt. 204 743rd Oak Leaves 19.2.45	15.5.43
Gebhardt, Rolf	Fhj. -Feldw., Zugf. 2./schw. Pz. Abt. 507	30.9.44
Frhr. Gedult v. Jungenfeld, Ernst-Wilhelm	Oberst d.R., Fhr. of a Kampfgruppe	11.1.45
Geelhaar, Arno	Lt. d.R., Fhr. 7./G. R. 151	16.4.44
Gehl, Paul	Oblt. d.R., Fhr. I./G. R. 453	9.5.45
Gehrke, Kurt	Oberstlt., Kdr. I./G. R. "GD" + 24.10.44 as Oberst	8.2.43

KNIGHT'S CROSS OF THE IRON CROSS

Gehrmann, Gerhard	Oblt. d.R., Chef 3./G. R. 422	15.4.44
Gehrmann, Johannes	Hptm. d.R., Staffelkpt. 6./Schlacht-Geschw. 1 + 27.1.44 at Winniza (Russia) as stv. Kdr. II./S.G. 77	31.12.43
Geiger, August	Oblt., Staffelkpt. 7./N. J.G. 1 416th Oak Leaves 2.3.44	22.5.43
Geiger, Georg	Obgefr., Gruppenfhr. in 10./G. R. 19 "List"	20.10.44
Geiger, Herbert	Ofw., Kp. Tr. Fhr. in 1./G. R. 380	8.8.44
Geisberg, Wilhelm	Oblt., Chef 3./Führer-Pz. Rgt. I (Führer-Begleit-Div.) + 22.4.45 at Neu-Petershain (Krs. Spremberg)	14.4. 45
Geisler, Hans	Gen.Lt., Kom.Gen. X. Fliegerkorps	4.5.40
Geisler, Herbert	Ofw., Flugzeugfhr. in Stabsstaffel/K.G. 4 "General Wever"	24.10.44
Geisler, Kurt	Hptm., Kdr. Lufttransportgruppe Don + 6./7. Sept. 43 over Cambridge, England as Kdr. III./Z.G. 1	24.1.43
Geisler, Rudolf	Major, Kdr. Pi. Btl. 662 455th Oak Leaves 13.4.44	7.12.43
Geisler, Siegfried	Hptm., Kdr. II./K.G. 76	20.7.44
Geismann, Johannes	Lt., Flugzeugfhr. in 1./K.G. 77	21.12.42
Geißhardt, Friedrich	Lt., Flugzeugfhr. in I./J.G. 77 101st Oak Leaves 23.6.42	30.8.41
Geißler, Erich	Oberst, Kdr. I.R. 200 (mot.) in DAK	29.7.42
Geißler, Gottfried	Oblt., Chef 3./St. Gesch. Abt. 185	21.8.41
Geißler, Helmut	Oberst, Kdr. Gren. Rgt. 187 + 15.12.43 at Janowitschi (Russia)	7.1.44
Geißler, Karl	Oblt. d.R., Chef 5./G. R. 46	1.2.45
Geißler, Willy	Uffz., Gruppenfhr. in 5./Pz. Aufkl. Abt. 7	14.5.44
Gelbhaar, Rudi	Oblt. (M. A.) d.R., Chef d. Marine-Batterie "Hamburg" der M. A.A. 604	26.6.44
Gelhaus, Harald	Kaptlt., Kdt. "U 107"	26.3.43
Gelhausen, Hans	Hptm., Fhr. I./G. R. 457	28.3.45
Gellert, Christian	Oblt., Bttr. Fhr. in I./Flak-Rgt. 43 (mot.)	11.6.44
Gellhorn, Roland	Major, Adj. 75. I.D.	14.2.45
Geltinger, Dionys	Major, Kdr. III./A.R. 251	2.9.44
Gemsjäger, Alfred	Lt., Beob. in 6. (F)/Aufkl. Gr. 122 + 2.9.44 at Brescia (Italy)	16.12.44
Gemünden, Otto	Wachtm., Geschützfhr. in I./Flak-Rgt. 49 in Flak-Rgt. 37	12.10.42
Genrich, Oskar	Oblt., Flugzeugfhr. in 2. (F)/Aufkl. Gr. 11 + 10.1.43 in Kurland	3.11.42
Gensberger, Ludwig	Oblt., Chef 13. (I. G.)/G. R. 544 + 23.2.45	5.4.45
Genz, Alfred	Oblt., Chef I./Fsch. Jäg. Sturm-Rgt.	14.6.41

Name	Rank/Unit	Date
Genzel, Karl-Heinz	Hptm., Fhr. I./G. R. 32	26.11.44
Genzow, Joachim	Oblt., Staffelkpt. 4./K.G. 2	23.3.41
Geppert, Erich	Oblt., Fhr. 3./St. Gesch. Abt. 209	14.4. 43
Gerber, Arthur	Feldw., Zugf. in Stabskp./G. R. 401	18.2.45
Gerdes, Hinrich	Ofw., Zugf. in 3./Pz. Rgt. 36	21.1.45
Gerdts, Hans	Obgefr., Funker in 3./A.R. 196	9.12.44
Gerhardt, Rudolf	Major, Kdr. II./Pz. Rgt. 7	22.9.41
Gerhold, Walther	Marine-Schreiber-Obgefr., Einmanntorpedofahrer in K1. Kampf-Flottille 361	6.7.44
Gericke, Walter	Hptm., Kdr. IV./Fsch. Jäg. Sturm-Rgt. 585th Oak Leaves 17.9.44	14.6.41
Gerke, Siegfried	Lt. d.R., Zugf. in 3./Pz. Pi. Btl. 16	2.12.42
Gerl, Franz	Ofw., Zugf. in 13. (I. G.)/G. R. 110	8.5.43
Gerlach, Heinrich	Hptm., Flugzeugfhr. at Kom.Gen. d. XI. Fliegerkorps Awarded in relation to the liberation of Mussolini	19.9.43
Gerlach, Dr. Julius	Hptm. d.R., Kdr. III./I.R. 507 + 18.9.43 in Russia as Oberstlt. d.R. of wounds	10.2.42
Gerlach, Karl (19)	Oblt., Chef 4./Pz. Rgt. 35 (Awarded in Danzig-Nehrung area)	3.5.45
Gerlach, Ludwig	Hptm., Kdr. I./G. R. 409	23.3.45
Gerlach, Waldemar	Oblt., Chef 2./M. G. Btl. 13	9.5.40
Gerloch, Bruno	Obstlt., Kdr. A.R. 90	4.9.40
Germer, Alfred	Oblt., Chef I./Pi. Btl. 171 + 5.8.44 in Russia as Major i.G.	26.5.40
Germer, Ernst	Fhj. -Feldw., Fhr. Radf. Zug in Stabskp./Fsch. Jäg. Rgt. 1	29.10.44
Frhr. v. Gersdorff, Rudolf-Christoph	Oberst i.G., Chef d. Gen. St. 7. Armee	26.8.44
Gerstenberg, Wilhelm	Feldw., Zugf. in 4./G. R. 287 + 26.4.44 east of Chmiclowa (Russia)	4.5.44
Gersteuer, Günter	Major, Kdr. Fsch. St. Gesch. Brig. 12	28.4.45
Gerstner, Siegfried	Major, Kdr. II./Fsch. Jäg. Rgt. 7	13.9.44
Gerth, Walter	SS-Obersturmfhr. d.R., Chef 7./SS-Pz. A.R. 3 "Totenkopf"	31.3.43
Gerth, Werner	Oblt., Staffelkpt. Sturmstaffel in IV./J.G. 3 "Udet" + 2.11.44 at Eisleben; posthumously promoted to Hptm.	29.10.44
Gertler, Gerhard	Ofw., Kp. Truppf in 7./Jäger-Rgt. 83	18.9.43
Geschwill, Heinz	Lt., Flugzeugfhr. in 9./K.G. 3 "Lützow"	23.3.41
Gesele, Karl	SS-Obersturmbannfhr., Kdr. SS-Sturmbrigade "RFSS" (later 16. SS-Pz. Gr. Div.)	4.7.44

KNIGHT'S CROSS OF THE IRON CROSS

Geskens, Franz	Feldw., Zugf. in 3./Pz.Jäg. Abt. 187 + 3.11.44 in Russia	9.12.44
Geßner, Harald	Lt., Fhr. 10./G. R. 61 + 18.3.44 during bombing raid on München as Oblt.	13.9.43
Gewehr, Hans	Hptm. d.R., Rgt. Adj. G. R. 698 + 4.8.44 in Russia	4.6.44
Gey, Joachim	Oblt., Staffelkpt. in II./K.G. 3 "Lützow"	21.6.43
Geyer, Heinrich	Feldw., Zugfhr. in 2./Pz. G. R. 6 + 8.11.1944 as Ofw. of wounds	22.10.44
Geyer, Hermann	Gen.D.Inf. z. V., Kom.Gen. IX. A.K. + 10.4.1946 on Wildsee – Suicide	25.6.40
Reichsfrhr. Geyr v. Schweppenburg, Leo	Gen. d. Pz.Tr., Kom.Gen. XXIV. A.K. (mot.)	9.7.41
Gidion, Dr. phil. Hans	Hptm. d.R., Fhr. II./I.R. 154	7.8.42
Giehrl, Walter	Oblt., Fhr. 7./Geb.Jäg. Rgt. 138 + 23.11.44 at Hernad (Hungary) as Hptm. & Kdr. I./G. J. R. 138	31.7.42
Gielnik, Albert	Lt., Kp. Fhr. in Gren. Ers. & Ausb. Btl. 318 + 23.2.1945 of wounds	24.2.45
Gierga, Kurt	Hptm., Chef 5./Pz. Rgt. 5	30.6.41
Gierster, Franz	Hptm., Fhr. InfBtl. z.b.V. 540	15.5.44
Gies, Alfred	Ofw., Flugzeugfhr. in 1./Schlacht-Geschw. 2 "Immelmann"	16.12.44
Giese, Horst	Lt., Fhr. 2./Pz. Abt. 5	17.4.45
Gieseke, Otto	SS-Standartenfhr. & Oberst d. Schupo, Kdr. SS-Pol. Schtz. Rgt. 1	30.9.42
Giesen, Gerhard	Oberst, Kdr. G. R. 123 + 5.2.45 aat Loschen (East Prussia)	11.3.45
Giffhorn, Karl-Heinz	Lt. d.R., V. B. in 6./A.R. 190 (mot.)	18.11.44
Gilbert, Erich	Hptm., Kdr. II./G. R. 116	30.4.45
Gildner, Paul	Ofw., Flugzeugfhr. d. 3./NJ.G. 1 196th Oak Leaves 26.2.43	9.7.41
Gille, Herbert	SS-Oberfhr., Kdr. SS-A.R. 5 "Wiking" 315th Oak Leaves 1.11.43 47th Swords 20.2.44 12th Diamonds 19.4.44	8.10.42
Gillis, Léon	SS-Untersturmfhr., Zugf. in 5. SS-Freiw. - Sturmbrigade "Wallonie"	30.9.44
Gilow, Peter	Oblt., Fhr. 2./Pz. Rgt. 1	14.9.42
Frhr. von & zu Gilsa, Werner-Albrecht	Oberst, Kdr. I.R. 9 68th Oak Leaves 24.1.42	5.6.40
Girg, Walter	SS-Untersturmfhr., Zugfhr. 1./SS-Jäg. Btl. 502 814th Oak Leaves 1.4.45	4.10.44
Gladewitz, Herbert	Lt. d.R., Fhr. 7./Ski-Jäg. Rgt. 1	20.10.44
Gläsche, Dieter	Oblt., Kp. Fhr. in Pz. G. R. 11	17.4.45

Glaesemer, Wolfgang	Oberst, Kdr. Pz. G. R. 6	12.2.43
Gläser, Alexander	Oblt., Staffelkpt. 4./Stuka-Geschw. 77 811th Oak Leaves 28.3.45	19.2.43
Glaeser, Erich	Major, Kdr. II./I.R. 484	20.8.42
Glätzer, Karl	Hptm., Fhr. I./G. R. 426	9.4.44
Glander, Erwin	Lt. d.R., Fhr. 2./Sturmgesch. Brig. 210 + 2.8.44 at Ostrowitsche (Russia); posthumously promoted to Oblt. d.R.	21.9.44
Glaser, Friedrich	Obgefr., Richtschtz. in 14. (Pz.Jäg.)/G. R. 253	2.11.43
Glaser, Wilhelm	Oblt. d.R., Zugf. in III./G. R. 35 (mot.)	17.8.43
Glasl, Anton	Oberst, Kdr. Geb.Jäg. Rgt. 100	11.10.43
Glasner, Günter	Ofw., Bordschtz. i. Stab/K.G. 6	31.12.43
Glatz, Josef	Lt., Fhr. I./Pz.Jäg. Abt. 46	12.1.45
Glettenberg, Ludger (Lutz)	Major d.R., Kdr. I./I.R. 549 + 14.8.42 Rshew (Russia)	24.9.42
Gliemann, Paul	Obstlt., Kdr. G. R. 481 + 20.2.45 at Dittlingen (Saarland)	24.12.44
Gloger, Dr. med. dent. Paul	Major, Kdr. St. Gesch. Abt. 244 + 18.1.43 in Stalingrad (Russia); posthumously promoted to Oberstlt.	25.1.43
Glunz, Adolf	Ofw., Flugzeugfhr. in 4./J.G. 26 "Schlageter" 508th Oak Leaves 24.6.44	29.8.43
Gnaden, Franz	Major, Kdr. I./Geb.Jäg. Rgt. 85 + killed in action as Obstlt.	8.8.41
Gneikow, Fritz	Uffz., Gruppenfhr. in 3./G. R. 12 + 12.12.44 south of Prekuln (East Prussia) as Feldw.	26.11.44
Gobert, Ernst-Ascan	Hptm., Staffelkpt. 2./K.G. 53 "Legion Condor" + 2.11.44 at Bad Kösern as Hptm. & Staffelkpt. 10./J.G. 27	3.4.44
Godde, Johannes	Major, Kdr. III./A.R. 18 (L)	24.1.45
Goden, Emil	Ofw., Zugf. in 3./G. R. 407	26.8.43
Godenau, Arthur	Stabsobersteuermann, Kdt. "R 5 1" in 1. Räumbootsflottille	31.5.40
Goebel, Günter	Oblt., Rgt. Adj. I.R. 208 180th Oak Leaves 18.1.43	18.10.41
Goebel, Günther	Hptm., Chef 1./Art. -Pak-Abt. 1064 (mot.)	3.11.44
Göbel, Hans	Hptm., Kdr. II./G. R. 1226	29.4.45
Göbel, Herbert	Oblt., Chef 11./I.R. 461 + 11.10.41, main dressing station at Rusanowo, near Wiasma (Russia) of wounds	19.3.41
Göbel, Karl	Major, Kdr. III./I.R. 420 252nd Oak Leaves 8.6.43	10.9.42
Göbel, Kilian	Ofw., Zugf. in I./PzjHg. Abt. 49 + 29.10.44	26.11.44
Göbel, Siegfried	Oblt., Staffelkpt. in III./Stuka-Geschw. 3	3.2.43

Göbel, Werner	Gefr. in 7./G. R. 670	30.9.44
Göhler, Johannes	SS-Obersturmfhr., Chef 4./SS-R. R. 1 "Florian Geyer"	17.9.43
Göller, Sigwart	Hptm. d.R., Kdr. II./Geb.Jäg. Rgt. 98	9.5.45
Göller, Dr. Wilhelm	Oberst, Kdr. Festg. Pi. Stab 30	27.12.42
Gölz, Ludwig	Hptm., Kdr. Feldersatz-Btl. 208	5.4.45
Göring, Hermann	Gen. Feldm., Reichsminister der Luftfahrt & Oberbefehlshaber der Luftwaffe Großkreuz 19.7.40	30.9.39
Goeritz, Werner	Gen.Lt., Kdr. 291. I.D.	6.11.43
Goerke, Rudolf	Lt. d.R., Fhr. 11./G. R. 410	9.6.44
Görlich, Richard	Uffz., Gruppenfhr. in 1./Pz. G. R. 394	4.7.44
v. Goerne-Plaue, Jürgen	Hptm., Kdr. Aufkl. Abt. 29 (mot.)	20.10.41
Görsch, Ewald	Ofw., Zugf. in 8./Pz. G. R. 13	15.3.43
Görtler, Horst	Feldw., Flugzeugf. Stab/S.G. 77	28.3.45
Görtz, Helmut	Feldw., Zugf. in 3./Fsch. Jäg. Rgt. 1	24.5.40
Gößmann, Franz	Ofw., Zugf. in 2./G. R. 199 "List"	14.5.44
Göstl, Erich	SS-Pz. Gren., MG-Schtz. 1. in 6./SS-Pz. G. R. 1 "LSSAH"	31.10.44
Göttert, Oswin	Obgefr., Gruppenfhr. in 11./G. R. 445	7.9.43
Göttinger, Rudolf	Oblt., Chef 13. (1. G.)/Geb.Jäg. Rgt. 91	14.12.43
Göttler, Johann	Ofw., Zugfhr. in 6./Pz. Gren. Rgt. 63	1.9.43
Goettler, Waldemar	Feldw., Zugf. in Abwehrkdo. 201 (Inf.)	2.8.43
Götz, Franz	Oblt., Staffelkpt. 9./J.G. 53	4.9.42
Götz, Hans	Oblt., Flugzeugfhr. in 2./J.G. 54 + 4.8.43 shot down at Karatschew (Russia) as Hptm. & Staffelkpt.	23.12.42
Götz, Heinrich	Obstlt., Kdr. I.R. 466 765th Oak Leaves 5.3.45	3.5.42
Götze, Karl	Oblt., Chef 1./Flak-Rgt. 37 (mot.)	21.7.40
Goetze, Manfred	Oblt., Staffelfhr. 8./Schl. G. 10 + 4.1.45 at Papa (Hungary) as Hptm. & Staffelkpt.	19.8.44
Goetzke, Axel	Lt. z. See d.R., Kdt. "R 16" in 5. Räumbootsflottille + 14.9.41 Finnischen Meerbusen	27.12.41
Gohde, Otto	Ofw., stv. Fhr. 3./G. R. 368	6.2.44
Golbach, Paul	Owm., Zugf. in 5./A.R. 263	13.10.41
Goldammer, Friedrich	Hptm., Kdr. Schnelle Abt. 306	22.8.43
Goldberg, Heinz	Gefr., Richtkan. in 6./A.R. 333	27.9.43
Goldbruch, Kurt	Oblt., Staffelkpt. 8./Schl. G. 1 + 19.4.45 at Kunersdorf (Krs. Wriezen) as Hptm.	28.1.45
Goldbrunner, Jakob	Feldw., Zugf. in 5./I.R. 19	17.9.41

ELITE OF THE THIRD REICH

Golinski, Heinz	Uffz., Flugzeugfhr. in 3./J.G. 53 + 16.10.42 south of Malta; posthumously promoted to Feldw.	30.12.42
Goll, Eitel	Rittm., Kdr. Radf. Abt. 117 + April 1945 at Budapest (Hungary) as Major	13.9.42
Gollas, Josef	Feldw., Zugf. in 6./I.R. 106	18.11.41
Gollé, Josef	Major, Kdr. 1./I.R. 339	19.7.40
Gollert-Hansen, Hans-Detlef	Oblt. d.R., Chef Radf. Aufkl. Schwadron 173 699th Oak Leaves 14.1.45	31.7.43
Golles, Karl	Ofw., Flugzeugfhr. in 9./S.G. 4 + 7.7.44 at Michaliszki (Kurland)	9.6.44
Gollnick, Hans	Gen. Major, Kdr. 36. I.D. (mot.) 282nd Oak Leaves 24.8.43	21.11.42
Gollnick, Klaus	Hptm., Fhr. Div. Füs. Btl. 371	7.10.44
Gollob, Gordon	Hptm., Kdr. II./J.G. 3 38th Oak Leaves 26.10.41 13th Swords 23.6.42 3rd Diamonds 30.8.42	18.9.41
Gollwitzer, Friedrich	Gen.Lt., Kdr. 88. I.D.	8.2.43
Graf v. d. Goltz, Albert	Major d.R., Kdr. I./I.R. 415 316th Oak Leaves 2.11.43	7.5.42
Goltzsch, Kurt	Lt., Flugzeugfhr. in 5./J.G. 2 "Richthofen" + 26.9.44 Glauchau (Silesia) as Oblt. & Staffelkpt. of wounds	5.2.44
Golz, Herbert (19)	SS-Standartenfhr. & Oberst der Schupo, Chef d. Gen. St. X. SS-A.K. & Fhr. e Kampfgr.	3.5.45
Gombert, Richard	Oblt. d.R., Fhr. 6./Jäg. Rgt. 83	23.2.44
Gomille, Herbert	Hptm., Kdr. II./Pz. Rgt. 4	25.10.42
Goriany, Wilhelm	Major, Kdr. II./Geb. Art.Rgt. 85	18.7.43
Gorn, Walter	Major, Kdr. I./Schtz. Rgt. 10 113th Oak Leaves 17.8.42 30th Swords 8.6.43	20.4.41
Gorski, Alfred	Uffz., Gruppenfhr. in 4. (M. G.)/G. R. 576	21.1.45
Gorski, Artur	Uffz., Gruppenfhr. in 3./G. R. 30 (mot.)	28.11.43
Gosewisch, Ferdinand	Oberst d.R., Kdr. A.R. 362	4.7.44
Gossow, Heinz	Ofw., Flugzeugfhr. in 1./J.G. 302	28.10.44
v. Gottberg, Curt	SS-Gruppenfhr. & Gen.Lt. d. Pol., Fhr. d. Kampfgr. "v. Gottberg" + 31. May 45 at Grundhof, Camp Leutzhöft (Holstein) suicide in British captivity; final post SS-Obergruppenfhr. & Gen. d. Waffen-SS & der Polizei	30.6.44
Gottke, Heinrich	SS-Unterscharfhr., V. B. in 3./SS-Flak-Abt. 17 "Götz v. Berlichingen"	27.12.44
Gottstein, Rainer	SS-Obersturmbannfhr., Kdr. Sipo & SD. Budapest & Führ. of a Kampfgr. + 13.2.45 at Tök, near Budapest (Hungary)	6.2.45

Graber, Heinz	Lt., Staffelfhr. 7./Stuka-Geschw. 2 "Immelmann" + 30.1.43 at Wassilkowo (Russia) as Staffelkpt.	19.6.42
Grabert, Siegfried	Oblt. d.R., Fhr. a Sonderkdos. in Bau-Lehr-Btl. z.b.V. 800 "Brandenburg" 320th Oak Leaves 6.11.43	10.6.41
Grabmann, Walter	Obstlt., Kmdre. Z.G. 76	14.9.40
Grabowski, Josef	Lt., Fhr. 4./Pz. G. R. 110	18.1.44
Gradl, Hans	Major, Kdr. I./Pz. Rgt. 39	15.11.41
Graeber, Heinz	Ofw., Bordfunker in 15./K.G. 2	30.9.43
Gräbner, Viktor-Eberhard	SS-Hptsturmfhr. d.R., Kdr. SS-Pz. -Aufkl. Abt. 9 "Hohenstaufen" + 18.9.44 Arnhem (Holland)	23.8.44
Gräbner, Werner	Ofw., Zugf. in 4./Füs. Rgt. 22 + 16.10.44 south of Schirwindt	30.9.44
Graebsch, Heinz	Hptm. d.R., Chef 14. (Pz.Jäg.)/G. R. 7 + 14.7.44 at Ulla, on the Düna (Russia)	20.7.44
Graefe, Hans	Fhj. -Ofw., Beobachter in 2. (H)/Aufkl. Gr. 6	26.12.44
Gräser, Fritz-Hubert	Oberst, Kdr. I.R. 29 (mot.) 517th Oak Leaves 26.6.44 154th Swords 8.5.45	19.7.40
Graeßner, Walther	Gen.Lt., Kdr. 298. I.D. + 16.7.43 in hospital at Troppau (Silesia) as Gen.D.Inf. & Kom.Gen. XII. A.K.	27.10.41
Grätz, Erich	SS-Hptsturmfhr., Chef 18. (Pz.Jäg.)/SS-Pz. G. R. 1 "LSSAH"	14.5.44
Graf, Alois	Obstlt., Kdr. G. R. 1082 + 8. April 1945 in Annaberg (Upper Silesia); posthumously promoted to Oberst	30.4.45
Graf, Hermann	Lt. d.R., Flugzeugfhr. 9./J.G. 52 93rd Oak Leaves 17.5.42 11th Swords 19.5.42 5th Diamonds 16.9.42	24.1.42
Graf, Rudolf	Oblt., Chef 1./Flak-Rgt. (mot.) "General Göring" + 21.1.45 at Hohenkirch/Graudenz as Obstlt. & Kdr. Fsch. Pz. Gr. Rgt. 2 "H. G."	6.10.41
v. Graffen, Karl	Gen. Major, Fhr. 58. I.D.	13.8.42
Grammel, Friedrich	Lt., Fhr. 3./G. R. 544 + 17.2.44 at Tscherkassy (Russia)	4.5.44
Granitza, Bruno	Hptm., Chef 12./A.R. 329 + 8.5.45 at Frauenburg-Goldingen (Kurland)	21.9.44
Gransee, Georg	Feldw., Zugf. in 7./Pz. Rgt. 31	19.9.43
Grascher, Simon	SS-Unterscharfhr., Zugtruppfhr. in 9./SS-Pz. G. R. 4 "Der Führer" + 14.7.43 north of Bjelgorod (Russia)	14.8.43
Grase, Martin	Oberst, Kdr. I.R. 1 248th Oak Leaves 23.5.43	18.10.41

Name	Details	Date
Grasel, Anton	Owm., Zugf. in a le. Flak-Abt. (mot.) + 16.9.44 in Russia	24.10.44
Grasemann, Walter	Oblt., Staffelkpt. 9./K.G. 27 "Boelcke"	9.10.43
Grassau, Fritz	Hptm., Kdr. II./I.R. 188 + 20.4.45 in Wienrode (Harz) as Oberst & Kdr. G. R. 267	16.7.41
Grasser, Anton	Obstlt., Kdr. I.R. 119 344th Oak Leaves 5.12.43	16.6.40
Grasser, Hartmann	Oblt., Flugzeugfhr. in II./J.G. 51 288th Oak Leaves 31.8.43	4.9.41
Grasser, Rudolf	Feldw., Zugf. 8./G. R. 191	29.11.44
Graßmann, Dietrich	Oblt., Staffelkpt. 1./K.G. 4 "General Wever"	12.3.45
Graßmann, Josef	Major, Kdr. II./G. R. 326	9.11.42
Graßmel, Franz	Major, Kdr. III./Fsch. Jäg. Rgt. 4 868th Oak Leaves 8.5.45	8.4.44
Graßmuck, Berthold	Ofw., Flugzeugfhr. in 2./J.G. 52 + 28.10.42 at Pitomnik (Stalingrad/Russia), shot down by flak	19.9.42
Gratz, Karl	Uffz., Flugzeugfhr. in 8./J.G. 52	1.7.42
Graubner, Reinhard	Hptm., Kdr. II./K.G. 4 "General Wever"	3.9.43
Grauert, Ulrich	Gen. d. Flg., Kom.Gen. I. Flg. Korps + 15.5.41 in France as Gen. Oberst	29.5.40
Grauting, August	Feldw., Zugf. in I.R. 16 + 4.7.41 at Parjota (Bessarabia) as Oblt. & Kp. Chef 10./I.R. 16	29.5.40
Frhr. v. Gravenreuth, Sigmund-Ulrich.	Oblt., Flugzeugfhr. in I./K.G. 30 692nd Oak Leaves 9.1.45	24.11.40
Grebarsche, Gerhard	SS-Hptscharfhr., Zugfhr. in 3./SS-Pz. G. R. 2 "LSSAH"	24.1.44
Greck, Franz	Uffz., Kp. Tr. Fhr. in 4./Pz. Aufkl. Abt. 8	5.2.45
Greese, Otto	Obgefr., MG-Schtz. 1 in 6./G. R. 487 + 2.11.43 at Kritschew (Russia); posthumously promoted to Uffz.	24.11.43
Grehl, Heinz	Oblt. d.R., Kp. Fhr. in Fest. Gren. Rgt. "Mohr" in Fest. Breslau	30.4.45
v. Greiffenberg, Hans	Gen. Major, Chef d. Gen. St. 12. Armee	18.5.41
Greim, Alfred	Obstlt., Kdr. II./I.R. 1 "GD" + 19.5.43 of spotted fever	4.6.42
Ritter v. Greim, Robert	Gen.Lt., Kom.Gen. V. Flg. Korps 216th Oak Leaves 2.4.43 92nd Swords 28.8.44	24.6.40
Greiner, Andreas	Objäg., Zugf. in 8./Jäg. Rgt. 75	6.2.44
Greiner, Erwin	Major, Fhr. G. R. 307	29.11.44
Greiner, Heinz	Oberst, Kdr. I.R. 499 572nd Oak Leaves 5.9.44	22.9.41
Greiner, Hermann	Oblt., Staffelkpt. II./N. J.G. 1 840th Oak Leaves 17.4.45	27.7.44
Greiter, Hans	Uffz., Meldestaffelfhr. in I./G. R. 165	13.1.45

Grenzel, Gerhard	Uffz., Flugzeugfhr. in 2./Stuka-Geschw. I + 10.1.44 Malta as Lt.	8.5.40
Gresiak, Horst	SS-Obsturmfhr., Fhr. 7./SS-Pz. Rgt. 2 "Das Reich"	25.1.45
Gretschmann, Josef	Ofw., Zugf. in 6./Schtz. Rgt. 40	11.8.41
Greve, Carl-Heinz	Lt., Flugzeugfhr. in 3./Kampf-Gr. 606	7.10.42
Greve, Prof. Dr. med. dent. Karl	Hptm. d.R. z. V., Kdr. I./Jäg. Rgt. 49 + 13.10.42 in Russia of wounds; posthumously promoted to Major d.R. z. V.	18.5.42
Grewe, Josef	Ofw., Flugzeugfhr. in 9./S.G. 77	20.7.44
Griebel, Osmar	Feldw., Flugzeugfhr. in 2./Stuka-Geschw. 77 + 9.3.44 north of Porochnja (Russia) as Fhj.-Feldw.	5.12.43
Grieme, Willy	SS-Obersturmfhr d.R., Fhr. 6./SS-Pz. G. R. 4 "Der Führer"	17.9.43
Griesbach, Franz	Major, Kdr. I./I.R. 391 242nd Oak Leaves 17.5.43 53rd Swords 6.3.44	14.3.42
Griese, Bernhard	SS-Sturmbannfhr. & Major der Schupo, Kdr. Pol. Schtz. Btl. 323	3.5.42
Grieser, Max	Lt., Fhr. 2./Pz. G. R. 114 + 5.8.44	14.8.44
Grieshammer, Fritz	Gen. Major, Kdr. 24. Flak-Div.	12.4.45
Griesinger, Herbert	Objäg., Gruppenfhr. in Jäger-Rgt. 56	2.9.44
Grießbauer, Hans-Christoph	Rittm. d.R., Chef 4./Füs. Btl. 58 + 16.11.43 at Nevel (Russia)	14.11.43
Grimberg, Heinz	Hptm., Kdr. Pz. Pi. Btl. 19	14.4. 45
Grimm, Heinz	Lt., Flugzeugfhr. in IV./N. J.G. 1 + 13.10.43 in hospital at Bremen of wounds	5.2.44
Grimminger, Johannes	Hptm. d.R., Fhr. Pz. Gren. Feld-Ers. Btl. 25 776th Oak Leaves 11.3.45	23.8.44
Grislawski, Alfred	Feldw., Flugzeugfhr. in 9./J.G. 52 446th Oak Leaves 11.4.44	1.7.42
Grodde, Werner	Hptm., Kdr. II./A.R. 13 (L)	6.4.44
v. Groddeck, Karl-Albrecht	Oberst, Kdr. I.R. 120 (mot.) + 10.1.44 in hospital at Breslau as Kdr. 161. I.D. of wounds; posthumously promoted to Gen.Lt.	8.9.41
Groebe, Manfred	Lt., Pi. Zugf. in Stabskp./G. R. 278	17.3.45
Gröschke, Kurt	Major, Kdr. II./Fsch. Jäg. Rgt. 1 693rd Oak Leaves 9.1.45	9.6.44
Grözinger, Ludwig	Hptm., Staffelkpt. 3./K.G. 53 "Legion Condor" + 15.2.45 as Major & Kdr. III./K.G. 53	25.11.42
Grohe, Walter	Hptm. d.R., Fhr. I./Pz. Rgt. 35 + 25.10.44 in hospital at Königsberg (East Prussia) of wounds	22.10.44

Grohmann, Franz	SS-Obersturmfhr., Chef I./SS-Pz. G. R. 3 "Deutschland"	23.8.44
Grollmus, Helmut	Lt., Flugzeugfhr. in II./J.G. 54 + 19.6.44 at Viipuri (Finland)	6.10.44
Gromeike, Gustav	Obgefr. in 2./Pi. Btl. 1 + 16.10.44 at Schirwindt	19.6.42
Gromotka, Fritz	Lt., Staffelkpt. 9./J.G. 27	28.1.45
Grons, Josef	Major, Kdr. I./Transport-Geschw. 2	20.4.44
Gropp, Heinz (6)	SS-Obersturmfhr. d.R., Fhr. 2./SS-Flak-Abt. 9 "Hohenstaufen"	6.5.45
Gros, Karl	Ofw., Zugf. in 1./Pz. Rgt. 2	14.12.43
Grosan, Erhard	Oberst, Kdr. Kampfgr. "Grosan" Tactical instructor at the Pz. Truppenschule Bergen	9.5.45
Groscheck, Johann	Ofw., Fhr. Reiterzug in Stabskp./G. R. 422	21.1.45
Groß, Alfred	Lt., Staffelfhr. 5./J.G. 26 "Schlageter"	20.4.45
Groß, Helmut	Major, Kdr. Div. Füs. Btl. 129	31.8.43
Groß, Martin	SS-Sturmbannfhr., Kdr. II./SS-Pz. Rgt. 1 "LSSAH"	22.7.43
Grosse, Gert	Major, Kdr. II./G. R. 529	3.1.44
Grossendorfer, Hans	Oblt., Beobachter in 7./K.G. 53 "Legion Condor" + 20.11.43 in Russia	26.3.44
Großjohann, Georg	Major, Fhr. G. R. 308	26.12.44
Großkreutz, Friedrich-Karl	Major, Kdr. St. Gesch. Abt. 244	22.11.43
Großmann, Horst	Oberst, Kdr. I.R. 84 292nd Oak Leaves 4.9.43	23.8.41
Großmann, Hugo	Feldw., stv. Fhr. 3./G. R. 252 + 29.1.44 in Russia of wounds	26.3.44
Großrock, Alfred	SS-Untersturmfhr., Zugf. in 6./SS-Pz. Rgt. 5 "Wiking" + 5.4.45 in Hungary in Soviet captivity of wounds	12.8.44
Grote, Ernst-Albert	Major, Fhr. G. R. 12	11.3.45
Frhr. Grote, Horst	Oblt., Staffelkpt. 4./(S.)Lehr-Geschw. 2	21.7.40
Groth, Erich	Hptm., Kdr. II./Z.G. 76 + 11.8.41 at Stavanger (Norway) as Major & Kommodore Z.G. 76	1.10.40
Groth, Heinz	Major d.R., Div. Adj. 1. Geb. Div. & Fhr. Geb.Jäg. Rgt. 99	9.5.45
Grothaus, Hermann	Oblt., Chef 11./A.R. 389	10.9.44
Grotheer, Siegfried	Obstlt., Kdr. G. R. 464	6.11.43
Gruber, Helmut	Oblt. d.R., Adj. II./Pz. G. R. 125	15.1.43
Gruber, Rupert	Major, Kdr. St. Gesch. Abt. 209	14.8.43
Grubinger, Adolf	Objäg., MG. -Fhr. in 9./Jäger-Rgt. 227	28.2.45
Grübl, Peter	Obgefr., Gruppenfhr. in 11./Geb.Jäg. Rgt. 98	20.12.41

Grün, Werner	Hptm., Fhr. I./Pz. Rgt. 5	8.2.43
Grünberg, Hans	Lt., Flugzeugfhr. 5./J.G. 3 "Udet"	9.6.44
Grüner, Georg	Oblt., Chef 1./Pz. Rgt. 33 "Prinz Eugen" 436th Oak Leaves 26.3.44	25.11.41
Grünert, Anton	Oblt. d.R., Chef 3./St. Gesch. Abt. 201 + 8.8.44 between the San and Vistula (Russia); posthumously promoted to Hptm. d.R.	15.3.43
Grünert, Richard	Oblt. d.R., Fhr. 3./Kradschtz. Btl. 7 244th Oak Leaves 17.5.43	14.10.41
Grünewald, Georg	Ofw., Zugf. in 1./Fsch. Jäg. St. Gesch. Brig. 12	29.10.44
Grünner, Rudolf	SS-Unterscharfhr., Gruppenfhr. in Rgt. "Mohr" in Festung Breslau	10.3.45
Grünwald, Harry	Oblt., Chef 2./A.R. 18 (mot.)	6.2.44
Grünwaldt, Wilhelm	Hptm. d.R., Kdr. I./Pz. G. R. 126	17.9.44
Gruhl, Herbert	Hptm., Chef 11./G. R. 133	5.4.44
Grumbt, Otto	Hptm., Kdr. II./Pz. G. R. 111	28.10.44
Grunau, Ernst	Oblt., Fhr. d. Begleitkp. d. 14. Pz-Div.	4.10.44
Grund, Julius	Hptm., Kdr. I./Geb.Jäg. Rgt. 138	30.10.43
Grundmann, Erich	Kaptlt. (Ing.), Flottillen-Ing. der 1. Räumbootsflottille	31.5.40
Grunge, Wilhelm	Obgefr., Gruppenfhr. in 4./Pz. G. R. 93	3.7.44
Grunhold, Werner	Uffz., Kp. Truppf. in 3./Fsch. Pz. G. R. 2 "HG"	30.11.44
Grunwald, Horst	Feldw., Zugf. in 4./G. R. 457	14.5.44
Gschwendtner, Karl-Georg	Ofw., Flugzeugfhr. in 7./Stuka-Geschw. 77 + 5.4.45 Prague (Czechoslovakia) as Lt. & Flugzeugfhr. in 1./S.G. 103	5.2.44
Gsell, Karl-Heinrich	Lt. d.R., Fhr. 2./Pz. Rgt. 35 + 25.2.45	23.2.44
Gsinn, Josef	Ofw., Zugf. in 4./Hochgebirgs-Jäg. -Btl. 3	20.7.44
Guckenberger, Rudolf	Hptm., Kdr. II./I.R. 481 + 14.1.45 west of Radom (Poland) as Oberstlt. & Kdr. Gren. Rgt. 21	20.8.42
Gudelius, Alfred	Major, Kdr. II./Schtz. Rgt. 14 + 25.3.44 Tarnopol, Lemberg (Poland) as Oberst & Kdr. Pz. Gr. Rgt. 8	10.2.42
Guderian, Heinz	Gen. d. Pz.Tr., Kom.Gen. XIX. A.K. 24th Oak Leaves 17.7.41	27.10.39
Guderian, Heinz-Günther	Major i.G., Ia 116. Pz.Div.	5.10.44
Gümbel, Karl	Oberst, Kdr. I.R. 516	30.10.41
Gümbel, Ludwig	Oberst, Fhr. Div. Gruppe "Gümbel" (Gren. Rgt. 308)	29.11.44
Günter, Wilhelm	Feldw., Zugf. in 13. (I. G.)/G. R. 508	5.3.45

ELITE OF THE THIRD REICH

Günther, Alfred	SS-Oberscharfhr., Zugf. In 1./SS-St. Gesch. Abt. 1 "LSSAH" + 26.6.44 in Normandy, France as SS-Hptscharfhr.	3.3.43
Günther, Heinrich-Albrecht	Hptm., Staffelkpt. 7./K.G. 27 "Boelcke" + 10.1.44 in Russia	9.6.44
Günther, Paul	Fhj. -Ofw., Flugzeugfhr. in 9./S.G. 10	2.2.45
Günther, Wilhelm	Feldw., Zugf. in 8./Pz. Rgt. 2 + 1944 as Ofw.	18.12.42
Günzel, Reinhard	Hptm., Kdr. II./K.G. 27 "Boelcke" 184th Oak Leaves 21.1.43	17.9.41
Gürke, Ernst	Major, Kdr. I./Flak-Rgt. 43	3.11.42
Gürz, Martin	SS-Hptsturmfhr., Fhr. III./SS-Freiw. -Pz. G. R. 23 "Norge" + 26.9.44 at Narva (Kurland); posthumously promoted to SS-Sturmbannfhr. d.R.	23.10.44
Gütschow, Hans	Lt. d.R., Kp. Fhr. in I./I.R. 545	25.10.42
Gugganig, Alois	Feldw., Zugf. in 12./Geb.Jäg. Rgt. 91 + 6.1.44 in Salzburg (Austria) of wounds	3.4.43
Guggenberger, Friedrich	Kaptlt., Kdt. "U 81" 171st Oak Leaves 8.1.43	10.12.41
Guhl, Paul	SS-Hptsturmfhr., Fhr. III. (gep.)/SS-Pz. G. R. 2 "LSSAH"	4.6.44
Guhr, Hans	Oblt., Rgt. Adj. I.R. 513	10.9.42
Guhrke, Heinz	Oblt. z. See d.R., Kdt. Torpedoboot "TA 20" + 31.10.44 during action in the Adriatic	5.11.44
Gumprich, Günther	Kapt. z. See, Kdt. Hilfskreuzer "Thor" (HSK 4) + 17.10.43 in Pacific Ocean as Kdt. Hilfskreuzer "Michel"	31.12.42
Gunzert, Ulrich	Oblt., Chef 3./Pi. Btl. 258	20.12.41
Gurran, Paul	Oberst, Kdr. I.R. 50 + 22.2.44 in a field hospital in Russia as Gen. Major & Kdr. 23. of wounds; posthumously promoted to z. Gen.Lt.	12.9.41
Guschker, Ernst	Hptm., Fhr. II./G. R. 587 + 13.12.43 in Russia of wounds as Major & Btl. Kdr.	3.8.43
Gust, Werner	Hptm., Kdr. III./G. R. 477 624th Oak Leaves 18.10.44	7.2.44
Gutheit, Helmut	Lt. d.R., Fhr. Jagdpanzer-Kp. 1011	17.4.45
Gutmacher, Gerhard	Hptm., Fhr. I./G. R. 178	14.1.45
Gutmann, Heinz	Oblt., Staffelfhr. 3./K.G. 53 "Legion Condor" + 3.3.45 at Üfingen, near Braunschweig as Hptm. & Staffelkpt. 9./J.G. 7	5.4.44
Gutmann, Joachim	Obstlt., Fhr. Pz. G. R. 11	18.9.42
Gutzmann, Erwin	Feldw., Flugzeugfhr. in II./S.G. 2 "Immelmann" + 10.4.45 at St. Pölten (Austria) as Oberfähnrich & Flugzeugfhr. in 8./S.G. 10	26.3.44

Gutzmer, Hans	Hptm., Staffelkpt. 3./K.G. 51	29.2.44
Gutzschhahn, Helmut	Hptm., Kdr. I./Pz. G. R. 6	8.5.43
Györy, August	Oblt., Flugzeugfhr. in 4. (F)/Aufkl. Gr. 122 + 1.1.45 as Staffelfhr. 4./N. J.G. 3	26.3.44
Gysae, Robert	Kaptlt., Kdt. "U 98" 250th Oak Leaves 31.5.43	31.12.41

H

Haag, Heinz	Oblt. z. See, Kmdt. "S 60" in 3. Schnellbootsflottille	25.11.44
Haarhaus, Walter	Major, Kdr. I./I.R. 477	1.2.42
Haas, Friedrich (17)	Lt., Staffelfhr. 5./J.G. 52 + 9.4.45 over Vienna (Austria)	26.4.45
Haas, Josef	Oberst, Kdr. G. R. 485 + 22.5.44 northern sector of the Eastern Front, Lake Swiblo (Russia) of wounds	14.11.43
Haas, Robert	Lt. d.R., Fhr. 1./St. Gesch. Brig. 244 + 23.12.44 in the Ardennes Offensive	25.1.45
Haase, Alfred	Major, Kdr. Pi. Lehr-Btl. 2 & Fhr. of a Kampfgr.	1.4.42
Haase, Curt	Gen. d. Art., Kom.Gen. III. A.K. + 9.2.43 in Berlin as Gen. Ob. & OB 15. Armee	8.6.40
Haase, Heinz-Georg	Ofw., Zugf. in 11./G. R. 122 + 25.11.43 Tarchau (Crimea)	2.9.43
Haase, Hermann	Hptm., Fhr. I./G. R. 423 + 30.7.44 in Russia; posthumously promoted to Major	5.9.44
Haase, Horst	Hptm., Kdr. IV./J.G. 3 "Udet" + 26.11.44 shot down at Erkelenz following an alarm to scramble; posthumously promoted to Major	24.10.44
Haase, Horst	Oblt. d.R., Fhr. Pz.Jäg. Kp. 1162	1.2.45
Haccius, Ernst	Gen.Lt., Kdr. 46. I.D. + 10.2.43 in northern Caucasus (Russia)	2.4.43
Hachfeld, Wilhelm	Hptm., Kdr. III./Z.G. 2 + 2.12.42 Bizerta (North Africa) accidentally	29.10.42
Hachtel, August	Ofw., Flugzeugf. in 4./Stuka-Geschw. 1	6.1.42
Hachtel, Georg	Oberst, Kdr. Jäger-Rgt. 56 + 20.7.43 in a base hospital at Konstanz of wounds; posthumously promoted to Gen. Major	30.4.43
Hack, Franz	SS-Sturmbannf., Kdr. III. (gep.)/SS-Pz. G. R. 9 "Germania" 844th Oak Leaves 18.4.45	14.5.44
Hackbarth, Willi	Gefr., Funker in 4./A.R. 32 + 27.7.44 at Purnawa/Kudupe, northern Russia, as Uffz.	18.4.43
Hackl, Anton	Oblt., Staffelkpt. 5./J.G. 77 109th Oak Leaves 9.8.42 78th Swords 9.7.44	25.5.42
Hackl, Leopold (17)	Fhj. -Oberfeldw., Flugzeugf. Stab/N.S.G. 3	20.3.45

Name	Details	Date
Hackl, Dr. Martin	Lt. d.R., Fhr. 2./Geb. Aufkl. Abt. 94	7.12.43
Hackler, Heinz	Fhj. -Ofw., Flugzeugf. in III./J.G. 77 + 1.1.45 missing near Antwerp as Lt. & Staffelfhr. 11./J.G. 77	19.8.44
Hadeball, Heinz-Martin	Hptm., Kdr. I./NJ.G. 6	27.7.44
Hadenfeldt, Friedrich	Obstlt., Kdr. A.R. 1818	17.3.45
Haderecker, Hermann	Major, Fhr. G. R. 20 (mot.)	4.5.44
Häberlen, Klaus	Hptm., Kdr. I./K.G. 51	20.6.43
Haeckel, Ernst	Gen.Lt., Kdr. 16. V.G.D.	28.10.44
Haecker, Franz	Ofw., Zugf. in 5./G. R. 211	16.3.44
Häfele, Josef	Ofw., Zugf. in 11./Geb.Jäg. Rgt. 99 + 17.5.42 at Fedorowka, during the battle for Kharkov (Russia)	18.11.41
Häfner, Ludwig	Lt., Flugzeugf. in 6./J.G. 3 "Udet" + 10.11.42 shot down over Stalingrad (Russia)	21.12.42
Hägele, Willi	Hptm., Chef 9./Flak-Rgt. 14	30.9.44
Haehing, Kurt	Gen. Major, Kdr. 126. I.D.	2.3.45
Haehnel, Wilhelm	Lt., Fhr. 4./A.R. 157	21.2.44
Haellmigk, Hartwich	Oberst, Kdr. G. R. 301	19.11.43
Hämel, Heinz	SS-Hptsturmf., Fhr. II./SS-Freiw. Pz. G. R. 24 "Danmark"	16.6.44
Haen, Rudolf	Hptm., Chef 1./Pz. Abt. 103 590th Oak Leaves 21.9.44	18.12.42
Hänert, Karl	Oblt., Chef 4. (MG.)/I.R. "Großdeutschland" (mot.) + 14.10.41 east of Brjansk (Russia); posthumously promoted to Hptm.	23.8.41
Haenicke, Siegfried	Gen.Lt. z. V., Kdr. 61. I.D. + 19.2.46 in Soviet captivity, at Camp Mühlberg a. d. Elbe; final post Gen.D.Inf. z. V. & W. K. Befehlsh. in general gouvernement	17.9.41
Haeuseler, Helmut	Obstlt., Kdr. G. R. 399 + 25.2.45 at Hoppenkind (East Prussia)	14.2.45
Häußler, Ernst	SS-Sturmbannf., Kdr. II./SS-Pz. G. R. 5 "Totenkopf"	15.8.43
Hafner, Anton	Feldw., Flugzeugf. in 6./J.G. 51 "Mölders" 452nd Oak Leaves 11.4.44	23.8.42
Hafner, Otto	Hptm. d.R., Chef 4./G. R. 61	23.9.43
Hagemann, Wolf	Obstlt., Kdr. III./Geb.Jäg. Rgt. 139 484th Oak Leaves 4.6.44	4.9.40
Hagen, Walter	Major, Kdr. III./Stuka-Geschw. 1 77th Oak Leaves 17.2.42	21.7.40
v. Hagen, Wilhelm	Hptm., Fhr. II./I.R. 267 + 15.3.45; posthumously promoted to Oberst	2.9.42
Hagena, Gottfried	Oblt., Flugzeugf. in 1./Nahaufkl. Gr. 15	17.4.45

KNIGHT'S CROSS OF THE IRON CROSS

Hager, Johannes	Hptm., Staffelkpt. in II./N. J.G. 1	12.3.45
Hager, Karl	Fw., Flugzeugf. in 4./Stuka-G. 2 "Immelmann" + 4.2.44 at Pancevo (Yugoslavia) as Fluglehrer 4./S.G. 151	29.2.44
Hagl, Andreas	Oblt., Zugf. in 2./Fsch. Jäg. Rgt. 3 + 28.7.44 in Italy as Hptm. d.R. & Führer d. Nachkomds. 1. Fsch. Jäg. Div	9.7.41
Hahlbohm, Adolf	Hptm., Kdr. II./G. R. 956 + 13.2.45 on the Po (north Italy) as Major & stv. Fhr. G. R. 1060	8.8.44
Hahm, Constantin	Major, Kdr. II./Fsch. Pz. Rgt. "HG"	9.6.44
Hahm, Walther	Oberst, Kdr. I.R. 480 676th Oak Leaves 9.12.44	15.11.41
Hahn, Hans (Assi)	Oblt., Flugzeugf. in 4./J.G. 2 "Richthofen" 32nd Oak Leaves 14.8.41	24.9.40
v. Hahn, Hans	Hptm., Kdr. I./J.G. 3	9.7.41
Hahn, Hans	Lt., Flugzeugf. in I./N. J.G. 2 + 11.10.41 shot down over England	9.7.41
Hahn, Joachim	Major, Kdr. Kampf-Gruppe 606 + 3.6.42 as Obstlt. & Kdr. K. Gr. 606	21.10.40
Hahne, Hans	Oberst, Kdr. I.R. 507 + 24.6.44 at Witebsk (Russia) as Kdr. 197. I.D. posthumously promoted to Gen. Major	10.2.42
Hailböck, Josef	Hptm., Kdr. I./J.G. 3 "Udet"	9.6.44
Haidle, Paul	Lt., Staffelfhr. in III./S.G. 77	16.2.45
Hain, Horst	Oblt., Chef 3./Pz. Aufkl. Abt. 23	28.3.45
Hainle, Adolf	Obwachtm., Fhr. a MG-Staffel in 2./Aufkl. Abt. 5 + 22.5.42 south- east of Lake Ilmen (Russia) of wounds	22.9.41
Haizmann, Richard	Obstlt. i.G., Ia 9. Flak-Div. (mot.) + January 1943 at Stalingrad (Russia)	28.1.43
v. Hake, Friedrich-Erdmann	Oberst, Kdr. Pz. Rgt. 4	23.11.43
Hakenholt, Hans	Hptm., Kdr. II./Flak-Rgt. 43 (mot.)	9.6.44
Haker, Theodor	Oblt., Staffelkpt. 6./Stuka-G. 77 + 26.7.44 at Lemberg (Poland) killed by partisans	29.2.44
Halbeck	SS-Untersturmfhr., Fhr. of a Kampfgruppe in V. SS-Gebirgskorps	17.4.45
Halder, Franz	Gen. of Art., Chef of the Generalstabes des Heeres	27.10.39
Hallauer, Hellmuth	Hptm., Chef 1./Pi. Btl. 59 (mot.) + 24.6.41 north of Kowno (Russia) of wounds	24.6.41
Hallensleben, Rudolf	Major, Kmdre. K.G. 76 + 19.4.45 at Leipheim (Danube) as Obstlt.	5.11.43

ELITE OF THE THIRD REICH

Halm, Günther	Gren., Richtschtz. in Pakzug Stabskp./Pz. G. R. 104, also awarded E. K. I. & II. Klasse simultaneously	29.7.42
Halten, Hans	Uffz., Gruppenfhr. in 3./G. R. 43	4.6.44
Hamann, Herbert	Major, Fhr. Pz. Feldersatz-Rgt. 63	28.2.45
Hamberger, Karl	Feldw., stellv. Fhr. 2./G. R. 62	8.11.44
Hamburger, Michael	Feldw., Zugf. in 4. (MG.)/G. R. 957	14.4. 45
Hamburger, Otto	Fhj. -Stabsfeldw., Fhr. 8. (MG.)/G. R. 426	4.10.44
Hamel, Heinz	Oblt. d.R., Fhr. 5./G. R. "Feldherrnhalle"	14.2.45
Hamer, Reino	Hptm., Kdr. I./Fsch. Jäg. Rgt. 7	5.9.44
Hamester, Bernhard	Hptm., Staffelkpt. in III./Stuka-G. 3 + 22.4.45 at Trebbin as Major & Fhr. S.G. 3	3.9.42
Hammer, Ernst	Gen.Lt., Kdr. 75. I.D.	20.12.41
Hammer, Ludwig	Lt., Flugzeugf. & Beob. in 4. (H)/Aufkl. Gr. 12	29.10.43
Hammerich, Willi	Oblt. d.R., Chef 4. (MG.)/G. R. 501	9.12.44
Hammerl, Karl	Ofw., Flugzeugf. in 1./J.G. 52 + 2.3.43 in Russia as Lt.	19.9.42
Hammerschmidt, Josef	Lt., stellv. Fhr. 8./Pz. Art.Rgt. 74	28.3.45
Hammon, Erich	Obstlt., Kdr. Pz. A.R. 119	1.2.45
Hampe, Herbert	Ofw., Flugzeugf. in II./K.G. 3	5.4.44
Hampel, Desiderius (15)	SS-Brigadefhr. & Gen. Major d. Waffen-SS, Kdr. Kampfgr. 13. Waffen-Gebirgs-Div. der SS	3.5.45
Hampl, Josef	Oblt. d.R., Chef 3./Geb.Jäg. Rgt. 85	10.9.43
Hanbauer, Heinrich	Oblt., Fhr. 2./Schtz. Rgt. 86 + 3.7.41 in Russia as Kp. Chef	7.3.41
Handke, Erich	Fhj. -Feldw., Bordfunker in IV./NJ.G. 1	27.7.44
Handke, Hermann	Hptm., stellv. Fhr. II./Jäg. Rgt. 49 + 14.9.44 at Matwica (Russia); posthumously promoted to Major	28.10.44
Handler, Johann	Lt., Fhr. 1./G. R. 958	14.4. 45
Hankamer, Wolfgang	Oblt., Staffelkpt. 6./K.G. 2 + 14.1.45 at Kyritz (Mark) as Hptm. & Staffelkpt. in I./J.G. 301	29.10.44
Hanke, Georg	Ofw., Flugzeugf. in 6./K.G. 76 SS-Obersturmbannfhr., Kdr.	26.3.44
Hanke, Hans (15)	Waffen-Geb. -Jäger-Rgt. 28	3.5.45
Hannak, Günther	Lt., Flugzeugf. in I./J.G. 77	1.7.42
Hanne, Erich	Lt., Flugzeugf. in 7./Stuka-Geschw. I + 5.9.42 at Leningrad (Russia) as Staffelf.	13.8.42
Hannibal, Heinrich	SS-Standartenf. & Oberst d. Schupo., Kdr. SS-Pol. Schtz. Rgt. 31	23.8.44
Hannig, Felix	Major d.R., Kdr. I./I.R. 9 + 23.7.41 during street fighting at Mogilew (Russia); posthumously promoted to Oberstlt. d.R.	17.9.41

Name	Rank/Unit	Date
Hannig, Horst	Lt., Flugzeugf. in 6./J.G. 54 364th Oak Leaves 3.1.44	9.5.42
Hans, Heinrich	Ofw., Zugf. in 3./G. R. 426	5.4.45
Hansen, Christian	Gen. d. Art., Kom.Gen. X. A.K.	3.8.41
Hansen, Erik Oskar	Gen. d. Kav., Kom.Gen. LIV. A.K.	4.9.41
Hansen, Hans-Christian	Hptm. d.R., Fhr. II./Fsch. Pz. G. R. 3 "HG"	11.2.45
Hansen, Josef	Uffz., Gewehrfhr. in 6. (MG.)/G. R. 317 + 2.4.44 north of Kovel (Russia) of wounds	15.4.44
Hansen, Max	SS-Sturmbannf., Kdr. II./1. Pz. Gren. Rgt/Pz. Gren. Div. "LSSAH" 835th Oak Leaves 17.4.45	28.3.43
Hansen, Walter	Oberst, Kdr. G. R. 554	16.10.44
v. Hanstein, Jobst	Oberst, Kdr. G. R. 109	13.9.43
Hantke, Konrad	Uffz., Gr. Fhr. in Inf. Nachr. Ersatz- & Ausb. Kp. 208	28.3.45
Hanusch, Erwin	Hptm. d.R., Kdr. I./G. R. 438 + 16.8.44 in Russia	8.8.44
Harang, Jürgen	Oblt., Staffelkpt. in II./J.G. 77 + 20.1.45 at Wielun (Poland)	2.2.45
v. Harbou, Joachim	Hptm., Fhr. I./S. R. 5 + 24.2.44 in Italy in Wehrmachtführungsstab; posthumously promoted to Obstlt.	15.11.41
Hardegen, Reinhard	Kaptlt., Kdt. "U 123" 89th Oak Leaves 23.4.42	23.1.42
Harden, Alfred	Hptm., Kdr. II./Pz. Rgt. 29 + 19.3.45 at Sili, near Frauenburg (Kurland)	10.2.45
Frhr. v. Hardenberg, Klaus	Major, Chef 11./I.R. 25 (mot.) + 3.11.42 accidentally at El Alamein (North Africa) as Obstlt. & Kdr. Pz. Gren. Rgt. 125; posthumously promoted to Oberst	30.11.40
Harder, Jürgen	Hptm., Staffelkpt. in III./J.G. 53 727th Oak Leaves 1.2.45	5.12.43
Harlinghausen, Martin	Major i.G., Chef d. Gen. St. X. Fliegerkorps 8th Oak Leaves 30.1.41	4.5.40
Harmel, Heinz	SS-Obersturmbannf., Kdr. SS-Pz. G. R. 3 "Deutschland" 296th Oak Leaves 7.9.43 116th Swords 15.12.44	31.3.43
Harms, Wilhelm	Obstlt. d.R., Kdr. G. R. 390	1.2.45
v. Harnack, Helmut	Oblt., Fhr. 10./Pz. Rgt. 21 + 21.1.42 in Russia	17.1.42
Harnoth, Josef	Hptm., Kdr. II./G. R. 313	14.2.45
Harpe, Josef	Gen. Major, Kdr. 12. Pz.Div. 55th Oak Leaves 31.12.41 36th Swords 15.9.43	13.8.41
Harras, Horst	Oblt., Zugfhr. in I./Flak-Rgt. 18	14.6.40
Harrendorf, Hermann	Hptm., Kdr. III./I.R. 469	16.2.42
Harries, Friedrich	Oblt., Staffelfhr. 7./K.G. 76	24.3.43
Harscheidt, Kaspar	Fhj. -Ofw., Zugf. in 3./G. R. 253	31.8.43

Name	Details	Date
Hart, Rolf	Lt., Beobachter in 9./K.G. 1 "Hindenburg" + 9.3.43 in Russia	15–10.42
Hartelt, Wolfgang	Oberfähnr., Zugf. in 2./Fsch. Pz. Rgt. "HG"	23.2.45
Harteneck, Gustav	Gen. d. Kav., Kom.Gen. I. Kav. Korps	21.9.44
Hartenstein, Werner	Korv. Kpt., Kdt. "U 156" + 12.3.43 in the Atlantic, east of Barbados	17.9.42
Harth, Helmuth	Uffz,., Pz. Kdt. in 12./Pz. Rgt. 21	22.1.43
Harthan, Lorenz	Ofw., Pi. Zugf. in 5./Pz. Aufkl. Abt. 11	12.6.44
Hartig, Walter	Oblt., Chef 3./le. Flak-Abt. 91 (mot.) + 1945 as Hptm.	4.2.42
v. Hartmann, Alexander	Gen. Major, Kdr. 71. I.D. + 26.1.43 in Stalingrad (Russia); posthumously promoted to Gen.D.Inf.	8.10.42
Hartmann, Alfred	Feldw., Zugf. in 11./G. R. 337	12.3.43
Hartmann, Erich	Lt., Flugzeugf. in 9./J.G. 52 420th Oak Leaves 2.3.44 75th Swords 2.7.44 18th Diamonds 25.8.44	29.10.43
Hartmann, Hermann	Feldw., Zugfhr. in 3./Pi. Btl. 34	31.8.43
Hartmann, Leo	Lt. d.R., Fhr. Pz.Jäg. Abt. Breslau	30.4.45
Hartmann, Otto	Gen. d. Art., Kom.Gen. XXX. A.K.	5.8.40
Hartmann, Walter	Oberst, Art. Kdr. 140 340th Oak Leaves 30.11.43 139th Swords 18.3.45	10.8.41
Hartmann, Werner	Korv. Kpt., Kdt. "U 37" 645th Oak Leaves 5.11.44	9.5.40
Hartmann, Werner	Hptm. d.R., Kdr. Pi. Btl. 8	4.10.44
Hartrampf, Kurt (8)	SS-Sturmbannführer, Kdr. (s) SS-Pz. Abt. 502	28.4.45
Harttrumpf, Paul	Lt., Fhr. 1./G. R. 12	8.5.45
Hartz, Walter	Ofw., Zugf. in 6./G. R. 431	6.2.44
Harzenmetter, Johann	Hptm., Kdr. II./G. R. 331	9.5.45
Harzer, Walter	SS-Obersturmbannf., Ia 9. SS-Pz.Div. "Hohenstaufen"	21.9.44
Haschberger, Max	Oberfähnrich, Ord.Offz. in I./G. R. 481	27.8.43
Hasche, Wolfgang	Hptm. d.R., Kdr. I./G. R. 987 6.2.45 posted missing	3.11.44
v. Hase, Karl-Günther	Major, Gen. St. Offz. b. Kdt. d. Festg. Schneidemühl (Ia Pz.Div. "Holstein")	12.2.45
Haselbach, Hans	Lt., Flugzeugf. in 14. (Eis.)/K.G. 27 "Boelcke" + 28.12.43 in Russia	12.11.43
Hasenbeck, Günter	Oblt., Kp. Fhr. in Pz. Aufkl. Abt. 6	26.8.43
Hasenpusch, Rudolf (11)	Lt., Fhr. Brüko. in Pz. Pi. Btl. 16	27.4.45
Haß, Siegfried	Gen.Lt., Kdr. 170. I.D.	18.2.45
Hasse, Frank	SS-Obersturmf, Fhr. 11./SS-Pz. G. R. 1 "LSSAH" + 24.12.44 in the Ardennes at Petit Coe (Belgium) by partisans, as Kp. Chef	6.8.44

Hasse, Wilhelm	Gen.Lt., Kdr. 30. I.D. 698th Oak Leaves 14.1.45	12.8.44
Haßel, Kurt	Major, Kdr. Pz. Verb. 700	17.6.43
Hauber, Friedrich	Hptm., Kdr. II./Fsch. Jäg. Rgt. 12 + 5.10.44 in Italy, motor vehicle accident	5.9.44
Hauck, Friedrich-Wilhelm	Gen.Lt., Kdr. 305. I.D.	11.6.44
Haude, Kurt	Oblt. d.R., Chef 6./Pz. G. R. 112 + 18.10.43 south of Rosslawl (Russia)	24.11.43
Ritter v. Hauenschild, Bruno	Oberst, Kdr. 4. Pz. Brig. 129th Oak Leaves, 27.9.42	25.8.41
v. Hauff, Ulrich	Hptm., Kdr. III./Jäg. Rgt. 75 + 3.1.44 north-west of Witebsk (Russia); posthumously promoted to Major	31.1.44
Hauffe, Arthur	Gen.Lt., Kdr. 46. I.D. + 22.7.44 at Lemberg (Poland) as Gen.D.Inf. & Kom.Gen. XIII. A.K.	25.7.43
Haugk, Helmut	Ofw., Flugzeugf. in 9./Z.G. 26 "Horst Wessel"	21.12.42
Haugk, Werner	Fhj. -Ofw., Flugzeugf. in 4./Z.G. 76 + 18.10.44 shot down over Aalborg (Denmark); posthumously promoted to Lt.	8.8.44
Haukelt, Edgar (10)	SS-Obersturmfhr., Chef 1./SS-Jagdpanzer-Abt. 561	28.4.45
Haun, Helmut	Oblt., Rgt. Adj. I.R. 77 + 26.11.41 of wounds	8.8.41
Haupt, Karl	Ofw., Flugzeugf. in 8./K.G. 3 "Lützow" + 3.1.44 over England	3.2.43
Hauptmann, Hans	Hptm., Fhr. Kradschtz. Btl. 55	15.3.43
Hauptmann, Heinrich	Hptm., Kdr. III./Pz. Gren. Rgt. 115	20.11.42
Haus, Georg	Oberst. Kdr. G. R. 55 + 16.4.45 at Pillau (East Prussia) as Gen.Maj. & Kdr. 50. I.D.; posthumously promoted to Gen.Lt.	12.2.44
Hauser, Eduard	Oberst,. Kdr. Pz. Rgt. 25 376th Oak Leaves 26.1.44	4.12.41
Hauser, Hans	SS-Sturmbannf & Major in der Schutzpolizei, Kdr. I./SS-Pz. G. R. 4 "Der Führer"	6.5.45
Hauser, Hansjörg	Hptm., Kdr. II./G. R. 35 (mot.) + 30.8.44 at Orscha (Russia)	17.8.43
Hauser, Hellmuth	Hptm., Staffelkpt. in I./K.G. 51	23.12.42
Frhr. v. Hauser, Paul	Hptm., Kdr. Kradschtz. Btl. 61 635th Oak Leaves 28.10.44	25.1.43
Hausmann, Karl	Ofw., Fhr. 3./Jäg. Rgt. 28	15.5.42
Haussels, Arthur	Major, Kdr. II./Geb.Jäg. Rgt. 139 + 13.2.43 in North Africa as Rgt. Kdr. of wounds; posthumously promoted to Oberst	4.9.40

Hausser, Paul	SS-Gruppenf. & Gen.Lt. of the Waffen-SS, Kdr. SS-Div. "Reich" 261st Oak Leaves 28.7.43 90th Swords 26.8.44	8.8.41
Haut, Erich	Hptm. d.R., Kdr. 1./Pz. G. R. 86 + September 1944 at Raska (Serbia)	10.5.43
Havik, Hans	SS-Untersturmf., Zugf. in 1./SS-Pol. Pz. Abt. 4	9.5.45
Hawelka, Heinrich	Oblt. d.R., Adj. IR./G. R. 413	22.1.44
Hax, Heinrich	Oberst, Fhr. 8. Pz.Div. 855th Oak Leaves 30.4.45	8.3.45
Haxter, Wilhelm	Ofw., Fhr. Radf. Zug in Stabskp./G. R. 691	14.8.43
v. Haxthausen, Elmershaus	Kaptlt., Chef 2. Artillerieträgerflottille	3.7.44
Hechler, Ernst	Korv. Kpt., Kdt. "U 870"	21.1.45
Hecht, Dietrich	Lt. d.R., Fhr. 5./G. R. 666	27.10.43
Hecht, Max	Major, Kdr. Flak-Rgt. 135 (mot.)	7.3.42
Heckelmann, Reinhold	Oblt., Ord.Offz. in G. R. 1091	11.3.45
Hecker, Hans	Obstlt., Kdr. Pi. Btl. 29 (mot.)	5.8.40
Heckmann, Alfred	Ofw., Flugzeugf. in 4./J.G. 3 "Udet"	19.9.42
Hedderich, Fritz	Ofw., Zugf. in 3./G. R. 487 + 8.3.45	28.12.43
Heder, Eberhard	SS-Hptsturmf., Fhr. SS-Pz. Pi. Btl. 5 "Wiking"	18.11.44
Heer, Karl	Hptm., Fhr. I./Volks-Art.Rgt. 178 + 22.3.45 at Leobschütz (Silesia)	30.4.45
Heesemann, Wolfgang	Oberst, Kdr. Pz. G. R. "GD" + 6.2.45 at Königsberg (East Prussia)	17.2.45
te Heesen, Paul	Hptm., Kdr. Pz. Abt. 106 "Feldherrnhalle" + 9.1.45 in Alsace	13.1.45
Hefter, Balthasar	Ofw., Zugf. in 3./Pz. Abt. 18 + 28.7.43 at Orel (Russia) of wounds	8.10.43
Heger, Otto	Hptm. d.R., Kdr. II./Jäg. Rgt. 227	21.9.44
Heger, Rudolf	Oblt., Fhr. 4./A.R. 96 + 31.1.44 south of Cassino (Italy) as Hptm.	20.1.43
Hegewald, Rudolf	Feldw., Zugf in 5./G. R. 428	28.10.44
Hehmeyer, Hermann	Hptm., Kdr. III./G. R. 216	10.12.42
Heibel, Ernst	Uffz., Gruppenf. in G. R. 1092 + 7.4.45	17.4.45
Heichele, Josef	Hptm., Fhr. Div. Füs. Btl. (A.A.) 129 742nd Oak Leaves 17.2.45	31.1.44
Heidbrink, Wilhelm	Major d.R., Fhr. G. R. 435 + 21.9.44 at Bauske (Lithuania) as Oberstlt. d.R.	6.3.44
Heidelberg, Friedrich	Hptm., kdrt. z. Gen. St. Ausb. in Stab 336. I.D. + 13.4.44 Crimea (Russia)	14.5.44
v. d. Heiden, Walter	Hptm., Kdr. Pi. Btl. 150	11.3.45
Heidenreich, Fritz	Oblt., Beobachter in 1. (F)/Aufkl. Gr. 120 + 30.5.44 in Norway as Hptm. & Staffelkpt.	3.6.41

KNIGHT'S CROSS OF THE IRON CROSS

Heidkämper, Otto	Oberst i.G., Chef d. Gen. St. XXIV. Pz.K.	8.2.43
Heidrich, Kurt	Oblt., Chef Fhr. 5./gem. Flak-Rgt. 314 (mot.) + 9./10.3.45 at Ohlenberg/Rhein	24.10.44
Heidrich, Manfred	Oblt., Chef 2./G. R. 232 + 4.2.45	5.4.45
Heidrich, Richard	Oberst, Kdr. Fsch. Jäg. Rgt. 3 382nd Oak Leaves 5.2.44 55th Swords 25.3.44	14.6.41
Heidschmidt, Joachim	Major, Fhr. G. R. 509	27.8.44
Heidtmann, Hans	Kaptlt., Kdt. "U 559"	12.4.43
Heiduschka, Alfred	Feldw., Flugzeugf. in 3./S.G. 2 "Immelmann" + 21.3.45 at Papa airfield (Hungary) as Ofw.	8.8.44
Ritter v. Heigl, Hubert-Maria	Obstlt., Kdr. Pi. Btl. 70 (mot.)	13.1.42
Heiland, Hans	Lt., Fh-r. 5./Pz. G. R. 126	9.5.45
Heiland, Karl	Hptm., Fhr. III./G. R. 55	27.10.43
Heilbronn, Gerhard	Hptm., Fhr. II./Schtz. Rgt. 7 + 1944; posthumously promoted to Oberst	12.4.42
Heilmann, Ludwig	Major, Kdr. III./Fsch. Jäg. Rgt. 3 412th Oak Leaves 2.3.44 67th Swords 15.5.44	14.6.41
Heilmann, Nicolaus	SS-Oberf., Kdr. 15. Waffen-Gren. Div. d. SS + 28.1.45 in Russia; final post: SS-Brigadefhr. & Gen. Major d. Waffen-SS & der Polizei	23.8.44
Heilmann, Otto	Oberst, Kdr. G. R. 671	9.6.44
Heim, Ferdinand	Gen. Major., Kdr. 14. Pz.Div.	30.8.42
Heim, Herbert	Uffz., Truppf. in 1./G. R. 116	3.7.44
Heim, Walther	Hptm., Fhr. Pz.Jäg. Abt. 10 (mot.)	5.12.43
Heimann, Heinrich	SS-Hptsturmf., Kdr. SS-St. Gesch. Abt. 1 "LSSAH" + 20.8.44 at Chambois (France) as SS-Sturmbannf.	23.2.44
Hein, Gerhard	Uffz., Zugf. in 10./I.R. 209 120th Oak Leaves 6.9.42	3.9.40
Hein, Kurt	Uffz., Gesch. Fhr. in 1./Pz.Jg. abt. 12	18.12.44
Hein, Willi	SS-Obersturmf. d.R., Chef 2./SS-Pz. Rgt. 5 "Wiking"	4.5.44
Heindl, Josef	Hptm. d.R., Kdr. I./G. R. 199 "List" 328. Oak Leaves 18.11.43	9.2.43
Heindorff, Hans	Oblt., Flugzeugf. & Beobachter in Fern-Aufkl. Gruppe des Ob. d. Luftwaffe	21.10.42
Heine, Werner	Major, Kdr. I./G. R. 499	1.5.43
Heinemann, Anton	Fhj. -Feldw., Bordfunker in 1./N. J.G. 2	17.4.45
Heiner, Engelbert	Ofw., Flugzeugf. in 9./K.G. 27 "Boelcke" + 18.3.45	9.12.42
Heinke, Martin	Oblt. d.R., Chef 1./Pz. Zerst. Abt. 156	28.2.45
Heinkel, Hugo	Ofw., Zugtruppin in 15./G. R. 361 (mot.)	16.11.44

Heinrich, Herbert	Oblt., Chef 3./A.R. 267	15.3.44
Heinrich, Horst	Oblt., Fhr. 2./Geb. Pi. Btl. 83	30.12.43
Heinrich, Otto	Feldw., Flugzeugf. in 3./S. K.G. 10 + 22.5.44 shot down over the English Channel; posthumously promoted to Ofw.	20.7.44
Heinrich, Willi	Lt., Fhr. 1./Pz. Abt. Führer-Gren. Brig.	9.12.44
Heinrichs, Conrad-Oskar	Oberst, Kdr. Inf.Rgt. 24 + 8.9.44 at Lüttich (Belgium) as Gen.Lt. & Kdr. 89. Inf. Div.	13.9.41
Heinrichs, Erich	Oblt., Flugzeugf. in II./K.G. 54 + 28.5.41 west of Ireland	22.6.41
Heinrichs, Josef	Feldw., Zugf. in 2./G. R. 328	10.6.43
Heinrici, Gotthard	Gen. d. Inf, Kom.Gen. XXXXIII. A.K. 333rd Oak Leaves 24.11.43 136th Swords 3.3.45	18.9.41
Heinrici, Hans-Joachim	Hptm., Fhr. II./G. R. 431	14.2.45
Heintz, Kurt	Hptm., Staffelkpt. 9. (K.)/L.G. 1 + 21.1.44 over Südostengland	17.10.42
Heintze, Erich	Uffz., Geschützf. in 3./Flak-Rgt. 33(mot.) in DAK	7.3.42
Heinze, Horst	Oblt., Fhr. 2./Pi. Btl. 169	30.9.44
Heinze, Otto	Ofw., Zugf. in 2./Pi. Btl. 3 (mot.)	6.11.42
Heinzmann, Georg	Ofw., Zugf. in 12. (MG)/I.R. 42	3.5.42
Heise, Hanns	Hptm., Kdr. IV./K.G. 76	3.9.42
Heisel, Johannes	Oblt., Chef 2./Pz.Jäg. Abt. 161 + 24.1.45 south-east of Allenburg (East Prussia)	9.12.44
Heisterman v. Ziehlberg, Gustav	Gen.Lt., Kdr. 28. Jäger-Div. + 22.2.45 hanged in Berlin-Spandau (related to the events of 20.7.44)	27.7.44
Heitmann, Hermann	Hptm. d.R., Fhr. III./A.R. 241	15.10.42
Heitz, Walter	Gen. d. Art., Kom.Gen. VIII A.K. 156th Oak Leaves 21.12.42	4.9.40
Hektor, Albert	SS-Oberscharf., Zugf. in 7./SS-Freiw. Pz. G. R. 24 "Danmark" + 9.4.45 at Hartberg/Steiermark	23.8.44
Helbig, Joachim	Hptm., Staffelkpt. 4. (K.)/Lehr-Geschw. I 64th Oak Leaves 16.1.42 20th Swords 28.9.42	24.11.40
Held, Felix	Lt., Zugf. in 1./Ers. Btl. Luftw. Kdo. Don + 18.1.43 in Russia	3.4.43
Held, Heinrich	Ofw., Zugf. in 2./Füs. Rgt. 22	12.12.44
Heldmann, Johann	Obstlt., Kdr. G. R. 53	17.3.45
Heldt, Max	Hptm. d.R., Fhr. II./G. R. 353 + 23.12.44 south of Frauenburg (East Prussia)	16.11.44
Helemann, Heinz	Oblt. d.R., Fhr. 7./G. R. 361 (mot.)	5.9.44
Hell, Ernst-Eberhard	Gen. d. Art., Kom.Gen. VII. A.K. 487th Oak Leaves 4.6.44	1.2.43

Name	Details	Date
Heller, Richard	Ofw., Flugzeugf. in III./Z.G. 26 "Horst Wessel" + 5.4.45 shot down over Wülfingerode (Harz) as Lt. & Staffelkpt. 2./J.G. 11	21.8.41
Heller, Siegfried	Hptm., Chef 1./Pi. Btl. 371	25.7.42
v. Hellermann, Vollrath	Obstlt., Kdr. Pz. G. R. 21	21.11.42
Hellmann, Erich	Lt., Fhr. 1./Fsch. Jäg. Rgt. 3	6.10.44
Hellmann, Paul	Kapt. d. Handelsmarine, Kapt. d. Blockadebrechers Motorschiff "Osorno"	6.1.44
Hellmers, Johannes	SS-Obersturmf. d.R., Chef 6./SS-Freiw. Pz. G. R. 49 "de Ruyter"	5.3.45
Hellmich, Günther	Oblt., Fhr. 2./St. Gesch. Abt. 270	20.12.43
Hellmich, Heinz	Gen.Lt., Kdr. 243. I.D. + 17.6.44 Cherbourg (France)	2.9.44
Hellriegel, Hans-Jürgen	Kaptlt., Kdt. "U 543" + 2.7.44 in Atlantic	3.2.44
Helmer, Karl	Lt., Ord.Offz. in II./Geb.Jäg. Rgt. 13	5.11.42
Helmich, Paul	Hptm. d.R., Kdr. I./G. R. 94	4.10.44
Helmling, Hans	Hptm. d.R., Kdr. II./Gren. Rgt. 480 + 4.12.43 near Mogilew (Russia) as Major d.R.; posthumously promoted to Obstlt. d.R.	13.9.43
Helms, Götz	Major, Kdr. I./I.R. 695 + 28.7.42 at Woronesh (Russia)	14.9.42
Hemmann, Alfred	Obstlt., Kdr. I.R. 426	21.8.41
Hemmer, Hermann	Lt., Flugzeugf. in 3. (F.)/Aufkl. Gr. 122	19.9.42
Hemmer, Wilhelm	Hptm. d.R. z. V., Fhr. 2./Feldzeug-Btl. 16 + 12.7.44 as Major d.R. z. V. of wounds	18.7.43
Hemmerich, Erwin	Hptm., Kdr. Pi. Btl. 326	28.3.45
Hempel, Adolf	Hptm., Chef Stabsbttr./Flak-Lehr-Rgt. (mot.)	30.12.42
Hempel, Alfred	Lt. d.R., Btl. Fhr. beim Festg. Kdt. Kolberg (Pomerania)	30.4.45
Hendricks, Heinrich	Uffz., Pz. Fahrer in 9./Pz. Rgt. 33 + 25.11.43	26.3.43
Henger, Wolfgang	Oberst, Kdr. Art.Rgt. 21	17.3.45
Ritter v. Hengl, Georg	Obstlt., Kdr. Geb.Jäg. Rgt. 137	25.8.41
Hengst, Max	Ofw., Flugzeugf. in 2./Transp. G. 3	9.6.44
Hengstler, Friedrich	Ofw., Zugf. in 3./Geb.Jäg. Rgt. 98	12.9.41
Hengstler, Richard	Hptm., Chef 1./Fsch. St. Gesch. Brig. 12	28.4.45
Henke, Fritz	SS-Oberscharf., Zugf. in 3./SS-St. Gesch. Abt. 1 "LSSAH"	12.2.44
Henke, Fritz	Ofw., Zugf. in 4./G. R. 306	15.5.44
Henke, Günther	Lt., Zugf. in 7./Reit. Rgt. 41	6.10.44
Henke, Karl	Oberst, Kdr. Pi. Landungs-Rgt. 770 (mot.) + 27.4.45 at Pillau (East Prussia) as Gen. Major & Pi. Kdr. 4. Armee bzw. Kdr. 290. I.D.	4.8.43

Henke, Max	Stabsfeldw., Zugf. in 1./Pz. Abt. 118	26.12.44
Henke, Werner	Oblt. z. See z. V., Kdt. "U 515" 257th Oak Leaves 4.7.43	17.12.42
Henkenschuh, Hans	Feldw., Zugf. in 7./G. R. 390	10.9.44
Henle, Hermann	Hptm., Fhr. II./Werfer-Rgt. 70	19.9.43
Henne, Rudolf	Hptm., Staffelkpt. 9./K.G. 51	12.4.42
Hennecke, Walter	Konteradm., Seekommandant Normandie	26.6.44
Hennemann, Konrad	Lt., Flugzeugf. in 1./K.G. 26 + 4.7.42 in the North Sea (PQ 17)	3.9.42
Hennicke, Hermann	Obstlt., Kdr. I.R. 37 + 27.8.41 north of Smolensk (Russia)	21.8.41
Hennig, Heinrich	Ofw., Zugf. in Stabskp./Füs. Rgt. 22	9.6.44
Henning, Horst	Ofw., Flugzeugf. in 1./K.G. 77 + 7.10.44 as Oblt. & Flugzeugf. in N. J.G. 3; posthumously promoted to Hptm.	22.5.42
Hennings, Eberhard	Hptm., Staffelkpt. 1./K.G. 4 "General Wever" + 28.4.42 in Russia	14.5.42
Henrich, Walter	Obstlt., Kdr. Pz. G. R. 40 + 30.7.43 at Kovel (Russia) as Oberst of wounds	8.2.43
Henrici, Friedrich-Karl	Hptm., Kdr. II./Pz. G. R. 13 + 11.10.43 in Jannowka (Russia) as Major	14.4. 43
Henrici, Sigfrid	Gen.Lt., Kdr. 16. I.D. (mot.) 350th Oak Leaves 9.12.43	13.10.41
Hensel, Gerhard	Ofw., Zugf. in 2./Pz. Rgt. 15 + 26.1.43 in Russia	26.12.41
Hensel, Herbert	Hptm., Kdr. Pz. Füs. Btl. der Führer-Gren. Brig.	5.3.45
Henssler, Walter	Oblt. d.R., Rgt. Adj. Pz. G. R. 126	8.8.44
Hentschel, Erwin	Ofw., Bordfunker in III./Stuka-Gesch. 2 "Immelmann" + 20.3.44 in Dnjestr (Russia) ertrunken	25.11.43
Hentschel, Otto	Feldw., Zugf. in 8. (MG.)/I.R. 418 missing July 1944 as Feldw.	18.9.42
Hentschel, Otto	Hptm., stellv. Kdr. Le. Flak-Abt. 94	9.6.44
Hentschel, Walter	Oblt., Fhr. II./G. R. 1095	31.10.44
Henz, Wilhelm	Lt., Fhr. 2./Kradschtz. Btl. 29 + 30.1.43 at Stalingrad (Russia) as Hptm. & Btl. Kdr.	8.8.41
Henze, Albert	Oberst, Kdr. Pz. G. R. 110 709th Oak Leaves 21.1.45	15.1.44
Henze, Karl	Oblt., Staffelkpt. 1./Stuka-Geschw. 77 481st Oak Leaves 20.5.44	15.7.42
Henze, Richard	Major d.R., Kdr. II./I.R. 518 703rd Oak Leaves 18.1.45	2.10.42
Herb, Wilhelm	Hptm., Kdr. I./I.R. 517 + 11.9.42 in Russia of wounds	10.9.42

Name	Details	Date
Herb, Wilhelm	Obstlt. d.R., Kdr. G. R. 380	12.8.44
Herbert, Josef	Lt., Fhr. 7./G. R. 289	24.12.44
Herbst, Erhard (7)	Ofw., Zugf. in II./Fallsch. Pz. Rgt. "HG"	26.3.45
Herbst, Josef	Oblt. d.R., Fhr. II./Füs. Rgt. "GD"	30.9.43
v. Herff, Maximilian	Oberst, Fhr. Kampfgr. v. Herff (Schtz. Rgt. 115) in DAK, + 6.9.45 at Ulverstone (England) as SS-Obergruppenf. & General d. W-SS in British captivity; final post Chef des Personalamtes der W-SS	13.6.41
Herfurth, Heinz	Major, Kdr. II./G. R. 189	16.4.44
Herfurth, Otto	Oberst, Kdr. I.R. 117 + 29.9.44 hanged in Berlin (related to 20.7.1944); final post Gen. Major & Chef d. St. Wehrkreis III (Berlin)	14.9.42
Herget, Wilhelm	Hptm., Kdr. 1./N. J.G. 4 451st Oak Leaves 11.4.44	20.6.43
Herkelmann, Rudolf	Oblt. d.R., Chef 6./G. R. 426	30.4.43
Herkner, Erich	Lt., Flugzeugf. in 14. (Eis.)/K.G. 55 + 17.1.45 over Litzmannstadt	6.12.44
Herling, Wilfried	Oblt., Staffelfhr. 7./Stuka-Geschw. 2 "Immelmann" + 28.11.43 on Bolsch. Kostromka-Nord (Russia) as Staffelkpt.; posthumously promoted to Hptm.	4.4. 43
Herlt, Ernst	Hptm., Chef 9./A.R. 253	17.4.45
Hermann, Alfred	Oberst, Kdr. I.R. 3 + 4.8.42 at the Volkhov bridgehead, Kirischi (Russia)	24.9.42
Hermann, Helmut	Hptm., Kdr. I./Geb.Jäg. Rgt. 100	18.12.44
Hermann, Horst	Feldw., Flugzeugf. in 2./S.G. 2 "Immelmann"	6.12.44
Hermann, Dipl.-Ing. Karl	Oberst d.R., Kdr. Gren. Rgt. 384 (kroat.)	24.12.44
Hermes, Otmar	Gefr., Kp. Melder 6./G. R. 464	11.6.44
Hermichen, Rolf	Hptm., Kdr. I./J.G. 11 748th Oak Leaves 19.2.45	26.3.44
Herold, Walter	Obstlt., Kdr. A.R. 10 (mot.) + 28.11.44 in Russia as Kdr. 10. Pz. Gren. Div.; posthumously promoted to Gen. Major	13.10.41
Herold, Wilhelm	Hptm., Kdr. I./G. R. 21	26.3.44
Herr, Traugott	Oberst, Kdr. 13. Schtz. Brigade 110th Oak Leaves 9.8.42 117th Swords 18.12.44	2.10.41
Herrlein, Friedrich	Gen. Major, Kdr. 18. I.D. (mot.)	22.9.41
Herrmann, Benno	Oblt., Flugzeugf. in 4./K.G. 76	19.6.42
Herrmann, Ernst	Oberst, Kdr. Flak-Rgt. 25 (mot.)	18.7.44
Herrmann, Fritz	Major, Kdr. I./I.R. 36	26.12.41
Herrmann, Georg	Oblt., Fhr. I./Jäg. Rgt. 38	31.12.44
Herrmann, Hajo	Oblt., Staffelkpt. 7./K.G. 4 "General Wever" 269th Oak Leaves 2.8.43 43rd Swords 23.1.44	13.10.40

Herrmann, Harry	Oblt., Chef 5./Fsch. Jäg. Rgt. 1	9.7.41
Herrmann, Kurt	Major, Kdr. Pi. Btl. 28	26.3.44
Herrmann, Richard	Ofw., Zugf. in Stabskp./Jäg. Rgt. 49	16.1.44
Herrmann, Wilhelm-Karl	Obstlt., Kdr. G. R. 273	9.6.44
Hertel, Rüdiger	Hptm., Fhr. I./Pz. G. R. 12	28.10.44
Hertwig, Hubertus	Major, Kdr. I./Pz. G. R. 66 + 25.1.44 in Russia; posthumously promoted to Obstlt.	5.1.44
Hertz, Gustav	Major, Kdr. I./A.R. 258	29.9.40
Hertzsch, Fritz	Oberst, Kdr. I.R. 77 + 15.7.41 in Russia; posthumously promoted to Gen. Major	8.8.41
Herwig, Hans-Erich	Oblt. d.R., Chef 7./G. R. 511	25.1.43
Herzbach, Max	Hptm., Chef 7./Fsch. Jäg. Rgt. 7	13.9.44
Herzer, Heinz	Ofw., Pi. -Zugfhr. in 10./S. R. 25 + 7.9.44	21.8.41
Herzig, Friedrich (7)	SS-Sturmbannf, Kdr. s. SS-Pz. Abt. 503 in III. (germ.) SS-Pz. Korps	29.4.45
Herzog, Hans-Georg	Major d.R., Kdr. II./Pz. G. R. 14 798th Oak Leaves 23.3.45	6.4.44
Herzog, Karl	Obstlt., Kdr. He. Sturm-Pi. Brig. 627 (mot.) simultaneously promoted to Oberst	17.4.45
Herzog, Kurt	Gen.Lt., Kdr. 291. I.D. 694th Oak Leaves 12.1.45	18.10.41
Herzog, Otto	SA-Obergruppenf., Führer der Volkssturm-Einheiten in Festung Breslau & Fhr. of a Kampfgr. in Festung Breslau + 6.5.45 during breakout attempt in Breslau	15.4.45
Hess, Ernst	Oblt., Fhr. 4./le. Flak-Abt. 192 (v) 19.6.44 Elba posted missing	30.9.44
Heß, Hans-Georg	Oblt. z. See d.R., Kdt. "U 995"	11.2.45
Hesse, Georg	Major, Fhr. III./I.R. 120 (mot.) + 22.9.42 north of Stalingrad (Russia) as Kdr. Kradsch. Btl. 160	31.12.41
Hesse, Heinrich	Oblt. d.R., Fhr. 1./G. R. 366	10.9.44
Hesse, Joachim	Oberst, Kdr. Pz. G. R. 64	6.4.44
Hesse, Rudolf	Lt., Fhr. 2./G. R. 165	9.5.45
Hessinger, Franz	Oblt., Flugzeugf. in 2. (F.)/Aufkl. Gruppe 123	8.8.44
Hessler, Günter	Kaptlt., Kdt. "U 107"	24.6.41
Hethey, Emil	Major, Kdr. Kampfgr. "Hethey" in Festung Küstrin	14.4. 45
Hettinger, Franz	Ofw., Bordfunker & Fliegerschütze in Stabsstaffel/S.G. 77	27.7.44
Hetzel, Ernst (17)	Major in Stab K.G. 100	20.4.45
Hetzenauer, Matthäus	Gefr., Scharfschütze in 7./G. J. R. 144	17.4.45
Heubeck, Konrad	SS-Untersturmf, Fhr. 1./SS-Pz. Rgt. 1 "LSSAH"	17.4.45

Name	Details	Date
Heubuch, Otto	Oberjäger, Geschützf in 16./Geb.Jäg. Rgt. 13 + 12.5.44 on Dnjestr at Griguripol (Russia)	8.2.44
Heuer, Heinz (8)	Ofw. (Feldgend.) in Kampfgr. z.b.V. Berlin 5 simultaneously promoted to Lt.	22.4.45
Heuer, Robert	Oblt., Flugzeugf. in 4. (Fl.)/Aufkl. Gr. 14	5.4.44
Heun, Wilhelm	Gen. Major, Kdr. 83. I.D.	9.12.44
Heuß, Conrad	Hptm., Fhr. II./I.R. 109 + March 1945 at Danzig as Oberstlt. & Kdr. Füs. Rgt. 34	27.3.42
Heute, Wilhelm	Oblt., Staffelkpt. in III./K.G. 54 + 3.7.44 in France as Hptm.	5.2.44
Heutling, Helmut	Uffz., Richtschtz. in 9. (I. G.)/Pz. G. R. 59	22.8.43
v. Heydebreck, Georg-Henning	Oberst, Kdr. Fsch. Pz. Rgt. 1 "HG"	25.6.44
Heydemann, Günther	Kaptlt., Kdt. "U 575"	3.7.43
Frhr. v. d. Heydte, Dr. jur. Dr. rer. pol. Friedr. -August	Hptm., Kdr. I./Fsch. Jäg. Rgt. 3 617th Oak Leaves	9.7.41 30.9.44
Heyduck, Werner	Oblt., Chef 1./G. R. 44 + May 1945 in Mecklenburg as Hptm.	3.3.45
Heye, Hellmuth	Kapt. z. See, Kdt. Schwerer Kreuzer "Admiral Hipper"	18.1.41
Heyen, Johann	Oblt. d.R., Chef 4. (MG.)/G. R. 377	27.8.44
Heyer, Hans-Joachim	Lt., Flugzeugf. in IR./J.G. 54 + 9.11.42 shot down over Leningrad	25.11.42
Baron v. Heyking, Ernst-Georg	Rittm., Kdr. III./G. R. 15 (mot.)	6.4.44
Heymann, Otto	Lt., Fhr. 8./Pz. Rgt. 31	17.3.45
Heymer, Otto	Major, Staffelkpt. 2. (H)/Aufkl. Gr. 14 + 25.2.43 in Russia as Oberst i.G. & Chef d. St. eines Luftw. Kdo. in Osten	13.4.41
Heyn, Alfred	Lt. d.R., Zugf. in 7./G. R. 267	12.8.44
Heyne, Hans-Walter	Oberst, Kdr. Art.Rgt. 182	16.4.43
Heynsen, Rudolf	Korv. Kpt. d.R. z. V., Chef 27. Minensuchflottille	20.4.45
Heyrowsky, Herbert	Rittm., Kdr. Radf. Abt. 248 + 4.7.42 at Stary Oskol on Don (Russia)	14.9.42
Heyse, Ulrich	Kaptlt., Kdt. "U 128"	21.1.43
Heyser, Kurt	Oberst, Kdr. I.R. 47	26.5.40
Hieber, Karl	Hptm., Fhr. I./I.R. 522 + 18.1.43 as Major & Btl. Kdr.	20.2.42
Hielscher, Otto	Oblt., Chef 5./A.R. 168	23.8.44
Hildebrand, Walter	Hptm., Flugzeugf. in 3./K.G. 26 + 21.10.43 shot down over the Mediterranean area	5.4.44

Name	Details	Date
Hilgermann, Dr. med. vet. Klaus	Oblt., Chef 13. (I. G.)/I.R. 422 641st Oak Leaves 29.10.44	8.10.42
Hilgendorff, Kurt	Obstlt., Kdr. G. R. 3	5.4.44
Hilgers, Wilhelm	Lt., Fhr. 6./Sturm-Rgt. 215 + 11.7.43 south of Orel (Russia)	31.7.43
Hille, Alfred	Hptm. d.R., Fhr. of a Kampfgr. in V. SS-Geb. Korps (Kdr. I./Fhj. G. R. 1237)	21.4.45
Hille, August	Lt. d.R., Fhr. 6./Pz. G. R. 33	9.6.44
Hillebrand, Franz	Oberjäger, Gruppenf. in 1./Geb.Jäg. Btl. 94 + 8.1.44 east of Winniza (Russia)	5.4.44
Hilpert, Carl	Gen.D.Inf., Kom.Gen. LIV. A.K. 542nd Oak Leaves 8.8.44	22.8.43
Hilheimer, Richard	Major d.R., Kdr. I./A.R. 20 (mot.)	28.11.43
Hilss, Willi	Uffz., Geschützf. in Pz.Jäg. Abt. 46	19.1.41
Hilt, Günther	Oblt. d.R., Fhr. 7./Jäg. Rgt. 56 386th Oak Leaves 8.2.44	14.9.42
Hiltensperger, Gottfried	Feldw., Zugf. in 4. (MG.)/G. R. 190	18.2.45
Himmelskamp, Bernhard	Obgefr., Richtschtz. in 4./Pz. Rgt. 35 + 28.8.43 south of Orel (Russia) of wounds	13.9.43
Hindelang, Hans	Ofw., Zugf. in 14. (Pz.Jäg.)/I.R. "GD" (mot.)	4.9.40
Hinerasky, Wilhelm	Obstlt., Kdr. G. R. 528 22.6.44 missing at Witebsk (Russia) as Oberst	23.12.43
Hinkelbein, Claus	Hptm., Kdr. II./K.G. 30	14.6.40
Hinkes, Heinz	Hptm., Flugzeugf. & Techn. Offz. in IV./Transp. Geschw. 4	20.4.44
Hinrichs, Ernst	Oblt., Flugzeugf. in 2./K.G. 51	25.7.42
Hintz, Erwin	Obgefr., Kdt. e. SPW in 8./s. Pz. G. R. 6 (gep.)	11.3.45
Hintz, Johannes	Oberstlt., Kdr. Flak-Rgt. 101 (mot.) simultaneously promoted to Oberst ; + 14.5.44 in Paris (France), as a result of a motor vehicle accident, as Kom.Gen. III./Flak-Korps; posthumously promoted to Gen.Lt.	29.7.40
Hintz, Kurt	Hptm., Kdr. I./Flak-Rgt. 40 (mot.)	6.2.45
Hintze, Ingfried	Hptm., Kdr. I./Pz. A.R. 103	20.10.44
Hintze, Otto	Oblt., Staffelkpt. 3./E-Gruppe 210 (J.G.)	24.11.40
Hinz, Bruno	SS-Untersturmf., Fhr. 2./SS-Pz. G. R. 10 "Westland" 559th Oak Leaves 23.8.44	2.12.43
Hippel, Ferdinand	Oberst, Kdr. G. R. 253	22.10.43
v. Hippel, Walter	Oberstlt., Kdr. Flak-Rgt. 102 (mot.) simultaneously promoted to Oberst	29.7.40
Hippler, Gustav	Oblt. d.R., Fhr. 5./I.R. 74 (mot.) + 22.8.42 in Russia as Hptm. d.R. & Btl. Kdr. of wounds	4.9.40
Hirn, Johannes	Oblt., Flugzeugf. in Nahaufkl. Gr. 32	7.4.45

KNIGHT'S CROSS OF THE IRON CROSS

Hirning, Hans	SS-Rottenf, Granatwerfertruppf. I.D. 6./SS-Totenkopf-Inf. -Rgt. 1 + 30.4.45 at Dürnholz (Czechoslovakia) as SS-Oberscharf. & Zugfhr. in Kampfgr. Böhmen-Mähren	23.10.42
Hirsch, Karl	Feldw., Zugf. in 3./Schtz. Rgt. 4 + 3.12.41 at Jasikowo/Moskau (Russia)	18.10.41
Hirschfeld, Ernst-Erich	Oblt., Flugzeugf. in 5./J.G. 300 + 28.7.44 at Erfurt (Thür.) as Staffelkpt.	24.10.44
v. Hirschfeld, Harald	Oblt., Chef 7./Geb.Jäg. Rgt. 98 164th Oak Leaves 23.12.42	15.11.41
Hirschmann, Ludwig	Lt. in 11./A.R. 29 (mot.)	19.1.43
Hißbach, Heinz-Horst	Hptm., Kdr. II./N. J.G. 2 + 14.4. 45 shot down over Gelnhausen (Hessen)	15.4.45
Hißmann, Josef	Major, Kdr. Heeres-Fla. -Btl. 617	13.5.43
Hitschhold, Hubertus	Hptm., Kdr. I./Stuka-Geschw. 2 "Immelmann" 57th Oak Leaves 31.12.41	21.7.40
Hitter, Alfons	Oberst, Kdr. A.R. 178 488th Oak Leaves 4.6.44	14.12.41
Hitz, Günter	Hptm., Staffelkpt. 2./Stuka-Geschw. 77 + 11.4.44 at Chodaczkow (Russia)	22.11.43
Hitzfeld, Otto	Obstlt., Kdr. I.R. 213 65th Oak Leaves 17.1.42 158th Swords 9.5.45	30.10.41
Hlauschka, Johann	Uffz., Gruppenf. in 3./G. R. 462	3.4.43
v. Hobe, Cord	Obstlt., Fhr. of a Kampfgr. XIII. SS-A.K.	9.5.45
Hoch, Johann	Uffz., Zugf. in 9./G. R. 1070	17.9.44
Hochbaum, Friedrich	Gen.Lt., Kdr. 34. I.D. 486th Oak Leaves 4.6.44	22.8.43
Hochgartz, Günther	Hptm., Fhr. II./G. R. 187	15.4.44
Hocke, Franz-Rainer	Obergefr., Gruppenfhr. in 7./G. R. 200 (mot.) + 20.10.44 in Italy	5.11.44
Hockenjos, Fritz	Hptm. d.R., stellv. Fhr. II./G. R. 380	2.9.44
Hodurek, Herbert	Hptm., Fhr. III./Geb.Jäg. Rgt. 144	15.4.44
Höcker, Hanskurt	Gen.Lt., Kdr. 258. I.D.	14.4. 43
Hoeckner, Walter	Hptm., Kdr. I./J.G. 4 + 25.8.44 Ziegenhain (Hessen) in an accident, as Major	6.4.44
Hoefeld, Robert	Oblt., Fhr. 4./Fsch. Jäg. Rgt. 5	18.5.43
Höfemeier, Heinrich	Ofw., Flugzeugf. in 1./J.G. 51 "Mölders" + 7.8.43 shot down over Karatschew (Russia) as Lt. & Staffelfbr. 3./J.G. 51 "Mölders"	5.4.42
Höfer, Dirk	Hptm., Kdr. Pi. Btl. 256	14.4. 45
Höfer, Heinrich	Hptm., Kdr. II./K.G. 55 656th Oak Leaves 18.11.44	3.9.43
Höfl, Hugo	Gen.Lt., Kdr. 206. I.D.	4.12.41
Höflinger, Karl	Lt. d.R., Flugzeugf. in 9./K.G. 77 + 18.4.41 over England	7.3.41

ELITE OF THE THIRD REICH

Högl, Franz-Josef	Major, Kdr. Pz. Pi. Btl. 220	26.11.44
Höhle, Karl	Major, Kdr. III./G. R. 378	11.3.45
Höhne, Friedrich	Hptm., Kdr. III./Jäger-Rgt. 204 253rd Oak Leaves 8.6.43	3.5.42
Höhne, Georg	Major, Fhr. Pz. G. R. 26 + 19.2.45	18.2.45
Höhne, Gustav	Gen. Major, Kdr. 8. I.D. 238th Oak Leaves 17.5.43	30.6.41
Höhne, Otto	Obstlt., Kmdr. K.G. 54	5.9.40
Höhne, Helmut	Lt., Zugf. in schw. Pz. Abt. 510	9.12.44
Höke, Stefan-Heinrich	Obstlt., Kdr. G. R. 18 + 28.6.44 at Bobruisk (Russia) as Oberst	28.7.43
Hölter, Hermann (16)	Gen.Lt., Chef Gen. Stab 20. Gebirgs-Armee	3.5.45
Hölz, Johannes	Oberst i.G., Chef d. Gen. St. LV. A.K. + 29.4.45 on the Elbe as Gen. Major & Chef d. Gen. St. A.O.K. 9	10.10.44
Hölz, Walter	Hptm., Kdr. III./Geb.Jäg. Rgt. 98	26.12.44
Hölzerkopf, Arnulf	Korv. Kpt., Chef 8. Minensuchflottille + 11.8.44 at the mouth of the Gironde (France); posthumously promoted to Fregattenkapt.	15.5.44
Hölzl, Hans	Hptm., kdrt. z. Gen. Stabsausbildg. beim VI. A.K. & Fhr. a Kampfgr. + 26.12.43 in Russia	23.2.44
Hoene, Karl-Friedrich	Lt. d.R., Fhr. 5./G. R. 755	26.11.44
Höner, Werner	Uffz., Gruppenf. in 2./Pi. Btl. 245 + 5.9.44 in France	30.9.44
Hönig, Justin	Feldw., Zugf. in 3./Pz. G. R. 41	18.2.45
Hönniger, Theodor	Ofw., Zugf. in 3./Pz. Rgt. 25	9.5.45
Graf von & zu Hoensbroech, Ignaz	Hptm., Kdr. II./Pz. G. R. 4	4.6.44
Hönscheid, Hanns	Ofw., Kriegsberichterstatter der Fallschirmtr.	12.3.45
Höper, Ahrend	Lt. d.R., Zugf. in 1./St. Gesch. Brig. 202	26.11.44
Hoepner, Erich	Gen. d. Kav., Kom.Gen. XVI. A.K. + 8.8.44 hanged in Berlin-Plötzensee (related to 20.7.44); final post Gen. Oberst & OB Pz. Gr. 4 (4. Pz. Armee) until winter 1941/42	27.10.39
Hoering, Johann	Oblt., Chef 2./St. Gesch. Brig. 277 + 19.10.44 at Schloßberg (East Prussia) as Hptm.	8.8.44
Hörl, Ludwig	Oberst, Kdr. Geb.Jäger-Rgt. 91	6.4.44
Hörner, Willi	Lt., Staffelkpt. 9./Stuka-Geschw. 2 "Immelmann" + 21.7.43 at Lomowez, near Orel (Russia) as Oblt. & Staffelkpt. 7./Stuka-Geschw. 2	10.5.43
Hörnicke, Werner	SS-Sturmbannf. d.R., Kdr. I./SS-G. R. 10 (mot.) in 1. SS-Inf. Brigade (mot.)	1.12.43

Hörning, Reinhard	Hptm. d.R., Kdr. I./G. R. 546 + 17.10.42 in Russia; posthumously promoted to Major d.R.	22.8.43
Hoernlein, Walter	Oberst, Kdr. Inf.Rgt. 80 213th Oak Leaves 15.3.43	30.7.41
Hörstermann, Johann	Major, Kdr. Kampfgr. G. R. 473	28.3.45
Hörwick, Anton	Ofw., Flugzeugf. in 7./N. J.G. 2 19.2.45 posted missing near Posen	8.8.44
v. Hößlein, Hartmut	Hptm., Kdr. II./A.R. 7	17.4.45
v. Hößlin, Roland	Hptm., Fhr. Pz. Aufkl. Abt. 33 + 13.10.44 as Major hanged(relating to 20.7.44)	23.7.42
Hoeth, Hans-Lothar	Hptm., Kdr. I./G. R. 311	6.4.44
Hofbauer, Franz	Feldw., Zugf. in 3./Div. Füs. Btl. 72	20.1.44
Hofbauer, Karl	Hptm., Fhr. I./I.R. 154	7.8.42
Hofer, Karl	Uffz., Zugf. in 3./Pz.Jäg. Abt. 49	26.10.43
Hofer, Lothar	SS-Sturmbannf, Kdr. III./SS-A.R. 54 "Nederland"	5.4.45
Hoff, Carl	Kaptlt., Chef 1. Areabootsflottille	6.5.45
Hoffend, Jakob (1)	Volkssturmmann, Feuerwerker & Bombenräumer in Luftgau VI, Köln	7.2.45
v. Hoffer, Herbert	Lt., Staffelfhr. in 5./S.G. 77	8.8.44
Hoffmann, Albert	Obgefr., MG. -Schtz. in 4./Kradschtz. Btl. 55	3.4.43
Hoffmann, Ernst	Hptm. d.R., Chef 2./G. R. 698	4.5.44
Hoffmann, Ernst-Wilhelm	Major, Chef I./Schtz. Rgt. 12 494th Oak Leaves 9.6.44	4.9.40
Hoffmann, Gerhard	Fhj. -Feldw., Flugzeugf. in 4./J.G. 52 + 17.4.45 shot down over Breslau as Lt. & Staffelfhr. 11./J.G. 52	14.5.44
Hoffmann, Heinrich	Ofw., Flugzeugf. in 12./J.G. 51 36th Oak Leaves 19.10.41	12.8.41
Hoffmann, Heinrich	Korv. Kpt., Chef 5. Torpedobootsflottille 524th Oak Leaves 11.7.44	7.6.44
Hoffmann, Heinz-Joachim	Major, Kdr. III./I.R. 44	15.4.42
Hoffmann, Herbert	Ofw., Fhr. 7./G. R. 426	15.4.44
Hoffmann, Dipl.-Ing. Kuno	Hptm., Kdr. I./(K)L.G. 1 + 25.1.44 in Berlin as Major & Abt. Chef in R.L.M.	14.6.41
Hoffmann, Kurt	Feldw., Zugf. in 3. (mot.)/Pi. Btl. 28 + 20.3.42 as Lt. in Russia	8.6.40
Hoffmann, Kurt-Caesar	Kapt. z. See, Kdt. Schlachtschiff "Scharnhorst"	21.3.42
Hoffmann, Ludwig (19)	SS-Hptsturmfhr., Fhr. III./SS-Pz. Gr. Rgt. 23 "Norge"	11.5.45
Hoffmann, Otto	Oblt., Fhr. 3./St. Gesch. Brig. 901 + 5.3.44 Nowo Archangelsk (Russia) as Hptm. & Kdr. St. Gesch. Abt. 911	31.7.42

ELITE OF THE THIRD REICH

Hoffmann, Paul	Ofw., Fhr. Pi. Zug in Stabskp./G. R. 211	2.3.44
Hoffmann, Reinhold	Lt., Flugzeugf. in 6./J.G. 54 + 24.5.44 at Friesack (Mark Brandenburg) during a forced landing	28.1.45
Hoffmann, Walter	Lt., Flugzeugf. in 8./S.G. 1	16.6.44
Hoffmann, Werner	Hptm., Kdr. I/N. J.G. 5	4.5.44
Hoffmann, Werner	Hptm., Staffelkpt. I./S.G. 1 + 7.2.45 at Frankfurt/Oder	8.8.44
Hoffmann-Schönborn, Günther	Major, Kdr. St. Gesch. Abt. 191 49th Oak Leaves 31.12.41	14.5.41
Hoffmann v. Waldau, Otto	Gen.Lt., Fliegerführer Afrika + 17.5.43 Balkans in an accident, as Gen. d. Flieger & Befehlsh. des Luftw. Kdo. Südost	28.6.42
Hoffmeister, Edmund	Gen. Major. Kdr. 383. I.D. + 1947 hanged in Soviet. captivity in Kiev (Russia), final post Gen.Lt. & K.G. XXXXI. Pz.K.	6.10.43
Hoffmeister, Heinrich	Major, Fhr. G. R. 915	31.1.45
Hoffmeister, Henning	Major, stellv. Fhr. G. R. 6	30.9.44
Hoffritz, Hans	Feldw., Zugf. in 14. (Pz.Jäg.)/I.R. 268	4.9.41
Hofmann, Adolf	Oblt., Chef 6./Geb.Jäg. Rgt. 100 + 18.1.43 in Russia as Hptm. & Btl. Kdr.	15.11.41
Hofmann, Bernhard	Major d.R., Kdr. I./I.R. 427	26.9.42
Hofmann, Horst	Obersteuerm., Steuermann & Wachoffz. auf "U 672"	20.5.44
Hofmann, Karl-Joachim	Hptm., Fhr. I./Pz. G. R. 108	4.7.44
Hofmann, Karl-Wihelm	Lt., Flugzeugf. in 8./J.G. 26 "Schlageter" + 26.3.45 over Bissel (Oldenburg) as Oblt. & Staffelkpt. 5./J.G. 26	24.10.44
Hofmann, Paul	Lt., Fhr. 6./G. R. 352	9.5.45
Hofmann, Rudolf	Gen.D.Inf., Chef d. Gen. St. OB. Nord	7.5.45
Hofmann, Willy	Ofw., Flugzeugfhr. in 2./Nahaufkl. Gr. 5	12.3.45
Hofsäss, Richard	Hptm., Staffelkpt. 1./Nahaufkl. Gruppe 2	9.1.45
Hogeback, Hermann	Oblt., Staffelkpt. 9. (K)/L.G. 1 192nd Oak Leaves 19.2.43 125th Swords 26.1.45	8.9.41
Hogrebe, Heinrich	Oblt. d.R., Chef 5./I.R. 422 454th Oak Leaves 13.4.44	17.8.42
Hohagen, Erich	Oblt., Staffelkpt. 4./J.G. 51	5.10.41
Hohen-Hinnebusch, Werner	Lt., Fhr. 3. (gem.)/Flak-Abt. 442	11.2.45
Hohenhausen, Richard	Oblt. d.R., Chef 2./St. Gesch. Abt. 184	11.5.42
Frhr. v. Hohenhausen & Hochhaus, Oskar (4)	Obstlt., Kdr. Pz. G. R. 9	11.5.45
Hohmann, Hans	Oblt. d.R., Fhr. I./Pz. Rgt. 31 + 21.1.45	5.3.45
Hohmeier, Heinrich	Fw., Zugfhr. in Stabs Kp./G. R. 994	9.5.45

Name	Details	Date
Hohmuth, Walter	Ofw., Fhr. 7./Pz. G. R. 6	14.5.44
Hohn, Dr. rer. pol. Hermann	Oberst, stv. Fhr. 72. Inf. Div. 410th Oak Leaves 1.3.44 109th Swords 31.10.44	28.11.43
Hohoff, Alfred	Hptm., Kdr. II./G. R. 1084	10.2.45
Hoinka, Alfred	Hptm., Fhr. Pz. Zerst. Abt. 156 + early February 1945 at Breitenstein/East Prussia	11.3.45
Hollaender, Walter	Obstlt., Kdr. Sturm-Rgt. 195	18.7.43
Holle, Alexander	Oberst, Fliegerführer Nord	23.12.42
Holle, Georg	Oblt., Staffelfhr. 2./K.G. 51 + 27.2.43 at Polltodeiskoje (near Rostov/Russia) as Hptm.	3.4.43
Hollekamp, Josef	Obgefr., Gruppenfhr. in 2. (Radf.)/Aufkl. Abt. 36	23.7.43
Hollenweger, Heinrich	Oblt., Chef 8./Pz. G. R. 108 + 4.1.43 Stalingrad (Russia) accidentally	1.11.42
Holler, Alfred	Major, stellv. Fhr. G. R. 426 + 19.9.44 Mirki, near Wenden (Baltic) as Fhr. G. R. 424	5.4.44
Hollermeier, Josef	Major, Fhr. Gr. Rgt. 1213 + 4.12.44 at the Siegoldsheimer Höhe at Colmar; posthumously promoted to Obstlt.	9.5.45
Hollidt, Karl-Adolf	Gen.Lt., Kdr. 50. I.D. 239rd Oak Leaves 17.5.43	8.9.41
Hollmann, Ernst	Hptm. d.R., Kdr. II./G. R. 1221	9.5.45
Holm, Max	Owm., St. Gesch. Kdt. in II./Pz. Rgt. Fhr. Begl. Div.	19.1.45
Holm, Norbert	Oberst, Kdr. Inf.Rgt. 156 (mot.)	20.12.41
Holst, Waldemar	Korv. Kpt., Chef 4. Räumbootsflottoille	3.12.42
Holste, Rudolf	Oberst, Kdr. A.R. 73 561st Oak Leaves 27.8.44	6.4.42
Holstein, Johann	Obgefr., Melder in 2./G. R. 698	16.10.44
Holte, Josef	SS-Oberscharf. d.R., Zugf. in 2./SS-Pz. Rgt. 9 "Hohenstaufen" + 20.8.44 at Livarot north of Laigle (France)	27.8.44
Holz, August	Feldw., Zugf. in 7./G. R. 16	18.12.44
Holz, Günther	Rittm. d.R., Chef 3./Pz.Jäger-Abt. 258	6.4.43
Holz, Hermann	Ofw., Fhr. 3./G. R. 9	14.4. 45
Holzapfel, Egon	Oblt. d.R., Rgt. Adj. G. R. 2	14.8.43
Holzapfel, Hans	Ofw., Zugf. in 11./G. R. 316	6.4.44
Holzapfel, Karl-Heinz	Hptm., Kdr. Pi. Btl. 29 (mot.)	11.9.43
Holzer, Friedrich	SS-Hptsturmf., Chef 1./SS-Pz. Rgt. 2 "Das Reich"	10.12.43
Holzhäuer, Fritz	Major, Kdr. III./Pz. Rgt. 29	6.8.41
Holzinger, Anton	Major, Kdr. I./Geb.Jäg. Rgt. 138	11.1.41
Holzinger, Franz	Lt. d.R., Zugf. in 1./Geb. Pz. -Jäger-Abt. 95	13.4.44
Holzmann, Leopold	Hptm., Kdr. I./G. R. 1059	16.11.44

Hombitzer, Walter	Hptm., Kdr. III./Volks-Artilleriekorps 405	30.4.45
Homburg, Heinrich	Hptm., Fhr. II./Jäg. Rgt. 83 + 23.3.45 at Balga (East Prussia)	25.7.44
v. Homeyer, Friedrich	Rittm., Fhr. gem. Aufkl. Kp. 580 in 90. le. Afrika-Div. + 3.7.42 at El Alamein (North Africa)	6.7.42
Homuth, Gerhard	Oblt., Staffelkpt. 3./J.G. 27 + 3.9.43 at Orel as Major & Kdr. I./J.G. 54	14.6.41
Honnefeller, Günter	Lt., Staffelfhr. 7./S.G. 10	17.10.44
Honsberg, Werner	Ofw., Flugzeugf. in 1./S.G. 77	20.7.44
Hopf, Theodor	Oblt., Chef 1. (Radf.)/I.R. 170	21.9.41
Hopf, Willi	Obgefr., Gruppenfhr. in 5./Schnelle Abt. 123	15.1.43
Hoppe, Gerhard	Uffz., Vorgesch. Beob. 9./A.R. 81	4.7.44
Hoppe, Gerhard	Major, Kdr. St. Gesch. Brig. 279 + 18.10.44 at Debilai east of Schloßbach (East Prussia)	29.11.44
Hoppe, Hans	Major, Kdr. II./Flak-Rgt. 46 (mot.)	9.5.45
Hoppe, Harry	Oberst, Kdr. Inf.Rgt. 424 682nd Oak Leaves 18.12.44	12.9.41
Hoppe, Johannes	Obstlt., Fhr. Pz. G. R. 12 + 26.1.44 in Russia as Oberst	26.10.43
Hoppe, Wolf-Horst	Major, Kdr. s. Pz.Jäg. Abt. 519	15.7.44
Horak, Erich	Ofw., Zugf. in 6./Füs. Rgt. 68	24.9.43
Horlbeck, Max	Major, Kdr. II./G. R. 435 + 26.3.45 at Gotenhafen	12.8.44
Hormann, Hans	Ofw., Beob. in 1./K.G. 100	5.12.43
Horn, Gerhard	Owm., Zugf. in 2. (Radf.)/Div. Füs. Btl. (A.A.) 218	23.8.44
Horn, Karl	Lt., Fhr. 6./G. R. 587 + 24.8.44 posted missing as Oblt.	10.2.44
Hornung, Walter	Major, Kdr. III./T. G. 2	9.6.44
Horten, Herbert	Lt. d.R., Chef 12./Art.Rgt. 81	2.9.43
Hortian, Kurt	Obstlt., Kdr. Flak-Rgt. 133 (mot.)	18.11.41
Hortmeyer, Siegfried	Oblt., Kp. Chef in G. R. 130	14.2.45
Hoßbach, Friedrich	Oberst, Kdr. Inf.Rgt. 82 298th Oak Leaves 11.9.43	7.10.40
Hoßfeld, Hans	Kaptlt. (MA), Kdr. Marine-Art. Abt. 531 659th Oak Leaves 25.11.44	6.10.44
Hoth, Hermann	Gen.D.Inf., Kom.Gen. XV. A.K. 25th Oak Leaves 17.7.41 35th Swords 15.9.43	27.10.39
Hotzy, Theodor	Wachtm., Zugf. in 3./Div. Füs. Btl. (A.A.) 7	9.6.44
van Houten, Rudolf	Ofw., Fhr. 1./Feld-Ers. Btl. 1 (56. I.D.)	5.4.45
Hoyer, Adolf	Oblt. d.R., Chef 4./Pz. Aufkl. Abt. 120 + 4.11.43 on western outskirts of Kiev (Russia) as Hptm. d.R.	8.10.43

KNIGHT'S CROSS OF THE IRON CROSS

Hoyer, Ludwig	Hptm. d.R., Kdr. III./G. R. 278 23.6.44 posted missing as Major d.R.	23.2.44
Hozzel, Paul-Werner	Hptm., Kdr. I./Stuka-Geschw. 1 230th Oak Leaves 14.4. 43	8.5.40
Hrabak, Dietrich	Hptm., Kdr. II./J.G. 54 337th Oak Leaves 25.11.43	21.10.40
Hrdlicka, Franz	Hptm., Staffelkpt. 5./J.G. 77 + 25.3.45 at Betzenrod (Hessen) as Kdr. I./J.G. 2 "Richthofen"	9.8.44
Hrustak, Martin	Ofw., Zugf. in 7./G. R. 162 473rd Oak Leaves 14.5.44	11.12.43
Hube, Hans	Gen. Major, Kdr. 16. Pz.Div. 62. Oak Leaves 16.1.42 22. Swords 21.12.42 13. Diamonds 20.4.44	1.8.41
Huber, Gustav	Hptm., Kdr. I./A.R. 115	26.11.44
Huber, Josef	Ofw., Flugzeugf. in 8./S.G. 77	20.7.44
Huber, Karl	Feldw., Stoßtruppf. in Aufkl. Abt 20 (mot.)	30.7.40
Huber, Siegfried	Ofw., Flugzeugf. in 7./Stuka-G. 2 "Immelmann" + 19.1.43 at Nowoposkow (Russia)	3.4.43
Ritter v. Hubicki, Dr. jur. Alfred	Gen.Lt., Kdr. 9. Pz.Div.	20.4.41
Hudel, Helmut	Hptm., Chef 1./Pz. Rgt. 7 219th Oak Leaves 2.4.43	27.5.42
Hübbe, Karl	Hptm., Kdr. I./G. R. 270 + 19.7.44 in Russia; posthumously promoted to Obstlt.	31.3.43
Hübner, Alois	Ofw., Zugf. in I./Pz. G. R. 129 + 23.9.44 in NW Europe	5.12.43
Huebner, Arnold	Gefr., Richtkan. in 3./Flak-Rgt. 33 (mot.) in DAK	7.3.42
Hübner, Eduard	Hptm., Kdr. Sturmbtl. Fallsch. A.O.K. 1	17.3.45
Hübner, Ekhard	Lt., Flugzeugf. in III./J.G. 3 "Udet" + 28.3.42 on Lake Ilmen at Staraja Russa (Russia)	3.5.42
Hübner, Ernst-August	Hptm., Chef 12. (MG.)/G. R. 122 + 7.11.43 'Tartar Wall' at Perekop, Crimea (Russia)	9.12.43
Hübner, Herbert	Feldw., Zugf. in 1./Pz.Jäg. Abt. 171	28.10.44
Hübner, Dr. med. dent. Rudolf	Gen. Major, Fhr. G. R. 529	9.3.45
Hübner, Walter	Uffz., V. B. in 3./A.R. 28	18.2.45
Hübner, Wilhelm	Lt., Flugzeugf. in Stabsstaffel/J.G. 51 "Mölders" + 7.4.45 by a direct hit from flak over Neukuhren (East Prussia) as Staffelfhr.	28.2.45
Hübsch, Anton	Ofw., Flugzeugf. in 2./S.G. 2 "Immelmann"	8.8.44
Hübscher, Erich	Uffz., Gruppenf. in 7./G. R. 914	23.8.44
Hückel, Ernst-Albrecht	Hptm., Kdr. Pz. Pi. Btl. "GD"	27.9.43

Hüfing, Hermann	Feldw., Zugf. in 8./G. R. 1076 + 15.1.45	23.10.44
Hühner, Werner	Gen.Lt., Kdr. 61. I.D.	18.4.43
Hüls, Dr. med. Heinrich	Oberarzt, Hilfsarzt in II./Pz. Rgt. 11 + 16.8.44 at Raseinen (East Prussia)	21.9.44
Hülsmann, Bernhard	Uffz., Geschützf. in 8./Flak-Rgt. 4 (mot.) + April 1945 as Lt.	22.1.43
v. Hülst, Dr. rer. pol. Hans-Franz	Major d.R., Fhr. Gren. Rgt. 378	9.2.43
Hümmerich, Willi	Lt. d.R., Zugf. in 14. (Pz.Jäg.)/I.R. 80	18.10.41
Hünemörder, Otto	Uffz., Geschützf. in 14. (Pz.Jäg.)/I.R. 309	16.4.43
v. Hünersdorff, Walther	Oberst, Kdr. Pz. Rgt. 11 259th Oak Leaves 14.7.43	22.12.42
Hünger, Georg	Oblt., Fhr. I./Pz. G. R. 26 + 26.8.44	6.10.44
Hüttebräucker, Hermann (12)	Hptm., Lehrer a. d. Panzertruppenschule Milowitz at Prag	6.5.45
Hütten, Karl	Hptm. d.R., Staffelkpt. 5. (F)/Aufkl. Gr. 122	24.10.44
Hütten, Theodor	Oblt., Fhr. Div. Versorg. Kolonne 349. I.D.	14.4. 45
Hüttner, Hans	Oberst, Kdr. I.R. 520	4.9.42
Hüttner, Hartmut	Hptm., Kdr. III./Jäger-Rgt. 228	15.3.43
v. Hütz, Leopold	Hptm., Kdr. III./G. R. 1054	5.9.44
Hufenbach, Helmuth	Obstlt., Kdr. G. R. 667 807th Oak Leaves 28.3.45	30.10.43
Huffmann, Heinz	Major, Kdr. St. Gesch. Abt. 201 + 15.3.45 as Obstlt. z.b.V. in OKH	14.4. 43
Huffmann, Helmuth	Gen.Lt., Kdr. 62. I.D.	30.9.43
Hug, Eduard	Obergefr., MG-Schütze in 1./Jäg. Rgt. 75	2.9.44
Huhn, Kurt	Hptm., Kdr. II./S.G. 77	17.3.43
Hulha, Alois	Oblt., Flugzeugf. in 6./K.G. 53 "Legion Condor"	17.3.45
Hulsch, Otto	Oblt., Flugzeugf. in 8./S.G. 1 + 16.1.45 at Warsaw (Poland) as Staffelkpt. 7./S.G. 1	5.2.44
Humke, August	Wachtm., Zugf. in 4./Div. Füs. Btl. (A.A.) 15 missing as Oberwachtm.	4.5.44
Hummel, Fritz	Hptm. d.R., Kdr. Jagdverb. Leitstelle West (Frontaufkl. Verb. II. West)	19.10.44
Hummel, Kurt	Oberst, Kdr. G. R. 124	15.5.44
Hund, Willy (19)	SS-Obersturmf., Fhr. of a Kampfgr. z.b.V. formed from 6. & 7./SS-Freiw. Pz. G. R. 23 "Norge" + 1945 in Berlin area	11.5.45
Hundert, Joachim	Lt. d.R., Fhr. 5./G. R. 124 + 9.8.44 in Russia	15.1.43
Hundertmark, Gerhard	Oblt., Chef 1./gem. Flak-Sturm-Abt. 802 (v)	22.12.44
Hundt, Gustav	Gen.Lt., Kdr. 1. Ski-Jäger-Div. + died in Soviet captivity	15.4.45

KNIGHT'S CROSS OF THE IRON CROSS

Hunger, Hans-Joachim	Lt. d.R., B. -Offz. in schw. Art. Abt. 526 (mot.)	9.4.44
Hunger, Heinrich	Lt., Flugzeugf. in Stabsstaffel/K.G. 2 + 14.8.41 at Nowgorod (Russia)	5.7.41
Huntemüller, Richard	Oblt., Chef 2./le. Flak-Sturm-Abt. 76 (mot. s.)	5.9.44
Hupfer, Konrad	Hptm., Chef 14./I.R. 72 136th Oak Leaves 28.10.42	21.9.41
Huppert, Helmut	Major, Kdr. Pz. Aufkl. Abt. 1	23.8.44
Huppertz, Herbert	Lt., Flugzeugf. in 12./J.G. 51 512th Oak Leaves 24.6.44	30.8.41
Hurdelbrink, Georg	SS-Obersturmf, Fhr. 1./SS-Pz.Jäg. Abt. 12 "Hitlerjugend"	16.10.44
Hurlebaus, August	Obergefr., Richtschtz. in 2./schw. Pz.Jäg. Abt. 665	23.2.44
Hurrle, Wilhelm	Uffz., V. B. in 13./G. R. 358	17.3.45
Husemann, Werner	Major, Kdr. I./N. J.G. 3	30.9.44
Husenett, Freimut	Oblt., Chef 2./G. R. 7 + 23.3.45 at Danzig of wounds	28.10.44
Huß, Walter	Hptm. d.R., Kdr. I./A.R. 240 (mot.) + 29.1.45 at Schönfeld (East Prussia) as Major d.R.	21.9.44
Huth, Joachim-Friedrich	Obstlt., Kmdre. Z.G. 26 "Horst Wessel"	11.9.40
Huy, Wolf-Dietrich	Oblt., Staffelkpt., 7./J.G. 77 83rd Oak Leaves 17.3.42	5.7.41
Huzel, Hans	Major, Fhr. Sturm-Rgt. 215	18.2.45
Hyza, Josef	Major, stv. Fhr. G. R. 579 1945 posted missing	9.6.44

I

Ibel, Max	Oberst, Kmdre. J.G. 27	22.8.40
Iden, Arthur	Owm., St. Gesch. Fhr. in Festung Schneidemühl 14/16.2.45 in Festung Schneidemühl	10.2.45
Iffland, Ulrich	Oberst, Kdr. Füs. Rgt. 22 + 18.11.43 in Russia	3.10.43
Ihde, Rudolf	Major, Kdr. I./Sturm-Rgt. 195 + 8.2.45	23.9.43
Ihlefeld, Herbert	Oblt., Flugzeugf. in 1./J.G. 77 16th Oak Leaves 27.6.41 9th Swords 24.4. 42	13.9.40
Ihrig, Ernst-Wilhelm	Oblt., Staffelfhr. 3./K.G. 3 "Lützow" + 30.11.42 in Russia as Hptm. & Gruppenkdr. I./K.G. 3	23.8.41
Ilk, Iro	Oblt., Flugzeugf. in 1. (K)/Lehr-Geschw. 1 + 25.9.44 at Moers (Rhineland) as Major & Kdr. III./J.G. 300	21.10.42

Illg, Wilhelm-Friedrich	Ofw., Flugzeugf. & Bordmech. in 9./K.G. 76 simultaneously promoted to Lt. d.R.	1.10.40
Imgenberg, Fritz	Stabsfeldw., Zugf. in Stabskp./G. R. 671	9.6.44
Imminger, Bernhard	Ofw., Zugf. In 3./Pz. G. R. 67	4.10.44
Indlekofer, Fritz	Hptm., Kdr. II./G. R. 1050	27.7.44
Ingenhoven, Peter	Hptm. d.R., stv. Kdr. KampfGr. z.b.V. 103 + 1.11.42 in Russia as Major d.R. & Kdr. K. Gr. z.b.V. 900	11.5.40
Ritter v. Ingram, Hermann	Uffz., Kp. Truppf. in 4. (MG.)/I.R. 309	16.6.40
Ippisch, Josef	Feldw., Zugf. in 12. (MG.)/G. R. 123	10.5.43
Isachsen, Herbert	Ofw., Flugzeugf. in 3. (K)/L.G. 1	3.9.43
Isczinsky, Richard	Ofw., Zugf. in 3./Div. Füs. Btl. (A.A.) 102	17.3.45
Iselhorst, Otto	Uffz., Gruppenf. in Stabskp./Jäg. Rgt. 24 (L)	14.4. 45
Isken, Eduard	Ofw., Flugzeugf. in 13./J.G. 53	14.1.45
Ißbrücker, Heinz-Jürgen	Oblt., Chef 3./Pz. Aufkl. Abt. 7	12.9.41
Isselhorst, Wilhelm	Oblt., Chef 7./G. R. 258	21.2.44
Issermann, Friedrich	Hptm., Kdr. I./G. R. 102	8.2.44
Ites, Otto	Oblt. z. See, Kdt. "U 94"	28.3.42
Itzen, Dirk	Lt., Erkundungsoffz. in 3./Flak-Rgt. "GG" (mot.) + 12.7.41 at Berditschew (Russia)	23.11.41
Ivers, Hans-Henning	Oblt., Fhr. III./I.R. 46	17.10.42
Iwand, Fritz	Obstlt., Kdr. I./Schtz. Rgt. 10 + 27.7.41 vor Bjeloj (Russia) as Kdr. Schützen-Rgt. 74; posthumously promoted to Oberst	15.5.40
Iwannek, Otto	Obgefr., Melder in 2./G. R. 45	17.3.45

J

Jabs, Hans-Joachim	Oblt., Flugzeugf. & Staffeloffz. in 2./Zerst. Geschw. 76 430th Oak Leaves 24.3.44	1.10.40
Jacob, Eberhard	Hptm., Kdr. III./Stuka-Geschw. 3	29.2.44
Jacob, Georg-Rupert	Oblt., Chef 1./Fsch. Jäg. Rgt. 7	13.9.44
Jacob, Karl-Peter	Oblt., Chef 2./G. J. K 143	13.6.41
Jacob, Paul	Oblt., stv. Fhr. I./Jäg. Rgt. 204	10.3.43
Jacobeit, Fritz	Gefr., Gruppenf. in 6./Füs. Rgt. 22	11.3.45
Jacobi v. Wangelin, Hans-Joachim Jacobs, Martin	Oblt., Staffelfhr. 1./K.G. 77 + 8.10.42 in Russia	19.9.42
	Obgefr., Gruppenf. in 2./G. R. 431	26.12.43
Jacoby, Fritz	Oblt. d.R., Chef 7./Pz. Gren. Rgt. 11 + 19.3.43 in Russia	3.4.43

KNIGHT'S CROSS OF THE IRON CROSS

Jaeckel, Egbert	Lt., Flugzeugf. in 3./Stuka-Geschw. 2 "Immelmann" + 17.7.43 at Orel (Russia) as Oblt. & Staffelkpt.; posthumously promoted to Hptm.	14.5.42
Jaedtke, Alfred	Hptm., Kdr. I./Pz. G. R. 14	21.9.44
Jäger, Erich	Oblt., Zug. in I./Flak-Rgt. 23 (mot.)	5.7.41
Jäger, Fritz	Major, Kdr. II./I.R. 8 + 21.8.44 hanged Berlin-Plötzensee (related to 20.7.44); final post Oberst & Kdr. Pz.Tr. II. & XXI.	26.5.40
Jaeger, Gerhard	Feldw., Zugf. in 7./I.R. 418 + 18.9.42 at Pustynja (Russia) as Lt. & Kp. Fhr.	23.2.42
Jaeger, Karl-Heinz	Lt. d.R., Fhr. 1./G. R. 167 786th Oak Leaves 16.3.45	4.8.43
Jäger, Dr. med. Rolf	Oberarzt, Truppenarzt in Fallsch. Jäg. Sturm-Abt. "Koch" (Eben Emael) simultaneously promoted to Stabsarzt	13.5.40
Jähde, Willy	Major, Kdr. schw. Pz. Abt. 502	16.3.44
Jähnert, Erhard	Lt., Flugmugf. in III./Stuka-Geschw. 3	18.5.43
Jäkel, Adolf	Oberst, Kmdre. Transp. Geschw. 1 + February 1945 during an Allied bombing raid as Oberst & Inspekteur beim Stab d. Lufttransportchefs der Wehrmacht	19.8.44
Jaenecke, Erwin	Gen.Lt., Kdr. 389. I.D.	9.10.42
Jäschke, Hans-Joachim	Oblt., Staffelfhr. 4./S.G. 1 + 21.7.44 at Kleszcsele (Hungary)	28.3.44
Jagusch, Bruno	Uffz., Pz. Kdt. in Pz.Jäg. Kp. 1349	5.3.45
Jahn, Gunter	Kaptlt., Kdt. "U 596"	30.4.43
Jahncke, Paul	Ofw., Zugf. in 1./Pz.Jäg. Abt. 53	18.2.45
Jahnke, Arthur	Lt. d.R., Fhr. 5./GR. 572	20.4.44
Jahr, Arno	Gen.Lt., Kdr. 387. I.D. + 21.1.43 at Podgornoje (Russia) (suicide)	22.12.42
Jas, Maximilian	Oberst, Kdr. Geb.Jäg. Rgt. 141	17.9.41
Jakob, Friedrich	Hptm., Fhr. II./I.R. 105 681st Oak Leaves 18.12.44	4.3.42
Jakob, Georg	Oblt., Staffelkpt. 2./Stuka-Geschw. 77 615th Oak Leaves 30.9.44	27.4.42
Jakob, Willy	Uffz., Zugf. in 7./I.R. 391 + 27.1.42 at Feodosia (Russia)	4.3.42
Jakwert, Josef	Ofw., Zugf. in Div. Pz.Jäg. Kp. 361 752nd Oak Leaves 24.2.45	14.5.44
Jamrowski, Siegfried	Oblt., Chef 6./Fsch. Jäg. Rgt. 3	9.6.44
Jander, Arthur	Major, Fhr. of a Kampfgr. from 62. I.D.	15.6.43
Janke, Hans	Obstlt., Kdr. G. R. 159	23.2.44
Janke, Karl	Hptm., Staffelkpt. 7./Stuka-Geschw. 2 "Immelmann"	16.11.42

ELITE OF THE THIRD REICH

Jannes, Ewald	Obgefr. in 9./Pz. G. R. 28	30.4.45
Jansa, Ernst (17)	Obstlt., Kdr. Flak-(Sturm-)Rgt. 12 (mot.) 726th Oak Leaves 1.2.45	31.10.44
Jansen, Willi	Oblt., Ord.Offz. in Pz. G. R. 128	15.5.44
Jansing, Theodor	Uffz., Kp. Truppf. in 3./G. R. 480 2.11.43 posted missing	26.1.44
Jansky, Paul-Vincenz	Oblt. d.R., Chef 7./Jäg. Rgt. 49	12.8.44
Janssen, Ewald (17)	Major, Kmdre. Schlacht-Geschw. 4	31.10.44
Janz, Siegfried	Obgefr., Gruppenf. in 1./Jäg. Rgt. 42 (L)	5.11.44
Jaquet, Fritz	Lt., Adj. I./G. R. 62	9.5.45
Jarosch, Alfred	Lt., Fhr. 8./Jäg. Rgt. 38	24.9.42
Jaschinski, Erich	Ofw., Flugzeugf. in I./T. G. 3	9.2.45
Jaschke, Erich	Oberst, Kdr. I.R. 90 (mot.) 295th Oak Leaves 7.9.43	4.12.41
Jaschke, Herbert (9)	Hptm., Kdr. St. Gesch. Brig. 249	23.4.45
Jasiek, Franz	Uffz., Zugf. in 5./Pz. G. R. 5	22.4.43
Jass, Georg	Major, Kdr. Div. Füs. Btl. 30	9.6.44
Jauer, Georg	Gen.Lt., Kdr. 20. Pz. Gr. Div. 733rd Oak Leaves 10.2.45	4.5.44
Jauernik, Georg	Stfeldw., Flugzeugf. in II/Stuka-Geschw. 77 + 8.2.45 at Sprottau airfield (Oberlausitz) as Lt. & Staffelfhr. 6./S.G. 77	27.11.42
Jeckeln, Friedrich	SS-Obergruppenf. & Gen. d. Pol. & d. Waffen-SS, Höherer SS- & Polizeifhr. Ostland & Rußland-Nord & Fhr. of a Latvian 802nd Oak Leaves 8.3.45 SS-Pol. Kampfgr.	27.8.44
Jeckstat, Erich	Feldw., Flugzeugf. in 1./K.G. 100	14.3.43
Jedele, Ernst	Ofw., Truppf. in 6./Sturm-Rgt. 14 + 8.3.44 west of Smolensk (Russia)	15.4.44
Jedermann, Otto	Hptm., Kdr. I./Pz. G. R. 146	14.5.44
Jenatschek, Josef	Lt., Fhr. 1./Pz. G. R. 14	4.5.44
Jenisch, Hans	Oblt. z. See, Kdt. "U 32"	7.10.40
Jenisch, Roland	Oberst d.R., Kdr. G. R. 756	9.12.44
Jenne, Peter	Hptm., Staffelkpt. 12./J.G. 300 + 2.3.45 at Belzig (Mark Brandenburg)	2.2.45
Jennewein, Josef	Lt., Flugzeugf. in 1./J.G. 51 "Mölders" + 26.7.43 east of Orel (Russia); posthumously promoted to Oblt.	5.12.43
Jenninger, Karl	Oblt., Chef 2./Festg. Inf. Btl. VI./999	26.11.44
Jenschke, Walter	SS-Kan., Funktruppf in 5./SS-Freiw. -A.R. 54 "Nederland" + in March 1945 in Festung Breslau	18.12.44
Jensen, Max	Feldw., Zugf in Stab I./G. R. 502	29.4.45

Name	Rank/Unit	Date
Jenster, Jakob	Ofw., Flugzeugf. in 6./Stuka-Geschw. 2 "Immelmann"	29.2.44
Jente, Heinz	Oblt., Staffelkpt. 2./K.G. 26	29.10.43
Jentzsch, Erich	Feldw., Zugf. in 4./G. R. 446	8.8.44
Jentzsch, Hans	Hptm., Kdr. I./Flak-Rgt. 291 (mot.)	25.11.44
Jerschke, Wilhelm	Stabsgefr., Melder in 2./Pz. G. R. 12	7.10.44
Jescheck, Hans-Heinrich	Hptm. d.R., Fhr. Pz. Aufkl. Abt. 118	5.3.45
Jeschonnek, Hans	Gen. Major, Chef d. Gen. Stabes der Luftwaffe + 19.8.43 in H. Quartier des Ob. d. L. at Goldap (East Prussia) as Gen. Oberst (suicide)	27.10.39
Jeserer, Helmut	Hptm., Kdr. II./Sturm-Rgt. 215	30.4.45
Jesse, Rudolf	Oblt. z. See d.R., Kommandant in der 8. Minensuchflottille	5.9.44
Jesser, Curt	Oberst, Kdr. Pz. Rgt. 36	18.1.42
Jetting, Ernst	Ofw., Zugf. in 1./G. R. 29 (mot,)	4.6.44
Jobelius, Hermann	Major, Kdr. II./G. R. 432	28.2.45
Jochems, Hermann	Ofw., Flugzeugf. i. Stab/Stuka-Geschw. 2 "Immelmann"	3.9.42
Jochims, Hermann-Gustav	Hptm., Chef 7./Gren. Rgt. 90 (mot.) + 28.4.45 in Berlin as Oberstlt. & Kdr. Pz. Gr. Rgt. 51	19.9.43
Jochimsen, Bernhard	Uffz. d.R., Gr. Fhr. in 1./Pi. Btl. 290	28.4.45
Jodl, Alfred	Gen. Oberst, Chef des Wehrmachtsführungstabes in OKW 865th Oak Leaves 10.5.45	6.5.45
Jodl, Ferdinand	Gen. d. Geb. Tr., Kom.Gen. XIX. Geb. Korps	13.1.45
Joecks, Martin	Hptm. d.R., Kdr. Le. Art. Abt. 426 (mot.)	14.5.44
Jödicke, Wolf-Joachim	Major, Kdr. I./K.G. 3 "Lützow"	5.2.44
Joerchel, Wolfgang	SS-Obersturmbannf., Kdr. niederländ. SS-Freiw. Pz. G. R. 48 "General Seyffardt" + early May 45 in Prague (Czechoslovakia) as SS-Standartenfhr. & Kdr. SS-Junkerschule Prag	21.4.44
Jörß, Karl	Bootsmannsmaat d.R., Flakleiter on a Transporter in the Mediterranean	17.2.43
Józwiak, Gerhard	Uffz., Zugf. in 12./Pz. G. R. 104	17.3.45
Johannes, Bernhard	Feldw., Flugzeugf. in 1./S.G. 10 + 11.7.44 Kaunas airfield (Lithuania); posthumously promoted to Ofw.	29.10.44
Johannesson, Rolf	Kapt. z. See, Kdt. Zerstörer "Hermes"	7.12.42
Johannmeyer, Willy	Oblt., Fhr. II./I.R. 503 329th Oak Leaves 18.11.43	16.5.42
Johanns, Günther	Major, Kdr. Pi. Btl. 292	9.1.44
Johannsen, Hans	Oblt. (Ing.), Leit. Ing. auf "U 802"	31.3.45

Johannsen, Kurt	Kaptlt., Chef 5. Schnellbootsflottille + 14.6.44 off Le Havre (France)	14.6.44
Johanssen, Karl-Ludwig	Lt., Bordfunker in I./N. J.G. 6	20.3.45
John, Dipl.-Ing. Richard	Gen. Major, Kdr. 292. I.D.	20.12.43
John, Richard	Feldw., Kp. Truppf in 2./G. R. 445	4.5.44
John, Wolfram	Oblt. d.R., Chef 2./St. Gesch. Brig. 209 + 27.4.45 in Samland (East Prussia)	18.11.44
Johne, Max	Oblt. d.R., Chef 9./G. R. 667 + 2.4.45 Medveziel (Slovakia) as Hptm. d.R. & Kdr. I./Gr. Rgt. 587	30.10.43
Johnen, Wilhelm	Oblt., Staffelkpt. 8./N. J.G. 6	29.10.44
Jokisch, Fritz	Feldw. d.R., Zugf. in 3./Pz. Gren. Rgt. 110 + 14.7.43 north of Bjelgorod (Russia) of wounds	28.7.43
Jolitz, Günter	Oblt., Staffelfhr. 9. (K)/L.G. I + 12.2.44 in Russia; posthumously promoted to Hptm.	5.6.44
Jollasse, Erwin	Oberst, Kdr. Schtz. Rgt. 52	2.11.41
Jooss, Ludwig	Major d.R., Kdr. I./Gren. Rgt. 21	17.3.45
Jope, Bernhard	Oblt., Flugzeugf. in 2./K.G. 40 431st Oak Leaves 24.3.44	30.12.40
Jopplen, Hermann-Friedrich	Oblt., Staffelkpt. 1./J.G. 51 11th Oak Leaves 23.4.41	16.9.40
Jordan, Adolf	Major, Kdr. 1./I.R. 203 + 21.8.42 Stalingrad (Russia) as Btl. Kdr. Inf.Rgt. 178; posthumously promoted to OTL	27.5.42
Jordan, Günther	Oberst d.R., Kdr. Jäger-Rgt. 25 (L)	17.3.45
Jordan, Hans	Oberst, Kdr. Inf.Rgt. 49 59th Oak Leaves 16.1.42 64th Swords 20.4.44	5.6.40
Jordan, Hans	Obstlt. i.G., la 72. I.D.	22.2.45
Jordan, Herbert	Hptm., Chef 4./A.R. 32 + 17.3.45 at Gotenhafen (Gdingen/Poland)	10.9.44
Jordan, Hermann	Hptm., Fhr. III./G. R. 9 + 2.8.43 at Mga, Lake Ladoga (Russia)	16.8.43
Jordan, Manfred	San. Uffz., Zugfhr. in 4./Pz. G. R. 66 + 10.5.44 in Russia as San. Feldw.	11.1.44
Joseph, Walter	Lt. d.R., Fhr. 4./Feldersatz-Btl. 107	24.6.44
Jost, Hans	Feldw., Zugfhr. in 2./Pz.Jäg. Abt. 256 + 23.2.44 south-east of Witebsk (Russia)	5.4.44
Jost, Walter	Oberst, Kdr. Inf. Rg. 75 + 22.4.45 at Villadosa (Italy) as Gen.Lt. & Kdr. 42. Jäger-Div.	31.3.42
Josten, Günther	Ofw., Flugzeugf. in 3./J.G. 51 "Mölders" 810th Oak Leaves 28.3.45	5.2.44
Joswig, Wilhelm	Ofw., Flugzeugf. in 9./Stuka-Geschw. 2 "Immelmann"	29.2.44

KNIGHT'S CROSS OF THE IRON CROSS

Juchem, Hans	SS-Hptsturmf, Kdr. II./SS-Pz. G. R. "Germania" + 13.8.43 on Donez (Russia)	12.9.43
Juditzki, Georg (17)	Lt., Flugzeugf. in Stab I./K.G. 53 "Legion Condor"	9.11.44
Jünemann, Walter	Feldw., Kp. Truppf. in 4./Pz. G. R. 104 + February 1945 in Italy	4.10.44
Jürgen, Friedrich-Wilhelm	Major, Kdr. II./Schtz. Rgt. 2 + in late summer 1954 in a hospital in Stalingrad (Russia) in Soviet captivity; final post Oberst	16.6.40
Jürgens, Heinz	SS-Hptsturmf, Kdr. SS-Pz. Aufkl. Abt. 4	9.5.45
Jürgens, Karl	Feldw., Zugf. in 2./I.R. 73 + 16.10.41 at Iljinskoje (Russia) as Ofw.	4.9.40
Jürgens, Wilhelm	Major, Kdr. II./Flak-Rgt. 23 (mot.)	9.6.44
Jürgensen, Arnold	SS-Sturmbannf., Kdr. I./SS-Pz. Rgt. 12 "Hitlerjugend" + 23.12.44 in the Ardennes	16.10.44
Jürgensen, Justus	Bau-Pionier in 5./Pi. Bau-Ers. &Ausb. Btl. 3 Crossen (Oder) + 5.2.45 detonation of a bridge at Fürstenberg, Frankfurt (Oder)	5.2.45
Jürgensen, Klaus	Hptm., Fhr. I./G. R. 46	2.2.44
Jüttner, Arthur	Hptm., Kdr. III./Inf.Rgt. 38 622nd Oak Leaves 18.10.44 141st Swords 5.4.45	14.12.41
Junck, Werner	Gen. Major, Kom.Gen. II. Jagdkorps	9.6.44
Jung, Heinrich	Hptm., Kdr. II./J.G. 54 + 30.7.43 over Mga (northern sector of Russia) in combat with Soviet fighters	12.11.43
Jung, Valentin	Hptm., Kdr. Feldersatz-Btl. 92 & Div. Kampfschule	28.12.43
ter Jung, Dietrich	Oblt. d.R., Fhr. II./Pz. G. R. 79	4.5.44
Jungclausen, Heinz	Oblt., Staffelkpt. 3./S.G. 4 "Immelmann" + 26.12.44 at Boppard (Rhine) as Hptm. & Staffelkpt. 3./J.G. 4	9.10.43
Junge, Herbert	Uffz., Kdt. einer 8.8 Flak in Greifenhagen (knocked out 7 tanks)	13.3.45
Junge, Wilhelm	Oblt. d.R., Chef 5./A.R. 1542 + 29.3.45	9.12.44
Jungkaus, Siegfried	Hptm., Kdr. III. (Eis.)/K.G. 3 "Lützow" + 22.4.43 over Poti harbour (Russia)	3.9.43
Jungkunst, Johann	Feldw., Zugf. in 11./I.R. 41 (mot.)	30.8.41
Jungnickel, Edgar	Oblt. z. See, Kdt. "U-Jäger 1430"	10.9.44
Jungwirth, Hans	Major, Kdr. Fsch. Aufkl. Abt. 12	9.5.45
Junker, Heinz	Lt., Zugf. in St. Gesch. Abt. 1026	14.1.45
Jura, Georg	Stabsfeldw., Fhr. 14./Jäger-Rgt. 49	28.4.43
Jursa, Franz	Uffz., Zugf. in 3./G. R. 482	2.8.43
Juschkat, Franz	Feldw., Zugf. in Stabskp./G. R. 43	17.2.43

K

Kachel, Georg	Hptm., Kdr. I./G. R. 670 + 18.10.44 in Russia as Major & Rgt. Fhr.	4.5.44
Kaden, Wolfgang	Kaptlt. d.R., Kdt. "U-Jäger 116" + 9.7.42 off Hammerfest (Norway) as Kdt. "UJ 1110"; posthumously promoted to Korv. Kpt. d.R.	18.12.40
Kadenbach, Herbert	Feldw., Zugf. in 12./Jäger-Rgt. 28 + 27.12.44 in Hungary	16.9.42
Kaeber, Hellmut	Oblt., Staffelkpt. 1. (N)/Aufkl. Gr. 13	28.1.45
Käding, Walter	Obersteuermann, III. W. O. & Steuermann on "U 123"	15.5.44
Kähler, Otto	Kapt. z. See, Kdt. Hilfskreuzer "Thor" (HSK 4) 583rd Oak Leaves 15.9.44	22.12.40
Kaehne, Edgar-Karl	Hptm., Kdr. I./I.R. 135	2.2.42
Källner, Hans	Oberst, Kdr. Schtz. Rgt. 73 392nd Oak Leaves 12.2.44 106th Swords 23.10.44	3.5.42
Kämmerer, Edmund	Ofw., Kp. Tr. Fhr. in 6./Pz. G. R. 76	5.4.45
Kämpfe, Helmut	SS-Sturmbannf. d.R., Kdr. III. (gep.)/SS- Pz. G. R. 4 "Der Führer" + 10.6.44 shot by Maquis in Limoges area (N France); posthumously promoted to SS-Obersturmbannf. d.R.	10.12.43
Kaeppel, Rudolf	Hptm., Chef Div. Begl. Kp. 11. Pz.Div. + 25.1.45	1.2.45
Käs, Josef	Ofw., Zugf. in 2./G. R. 19	18.7.43
Käseberg, Herbert	Lt., Fhr. in 5./Pz. G. R. 156	14.4. 45
Kaessler, Werner	Oblt. d.R., Chef 2./Pz. G. R. 108 + 23.8.44	27.8.44
Kästner, Robert	Major, Fhr. Gren. Rgt. 105 401st Oak Leaves 21.2.44	11.12.43
Kaether, Ernst	Obstlt. d.R., Kdr. I.R. 14	10.12.42
Graf v. Kageneck, Clemens-Heinrich	Hptm., Kdr. schw. Pz. Abt. 503 (Tiger) 513th Oak Leaves 26.6.44	4.8.43
Graf v. Kageneck, Erbo	Oblt., Staffelkpt. 9./J.G. 27 39th Oak Leaves 26.10.41	30.7.41
Kahl, Bruno	Hptm., Kdr. III./PZ. Rgt. 21 270th Oak Leaves 8.8.43	8.2.43
Kahl, Konrad	Hptm., Kdr. I./K.G. 30	13.8.42
Kahle, Helmuth	Ofw., Beob. in 3./K.G. 4 "General Wever"	9.6.44
Kahle, Rudolf	Hptm., Kdr. Pz. Pi. Btl. 40	2.9.44
Kahler, Hans-Joachim	Major, Kdr. Kradschützen-Btl. 34 355th Oak Leaves 17.12.43	14.4. 43

KNIGHT'S CROSS OF THE IRON CROSS

Kahsnitz, Erich	Oberst, Kdr. Füs. Rgt. "GD" + 29.7.43 in hospital in Breslau of wounds; posthumously promoted to Gen. Major	15.7.43
Kainz, Karl	Hptm. d.R., Chef 11./Jäg. Rgt. 25	31.1.45
Kaiser, Albert	Hptm., Chef 1./Geb. Pz.Jäg. Abt. 44 + 6.8.41	21.8.41
Kaiser, Erich	Oblt., Chef 6./Pz. Rgt. 39 + 26.8.42 of wounds, in Russia as Hptm. & Abt.Kdr.	26.2.42
Kaiser, Herbert	Ofw., Flugzeugf. in 8./J.G. 77 (later J.G. 1)	14.3.43
Kaiser, Vinzenz	SS-Hauptsturmf., Fhr. III. (gep.)/SS-Pz. G. R. 4 "Der Führer" missing 20.4.45 in the Nürnberg area as SS-Obersturmbannf.	6.4.43
Kaiser, Wilhelm	Oblt., Adj. III./Stuka-Geschw. 2 "Immelmann"	4.2.42
Kalb, Hans	Hptm. d.R., Kdr. II./G. R. 320	29.2.44
Kalbitz, Helmut	Oblt., Chef 1./Pi. Btl. 125 366th Oak Leaves 7.1.44	23.8.41
Kalden, Peter	Lt., Staffelf. 13./J.G. 51 "Mölders"	6.12.44
Kaldrack, Rudolf	Hptm., Kdr. III./Z.G. 76 70th Oak Leaves 9.2.42	2.11.40
Kaletsch, Georg	Oblt. d.R., Fhr. II./G. R. 283 + 6.3.44 at Schepetowka (Russia)	26.3.44
v. Kalinowsky, Herbert	Oberst, Kdr. Volks-Werfer-Brigade 8	30.4.45
Kalkgruber, David	Uffz., Gruppenf. in 5./G. R. 3	19.8.44
Kalkhoff, Walter	Uffz., Gruppenf. In I./I.R. 67 (mot.)	26.5.40
Kalls, Alois	SS-Obersturmf., Fhr. 1./schw. SS-Pz. Abt. 502 + 2.5.45 in Kummersdorf area south of Berlin as SS-Hptsturmfhr.	23.8.44
v. Kalm, Hennig-Tile	Major, stellv. Fhr. G. R. 24 + 25.3.45 at Helligenbeil (East Prussia) as Obstlt. & Rgt. Kdr.	17.9.44
Kalow, Siegfried	Uffz., Gruppenf. in 10./Fsch. Pz. G. R. 2 "Hermann Göring" + 12.8.44	29.10.44
Kals, Ernst	Korv. Kpt., Kdt. "U 130"	1.9.42
Kam, Soeren	SS-Untersturmf., Fhr. 1./SS-Pz. G. R. 9 "Germania"	7.2.45
Kamecke, Hans	Gen.Lt., Kdr. 137. I.D. + 16.10.43 south of Kolpen, west of the Dnjestr (Russia)	27.10.43
Kaminski, August	Ofw., Zugf. in 3./schw. Pz.Jäg. Abt. 655	6.10.44
Kaminski, Herbert	Hptm., Kdr. I./Z.G. 26 "Horst Wessel"	6.8.41
Kaminski, Werner (3)	Obstlt., Ia Festg. Div. Kreta	6.5.45
Kaminsky, Emil	Ofw., Zugf. in I.R. 446 497th Oak Leaves 12.6.44	15.10.42
Kamischke, Werner	Hptm., Kdr. II./G. R. 4	9.1.45
Kammhuber, Josef	Gen. Major, Kdr. 1. Nachtjagd-Div.	9.7.41

v. Kamptz, Gerhard	Korv. Kpt., Chef 2. Räumbootsflottille 225nd Oak Leaves 14.4. 43	6.10.40
Kamski, Johann	Obgefr. in 14./G. R. z.b.V. 1. Pz. Armee	30.4.45
Kannenberg, Kurt	Stabsfeldw., Zugf. in 3./schw. Pz. Abt. 506 + 17.11.44 at Puffendorf, Geilenkirchen	9.12.44
Kapp, Wolfganiz	Major, Kdr. St. Gesch. Lehr-Brig. 920	3.3.45
Kappis, Hans-Joachim	Oblt. d.R., stv. Fhr. I./G. R. 45 849th Oak Leaves 28.4.45	18.2.45
Kapsreiter, Franz	Ofw., Zugf. in 4. (Sturmg.)/Führer-Gren. Brig.	14.1.45
Karau, August	Ofw., Fhr. 9./G. R. 46	12.1.45
Karbe, Adalbert	Oblt., Staffelkpt. 3./K.G. 55 + 30.7.42 over England as Hptm.	12.11.41
Karch, Fritz (17)	Hptm., Kdr. II/J.G. 2 "Richthofen"	17.4.45
Karcher, Karl-Ehrhart	Oblt. z. See, Kdt. "S 87" in 4. Schnellbootsflottille	12.8.43
Karck, Georg	SS-Obersturmf., Fhr. 9./SS-Pz. G. R. 2. "LSSAH" + 3.7.44 accidentally as SS-Hptsturmf. & Fhr. II./SS-Pz. G. R. 2 "LSSAH" in Normandy; posthumously promoted to SS-Sturmbannfhr.	3.8.43
Karczewski, Bruno	Major, Kdr. I./G. R. 162 767th Oak Leaves 5.3.45	12.3.44
Kardel, Hennecke	Lt. d.R., Adj. III./G. R. 399	23.2.44
Karg, Ulrich	Objäg., Fhr. Radf. Zug in 17./GJ. R. 91	5.7.43
Karl, Franz	Gen.Lt., Kdr. 263. I.D.	5.8.40
Karl, Friedrich-Wilhelm	SS-Obersturmbannf., Kdr. SS-Freiw. Pz. A.R. 11 "Nordland"	26.12.44
Karl, Josef	Uffz., Geschützf. in 2./Pz.Jäg. Abt. 49 397th Oak Leaves 16.2.44	26.8.43
Karl, Otto	Oblt. z. See d.R., Kdt. Artillerie-Leichter "AF 65"	21.3.45
Karow, Gustav	Oberst d.R., Kdr. G. R. 322	19.8.44
Karrenberg, Albert	Oblt., Chef 2./Pz. G. R. 9	11.12.44
Karst, Friedrich	Oberst, Kdr. I.R. 461	28.8.42
Kassner, Helmut	Oberst, Kdr. G. R. 975	14.4. 45
Kastl, Andreas	Feldw., Zugf. in 11./G. R. 20 (mot.)	14.5.44
Kastner, Gustav	Oblt. d.R., Fhr. 2./A.R. 389	12.12.44
Kastner, Josef	Objäg., Zugf. in 7./Jäg. Rgt. 207 + 9.12.44 at Silwas (eastern Slovakia)	2.6.43
Katzenmeier, Hans	Uffz., Zugf. in 6./G. R. 698	9.6.44
Kaubisch, Horst	Hptm., Staffelkpt. 9./Stuka-Geschw. 77 505th Oak Leaves 24.6.44	16.11.42
Kauermann, Helmut	Ofw., Zugf. in 7./Pz. Rgt. 2	20.3.44
Kauffmann, Gerhard	Gen.Lt., Kdr. 256. I.D.	9.7.41

KNIGHT'S CROSS OF THE IRON CROSS

Kaup, Heinrich	Obgefr. in 3./G. R. 184	19.9.43
Kausch, Paul-Albert	SS-Obersturmbannf., Kdr. SS-Pz. -Abt. 11 "Hermann von Salza" 845th Oak Leaves 23.4.45	23.8.44
Kautz, Oskar	Oblt., Chef 7./Gren. Rgt. 156 + 22.7.43 on the Mius front (Russia)	28.7.43
Kayß, Alfred	Oblt., Kp. Chef in Feldersatz-Btl. 267 + 5.1.44 south-west of Propoisk (Russia); posthumously promoted to Hptm.	18.1.44
Kazmeier, Paul	Hptm. d.R., Fhr. II./G. R. 420	26.10.43
Kecht, Franz	Oblt., Fhr. III./G. R. 70 + 25.10.43 in Russia of wounds; posthumously promoted to Hptm.	18.10.43
Keck, Johannes	Lt. d.R., Fhr. 2./Pz. Aufkl. Abt. 23	18.2.45
Keck, Karl	SS-Hptsturmf. & Hptm. d. Schutzpolizei, Fhr. 15. (Pi.)/SS-Pz. G. R. 21 "Frundsberg" + 11.7.44 in Normandy at Avenay (France)	23.8.44
Kedzia, Ernst-Georg	Hptm., Fhr. II./G. R. 272 794th Oak Leaves 23.3.45	26.11.44
Keese, Heinrich	Oblt. d.R., Chef 2./Pi. Btl. 20 (mot.) 805th Oak Leaves 28.3.45	20.10.44
Kegel, Karl-Ludwig	Lt., Fhr. 5./Pz. Rgt. 18 + 1.1.43 at Tschertkowo on Don (Russia) as Hptm. & Chef 5. (Pz.)/Fhr. -Begl. -Btl.	25.8.41
Keichel, Otto	Ofw., Spähtruppf in 1./Pz. Aufkl. Lehr-Abt. 130	18.1.45
Keil, Anton	Hptm., Kdr. II./Stuka-Geschw. 1 + 29.8.41 at Skalowa (Russia)	19.8.40
Keil, Günther	Obstlt. d.R., Kdr. G. R. 919	27.6.44
Keil, Max	Oblt., stellv. Fhr. 1./Pz. Rgt. 8 in DAK + 8.4.43 in North Africa	20.4.43
Keiling, Siegfried	Hptm., Kdr. Art. Abt. 62 (russ.)	4.10.44
Keiner, Walter	Gen.Lt., Kdr. 62. I.D.	17.7.41
Keipp, Willy	Feldw., Zugf. in 6./G. R. 124	30.10.43
Keiser, Paul	Oberst, Kdr. G. R. 326	6.11.43
Keitel, Wilhelm	Gen. Oberst, Chef OKW + 16.10.46 hanged at Nürnberg; final post Gen. Feldmarschall	30.9.39
Kelbch, Albert	Ofw., Flugzeugf. in 1. (F)/Aufkl. Gr. 120 + 8.11.43 north of Pescaria (Adria/Italy)	12.11.43
Kelbling, Gerd	Kaptlt., Kdt. "U 593"	18.8.43
Keller, Alfred	Gen. d. Fl., Kom.Gen. IV. Fliegerkorps	24.6.40
Keller, Lothar	Hptm., Kdr. II./J.G. 3 + 26.6.41 accidentally at Wladimierz (Poland)	9.7.41
Kellermann, Ortwin	Oblt. d.R., Chef 1./Div. Füs. Btl. (A.A.) 72	30.9.44
Kellner, Wolfgang	Oblt., Chef 1./Pz.Jäg. Abt. 24	14.4.45

Kemethmüller, Heinz	Feldw., Flugzeugf. in 8./J.G. 3 "Udet"	2.10.42
Kemler, Heinrich	Hptm., Kdr. II./G. R. 78	14.4. 45
Kemnade, Friedrich	Kaptlt., Chef 3. Schnellbootsflottille 249th Oak Leaves 27.5.43	23.7.42
Kempas, Traugott	Hptm., Kdr. I./G. R. 176 757th Oak Leaves 28.2.45	9.12.44
Kempe, Walter	Feldw., Zugf. 2./Pi. Btl. 248	14.5.44
Kempf, Karl	Ofw., Flugzeugl. in 7./J.G. 54 + 3.9.44 accidentally at Bael (Belgium) as Lt. in 6./J.G. 26 "Schlageter"	4.2.42
Kempf, Werner	Gen.Lt., Kdr. 6. Pz.Div. 111th Oak Leaves 10.8.42	3.6.40
Kempin, Günther	Feldw., Flugzeugf. in 14./K.G. 27 "Boelcke"	17.4.45
Kempke, Wilhelm	Feldw., Gruppenf. in 1./Fallsch. Jäg. Sturm-Rgt. (7. Flieger-Div.) + 2.12.44 over the Reich as Oblt. & Staffelfhr. in d. II./K.G. 200	21.8.41
Kempken, Heinrich	Fhj. -Feldw., Flugzeugf. in 7./S.G. 3	29.10.44
Kendler, Rudolf	Hptm. d.R., m. d. F. b. Pz. Aufkl. Abt. 4	2.9.44
Kennel, Karl	Hptm., Staffelkpt. 5./S.G. 1 666th Oak Leaves 25.11.44	19.9.43
Kentrat, Eitel-Friedrich	Kaptlt., Kdt. "U 74"	31.12.41
Keppel, Wilhelm	Uffz., Hilfs-V. B. in 7./A.R. 227	9.6.44
Keppler, Georg	SS-Oberführer, Kdr. SS-Inf. Rgt. (mot.) "Der Führer" in SS-Verfügungs-Div., later "Das Reich"	15.8.40
Keppler, Hans	Major, Kdr. III./K.G. 1 "Hindenburg" + 3.9.42	20.8.42
Kepplinger, Ludwig	SS-Hptscharf., Stoßtruppf. & Zugfhr. in 11./SS-Inf.Rgt. "Der Führer" + 6.8.44 shot by Maquis south-east of Laval (France) as SS-Sturmbannfhr. & Kdr. SS-Pz . Abt. 17	4.9.40
Kercher, Fritz	Lt., Zugf. in 1. (St. Gesch.)/Pz.Jäg. Abt. 5	6.3.44
Kerfin, Horst	Oblt., Chef 11./Fsch. Jäg. Rgt. 1 + 22.1.43 at Alexejewska (Orel, Russia) as Hptm. & Rgt. Adj. Fsch. Jäg. Rgt. 1	24.5.40
Kern, Friedrich	Hptm. d.R., Kdr. III./A.R. 198	30.12.43
Kern, Karl	Ofw., Flugzeugf. in 6./T. G. 3	9.6.44
Kern, Wilhelm	Oblt., Chef 10./G. R. 44	5.4.44
Kerscher, Albert	Feldw., Pz. Kdt. in 2./schw. Pz. Abt. 502	23.10.44
Kertz, Wolfram	Oblt. d.R., Fhr. 8./Kampfgr. "Bruhn" (11./SS-Pz. Korps)	4.10.44
Kerutt, Hellmut	Major, Kdr. Fsch. Jäg. Btl. "Kerutt"	2.2.45
Kessel, Karl	Obstlt., Kmdr. K.G. 2	23.1.44

KNIGHT'S CROSS OF THE IRON CROSS

v. Kessel, Mortimer	Gen. Major, Kdr. 20. Pz.Div. 611th Oak Leaves 16.10.44	28.12.43
Kessel, Wilhelm	Owm., Zugfhr. in 3./Pz. Aufkl. Abt. "GD"	23.2.44
Keßelring, Albert	Gen. d. Flieger, Chef Luftflotte 1 78th Oak Leaves 25.2.42 15th Swords 18.7.42 14th Diamonds 19.7.44	30.9.39
Kessler, Arnold	Major, Kdr. Pz.Jäg. Abt. 61	4.10.44
Keßler, Hermann	Oberst, Kdr. G. R. 192	17.9.43
Kessler, Ulrich	Gen.Lt., Fliegerführer Atlantic	8.4.44
Kessler, Wolfgang	Oblt. d.R., stellv. Fhr. I./A.R. 181	16.4.44
Kesten, Dieter	SS-Hptsturmf., Fhr. 6./SS-Pz. Rgt. 2 "Das Reich" + 7.4.45 south of Vienna (Austria) as SS-Sturmbannf. & Abt.Kdr.	12.11.43
Frhr. v. Ketelhodt, Gerd	Oblt., Chef 9./I.R. 472	13.7.40
Ketscher, Hans	Hptm., Beob. in 1. (F)/Aufkl. Gr. 121	24.11.44
Ketterer, Karl	Ofw., Zugf. in 7./Pz. Rgt. 15 KIA	24.3.43
Ketterl, Franz	Oblt., Chef 1./I.R. 438	12.1.42
Kettgen, Hans	SS-Hptsturmf., Kdr. I./SS-Pz. G. R. "Schill"	14.2.45
Kettmann, Rudolf	Uffz., St. Gesch. Fhr. in Pz.Jäg. Kp. 1122	17.4.45
Keup, Dr. med, Walter	Ass. Arzt, Btl. Arzt I./Füs. Rgt. 202	21.3.44
v. Keußler, Friedrich	Oberst, Kdr. G. R. 1 + 9.7.44 in Russia during defensive fighting	23.2.44
Kiefer, Eduard	Hptm., Chef 2./Pz. Aufkl. Abt. "HG"	18.5.43
Kiefer, Hermann	Oblt., Kdr. Stell. Kampfgr. XII./2 (416. I.D.)	5.4.45
Kiefer, Martin	Uffz., Gruppenf. in 7./G. R. 320	12.8.44
Kieffer, Dr. phil. Emil	Korv. Kpt. d.R., Chef 3. Minensuchflottille	3.12.44
Kiehl, Rudolf	Hptm., Fhr. d. Kampfstaffel in DAK Begleitkdo. Rommel-Fhr. Kampfgr. Kiehl + 4.9.42 at Alam Halfa (North Africa)	6.7.42
Kiel, Johannes	Oblt. d.R., Flugzeugf. in I./Z.G. 26 "Horst Wessel" + 29.1.44 shot down over Kirchheimbolanden (Pfalz); final post Hptm. d.R. & Kdr. III./Z.G. 76	18.3.42
Kiel, Rudolf	Hptm., Kdr. I./K.G. 55	20.12.41
Kienast, Fritz	Oblt., Fhr. 1./Füs. Btl. "Demba" + 1944 as Hauptm.	9.4.44
Kiene, August	Lt., Fhr. 7./Pz. G. R. 14 + 5.8.44 in Russia; posthumously promoted to Oblt.	4.5.44
Kienitz, Werner	Gen. d. Inf, Kom.Gen. XVIII. A.K.	31.8.41
Kientsch, Willy	Lt., Staffelfhr. 6./J.G. 27 527th Oak Leaves 20.7.44	22.11.43
Kiermeier, Heinrich	Uffz., Gruppenf. in 8./G. R. 423	23.8.44
Kieser, Wilhelm	Major d.R., Kdr. II./G. R. 313	16.9.43

Name	Details	Date
Kieseritzky, Gustav	Vizeadmiral, Kom. Adm. Black Sea + 19.11.43 in Russia	20.11.43
Kiesgen, Peter	Lt., Fhr. 1./I.R. 239	5.10.41
Kieslich, Franz	Oblt., Staffelkpt. 7./Stuka-Geschw. 77 619th Oak Leaves 18.10.44	5.1.43
Kiesling, Heinrich	Major, Kdr. III./G. R. 768 321st Oak Leaves 7.11.43	10.6.43
Kiesling, Helmut	Hptm. d.R., Fhr. II./G. R. 336 + 12.4.44 in Russia as Major d.R. & Fhr. e. Kampfgr.	1.9.43
Kiess, Walter	Oblt., Chef Lastenseglerkdo. in Fallsch. Jäg. Sturmabt. "Koch"; simultaneously promoted to Hptm.	12.5.40
Kilian, Gunter	Lt., Staffelfhr. 2./S.G. 77	2.4.45
Kilian, Gustav	Hptm. d.R., Fhr. 1./Inf. Wach-Btl. 591	15.5.42
Kilian, Wilhelm	Major, Kdr. Div. Füs. Btl. (A.A.) 102	8.2.45
Kimmich, Friedrich	Major d. Landwehr, Fhr. II./G. R. 554	11.12.42
Kimmich, Hans-Jörg	Hptm., Rgt. Adj. G. R. 119 (mot.)	25.1.45
Kinder, Georg	Hptm., Kdr. II./G. R. 102	8.2.44
Kindler, Alfred	Hptm., Staffelkpt. 6./K.G. 2	24.9.42
Kinz, Helmut (15)	SS-Hptsturmf., Kdr. Waffen-Geb. Aufkl. Abt. 13 der SS	3.5.45
Kinzel, Eberhard	Oberst i.G., in Gen. Stab des Heeres + 11. May 45 Idstedt, Flensburg (suicide); final post Gen. d. inf. & Chef d. Gen. St. OB Nord	23.12.42
Kinzinger, Rudi	Oblt., Chef Pi. Kp./Jäg. Rgt. 49 + 16.2.45 Zagern (Pr. Holland)	18.2.45
Kipfmüller, Walter	Hptm., Staffelkpt. 2./K.G. 77	29.10.43
Kirchheim, Heinrich	Gen. Major, Leiter der Sonderstelle Libyen, Fhr. ital. Div. "Brescia"	14.5.41
Kirchlehner, Ernst	Uffz., Gruppenf. in 2./Füs. Btl. 126 + 14.7.44 at Dünaburg (Russia)	23.10.44
Kirchner, Friedrich	Gen.Lt., Kdr. 1. Pz.Div. 391st Oak Leaves 12.2.44 127th Swords 26.1.45	20.5.40
Kirchner, Heinz	Lt. d.R., Zugf. in 1./Schtz. Rgt. 113 + 27.11.42 at Belyj (Russia) as Oblt. d.R. & Kp. Chef	29.9.41
Kirchner, Kurt	Wachtm., Geschützf. in St. Gesch. Bttr. 667 + 31.7.44 at Avranches (France) as Ofw. & Zugf. in St. Gesch. Brig 341	20.2.42
Kirchner, Otto	SS-Untersturmf., Fhr. in Stabsschwadron/SS-Reiter-Rgt. 16 + 3.5.45 Prague (Czechoslovakia) in Czech captivity; final post SS-Obersturmfhr.	21.4.44
Kirn, Dietrich	Hptm., Fhr. Frontaufkl. Kdo. 202	12.12.44
Kirn, Hans	Ofw., Flugzeugf. in 8./K.G. 6	29.2.44

KNIGHT'S CROSS OF THE IRON CROSS

Kirn, Julius	Hptm., Chef 1./Pz. Rgt. 18 + 16.7.41 in northern sector of Russia	17.7.41
Kirsch, Walter	Oblt. d.R., Chef 7./G. R. 161 + 16.9.44 in hospital as Hptm. d.R. of wounds	6.3.44
Kirsche, Heinz	Oblt. d.R., Fhr. 2./Pi. Btl. 658 + 14.2.44 in Russia as Major & Btl. Kdr.	13.10.42
Kirschenmann, Wilhelm	Uffz., Gruppenf. in 7./G. R. 82	12.3.43
Kirschner, Joachim	Lt., Staffelfhr. 5./J.G. 3 "Udet" 267th Oak Leaves 2.8.43	23.12.42
Kirschner, Ludwig	Major, Kdr. I./I.R. 436 135th Oak Leaves 28.10.42	18.1.42
Kirsten, Ernst	Lt. d.R., Fhr. 4./G. R. 410 + 19.4.44 in Narva area (Russia); posthumously promoted to Oblt. d.R.	15.5.44
Kirsten, Rudi	Hptm., Fhr. Pz. Gren. Ers. & Ausb. Abt. "GD"	28.3.45
Kissel, Hans	Oberst, Kdr. G. R. 683	17.3.44
Kitta, Paul	Feldw., Zugf. in 1./G. R. 439	23.2.44
Kittel, Dipl-Ing., Friedrich	Gen. Major, Kdr. 62. V.G.D.	9.1.45
Kittel, Heinrich	Gen. Major, Kampfkdt. von Lemberg	12.8.44
Kittel, Kurt	Obgefr., Granatwerfer-Truppf. 5./G. R. 88	29.11.44
Kittel, Otto	Ofw., Flugzeugf. d. 2./J.G. 54 449th Oak Leaves 11.4.44 113th Swords 25.11.44	29.10.43
Klärmann, Hans	Hptm., Fhr. II./Pz. Gren. Rgt. 361 + 6.9.44 in Russia	9.9.42
Klaiber, Hans	Lt., Zugf. in 3. (l.)/Flak-Rgt. 11 (mot.) + 9.5.45 at Dauba, near Prague, of wounds as Hptm. & Bttr. Chef	26.7.42
Klammeck, Hans	Ofw., Zugf. in 4. (MG.)/G. R. 1082	10.2.45
Klappich, Günter	Oblt., Chef 11./I.R. 6C) (mot.) 254th Oak Leaves 8.6.43	31.7.42
Klar, Eduard	Wachtm., V. B. in 3./A.R. 122	17.6.43
Klasing, Fritz	Obstlt. d.R., Kdr. G. R. 446 745th Oak Leaves 19.2.45	12.8.44
Klassmann, Helmut	Kaptlt., Chef 3. Räumbootsflottille	22.12.43
Klatt, Paul	Oberst, Kdr. Geb.Jäg. Rgt. 138 686th Oak Leaves 26.12.44	4.1.43
Klaucke, Werner	Lt. d.R., Zugf. in 3./Pz.Jäg. Abt. 200 + 14.9.44 at Epinal (France)	4.7.44
Klaus, Johann-Alfred	Oblt., Staffelf. 6./S.G. 1	26.3.44
Klaus, Ludwig	Major, Kdr. Pz.Jäg. Abt. 340 + 26.1.45 in Westen as Rgt. Kdr.	7.10.44
Klaus, Otto	Hptm., Kdr. II./G. R. 333	17.9.44

Klausgraber, Franz	Hptm., Kdr. III./Inf.Rgt. 227 + 11.6.44 at Stanislau (Russia) as Kdr. Gr. Rgt. 975 of wounds; posthumously promoted to Oberst	13.3.42
Klawe, Erich	Hptm., Fhr. I./I.R. 23 227th Oak Leaves 14.4.43	12.7.42
Kleber, Ludwig	Oblt., Chef 1./Feld-Ers. Btl. 212	5.4.45
Klee, Friedrich	Uffz., Fhr. Sturmzug/Füs. Btl. 126	21.1.45
Kleeberger, Karl	Uffz., Gruppenf. in 1./Gren. Rgt. Gruppe 554	9.6.44
Kleemann, Ulrich	Oberst, Kdr. 3. Schützen-Brigade 304th Oak Leaves 16.9.43	13.10.41
Kleemann, Willy	Oberfähnr., Fhr. 2./Pz. Pi. Btl. 51	11.1.45
Kleffel, Paul-Georg	Oblt. d.R., Chef 4./Pz. Aufkl. Abt. 3	14.5.44
Kleffel, Philipp	Gen.Lt., Kdr. 1. I.D.	17.2.42
Kleffner, Franz	SS-Sturmbannf., Kdr. SS-Krdschtz. Btl. "Totenkopf" + 16.3.45 Sakarestis (Hungary); final post SS-Obersturmbannf. & Kdr. SS-Pz. G. R. 6 "Theodor Eicke"	19.2.42
Kleim, Fritz	Uffz., Gruppenf. in 5./Gren. Brig. 388	3.11.44
Kleimann, Hans	Uffz., Zugf. in 8. (M. G.)/G. R. 426 Simultaneously promoted to Feldw.	5.4.45
Klein, Alfons	Oblt., Staffelkpt. 10./J.G. 11	27.4.45
Klein, Armin (17)	Lt., Fhr. 15./Fsch. Flak-Rgt. "HG"	12.3.45
Klein, Georg	Feldw., Zugf. in 15./Jäg. Rgt. 204	27.8.43
Klein, Gerhard	Obstlt., Kdr. Waffenschule AOK 9	30.12.43
Klein, Heinrich	Hptm., Staffelkpt. 2./K.G. 27 "Boelcke"	10.6.43
Klein, Dr. Herbert	Oblt., Flugzeugf. in Stabsstaffel I./K.G. 100	29.2.44
Klein, Hermann	Oblt. d.R., Rgt. Adj. G. R. 551 567th Oak Leaves 2.9.44	15.4.44
Klein, Kurt	Ofw., Zugf. in 12. (MG.)/G. R. 424	16.4.44
Klein, Max	Feldw., Zugf. in 2./G. R. 485 + 12.11.44 at Saarburg	9.4.44
Klein, Walter	Major, Kdr. III./I.R. 193 + 22.3.41 west Norway by an avalanche	9.5.40
Kleindienst, Erhard	Lt., Fhr. 8./Jäg. Rgt. 28 + 11.10.44 at Kunsenburg (East Prussia); posthumously promoted to Oblt.	18.12.44
Kleinheisterkamp, Matthias	SS-Brigadef. & Gen. Major d. W-SS, Kdr. SS-Div. "Reich" 871st Oak Leaves 9.5.45	31.3.42
Kleinmann, Alfons	Hptm., Fhr. I./G. R. 118	14.8.43
Kleinschmidt, Ernst	Lt. d.R., Btl. Adj. in Pz. G. R. 111	30.9.43
Kleinschmidt, Werner	Hptm., Kp. Chef. in Aufkl. Abt. 341 (mot) + 15.3.45	14.12.41

Name	Rank/Unit	Date
v. Kleist, Ewald	Gen. d. Kav., Kom.Gen. XXII. A.K. (Pz. Gruppe "Kleist") 72nd Oak Leaves 17.2.42 60th Swords 30.3.44	15.5.40
v. Kleist-Retzow, Jarislaff	Major, Kdr. II./A.R. 161 + 25.3.45 at Balga (East Prussia) as Rgt. Fhr.	14.2.45
Klemann, Helmut	Oblt., Fhr. 2./Pz. G. R. 59	28.10.44
Klemm, Hans	Uffz., Gruppenf. in 2./I.R. "GD" (mot.) + in Camp Tiflis (Russia) in Soviet captivity	10.12.42
Klemm, Rudolf	Hptm., Staffelkpt. 10./J.G. 54	18.11.44
Klemt, Heinrich (8)	Hptm., Fhr. Pz. Pi. Btl. II./Führer-Gren. Brigade	2.5.45
Klemz, Bernhard	Hptm., Chef 5./Pz. Rgt. "GD"	4.6.44
Kless, Friedrich	Major, Kdr. II./K.G. 55	14.10.40
Klett, Albert	SS-Obersturmf. d.R., Chef 6./SS-Kav. Rgt. 15 "Florian Geyer" + 14.2.45 at Szambek, near Tata (Hungary) as Hptsturmfhr. d.R.	16.10.44
Klette, Hans Dietrich	Major, Kdr. Fernaufkl. Gruppe 4	5.4.44
Kliemann, Nikodemus	Oberst, Kdr. G. R. 410	9.5.45
Klien, Heinz	Oblt., Staffelkpt. in II./K.G. 27 "Boelcke"	12.11.41
Klier, Erich	Oblt. d.R., Chef 5./Jäg. Rgt. 56	4.5.44
Klima, Robert	Lt. d.R., Fhr. 6./G. R. 1	10.8.43
Klimek, Helmut	Ofw., Bordfunker in 14. (Eis.)/K.G. 27 "Boelcke" + 9.12.44 missing over France	9.6.44
Kling, Heinrich	SS-Hptsturmf., Chef 13. (schw.)/SS-Pz. Rgt. 1 "LSSAH"	23.2.44
Klingenberg, Fritz	SS-Hptsturmf., Chef 2./SS-Kradsch. Btl. "Reich" + 22.3.45 at Herxheim (Rheinpfalz) as SS-Oberführer & Fhr. 17. SS-Pz. Gr. Div. "Götz v. Berlichingen"	14.5.41
Klinger, Kurt	Oblt., Chef 15. (Radf.)/G. R. 89 + 3.1.44 as Major & Btl. Kdr.	19.1.43
Klinke, Walter	Major, Kdr. I./G. R. 31 + 18.10.44 in Latvia	30.9.44
Klischat, Friedrich	Feldw., Zugf. in 3./Füs. Rgt. 27 + 2.7.44 in Russia as Ofw.	12.3.44
Klitsch, Franz	Oblt. d.R., Kp. Fhr. in G. R. 120 (rnot.)	22.1.43
Klocke, Walter	Obstlt., Kdr. Sturm-Rgt. 215 + 18.1.45 Gorlice (Galicia) as Oberst	20.4.44
Klöpper, Heinrich	Ofw., Flugzeugf. in 11./J.G. 51 "Mölders" + 29.11.43 posted missing after aerial combat over the Zuider-See (Holland) as Oblt. & Staffelkpt. 7./J.G. 1	4.9.42
Klöpping, Wilhelm	Obgefr., MG-Schtz. in 5./Pz. G. R. 4	15.5.43
Kloos, Hermann	Hptm. d.R., Chef 3. (sPW)/Pz. Aufkl. Abt. 8 + 10.12.43 in Russia of wounds; posthumously promoted to Major	13.12.43
Klos, Otto	Hptm., Fhr. Jäg. Rgt. 41 (L)	9.12.44

Klose, Erwin	Hptm., Fhr. II./Jäg. Rgt. 28	9.1.45
Klose, Friedrich	Uffz., Geschützf. in 14. (Pz.Jäg.)/I.R. 240 13. - 30.8.44 posted missing	20.8.42
Klose, Helmut	Ofw., Kp. Truppf. in 6./Pz. G. R. 115	16.11.44
Klose, Paul	Major d.R., Kdr. I./Fest. G. R. "Hanf" Breslau	30.4.45
Klosinski, Werner	Obstlt., Kmdre. K.G. 4 "General Wever"	9.6.44
Kloskowski, Karl	SS-Hptscharf., Zugf. in 4./SS-Pz. Rgt. 2 "Das Reich" 546th Oak Leaves 11.8.44	11.7,43
Kloß, Max	Major, Kdr. II./Geb.Jäg. Rgt. 144 + 2.12.44 Hernad (Hungary)	26.11.44
Klossek, Ernst	Oblt., Chef 12./I.R. 422 + 2.3.42 Semtizy (Volkhov, /Russia) as Kdr. III./I.R. 422 & Hptm. of wounds	23.2.42
Klosterkemper, Bernard	Oberst, Kdr. G. R. 920	4.7.44
Klotz, Ludwig	Oblt. d.R., Chef 9./I.R. 423 + 14.2.44 at Lopanez, south of Luga (Russia) as Major d.R. & Kdr. III./Gr. Rgt. 423	4.7.40
Klotzsche, Hans	Major, Kdr. I./Pz. A.R. 80	28.12.43
Klüber, Wilhelm	Oblt., Staffelkpt. 8./Stuka-Geschw. 1 + 19.7.44 at Bialystok (Russia) as Hptm.	16.4.43
Klümper, Werner	Major, Kmdr. K.G. 26	29.8.43
Klünder, Erich	Korv. Kpt., Chef 5. Minensuchflottille	12.8.44
Klüser, Ewald	Hptm., Chef 2./Pi. Btl. 12	10.2.45
Klüver, Max	Hptm. d.R., Kdr. I./Pz. G. R. 40	12.10.43
Klug, Bernd	Kaptlt., Kdt. "S 28" in 1. Schneflbootsflottille 361st Oak Leaves 1.1.44	12.3.41
Kluge, Ernst	Feldw., Zugf. in 6./Pz. G. R. 25	7.10.44
Kluge, Gerhard	Oblt. d.R., Fhr. II./G. R. 586 + 4.3.45 at Euskirchen (Rhineland)	9.6.44
v. Kluge, Günther	Gen. d. Art., OB 4. Armee simultaneously promoted to Gen. Oberst 181st Oak Leaves 18.1.43 40th Swords 29.10.43	30.9.39
Kluge, Waldemar	Major, Kdr. I./Fallsch. -Pz. G. R. 2 "HG"	2.8.43
v. Kluge, Wolfgang	Gen.Lt., Kdr. 292. I.D.	29.8.43
Klußmann, Hans-Jürgen (17)	Oblt., Techn. Offz. in I./S.G. 1	9.11.44
Kluth, Bernhard	Feldw., Zugf. in 12./Schtz. Rgt. 4	28.11.40
Kmitta, Lothar	Lt., Flugzeugf. in Nahaufkl. Gr. 5	18.11.44
Knaack, Kurt	Oblt. d.R., Fhr. 2./I.R. 410 + 6.4.44 in Russia as Div. Adj. 122. Inf. Div. of wounds; posthumously promoted to Major d.R.	5.11.42
Knaak, Hans-Wolfram	Oblt., Chef 8./Lehr-Rgt. z.b.V. 800 "Brandenburg" + 26.6.41 Dünaburg (Russia); posthumously promoted to Rittm.	3.11.42

Knabe, Gustav-Georg	Obstlt., Kdr. Kradschtz. Btl. 15	1.6.41
Knabe, Konrad	Hptm., Kettenfhr. in Fernaufkl. Staffel Lappland (l. (F)/Aufkl. Gr. 124) (AOK 20. Geb. Armee)	16.4.43
Knacke, Reinhold	Oblt., Flugzeugf. in 3./N. J.G. 1 190th Oak Leaves 7.2.43	1.7.42
Knaf, Walter	Lt., Zugf. in 8./Fsch. Pz. G. R. 2 "HG" + 8.12.43 in Italy	4.4. 44
Knapp, Franz	Major, Kdr. s. Pz.Jäg. Abt. 663	10.9.44
Knapp, Wilhelm	Hptm., Staffelkpt. 3. (F)/Aufkl. Gr. 123 + 10.6.44 NW Europe as Major & Gruppenkdr.	2.11.40
Knappe, Herbert	Ofw., Zugf. in 14./Jäg. Rgt. 83	15.5.44
Knappe, Kurt	Uffz., Flugzeugf. in 5./J.G. 51 "Mölders" + 3.9.43 shot down over France as Ofw. & Flugzeugf. in 7./J.G. 2 "Richthofen"	3.11.42
Knaul, Ernst	Uffz., Gewehrfhr. in 4. (schw.)/Div. Füs. Btl. 96 + 6.4.45 Engelhartstetten, near Hainburg a. d. Donau as Feldwebel	6.3.44
Knaup, Ludwig	Hptm. d.R., Chef 2./St. Gesch. Brig. 904 + 18.3.45 in Ermland as Btl. Fhr. in Pz. Gr. Div. "GD"	4.10.44
Knaust, Hans-Peter	Major, Kdr. Kampfgr. "Sonnenstuhl" in II. SS-Pz. Korps 843. Oak Leaves 17.4.45	28.9.44
Knauth, Dr. Wilhelm	Lt. d.R., Fhr. 3./Pz. Abt. 505	14.11.43
Knebel, Ernst	Oberst, Kdr. Feld. Ers. Rgt. Pz. AOK 3 & Anneewaffenschule 744. Oak Leaves 19.2.45	27.8.44
v. Knebel-Doeberitz, Rudolf (19)	Major i.G., Ia 24. Pz.Div.	11.5.45
Knemeyer, Siegfried	Major in Stabsamt des RLM, Kdr. Aufkl. Lehr-Gr. des Ob. d. Luftw.	29.8.43
von dem Knesebeck, Wasmod	Oberstlt. i.G., Ia 306. I.D. + 6.3.45 at Lepseny (Hungary) as Kdr. R. R. 3	14.5.44
Knetsch, Wilhelm	Major, Kdr. I.R. 545	8.10.42
Kniep, Walter	SS-Sturmbannf., Kdr. SS-St. Gesch. Abt. 2 "Das Reich" + 22.4.44 accidentally at Thouars (France) as Kdr. SS-Pz. Abt. 17 "Götz v. Berlichingen"	14.8.43
Knirsch, Walter	Feldw., Zugf. in 14./G. R. 89	21.12.44
Knittel, Gustav	SS-Sturmbannf., Kdr. SS-Pz. Aufkl. Abt. 1 "LSSAH"	4.6.44
v. Knobelsdorff, Otto	Gen.Lt., Kdr. 19. Pz.Div. 322nd Oak Leaves 12.11.43 100th Swords 21.9.44	17.9.41
Knobloch, Leo	Uffz., Kp. -Truppf. in 1./Reiter-Rgt. 32	30.9.44
Knoche, Heinz	Major, Fhr. Pz. G. R. 33	5.4.45

ELITE OF THE THIRD REICH

Knöchlein, Fritz	SS-Obersturmbannf, Kdr. SS-Freiw. -Pz. G. R. 23 "Norge" + 21.1.49 condemned to death by a British court, hanged at Hameln	16.11.44
Knörrchen, Egon	Hptm. d.R., Chef 4./A.R. 218	28.3.45
Knoespel, Walter	Hptm., Kp. Chef in I.R. 156 (mot.)	17.1.42
Knoke, Heinz (17)	Hptm., Kdr. III./J.G. 11	27.4.45
Knollmann, Karl-Heinz	Lt. d.R., Kp. Fhr. in G. R. 45	21.3.44
Knoop, Dr. med. dent. Rolf	Major, Kdr. I./G. R. 377	26.7.44
v. Knoop, Waldemar	Major d.R., Kdr. Radf. Abt. 8	26.3.43
Knop, Albert	Hptm., Kdr. III./G. R. 118	17.8.43
Knorr, Karl-Heinz	Hptm., Kdr. Flak-Sturm-Abt. 7	28.2.45
Knorr, Walter	Uffz., Gruppenf. in 6./Pz. G. R. 108 + 30.1.45	6.3.44
Knostmann, Georg	Hptm. d.R., Rgt. Adj. G. R. 266	4.5.44
Knotzer, Josef	Major, Fhr. of a Alarmeinheit/9. Pz.Div.	23.3.45
Knüppel, Heinrich	Major, Kdr. II./I.R. 256	7.8.42
Knüppel, Karl-Günther	Lt. d.R., Zugf. in Stabskp./G. R. 51 (mot.)	17.12.43
Knüttel, Karl	Ofw., Zugf. in 1./Pz.Jäg. Abt. 200	3.11.44
Knust, Friedrich-Karl	Obstlt., Kmdre. (K)Lehr-Geschw. 1	3.5.42
Knuth, Friedrich-Wilhelm	Major, Fhr. G. R. 211 + 10.3.44 at Cassino (Italy) as Rgt. Fhr.; posthumously promoted to Obstlt.	6.3.44
Knuth, Hermann	Kapt. z. See, Chef 1. Sicherungsdivision	24.9.44
Koall, Gerhard	Hptm., Kdr. IV./J.G. 54 + 27.4.45 shot down over Anklam (Mecklenburg) as Kdr. IV./J.G. 3 "Udet"	10.10.44
Koberling, Horst	Oblt. d.R., Fhr. II./Pz. G. R. 25	30.4.45
Kobersky, Herbert	Uffz., Zugf. in Rgt. -Gruppe 481 + 5.1.45 in a field hospital at Memel as Feldw. IL./Gr. Rgt. 280 of wounds	4.10.44
Koch, Alfred (6)	SS-Obersturmf., Fhr. II./SS-Pz. G. R. 3 "Deutschland"	6.5.45
Koch, Alfred (17)	Oblt., Fhr. 2./le. Flak-Abt. 71 + 20.6.45 shot by the French at Vaucouleurs (France)	7.4.45
Koch, August	Hptm., Fhr. of a Kampfgr. in Festg. Posen	20.2.45
Koch, Dr. rer. pol. Dietrich	Feldw., Zugf. in 3./Pz.Jäg. Abt. 88	23.2.42
Koch, Erwin	Major, Kdr. II./G. R. 447	28.5.43
Koch, Friedrich	Gen.D.Inf. z. V., Kom.Gen. XXXXIV. A.K.	13.10.41
Koch, Karl	Ofw., Zugf. in III./Fsch. Jäg. Rgt. 15 + 26.7.44 at St. Lo (Normandy/France)	24.10.44
Koch, Max	Obstlt. d.R., Kdr. G. R. 585 + 15.4.44 between the Dnjestr and Pruth (Russia); posthumously promoted to Oberst d.R.	4.6.44

Koch, Theodor	Oblt., Chef 6./A.R. 36 (mot.)	2.9.44
Koch, Walter	Hptm., Kdr. Fsch. Jäg. Sturmabt. "Koch" simultaneously promoted to Major; + 23.10.43 in a Berlin hospital, as a result of an accident, as Obstlt. & Kdr. Fsch. Jäg. Rgt. 5	10.5.40
Koch, Willi	Feldw., Fhr. 6./G. R. 32 612th Oak Leaves 16.10.44	16.4.44
Koch, Willi	Ofw., Zugf. in 3./Fsch. Jäg. Rgt. 1	9.6.44
Koch-Erpach, Rudolf	Gen.Lt., Kdr. 8. I.D.	24.6.40
Kochanowski, Johann	Owm., Zugf. in 2./St. Gesch. Abt. 201	15.10.42
Kochendörfer, Karl	Uffz., Gesch. Fhr. in 3. (schw.)/Schnelle-Abt. 296	18.9.42
Kociok, Josef	Ofw., Flugzeugf. in 10. (NJ)/Z.G. 1 + 26.9.43 over Kertsch (Russia) following a collision with a Soviet aircraft, as Flugzeugfhr. in N. J.G. 200; posthumously promoted to Lt.	31.7.43
Kodré, Heinrich	Major, Kdr. II./I.R. 123	14.5.41
Köchle, Ludwig	SS-Oberscharf., Stoßtruppf. & Zugfhr. In 5./SS-Totenkopf-Inf.Rgt. 1 + 9.6.42 south of Lake Ilmen at Polizo (Russia)	28.2.42
Köchling, Friedrich	Gen. Major, Kdr. 254. I.D.	31.7.42
Köck, Reinhold	Hptm. d.R., Kp. Chef in G. R. 469	5.1.45
Köckerbauer, Hans	Ofw., Zugf. in 13./Geb.Jäg. Rgt. 91 + 28.7.42 at a crossing of the Don south of Batask (Russia)	18.11.41
v. Koeckritz, Hans-Joachim	Rittm. d.R., Kdr. Div. Füs. Btl. (A.A.) 32 + 4.2.44 at Pustoschka (Russia); posthumously promoted to Major d.R.	10.2.44
Koeditz, Alfred	Lt. d.R., Flugzeugf. in Stab/K. Gr. z.b.V. 100	23.12.42
Köhler, Armin	Hptm., Kdr. III./J.G. 77	7.2.45
Koehler, Carl-Erik	Gen.Lt., Kdr. 306. I.D.	4.5.44
Köhler, Fritz	Obstlt., Kdr. Fern-Aufkl. Gruppe 122	4.11.41
Köhler, Georg	Lt., Fhr. 3./Pz. G. R. 26	3.1.43
Köhler, Hans-Joachim	Rittm., Kdr. I./Reiter-Rgt. 31	5.3.45
Köhler, Heinrich	Lt. d.R., Zugf. in 3./He. St. Gesch. Brig. 210	20.4.45
Köhler, Dr. jur. Helmut	Hptm. d.R., Fhr. Pz. Aufkl. Abt. 1	3.11.44
Köhler, Helmut	Hptm., Fhr. II./G. R. 154	18.2.45
Köhler, Rudolf	Major, Kdr. I./Schtz. Rgt. 73 + 7.7.43 Bjelgorod (Russia) as Oberst & Kdr. Pz. Gren. Rgt. 73	27.7.41
Köhler, Siegfried	Uffz., Meldestaffelfhr. d. I./Pz. G. R. 108	17.3.45
Koehler, Walter (4)	Ofw., Zugfhr. In 3./schw. Heeres-Pz.Jäg. Abt. 525	11.5.45

Köhler, Werner	Hptm., Btl. Kdr. in Füs. Rgt. 26	13.2.45
Koehne, Hans-Günther	Hptm., Staffelkpt. Stabsst./Stuka-G. 2 "Immelmann"	3.11.42
Köhnen, Hermann	Hptm., Fhr. I./G. R. 1145	28.2.45
Köhnke, Otto	Hptm., Kdr. II./K.G. 54	1.8.42
Kölbel, Otto	Obgefr., Gruppenf. in 2./G. R. 542	1.6.43
Köllner, Jürgen	Hptm., Kdr. II./G. R. 671 + 8.10.44 in Russia	4.5.44
Kölsch, Erich	Uffz., Gruppenf. in 3./Pi. Btl. 263	18.11.44
v. Koenen, Friedrich	Hptm., Kdr. III./4. Rgt. "Brandenburg" (Einheit der Abwehr) + 20.8.44 Vizegrad (Croatia) as Obstlt. & Kdr. 4. Jäger-Rgt. "Brandenburg"	16.9.43
König, Alfons	Oblt. d.R., Chef 6./I.R. 199 194th Oak Leaves 21.2.43 70th Swords 9.6.44	21.12.40
König, Christian	Hptm., Fhr. II./G. R. 41 (mot.)	5.1.43
König, Ernst	Major, Fhr. G. R. 12 598th Oak Leaves 21.9.44	16.9.43
König, Eugen	Major, m.F.b. I.R. 352 318th Oak Leaves 4.11.43	1.8.42
König, Georg	Feldw., Zugl. in 1./Pz. Abt. 18	13.9.43
Koenig, Hans-Heinrich	Oblt., Fhr. I./J.G. 11 + 24.5.44 shot down over Kahenkirchen (Holstein); posthumously promoted to Hptm.	19.8.44
König, Heinrich	Hptm., Kdr. I./G. R. 915	14.2.45
Koenig, Heinz	Lt., Fhr. 3./Fsch. St. Gesch. Abt. "HG"	8.2.45
König, Herbert	Ofw., Flugzeugf. in 12./T. G. 1	9.6.44
König, Reinhard	Oblt. (Ing.), Leit. Ing. auf "U 123"	8.7.44
König, Rudolf	Feldw., Zugf. in 2./Pz. G. R. 74	17.12.42
König, Viktor	Feldw., Beob. in 14. (Eis.)/K.G. 55 + 29.8.44 over the Bucht of Riga	6.10.44
König, Wilhelm	Oblt. d.R., Chef 1./Kav. Rgt. "Atte" + 15.8.44 at a main dressing station in Russia as Rittm. d.R. of wounds	10.9.43
Koeppel, Walter	Uffz., Geschf. in 14. (Pz.Jäg.)/G. R. 111	15.2.43
Köppen, Eckhardt (17)	Uffz., Kp. Truppf. in 1./Fsch. Pz. Pi. Btl. 2 "HG"	15.3.45
Köppen, Gerhard	Feldw., Flugzeugf. in 7./J.G. 52 79th Oak Leaves 27.2.42	18.12.41
Koepsell, Herbert	Uffz., Kp. Truppf. in 1./Fsch. Pz. Pi. Btl. 2 "HG"	7.2.45
Körner, Adolf	Oblt. d.R., Fhr. 7./A.R. 168	20.1.45
Körner, Friedrich	Lt., Staffelfhr. 2./J.G. 27	6.9.42

KNIGHT'S CROSS OF THE IRON CROSS

Körner, Helmut	Lt. d.R., Zugf. in 2./Pz.Jäg. Rgt. 656 + 22.4.45 between Neu-Petershain & Greifenhain near Cottbus	3.12.43
Körner, Karl (10)	SS-Hptscharfhr., Zugfhr. in 2./schw. SS-Pz. Abt. 503	29.4.45
Körner, Martin	Oblt., Staffelkpt. 4./Kampfgr. z.b.V. 9	14.3.43
Körner, Walter (19)	SS-Hptsturmfhr., Rgt. -Adjut. SS-Freiw. Pz. Gren. Rgt. 23 "Norge"	11.5.45
Körte, Peter	Oberst, Kdr. Füs. Rgt. 26	27.9.43
Köster, Alfons	Ofw., Flugzeugf. in 3./N. J.G. 2 + 7.1.45 shot down over Varel/Oldenburg as Staffelkpt. in IV./N. J.G. 3; nachträgl. zum Hptm.	29.10.42
Koester, Alfred	Oberst, Kdr. Pz. G. R. 200	10.5.43
Köster, Helmut	Feldw., Flugzeugf. in 1./S.G. 2 "Immelmann" + 8.8.44 at Sächs. -Regen (Hungary); posthumously promoted to Ofw.	8.8.44
Köster, Walter	Hptm., Kdr. III./I.R. 156 (mot.) + 31.7.42 on the Don (Russia) as Major	30.10.41
Köther, Wilhelm	Oblt., Chef 1./Div. Aufkl. Abt. 257	27.5.42
Kötke, Werner	Hptm., Kdr. I./G. R. 994 + 17.7.44 at Ancona (Italy); posthumously promoted to Major	23.8.44
Koetz, Karl	Hptm., Kdr. II./I.R. 463 374th Oak Leaves 24.1.44	2.10.41
Kofler, Florian	Major, Kdr. II./Jäg. Rgt. 56 + 31.10.44	16.11.44
Kohl, Christoph	Uffz., Kp. Truppf in 2./Pz. G. R. 12 + 20.8.44 in Russia as Ofw.	14.5.44
Kohla, Helmut	Ofw., Zugf. in 4./Pz. Abt. 21 + 25.6.44 at Werch Lesslje, 35 km south of Bobruisk (Russia)	16.8.43
Kohlauf, Franz	Korv. Kpt. Chef 4. Torpedobootsflottille + 26.4.44 off St. Malo (France) on "T 29"; posthumously promoted to Freg. Kpt.	29.10.43
Kohler, Wilhelm	Hptm., Fhr. of a Kampfgr. im I.R. 195 607th Oak Leaves 4.10.44	10.12.42
Kohlermann, Otto	Oberst, Arko 129	22.2.42
Kohlhaas, Karl	Uffz., Zugf. in 7./G. R. 485	4.5.44
Kohlhaas, Ludwig	Obstlt., Kdr. III./Füs. Rgt. "GD" + 30.11.42 at Morosowo (Russia)	21.11.42
Kohlhagen, Kurt	Lt., Flugzeugf. & Beob. in 1. (N)/Aufkl. Gr. 2 + 25.3.45 at Oderberg as Oblt.	30.9.44
Kohmann, Hanns	Hptm., Flugzeugf. in Fliegerstaffel des Führers + 21.4.45	28.2.45

219

Kohnz, Bruno	Ofw., Zugf. in 11./Jäg. Rgt. 207 207th Oak Leaves 6.3.43	17.12.42
Kohout, Franz-Josef	Hptm., Fhr. II./Pz. Rgt. 33	4.12.41
Koltschka, Siegfried	Oblt. z. Sce, Kdt. "U 616"	27.1.44
Koj, Ewald	Hptm., Chef 3./Geb. A.R. 8 (8. Jäg. Div.) + 11.3.45 at Teplice	9.5.45
Kokott, Heinz	Oberst, Kdr. G. R. 337	17.3.43
Kolb, Fritz	Fhj. -Feldw., Flugzeugf. in 5./T. G. 3	9.6.44
Kolb, Richard	Major d.R., Kdr. Le. Flak-Abt. 91 (mot.)	12.11.41
Kolb, Werner	Major d.R., Kdr. II./I.R. 36 514th Oak Leaves 26.6.44	27.6.42
Kolbeck, Hans	Ofw., Zugf. in 1./G. R. 1083 + 17.2.45	24.2.45
Kolbeck, Dr. med. dent. Rudolf	Obstlt. d.R., Kdr. G. R. 316 403rd Oak Leaves 22.2.44	20.4.43
Kolbow, Hans	Oblt., Staffelkpt. 6./J.G. 51 + 16.7.41 Russia, by Soviet AA fire	27.7.41
Kolbus, Friedemann	Oblt., Chef 3./Pz.Jäg. Abt. 161	9.12.44
Kolczyk, Heinz	Rittm., Kdr. Pz. Aufkl. Abt. 7	6.4.44
Koll, Johannes	Lt., Fhr. 2./G. R. 696	24.12.44
Koll, Richard	Oberst, Kdr. Pz. Rgt. 11	15.7.41
Kollak, Reinhard	Ofw., Flugzeugf. in 8./N. J.G. 4	29.8.43
Kollberg, Botho	Obstlt., Kdr. I.R. 23 384th Oak Leaves 8.2.44	6.9.42
Kollehn, Gerhard	Major, Fhr. Jäg. Rgt. 38	11.12.44
Koller, Albert	Oblt., Staffelkpt. 4./K.G. 55	13.11.42
Koller, Gustav	Obgefr., Gruppenf. in 1./Pz. G. R. 21 + 10.11.44 south of Besenyvetelek (Ungarn)	8.8.44
Koller, Karl	Oberst i.G., Chef d. Gen. St. Luftflotte 2	10.4.42
Kollewe, Gerhard	Hptm., Kdr. II./(K.)Lehr-Geschw. 1 112th Oak Leaves 12.8.42	5.7.41
Kollhofer, Josef	Obgefr., Geschf. in 4./Pz. G. R. 26 + 24.11.44	14.8.44
Kollmann, Fritz	Lt. d.R., Zugf. in Pz. G. R. 59	6.10.44
Kolodziejczyk, Georg	Ofw., Zugf. in 3./Pz. Rgt. 15	5.3.45
Koltermann, Wolfgang	Oblt., Chef 3./schw. Pz. Abt. 507	11.3.45
Kompch, Herbert	Hptm., Kdr. I./Flak-Rgt. 4 (mot.) + 25.3.44 in Kamenez-Podolsk (Russia)	11.3.44
Konopacki, Gänther	Oblt., Fhr. Aufkl. Abt. 168 797th Oak Leaves 23.3.45	19.12.43
Konopka, Gerhard	Oblt. d.R., Fhr. II./G. R. (mot.) "Großdeutschland"	29.8.43
Konrad, Alfred	Owm., Zugf. in 1./Aufkl. Abt 7 + 10.1.44 in Russia of wounds	8.8.43
Konrad, Rudolf	Gen. d. Geb. Tr.,1 Kom.Gen. XXXXIX. Geb. Korps	1.8.42

KNIGHT'S CROSS OF THE IRON CROSS

Konschegg v. Pramburg, Dr. jur. Lambert	Major, Kdr. III./K.G. 40	28.2.45
van Koolwijk, Wilhelm	Oberst, Kdr. Flak-Rgt. 37 (mot.)	8.8.44
Koopmann, Erwin	Major, Fhr. G. R. 76 + 8.11.43 south-east of Kiev (Russia); posthumously promoted to Obstlt.	28.11.43
Kopatzki, Lothar	Lt., Fhr. Pz.Jäg. Kp. 1212	5.4.45
Kopp, Helmut	Oblt., Fhr. 1./I.R. 151 + 18.1.43 at Gorodok south of Lake Ladoga (Russia) as Chef 6./G. R. 151	2.6.42
Kopp, Karl	Feldw., Zugf. in 11./I.R. 512	15.11.41
Kopp, Walter	Hptm., Kdr. I./Geb.Jäg. Rgt. 99	6.11.42
Kopp, Walter	Major, Fhr. G. R. 1077	9.2.45
Koppe, Rudolf	Hptm., Kdr. Pz. Aufkl. Abt. 23	18.11.44
Koppenwallner, Karl	Oberst, Kdr. G. R. 97	1.1.44
Kordemann, Martin	Ofw., Zugf. in 6./G. R. 577	11.5.45
Korfes, Dr. rer. pol. Otto	Gen. Major, Kdr. 295. Inf. Div.	77.1.43
Korn, Heinz	Feldmeister in RAD, Meßoffz. in 4./schw. Flak-Abt. 232 (RAD 8/60)	14.1.45
Kornblum, Dietrich	Oblt., Staffeffhr. 4./K.G. 53 "Legion Condor" + 27.11.44 shot down over Juist island (North Sea) as Hptm. & Staffelkpt. 9./N. J.G. 2	9.6.44
Kornmeyer, Hans	Major, Kdr. II./I.R. 109	9.5.42
Kornprobst, Franz	Oberst, Kdr. G. R. 320	5.4.45
Kornprobst, Otto	Lt., Zugf. in Pz. Abt. 118 + 2.5.45 in Berlin	23.3.45
Korol, Anton	Lt. d.R., Staffelfhr. 10. (Pz.)/S.G. 2 "Immelmann"	12.3.45
Korte, Hans	Gen. Major, Kdr. 2. (Torpedo-)Flieger-Div.	30.9.44
Korten, Günther	Gen. Major, Chef d. Gen. St. Luftflotte + 22.7.44 as a result of severe wounds received on 20.7.44 in Fhqu. in Rastenburg (East Prussia) as Chef Gen. St. d. Luftwaffe; posthumously promoted to Gen. Oberst	13.5.41
Korth, Claus	Kaptlt., Kdt. "U 93"	29.5.41
Korth, Siegfried	SS-Obersturmfhr., Chef 3./SS-Kav. Rgt. 18 "Florian Geyer"	9.2.45
Korthals, Gerhard	Hptm., Staffelkpt. 8./K.G. 51 + 3.11.42 shot down over Russia as Kdr. II./K.G. 51	2.10.42
Korts, Berthold	Lt., Flugzeugf. in 9./J.G. 52 29.8.43 failed to return from a mission over Kharkov (Russia) as Staffelfhr.	29.8.43

v. Kortzfleisch, Joachim	Gen.D.Inf., Kom.Gen. XI. A.K. + 20.4.45 at Wülwesort (Krs. Olpe/Westf.); final post z. V. II. Gr.B	4.9.40
Korupkat, Günther	Ofw., stellv. Fhr. 6./G. R. 1077 + 11.2.45 in East Prussia	9.2.45
Kosar, Karl	Lt. d.R., Zugf. in 2./Pz. Abt. 7	7.2.44
Kosch, Benno	Obstlt., Kdr. II./K.G. 1 "Hindenburg"	1.10.40
Koser, Christian	Ofw., Fhr. 4./G. R. 273	2.9.44
Koske, Dr. Karl	Gen. Major, Kdr. 212. I.D. + 8.4.45 in Vienna, during an Allied bombing raid	15.3.44
Koslinko, Otto	Uffz., Zugfhr. in 8./G. R. 504 + 28.3.44; posthumously promoted to Feldw.	4.6.44
Kossack, Siegfried	Oberst, Kdr. G. R. 1051	18.11.44
Koßmala, Georg	Oberst, Kdr. Sich. Rgt. 3 435th Oak Leaves 26.3.44	13.3.42
Koßmann, Karl-Richard	Oberst, Kdr. Pz. G. R. 74	23.3.45
Kostka, Franz	Obgefr., Stoßtruppf. in 6./G. R. 399	10.5.43
Kotlowski, Franz	Obgefr., Gruppenf. in 7./G. R. 411	16.11.44
Kotz, Richard	Oberst, Kdr. G. R. 389	21.10.43
Kowalewski, Robert	Hptm., Flugzeugf. in Stabsstaffel/X. Fliegerkorps	24.11.40
Kox, Peter	Ofw., Zugf. in 1./Pz.Jäg. Abt. 169	5.4.45
Kraas, Boris	SS-Sturmbann£, Kdr. SS-Pz.Jäger-Abt. 3 "Totenkopf" + 13.2.45 in a base hospital at Linz/Danube of wounds	28.2.45
Kraas, Hugo	SS-Sturmbannf, Kdr. I./2. Pz. Gren. Rgt/Pz. Gren. Div. "LSSAH" 375th Oak Leaves 24.1.44	28.3.43
Kracht, Hermann	Ofw., Zugf. in 12. (MG)/G. R. 29 (mot.) + 2.6.44 east of Aprilia (Italy)	25.12.44
Krämer, Christoph	Ofw., Zugf. in 5./Pz. G. R. 7	14.5.44
Kraemer, Fritz	Obstlt. i.G., Ia 13. Pz.Div.	17.12.42
Krämer, Paul	Obstlt., Kdr. Pz. G. R. 93 + 9.3.45	7.2.45
Krämer, Richard	Lt., Zugf. in 1./St. Gesch. Brigade 232	30.9.44
Kräussel, Oskar	Feldw., Flugzeugf. in K.G. z.b.V. 172 + 6.3.43 as Ofw. in south Russia	24.12.42
Krafft, Heinrich	Oblt. d.R., Staffelkpt. 3./J.G. 51 "Mölders" + 14.12.42 over Bjeloi (Russia) by Soviet flak; final post Hptm. d.R. & Kdr. I./J.G. 51 "Mölders"	18.3.42
Krafft, Horst	Oblt., Chef 2./St. Gesch. Abt. 185	29.9.41
Kraft, Alfred	Uffz., Zugf. in 2./Pz. Rgt. 27 + 20.6.43 in Russia as Feldw. of wounds	22.1.43
Kraft, Gerhard	Hptm., Kdr. I./Pz. G. R. 112	23.2.44

Name	Details	Date
Kraft, Josef	Oblt., Flugzeugf. in II./N. J.G. 6 838th Oak Leaves 17.4.45	30.9.44
Kraft, Karl	Major, Kdr. I./I.R. 42 + 28.1.42 as Obstlt. of wounds	18.1.42
Krag, Ernst-August	SS-Sturmbannf, Kdr. SS-Pz. Aufkl. -Abt. 2 "Das Reich" 755th Oak Leaves 28.2.45	23.10.44
Krah, Hans	Major, Kdr. I./Füs. Rgt. 34 + 21.7.44 as Rgt. Kdr., posthumously promoted to Oberst	11.10.43
Krahl, Karl-Heinz	Hptm., Fhr. I./J.G. 2 "Richthofen" + 14.4. 42 over Malta by flak as Kdr. II./J.G. 3 "Udet"; posthumously promoted to Major	13.11.40
Krainz, Walter	Obgefr. in III./Jäg. Rgt. 75	17.4.45
Kraig, Dietrich	Gen. Major, Kdr. 168. I.D. 549th Oak Leaves 11.8.44	23.7.42
Krakau, August	Oberst, Kdr. Geb.Jäg. Rgt. 85	21.6.41
Kral, Rupprecht	Uffz., Geschützf. in 14. (Pz.Jäg.)/G. R. 19	15.5.44
Kralemann, Friedrich	Ofw., Flugzeugf. in II./K.G. 3 "Lützow" + 1.12.43 shot down over Russia	29.10.43
Kramer, Heinz	Uffz., Richtschtz. in 2./schw. Pz. Abt. 502 + 1.45 at Prawten (East Prussia)	6.10.44
Kramer, Rudolf	Hptm., Staffelkpt. in K.G. 26	18.3.45
Krancke, Theodor	Kapt. z. See, Kdt. Schwerer Kreuzer "Admiral Scheer" 614th Oak Leaves 18.10.44	21.2.41
van Kranenbrock, Wolfgang	Hptm., Kdr. II./I.R. 102	25.9.42
Kranz, Bernhard	Oblt. d.R., Chef 15./Jäg. Rgt. 83	5.11.44
Kranz, Rudolf	Major, Kdr. St. Gesch. Brig. 249	23.10.44
Krappe, Günther	Gen.Lt., Kdr. 61. I.D.	11.4.44
Krappmann, Heinrich	Obgefr., Geschützkan. in 19./Fsch. Pz. Flak-Rgt. "HG"	28.2.45
Kratsch, Dr. Günther	Major, Kdr. I./A.R. 65 (mot.)	29.9.40
Kratzenberg, Hans	Major, Kdr. III./Schtz. Rgt. 3	15.8.40
Kratzert, Rudolf	Hptm., Kdr. III./Fsch. Jäg. Rgt. 3	9.6.44
Kraus, Adolf	Ofw., Flugzeugf. in 4./K.G. 1 "Hindenburg" + 30.9.42 in Russia	25.11.42
Kraus, Eduard	Oblt. d.R., Fhr. 6./Pz. G. R. 14	25, 1.43
Kraus, Ewald	Major, stellv. Fhr. Pz. A.R. 102	26.3.44
Kraus, Hans-Werner	Kaptlt., Kdt. "U 83"	19.6.42
Kraus, Rupert	Oblt., Fhr. 2./Fsch. Pz. Rgt. 1 "HG"	30.11.44
Krause, Bernhard	SS-Sturmbannf., Kdr. I./SS-Pz. G. R. 26 "Hitlerjugend" + 19.2.45 on Granbrückenkopf (Hungary) as SS-Obersturmbannf. & Rgt. Kdr.	18.11.44

ELITE OF THE THIRD REICH

Krause, Fritz	Oberst, Kdr. Flak-Rgt. 91 (mot.) + 25.1.43 in Stalingrad (Russia)	24.3.43
Krause, Johannes (Hans)	Hptm., Kdr. II./N. J.G. 101 + März 1945 as Kdr. I./N. J.G. 4	7.2.45
Krause, Max	Major, Fhr. G. R. 106	18.11.44
Krause, Richard	Hptm., Kdr. II./G. R. 848 12.10.44 missing as Kdr. I./G. R. 1073	4.5.44
Krause, Walther	Gen. Major, Kdr. 170. I.D.	10.6.43
Krauss, Bernhard	Uffz., I. G. -Fhr. in 2./Pz.Jäg. Abt. 128	9.1.45
Krauss, Oswald	SS-Sturmbannf., Fhr. SS-Kav. Rgt. 15 "Florian Geyer" + 9.3.45 missing in Hungary as SS-Obersturmbannfhr.	27.1.45
Krauß, Walter	Oblt., Flugzeug. i. d 2. (H)/Aufkl. Gr. 21 363rd Oak Leaves 3.1.44	29.7.40
Krebs, Erich	Hptm., Chef 1./Flak-Rgt. 11 (mot.)	16.2.42
Krebs, Günther-Wolfgang	Lt., Fhr. of a Kampfgr. d. Heeres-Geb.Jäger-Btl. 201 + 14.12.44 in Russia	26.12.44
Krebs, Hans	Gen.Lt., Chef d. Gen. St. H.Gr. Mitte 749th Oak Leaves 20.2.45	26.3.44
Krech, Günther	Kaptlt., Kdt. "U 558"	17.9.42
Kreckow, Günther	Lt., Battr. Offz. in A.R. 6	6.11.44
Krei, Werner	Oberfähnrich, Zugf. in 5./Pz. A.A. 19	10.2.44
Kreiner, Herbert	Hptm., Btl. Kdr. in G. R. 261 Missing at Stalingrad	28.1.43
Kreipe, Heinrich	Obstlt., Kdr. I.R. 209	13.10.41
Kreitmair, Rudolf	Hptm. d.R., Fhr. 7./G. R. 282 + 28.9.43 south of Woroshdenije (Kuban bridgehead/Russia) as Btl. Kdr.	31.3.43
Kremer, Hermann	Major d.R., Kdr. II./A.R. 129	23.3.45
Krems, Gerhard	Lt., Flugzeugf. in 2./K.G. 27 "Boelcke"	25.5.42
Krenz, Wilhelm	Feldw., Zugf. in 3./Div. Füs. Btl. 96	4.5.44
Krenzer, Hermann	Oblt., Chef 2./I. K 379	14.12.41
Kreß, Hermann	Oberst, Kdr. Geb.Jäg. Rgt. 99 + 11.8.43 at Noworossijsk (Russia) as Gen.Lt. & Kdr. 4. Geb. Div.	20.12.41
Kreß, Ulrich	Lt. d.R., Zugf. in 1./Aufkl. Abt. 20 + 15.1.43 in Russia as Oblt. d.R. & Kp. Chef	22.9.41
Kresse, Ludwig-Hilmar	Major d.R., Kdr. Feld-Ers. Btl. 94	18.11.44
Kressel, Wilhelm	Lt. d.R., Fhr. 5./Sturm-Rgt. d. Pz. AOK 4	16.10.44
Kreßmann, Erwin	Hptm., Chef 1./schw. Pz.Jäg. Abt. 519	9.12.44
Kretschmer, Franz	Lt. d.R., Zugf. in 1./schw. Pz.Jäg. Rgt. 656	17.12.43
Kretschmer, Otto	Kaptlt., Kdt. "U 99" 6th Oak Leaves 4.11.40 5th Swords 26.12.41	4.8.40

Name	Rank/Unit	Date
Kretschmer, Theodor	Oberst, Fhr. 17. Pz.Div.	8.3.45
Krettek, Heinz	Lt. d.R., Fhr. 5./G. R. 423	12.8.44
Kretzschmar, Wolfgang	Major, Kdr. Gen. -Btl. 540 z.b.V. 600th Oak Leaves 30.9.44 121st Swords 12.1.45	15.5.43
Kreutz, Karl	SS-Standartenf., Kdr. SS-Pz. A.R. 2 "Das Reich" 863rd Oak Leaves 6.5.45	27.8.44
Kreutzberg, Anton	Uffz., Geschützf. in 2./schw. Pz.Jäg. Abt. 525	21.9.44
Kreuzer, Eduard	Obstlt., Kdr. Jäger-Rgt. 24 (L) + 22.2.45	17.3.45
Kreuzer, Franz	Uffz., Gruppenf. in 3./G. R. 89	15.1.43
Kreuzinger, Othmar	Oblt. d.r., Chef 4./Pz. A.A. 19 625th Oak Leaves 18.10.44	14.5.44
Krey, Heinz	Lt. (Ing.), Leit. Ing. on "U 752" + 23.5.43 in Atlantic	4.9.43
Krey, Hermann	Fhj. -Wachtm., Zugf. in 2./Div. Füs. Btl. 30	17.9.44
Kreysing, Hans	Oberst, Kdr. I.R. 16 183rd Oak Leaves 20.1.43 63rd Swords 13.4.44	18.5.40
Kriebel, Karl	Gen. Major, Kdr. 56. I.D.	4.7.40
Krieg, Gerhard	Oberwachtm., Zugf. in 1./Heeres-Sturm-Geschütz-Brig. 243	28.3.45
Krieg, Harald	Oblt., Chef 4./Schtz. Rgt. 1	15.7.41
Krieg, Johann	Oblt. z. See, Chef d. Kleinkampfflottille 361	8.7.44
Krieger, Friedrich-Wilhelm	Hptm., Kdr. II./G. R. 87 + 1.9.43	7.9.43
Krieger, Werner	Major, Kdr. I./G. R. 17	31.10.44
Krieger, Wilhelm	Feldw., Zugf. in 1./G. R. 168	4.6.44
Kriening, Herbert	Feldw., Zugf. in 12. (MG)/G. R. 234	23.8.43
Krings, Josef	Ofw., Kp. Truppf in 2./G. R. 412	4.5.44
Krink, Heinz	Lt., Adj. II./Fsch. Jäg. Rgt. 3	9.6.44
Kroeg, Helmut	Oblt., Fhr. II./G. R. 45	28.3.45
Kröhne, Wilhelm	Major, Kdr. St. Gesch. Brig. 190	24.2.45
Krogmann, Otto	Uffz., Zugf. in 1./Inf.Rgt. 668	9.11.42
Kroh, Hans	Major, Kdr. I./Fsch. Jäg. Rgt. 2 443rd Oak Leaves 6.4.44 96th Swords 12.9.44	21.8.41
Krohn, Ernst	Ofw., Zugf. in 1./G. R. 505	27.10.43
Krohn, Hans	Gefr., Richtschtz. in 1./Pz.Jäg. Abt. 20	6.4.42
Krohn, Hans	Ofw., Bordfunker in 6./Stuka-G. 2 "Immelmann"	26.3.44
Kroj, Theo	Hptm., Fhr. II./G. R. 87	24.11.43
Kroll, Hermann	Ofw., Flugzeugf. in 7. (F)/Lehr-Geschwader 2 + 1944	5.4.42
Krombholz, Franz-Josef	SS-Hptsturmf., Kdr. III./SS-Freiw. -Geb.Jäg-Rgt. 14 "Prinz Eugen"	28.3.45
Kron, Otto	SS-Hptsturmf., Fhr. SS-Flak-Abt. "Totenkopf'	28.6.42

Name	Details	Date
Kroner, Max-Georg	Hptm., Kdr. III./G. R. 463	17.10.43
Kropp, Fritz	Uffz., Gruppenf. in 2./G. R. 48 + 10.2.45 at Arnswalde (Pomerania)	12.3.44
Kroschinski, Hans-Joachim	Ofw., Flugzeugf. in 3./J.G. 54	17.4.45
Kroseberg, Heinz	Hptm. d.R., Staffelkpt. Wüstennotstaffel + 12.5.42 missing over the Mediterranean	9.6.42
v. Krosigk, Dedo	Hptm., Chef 1./I.R. 51 (mot.)	15.5.42
v. Krosigk, Ernst-Anton	Gen. Major, Kdr. 1. I.D. 827th Oak Leaves 12.4.45	12.2.44
Kruck, Kurt	Oblt., Chef 4./Div. Füs. Btl. 96	20.10.44
Krück, Fritz	Oblt., Fhr. II./G. R. 226	5.3.45
Krüder, Ernst-Felix	Kapt. z See, Kdt. Hilfskreuzer "Pinguin" (HSK 5) 40th Oak Leaves 15.11.41	22.12.40
Krügel, Albrecht	SS-Sturmbannf., Kdr. II./SS-Freiw. -Pz. G. R. 23 "Norge" 651st Oak Leaves 16.11.44	12.3.44
Krüger, Erwin	Oberfähnrich, Spähtruppf. in Pz. Späh-Schwadron/Pz. A.A. 24	17.9.44
Krüger, Felix	Ofw., Spähtruppf. in Stabskp./Pz. Aufkl. Abt. 6	9.12.44
Krüger, Friedrich-Wilhelm	SS-Obergruppenf. & General der W-SS & Pol., Kdr. 6. SS-Geb. Div. "Nord" + 10.5.1945 in Austria as Kom.Gen. V. SS-Geb. Korps (suicide)	22.10.44
Krüger, Fritz	Stabswachtm., Bttr. Offz. d. 1./A.R. 37	17.3.45
Krüger, Hans-Heinrich	Major i.G., Fhr. a Kampfgr. d. 321. I.D.	3.12.43
Krüger, Helmut	Hptm. d.R., Kdr. I./G. R. 151	11.4.44
Krüger, Horst	Oblt., Beob. in 3. Nacht-Aufkl. -Staffel	4.11.41
Krüger, Joachim	SS-Untersturmf., Fhr. 10./SS-Pz. G. R. 4 "Der Führer" + 14.8.43 Kharkov, Bjelgorod (Russia) of wounds; posthumously promoted to SS-Obersturmfhr.	24.6.44
Krüger, Kurt	Lt. d.R., Zugf. in Pz. Abt. 8	7.2.44
Krüger, Kurt	Oberwachtm., Bttr. Offz. in 2./A.R. 156 + 12.7.43 Orel (Russia) of wounds	31.7.43
Krüger, Rudolf	Ofw., Zugf. in 6./I.R. 32	5.10.41
Krüger, Walter	Gen. Major, Kdr. 1. Schtz. Brig. 373rd Oak Leaves 24.1.44	15.7.41
Krüger, Walter	SS-Brigadef. & Gen. Major der W-SS, Kdr. SS-Polizei-Div. 286th Oak Leaves 31.8.43 120th Swords 11.1.45	13.12.41
Krüger, Walther	Obstlt., Kdr. Pz. G. R. 71	27.8.43
Krützmann, Friedrich-Karl	Hptm., Kdr. I./Pz. G. R. 5	3.3.44
Krugner, Leopold	Uffz., Geschützf. in 1./Pzjäg. Abt. 17	14.2.45

Krumminga, Hans	Lt., Flugzeugf. in 9./Stuka-Geschw. 2 "Immelmann" posthumously promoted to Oblt. + 28.11.43 at Kriwoi Rog (Russia) as Techn. Offz. in III./Stuka-Geschw. 2;	19.9.43
Krupinski, Walter	Lt., Flugzeugf. in 6./J.G. 52 415th Oak Leaves 2.3.44	29.10.42
Kruse, Ernst	Ofw., Zugf. in 7./Pz. G. R. 3 245th Oak Leaves 17.5.43	6.10.42
Kruse, Gerhard	Hptm. d.R., Fhr. I./G. R. 48 534th Oak Leaves 27.7.44	23.2.44
Kruse, Heinrich	Hptm., Fhr. Gren. Rgt. Gruppe 311	26.3.44
Kruse, Heinz	Feldw., Zugf. in schw. Pz. Abt. 655	23.3.45
Krutemeier, Gustav	Ofw., Zugf. in 1./Geb. Pi. Btl. 99	3.10.42
Ksiag, Johann	Feldw., Zugf. in 2./Pz.Jäg. Abt. 176	15.1.43
Kubel, Wilhelm	Hptm. d.R., Fhr. II./G. R. 162	30.9.44
Kubisch, Walter	Ofw., Bordfunker in N. J.G. 3 + 6.10.44 over Paderborn with OTL Lent; posthumously promoted to Lt.	31.12.43
Kuchar, Jakob	Gefr. in 8./Jäg. Rgt. 228	11.5.45
Kübler, Ludwig	Gen. Major, Kdr. 1. Geb. Div. + February 1947 hanged in Lubljana (Yugoslavia); final post Gen. d. Geb. Tr. & Befehlsh. Sich. Gebiet Adriatisches Küstenland	27.10.39
v. Küchler, Georg	Gen. d. Art., OB 3. Armee 273rd Oak Leaves 21.8.43	30.9.39
Kühl, Dr. jur. Ernst	Oberst d.R., Kmdre. K.G. 55 356th Oak Leaves 18.12.43	17.10.42
Kühl, Hermann	Hptm., Staffelkpt. 2./K.G. 4 "General Wever" + 22.7.42 shot down over Kharkov (Russia) as Kdr. III./K.G. 41; posthumously promoted to Major	24.11.40
Kühme, Kurt	Major, Kdr. St. Gesch. Brig. 280	9.12.44
Kühn, Friedrich (Fritz)	Gen. Major, Kdr. 3. Pz. Brigade + 15.2.44 in Berlin during an Allied bombing raid as Gen. d. Pz.Tr. & Chef of Kraftfahrwesens in OKW & of Heeresmotorisierung	4.7.40
Kühn, Hans-Jochen	Lt. d.R., Chef 9./Pz. Rgt. 36	12.1.44
Kühne, Martin	Hptm., Kdr. I./Fsch. Jäg. Rgt. 2	29.2.44
Kühnfels, Rudolf	Oblt., Kp. Chef im Jäg. Rgt. 54	9.12.44
Kümmel, Johannes	Oblt., Chef 1./Pz. Rgt. 8 133rd Oak Leaves 11.10.42	9.7.41
Kümmling, Otto	Uffz., Gruppenf in 6./G. R. 530	4.5.44
Kündiger, Herbert	Major, Kdr. I./G. R. 978 708th Oak Leaves 21.1.45	9.12.44

Künkel, Christian	Lt., Flugzeugf. in 8./Stuka-Geschw. 3 + 27.1.44 at Kertsch (Russia); posthumously promoted to Oblt.	26.3.44
Künnecke, Heinz	Oblt., Chef 2./Inf. Btl. z.b.V. 500	16.11.43
Reichsfrhr. v. Künsberg-Weidenberg, Heino	Obstlt., Kdr. G. R. 188	16.9.43
Künzel, Hans-Joachim	Oblt., Fhr. 3./Schtz. Rgt. 10	22.9.41
Künzel, Karl-Friedrich	Oblt. z. See, Gruppenf. & Kdt. "S 28" in 1. Schnellbootsflottille	12.12.43
Kürsten, Hans	Lt. d.R., Zugf. in 1./Pz. Rgt. 7 + 6.12.42 in Tunisia as Oblt. d.R. & Kp. Fhr.	11.10.41
Küsel, Alfred	Rittm., Kdr. 1./G. R. 4	12.12.44
Küspert, Karl	Hptm., Chef 1./Pz. Rgt. 35 + 16.4.45 drowned, when the troop transporter ("Goya") on which he was travelling was sunk	16.10.44
Kuester, Ferdinand	Oblt., Chef 1./G. R. 58 + 14.1.45 at the Warka bridgehead as Hptm. & Kdr. I./Gr. Rgt. 18	27.10.43
Küster, Heinz	Lt., Fhr. 5./G. R. 108	15.7.43
Küster, Rudolf (Rolf)	Oblt., Flugzeugf. in 6./K.G. 53 "Legion Condor"	17.3.45
Küster, Wilhelm	Oblt., Flugzeugf. in Wettererkundungsstaffel 26 + 25.11.42 in North Africa	18.5.43
Kuffner, Andreas	Oblt., Staffelfhr. 4./Stuka-G. 2 "Immelmann" 684th Oak Leaves 20.12.44	16.4.43
Kugelstadt, Otto	Feldw., Zugf. in 6./G. R. 485	26.12.44
Kugler, Eugen	Hptm. d.R., Fhr. I./G. R. 19 "List"	5.4.45
Kugler, Josef	Uffz., Gruppenf. in 9./G. R. 200 (mot.)	3.11.44
Kuhenne, Helmut	Ofw., Bordfunker Stab/Fernaufkl. Gr. 3	20.1.45
Kuher, Josef	Oberwachtm., Bttr. Offz. & V. B. in 7./schw. Werfer-Rgt. 3 (mot.)	9.5.45
Kuhlmann, Herbert	SS-Sturmbannf., Kdr. I./SS-Pz. Rgt. 1 "LSSAH"	13.2.44
Kuhlmey, Kurt	Hptm., Kdr. II./Stuka-G. 3	15.7.42
Kuhlwilm, Wilhelm	Oblt., Kp. Fhr. in Fsch. Pz. G. R. 3 "HG"	30.11.44
Kuhn, Karl	Hptm., Fhr. Rückkampfgruppe "Kuhn" (ehem. G. R. 81)	26.11.44
Kuhn, Otto	Oblt. d.R., Chef 5./Pz. G. R. 13	7.3.43
Kuhn, Walter	Obgefr., Richtschtz. in 3./Pz.Jäg. Abt. 1	23.8.43
Kuhna, Bernhard	Oblt., Fhr. II./I.R. 508	12.1.42
Kuhnert, Alfred	Oberst, Kdr. G. R. 51 (mot.)	20.4.44
Kuhnert, Manfred	Gefr., Richtschtz. in 14. (Pz.Jäg.)/G. R. 442	22.1.44
Kuhnke, Günter	Kaptlt., Kdt. "U 28"	19.9.40
Kuhnle, Theophil	Hptm., Chef St. Gesch. Kp. 1014	18.2.45

Kujacinski, Norbert	Hptm. d.R., Chef 4./Pz. Rgt. 23	18.11.44
Kullmer, Arthur	Gen.Lt., Kdr. 296. I.D. 758th Oak Leaves 28.2.45	27.10.43
Kulot, Josef	Obgefr., Gruppenf. in 6./I.R. 60 (mot.)	24.9.42
Kulp, Karl	Feldw., Zugf. in 13./Fsch. Pz. G. R. 4 "HG" + 5.2.45 at Sollnicken (East Prussia) of wounds as Ofw.	5.9.44
Kuls, Wolfgang	Rittm., Kdr. III./PzRgt. 24	24.2.45
Kult, Josef	Lt. d.R., Fhr. 3./Jäg. Rgt. 228 212th Oak Leaves 15.3.43	7.10.42
Kumm, Otto	SS-Obersturmbannf., Kdr. SS-Inf.Rgt. (mot.) "Der Führer" 221st Oak Leaves 6.4.43 138th Swords 17.3.45	16.2.42
Kummer, Alfred	Fhj. -Ofw., Flugzeugf. in 11./T. G. 2 + March 1945 Breslau	18.11.44
Kummer, Gotthard	Feldw., Zugf. in 1./G. R. 45	11.3.43
Kummetz, Oskar	Konteradm., Fhr. Kampfgruppe Oslo	18.1.41
Kunert, Gerhard	Obgefr., Gruppenfhr. in 6./Pz. Gren. Rgt. 33 606th Oak Leaves 4.10.44	16.9.43
Kunert, Hans	Lt. d.R., V. B. in 4./A.R. 5	23.8.44
Kunert, Rudolf	Hptm. d.R., Fhr. II./G. R. 401	21.9.44
Kunkel, Kurt-Ernst (5)	Lt., Kp. Chef 2./F.J.R. 4	30.4.45
Kunkel, Rolf	Major, Kdr. Div. Füs. Btl. 26 + 29.11.44 at St. Etienne (France)	17.3.45
Kunsch, Erwin	Hptm., Kdr. II./G. R. 232 + 28.9.43 of wounds; posthumously promoted to Major	24.11.43
Kuntz, Albert	Hptm., Fhr. Pz. Aufkl. Abt. 2	6.2.44
Kuntz, Herbert	Lt. d.R., Flugzeugf. in 3./K.G. 100	14.3.43
Kuntze, Albrecht	Oblt., Flugzeugf. in 6./K.G. 26 + 5.7.43 in Russia as Hptm. & Gruppenkdr.	16.5.40
Kuntze, Walter	Gen. d. Pi., Kom.Gen. XXXXII. A.K.	18.10.41
Kuntzen, Adolf-Friedrich	Gen.Lt., Kdr. 8. Pz.Div.	3.6.40
Kunz, Hermann	Lt., Zugf. in 2./Pz.Jäg. Abt. 37	17.12.43
Kunz, Karl	Oberst, Kdr. G. R. 412 +31.1.44 south of Leningrad (Russia) of wounds	6.4.44
Kunz, Rudolf	Oblt. d.R., Fhr. Schnelle Abt. 306	10.6.43
Kunze, Erhard	Ofw., Zugf. in 2./Aufkl. Abt. 341 (mot.) + 6.1.42 in Area Rostow (Russia)	22.2.42
Kunze, Gottfried	Hptm. d.R., Fhr. 1./G. R. 211	20.4.45
Kunze, Herbert (17)	Ofw., Beobachter in a Kampf-Geschw.	31.10.44
Kunzmann, Karl	Ofw., Zugf. in 8./Pz. Rgt. 35 + 5.8.44 accidentally in Russia	21.9.44
Kupfer, Baptist	Gren., MG-Schtz. in 4. (MG.)/G. R. 544	25.7.44

Kupfer, Dr. jur. Ernst	Hptm., Staffelkpt. 7./Stuka-Geschw. 2 "Immelmann" 173rd Oak Leaves 8.1.43 62nd Swords 11.4.44	23.11.41
Kupka, Hans	Lt., Kp. Fhr. in G. R. 20 (mot.) + 15.10.43 south-eastwards Kiew (Russia) of wounds	14.11.43
Kupke, Georg	Obstlt., Kdr. G. R. 1075	18.11.44
Kuppinger, Ernst	Hptm., Fhr. II./G. R. 352 819th Oak Leaves 5.4.45	24.12.44
Kuppisch, Herbert	Kaptlt., Kdt. "U 94" + 27.8.43 in Atlantic as Kdt. "U 847"; posthumously promoted to Korv. Kapt.	14.5.41
Kupsch, Gottfried	Oblt. d.R., Fhr. 1./Radf. Abt. 72 + 16.6.42 Sevastopol, Crimea (Russia)	3.9.42
v. Kurowski, Eberhard	Oberst i.G., Chef d. Gen. St. XXXX. A.K.	23.1.42
Kurscheid, Hans	Lt., Fhr. 1./G. R. 426	28.10.44
v. Kursell, Claus	Hptm. d.R., Fhr. II./G. R. 3	17.10.44
Kurz, Hans	Hptm., Kdr. II./G. R. 994	9.12.44
Kurz, Karl	Oblt., Chef 9./Geb. Art.Rgt. 95	5.3.45
Kurz, Rudolf	Oberfähnr., Fhr. 2./Fsch. Jäg. Rgt. 12	18.11.44
Kurz, Wilhelm	Hptm. d.R., Kdr. II./Pz. G. R. 125	20.10.44
Kurze, Max	Major d.R., Kdr. Pz.Jäg. Abt. 187	20.9.44
Kusatz, Franz	Major, Staffelkpt. Nachtaufkl. Staffel + 25.10.42 shot down over Breslau	25.11.42
Kuske, Ortwin	SS-Untersturmf., Fhr. 3./SS-Pz. Aufkl. Abt. 17 "Götz v. Berlichingen"	26.11.44
Kutscha, Herbert	Lt. d.R., Flugzeugf. in II./S. K.G. 210	24.9.42
Kutscher, Alfred	Lt., Fhr. 2./Div. Füs. Btl. 35 + 25.8.44 at Rozan (Russia) as Btl. Fhr.; posthumously promoted to Hptm.	18.1.44
Kutschkau, Ernst	Ofw. d.R., Fhr. 6./G. R. 3 777th Oak Leaves 11.3.45	16.4.44
Kuzmany, Alfred	Obstlt., Kdr. I.R. 338	2.2.42
Kylling-Schmidt, Ekkehard	Lt., Fhr. 3./I.R. 26 150th Oak Leaves 4.12.42	20.10.41
Kynast, Paul	Obstlt., Kdr. G. R. 587 + 15.4.44 in Area Tarnopol (Russia); posthumously promoted to Oberst	4.6.44

L

Laage, Karl-Ernst	Lt. d.R., Fhr. 1./A.R. 66	26.11.44
Labenski, Helmut	Oblt., Chef 1./G. R. 409	9.4.44

KNIGHT'S CROSS OF THE IRON CROSS

Name	Details	Date
Labrenz, Erich	Hptm., Kdr. III./I.R. 480 + in summer 1949 in Workuta (Russia) in Soviet captivity; final post Obstlt. I. G.	31.12.41
Laebe, Heinz-Oskar	Obstlt., Kdr. I/G. R. 44 854th Oak Leaves 29.4.45	7.3.44
Lämmel, Walter	Oblt., Fhr. I./G. R. 366	17.3.45
Laengenfelder, Hanns	Obstlt., Kdr. G. R. 106 856th Oak Leaves 30.4.45	21.10.43
Lagois, Ehrenfried	Ofw., Flugzeugf. in 5./S.G. 2 "Immelmann" + 15.4.44 over Chersoness airfield (Crimea/Russia)	26.3.44
Laier, Gustav	Hptm. d.R., Fhr. II./G. R. 528	3.11.44
Lainer, Josef	SS-Oberscharf., Zugf. in 1./SS-Pz. G. R. "Der Führer"	8.10.43
Lais, Otto	Major d.R., Kdr. G. R. 858	30.9.44
Lambach, Helmut	Oblt. d.R., Chef 11./G. R. 88	6.3.44
Lambert, August	Lt., Flugzeugf. in 5./S.G. 2 "Immelmann" + 17.4.45 shot down at Kamenz (Saxony) as Oblt. & Staffelkapt. 8./S.G. 77	14.5.44
Lamey, Hubertus	Oberst, stellv. Fhr. 28. Jäger-Div.	12.2.44
Lammer, Karl	Uffz., Gruppenf. in Pi. Zug d. Stabskp./G. R. 105	13.1.44
Lammerding, Heinz	SS-Oberführer, Kdr. Pz. Kampfgruppe "Das Reich"	11.4.44
Lampart, Karl	Gren. in 5./G. R. 587	14.4. 45
Lampe, Hermann	Major d.R., stellv. Fhr. G. R. 419	16.11.43
Lampp, Wolfgang	Major, Kdr. Felders. -Btl. 104 + 23.10.43 south-west of Gomel (Russia)	19.12.43
Lamprecht, Herbert	Hptm., stellv. Kdr. le. Flak-Abt. 76 (mot.) 532nd Oak Leaves 25.7.44	22.1.43
Lancelle, Otto	Gen. Major, Kdr. 121. I.D. + 3.7.41 at the Kraslawa Düna bridgehead (Russia); posthumously promoted to Gen.Lt.	27.7.41
Lancier, Hubert	Uffz., Gruppenf. in 7./G. R. 399	18.2.45
von der Lancken, Dietrich	Major, Kdr. III./Pz. Rgt. 24 + 29.12.42 at Stalingrad (Russia) as Fhr. Pz. Rgt. 24; posthumously promoted to Obstlt.	29.10.42
Landau, Christian-Johannes	Gen. Major, Kdr. 176. I.D.	9.5.45
Landeck, Gustav	Lt. d.R., Kp. Fhr. in G. R. 423 + 1944	21.9.44
Landfermann, Carl-August	Oblt. (Ing.) d.R., Leit. Ing. on the "U 181"	27.10.43
Landgraf, Franz	Oberst, Kdr. 4. Pz. Brigade + 19.4.44 in Stuttgart; final post Gen.Lt. & Kdr. Pz.Div. Nr. 155	16.6.40

Landgraf, Paul	Lt., Flakkampftruppf. in I./Flak-Rgt. 19 (mot.)	22.1.43
Landwehr, Paul	Major d. Schupo, Kdr. II./SS-Pol. Rgt. 14 + 28.4.45 at Taubendorf (Spreewald)	17.3.45
Lang, Emil	Lt., Staffelfhr. 9./J.G. 54 448th Oak Leaves 11.4.44	22.11.43
Lang, Friedrich	Oblt., Flugzeugf. in 1./Stuka-G. 2 "Immelmann" 148th Oak Leaves 21.11.42 74th Swords 2.7.44	23.11.41
Lang, Georg	Ofw., Beobachter in II. (H)/12. (Nahaufkl. Gruppe 15)	20.12.44
Lang, Hermann	Rittm., Kdr. Div. Füs. Btl. 68	30.9.44
Lang, Hermann	SS-Unterscharf., Meldestaffelfhr. in I./SS-Pz. G. R. 5 "Totenkopf"	23.10.44
Lang, Joachim-Friedrich	Oberst, Kdr. G. R. 481 + 16.4.45 at Pillau (East Prussia) as Gen. Major & Kdr. 95. Inf. Div.	4.9.43
Lang, Joseph	Feldw., Stoßtruppf. in 2./Pi. Btl. 15 + 27.7.43 of wounds, in Russia, as Oblt. & Kp. Chef	4.7.40
Lang, Ludwig	Oblt., Chef 2./A.R. 7	6.10.44
Lang, Rudolf	Obstlt., Kdr. Geb. Pz.Jäg. Abt. 44	23.8.41
Langanke, Fritz	SS-Standartenoberjunker, Zugf. in 2./SS-Pz. Rgt. 2 "Das Reich"	27.8.44
Langbehn, Joachim	Hptm., Staffelkpt. 5./Stuka-Geschw. 2 "Immelmann" + 25.11.42 at Russka (great bend of the Don/Russia)	24.3.43
Lange, Erhard	Oblt. d.R., Kp. Chef in Kampfgr. des Sonderkdo. OKW-Abwehr II	15.1.43
Lange, Erich	Hptm. d.R., Fhr. Füs. Btl. 299	28.10.44
Lange, Erwin	Hptm., Kdr. II./G. R. 698	8.10.43
Lange, Gerhard	Hptm., Fhr. II./Pz. Rgt. 35	28.3.45
Lange, Günther (6)	SS-Sturmmann, Grfhr. in 16. (Pi.)/SS-Pz. Gren. Rgt. 4 "Der Führer"	6.5.45
Lange, Hans-Günther	Kaptlt., Kdt. "U 711 " 853rd Oak Leaves 29.4.45	26.8.44
Lange, Heinz	Hptm., Kdr. IV./J.G. 51 "Mölders"	18.11.44
Lange, Paul	Feldw., Zugf. in I./Pz. G. R. 13	7.9.44
Lange, Dr. med. dent. Walter	Obstlt. d.R., Kdr. G. R. 43 300th Oak Leaves 13.9.43	10.2.43
Lange, Werner	Vizeadmiral, Kom. Admiral Ägäis	28.10.44
Lange, Wolfgang	Gen. Major, Kdr. Korps-Abt. C	14.5.44
Langemeyer, Dr. med. habil. Carl	Stabsarzt d.R., Kdr. Fsch. San. Lehr-Abt.	18.11.44
Langendorf, Georg	SS-Untersturmf. d.R., Fhr. 5. (schw.)/SS-Freiw. Pz. Aufkl. Abt. 11 "Nordland"	12.3.44

KNIGHT'S CROSS OF THE IRON CROSS

v. Langenn-Steinkeller, Ernst-Hasse	Rittm., Kdr. Pz. Aufkl. Abt. 24	9.6.44
Langenohl, Willy	Lt., Fhr. 3./Pz. Pi. Btl. 57	30.4.45
Langenstraß, Ernst-Friedrich	Oblt., Chef 2./Pi. Btl. 28	5.6.40
Langer, Albert	Gefr., Gruppenf. i. I./G. R. 51 (mot.)	7.4.44
Langer, Günter	Lt. d.R., Fhr. Füs. Kp. 191	5.9.44
Langer, Karl-Heinz (17)	Major, Kdr. III./J.G. 3 "Udet"	20.4.45
Langer, Kurt	Oberst, Stabsoffz. f. Panzerbekämpfung beim Oberkdo. H.Gr.E	11.12.44
Frhr. v. Langermann & Erlencamp, Willibald	Gen. Major, Kdr. 29. (mot.) 75th Oak Leaves 17.2.42	15.8.40
Langert, Walter	Hptm., Kdr. I./G. R. 697 posted missing 17.7.44	9.6.44
Langesee, Karl	Hptm., Kdr. II./Jäger-Rgt. 207 211th Oak Leaves 15.3.43	10.8.42
Langfeldt, Kay	Oblt., Schwadr. Chef in Radf. Abt. 30	18.5.43
Langguth, Alfred	Lt. d.R., Fhr. 1./G. R. 351 + 13.1.44 in Russia as Oblt. d.R.	31.3.43
Langhart, Theodor	Oblt., Staffelkpt. 8./Stuka-Geschw. 77 + 22.12.42 by a Soviet ground-attack in the Don bend at Fissenkowo (Russia)	22.1.43
Langhorst, Bernhard	SS-Sturmbannf., Kdr. SS-Freiw. -Pz. jäg. Abt. 20 (estn. Nr. 1)	5.4.45
Langkeit, Willy	Major, Kdr. II./Pz. Rgt. 36 348th Oak Leaves 7.12.43	9.12.42
Langkopf, Paul	Ofw., Flugzeugf. in 1./Stuka-Geschw. 77	19.2.43
Langmaier, Matthias	Hptm. d.R., Kdr. III./Geb.Jäg. Rgt. 85	29.2.44
Lanz, Dr. jur., Dipl. -Ing. Albrecht	Major, Kdr. I./I.R. 396 + 27.1.42 in hospital at Smolensk (Russia) as Obstlt., of wounds	4.9.40
Lanz, Alfred	Uffz., Gruppenf. in 8. (MG.)/G. R. 44	9.1.45
Lanz, Hubert	Oberst i.G., Chef d. Gen. St. XVIII. A.K. 160th Oak Leaves 23.12.42	1.10.40
Lapp, Karl-Walter	Hptm., Kdr. Ski-Btl. 82	14.8.44
Larisch, Anton	Feldw., Zugf. in 8. (MG.)/I.R. 190	25.2.42
v. Larisch, Heribert	Gen.Lt., Kdr. 129. I.D.	26.12.44
Larsen, Rudolf	Uffz., Pz. Kdt. in 2./Pz. Rgt. "GD"	23.10.44
Lasch, Otto	Oberst, Kdr. Inf.Rgt. 43 578th Oak Leaves 10.9.44	17.7.41
Laschet, Ulrich	Fhj. -Oberjäg., Gruppenfhr. in 1./Jäg. Rgt. 54 (L)	15.4.44
Laskowski, Erwin (17)	Ofw., Flugzeugf. in 8./J.G. 11	27.4.45
Lasse, Kurt	Oblt., Staffelkpt. 9./J.G. 77 + 8.10.41 shot down over Perekop (Russia)	3.5.42

Lasse, Wilhelm	Uffz., Gruppenf. 5./G. R. 82 + 26.1.44 in Russia	12.3.44
Lassen, Georg	Oblt. z. See, Kdt. "U 160" 208th Oak Leaves 7.3.43	10.8.42
Latz, Albert	Oberst z. V., Fhr. Kampfgr. "Latz" + 6.11.43 at Kiev (Russia)	30.12.43
Lau, Fritz (17)	Hptm., Staffelkpt. 4./N. J.G. 1	28.4.45
Lau, Heinrich	Major, Kmdr. K.G. 1 "Hindenburg"	10.5.43
Lau, Kurt	Hptm., Staffelkpt. 1./Stuka-Geschw. 2 "Immelmann"	6.4.44
Lau, Lothar	Oblt., Staffelkpt. 8./Stuka-Geschw. 2 "Immelmann"	22.6.41
Lau, Werner	Lt. d.R., Zugf. in 5./Lehr-Rgt. z.b.V. 800 "Brandenburg"	9.12.42
Laubereau, Hugo	Obstlt., Kdr. G. R. 61	22.11.43
Laubmeier, Ludwig	Oblt. d.R., Chef 1./St. Gesch. Brig. 191	4.10.44
Lauch, Karl	Ofw., Zugf. in 8./Pz. G. R. 14	5.5.43
v. Lauchert, Meinrad	Major, Kdr. I./Pz. Rgt. 35 396th Oak Leaves 12.2.44	8.9.41
Laudenbach, Otto	Major, Kdr. III./G. R. 88 + 2.2.44 in Russia of wounds	14.12.43
Laue, Hermann	Obgefr., Gruppenf. in 9./Pz. G. R. 76 + 24.3.45	5.4.45
Laukat, Richard	Major, Kdr. II./A.R. 103 + 5.7.44 east of the Beresina (Russia) as Oberst & Kdr. A.R. 103	18.10.41
Launer, Kurt	SS-Sturmbannf, Kdr. II./SS-Pz. G. R. "Theodor Eicke"	15.8.43
Laupenmühlen, Oskar	Ofw., Fhr. 7./G. R. 399	9.5.45
Lauter, Wilhelm	Lt. d.R., Fhr. 3./A.R. 212	16.1.45
Lautz, Friedrich	Obstlt., Kdr. G. R. 1091	9.12.44
Laux, Paul	Gen.Lt., Kdr. 126. I.D. 237th Oak Leaves 17.5.43	14.12.41
Lawall, Dr. jur. Erich	Major d.R., Kdr. Radf. Abt. 54,	5.11.42
Lawrenz, Johannes	Hptm., Kdr. III./Jäg. Rgt. 38	14.5.44
Lay, Josef	Fhj. -Ofw., Zugf. in Fhj. Gren. Rgt. 1239 + 15.3.45 on the Oder	5.4.45
Leber, Heinz	Ofw., Flugzeugf. in 2./J.G. 51 "Mölders" + 1.6.43 shot down by flak at Orel (Russia); posthumously promoted to Lt.	29.2.44
Lechermann, Michael	Feldw., Zugfhr. in St. Gesch. Abt. 1007 + 18.7.44 in Russia	18.11.44
Lechl, Franz	Ofw., Zugf. in 5./G. R. 266	14.8.43

Name	Details	Date
Lechner, Alois	Hptm., Staffelkpt. I./N. J.G. 100 23.2.44 wounded at Mogilew, taken into Soviet captivity, since posted missing Major & Kdr. I./N. J.G. 100	5.2.44
Lechner, Friedrich	Major d.R., Kdr. Feldersatz-Btl. 212	27.7.44
Lechtenbörger, Dipl.-Ing. Willi	Oblt. (Ing.) d.R., Leit. Ing. auf "U 847" + 27.8.43 in the Atlantic; posthumously promoted to Kaptlt. (Ing.) d.R.	4.9.43
Lederer, Joachim	Hptm., Kdr. Pz.Jäg. Abt. 344	30.4.45
v. Leeb, Wilhelm Ritter	Gen. Oberst, OB H.Gr.C	24.6.40
Leesmann, Karl-Heinz	Oblt., Staffelkpt. 2./J.G. 52 + 25.7.43 shot down over the North Sea as Major & Kdr. III./J.G. 1	23.7.41
Lehmann, Christian	Major d.R., Kdr. II./G. R. 726 + 6.6.44 at St. Croix-Caen (France)	4.7.44
Lehmann, Hans	Oblt. z. See, Kdt. "U 997"	11.5.45
Lehmann, Hans-Georg	Oblt., Fhr. Sturmkp. d. Div. Kampfschule "HG" + 20.10.44 Trakehnen (East Prussia); posthumously promoted to Hptm.	10.10.44
Lehmann, Hans-Joachim	Oblt., Staffelkpt. 8./Stuka-Geschw. 2 "Immelmann"	23.11.41
Lehmann, Kurt	Oblt., Staffelkpt. 2./K.G. 53 "Legion Condor"	19.2.43
Lehmann, Paul	Oblt., Chef 8./Flak-Rgt. 24 (mot.)	5.4.42
Lehmann, Paul	Korv. Kpt. d.R. z. V., Chef 42. Minensuchflottille	24.9.44
Lehmann, Rudolf	SS-Obersturmbannf., Ia 1. SS-Pz.Div. "LSSAH" 862nd Oak Leaves 6.5.45	23.2.44
Lehmann, Waldemar	Hptm., Fhr. II./G. R. 3	19.8.44
Lehmann-Willenbrock, Heinrich	Kaptlt., Kdt. "U 96" 51st Oak Leaves 31.12.41	26.2.41
Lehner, Franz	Feldw., Kampfbeobachter in 6./K.G. 53 "Legion Condor"	22.5.43
Lehner, Wilhelm	Feldw., Zugf. in 5./Pz. G. R. 40	15.6.43
Lehnert, Willy	Ofw., Bordfunker i. Stab/K.G. 6	5.4.44
Lehnhoff, Ernst-Günter	Major, Kdr. Pz. Füs. Btl. d. Führer-Gren. Brigade	12.12.44
Lehrig, Herbert	Lt., Zugf. in II./G. R. 161	10.9.44
Lehrkinder, Alois	Feldw., Zugf. in 7./G. R. 447	3.4.43
Lehrter, Günther	Lt. d.R., Zugf. in 5./Pz. Rgt. 27	2.9.44
Lehweß-Litzmann, Walter	Obstlt., Kmdre. K.G. 3	29.10.43
Leibnitz, Gerhard	Oblt., Flugzeugf. & Beob. in 2. (N)/Aufkl. Gr. 5 + 1945 shot in Soviet captivity	14.1.45
Leicht, Helmut	Hptm., Staffelkpt. 2./Stuka-Geschw. 77 631st Oak Leaves 24.10.44	3.9.42

Leie, Erich	Oblt., Flugzeugf. i. Stab I./J.G. 2 "Richthofen" + 7.3.45 at Schwarzwasser/Hultschin in an accident as Kommodore J.G. 77; posthumously promoted to Oberstlt.	1.8.41
Leimbach, Karl	Ofw., Fhr. 7./G. R. 1	17.3.45
Leimkuhl, Helmut	Lt. d.R., Fhr. 7./G. R. 756 + 20.10.44 at Castel del Rio (Italy)	26.11.44
Leingärtner, Ludwig	Hptm., Staffelkpt. 2./Stuka-Geschw. 1 + 11.4.44 at Torgau (Elbe)	5.2.44
Leinhos, Ludwig	Oblt., Chef 6./Pz. Rgt. 18 + 21.8.42 at Gorki, 60 km east of Wjasma (Russia) as Hptm.	5.2.42
v. Leipzig, Hellmut	Lt. d.R., Zugf. in Pz. Aufkl. Abt. "Brandenburg"	28.4.45
Leitenberger, Helmut	Lt., Zugf. in 3./Fsch. Pz. Rgt. "HG"	17.4.45
Leitner, Dr. Leopold	Major, Fhr. G. R. 132	24.12.44
Lembke, Armin	Obstlt., Kdr. G. R. 220	5.3.45
Lemcke, Gerhard	Obstlt., Kdr. G. R. 89	12.1.45
Lemelsen, Joachim	Gen. d. Pz.Tr., Kom.Gen. XXXXVIII. Pz.K. 294th Oak Leaves 7.9.43	27.7.41
Lemke, Fritz	Hptm., Fhr. II./G. R. 3 + 24.6.44 in Russia	16.2.44
Lemke, Gerhard	Feldw., Kp. Truppf. in 7./G. R. 82	28.4.43
Lemke, Max	Major, Kdr. Aufkl. Abt. 17	18.10.41
Lemke, Siegfried	Lt., Staffelfhr. 1./J.G. 2 "Richthofen"	14.6.44
Lemke, Wilhelm	Lt., Staffelfhr. 9./J.G. 3 "Udet" 338th Oak Leaves 25.11.43	12.9.42
Lemm, Heinz-Georg	Hptm., Kdr. I./Füs. Rgt. 27 525th Oak Leaves 11.7.44 137th Swords 15.3.45	14.4. 43
Lemp, Fritz-Julius	Kaptlt., Kdt. "U 30" + 9.5.41 north of Iceland as Kdt. "U 110"	14.8.40
Lempp, Otto	Hptm. d.R., Chef 2./Pz. A.R. 75 + 11.8.44 in Poland	14.5.44
v. Lengerke, Wilhelm	Obstlt., Kdr. I./Reiter-Rgt. 1 + 26.8.42 at Krasnoarmeisk, southern edge of Stalingrad (Russia) as Oberst & Kdr. Pz. G. R. 21; posthumously promoted to Gen. Major	31.8.41
Lenkeit, Horst	Hptm., Kdr. I./G. R. 1076 + 1945	3.11.44
Lennartz, Hans	Hptm., Fhr. Alarm-Btl. Kolberg	9.5.45
Lent, Helmut	Oblt., Staffelkpt. 6./N. J.G. 1 98th Oak Leaves 6.6.42 32nd Swords 2.8.43 15th Diamonds 31.7.44	30.8.41
Lenz, Heinrich	Ofw., Zugf. in 1./G. R. 159	26.12.43
Lenz, Hermann	Obstlt., Kdr. G. R. 164 + 3.8.43 in Russia as Oberst	9.2.43
Lenz, Martin	Major, Kdr. I. (SPW)/Pz. G. R. 192	25.1.45

KNIGHT'S CROSS OF THE IRON CROSS

Leopold, Fritz	Oblt., Staffelkpt. 5./K.G. 3 "Lützow" + 5.11.43 in Russia; posthumously promoted to Hptm.	26.3.44
Leopoldsberger, Josef	Feldw., Zugf. in 1./I.R. 207 + 15.9.42 in the southern sector of the front (Russia) accidentally as Ofw.	14.3.42
Lepkowski, Erich	Lt., Fhr. 5./Fsch,Jäg. Rgt. 2	8.8.44
Lepper, Richard	Oberst, Fhr. Kampfgr. "Lepper" & Art. Kdr. 6 u. Fhr. e. Kampfgr. + 30.3.43 in Camp Frolow at Stalingrad (Russia) in Soviet. captivity; final post Gen. Major	17.12.42
Leppla, Richard	Hptm., Kdr. III./J.G. 51	27.7.41
Leroy, Jacques (8)	SS-Untersturmf., Fhr. 1./SS-Freiw. G. R. 69 "Wallonie"	20.4.45
Frhr. v. Lersner, Dipl.-Ing. Karl	Oberst, Kdr. G. R. 537 + 25.1.43 at Orel (Russia); posthumously promoted to Gen. Major	12.3.43
Leschke, Alexander	Major d.R., Kdr. II./I.R. 11 (mot.) + 7.12.42 in Leipzig (Saxony) as Oberst d.R. & Rgt. Kdr.	4.11.41
Leske, Martin	Hptm., Kdr. I./Jäg. Rgt. 49	19.8.44
Lestmann, Karl	Hptm., Kdr. II./Pz. Rgt. 15 + 26.2.43 in Donezbecken (Russia) of wounds; posthumously promoted to Major	25.1.43
Lethaus, Waldemar	Hptm., Kdr. Pz. Gren. Btl. 2103 + 28.12.44	9.12.44
Leukefeld, Karl-Otto	Oblt., Chef 1./I.R. 123	23.10.41
Leupert, Otto	Ofw., Flugzeugf. in I. (K)/L.G. 1 + 26.8.44 during landing at airfield in Brussels (Belgium) as Lt.	22.1.43
Leuschner, Alois	Lt., Fhr. Pi. Kp./Jäg. Rgt. 83	2.9.44
Leuschner, Kurt	Hptm., Fhr. III./S. R. 25	27.10.41
v. Lewinski, gen. v. Manstein, Fritz-Erich	Gen.D.Inf., Kom.Gen. XXXVII. A.K. 209th Oak Leaves 14.3.43 59th Swords 30.3.44	19.7.40
Lex, Alfred	SS-Hptsturmf. d.R., Fhr. I./SS-Pz. G. R. 4 "Der Führer" + 11.3.44 west of Shepetowka (Russia)	10.12.43
Lex, Hans	Oblt. d.R., Chef 7./Pz. Rgt. "GD"	10.9.43
Leyck, Siegfried	Hptm., Kdr. III./Pz. Füs. Rgt. "GD" + 7.7.43 north-west of Bjelgorod (Russia) of wounds	17.12.43
Leypold, Karl-Heinz	Hptm. d.R., Chef 4./G. R. 347 + 29.4.45 at Torgelow (Pomerania)	11.4.44
v. Leyser, Ernst	Gen. Major, Kdr. 269. I.D.	18.9.41
Leyser, Hans-Georg	Oberst, Kdr. I.R. 51 (mot.)	3.5.42
Lichel, Walter	Gen.Lt., Kdr. 123. I.D.	18.9.41
Lichte, Karl-Heinz (6)	SS-Hptsturmf., Chef 5./SS-Pz. Rgt. 5 "Wiking"	6.5.45

237

Lichtenberg, Philipp	Kaptlt. (Ing.), Leit. Ing. auf "U 516"	31.3.45
Lichtenberger, Hermann	Oberst, Kdr. Flak-Rgt. 104 (mot.)	12.11.41
Lieb, Theo-Helmut	Gen.Lt., Fhr. XXXXII. A.K. 400th Oak Leaves 18.2.44	7.2.44
Liebe, Heinrich	Kaptlt., Kdt. "U 38" 13th Oak Leaves 10.6.41	14.8.40
Frhr. v. Liebenstein, Dipl.-Ing. Gustav	Freg. Kpt. d.R., Chef 2. Landungsdivision & Seetransportchef Messina-Straße	3.9.43
Frhr. v. Liebenstein, Kurt	Gen. Major, Kdr. 164. Leichte Div.	10.5.43
Liebenwein, Josef	Oblt., Chef 7./Sturm-Rgt. 195 + 23.3.45 at Leobschütz (Upper Silesia) as Hptm. & Kdr. II./Sturm-Rgt. 14	7.4.44
Liebetrau, Gerhard	Uffz., Gruppenf. in 1./G. R. 399	11.3.45
Liebherr, Hans	Ofw., Bordfunker in I./N. J.G. 4	27.7.44
Liebig, Herbert	Lt., Fhr. 3./Pz. G. R. 103	9.12.44
Liebing, Walter	Major, Fhr. Fsch. Jäg. Rgt. 23	2.2.45
Liebisch, Franz	SS-Obersturrnfhr., Schwadr. Chef in 8. SS-Kav. Div. "Florian Geyer" + 12.2.45 during attempted breakout from Budapest	9.2.45
Liebmann, Emil	Major, stellv. Fhr. II./Jäg. Rgt. 228	18.11.44
Liecke, Karl (15)	SS-Obersturmbannf. & Obstlt. d. Schupo, Kdr. Waffen-Geb.Jäg. Rgt. 27 der SS	3.5.45
Liedtke, Albert-Gustav	Fhj. -Ofw. in 6./F. Jäg. Rgt. 1241 + 11.3.45 at the Seelower Höhen	15.3.45
Liedtke, Bruno	Lt., Fhr. 1./G. R. 151 + 8.2.45 In East Prussia	18.2.45
Liehl, Leopold	Uffz., Gruppenf. in 7./Pz. G. R. 10	31.3.43
Liehr, Franz	Uffz., Gruppenf. in Pz. Pi. Btl. 93	11.12.44
Lienau, Detlef	Hptm., Kdr. Pz. Aufkl. Abt. 33 + 22.6.43 of wounds; posthumously promoted to Major	9.5.43
Lier, Friedrich	Major, Kdr. Sturm-Btl. AOK 6 869th Oak Leaves 8.5.45	3.11.44
Liese, Heinrich	Wachtm., Zugf. in 2./A.R. 299	14.4. 43
Liese, Kurt-Günther	Hptm., Kdr. I./G. R. 309	16.4.43
Liesendahl, Frank	Hptm., Staffelkpt. 10./J.G. 2 "Richthofen" posted missing since 17.7.42 following an attack on a freighter off Brixham	4.9.42
Lieske, Kurt	Ofw., Zugf. in II./G. R. 508	2.9.44
Ließmann, Helmut	Hptm. d.R., Fhr. III./G. R. 731	3.11.44
Liethmann, Günter	Hptm., Chef 3./St. Gesch. Abt. 237	26.10.43
Lignitz, Arnold	Oblt., Kdr. III./J.G. 54 + 30.9.41 shot down at Siverska/Leningrad; probably died in Soviet captivity; died as Hptm.	5.11.40

v. Lilienhoff-Zwowitzki, Helmut	Oberst, Kdr. G. R. 439 + 30.6.44 at Walinowka (Russia) as Oberst	14.8.43
Lilienthal, Diedrich	Uffz., Pak-Geschüzf. in 1. (schw.)/Schnelle Abt. 290 + 28.8.44 at a hospital in Baldone south of Riga (Latvia), as Feldw. & Zugf., of wounds	2.4.43
Limbach, Johannes	Oblt. z. See, 1. Wachoffz. auf "U 181"	6.2.45
v. Limburg-Hetlingen, Enno-Erich (13)	Oberst, Kdr. G. R. 731	3.5.45
Limmer, Hans	Ofw., Spähtruppf. in 1. (Pz. Späh)/Pz. Aufkl. Abt. 7 + 1.2.45 in Russia as Lt.	27.10.41
Linde, Rudolf	Major, Kdr. U./G. R. 410	8.5.45
Lindemann, Ernst	Kapt. z. See, Kdt. Schlachtschiff "Bismarck" + 27.5.41 in the Atlantic off Iceland	27.12.41
Lindemann, Fritz	Oberst, Art. Kdr. 138 + 22.9.44 in Gestapo custody in Berlin, of wounds; final post Gen. d. Art. in OKH	4.9.41
Lindemann, Georg	Gen.Lt., Kdr. 36. I.D. 275th Oak Leaves 21.8.43	5.8.40
Lindemann, Gerhard	Oberst, Kdr. Inf.Rgt. 216 580th Oak Leaves 10.9.44	25.1.43
Lindemann, Karl-Wilhelm	Lt., Zugf. in 5./Pz. Rgt. 29	14.4. 45
Lindemann, Max	Rittm. d.R., Fhr. I./G. R. 48	11.3.45
Lindemann, Viktor	Lt., Adj. III./I.R. 124 + 9.9.42 at Dubakino, southern sector of the Eastern Front as Chef 4./Radf. -Abt. 72	21.9.41
Lindenau, Hans	Ofw., m.F.b. 1/G. R. 1	17.3,45
Lindenau, Usdau (14)	Obstlt. i.G., Chef d. St. IX. SS-Geb. Korps	10.2.45
Lindenberg, Friedrich	Oblt., Fhr. 5./Pz. G. R. 63	30.1.43
Lindenblatt, Herbert (16b)	Oberstlt., Kdr. Jäg. Rgt. 750 simultaneously promoted to Oberst	3.5.45
Linder, Hermann	Ofw., Zugf. & Ord.Offz. in II./Jäg. Rgt. 207 + 8.7.43 Kuban bridgehead (Russia)	19.6.43
Linderkamp, Heinrich	Major, Kdr. III. (Jäger)/G. R. 17 + 17.1.45 in Kurland as Major & Fhr. Gr. Rgt. 911	24.12.44
Lindhorst, Werner	Hptm. d.R., Chef 8. (MG)/G. R. 89	23.2.44
Lindig, Max	Gen.Lt., Höh. Art. Kdr. 307	27.7.44
Lindinger, Eduard	Feldw., Flugzeugf. in 7./K.G. 1 "Hindenburg"	9.12.42
Lindmayr, Alois	Hptm., Staffelkpt. 7./K.G. 76	21.7.40
Lindner, Alfred	Uffz., Zugf. in 9./G. R. 12	18.1.45
Lindner, Anton	Wachtm., Zugf. in 3./Div. Füs. Btl. 36	17.3.44
Lindner, Anton	Lt., Flugzeugf. in Stabsstaffel/J.G. 51 "Mölders"	8.4.44

Lindner, Gerhard	Gen. Major, Kdr. 346. I.D.	5.5.45
Lindner, Herbert	Uffz., Gruppenf. in 6./Pz. G. R. 60	28.7.43
Lindner, Kurt	Feldw., Zugf. in II./G. R. 1055	9.12.44
Lindner, Martin	Oblt., Chef 7./Jäg. Rgt. 741	21.1.45
Lindner, Otto	Major, Fhr. II./I.R. 60 (mot.) + in Summer 1944 as Oberst & Kdr. G. R. 53	19.3.42
Lingner, Hans	Oblt., Chef 7./I.R. 65 + 28.8.41 at Berislaw (Russia) of wounds	24.6.40
Linke, Gottfried	Hptm., Kdr. He. Pi. Btl. 44 (mot.)	1.3.45
Linke, Lothar	Oblt., Staffelfhr. 12./NJ.G. 1 + 14.5.43 over Holland in an accident	19.9.43
Linke, Richard	Hptm., Kdr. I./K.G. 54	17.9.41
Linke, Walter	Ofw., Bordfunker in 3./S.G. 2 "Immelmann"	16.12.44
Linz, Rudi	Lt., Flugzeugf. in 12./J.G. 5 + 9.2.45 at Meistad (Norway)	12.3.45
Lion, Karl-Hermann	Oblt., Staffelkpt. 9./Stuka-Geschw. 1	4.6.42
Lipfert, Helmut	Lt. d.R., Staffelfhr. 6./J.G. 52 837th Oak Leaves 17.4.45	5.4.44
Lipinski, Dr.-Ing., Hans	SS-Obersturmf. d.R., Fhr. I./SS-Flak-Abt. 18	2.1.45
Lipp, Hans-Hermann (17)	Hptm., Btl. Fhr. in Fsch. Jäg. Rgt. "Hübner" + 11.9.44 in Belgium	31.10.44
Lipp, Karl	Ofw., Flugzeugf. in 4./K.G. 55 + 19.11.42 in Stalingrad (Russia); posthumously promoted to Lt.	16.11.42
Lippe, Hans (17)	Lt., Zugf. in Fsch. Pz. G. R. 1 "HG"	26.3.45
zur Lippe-Weissenfeld, Prinz Egmont	Oblt., Staffelkpt. 5./NJ.G. 2 263rd Oak Leaves 2.8.43	16.4.42
Lippelt, Rudolf	Major, Kdr. II./A.R. 371	9.5.45
Lippelt, Walter	Hptm., Fhr. I./Pz. G. R. 8	8.5.45
Lippert, Rolf	Oberst, Kdr. Pz. Rgt. 31 + 1.4.45 at Bielefeld (Westf.) as Gen.Maj. & Kdr. 5. Pz.Div.	9.6.44
Lippert, Wolfgang	Hptm., Kdr. II./J.G. 27 + 3.12.41 as a result of of wounds suffered when shot down; died in British captivity, North Africa	24.9.40
Lippolt, Walter	Feldw., Zugf. in 1./Pz.Jäg. Abt. 240	4.3.42
Liss, Erhard	Hptm., Chef 5./Sturm-Rgt. 195	30.4.45
List, Franz	Hptm., Kdr. II./Geb.Jäg. Rgt. 144	3.3.43
List, Hans	Oblt. d.R., Kp. Fhr. in Feldersatz-Btl. 94	26.12.44
List, Wilhelm	Gen. Oberst, OB 14. Armee	30.9.39
Litjens, Stefan	Ofw., Flugzeugf. in 4./J.G. 53	21.6.43
Littmann, Walter	Hptm., Fhr. I./Pz. G. R. 8	17.4.45
Litzke, Erich	Ofw., Zugf. in 2./schw. Pz. Abt. 509	20.10.44

Name	Rank/Unit	Date
Lobmeyer, Jakob (8)	SS-Hptsturmf., Kdr. SS-Jagd-Pz. Abt. 561	28.4.45
Loch, Herbert	Gen.Lt., Kdr. 17. I.D.	16.6.40
Lodtka, Heinrich	Ofw., Zugf. in 8. (MG)/G. R. 82 + 4.1.44 in Russia of wounds	27.9.43
Loebel, Walter	Obstlt. i.G., Kmdre. K.G. 30	29.7.40
Frhr. Loebenstein v. Aigenhorst, Gottfried	Oblt. d.R., Chef 13. (I. G.)/G. R. 133 + 22.4.43 at Shamara (Russia); posthumously promoted to Hptm. d.R.	30.4.43
Löchner, Rudolf	Oblt. d.R., Fhr. 3. (schw.)/Schnelle Abt. 161 + 15.3.44 accidentally as Fhr. 3./St. Gesch. Abt. 361; posthumously promoted to Hptm. d.R.	5.7.43
Löffelbein, Günther	Oblt., Staffelkpt. in I./K.G. 51	19.9.43
Löffler, Alfred	Uffz., Zugf. in 1./G. R. 487	20.4.43
Löffler, Emil	Ofw., Zugf. in 4. (MG)/G. R. 460 + 25.10.43 in Russia	12.11.43
Löffler, Erich	Hptm., Kdr. II./I.R. 57 + 17.3.45 as Oberstlt. & Kampfkdt. of Frankfurt a. M.	7.10.42
Loeffler, Rolf	Hptm., Chef 10./I.R. 70 + 21.7.43 at Werchopenje (Russia) as Gen. Stabsoffz. in a Pz.Div.	14.9.42
Löhr, Alexander	Gen. d. Flieger, Chef Luftflotte 4 705th Oak Leaves 20.1.45	30.9.39
Löhr, Erich	Oberst, stellv. Fhr. 121. I.D.	12.8.44
v. Loeper, Friedrich-Wilhelm	Gen.Lt., Kdr. 10.1. b. (mot.)	29.9.41
Loer, Wilhelm	Oblt. d.R., Fhr. I./G. R. 311 + 25.8.44 as Hptm. d.R.	26.12.43
Löring, Heinrich	Lt. d-R., Adj. Pz. Aufkl. Abt. 118	7.4.44
Loerzer, Bruno	Gen.Lt., Kom.Gen. II. Fliegerkorps	29.5.40
Loesch, Ernst	Major, Kdr. I./Pz. G. R. 1	14.5.44
v. Lösecke, Hans	Hptm., Kdr. III./G. R. 90 (mot.)	8.2.43
Löser, Hans-Joachim	Hptm., Kdr. M./Füs. Rgt. 230	20.1.43
Lösing, Werner	Gefr., Gewehrfhr. in 12. (MG)/G. R. 67	29.2.44
Löwe, Erich	Hptm., Chef 3./Pz. Abt. 65 385th Oak Leaves 8.2.44	4.9.40
Loewer, Dipl.-Ing., Kurt	Korv. Kpt. d.R., Chef 11. Vorposten-Flottille	24.6.44
Löwrick, Karl	Obstlt., Kdr. III./I.R. 272 247th Oak Leaves 17.5.43	5.8.40
Lohmann, Hanns-Heinrich	SS-Sturrnbannf., Kdr. III./SS-Freiw. Pz. G. R. 23 "Norge" 872nd Oak Leaves 9.5.45	12.3.44
Lohmeyer, Hans-Georg	Lt., Staffelfhr. 6./S.G. 77 + 22.10.44 in Gumbinnen (East Prussia)	6.10.44

Lohmeyer, Karl	Oberst, Kdr. I.R. 505 + 4.1.42 at Leningrad (Russia); posthumously promoted to Gen. Major	15.7.41
Lohrey, Christian	Gefr., Kp. Tr. Melder in 3./Pz. G. R. 41	11.3.45
Lohß, Martin	Hptm., Kdr. I./Füs. Rgt. 34	28.7.44
Loibl, Lambert	Obgefr., Richtschtz. in 1./Pz. G. R. 33	9.6.44
Lombard, Gustav	SS-Obersturmbannf., Kdr. SS-Kav. Rgt. 1	10.3.43
Loos, Georg	Lt., Zugf. in I./Pi. Btl. 152	23.11.41
Loos, Gerhard	Lt., Staffelfhr. 8./J.G. 54 + 6.3.44 in the Oldenburg area in an accident following aerial combat, as Oblt.	5.2.44
Loos, Walter	Oblt., Fhr. III./G. R. 130 + 1.12.44 in Russia as Major	31.3.43
Loos, Walter	Ofw., Flugzeugf. in Stab/J.G. 300	20.4.45
Loos, Wilhelm	Oblt., Chef 10./G. R. 76 (mot.)	21.4.44
Loose, Otto	Uffz,., Geschützf. in 14. (Pz.Jäg.)/G. R. 507	4.11.43
Lorch, Anton	Obstlt., Kdr. Geb.Jäg. Rgt. 144	4.6.44
Lorch, Herbert	Major, Kdr. II./K.G. 1 "Hindenburg" + 19.8.42 in Russia	5.1.43
Lorenz, Alfred	Feldw., Ord.Offz. in 7./G. R. 485	4.10.44
Lorenz, Erich	Major d.R., Kdr. I./G. R. 287 467th Oak Leaves 4.5.44	14.11.43
Lorenz, Franz	Lt., Fhr. 5./G. R. 586	4.5.44
Lorenz, Friedrich	Hptm., Staffelkpt. 1./Stuka-Geschw. 1 + 17.7.43 at Strelnikowo (Russia)	31.7.43
Lorenz, Herbert	Ofw., Zugf. in 4. (MG)/G. R. 530	4.5.44
Lorenz, Karl	Major, Kdr. Pi. Btl. "GD" 395th Oak Leaves 12.2.44	17.12.42
Lorenz, Wilhelm	Oberst, Kdr. I.R. 376 + 2.1.43 in Demjansk (Russia) of wounds; posthumously promoted to Gen. Major	28.12.42
Lorenzen, Bernhard	Hptm. d.R., Kdr. I./G. R. 121	3.4.43
Lorenzen, Karl	Feldw., Zugf. in 7./G. R. 377	9.12.44
Lorfing, Artur	Obgefr. in 1./G. R. 956	9.5.45
Losigkeit, Fritz (17)	Major, Kmdr. J.G. 51 "Mölders"	28.4.45
v. Loßberg, Viktor	Major, Kdr. III./K.G. 26	17.10.41
Loth, Hans	Lt., Zugf. in 10./I.R. 203	25.7.42
Lotse, Christian	Oblt., Bttr. Chef in I./Flak-Rgt. 231 (mot.)	4.2.42
Lotter, Hans	Oblt., Beobachter in 11. (H)/Aufkl. Gr. 12	28.1.45
Lottner, Kurt	Oberst, Kdr. G. R. 111	14.10.43
Lotze, Gerhard	SS-Obersturmf., Fhr. 5./SS-Pz. G. R. 10 "Westland" + 13.10.44 at Modlin (Poland); posthumously promoted to SS-Hptsturmf.	1.2.45

Name	Details	Date
Lotze, Dr. Heinz	Hptm. d.R., Fhr. I./Pz. Gren. Rgt. "Kahle" (Pz.Tr. Schule Bergen) in Kampfgr. Grosan	9.5.45
Lublow, Willi	Obgefr., Gruppenf. in 14./G. R. 284 + 1.2.45	27.7.44
Lucas, Werner	Feldw., Flugzeugf. in 4./J.G. 3 "Udet" + 24.10.43 shot down over Leiden (Holland) as Hptm. & Staffelkpt.	19.9.42
Lucht, Ernst	Konteradmiral, Befehlshaber of the Sicherung in the Nordsee	17.1.45
Lucht, Walther	Gen.Lt., Kdr. 336. I.D. 691st Oak Leaves 9.1.45	30.1.43
Luchtenberg, Günter	Stabsfeldw., Beobachter in 2. (H)/Aufkl. Gr. 6	6.12.44
v. Luck & Witten, Hans-Ulrich	Major, Fhr. Pz. G. R. 125 (mot.)	8.8.44
v. Lucke, Claus	Lt., Zugf. in 9./Pz. Rgt. 18	31.8.41
Luckmann, Erich	Obgefr., Geschützf. in 3./Flak-Rgt. 241 (mot.) + 18.1.43 at Stalingrad (Russia)	21.12.42
Luczny, Alfons	Gen.Lt., Kdr. 2. Flak-Div. (mot.)	9.6.44
Ludigkeit, Günter	Oblt., Staffelkpt. 5./Stuka-Geschw. 77	26.3.44
Ludin, Hermann	Hptm. d.R., Fhr. II./G. R. 290 + 19.4.45 at Baura (Italy) as Major d.R. & Btl. Kdr.	23.10.44
Ludwig, Franz	Oblt., Chef 2./St. Gesch. Abt. 1346 + 14.8.44 in France	24.6.44
Ludwig, Hanns	Feldw., Flugzeugf. in 10. (Pz.)/S.G. 2 "Immelmann" + 19.1.45 at Loben (Upper Silesia) as Ofw.	8.8.44
Ludwig, Jürgen	Oblt., Chef 2./Pi. Btl. 74 + 22.10.43 in Russia as Hptm. i. e. Pi. -Rgt. Stab	20.2.43
v. Ludwiger, Hartwig	Obstlt., Kdr. I.R. 83 163rd Oak Leaves 23.12.42	15.7.41
Lübbe, Vollrath	Gen.Lt., Kdr. 2. Pz.Div.	17.8.43
Lübke, Robert	Ofw., Zugf. in 1./Pz. G. R. 25	7.1.44
Lücke, Max-Hermann	Oblt., Flugzeugf. in 9./J.G. 51 "Mölders" + 8.11.43 of wounds received on 23.10.43 at Mosyr (Russia)	6.4.44
v. Lücken, Theodor	Oblt., Fhr. II./I.R. 502 469th Oak Leaves 7.5.44	2.3.42
Lüdcke, Hugo	Lt. d.R., Fhr. 8./Jäger-Rgt. 28 simultaneously promoted to Oblt. d.R.	9.2.43
Lüddecke, Fritz	Ofw., Flugzeugf. in Stabsstaffel/J.G. 51 "Mölders" + 10.8.44 shot down at Wilkowischken/East Prussia	18.11.44
Lüdden, Siegfried	Kaptlt., Kdt. "U 188" + 13.1.45 accidentally, during a ship's fire on the "Daressalam" as Korv. Kapt. & Referent in Stab Kom. Adm. d. U-Boote	11.2.44
Lüdecke, Otto-Joachim	Gen. Major, Kdr. 56. I.D.	8.8.43

ELITE OF THE THIRD REICH

Lüders, Friedrich	Hptm., Chef 2./schw. Pz.Jäg. Abt. 654	30.9.44
Lüdke, Ernst	Oblt. d.R., Fhr. 2./gem. Flak-Abt. 241	5.9.44
Luedtke, Erwin	Fhj. -Ofw., Zugf. in 1./G. R. 502 + 14.7.44 in Russia as Lt. d.R. & Kp. Fhr.	15.5.44
Lühne, Richard	Uffz., Vorg. Beob. in A.R. 389	28.10.44
Lühr, Arthur	Owm., B-Offz. in 6./AR. 225	10.2.45
Luehrs, Wolfgang	Oblt., Staffelkpt. 2./K.G. 53 "Legion Condor" + 20.4.45 during the battle for Nürnberg as Hptm.	24.10.44
Lüke, Willi	Uffz., Gruppenf. in 3./Pi. Btl. 196	16.11.44
Lülfing, Harald	Hptm. d.R., Kdr. Füs. Btl. 7	28.10.44
Lüneburg, Paul	Oberst d.R., Kdr. A.R. 126	5.9.44
Lüngen, Siegfried	SS-Hptscharf., stellv. Fhr. 6./SS-Freiw. -Pz. G. R. 23 "Norge"	16.11.44
Lüth, Wolfgang	Oblt. z. See, Kdt. "U 138" 142nd Oak Leaves 13.11.42 29th Swords 15.4.43 7th Diamonds 9.8.43	24.10.40
Lütje, Heinz-Jürgen	Lt. d.R., Fhr. 2./I.R. 76 (mot.) + 14.11.41 in Leningrad (Russia)	18.10.41
Lütje, Herbert	Hptm., Staffelkpt. 8./N. J.G. 1 836th Oak Leaves 17.4.45	1.6.43
Lütjens, Günther	Vizeadmiral, Befehlshaber of the Aufklärungsstreitkräfte + 27.5.41 in Atlantic off Iceland on the "Bismarck" as Admiral & Flottenchef	14.6.40
v. Lüttichau, Hannibal	Hptm., Kdr. II./Pz. Rgt. 2	16.1.45
Frhr. v. Lüttwitz, Heinrich	Oberst, Kdr. Schtz. Rgt. 59 571st Oak Leaves 3.9.44 157th Swords 9.5.45	27.5.42
Frhr. v. Lüttwitz, Smilo	Oberst, Kdr. Schtz. Rgt. 12 426th Oak Leaves 16.3.44 76th Swords 4.7.44	14.1.42
Lützow, Günther	Major, Kmdr. J.G. 3 27th Oak Leaves 20.7.41 4th Swords 11.10.41	18.9.40
Frhr. v. Lützow, Kurt-Jürgen	Oberst, Kdr. I.R. 89 37th Oak Leaves 21.10.41	15.8.40
Lützow, Joachim	Oblt., Chef St. Gesch. Bttr. 667	4.11.41
Luhr, Hans	Ofw., Flugzeugf. in 7./Stuka-G. 77 + 20.9.44 at Novy-Dvor airfield (Czekoslovakia) as Flugzeugfhr. in 2./Schlacht-Geschwader 102	29.2.44
Luitjens, Walter	Oblt. d.R., Fhr. 6./G. R. 151 + 27.1.44 south of Lake Ladoga (Russia) of wounds as Hptm. d.R. & Kp. Chef	3.9.43
Lukas, Kurt	Ofw., Zugf. in 5./G. R. 1124	17.3.45
Lukesch, Dieter	Lt., Flugzeugf. in 7./K.G. 76 620th Oak Leaves 10.10.44	20.12.41
Lummel, Hans	Obgefr., Kp. Trupp-Melder in 1./G. R. 333	16.10.44

Name	Details	Date
Lumpp, Josef	Feldw., Zugf. in 2./G. R. 358	18.1.45
Lumpp, Karl-Willi	Oblt. d.R., Fhr. 3./G. R. 226	18.7.43
Luthardt, Hans	Lt. d.R., Fhr. Div. Stoßtrupp-Kp. 302	31.7.43
Lutsch, Waldemar	Oblt., Staffelkpt. 1. (F)/Aufkl. Gr. 121 + 4.9.43 in Russia	19.9.43
Lutter, Johannes (Hanns)	Ofw., Flugzeugf. in II./Schnell-K.G. 210	5.10.41
Lutz, Johannes (Hans)	Lt., Zugf. in Div. Begl. Kp. 116. Pz.Div.	9.12.44
Lutz, Martin	Hptm., Staffelkpt. 1./Zerst. Geschw. 1 +27.9.40 shot down during a raid on an aircraft factory at Bristol, UK, as Kdr. Erpr. Gr. 210	1.10.40
Lutz, Waldemar	Hptm., Chef 1./St. Gesch. Abt. 245 + 15.9.42 at Stalingrad (Russia)	2.10.42
Lutze, Helmut	Ofw., Zugf. in 1./Kradschtz. Btl. 64	2.10.42
Lutze, Werner	Hptm., Kdr. II./I.R. 169	24.7.41
Lux, Walter	Major, Fhr. G. R. 316	10.7.44
Luxenburger, Josef	Oblt., Beobachter in 4./K.G. 55	3.4.43
Luz, Helwig	Oberst, Kdr. S. R. 110	15.11.41
Luz, Karl	Hptm., Fhr. I./G. R. 850 + 24.4. 45 at Mährisch-Ostrau as Major & Fhr. Sturm-Rgt. 14	23.8.44
Lyhme, Konrad	Hptm., Fhr. III./I.R. 50	9.10.42

M

Name	Details	Date
Maas, Johann	Fhj. -Wachtm., V. B. in 12./A.R. 104 + 26.7.44 in Russia	25.10.44
Maaz, Heinz	Obgefr., Gruppenf. in 3./Pz. Aufkl. Abt. "GD"	4.10.44
Mach, Franz-Wilhelm	Major, Kdr. I./Kuban-Kosaken-Rgt. 4	30.4.45
Mach, Hans-Heinrich	Oblt., Chef 7./I.R. 220 + 10.11.43 during the battles at Nevel (Russia) as Hptm. & Btl. Kdr.	15.11.41
Macher, Heinz	SS-Untersturmf., Fhr. 16. (Pi.)/SS-Pz. G. R. "Deutschland" 554th Oak Leaves 19.8.44	3.4.43
Macher, Robert (2)	Gen. Major, Chef des Stabes AOK East Prussia + 22.10.49 in Soviet captivity	14.5.45
Machold, Werner	Ofw., Flugzeugf. in 7./J.G. 2 "Richthofen"	5.9.40
Macholz, Siegfried	Gen.Lt., Kdr. 49. I.D.	16.10.44
Machowsky, August	Oblt., Chef Pi. Kp./Jäger-Rgt. 28	30.4.45
v. Mackensen, Eberhard	Gen. d. Kav., Kom.Gen. III. A.K. (mot.) 95th Oak Leaves 26.5.42	27.7.41
Mader, Anton	Major, Kdr. II./J.G. 77	23.7.42
Mader, Anton-Josef	Feldw., Flugzeugf. & Beob. in 5. (H)/Aufkl. Gr. 11	26.3.44

Name	Details	Date
Mader, Franz	Major d.R., Kdr. I./G. R. 576	12.12.44
Mader, Hans	Oblt., Staffelkpt. 4./K.G. 54 + 3.7.44 over England as Major & Kdr. II./K.G. 54	3.9.42
Mäder, Hellmuth	Major, Kdr. III./I.R. 522 560th Oak Leaves 27.8.44 143rd Swords 18.4.45	3.4.42
Maek, Hermann	Oblt., Fhr. 5./I.R. 453	20.3.42
Maempel, Rolf	Oberst, Kdr. Pz. G. R. 125	5.12.43
Mänhardt, Manfred	Oblt., Beobachter in 4. (F)/Aufkl. Gr. 122	9.6.44
Frhr. v. Maercken zu Geerath, Jürgen	Oblt., Chef 1./Pz. Rgt. 36 + 14.2.45 at Grünberg (Silesia) as Major & Kdr. Pz. Ers. Abt. Sagan	17.9.41
Maerz, Xaver	Ofw., Zugf. in 6./I.R. 34 + 14.1.45	27.5.42
Maes, Friedrich-Wilhelm	Kaptlt. (M. A.), Bttr. Chef Batterie "Völtzendorf', i. d. Marine-Flak-Abt. 219 (9. Marine-Flak-Rgt.) + 19.3.45 at Gotenhafen (Gdingen)	25.3.45
Maetzel, Heinz	Hptm., Staffelkpt. 1./Femaufkl. Gr. 4	5.4.44
Magawly, Christoph	Hptm., Kdr. II./G. R. 287	15.3.44
Mager, Rolf	Hptm., Kdr. II./Fsch. Jäg. Rgt. 6 + 1.1.45 in a US hospital of wounds; posthumously promoted to Major	31.10.44
Magerfleisch, Friedrich-Wilhelm	Gefr. in 3. (schw.)/Schnelle Abt. 376 + 8.12.42 at Stalingrad (Russia)	20.1.43
Magg, Alois	Oblt., Flugzeugf. in 9./K.G. 2	5.9.44
Magold, Hanns	Oblt., Chef 1./St. Gesch. Abt. "GD" + 15.9.44 in Russia as Hptm. & Kdr. St. Gesch. Brig. 311	3.4.43
Mahler, Adolf	Oberst d.R., Kdr. A.R. 30	23.10.44
Mahlke, Helmut	Hptm., Kdr. III./Stuka-Geschw. 1	16.7.41
Mahlmann, Friedrich	Lt. d.R., Fhr. II./G. R. 587 posted missing 20.8.44 as Oblt.	17.3.44
Mahlstedt, Heinrich	Ofw., Zugf. in 3./Pz. Abt. 8 + 27.8.44 Bobruisk (Russia)	30.9.44
Mahn, Friedrich-Karl	Hptm., Offz. z.b.V. in 1./Nah-Aufkl. Gr. 5	24.1.45
Mahn, Werner	Ofw., Zugf. in 2./Pz. Rgt. 10	8.2.43
Mahnken, Heinrich	Rittm. d.R., Kdr. Aufkl. Abt. 299 + 10.7.44 in Russia as Kdr. of a Gren. Rgt.; posthumously promoted to Oberst d.R.	5.4.42
Mai, Emil	Lt. d.R., Zugf. in 1./G. R. 200 (mot.)	16.11.44
Maier, Kurt	Oblt., Beob. & Flugzeugkdt. in 3./K.G. 4 "General Wever" 674th Oak Leaves 6.12.44	16.11.42
Maisel, Eberhard	Ofw., Zugf. in 2./G. R. 118	23.7.43
Maisel, Ernst	Oberst, Kdr. Inf.Rgt. 42	6.4.42

KNIGHT'S CROSS OF THE IRON CROSS

Maitla, Paul	Waffen-Hptsturmf., Fhr. I./Waffen-G. R. 45 der SS (estn. Nr. 1) + in May 1945 in Bohemi, shot by the Soviets as Waffen-Sturmbannfhr.	23.8.44
Makrocki, Wilhelm	Hptm., Kdr. I./Z.G. 26 "Horst Wessel" posted missing since 21.5.41 following a flight over Crete, as Major	6.10.40
v. Malachowski, Wilhelm	Oblt., Chef 2./St. Gesch. Abt. 189 206th Oak Leaves 6.3.43	30.1.42
Frhr. v. Malapert Gen. v. Neufville, Robert-Georg	Oblt., Staffelkpt. 5./Stuka-Geschw. 1 99th Oak Leaves 8.6.42	6.1.42
Malguth, Einhart	Oblt., Rgt. Adj. Pz. Rgt. 35 + 15.6.40 at Chables (France)	11.5.42
Malkomes, Hans	SS-Obersturmf., Chef 2./SS-Pz. Rgt. 1 "LSSAH" + April 1945 at Veszprem (Hungary) as SS-Hptsturmfhr.	30.10.44
Mally, Karl	Hptm., Fhr. II./G. R. 191	12.3.44
v. Malotki, Wolfgang	Oblt. d.R., Chef 3./G. R. 45	7.3.43
Frhr. v. Maltzahn, Berndt-Joachim	Major, Kdr. Pz. G. R. 59	14.2.45
Frhr. v. Maltzahn, Günther	Hptm., Kdr. II./J.G. 53 29th Oak Leaves 24.7.41	30.12.40
Mangels, Hermann	Lt. d.R., Zugf. in Pi. Btl. 189	17.3.45
Manitius, Johannes	Obstlt., Kdr. I.R. 386	3.4.42
Manitz, Hans-Horst	Hptm. d.R., Kdr. 1./G. R. 274	23.8.44
Mann, Fritz	Lt., Zugf. Pi. Zug in Stabskp./G. R. 274	6.4.44
Mann, Martin	Obstlt., Kdr. G. R. 187	23.10.44
Manns, Werner v. Manstein	Hptm., Kdr. III./G. R. 96 see under v. Lewinski gen. v. Manstein	13.1.44
Mantel, Gerhard	Oblt., Chef 2./Pz.Jäg. Abt. 52	14.4. 45
v. Manteuffel, Hasso	Oberst, Kdr. Schtz. Rgt. 6 332nd Oak Leaves 23.11.43 50th Swords 22.2.44 24th Diamonds 18.2.45	31.12.41
Marbach, Karl-Heinz	Oblt. z. See, Kdt. "U 953"	22.7.44
Marbach, Paul	Major d.R., Kdr. I./G. R. 217	20.2.43
Marchel, Oskar	Uffz., Zugf. in 3./G. R. 45 + 10.3.44 south-east of Leningrad (Russia)	15.4.44
Marcks, Erich	Gen.Lt., Kdr. 101. Leichte Inf. Div. 503rd Oak Leaves 24.6.44	26.6.41
Marcks, Werner	Oberstlt., Fhr. Kgr. Marcks d. Pz. Armee Afrika Schtz. Rgt. 104 in DAK 593rd Oak Leaves 21.9.44	2.2.42

ELITE OF THE THIRD REICH

Marienfeld, Werner	Obstlt., Kmdr. K.G. 54 + 23.10.44 accidentally as Oberst & General der Kampfflieger	27.11.41
Marienfeld, Willy	Major d.R., Kdr. II./I.R. 123 482nd Oak Leaves 25.5.44	17.8.42
Maringgele, Hermann	SS-Hptscharf., Zugf. in 2./SS-Kav. Rgt. 15 "Florian Geyer"	21.2.45
Markgraf, Paul	Oblt., Fhr. Pz.Jäg. Abt. 40	3.1.43
Markworth, Friedrich	Kaptlt., Kdt. "U 66"	8.7.43
Markworth, Walter	Oblt., Fhr. II./G. R. 12	14.4. 45
Marquardt, Heinz	Fhj. -Ofw., Flugzeugf. in 13./J.G. 51 "Mölders"	18.11.44
Marre, Herbert	Oblt., Chef 13./G. R. 424	17.4.45
Marreck, Günther	Hptm. d.R., Fhr. II./G. R. 422	15.4.44
Marscholek, Hans (17)	Oblt., Bttr. Fhr. in Fsch. Flak-Abt. 5	31.10.44
Marseille, Hans-Joachim	Lt., Flugzeugf. in 3./J.G. 27 97th Oak Leaves 6.6.42 12th Swords 18.6.42 4th Diamonds 3.9.42	22.2.42
Martens, Alfred	Oblt. d.R., Fhr. I./G. R. 586	28.11.43
Martens, Egbert	Oberst, Kdr. Werfer-Rgt. 70 (mot.)	3.11.44
Martens, Otto	Hptm. d.R., Kdr. Pz.Jäg. Abt. 72	23.11.41
Martienssen, Ekkehard	Oblt. z. See d.R., Kdt. "Vp. 203" in 2. Vorpostenflottille	29.6.44
Martin, Christian	Hptm., Kdr. Pz.Jäg. Abt. 521	20.1.43
Martin, Heinz	Lt. d.R., Ord.Offz. in Stab I.R. 520 + 27.9.42 30 km north of Bolchow (Russia) as Oblt. d.R. & Chef 5./I.R. 520	20.12.41
Martin, Wolfgang	Ofw., Flugzeugf. in 6./K.G. 3 "Lützow" + 13.5.44 east of Frankfurt/Oder at Burschen as Ofw. & Flugzeugf. in 4./Z.G. 26 "Horst Wessel"	30.12.42
Martinek, Robert	Gen. Major, Kdr. 267. I.D. 388th Oak Leaves 10.2.44	26.12.41
v. der Marwitz, Egon	Oblt., Chef 3./G. R. 44	12.8.44
Marzluf, Xaver	Major, Kdr. II./Pz. G. R. 103 + 3.6.44 in sector of H.Gr. Südukraine	9.7.44
Masanrie, Lino (Arzelino)	SS-Hptsturmf., Fhr. SS-Pz. Aufkl. Abt. 3 "Totenkopf" + 9.8.44 at Radzymin (Poland) as SS-Sturmbannf. & Abt.Kdr.	3.4.43
Masemann, Willi	Uffz. in 4./Pzjdg. Abt. 15 (L)	25.6.44
Massa, Wilhelm	Oblt. d.R., Chef 5./G. R. 35 (mot.)	21.1.45
Frhr. v. Massenbach, Dipl.-Ing. Dietrich	Major, Kdr. II./K.G. 4 "General Wever"	27.8.40
Massow, Horst	Hptm., Kp. Chef in Fähnrichs-Rgt. 3 Div. "Märk. Friedland"	11.3.45

KNIGHT'S CROSS OF THE IRON CROSS

Matern, Alfred	Ofw., Zugf. in 5./Füs. Rgt. 22 784th Oak Leaves 16.3.45	4.9.43
Matern, Karl-Heinrich	Hptm., Kdr. II./Z.G. 1 + 8.10.43 shot down west of Brest (France)	9.10.43
Matern, Kurt	Major, Fhr. Inf.Rgt. 39 + 1.12.43 in Russia as Oberst & Kdr. Füs. Rgt. 39	14.9.42
Materna, Friedrich	Gen.Lt., Kdr. 45. I.D.	5.8.40
Matheja, Siegmund (19)	Uffz. in Pz. Haub. Abt. Führer-Gren. Div. "GD"	6.5.45
Mathes, Josef	Owm., Zugf. in 3./St. Gesch. Brig. 280 + 19.9.44 in Arnhem (Holland)	4.10.44
Mathes, Wolfgang	Lt. d.R., Fhr. 5./G. R. 42	9.1.45
Matoni, Walter	Hptm., Kdr. II./J.G. 2 "Richthofen"	16.12.44
Matschoß, Kurt (8)	Major, Fhr. of a Kampfgr. in Festg. Abschnitts-Kdo. "Bärenfänger" in Berlin + 29.4.45 in Berlin of wounds; posthumously promoted to Oberstlt.	28.4.45
Mattenklott, Franz	Gen.Lt., Kdr. 72. I.D.	23.11.41
Mattern, Walter	SS-Obersturmf., Fhr. 7./SS-Pz. Rgt. 3 "Totenkopf"	20.10.44
Matthess, Leopold	Oblt., Chef 4./M. G. Btl. 13	9.5.40
Matthis, Dr. rer. pol. Werner	Oberst, Kdr. G. R. 428	22.1.44
Mattusch, Walter (6)	SS-Hptsturmf., Kdr. II./SS-Pz. G. R. 3 "Deutschland"	6.5.45
Matuschewitz, Erich	Uffz. in 2./G. R. 232	30.9.44
Matzen, Ingwer (Jens)	Korv. Kpt., Chef 6. Schnellbootsflottille	2.5.45
Matzke, Othmar	Major, Kdr. Pi. Btl. 211	18.11.44
Matzky, Gerhard	Gen.Lt., Kdr. 21. I.D.	5.4.44
Frhr. v. Mauchenheim gen. Bechtolsheim, Theodor	Kapt. z. See, Chef 8. Zerstörerflottille "Narvik"	3.7.44
Maucke, Wolfgang	Oberst, Kdr. Pz. G. R. 115	18.2.45
Maurer, Heinrich	Obgefr., Gruppenfhr. in Stabskp./Pz. G. R. 125	6.10.44
Maurer, Otto	Korv. KPt., Chef 12. Raumbootsflottille	3.7.43
Maurer, Stefan	Ofw., Zugf. in 8./G. R. 35 (mot.) + July 1944 at Orscha (Russia) as Lt.	16.8.43
Maurus, Anselm	Lt., Zugf. in 10./le. Flak-Rgt. 411 (sf)	30.9.44
Maus, August	Kaptlt., Kdt. "U 185"	21.9.43
Mauss, Dr. med. dent. Karl	Obstlt., Kdr. II./Schtz. Rgt. 69 335th Oak Leaves 24.11.43 101st Swords 23.10.44 26th Diamonds 1 15.4.45	26.11.41
Mauz, Otto	Ofw., Zugf. 3./Heeres-Pi. Btl. 671 (mot.)	9.12.44

May, Johann	Oblt., Fhr. III./Geb.Jäg. Rgt. 138 + 5.9.43 south of Skelewatyi (Russia) as Hptm. & Btl. Kdr.	25.1.43
Maydorn, Otfried	Oberst, Kdr. G. R. 554	12.12.44
Mayer, Egon	Lt. d.R., Flugzeugf. in J.G. 2 "Richthofen" 232nd Oak Leaves 16.4.43 51st Swords 2.3.44	1.8.41
Mayer, Hans-Karl	Hptm., Staffelkpt. 1./J.G. 53 + 17.10.40 over the Channel as Kdr. I./J.G. 53	3.9.40
Mayer, Hermann	Lt. d.R., Zugf. in 2./G. R. 258	14.4. 43
Mayer, Isidor	Obgefr., Gewehrfhr. in 14./Geb.Jäg. Rgt. 91 + 19.9.44	19.11.43
Mayer, Dr. rer. pol., Dr.-Ing. Johannes	Oberst, Kdr. I.R. 501 453rd Oak Leaves 13.4.44 89th Swords 23.8.44	13.9.41
Mayer, Wilhelm	Lt., Staffelf. 5./J.G. 26 "Schlageter" + 4.1.45 over Emsland in aerial combat	12.3.45
Mayer, Willy	Hptm., Fhr. I./G. R. 196	18.11.44
Mayer zur Linde, Helmuth	Hptm., Fhr. III./G. R. 102 posted missing since 13.9.44 on the Düna	8.2.44
Mayerl, Maximilian	Oblt., Staffelkpt. 9./J.G. 51 "Mölders"	22.11.43
Mayr, Rudolf	Oblt., Staffelkpt. 9./K.G. 40	18.5.43
Mecke, Karl-Conrad	Kapt. z. See, Kdr. 22. Marine-Flak-Rgt.	11.4.43
Mecke, Walter	Major, Kdr. I./Pz. Rgt. 27 + 1.12.41 during an assault over the Narwa (Russia)	23.11.41
Meckel, Helmut	Oblt., Staffelkpt. in I./J.G. 3 + 8.5.43 accidentally in Tunis as Hptm. in Stab J.G. 77	12.8.41
Mecklenburg, Max	Major, Führer of a Kampfgr. in Jäg. Rgt. 28	18.11.44
v. der Meden, Carl-Friedrich	Obstlt., Kdr. Radf. Abt. 12	8.8.41
Meder, Albert	Major d.R., Kdr. Pz.Jäg. Abt. 33	5.11.44
Meder, Johannes	Major, Kdr. III./I.R. 19 + 7.4.43 in Russia as Oberst & Rgt. Kdr. of wounds	4.9.40
Medicus, Franz	Major, Fhr. Kampfstaffel OB H.Gr. Afrika + 4.4.45 west Hungary during an enemy strafing run as Kdr. Pz.Jäg. Abt. 543	16.4.43
Meendsen-Bohlken, Wilhelm	Konteradm., Befehlshaber d. Deutschen Marinekommandos Italy	15.5.44
Meentzen, Wilhelm	Kaptlt., Kdt. Torpedoboot "T 24"	30.10.44
Megow, Herbert	Hptm., in Pak. Art. Abt. 1037	9.12.44
Mehl, Waldemar	Kaptlt., Kdt. "U 371"	28.3.44
Mehring, Theodor	Obstlt. i.G., Chef d. Gen. St. 3. Geb. Div.	15.7.44
Mehrle, Hans	Oblt., Rgt. Adj. G. R. 380	15.4.44
Meier, Gerhard	Lt., Fhr. Pz.Jäg. Abt. 26	5.4.45
Meier, Hans	Hptm., Fhr. I./Pz. G. R. 74 874th Oak Leaves 9.5.45	30.9.44

Meier, Hans-Otto	Ofw., Flugzeugf. in 9./S.G. 77 + 2.5.44 at Pokropiwna (Russia)	9.6.44
Meier, Helmut	Oblt., Chef 14. (Pz.Jäg.)/I.R. 79 + 17.6.40 in France	7.3.41
Meier, Johann-Hermann	Lt., Staffelf. in 1./J.G. 26 "Schlageter" + 15.3.44 accidentally at Florennes (France)	16.12.44
Meierdress, Hubert-Erwin	SS-Obersturmf., Fhr. SS-St. Gesch. Bttr. "Totenkopf" 310th Oak Leaves 5.10.43	13.3.42
Meierkord, Gustav	Oblt. d.R., Chef 3./Pz. G. R. 64	9.12.43
Meimberg, Julius	Hptm., Kdr. II./J.G. 53	24.10.44
Meindl, Eugen	Gen. Major, Kdr. Fsch. Jäger-Sturm-Rgt. 564th Oak Leaves 31.8.44 155th Swords 8.5.45	14.6.41
Meinecke, Hans-Georg	Oblt. d.R., Chef 1./G. R. 667 since 28.8.44 missing as Hptm. d.R.	14.5.44
Meineke, Bruno	Major, Kdr. I./I.R. 407	19.6.42
Meiners, Ernst	Oberst d.R., Kdr. G. R. 161	17.12.43
Meiners, Dr. Otto	Major, Kdr. III./I.R. 477 + 3.7.44 on Dniestr in Russia as Oberst & Kdr. G. R. 467	22.2.42
Meinhardt, Rudolf	Obgefr., stellv. Gruppenf. Pi. Zug/G. R. 528 + 23.6.44 in Russia; posthumously promoted to Uffz.	15.5.44
Meinhold, Dr. Wolfgang	Oblt. d.R., Chef 8./G. R. 123	15.5.43
Meinicke, Johannes	Lt., Staffelf. 1./S.G. 1 + 4.9.43 at Bersinow (Russia) as Hptm. & Staffelkpt.	7.4.43
Meinigke, Alfred	Major, Kdr. I./G. R. 188 + 27.9.43	31.3.43
Meisel, Hans-Gustav	Fhj. -Ofw., Beob. & Kdt. in 5. (H)/Aufkl. Gr. 41	20.7.44
Meisel, Martin	Oblt., Flugzeugf. & Techn. Offz. in 2. (F)/Aufkl. Gr. 123	21.12.42
Meisel, Wilhelm	Kapt. z. See, Kdt. Schwerer Kreuzer "Admiral Hipper"	26.2.41
Meißner, Herbert	Owm., Zugf. in 3./St. Gesch. Abt. 244	8.8.43
Meißner, Joachim	Lt. d.R., stllv. Fhr. Sturmgruppe "Eisen" in Fsch. Jäg. Sturmabt. "Koch" simultaneously prmoted to Oberleutnant d.R. + 25.7.44 west of St. Lo (Normandy/France) as Hptm. & Kdr. III./Fsch. Jäg. Rgt. 14(mot.)	12.5.40
Meißner, Robert	Gen.Lt., Kdr. 68. I.D. + January 1953 in Soviet captivity; final post Chef des Reichskriegsgerichts	24.5.43
Meißner, Siegfried	Hptm., Kdr. 1II./I.R. 408 + 23.4.45 at Nieheim/Höxter as Obstlt.	25.9.42
Meister, Ludwig	Hptm., Staffelkpt. 1./N. J.G. 4	9.6.44
Meister, Rudolf	Gen.Lt., Kom.Gen. IV. Flieger-Korps	5.9.44

Meiswinkel, Heinrich	Feldw., Zugf. in 1./G. R. 392	5.3.45
Meitzel, Helmut	Hptm., Kdr. II./G. R. 15 (mot.)	27.7.44
Melchior, Ulrich	Stabsfeldw., Zugf. in 6./Pz. Rgt. 18 + 1.2.42 Suchinitschi (Russia) of wounds	7.2.42
v. Mellenthin, Horst	Gen.Lt., Kdr. 205. I.D. 815th Oak Leaves 4.4.45	10.10.44
Mellwig, Karl	Oberst, Kdr. G. R. 313	12.8.44
Meltzer, Walter	Oblt., Staffelkpt. in III./K.G. z.b.V. 1 + 15.8.43 shot down over Berlin-Schönwalde as Hptm.	23.12.42
Melzer, Reinhard	Uffz., GeschUtzf. in I./Flak-Rgt. 33 (mot.)	30.6.41
Melzer, Walter	Oberst, Kdr. I.R. 151 558th Oak Leaves 23.8.44	21.8.41
Memmert, Friedrich	Uffz., Zugf. in 2./Pi. Btl. 20 (mot.)	9.6.44
Menapace, Josef	Lt., Staffelf. 7./S.G. 1 + 6.10.43 at Stracholessje on Pripjet (Russia) as Hptm. & Staffelkpt.	20.8.42
Mende, Dr. jur. Erich	Major, Fhr. G. R. 216	28.2.45
Mendte, Rolf	Fhj. -Fw., Zugf. in 6./G. R. 31	24.12.44
Meng, Heinz	Lt. d.R., Kp. Fhr. in Pi. Btl. 292	5.3.45
Mengersen, Ernst	Kaptlt., Kdt. "U 101"	18.11.41
Menges, Otto	Ofw., Zugf. in 6./Fsch. Jäg. Rgt. 1 + 24.5.44 in Italy of wounds ; posthumously promoted to Lt.	9.6.44
Menke, August	Obgefr., MG-Schütze in 7./G. R. 501	16.4.44
Menke, Horstmar	Hptm. d.R., Kdr. I./G. R. 1099	17.3.45
Menny, Erwin	Oberst, Kdr. 15. Schtz. Brigade	26.12.41
v. Mentz, Franz	Major, Fhr. Pz. G. R. 40	22.9.43
Menzel, Joachim	Major d.R., Kdr. Heeres-Flak-Art. -Abt. (mot.) 277	10.9.44
Mergner, Eberhard	Major, Fhr. Jäger-Rgt. 207	1.2.45
Merk, Ernst	Oberst i.G., Chef d. Gen. St. III. Pz.K.	15.7.44
Merkel, Herbert-Dietrich	Hptm. d.R., Fhr. I./Pz. G. R. 304	8.8.43
Merker, Hans-Hermann	Oblt., Staffelf. in I./K.G. 3 "Lützow"	9.6.44
Merker, Ludwig	Oberst, Kdr. I.R. 215	18.11.41
Merks, Hans-Joachim	Kaptlt., Chef 2. Räumbootsflottille	6.5.45
Mersmann, Ernst Hermann	Hptm., Staffelkpt. 1./Kampfgr. z.b.V. 9	23.12.42
Merten, Karl-Friedrich	Korv. Kpt., Kdt. "U 68" 147th Oak Leaves 16.11.42	13.6,42
Merten, Peter	Ofw. d.R., Zugf. in 5./I.R. 124	15.10.42
Mertens, Ewald	Hptm., Chef 15./I.R. 204	22.2.42
Mertens, Helmut	Oblt., Flugzeugf. in I./J.G. 3 "Udet"	4.9.42

Name	Rank/Unit	Date
Mertens, Otto	Hptm. d.R., Fhr. III./Füs. Rgt. 68	11.4.44
Mertins, Gerhard	Hptm., Fhr. Fsch. Pi. Btl. 5	6.12.44
Meschede, Heinrich	Oblt. d.R., Fhr. I./G. R. 308	25.1.45
Meschkat, Gerhard	Uffz., Pz. Fahrer in I./Pz.Jäg. Abt. 72	4.10.44
Messer, Wilhelm	Lt., Flugzeugfhr. in II./Transp. -Geschw. 2	12.3.45
Messinger, Erich	Obstlt., Kdr. G. R. 559	16.10.44
Metelmann, Ernst	Hptm., Kdr. I./Pz. G. R. 11	22.8.43
Methner, Gerhard (5)	Hptm., Kdr. II./Fsch. Art.Rgt. 6	30.4.45
Mette, Fritz	Obgefr., Gruppenf. in 9./G. R. 92 (mot.)	5.1.43
Metz, Eduard	Gen. Major, Kdr. 5. Pz.Div.	5.1.43
Metz, Hans	Hptm., Bttr. Chef in Heeres-Art. Abt. 1042 (so	5.3.45
Metze, Walter	Owm., Zugf. in Flak-Rgt. 36 (mot.) + 6.10.44 in Russia	9.6.44
Metzger, Eugen	Lt. d.R., Zugf. in 1./St. Gesch. Abt. 203	29.9.41
Metzger, Richard	Major, Kdr. Inf. Btl. z.b.V. 561	12.10.43
Metzig, Rudolf	Oblt., Flugzeugf. & Techn. Offz. in Stab I./K.G. 4 "General Wever" + 25.2.44 in Russia	9.6.44
Metzler, Jost	Kaptlt., Kdt. "U 69"	28.7.41
Meurer, Manfred	Oblt., Staffelkpt. 3./N. J.G. 1 264th Oak Leaves 2.8.43	16.4.43
Meusgeier, Fritz	Ofw., Oberschirrmeister in 3./Pz.Jäg. Abt. 13	15.11.41
Mevissen, Kurt	Feldw., Flugzeugf. in 9./K.G. 1 "Hindenburg"	19.9.42
Meyer, Bruno	Oblt., Staffelkpt. 5./(S)L.G. 2	21.8.41
Meyer, Constantm	Obstlt., Fhr. I.R. 257	8.5.42
Meyer, Eduard	Lt., Flugzeugf. in I./Z.G. 26 "Horst Wessel" + 31.3.42 shot down at Welish (Russia)	20.12.41
Meyer, Elimar	Lt., Lastenseglerpilot in 12./Luftlandegeschw. 1	17.9.43
Meyer, Friedrich-August	Oberst, Kdr. Fsch. Pz. Ersatz- & Ausbildungs-Brigade "HG"	9.5.45
Meyer, Fritz	Gen. Major, Kdr. Oberbaustab 7	6.4.43
Meyer, Günter	Lt. d.R., Zugf. in 3./Pz. Aufkl. Abt. 12	5.3.45
Meyer, Hans	SS-Hauptsturmf., Fhr. I./SS-Freiw. Pz. G. R. 49 "De Ruyter"	2.9.44
Meyer zur Heyde, Hans	Oblt., Chef 3./Flak-Rgt. 34	7.4.45
Meyer, Hans-Adolf	Oblt., Staffelf. 8./S.G. 3 + 1.7.44 at Udetfelde	6.4.44
Meyer, Heinrich	Oblt., Beobachter in I./K.G. 2	15.10.42
Meyer, Heinz	Hptm. d.R., Chef 8./Fsch. Jäg. Rgt. 4 654th Oak Leaves 18.11.44	8.4.44
Meyer, Heinz	Hptm., Kp. Chef in II./Pz. Rgt. 22	4.10.44
Meyer, Heinz	Oberfähnrich, Flugzeugf. in 8./S.G. 2 " Immelmann"	17.4.45
Meyer, Jochen	Rittm., Kdr. II./Pz. G. R. 155	31.3.43

Meyer, Josef	Hptm., Fhr. II./G. R. 423 + 10.2.45	5.4.45
v. Meyer, Kuno	Major, Kdr. I./Pz. Rgt. 24 795th Oak Leaves 23.3.45	26.11.44
Meyer, Kurt	SS-Sturmbannf., Kdr. SS-Aufkl. Abt. "LSSAH" 195th Oak Leaves 23.2.43 91st Swords 27.8.44	18.5.41
Meyer, Otto	Ofw., Flugzeugf. in III./K.G. 55 + 23.2.45 at Eger (Sudetenland)	29.2.44
Meyer, Otto	SS-Obersturmbannf., Kdr. SS-Pz. Rgt. 9 "Hohenstaufen" 601st Oak Leaves 30.9.44	4.6.44
Meyer, Walter	Ofw., Stoßtruppf. in 7./I.R. 125	14.5.41
Meyer, Walter	Feldw., Zugf. in 5./G. R. 1221	11.3.45
Meyer, Walter	Hptm., Kampfkdt. von Lüben	23.3.45
Meyer, Werner	SS-Obersturmf., Fhr. 1./SS-Pz. G. R. 9 "Germania"	4.5.44
Meyer-Buerdorf, Heinrich	Gen.Lt., Kdr. 131. I.D.	15.11.41
Meyer-Rabingen, Hermann	Gen.Lt., Kdr. 197. I.D.	12.1.42
Meyering, Heinrich	Feldw., Flugzeugf. in 3./S.G. 2 "Immelmann"	6.4.44
Meyn, Wilhelm	Lt., Staffelf. 9./S.G. 3	24.10.44
Mez, Emil	Hptm., Kdr. 1./G. R. 290	6.3.44
Michael, Ernst	Oberst, Kdr. I.R. 2 + 22.1.44 at Tuganitzky (Russia) as Oberst & Fhr. 9. Luftw. Feld-Div.; posthumously promoted to Gen. Major	18.5.42
v. Michael, Friedrich-August	Hptm., Kdr. II./G. R. 172	10.2.45
Michael, Georg	Lt. d.R., Zugf. in 6./Reiter-Rgt. 22 187th Oak Leaves 25.1.43	19.1.41
Michael, Hermann	Hptm., Staffetkpt. 8./K.G. 1 "Hindenburg" + 5.7.43	9.10.43
Michaelis, Hans	Major, Fhr. G. R. 184	28.9.43
Michaelis, Herbert	Oberst, Kdr. G. R. 525 & Fhr. 298. I.D.	27.12.42
Michahelles, Hans	Konteradm., Festungskommandant Girondemündung Nord	30.4.45
Michalek, Georg	Oblt., Staffelkpt. 4./J.G. 3	4.11.41
Michalski, Erich	Major, Kdr. II./G. R. 578	6.2.44
Michalski, Gerhard	Oblt., Staffelkpt. 4./J.G. 53 667th Oak Leaves 25.11.44	4.9.42
Michel, Fritz	Hptm., Fhr. I./Pz. G. R. 200	18.12.44
Michelsen, Heinz	Hptm., Fhr. I./Pz. G. R. 11 + 2.3.45 in Löwen at Köln/Rhein	18.2.45
Mickl, Johann	Oberst, Kdr. Schtz. Rgt. 155 205th Oak Leaves 6.3.43	13.12.41

Mickley, Hubert	Hptm., Fhr. I./G. R. 4 540th Oak Leaves 4.8.44	26.12.43
Mickley, Karl	Oblt. d.R., Chef 7./Schtz. Rgt. 304	13.6.41
Mielke, Albert	Feldw., Zugf. in 6./G. R. 189	23.3.45
Mieth, Friedrich	Gen.D.Inf., Kom.Gen. IV. A.K. 409th Oak Leaves 1.3.44	2.11.43
Miethig, Rudolf	Lt., Staffelf. 3./J.G. 52 + 10.6.43 at Crimeaskaja (Russia) as Staffelkpt.; posthumously promoted to Hptm.	29.10.42
Mietusch, Klaus	Hptm., Kdr. III./J.G. 26 "Schlageter" 653rd Oak Leaves 18.11.44	26.3.44
Mikosch, Hans	Obstlt., Kdr. Pi. Btl. 51 201st Oak Leaves 6.3.43	21.5.40
Mikus, Bernhard	Lt. d.R., Fhr. I./Pz. G. R. 114	26.8.43
Milbradt, Gerhard	Lt. d.R., Fhr. 6./G. R. 532 + 1944 in Russia	1.10.43
Milch, Erhard	Gen. Oberst, Staatssekretär of the Luftfahrt in Reichsluftfahrtministerium	4.5.40
Milch, Dr. jur. Werner	Hptm. d.R., Kdr. Fsch. Granatwerfer-Lehr- & Versuchs-Btl.	9.1.45
Mildebrath, Werner	Obstlt., Kdr. I./Pz. Rgt. 5	12.8.42
Milek, Otto	Rittm., Fhr. Dlv. Füs. Btl. (A.A.) 11	10.9.44
Millahn, Karl-Hermann	Hptm., Staffelkpt. Stabsstaffel/K.G. 76	29.2.44
Miller, Hans	Lt. d.R., Zugf. in 14./G. R. 546 posted missing since 11.3.45 missing as Oblt., badly wounded	18.12.44
Millonig, Franz	Oblt., Fhr. 1./Pz. Pi. Btl. 57 + 14.1.42 vor Moskau (Russia) as Hptm. & Kp. Chef	18.10.41
v. Milovan, Berndtlubich	SS-Obersturmf., Fhr. 1./SS-St. Gesch. Abt. 3 "Totenkopf"	14.10.43
Mimra, Aegidius	Hptm., Kdr. I./Pz. Rgt. 31	18.2.45
Mink, Wilhelm	Ofw., Flugzeugf. in 5./J.G. 51 "Mölders" + 12.3.45 shot down at Hadersleben Nordschleswig/Dänemark) as Flugzeugf. in 1. (Erg.)/J.G. 1	19.3.42
Mintert, Franz	Obgefr., Richtschtz. in Pz.Jäg. Abt. 26	14.9.42
Mirau, Harry	Gefr., Richtschtz. in 3./Pz.Jäg. Abt. 3 + in Soviet captivity	13.11.42
Frhr. v. Mirbach, Götz	Oblt. z. See, Kdt. "S 21" in 1. Schnellbootsflottille 500th Oak Leaves 14.6.44	14.8.40
Mischke, Gerd	Lt., Zugf. in 2./Fsch. M. G. Btl. 1	18.5.43
Misera, Walter	Major, Kdr. II./G. R. 515 569th Oak Leaves 2.9.44	23.8.43
Mißner, Helmut	Ofw., Flugzeugf. i. d. I./J.G. 54 + 12.9.44 shot down at Sagan	10.10.44
Mitschke, Martin	Feldw., Zugf. in 2./G. R. 200 (mot.)	16.10.44

Mitterwenger, Lambert	Uffz. in 2. (Stu. Gesch.)/Pz.Jäg. Abt. 1548	18.12.44
v. Miitzlaff, Berndt	Major, Kdr. Pz. Aufkl. Abt. 8	20.12.43
Mix, Walter	Oblt. d.R., Chef 9./G. R. 174 405th Oak Leaves 22.2.44	18.12.42
Mlinar, Stefan	Gefr., Funktruppf. in 5./Geb.Jäg. Rgt. 13	24.6.44
Moch, Friedrich	Hptm., Fhr. I./I.R. 258 since 7.6.44 missing as Major & Kdr. 1./G. R. 1058	27.3.42
Mocken, Aloys	Hptm. d.R., Kdr. 1./G. R. 216	28.7.43
Model, Walter	Gen.Lt., Kdr. 3. Pz.Div. 74th Oak Leaves 17.2.42 28th Swords 2.4.43 17th Diamonds 17.8.44	9.7.41
Moder, Willy	Uffz., Gruppenf. in 6./Schtz. Rgt. 3 + 14.3.45	28.11.40
Modick, Johannes	Oblt. d.R., Chef 3./G. R. 670	5.2.45
Modrow, Ernst-Wilhelm	Hptm., Staffelkpt. 1./N. J.G. 1	19.8.44
Möbus, Martin	Lt., Flugzeugf. in 1./Stuka-Geschw. 1 463rd Oak Leaves 27.4.44	8.5.40
Möckel, Alexander	Obstlt., Kdr. I.R. 517 + 24.3.45 at Karlsruhe (Baden) as Gen.Maj. & Kdr. 16. V. Gr. Div.	6.2.42
Möckel, Hans-Hermann	Hptm., Fhr. E. Kampfgr. G. R. 226	17.4.45
Möhle, Artur	Oblt. d.R., Flugzeugf. & Beob. in 2. (H)/Aufkl. Gr. 12 + 19.4.42 at Malotoltuscha (Russia) of wounds	23.6.42
Moehle, Karl-Heinz	Kaptlt., Kdt. "U 123"	26.2.41
Möhlmann, Helmut	Kaptlt., Kdt. "U 571"	16.4.43
Möhring, Heinz	Hptm., Fhr. II./G. R. 255 simultaneously promoted to Major	6.3.44
Möhring, Kurt	Oberst, Kdr. G. R. 82 + 18.12.44 at Befort (France) as Gen. Major & Kdr. 276. I.D. (V. Gr. Div.); posthumously promoted to Gen.Lt.	18.7.43
Mölders, Werner	Hptm., Kdr. III./J.G. 53 2nd Oak Leaves 21.9.40 2nd Swords 22.6.41 1st Diamonds 15.7.41	29.5.40
v. Moellendorff, Leonhard	Rittm. d.R., Kdr. III./Führer-Begleit-Brigade + 1.1.45 at Houffalize (Ardennes/Belgium)	8.1.45
Möller, Emil	Hptm. d.R., Fhr. I./G. R. 266	26.10.43
Möller, Ernst	Major, Kdr. Div. Füs. Btl. 553 V.G.D.	30.4.45
Möller, Günther	Oblt., Chef 2./St. Gesch. Abt. 191 + 22.9.41 southeast of Kiew (Russia)	22.9.41
Möller, Hans	Oblt., Ord.Offz. (01) Stab 15. I.D.	15.8.40
Moeller, Hans	Oblt., Chef Jagd-Pz. Kp. 1181	14.4. 45
Möller, Hans	Uffz., Zugf. in 11./I.R. 58	6.9.42
Möller, Lorenz	Oblt., Staffelkpt. in II./K.G. z.b.V. 1 + 27.6.44 in hospital at Westerland (Sylt) as Hptm.	4.2.42

KNIGHT'S CROSS OF THE IRON CROSS

Möller, Werner	Hptm., stv. Fhr. I./Pz. G. R. 12	28.11.43
Mörgel, Kurt	Hptm., Kdr. II./G. R. 200 (mot.) + 1945 at Dresden as Major & Kdr. Fsch. Pz. Gr. Rgt. 1 "HG"	17.9.44
Möse, Walter	Objäg., Zugf. in 13./Jäger-Rgt. 49 390th Oak Leaves 10.2.44	11.3.43
Mösslacher, Erhard	SS-Obersturmfhr., Chef 6./SS-Kav. Rgt. 16 "Florian Geyer" + 1945 in Budapest (Hungary) as SS-Hptsturmfhr.	9.2.45
Möws, Gerhard	Oblt., Chef 3./Kradschtz. Btl. 22	1.11.42
Mohnke, Wilhelm	SS-Obersturmbannf., Kdr. SS-Pz. G. R. 26 "Hitlerjugend"	11.7.44
Mohr, Carl-Friedrich	Kaptlt., Chef 24. Minensuchflottille "Karl-Friedrich Brill"	11.3.45
Mohr, Johann	Kaptlt., Kdt. "U 124" 177th Oak Leaves 13.1.43	27.3.42
Mohr, Rolf	Uffz., Gr. Fhr. in 1./Pz. Gren. Rgt. 26	5.3.45
Mohr, Walter	Ofw., Zugf. in II./G. R. 313	28.9.43
Mohr, Walter-Peter	Major, Fhr. G. R. "Mohr" in Festung Breslau	9.4.45
Mohrmann, Hans	Hptm. d.R., Kdr. I./G. R. 892	24.6.44
Mokros, Gerhard	Lt., Fhr. 7./I.R. 331 860th Oak Leaves 5.5.45	18.11.41
Moldenhauer, Siegfried	Hptm., Fhr. II./G. R. 48	20.1.44
Molinari, Karl-Theodor	Major, Kdr. I./Pz. Rgt. 36	3.11.44
v. Moltke, Helmut	Rittm., kdrt. zur Gen. Stabs-Ausbildg. b. d. 19. Pz.Div. & Fhr. Pz. Aufkl. Abt. 19	22.9.43
Mondabon, Heinrich	Oblt., Kp. Chef in II./Schtz. Rgt. 114 + 12.12.41 at Borissowglebskaja northwest of Moskau	4.12.41
Mons, Rudolf	Oblt., Flugzeugf. in I./K.G. 40 + 26.11.43 in Mediterranean as Major & Kdr. III./K.G. 40	18 . 9.41
Monschau, Richard	Major, Kdr. III./Pz. G. R. 2	23.12.44
Montag, Alfred	Hptm. d.R., Chef 2./St. Gesch. Brig 909 873rd Oak Leaves 9.5.45	21.4.44
Montreal, Zeslaus	Ofw., Zugf. in 1./G. R. 445 + 21.1.45 in Kreis Ortelsburg (East Prussia)	6.11.43
Moormann, Gerhard	Obgefr., Gruppenf. in 6./Pz. G. R. 4 + 13.3.44; posthumously promoted to Uffz.	14.5.44
Mooyman, Gerardes	SS-Sturmmann, Geschützf. in 14./SS-Freiw.-Legion "Nederland"	20.2.43
Morawietz, Johannes	Oblt., Fhr. 1./Jäger-Rgt. 28	7.1.43
Morawietz, Willi	Ofw., Zugf. in 13./G. R. 3	5.11.43
Morgenstern, Erich	Ofw., Bordfunker in I./S.G. 5	4.5.44
Morich, Gerhard	Hptm., Staffelkpt. 4./K.G. 4 "General Wever"	20.7.44
Moritz, Georg-Friedrich	Rittm., Chef 2./Radf. Abt. 32	28.4.43

Moritz, Wilhelm	Major, Kdr. IV./J.G. 3 "Udet"	18.7.44
Morr, Hermann	Lt., Fhr. 1./Heeres-Pi. Btl. 746	31.12.44
Mors, August	Lt., Flugzeugf. in 1./J.G. 5 + 8.8.44 in France of wounds received 6.8.44	20.10.44
Morsche, Max	Gefr. in 14./G. R. 101	9.5.45
Morys, Georg	Ofw., Zugf. in 1./Pz.Jäg. Abt. 181 + 7.5.45 northwest of Tukkum in Lettland	2.9.44
Morzik, Friedrich-Wilhelm	Oberst, Kmdre. K.G. z.b.V. 1 & Lufttransportführer Ost d. Luftflotte 1	16.4.42
Mosandl, Anton	Lt. d.R., Zugf. in 6./Geb.Jäg. Rgt. 99 + 2.12.42 north of Tuapse (Russia) as Oblt. d.R. & Kp. Chef of wounds	28.11.40
v. der Mosel, Hans	Oberst, Kdr. I.R. 548 589th Oak Leaves 18.9.44	9.8.42
Moser, Oskar	Stabsfw., Zugf. in 2./Pz. Abt. 106 "Feldherrnhalle"	4.10.44
Moser, Wilhelm	Obgefr., Gruppenf. in 3./G. R. 24	5.9.44
Moser, Willi	Gen.Lt., Kdr. 299. I.D. + 1946 in Soviet captivity; final post Gen. d. Art. & Befehlsh. Feldjäger-Kdo. 11	26.10.41
Moshammer, Johann	Major, Kdr. II./I.R. 50 + 27.9.42 Terek (Caucasus/Russia); posthumously promoted to Oberstlt.	31.12.41
Mosler, Franz	Gefr., Richtschtz. in 9./I.R. 461 + 7.7.44 as Feldw. & Zugf.	9.5.42
Moßdorf, Martin	Oblt., Staffelkpt. 3./Stuka-Geschw. 3	3.9.42
Moßgraber, Hans-Theo	Oblt., Staffelkpt. 5./K.G. 3 "Lbtzow" + 27.11.42 in Russia	29.10.43
Most, Jakob	Feldw., Zugf. in 2./Pz. Aufkl. Abt. 9	23.10.44
Mothes, Heinz	Hptm., Fhr. I./G. R. 3	18.10.43
Moysies, Bruno	Ofw., Zugf. in 3./Füs. Rgt. 22	6.3.44
Mozer, Werner	Lt. d.R., Zugf. in 5./Feldersatz-Btl. 215	11.12.44
Mrkva, Rudolf	Oblt., Flugzeugf. in 2./S.G. 2 "Immelmann"	20.7.44
Mrousek, Ewald	Stabsfw., Zugf. in 2./Feld-Btl. Tunis 1	19.1.43
Mücke, Johannes	Oblt., Chef 3./I.R. 51 (mot.) + 5.7.44 southwest of Minsk (Russia) as Btl. Kdr. Gr. Rgt. 30 (mot.); posthumously promoted to Obstlt.	10.2.42
Mügge, Georg	Oblt., Fhr. II./I.R. 203	27.12.41
Mühlbauer, Rudolf	Oberbootsmannsmaat, Brückenmaat on "U 123"	10.12.44
Mühleck, Karl	SS-Untersturmf., Zugf. in 2./SS-Pz. Rgt. 2 "Das Reich" + 26.12.44 in the Ardennes offensive as SS-Obersturmf. & Fhr. 1./SS-Pz. Rgt. 2 "Das Reich"	4.6.44

v. zur Mühlen, Hans-Heinrich	Oblt. d.R., Staffelkpt. 2./T. G. 3	28.2.45
Frhr. v. Mühlen, Kurt-Hermann	Obstit., Fhr. Jäg. Rgt. 75 690th Oak Leaves 9.1.45	6.11.42
Mühlenkamp, Johannes-Rudolf	SS-Sturmbannf., Kdr. SS-Pz. Abt. 5 "Wiking" 596th Oak Leaves 21.9.44	3.9.42
Mühlke, Günter	Gefr., Melder in II./G. R. 959	14.4. 45
Müllensiefen, Peter-Eberhard (17)	Hptm., Staffelkpt. 1. (H)/Aufkl. Gr. 31	31.10.44
Müller, Albert	SS-Hptscharf., Pakzugf. in 4./SS-Pz. G. R. 10 "Westland"	4.8.43
Müller, Albert	Kaptlt., Kdt. "S 59" in 3. Schnellbootsflottille	13.12.43
Müller, Albert	Stabsgefr., Gruppenfhr. in 1./Füs. Rgt. 22	4.10.44
Müller, Albrecht	Oblt. d.R., Chef 1./G. R. 446	23.2.44
Müller, Alfred	Hptm., Chef St. Gesch. Lehr-Bttr. 901 354th Oak Leaves 15.12.43	20.2.43
Müller, Alfred	Feldw., Zugf. in 2./G. R. 256 + 26.6.44 at Losok south of Newel (Russia) as Ofw.	8.5.43
Müller, Alfred	Hptm., Fhr. Sturm-Btl. AOK. 9 + 6.7.44 in Russia; posthumously promoted to Major	12.8.44
Müller, Alois	Uffz., Gruppenf. in 4./G. R. 435 + 17.7.44 south of Dünaburg (Russia)	12.8.44
Müller, Anton	Hptm., Fhr. I./G. R. 501 738th Oak Leaves 14.2.45	10.9.44
Müller, Curt	Ofw., Zugf. in 9./G. R. 220 + 16.1.44 north of Newel (Russia)	7.2.44
v. Müller, Dietrich	Obstlt., Kdr. S. R. 5 272nd Oak Leaves 16.8.43 134th Swords 20.2.45	3.5.42
Müller, Eduard now Müller-Reinders	Owm., Zugf. in 2./St. Gesch. Abt. 244	25.1.43
Müller, Erich	Feldw., Flugzeugf. in Stabsstaffel S.G. 2 "Immelmann" +22.7.44 at Zilistea (Rumania)	6.12.44
Müller, Erwin	Ofw., Truppf. in 2./Pi. Btl. 122 + 21.12.43 in Russia of wounds	29.2.44
Müller, Friedrich	Ofw., Zugf. in 8. (MG)/G. R. 461 missing 26.6.44	27.8.43
Müller, Friedrich-Karl	Oblt., Staffelkpt. 8./J.G. 53 126th Oak Leaves 23.9.42	14.9.41
Müller, Friedrich-Karl	Hptm., Staffelkpt. 1./N. J.G. 10	27.7.44
Müller, Friedrich-Wilhelm	Obstlt., Kdr. I.R. 105 86th Oak Leaves 8.4.42 128th Swords 27.1.45	22.9.41
Müller, Fritz	Hptm., Kdr. II./Jäger-Rgt. 38 477th Oak Leaves 14.5.44	25.8.42
Müller, Georg	Oblt. d.R., Chef 2./I.R. 321	9.8.42
Müller, Gerhard	Oberst, Kdr. Pz. Rgt. 5	9.9.42

Müller, Gerhard	Major d.R., Kdr. Pi. Btl. 208 + 13.7.43	10.3.43
Müller, Gottlob	Gen. Major, Kom.Gen. & Befehlshaber Luftgau Tunis + 28.4.45 in Berlin as Gen.Lt. & Fliegerführer Berlin	8.6.43
Müller, Günter	Hptm., Kdr. II./G. R. 551 + 23.8.44 in Russia	19.8.44
Müller, Günther	Lt., Staffelfhr. 7./S.G. 1 + 23.6.44 at Ploesti (Rumania) as Hptm.	9.10.43
Müller, Hans	Hptm., Kdr. II./I.R. 111	18.1.42
Müller, Hans	Oblt., Flugzeugf. in Fern-Aufk. 1. Gr. 5	18.11.44
Müüer, Hans	Hptm., Kdr. I./G. R. 111	14.4. 45
Müller, Heinz	SS-Hptsturmf. d.R., Fhr. III./SS-Pz. G. R. 6 "Theodor Eicke"	23.3.45
Müller, Helmut	Oblt., Bttr. Chef in schw. Art. Abt. 624 (mot.)	23.10.44
Müller, Dr. Herbert	Major, Kdr. II./Schtz. Rgt. 394 + 14.7.42 on the Don at Millerowo (Russia) as Oberst & Kdr. S. R. 126	8.9.41
Müller, Horst	Oblt., Flugzeugf. in II./K.G. 76	3.5.42
Müller, Johann	Ofw., Zugf. in 5./G. R. 332	6.4.44
Müller, Johann	Feldw., Pz. Kdt. in 3./Panzer-Abt. 502 (mot.) + 24.10.44	23.10.44
Müller, Karl	Ofw., Flugzeugf. in 12./K.G. 2 + 8.2.43 in Russia	15.10.42
Müller, Karl	Kaptlt., Kdt. "S 52" in 5. Schnellbootsflottille	8.7.43
Müher, Klaus	Major, Kdr. Pz. Abt. 60	3.4.42
Müller, Klaus	Oblt., Chef 6./Pz. Rgt. 2 + 4.9.42 at Leningrad (Russia); posthumously promoted to Hptm.	7.10.42
Müller, Kurt	Oblt., Fhr. 6./Pz. Rgt. 4	14.2.45
Müller, Ludwig	Gen.Lt., Kdr. 97. Jäger-Div. 440th Oak Leaves 6.4.44	25.10.43
Müller, Martin	Ofw., Zugf. in 13. (I. G.)/I.R. 90	25.10.42
Müller, Peter	Oblt. d.R., Chef 2./G. R. 666	3.4.43
Müller, Philipp	Hptm., Staffelkpt. 1./K.G. 55	2.4.43
Müller, Richard	Gen.Lt., Kdr. 211. I.D. + 16.7.43 north-east of Orel (Russia)	7.3.43
Müller, Rudolf	Feldw., Flugzeuf. in 6./J.G. 5 missing since 19.4.43 during ditching off Murmansk as Ofw.	19.6.42
Müller, Rudolf	Hptm., Kdr. I./K.G. 27 "Boelcke"	1.7.42
Müller, Rudolf	Oblt., Fhr. 6./A.R. 24	30.4.45
Müller, Siegfried	SS-Sturmbannf., Kdr. SS-Pz. G. R. 25 "Hitlerjugend"	19.12.44
Müller, Vincenz	Gen.Lt., stellv. Fhr. XXVII. A.K.	7.4.44
Müller, Waldemar	Hptm., Kdr. II./G. R. 211	6.3.44

Müller, Walter	Major d.R., Kdr. II./G. R. 272	21.10.42
Müller, Walter	Hptm., Kdr. Pz.Jäg. Abt. 389	27.7.44
Müller, Werner	Oblt., Fhr. 7./Pz. G. R. 67	26.12.44
Müller, Wilhelm	Hptm., stv. Kdr. I./Flak-Rgt. 231(mot.)	9.1.45
Müller, Willi	Uffz., Gruppenf. in 2./G. R. 1060	25.1.45
Müller, Willy	Major, Kdr. Pz. Pi. Btl. 144	14.4. 45
Müller-Gebhard, Philipp	Gen.Lt., Kdr. 72. I.D.	3.9.42
Müller-George, Herbert	Hptm., Fhr. I./Jäger-Rgt. 741	18.2.45
Müller-Melahn, Erich	Oberst, Kdr. G. R. 151	5.4.44
Müller-Rochholz, Friedrich (19)	Hptm., Kdr. Pz. Stu. Pi. Btl. "Brandenburg"	8.5.45
Müller-Stöckheim, Günther	Kaptlt., Kdt. "U 67" + 16.7.43 in mid-Atlantic; posthumously promoted to Korv. Kapt.	27.11.42
Müncheberg, Joachim	Oblt., Staffelkpt. 7./J.G. 26 "Schlageter" 12th Oak Leaves 7.5.41 19th Swords 9.9.42	14.9.40
Münst, Thaddäus	Uffz., Truppf. in 1./Pz. A.A. 125	14.4. 45
Münster, Leopold	Feldw., Flugzeugf. in II./J.G. 3 "Udet" 471st Oak Leaves 12.5.44	21.12.42
Muenzner, Eberhard	Hptm., Rgt. Adj. Pz. G. R. 111	23.8.43
Mues, Alfred	Oblt., Chef 8./Schtz. Rgt. 64 + 26.11.42 Stalingrad (Russia) as Hptm. & Btl. Kdr. of wounds	31.12.41
Mütherich, Hubert	Oblt., Staffelkpt. 5./J.G. 54 + 9.9.41 Leningrad (Russia) accidentally during a forced landing	6.8.41
Mützelburg, Rolf	Kaptlt., Kdt. "U 203" 104th Oak Leaves 15.7.42	17.11.41
Muggenthaler, Alfons	Oblt. d.R., Beobachter in 1. (F)/Aufkl. Gr. 121	29.2.44
Mugler, Hermann	Oblt., Chef 5./Geb. Pi. Btl. 54 + 4.3.43 in Kuban bridgehead (Russia) as Hptm. & Btl. Kdr. of wounds	5.7.41
Muhr, Johann	Lt., Fhr. des Eisenb. Flak-Panzerzuges d. 5./Flak. -Abt. 505	22.11.43
Mulzer, Josef-Georg	Major, Kdr. Pi. Btl. 195 367th Oak Leaves 10.1.44	7.9.43
Mummert, Werner	Major d.R., Kdr. Aufkl. Abt. 256 429th Oak Leaves 20.3.44 107th Swords 23.10.44	17.8.42
Mund, Dieter	Lt. d.R., Fhr. 1./Pz.Jäg. Abt. 61 + 23.11.43 of wounds, in Russia as Führer Div. Begleit-Kp.; posthumously promoted to Oblt. d.R.	19.9.43
Mund, Franz	Obfw., Beobachter in 6./K.G. 53 "Legion Condor"	17.3.45

Mundt, Ulrich	Ofw., Flugzeugf. in 10. (Pz.)/S.G. 1 + 29.1.45 south of Bütow (Pomerania) as Flugzeugfhr. In 2. (Pz.)/S.G. 9	25.11.44
Munser, Rudolf	Hptm. d.R., Kdr. 11./G. R. 338	9.4.43
Munz, Johann	Hptm., Kdr. Pi. Bt. 387	18.11.43
Munzel, Oskar	Oberst, Fhr. 14. Pz.Div.	16.10.44
Murken, Heinrich	Major, Fhr. G. R. 124 + 30.1.44	21.2.44
Murr, Heinz	SS-Hauptsturmfhr., Fhr. III./SS-Pz. Gren. Rgt. 9 "Germania"	21.9.44
Musculus, Friedrich-Heinrich	Major d.R., Fhr. Pz.Jäger-Abt. 111	17.2.43
Muser, Alfred	Kaptlt., Chef 8. Räumbootsflottüle	12.8.44
Muster, Fritz	Feldw., Truppf. in Pz. Aufkl. Abt. 116	14.4. 45
Muth, Karl	Ofw., Zugf. in 7./G. R. 399	5.9.44
Muttenthaler, Franz	Feldw., Zugf. in 1./Pz. G. R. 10	11.12.44
Mylius, Wilhelm	Hptm., Staffelkpt. 6./K.G. 55	3.4.43

N

Nacke, Heinz	Hptm., Staffelkpt. 6./Z.G. 76	2.11.40
Nacke, Rudolf	Stabsfw., Flugzeugf. in III./K.G. 76	23.7.41
Naderwitz, Kurt	Oblt., Chef 1./Pz. G. R. 112	1.1.44
Nadolski, Werner	Oblt., Chef 3./Flak-Rgt. 61 (mot.)	31.12.43
Nädele, Wilhelm	Major, Kdr. II./G. R. 460 + 1944 as Oberst	4.11.43
Näfe, Walter	Ofw., Zugf. i. d. 5./G. R. 232	4.10.44
Nähring, Alfred	Major, Fhr. Pz. G. R. 73	4.10.44
Nagel, Helmut	Ofw., Zugf. in 2./Gren. Rgt. Gruppe 163	15.3.44
Nagel, Willy	Oberst, Kdr. G. R. 131	12.6.44
Nagengast, Georg	Major, Kdr. II./G. R. 119 (mot.) + 4.7.44	28.11.43
Najock, Karl-Heinz	Oblt., Flugzeugf. & Beob. in 1. (H)/Aufkl. Gr. 5	28.4.45
Namyslo, Bruno	Ofw., Zugf. in 6./Jäger-Rgt. 49	4.5.44
Naseband, Werner	Hptm., Kdr. I./G. R. 451	28.1.43
Nass, Walter	Obstlt., Kdr. G. R. 937	30.9.44
v. Natzmer, Oldwig	Oberst i.G., Ia Pz. Gren. Div. "GD"	4.9.43
Nau, Herbert	Kaptlt., Chef 10. Räumbootsflottille + 22.8.44 in Nord France; posthumously promoted to Korv. Kpt.	11.7.44
Naue, Herbert	Lt. d.R., Fhr. 2./I.R. 178 + 17.6.42 Sevastopol (Russia) as Hptm. d.R. & Btl. Fhr.	13.7.40
Naumann, Hans-Jörg	Hptm., Kdr. Feldersatz-Btl. 172 d. 72 I.D. + 13.10.43 south-west of Perejaßlaw (Russia)	12.11.43

KNIGHT'S CROSS OF THE IRON CROSS

Naumann, Helmut	Oblt., Staffelkpt. 3./Stuka-Geschw. 3	22.6.41
Naumann, Horst	Uffz., Geschützf. in 3./st. Gesch. Abt. 184	4.1.43
Naumann, Johannes	Hptm., Kdr. II./J.G. 6	9.11.44
Nebe, Werner	Major, Kdr. I./Schtz. Rgt. 59 + 12.7.44 north of Baranowitschi (Russia) as Oberst & Kdr. Gr. Rgt. 30	14.12.41
Nebel, Peter	Oblt., Chef 3./St. Gesch. Abt. 177	27.3.42
Nechansky, Leonhard	Oblt. d.R., Chef 1./G. R. 131 + 4.12.42 Stalingrad (Russia)	20.1.43
v. Necker, Hanns-Horst	Oberst, Kdr. Fsch. Pz. G. R. 2 "HG"	24.6.44
Nehring, Walther K.	Gen. Major, Kdr. 18. Pz.Div. 383rd Oak Leaves 8.2.44 124th Swords 22.1.45	24.7.41
Neibecker, Franz	Oberst; Kdr. Inf.Rgt. 227	16.2.42
Neidhöfer, Hans	Hptm. d.R., Fhr. II./G. R. 712	26.12.44
Neigl, Ludwig	Feldw., stv. Zugf. in Stabskp./s. Pz.Jäg. Abt. 519	27.7.44
v. Neindorff, Egon	Gen. Major, Kdt. v. Tarnopol 457th Oak Leaves 17.4.44	4.4. 44
Neise, Walter	Oberst d.R., Kdr. Armeewaffenschule PZ. AOK. 4	5.2.45
Neitzel, Karl	Korv. Kpt., Kdt. "U 510"	27.3.43
Neitzel, Walter	Hptm., Fhr. I./G. R. 409 576th Oak Leaves 5.9.44	2.6.43
Nelke, Herbert	Uffz., Geschützf. in 1./Flak-Rgt. 23 (mot.) + 30.1.41 Balkans accidentally as Owm. (w/7. Pz.Div.)	4.7.40
Nelles, Heinrich	Feldw., Zugf. in 4./G. R. 698	10.9.44
Nemecek, Ludwig	Oblt., Beobachter in 3. (F)/Aufkl. Gr. 122 + 13.4.43 at Wien during conversion to Flugzeugführer	19.9.42
Nemitz, Willi	Ofw., Flugzeugf. in 4./J.G. 52 + 11.4.43 shot down over Anapa (Caucasus); posthumously promoted to Lt.	24.3.43
Nemnich, Gerhart	Hptm., Kdr. Pz. Pi. Btl. 19 + 15.3.45 in Zepplin	15.7.43
Nentwig, Günther	Major, Kdr. I./A.R. 295 + 31.1.43 at Stalingrad as Oberst	21.1.42
Nestle, Karl	Feldw., Zugf. in 7./G. R. 35 (mot.) 30.7.43 north-west of Orel (Russia)	17.8.43
Neuber, Helmut	Stabsfw., Zugf. in 2./G. R. 176	25.1.45
Neubert Frank	Oblt., Staffelkpt. 2./Stuka-Geschw. 2 "Immelmann"	22.6.41

ELITE OF THE THIRD REICH

Neubert, Karl	Major, Kdr. Ski-Jäger-Btl. 1. + 15.4.45 at Troppau, died of his wounds in hospital	
Neubert, Rudolf	Hptm., Kdr. II./G. R. 32 817th Oak Leaves	29.2.44
Neubrandt, Rudolf	Lt. d.R., Zugf. in Pz. Aufkl. Abt. 37 + 11.10.41 during defensive fighting at Wiasma (Russia) as Oblt. d.R. & Kp. Chef	29.9.40
Neuer, Walther	Major, Führer of a Kampgr. in Ploesti (Romania)	5.11.44
Neuerburg, Hermann	Oblt. d.R., Fhr. Div. Füs. Btl. (A.A.) 121	8.2.44
Neufeld, Ernst	Ofw., Zugf. in 2./Kradschtz. Btl. 40	3.1.43
Neufellner, Karl	Oberst, Kdr. Art.Rgt. 86	6 4.44
Neuffer, Georg	Gen. Major, Kdr. 20. Flak-Div. (mot.)	1.8.43
v. Neufville, Georg	Oberst z. V., Kdr. I.R. 195 + 3.11.41 at main dressing station at Panowo (Russia), of severe wounds; posthumously promoted to Gen. Major z. V.	22.9.41
Neugebauer, Walter	Oblt., Fhr. 12./A.R. 12	16.10.44
Neuhierl, Josef	Uffz., Gr. Fhr. in 8./G. R. 3 + 25.3.45 at Heiligenbeil (East Prussia)	17.3.45
Neuhoff, Hermann	Lt., Staffelf. in III./J.G. 53	16.6.42
Neuhoff, Karl	Ofw., Stoßtruppf. in 6./Fsch. Jäg. Rgt. 3	9.6.44
Neuling, Ferdinand	Gen.Lt., Kdr. 239. I.D.	28.2.42
Neumann, Eggert	SS-Sturmbannf. d.R., Kdr. SS-Geb. Aufkl. Abt. 7 "Prinz Eugen"	3.11.44
Neumann, Ernst	Hptm., Fhr. Festg. Inf. Btl. XII/999	20.4.45
Neumann, Friedrich-Wilhelm	Gen.Lt., Kdr. 712. I.D.	16.10.44
Neumann, Dr. med. Heinrich	Oberstabsarzt, Truppenarzt Fallsch. Jäg. Sturm-Rgt.	21.8.41
Neumann, Helmut (17)	Lt., Staffelf. 14./J.G. 5	12.3.45
Neumann, Joachim	Major, Kdr. I./Pz. A.R. 103	23.2.44
Neumann, Johannes	Hptm. d.R., Chef 8./G. R. 852	17.9.44
Neumann, Jürgen	Oblt., Chef I./I.R. 5 (mot.) + 19.7.43 at Orel (Russia) as Hptm. & Btl. Kdr.; posthumously promoted to Major	1.11.41
Neumann, Klaus	Feldw., Flugzeugf. in 16./J.G. 3 "Udet"	9.12.44
Neumann, Otto	Lt., Fhr. 6./A.R. 126 + 22.2.45 in Kurland at Prekuln (Latvia)	5.4.45
Neumann, Rudolf	Hptm., Staffelkpt. 2./S.G. I	17.4.44
Neumann, Werner	Oberst, Kdr. G. R. 121	5.9.44

even
KNIGHT'S CROSS OF THE IRON CROSS

Neumann-Silkow, Walter	Oberst, Kdr. 8. Schtz. Brigade + 9.12.41 in hospital at Derna (North Africa) as Kdr. 15. Pz.Div. in DAK of wounds; posthumously promoted to Gen. L. t.	5.8.40
Neumayer, Hans	Oblt. d.R., Chef 12. (MG)/G. R. 282	20.1.44
Neumayr, Lorenz	Gefr., MG-Schütze in 1./G. R. 755	14.1.45
Neumeier, Hans	Feldw., Zugf. in 2./Pz. G. R. 64	6.4.44
Neumeister, Karl	Oberst, Kdr. Pz. G. R. 1	4.6.44
Neumeyer, Werner	Lt., Zugf. in 1./Pz. Rgt. 26	23.10.44
Neumüller, Ernst	Oblt., Fhr. 14. (Pz.Jäg.)/Div. Kampfgr. 216	5.10.44
Neumüller, Fritz	Lt., Flugzeugf. & Adj. II./Stuka-Geschw. 77 + 17.8.44 at Baranow (Russia) as Staffelfhr. 7./S.G. 10	4.5.44
Neunhoeffer, Lothar	Major, Kdr. Div. Füs. Btl. (A.A.) 292	3.1.44
Nibbe, Kurt	Oberfähnrich, Zugf. in 1./Pi. Btl. 20	17.3.45
Nickel, Heinrich	Obstlt., Kdr. III./I.R. 26 543rd Oak Leaves 8.8.44	16.6.40
Nicolussi-Leck, Karl	SS-Obersturmf., Chef 8./SS-Pz. Rgt. 5 "Wiking"	9.4.44
Niederländer, Horst	Hptm., Fhr. I./G. R. 686 491st Oak Leaves 9.6.44	10.2.43
Niedermeier, Heinrich	Lt. d.R., Zugf. in 5./Geb.Jäg. Btl. 94 + 7.11.43 Chersson bridgehead (Russia) of wounds	11.12.43
Niedzwetzki, Hans	Feldw., Zugf. in 2./G. R. 23	22.8.43
Niedzwitzki, Roman	Uffz. d.R., VB in 12./Art.Rgt. 290	28.4.45
Niegsch, Karl	Major d.R., Kdr. I./G. R. 223	30.4.45
Niehoff, Hermann	Gen.Lt., Kdr. 371. I.D. 764th Oak Leaves 5.3.45 147th Swords 26.4.45	15.6.4.4
Niehuus, Heinz	Hptm., Kdr. I./S.G. 77	17.4.45
Nielsen, Albert	Owm., Zugf. in 3./Div. Füs. Btl. 58	17.3.45
Niemack, Horst	Rittm., Kdr. Aufkl. Abt. 5 30th Oak Leaves 10.8.41 69th Swords 4.6.44	13.7.40
Niemann, August	Feldw., Zugf. in 3./Pi. Btl. 112 + 2.4.45 Pillau, as Lt., of wounds	4.5.44
Niemann, Eduard	Oberst d.R., Kdr. A.R. 212	29.2.44
Niemann, Heinrich	Lt. d.R., Fhr. 3./Pi. Btl. 196	30.4.43
Niemann, Willi	Uffz., Gesch. Fhr. in 9./A.R. 31	26.12.44
Niemeck, Gerhard	Feldw., Zugf. in 8./Pz. Rgt. 31	14.3.43
Niemeier, Ernst	Feldw., Zugf. in II./G. R. 431	18.2.45
Niemietz, Josef	Hptfw., Zugf. in Stab 3. (Fla)/Pz.Jäg. Abt. 332	24.7.43
Nießen, Peter	Lt., Ord.Offz. in G. R. 979	9.1.45
Nietert, Georg	Uffz., Geschützf. in 14./G. R. 994	10.2.45
Nietsche, Heinrich	Hptm., Kdr. III./I.R. 105 + 9.5,45 as Oberstlt.	13.6.41

Name	Details	Date
Niggemeyer, Wilhelm	Lt. d.R., Fhr. 2./Pi. Btl. 26 241st Oak Leaves 17.5.43	18.9.42
Nilshon, Hans	Major, Kdr. III./A.R. 26	28.3.45
Nippa, Erhard	Oblt., Flugzeugf. in 15./SKG. 10	26.3.44
Nippes, Kurt	Lt. d.R., Zugf. in 1./St. Gesch. Abt. 276 + 10.12.43 north-east of Kiev (Russia); posthumously promoted to Oblt. d.R.	29.1.44
Nitsch, Alfred	Ofw. Flugzeugf. in 2. (F)/Aufkl. Gr. 123	21.6.43
Nitsch, Hans-Joachim	Lt., Zugf. in Pz. Abt. 118	23.3.45
Nitsch, Hermann	Obgefr., VB-Funker in 6./A.R. 11	17.4.45
Nitsch, Martin	Oblt., Fhr. 6./G. R. 417 + 19.9.44	30.9.44
Nittler, Robert	Lt., Fhr. 3./G. R. 212 + 1943 in Stalingrad (Russia)	20.1.43
Noack, Karl	Oblt., Chef 1. (reit.)/Div. Aufkl. Abt. 168 + 5.1.44 in Russia as Rittm. & Abt.Kdr.	24.4. 43
Noak, Karl-Heinz	Lt., Zugf. in 2./Pz.Jäg. Abt. 46 63rd Oak Leaves 16.1.42	5.8.40
Nobis, Ernst	Hptm., Kdr. 11./I.R. 204 151st Oak Leaves 5.12.42	21.1.42
Nocken, Klaus	Major, Kdr. III./K.G. 26 + early May 1945 Prague (Czechoslovakia)	29.10.43
Nöbel, Kurt	Obgefr., Gruppenf. in 1. (reit.)/Aufkl. Abt. 7	30.11.43
Nökel, Friedrich-Karl	Hptm. d.R., Fhr. II./Pz. Rgt. 31	17.9.44
Noeldechen, Ferdinand	Gen. Major, Kdr. 96. I.D.	8.6.43
Noëll, Cornelius	Oblt., Flugzeugf. in 4. (F)/Aufkl. Gr. d. Ob. d. L.	22.10.41
Nölter, Herbert	Hptm., Staffelkpt. 2./K.G. 3 "Lützow" + 13.5.45 of wounds received at Halberstadt as Hptm. u. Kdr. 11./J.G. 301	5.9.44
Nöske, Klaus	Hptm., Staffelkpt. I./K.G. 4 "General Wever"	16.5.41
Nohr, Karl	Uffz., Gruppenf. in Stabskp./G. R. 453	9.5.45
Noller, Wilhelm	Fhj. -Feldw., Flugzeugf. in 2./S.G. 2 "Immelmann"	6.4.44
Nolte, Harro	Lt. d.R., Fhr. 4./G. R. 507	4.10.44
Nolte, Kurt	Hptm. d.R., Kdr. II./I.R. 213	6.9.42
Nolte, Walter	Hptm., Kdr. II./G. R. "Jütland"	5.4.45
Nordmann, Karl-Gottfried	Oblt., Staffelkpt. 12./J.G. 51 35th Oak Leaves 16.9.41	1.8.41
Nordmann, Theodor	Lt., Flugzeugf. in 8./Stuka-Geschw. I 214th Oak Leaves 17.3.43 98th Swords 17.9.44	17.9.41
Nordt, Otto	Kaptlt., Chef 14. Räumbootsflottille	6.9.44
Normann, Helmut	Oblt. d.R., Fhr. I./Jäger-Rgt. 83 + 23.3.45 at Balga (East Prussia)	23.2.44

KNIGHT'S CROSS OF THE IRON CROSS

Norz, Jakob	Ofw., Flugzeugf. in 6./J.G. 5 + 16.9.44 shot down at Kirkenes (Norway) as Lt.	26.3.44
Nossek, Rainer	Fhj. -Ofw., Flugzeugf. in 10. (Pz.)/S.G. 3 + 30.4.45 in aerial combat over Schwerin (Sylte) as Lt. & Staffelfhr. 3. (Pz.)/S.G. 9	29.10.44
v. Nostitz-Wallwitz, Gustav-Adolf	Oberst, Kdr. Pz. A.R. 89 + 31.5.45 at Eckernförde of wounds; final post Gen. Major & Kdr. 24. Pz.Div.	12.6.44
v. Nottbeck, Jürgen	Hptm., Kdr. I./G. R. 94	21.1.45
v. Notz, Friedrich-Wilhelm	Obstlt., Kdr. G. R. 1233	23.3.45
Nowak, Alfred	SS-Oberscharf. d.R., Zugf. in 3./SS-Reiter-Rgt. 1 "Florian Geyer" + 13.9.43 on Dnjepr at Klimenkowke (Russia)	1.11.43
Nowak, Paul	Lt. d.R., Fhr. 1./G. R. 273	10.9.44
Nowotnik, Heinz	SS-Untersturmf. d.R., Fhr. 14. (MG)/SS-Pz. G. R. 1 "LSSAH"	14.5.44
Nowotnik, Karl	San. Feldw. in Stab/Div. Füs. Btl. (A.A.) 212	15.3.44
Nowotny, Walter	Lt., Flugzeugf. in 9./J.G. 54 293rd Oak Leaves 4.9.43 37th Swords 22.9.43 8th Diamonds 19.10.43	4.9.42
Nowowieski, Gregor	Hptm., Kdr. II./G. R. 695	28.12.44
Nuckelt, Alfred	Major, Kdr. Div. Füs. Btl. 218	10.9.44
Nürnberger, Erich	Feldw., Zugf. in 12./I.R. 410 + 12.3.44 at the Narva front (Russia) as Kpt. Chef; posthumously promoted to Oblt.	4.12.42
Nugent, Carlos	Fhj. -Ofw., Bordfunker in 1./N. J.G. 2	17.4.45
Nugiseks, Harald	Waffen-Unterscharf., Zugf. in 1./estn. SS-Freiw. G. R. 46 7.5.45 at Hirschberg into Soviet captivity as SS-Waffen-Oberscharf., posted missing since then	9.4.44
Nuhn, Heinrich	Hptm., Kdr. Pz. Pi. Btl. in Führer-Gren. Div.	9.5.45

O

Obergethmann, Eduard	Obstlt., Kdr. Flak-Rgt. 99 (mot.) + in April 1943 in Soviet captivity; final post Oberst	24.1.43
Oberhofer, Hans	Hptm., Kp. Chef in II./Jäg. RgL 25 (L) + 20.2.45 of wounds	23.3.45
Oberkircher, Karl	Objäg., Gruppenfhr. in 6./Geb.Jäg. Rgt. 218	12.10.43
Oberländer, Werner	Oblt., Flugzeugf. in 2./K.G. 55	24.3.43
Oberloskamp, Walther	Lt. d.R., Zugf. in 3./St. Gesch. Brig. 667 + 25.6.44 in Russia as Oblt. d.R. & Fhr. 2./St. Gesch. Abt. 667	10.5.43

Graf v. Oberndorff, Dr. jur. Fritz	Major d.R., Kdr. Aufkl. Abt. 34	25.8.41
Oberweg, Herbert	Oberfähnrich, Beobachter in 11. (H)/Aufkl. Gr. 13. + 6./7.4.45 Fischhausen (Samland)	8.8.44
Oberwöhrmann, Erich	Hptm., Fhr. Pz. Abt. "Feldherrnhalle"	7.2.44
Obleser, Friedrich	Lt., Staffelf. 8./J.G. 52	23.3.44
Obschil, Alois	SS-Obersturmf., Fhr. 2./G. R. 1126	28.3.45
Obst, Walter	Lt., Fhr. 4./Pz. G. R. 66 + 10.10.43 at Oktoberfeld of wounds	30.11.43
v. Obstfelder, Hans	Gen.D.Inf., Kom.Gen. XXIX. A.K. 251st Oak Leaves 7.6.43 110th Swords 5.11.44	27.7.41
v. Obstfelder, Wolfgang	Hptm., Kdr. s. Pz.Jäg. Abt. 346 858th Oak Leaves 30.4.45	10.9.44
Ochs, Heinrich	Ofw., Zugf. in 1./Pz.Jäg. Abt. 101 360th Oak Leaves 30.12.43	2.6.43
Ochsner, Willifrank	Oberst, Kdr. 31. I.D. simultaneously promoted to Gen. Major	18.1.44
Ochßner, Heinrich	Major, Kdr. Div. Füs. Btl. 132 + 16.9.44 in Russia	19.8.44
Odebrecht, Job	Gen. d. Flakart., Kom.Gen. II. Fla-Korps (mot.)	5.9.44
Odenhardt, Wilhelm	Ofw., Beobachter in 4./K.G. 4 "General Wever"	29.10.44
Oeckel, Erich	Oblt., Chef 5./Schtz. Rgt. 4 + 13.7.43 north of Bjelgorod (Russia) as Hptm. & Kdr. II./Pz. Gr. Rgt. 4	24.6.40
Oehl, Heinz	Lt., Fhr. 1./G. R. 62 + 5.7.43 at Orel (Russia)	25.7.43
Oehmichen, Dr. Hermann	Obstlt., Fhr. Kampfgr. "Oehmichen"	27.12.42
Oehrn, Victor	Kaptlt., Kdt. "U 37"	21.10.40
Oekenpöhler, Johann-Peter	Ofw., Flugzeugf. in 8./K.G. 27 "Boelcke"	2.6.43
Oelker, Heinrich	Hptm., Fhr. Div. Füs. Btl. 21 (L)	26.3.44
Oepke, Karl	Hptm., Chef 6./A.R. 12	16.4.44
Oesau, Walter	Hptm., Staffelkpt. 7./J.G. 51 9th Oak Leaves 6.2.41 3rd Swords 15.7.41	20.8.40
Oesten, Jürgen	Kaptlt., Kdt. "U 106"	26.3.41
Oesterlin, Albert	Kaptlt. d.R., Chef Küstenschutzflottille "Attika" + 22.1.44 during an air raid on Athens(Greece); posthumously promoted to Korv. Kpt. d.R.	9.6.44
Österreicher, Karl	Gefr., MG-Schtz. in 11./G. R. 186	18.12.42
Oesterwitz, Karl-Heinz	Oblt., Chef 7./Lehr-Rgt. z.b.V. 800 "Brandenburg" 734th Oak Leaves 10.2.45	30.4.43
Ofenloch, Heinrich	Uffz., Gruppenf. in 1./Pi. Btl. 323	12.7.43

KNIGHT'S CROSS OF THE IRON CROSS

Name	Details	Date
Offschany, Karl	Feldw., Zugf. in 9./I.R. 191 + 4.10.44 at Götz as Hptm.	7.3.41
Ohlrogge, Walter	Feldw., Flugzeugf. in 5./J.G. 3	4.11.41
Ohmsen, Walter	Oblt. (MA), Chef Marinebatterie "Marcouf" (Mar. Art. Abt. 260)	14.6.44
Ohrloff, Horst	Oblt., Chef 11./Pz. Rgt. 25	27.7.41
Okrent, Wilhelm	Obgefr., Richtkanonier in 4./Pz. A.R. 116	2.4.43
Olboeter, Erich	SS-Sturmbannf., Kdr. III. (gep.)/SS-Pz. G. R. 26 "Hitlerjugend" + 2.9.44 in hospital Charleville (Belgium) of wounds	28.7.44
Olbricht, Friedrich	Gen.Lt., Kdr. 24. I.D. + 20.7.44 in Berlin (OKH) shot in connection with the July plot as Gen.D.Inf. & Chef Allg. Heeresamt in OKH	27.10.39
Olejnik, Robert	Oblt., Staffelkpt. 4./J.G. 1	27.7.41
Oll, Herbert	Hptm., Kdr. I./A.R. 78 +18.4.44 as Oberst & Amtschef in OKH/PA. Nach Unfall	23.8.41
Olschewski, Georg	Oblt. (Ing.), Leit. Ing. auf "U 66"	23.4.44
Omert, Emil	Lt., Flugzeugf. in III./J.G. 77 +24.4. 44 after bailing out over Ploesti (Rumania) as Hptm. & Kdr. III./J.G. 77	19.3.42
v. Ondarza, Leon	Oberst, Kdr. Pz. A.R. 2 +21.4.45 accidentally at Meyenburg (Ostprignitz)	2.9.44
Opdenhoff, Hermann	Oblt. z. See, Kdt. "S 31" in 2. Schnellbootsflottille + 21.3.45 off Texel (Holland) as Kor. Kpt. & Chef 2. Schnellbootsflottille on the "S 181"	16.5.40
Opitz, Heinz-Eberhard	Obstlt., Kdr. G. R. 911	11.3.45
v. Oppeln-Bronikowski, Hermann	Oberst, Kdr. Pz. Rgt. 204 536th Oak Leaves 142nd Swords 17.4.45	1.1.43 28.7.44
Oppenländer, Kurt	Gen. Major, Kdr. 305. I.D. + 17.3.47 in Garmisch-Partenkirchen in US captivity; final post Gen.Lt. & Fhr. 198. Inf. Div.	25.7.42
Oppermann, Walter	Feldw., Zugf. in 7./Jäger-Rgt. 38 +20.3.43	5.5.43
Orinschnig, Egon	Oblt., Chef 10./I.R. 266 + 11.9.42 south of Rshew (Russia) as Hptm. & Btl. Fhr.	13.6.41
Graf v. Oriola, Ralph	Gen.Lt., Kdr. 299. I.D.	23.12.43
Orlowski, Helmuth	Major, Kdr. Fern-Aufkl. Gr. 122 + 8.11.43 north of Pescaria (Adriatic/Italy)	19.9.43
Orth, Heinrich	Ofw., Zugf. in 4./Fsch. Jäg. Sturm-Rgt. + 10.3.42 at Schaikowka (Russia); posthumously promoted to Lt.	18.3.42
Orth, Karl	Gren., in 13./G. R. 453 simultaneously awarded the EK. II. & I. Klasse	3.3.44

Name	Details	Date
Orthofer, Alfons	Hptm., Kdr. II./Stuka-Geschw. 77 + 12.10.42 in hospital at Maikop (Russia) as Major & Kmdr. Stuka-Geschw. 77; posthumously promoted to Obstlt.	23.11.41
Ortlieb, Karl	Obstlt., Kdr. G. R. 754	10.9.44
Orzegowski, Ernst	Fhj. -Feldw., Flugzeugf. in 7./S.G. 10	14.1.45
Ossege, Theodor	Objäg., Gruppenfhr. in 1./Jäger-Rgt. 56 + 29.7.44 in Wolhynien (Russia)	5.9.44
Ostendorf, Werner	SS-Sturmbannf., Ia SS-Div. "Reich" 861st Oak Leaves 6.5.45	13.9.41
Oster, Dieter	Oblt., Chef 2./Flak-Rgt. 8 (mot.)	9.12.42
Osterhold, Wilhelm	Major, Kdr. III./Füs. Rgt. 27 732nd Oak Leaves 10.2.45	26.3.44
Osterkamp, Theodor	Gen. Major, Jagdfliegerführer Luftflotte 2	22.8.40
Ostermann, Felix	Hptm., Fhr. Div. Btl. 260	26.8.43
Ostermann, Max-Hellmuth	Lt., Flugzeugf. in 7./J.G. 54 81st Oak Leaves 12.3.42 10th Swords 17.5.42	4.9.41
Ostermeier, Hans-Arno	Hptm. d.R., Fhr. of a Kampfgr. in Pz. Gr. Div. FHH 834th Oak Leaves 15.4.45	23.8.44
Oswald, Franz	Hptm., Staffelkpt. 13. (Pz.)/S.G. 9	24.10.44
Otolsky, Oskar	Major, Kdr. (Fern)Aufkl. Gr. 2 +22.4.45 at Pardubitz	30.9.44
Ott, Eugen	Gen.D.Inf., Kom.Gen. LII. A.K.	25.12.42
Ott, Heinz (19)	Owm., Zugf. in 12./Pz. Rgt. 24	11.5.45
Ott, Helmuth	Oblt. d.R., Chef 3./G. R. 97	16.11.43
Ott, Joachim	Hptm. d.R., Fhr. I./Jäger-Rgt. 28	28.10.44
Ott, Rudolf	Oberst, Kdr. Jäger-Rgt. 56	28.2.45
Ottawa, Norbert	Hptm. d.R., Chef I./Füs. Rgt. 22	7.9.43
Otte, Albrecht	Oblt., Chef 2./Pz. Pi. Btl. 32	28.4.45
Otte, Friedrich-Wilhelm	Oberst, Kdr. Jäger-Rgt. 207 + 8.5.44 at Sevastopol (Russia) as Kdr. Jäg. Rgt. 213; posthumously promoted to Gen. Major	13.11.42
Otte, Dr. jur. Maximilian	Oblt., Flugzeugf. in 9./Stuka-Geschw. 2 "Immelmann" 433rd Oak Leaves 24.3.44	5.4.42
Ottenbacher, Otto-Ernst	Gen.Lt., Kdr. 36. I.D. (mot.)	13.8.41
Otto, Ernst	Hptm., Fhr. II./G. R. 454	10.2.43
Otto, Rudolf	Uffz., Gr. Fhr. in 6./G. R. 529	15.5.44
Otto, Werner	Uffz., Gruppenf. in 2./G. R. 529	6 4.44
v. Oven, Karl	Gen.Lt., Kdr. 56. I.D.	9.1.42
Overhagen, Theo	Feldw., Zugf. in 9./Pz. G. R. 9 + 23.5.44 at Pontecorvo (Italy)	1.1.44
Overhoff, Gerold	Oblt., Chef I./G. R. 11 (rpot.)	10.12.42

P

Pabst, Karl	Hptm., Kdr. III./Geb. Art.Rgt. 112	4.11.43
Pabst, Karl	Hptm., Chef 3./Pi. Btl. 296 + 1944 in Russia as Btl. Kdr.	19.12.43
Pabst, Kurt	Hptm. d.R., Kdr. Div. Füs. Btl. (A.A.) 81	13.4.44
Pacher, Alois	Obstlt., Kdr. G. R. 222	5.3.45
Pade, Gerhard (5)	Major, Kdr. I./Fsch. Jäg. Rgt. 4	30.4.45
Paege, Arno	Hptm. d.R., Chef 13. (IG.)/G. R. 461	27.7.44
Paegelow, Otto	Uffz., Gr. Fhr. in 2./Füs. Btl. 719 simultaneously promoted to Lt.	8.2.45
Paepcke, Heinrich	Oblt., Staffelkpt. 7./K.G. 30 154th Oak Leaves 19.12.42	5.9.40
Paetow, Heinz	Ofw., Zugf. in 6./G. R. 132	17.12.42
Paetsch, Otto	SS-Obersturmbannf., Kdr. SS-Pz. Rgt. 10 "Frundsberg" 820th Oak Leaves 5.4.45	23.8.44
Pätz, Erich	Ofw., Flugzeugf. in 7./S.G. 2 "Immelmann" + 25.10.43 north of Kriwoi-Rog (Russia)	29.2.44
Pagel, Georg	Oblt., Chef schw. Pz.Jäger-Kp. 1558	28.3.45
Pakebusch, Karl (9)	Btl. Fhr. in Volkssturm Berlin-Wedding	27.4.45
Paletta, Harry	SS-Obersturmf., Chef SS-St. Gesch. Batt. 1007 "Prinz Eugen" + 17.11.44 at the Danube bridgehead at Batina (Yugoslavia)	26.11.44
Palmgren, Karl	Korv. Kpt. d.R., Kdt. Sperrbrecher IX & I 523rd Oak Leaves 11.7.44	3.8.41
Pampus, Ferdinand	Oblt., Chef 14./I.R. 6 + 13.2.42 Demiansk (Russia)	16.2.42
Pandel, Alfred	Hptm., Fhr. I./G. R. 84 + 20.10.43; posthumously promoted to Major	19.12.43
Panknin, Herbert	Kaptlt. (Ing.), Leit. Ing. on "U 106"	4.9.43
Pankow, Georg	Obgefr., s. MG-Fhr. in 2./G. R. 338 simultaneously promoted to Uffz.	31.3.43
Pankow, Dr. med. dent. Werner	Hptm. d.R., Fhr. II./I.R. 151	20.9.41
Pannier, Rudolf	Major der Schupo, Kdr. 1./SS-Pol. Schtz. Rgt. 2	11.5.42
v. Pannwitz, Helmuth	Obstlt., Kdr. Aufkl. Abt. 45 167th Oak Leaves 23.12.42	4.9.41
Panse, Werner	Oblt., Staffelf. 9./S.G. 1	4.5.44
Pantel, Kurt	Hptm., Chef 8. (MG)/I.R. 96 + 23.5.42 Demiansk (Russia) of wounds	7.8.42
Pantzlaff, Dr. jur. Karl	Major d.R., Kdr. III./Pz. A.R. 2	8.8.43
Panusch, Peter	Feldw., Zugf. in 1./G. R. 286	26.2.45
Panzenhagen, Albert	Obstlt., Kdr. Pz. Gren. Rgt. 361	2.10.42

ELITE OF THE THIRD REICH

Papas, Fred	SS-Untersturmf, Kp. -Fhr. in SS-Pz. A.A. 17 "Götz v. Berlichingen"	27.12.44
Pape, Günther	Major, Kdr. Kradschtz. Btl. 3 301st Oak Leaves 15.9.43	10.2.42
Pape, Kurt-Albert	Hptm., Staffelkpt. 3./Stuka-Geschw. 5 + 7.7.43 at Ssamodurowka (Russia)	20.6.43
Pape, Walter	Uffz., Gruppenf. in 5./I.R. 211	7.3.41
Pape, Werner	Hptm., Kdr. Feldersatz-Btl. 158	5.3.45
Papesch, Josef	Feldw., Zugf. Radfahrzug in G. R. 2	7.3.44
Papst, Gerhard	Rittm., Fhr. Pz. Aufkl. Abt. 13	15.1.45
Pardon, Willi	Wachtm., Zugf. in 1./Aufkl. Abt. 15	9.12.44
Parisius, Heinrich	Feldw., Flugzeugf. in 12. (H)/Aufkl. Gr. 13 + 11.2.45 as Ofw.	18.11.44
Paschke, Werner	Oblt. d.R., Chef 3./G. R. 161	19.8.44
Pasold, Heinrich	Oblt. d.R., Chef 4./Geb.Jäg. Rgt. 13	10.9.44
Passegger, Hans	Uffz., Fernsprechtruppf. in Nachr. Staffel II./G. R. 480	27.8.43
Pasternack, Eberhard	Oblt. d.R., Fhr. 7./I.R. 506	22.9.41
Pasternak, Arthur	Oblt. d.R., Chef 2./Pi. Btl. 8 (mot.) + 15.9.44 at Ergli/Kurland as Hptm. d.R. & Fhr. Pz. Pi. Btl. 13	24.3.43
Patry, Walter	Feldw., Flugzeugf. in 3. (F)/Aufkl. Gr. 22 + in January 1945	28.2.45
Patuschka, Dr. Horst	Hptm., Kdr. II./N. J.G. 2 + 6.3.43 failed to return from a mission	10.5.43
Paukner, Ernst	Hptm. d.R., m. d. F. b. II./G. R. 407	18.7.44
Paul, Friedrich-Karl	Korv. Kpt., Chef 2. Torpedobootsflottille	4.3.45
Paul, Hugo	Hptm., Fhr. Fsch. Jäg. Btl. Paul	18.11.44
Paul, Karl	Hptm. d.R., Fhr. I./G. R. 1073 + 3.9.44 on the East Prussian border at Walka	20.10.44
Paul (9)	Uffz. in Kampfgruppe Wach-Rgt. "GD" in Festung Berlin	25.4.45
Pauls, Rolf	Major i.G., Ia 363. Volks-Gren. Div.	18.11.44
Pauls, Werner	Oblt., Chef 9./I.R. 45	23.11.41
Paulsen, Karl-August	Oblt., Staffelkpt. 9./K.G. 30	29.2.44
Paulus, Friedrich	Gen. d. Pz.Tr., OB 6. Armee 178th Oak Leaves 15.1.43	26.8.42
Paulus, Dr. rer. pol. Walter	Lt. d.R., Fhr. 3./Pz.Jäg. Abt. 263	31.3.42
Paulussen, Heinz	Hptm., Fhr. Pz. Aufkl. Abt. 18 + 7.9.43 west of Wjasma (Russia)	18.9.43
Pausinger, Joseph	Obstlt. d.R., Kdr. Inf.Rgt. 339	16.2.42
Peek, Wilhelm	Major, Kdr. II./G. R. 953 + 23.10.44	4.10.44

Peichl, Adolf	SS-Hptscharf., Zugf. in 12. (gep.)/SS-Pz. G. R. 4 "Der Führer"	16.10.44
Pein, Friedrich	Objäg., Scharfschtz. in 2./Jäger-Rgt. 227	28.2.45
Peiper, Joachim	SS-Sturmbannf., Kdr. III. (gep.)/SS-Pz. G. R. 2 "LSSAH" 377th Oak Leaves 27.1.44 119th Swords 11.1.45	9.3.43
Peitsch, Herbert	Gefr., Gewehrgranatschtz. in 7./Fsch. Jäg. Rgt. 6 + August 1944 in France of wounds	29.10.44
Peitsmeyer, Wolfdietrich	Oblt., Staffelkpt. 6./(S) L.G. 2 + 10.12.42 in Mediterranean area as Hptm. & Kdr. I./S.G. 2 "Immelmann"	21.7.40
Pekrun, Dietrich	Oblt., Flugzeugf. & Adj. 1./Stuka-G. 2 "Immelmann"	22.6.41
Pellengahr, Richard	Gen.Lt., Kdr. 196. I.D.	9.5.40
Peltz, Dietrich	Oblt., Staffelkpt. 1./Stuka-Geschw. 3 46th Oak Leaves 31.12.41 31st Swords 23.7.43	14.10.40
Pelz, Erich	Ofw., Zugf. in 5./Pz. G. R. 10	6.10.44
Pelzer, Jakob	Gefr. in 1./I.R. 61 + 2.9.42 of wounds	15.1.42
Pemsel, Max-Josef	Gen. Major, Kdr. 6. Geb. Div.	9.12.44
Penkert, Oskar	Feldw., Zugf. in 3./Pz. G. R. 108	23.2.44
Penth, Paul	Major d.R., Kdr. Pi. Rgt. Stab 677	14.5.44
Pentzien, Hans	Hptm. d.R., Staffelkpt. 1. (F)/Aufkl. Gr. 124	2.2.45
Pergande, Werner	Lt., Kp. Fhr. in G. R. 108	22.11.43
Persson, Joachim	Oblt. d.R., Chef 14. (Pz.Jäg.)/G. R. 501 + 25.3.44 Nevel (Russia) of wounds; posthumously promoted to Hptm. d.R.	26.3.44
Pesch, Erwin	Hptm., Fhr. I./G. R. 239	30.7.43
Peschel, Georg (18)	Ofw., Zugf. in 10./Jg. Rgt. 49	11.5.45
Peschel, Rudolf	Gen.Lt., Kdr. 6. Luftw. -Feld-Div. + 30.6.44 at Witebsk (Russia)	20.1.44
Peschke, Gustav	Major, Kdr. II./Pz. G. R. 394 + 10.12.43 in Tscherkassy (Russia) of wounds	15.1.44
Peschke, Otto	Uffz., Kp. Tr. Fhr. in 2./G. R. 132	5.3.45
Pestke, Hans-Gotthard	Oblt., Chef 3./I.R. 176 311th Oak Leaves 14.10.43	15.11.41
Pete-Nemeth, Ernst	Uffz., Meldestaffelfhr. in II./G. R. 401	17.3.45
Peteani, Josef	Oblt., Flugzeugf. in 7./L.G. 2 + 4.9.42 Stalingrad (Russia) (Nahaufkl. Gruppe 12)	21.10.42
Peter, Erich	Uffz., Flugzeugf. in Stabsst./Stuka-G. 2 "Immelmann" + 25.4.45 at Strausberg (Mark) as Ofw. & Flugzeugfhr. In Stab II./S.G. 151	22.7.43
Peter, Gerhard	Oblt., Chef 3./Pz. Pi. Btl. 16	15.11.41
Peter, Rudolf	Obergefr., Gruppenf. in 2./G. R. 307	16.11.44

ELITE OF THE THIRD REICH

Ritter & Edler v. Peter, Wilhelm	Major, Kdr. I./Pz. Rgt. 36 + 26.9.41 during assault on Mirgorod (Russia) of wounds; posthumously promoted to Oberstlt.	15.7.41
Peterburs, Hans	Ofw., Flugzeugf. in II./Z.G. 1 + 11.1.44 at Salerno (Italy) as Flugzeugf. in II./Schlacht-Geschwader 4	25.11.42
Petereit, Max-Eugen	Oblt. d.R., Fhr. 3./A.R. 240 + 29.9.42 in defensive fighting at Neva south of Lake Ladoga (Russia)	7.10.42
Peterhänsel, Horst-Egon	Major, Kdr. I./G. R. 272	6.4.44
Petermann, Erich	Ofw., Zugf. in 4./Kradschtz. Btl. 64 + 18.9.42 during advance on Stalingrad (Russia) as Lt. & Fhr. 4./Kradschtz. Btl. 64 of wounds	17.8.42
Petermann, Viktor	Lt., Flugzeugf. in III./J.G. 52	29.2.44
Peters, Alfred	Ofw., Zugf. in 14. (Pz.Jäg.)/G. R. 348	3.8.44
Peters, Josef	Oblt., Beob. in 12./K.G. 26	6.4.44
Peters, Karl (17)	Hptm., Kdr. II. (Kampf/Lehr-Geschw. 1	9.4.45
Peters, Kurd	Major, Kdr. II. (Sturm)/J.G. 300	29.10.44
Peters, Reinhard	Lt. d.R., Fhr. 4./Pz. Rgt. 35	29.2.44
Peters, Werner	Oblt. d.R., Fhr. II./G. R. 587 posted missing 24.8.44 as Major & Bt. Kdr. II./G. R. 587	16.11.43
v. Petersdorff, Horst	Hptm. z. V., Kdr. III./I.R. 189	29.6.40
v. Petersdorff, Manfred	Major, Kdr. I./I.R. 529	9.2.42
Petersen, Carl-August	Hptm., Staffelkpt. 9./K.G. 27 "Boelcke"	7.3.42
Petersen, Edgar	Major, Kdr. I./K.G. 40	21.10.40
Petersen, Fritz	Wachtm., Geschützf. in 6./Flak-Rgt. 4 (mot.) 438th Oak Leaves 26.3.44	16.11.42
Petersen, Heinrich	Stabsobersteuermann, Wachoffz. & Steuermann on "U 99"	5.11.40
Petersen, Heinrich	Hptm., Kdr. I./I.R. 184 + 7.8.43 in Russia as Major & Rgt. Fhr.	6.2.42
Petersen, Heinrich	SS-Obersturmbannf., Kdr. SS-Geb.Jäg. Rgt. 1 "Prinz Eugen" + 9.5.45 between Tabor & Pilsen in Bohemia-Moravia (suicide) as SS-Standartenf. & Fhr. 18. SS-Pz. Gren. Div. "Horst Wessel"	13.11.43
Petersen, Otto	SS-Hptsturmf., Kdr. II./SS-Freiw. Pz. G. R. 49 "De Ruyter"	11.12.44
Petersen, Rudolf	Korv. Kpt., Chef 2. Schnellbootsflottille 499th Oak Leaves 13.6.44	4.8.40
Petershagen, Rudolf	Obstk., Kdr. II./I.R. 92 (mot.)	20.7.42
Peterson, Georg	Hptm. d.R., Fhr. Art. Abt. 929	27.8.44
Petzold, Ernst	Oblt., Flugzeugf. in 5./K.G. 54	17.9.41
Petzold, Joachim	Hptm., Kdr. I./K.G. 27 "Boelcke"	18.5.43

KNIGHT'S CROSS OF THE IRON CROSS

Name	Details	Date
Pfaffendorf, Armin	Oblt., Flugzeugf. in 1. (H)/Aufkl. Gr. 13 + 18.1.44 in Russia as Chef I./St. Gesch. Abt. 184; posthumously promoted to Hptm.	22.5.42
Pfalzgraf, Oskar	Uffz., Zugf. in 5./I.R. 695	7.10.42
Pfannkuche, Karl	Major, Kdr. II./Pz. Rgt. 33	17.3.45
Pfattischer, Josef	Uffz., Gruppenf. in 8./G. R. 61	4.10.44
Pfau, Otto	Hptm., Fhr. I./Pz. G. R. "GD"; missing March 1945 in East Prussia	23.3.45
Pfeffer, Max	Gen.Lt., Kdr. 297. I.D. + 3.1.56 in Soviet captivity in Camp Wolkowo (Russia); final post Gen. d. Art. & Kom.Gen. IV. A.K.	4.12.41
Pfeffer-Wildenbruch, Karl	SS-Obergruppenf. & Gen. d. W-SS, Kom.Gen. IX. SS-Geb. Korps 723rd Oak Leaves 1.2.45	11.1.45
Pfeifer, Hellmuth	Obstlt., Kdr. Inf.Rgt. 185 574th Oak Leaves 5.9.44	26.11.41
Pfeiffer, Franz	Hptm., Chef 15./Geb.Jäg. Rgt. 100	13.6.41
Pfeiffer, Dr. Georg	Gen.Lt., Kdr. 94. I.D. + 28.6.44 at Beresina (Russia) as Gen. d. Art. & Kom.Gen. VI. A.K.	15.1.43
Pfeiffer, Hans	Lt. d.R., Fhr. 2./Pi. Btl. 97	26.1.42
Pfeiffer, Hellmut	Hptm., Kdr. II./I.R. 671 + 12.11.42 at Stalingrad (Russia)	19.9.42
Pfeiffer, Horst	Oblt., Fhr. I./G. R. 755	12.1.45
Pfeiffer, Johannes	Oblt., Staffelkpt. 12. (Stuka)/L.G. 1	10.10.41
Pfeiffer, Karl	Oblt., stv. Fhr. I./G. R. 435	15.3.44
Pfeil, Johann	Hptm., Kdr. I./G. R. 80 + 13.2.44 at Tinowka east of Schaschkoff (Russia)	29.2.44
Pfennig, Herbert	Lt. d.R., Zugf. in 4./Pz. G. R. 25	21.9.44
Pfeuffer, Arno	Rittm., Kdr. Aufkl. Abt. 332	7.8.43
Pfitzer, Werner	Lt., Stoßtruppf. in 3./Schtz. Rgt. 113	19.7.41
Pfitzner, Heinz	Oblt. d.R., Chef 2./Pi. Btl. 290	15.1.43
Pfizenmayer, Paul	Hptm. d.R., Chef 3./A.R. 215	3.11.44
Pflanz, Rudolf	Oblt., Flugzeugf. in 1./J.G. 2 "Richthofen" + 31.7.42 at Abbeville (France) during aerial combat as Staffelkpt. 1./J.G. 2 "Richthofen"; posthumously promoted to Hptm.	1.8.41
Pflieger, Kurt	Gen.Lt., Kdr. 416. I.D.	10.2.45
Pflugbeil, Johann	Gen.Lt., Kdt. of Mitau (Latvia)	12.8.44
Pflugbeil, Kurt	Gen.Lt., Kom.Gen. IV. Fliegerkorps 562nd Oak Leaves 27.8.44	5.10.41
Pförtner, Helmut	SS-Untersturmf., d.R., Fhr. 6./SS-Rgt. "Germania" + 28.2.43 at Isjum (Russia) as SS-Hptsturmf. d.R. & Kp. Chef	18.1.42
Pfreudtner, Karl	Owm., Zugf. in 2./St. Gesch. Abt. 244 + 26.6.44 Rogatschew bridgehead (Russia)	10.9.42

Pfühl, Heinz	Wachtm. d.R., Schwadronstruppf. in 3./Div. Füs. Btl. 362	5.2.45
v. Pfuhlstein, Alexander	Oberst, Kdr. I.R. 154	17.8.42
Philipp, Christian	Gen.Lt., Kdr. 8. Jäger-Div.	11.3.45
Philipp, Ernst	Oblt., Chef 4./Pz. Rgt. 1 599th Oak Leaves 30.9.44	28.11.40
Philipp, Hans	Oblt., Staffelkpt. 4./J.G. 54 33rd Oak Leaves 24.8.41 8th Swords 12.3.42	22.10.40
Philipp, Hans-Otto	Korv. Kpt. d.R., Chef 1. Küstensicherungsverband	31.12.44
Philipp, Wilhelm	Ofw., Flugzeugf. in 3./J.G. 54	26.3.44
Philippi, Alfred	Oberst, Kdr. G. R. 535	14.5.44
Philippi, Karl	Oberst, Kdr. Inf.Rgt. 207 + 30.10.41 at Artemowsk (Russia)	2.11.41
Philipps, Karl	Oblt., Chef 5./Pz. Gren. Lehr-Rgt. 901	7.4.44
Philipps, Dipl.-Ing. Wilhelm	Gen.Lt., Kdr. 3. Pz.Div.	5.3.45
Phleps, Arthur	SS-Gruppenf. & Genlt. d. W-SS, Kdr. SS-Div. "Prinz Eugen" 670th Oak Leaves 24.11.44	4.7.43
Phönix, Harry	SS-Hptsturmf., Kdr. II./SS-A.R. 8 "Florian Geyer"	21.2.45
Pichler, Johann	Fhj. -Ofw., Flugzeugf. in 7./J.G. 77	19.8.44
Picht, Alfred	Major d.R., Kdr. III./Pz. A.R. 78	9.12.44
Pick, Gerhard	Hptm., Kdr. II./I.R. 490 553rd Oak Leaves 19.8.44	2.11.41
Picker, Egbert	Oberst, Kdr. Geb.Jäg. Rgt. 98	18.11.41
Pickert, Wolfgang	Gen. Major, Kdr. 9. Flak-Div. (mot.) 489th Oak Leaves 5.6.44	11.1.43
Picus, Karl	SS-Obersturmf. in SS-Pz. Rgt. 5 "Wiking"	17.4.45
Piechulla, Alois	Gefr., MG-Schütze in 2./Pz. G. R. 33	11.4.43
Piefer, Friedrich	Fhj. -Ofw., stellv. Fhr. 2./G. R. 464	2.9.44
Piehler, Franz	Hptm., Kdr. I./Jäg. Rgt. 25 (L)	6.10.44
Piekenbrock, Heinz	Gen. Major, Kdr. 208. I.D.	4.5.44
Pielmeier, Hans	Hptm., stellv. Kdr. Le. Flak-Abt. 89 (mot.)	20.7.44
Piening, Adolf	Kaptlt., Kdt. "U 155"	13.8.42
Pieper, Claus	Oblt. d.R., Fhr. 2./Pz.Jäg. Abt. 161	24.2.45
Pieper, Heinz	Ofw., Zugf. in Gren. Rgt. 230 + 16.1.43 Stalingrad (Russia)	20.1.43
Pieper, Heinz	Uffz., Geschützf. in I./Pz.Jäg. Abt. 19 + 7.9.43 of severe wounds during withdrawals following Op Zitadelle (Russia)	17.9.43
Pieper, Willi	San. -Uffz. in Stabskp. (Pi. Zug)/G. R. 478 + 13.7.43 in Kursk-Orel area (Russia); posthumously promoted to San. Feldw.	8.4.43

Pietsch, Werner	Hptm. d.R., Chef 6./Pz. Rgt. 39	16.11.43
Pietschmann, August	Owm. d.R., Nachr. Staffelfhr. in 8./A.R. 24	20.10.44
Pietschmann, Karl	Feldw., Zugf. Pi. Zug in Stabskp./G. R. 57 + 19.3.44 southern sector of the Eastern Front (Russia)	9.6.44
Pietzonka, Erich	Obstlt., Kdr. Fsch. Jäg. Rgt. 7 584th Oak Leaves 16.9.44	5.9.44
Piffer, Rudolf-Anton	Ofw., Staffelf. 2./J.G. 1 "Oesau" + 17.6.44 at Calvados (France); posthumously promoted to Lt.	20.10.44
Pikrot, Hans	Lt., Fhr. 2./Pi. Btl. 158	2.9.44
Pilarski, Hubert	Ofw., Zugf. in 8. (MG)/G. R. 511 493rd Oak Leaves 9.6.44	4.8.43
Pilat, Karl	Major, Kdr. III./G. R. 53	14.11.43
Pilz, Walter	Feldw., Flugzeugf. in 5./K.G. 55	24.3.43
Pingel, Rolf	Hptm., Kdr. I./J.G. 26 "Schlageter"	14.9.40
Pinkepank, Georg	Korv. Kpt., Chef 2. Räumbootsflottille	12.8.44
Pintschovius, Johannes	Hptm., Kdr. III./I.R. 202 + 4.1.45 as Obstlt. +20.1.45 at Konin (West Prussia) as Obstlt. & Kdr. Heeres-Uffz. Schule 14 Kosten (Warthe)	5.5.42
Pipan, Artur	Oblt., Staffelkpt. 5./Stuka-Geschw. I	6.4.44
Pirch, Wilhelm	Hptm., Fhr. Pz. Aufkl. Abt. 11	13.9.43
Pirhofer, Ernst	Obgefr., Richtkan. in 7./Flak-Rgt. 43 (mot.)	4.5.44
Pirner, Karl	Feldw., Zugf. in 10./G. R. 520 + 13.3.43 in Russia	21.5.43
Piske, Herbert	Oblt., Staffelkpt. 3./S.G. 10	15.3.45
Pitsch, Walter (6)	SS-Hptscharf., Zugf. in 4./SS-Flak-Abt. 1 "LSSAH"	6.5.45
Pittschellis, Adolf	SS-Sturmbannf., Kdr. SS-Pz.Jäg. Abt. 3 "Totenkopf" + 26.1.45 Stuhlweißenburg (Hungary)	23.8.44
Pizala, Josef	Hptm., Chef 2./Flak-Rgt- 111 (mot.) + 14.10.41 in Russia of wounds	17.10.41
Placzek, Franz	Ofw., Beobachter in 2./K.G. 55	3.4.43
v. der Planitz, Max Edler	Major d.R., Fhr. Pz.Jäg. Abt. 161	14.2.45
Plapper, Albert	Gefr., Gruppenf. in 4./Fsch. Pz. Gr. Rgt. 2 "HG" + 28.1.45 at Arnfelde (East Prussia)	30.11.44
v. Plato, Anton-Detlev	Obstlt. i.G., Ia 5. Pz.Div.	19.8.44
Platta, Reinhold	Obgefr., MG-Schtz. in 1./G. R. 309	12.12.44
Platz, Hubert (19)	Major, Kdr. Pz. A.R. 89	11.5.45

Platzer, Friedrich	Oblt., Staffelf. 3./Stuka-Geschw. 2 "Immelmann" + 16.3.42 at Doworez on Lake Ilmen (Russia); posthumously promoted to Hptm.	5.4.42
Plein, Josef	Obgefr., Gr. Fhr. in 6./G. R. 545 + 20.4.45 in Klettkau (Danziger Bucht)	14.4. 45
Pleiß, Gerhard	SS-Obersturmf., Chef 1./"LSSAH" (mot.) + 17.11.41 Rostov (Russia) as SS-Hptsturmf.	20.4.41
Plenzat, Kurt	Ofw., Flugzeugf. in 2./Stuka-Geschw. 2 "Immelmann" 712th Oak Leaves 24.1.45	19.9.43
Plesch, Hans	Lt. d.R., Fhr. 12./I.R. 6	21.3.42
Pleß, Helmut	Lt., Flugzeugf. in 4. (H)/Aufkl. Gr. 31	9.6.44
Graf v. Plettenberg, Georg	Rittm., Kdr. schw. Kav. Abt. 4 730th Oak Leaves 5.2.45	12.8.44
Plettner, Erich	Hptm. d.R., Fhr. I./G. R. 507	1.1.44
Plewig, Waldemar	Hptm., Kdr. II./Stuka-Geschw. 77	14.12.40
Plickat, Fritz	Feldw., Zugf. in 8./Pz. Rgt. "GD"	9.12.44
Plinzner, Peter-Paul	Oblt., Chef 5./Pz. Rgt. 27 + 17.10.41 near Moscow (Russia) of wounds	20.10.41
Pliska, Fritz	Ofw., Zugf. in 3./Pz. Pi. Btl. 19	26.3.44
Plocher, Hermann	Gen. Major, Chef d. Gen. St. Luftflotte 3 867th Oak Leaves 8.5.45	22.11.43
Plöger, Karl-Heinrich	Oblt., Chef 6./Pz. G. R. 14	23.3.45
Plönzke, Werner	Gefr., MG-Schtz. in 5./Pz. G. R. 103	4.7.44
Plümer, Friedrich-Hans	Hptm., Kdr. I./G. R. 268	28.1.43
Pochat, Karl-August	Obstlt., Kdr. Aufkl. Abt. 29 (mot.) + 30.6.42 in Kursk-Charkow area (Russia) as Oberst & Kdr. Pz. Rgt. 201	5.8.40
Podehl, Erich	Ofw., Zugf. in Pz.Jäg. Abt. 349	5.4.45
Podrasa, Reinhold	Ufw., Zugf. in 3./G. R. 551	31.1.45
Pöhler, Heinz	Ofw., Zugfhr. in 1./G. R. 32	2.9.44
Poehlmann, Hermann	Hptm., Kdr. I./Flak-Rgt. 33	11.2.45
Pöhner, Georg	Uffz., Kp. Truppf. in 6./Pz. G. R. 33	21.9.44
Pöhs, Josef	Lt. d.R., Flugzeugf. in 5./J.G. 54 + 30.12.43 shot down over Bad Zwischenahn (Oldenbg.) as Oblt. d.R. in Erprob. Kdo. 16 (Me 163)	6.8.41
Poel, Gerhard	Gen. Major, Oberfeldkdt. 400 & Kdt. v. Wilna + 8.5.45 at Brünn (Czechoslovakia) as Gen.Lt.	16.10.44
Poel, Gustav	Kaptlt., Kdt. "U 413"	21.3.44
Pöllath, Konrad	Ofw., Flugzeugf. in 2. (H)/Aufkl. Gr. 12	14.1.45
Pölz, Hubert	Lt. d.R., Staffelf. 7./Stuka-Geschw. 3 661st Oak Leaves 25.11.44	5.2.44
Pöppel, Julius	Wachtm., Zugf. in 5./Pz. G. R. 26	31.12.44
Poerschke, Fritz	Hptm. d.R., Fhr. III./I.R. 446	26.8.42

Name	Details	Date
Pörschmann, Johannes	Hptm., Kdr. Pz. Pi. Btl. 13 + 13.3.45	11.3.45
Pöschl, Franz	Hptm., Kdr. I./Gebjäg. Rgt. 100	23.2.44
Pössinger, Michael	Lt. d.R., Zugf. in 16./Geb.Jäg. Rgt. 98 759th Oak Leaves 28.2.45	19.7.40
Pössl, Walter	Major, Kdr. I./Pz. Rgt. "GD" + 25.9.44 Warsaw (Poland) as Rgt. Fhr.; posthumously promoted to Oberstlt.	20.4.43
Pöthig, Georg	Ofw., Bordfunker in 8./S.G. 2 "Immelmann"	5.9.44
Pötschke, Werner	SS-Hptsturmf., Chef I./SS-Pz. Rgt. 1 "LSSAH" 783rd Oak Leaves 15.3.45	4.6.44
Poetter, Joachim	Hptm., Kdr. I./K.G. 77	16.4.42
Pohl, Eberhard	Major, Kdr. I./I.R. 134	17.12.42
Pohl, Franz	Uffz., Geschützf. in 14. (Pz.Jäg.)/G. R. 220	10.9.44
Pohl, Günther	Hptm., Kdr. Pz.Jäg. Abt. 712	24.2.45
Pohl, Max Ritter	Gen. d. Flg., Kom.Gen. of the Luftw. in central Italy	15.6.44
Pohlmann, Wilhelm	Hptm., Kgr. Fhr. Führer-Begleit-Btl. + 10.10.43 in Russia of wounds as Major & Kdr. III./Pz. Füs. Rgt. "GD"	14.3.43
Pohrig, Heinrich	Lt. d.R., Zugf. in 3./Pz. G. R. 12	15.4.44
Polack, Dr. rer. pol. Fritz	Oberst, Kdr. A.R. 29 (mot.)	27.8.43
Polewacz, Harry	SS-Sturmbannf., Kdr. III./SS-Pz. G. R. "Nordland" + 12.1.43 Rostov (Russia) as SS-Obersturmbannfhr. Rgt. Kdr.	23.12.42
Poll, Matthias	Obgefr., Kp. Tr. Fhr. in 2./Pi. Btl. 186	8.8.43
Pollak, Johann	Obgefr., Fernsprecher in Stab I./G. R. 434 + 1.4.44 in Russia	4.5.44
Pollmann, Othmar	Major, Kdr. II./G. R. 481 760th Oak Leaves 28.2.45	27.8.43
Pollmann, Otto	Lt. z. See d.R., Kdt. "U-Jäger 2210" (22. Ujagd-Flottille) 461st Oak Leaves 25.4.44	19.5.43
Pollner, Georg	Ofw., Zugf. in 3./Pz. Aufkl. Abt. 110	3.11.44
Pollow, Dr. jur. Herbert	Oblt. d.R., stv. Fhr. II./I.R. 479 + 14.8.42 at Trysseli east of Wjasma (Russia); posthumously promoted to Hptm. d.R.	1.8.42
Polz, Heinz	Owm Geschützstaffelf. im Flak-Sturm-Rgt. 241 (mot)	1.12.44
Pommer, Hellmut	Oblt. d.R., Chef 1./G. R. 179 + 17.7.43 at Donets (Russia), of wounds	25.7.43
Ponath, Gustav	Obstlt., Kdr.	13.4.41
v. Poncet, Hans	Oberst, Kdr. G. R. 358	8.8.44
Pongratz, Johann	Ofw., Zugf. in 2./I.R. 74	4.9.40
Poppe, Hermann	Ofw., Zugf. in 13./G. R. 216	23.3.45

ELITE OF THE THIRD REICH

Poppinga, Hinrich	Obstlt., Kdr. I.R. 131	5.2.42
Populo, Theodor	Lt., Fhr. 7./Schtz. Rgt. 4	27.7.41
Porath, Rudolf	Lt. z. See d.R., Kdt. "Vp 1806" (18. Vorposten-Flottille)	8.10.41
Porsch, Günther	Ofw., Flugzeugf. & Beob. in 1. (H)/Aufkl. Gr. 2	20.7.44
Port, Johann	Feldw., Zugf. in 8. (MG)/I.R. 266	25.8.42
Portsteffen, Josef	Ofw., Stoßtruppfhr. in 1./Pi. Btl. 51 (mot.)	21.5.40
v. Poschinger, Joachim Ritter	Major, Fhr. Pz. Gren. Lehr-Rgt. 902 + 4.4. 45 at Silbach (Westf.) as Obstlt. & Rgt. Kdr.	25.1.45
Poschusta, Leopold	Uffz., Zugf. in 2./Pz. Füs. Rgt. "GD" + 15.11.43 Krivoi-Rog at Kommunar (Russia)	12.11.43
Poske, Fritz	Korv. Kpt., Kdt. "U 504"	6.11.42
Post, Eduard	Hptm. d.R., Kdr. III./G. R. 744	28.2.45
Post, Martin	Feldw., Zugf. in 6./Pz. G. R. 12	21.9.44
Post, Otto	Oblt., Chef 1./Div. Füs. Btl. 94	29.2.44
Postel, Georg-Wilhelm	Oberst, Kdr. I.R. 364 215th Oak Leaves 28.3.43 57th Swords 26.3.44	9.8.42
Potschka, Hermann	SS-Sturmbannf. d.R., Kdr. II./SS-Freiw. Pz. A.R. 11 "Nordland" + in spring 1945 on the Eastern Front	26.12.44
Prager, Fritz	Hptm., Kdr. II./Fsch. Jäg. Rgt. 1 + 3.12.40 of wounds in hospital at Braunschweig, as Major	24.5.40
Prager, Otto	SS-Sturmbannf. & Major d. SchutzPol., Fhr. SS-Pol. Pz. G. R. 7 + 28.4.45 at Neubrandenburg as SS-Obersturmbannfhr. & Oberstlt. d. Schutzpolizei & Rgt. Kdr.	9.12.44
Praßdorf, Heinrich	Obermaschinist auf "U 1203"	21.4.45
Praun, Albert	Gen.Lt., Kdr. 129. I.D.	27.10.43
Prchal, Johann	Uffz., Gruppenf. in 7./G. R. 448 posted missing 17.10.43	12.11.43
Preinfalk, Alexander	Uffz., Flugzeugf. in 5./J.G. 77 + 12.12.44 at Bruchsal (Baden) when bailing out as Ofw. & Flugzeugf. in 6./J.G. 53	14.10.42
Preiss, Armin	Oblt. d.R., Chef 9./G. R. 520 + 30.9.43 north of Brjansk (Russia); posthumously promoted to Hptm. d.R.	2.11.43
Preiß, Josef	Objäg., Gruppenf. in 15./Jäger-Rgt. 227	20.4.45
Prentl, Josef	Oblt., Chef 2./Flak. Rgt. 231 851st Oak Leaves 28.4.45	21.10.42
Press, Heinrich	Hptm., Kdr. II./G. R. 105	16.10.44
Pressler, Gustav	Hptm., Kdr. III./Stuka-Geschw. 2 "Immelmann" 188th Oak Leaves 26.1.43	4.2.42
Preu, Theodor	Oberst, Kdr. G. R. 21	9.1.44
Preuß, Carl	Oblt., Fhr. 6./G. R. 272	14.2.45

Name	Rank/Unit	Date
Preuß, Ernst	Stabsfw., Ord.Offz. in III./G. R. 53	17.12.43
Preuß, Georg	SS-Obersturmf, Fhr. 10. (gep.)/SS-Pz. G. R. 2 "LSSAH"	5.2.45
Pressler, Wilhelm	Ofw., Zugf. in 12./G. R. 12 + 9.4.44 in Russia	9.6.44
Priem, Otto	Oblt., Chef 10./G. R. 501	16.4.43
Prien, Günther	Kaptlt., Kdt. "U 47" 5th Oak Leaves 20.10.40	18.10.39
Prien, Peter	Oblt. d.R., Fhr. Stabskp. 2. Pz.Div.	9.5.45
Prieß, Helmuth	Gen.Lt., Kdr. 121. I.D. + 21.10.44 at Hasenrode (East Prussia) as Gen.D.Inf. & Kom.Gen. XXVII. A.K.	7.3.44
Prieß, Hermann	SS-Oberführer, Kdr. A.R. d. SS-Pz. Gren. Div. "Totenkopf" 297th Oak Leaves 9.9.43 65th Swords 24.4. 44	28.4,43
Prill, Günter	Oblt., Chef 3./G. R. 51 (mot.)	18.1.44
Priller, Josef	Oblt., Staffelkpt. 6./J.G. 51 28th Oak Leaves 20.7.41 73rd Swords 2.7.44	19.10.40
Primozic, Hugo	Wachtm., Zugf. in 2./St. Gesch. Abt. 667 185th Oak Leaves 25.1.43	19.9.42
Prinner, Josef	Gen.Lt., Höll. Art. Kdr. 311	11.1.45
Prinz, Karl-Heinz	SS-Sturmbannf., Kdr. 11./SS-Pz. Rgt. 12 "Hitlerjugend" + 14.8.44 in Normandy (France) at Hill 159	11.7.44
Prinz, Kurt	Oblt., Fhr. 1./G. R. 164	14.4. 45
v. Prittwitz & Gaffron, Bernhard	Obstlt.,Fhr. G. R. 586 + 25.4.44 at Grigoropol (Russia); posthumously promoted to Oberst	24.6.44
Pritzel, Klaus	Hptm., Staffelkpt. 2. (F)/Aufkl. Gr. des Ob. d. Luftw.	15.10.42
Probst, Heinz (17)	Uffz., Zugf. in Fsch. Pz. G. R. 1 "HG"	26.3.45
Probst, Theodor	Ofw., Zugf. in 12. (MG)/G. R. 519	20.4.43
Prochaska, Ernst	Lt. d.R., Fhr. 8./Lehr-Rgt. z.b.V. 800 "Brandenburg" + 9.8.42 at Maikop bridge (Russia)	16.9.42
Prochazka, Alois	Lt., Fhr. 10./I.R. 38	24.6.40
Frhr. v. Prochazka, Robert	Hptm., Abt. Fhr. in Werfer-Rgt. 55	19.12.43
Proehl, Georg	Rittm., Chef 2./Jäg. Rgt. 39 (L)	9.12.44
Pröhl, Günther	Hptm. d.R., Fhr. Pz.Jäg. Abt. 290	10.1.42
Pröll, Karl	Hptm., Kdr. II./Pz. G. R. 63 715th Oak Leaves 25.1.45	30.1.43
Prössl, Erwin	Lt., Flugzeugf. in 4. (H)/Aufkl. Gr. 31	29.2.44
Proetzel, Bodo	Oblt., Beobachter in 2. (F)/Aufkl. Gr. 11	4.8.44
Proll, Herbert	Hptm., Kdr. I./G. R. 106 + 20.7.44 in Bessarabia (Rumania)	9.6.44

ELITE OF THE THIRD REICH

Promesberger, Ludwig	Obgefr., MG-Schtz. in 8./Pz. G. R. 103	14.5.44
Prominski, Hans	Oblt., Beobachter in 2. (F)/Aufkl. Gr. 22	8.8.44
Proske, Friedrich-Wilhelm	Oblt., Chef 1. (Radf.)/I.R. 84 + August 1944 as Major & Rgt. Fhr.	12.4.42
Pross, Emil	Hptm., Fhr. II./G. R. 62	30.9.44
Prüger, Walter	Oblt., Staffelf. 2./K. Gr. 606 + 6.7.42 over Malta; posthumously promoted to Hptm.	5.1.43
Prümm, Karl	Oblt., Chef 7./G. R. 105	21.5.43
Prüß, Walter	Lt., Fhr. 6./G. R. 76 (mot.) 796th Oak Leaves 23.3.45	10.9.44
Pruß, Willi	Oberst, Kdr. G. R. 670	5.2.45
Przedwojewski, Felix	SS-Unterscharf., Geschützf. i. d. 2./SS-St. Gesch. Abt. 3 "Totenkopf"	16.12.43
Przyklenk, Kurt	Ofw., Spähtruppf. in 1./Pz. Aufkl. Abt. 40 + 10.1.43 in Stalingrad (Russia) as Lt. & Ord.Offz. in Kradschütz. -Btl. 64	1.8.41
Puchinger, Rudolf	Oblt., Staffelkpt. 8./K.G. 6 + 19.6.44 as Major & Gruppenkdr., over England	24.1.43
Püchler, Karl	Oberst, Kdr. Inf. -Rgt. 228	20.12.41
Pültz, Theodor	Lt. d.R., Zugf. in 5./Pz. Aufkl. Abt. 9	10.8.43
Püschel, Dr. Martin	Major, Kdr. II./Schtz. Rgt. 33	8.8.41
Püttcher, Heinrich	Lt. d.R., Kp. Fhr. in Pz. Pi. Btl. 86	14.4. 45
Pulst, Günther	Oblt. z. See, Kdt. "U 978"	21.12.44
Punkt, Paul	Oblt., Chef 3./Heeres-Pi. Btl. 753 + 30.1.45 of wounds	11.3.45
Purklis, Nikolaus	Uffz., Gruppenf. in 6./G. R. 430 + 14.1.45 at Rogan	28.10.44
Puschmann, Herbert	Hptm., Staffelkpt. 6./J.G. 51 "Mölders" + 3.2.44 shot down at Civitavecchia (Italy)	5.4.44
Puttfarken, Dietrich	Oblt., Flugzeugf. in 1./K.G. 51 + 23.4.44 over Cambridge (England) as Hptm. & Staffelkpt. Fernnachtjagdstaffel K.G. 51 (Me 410); posthumously promoted to Major	7.10.42
Putz, Helmut	Oblt., Flugzeugf. in II./K.G. 27 "Boelcke"	19.9.42
Putzka, Erich	Hptm., Staffelkpt. 3. (F)/Aufkl. Gr. 121 posted missing 23.12.44 south of Lüttich (Belgium); final post Stab III./J.G. 11; posthumously promoted to Major	9.12.42

Q

Quaet-Faslem, Klaus	Major, Kdr. I./J.G. 3 "Udet" + 30.1.44 shot down over Elm-Gebirge at Brunswick; posthumously promoted to Oberstlt.	9.6.44

Quassowski, Joachim	Hptm., Kdr. II./G. R. 484 + posted missing April 1945 as Major	18.10.43
Quast, Werner	Fhj. -Ofw., Flugzeugf. in 4./J.G. 52	31.12.43
Quednau, Horst	Oblt., Flugzeugf. in III./K.G. 27 "Boelcke"	3.9.42
Quednow, Fritz	Hptm., Kp. Chef in Fsch. Pz. Rgt. "HG" + 27.4.44 in Italy	5.4.44
Quentin, Friedrich	Major, Kdr. Kradschtz. Btl. 6	8.2.43
Quest, Ewald	Oblt. d.R., Chef 1./Flak-Rgt. 33 (mot.)	4.5.44

R

Raab, Alexander	Oblt., Staffelkpt. in I./K.G. 77	5.9.44
Raab, Josef	Hptm., Fhr. a Kampfgr. des G. R. 77	16.10.44
Raabe, Günter	Lt. d.R., V. B. in 6./A.R. 161	10.9.44
Raaf, Friedrich	Lt. d.R., Chef 7./Pz. G. R. 21	18.1.45
Rab, Johann	Oblt., Chef 1./Pz. Pi. Btl. 79 + 30.3.43 posthumously promoted to Hptm.	10.6.43
Rabben, Herbert	Ofw., Flugzeugf. in 3./S.G. 77	4.5.44
Rabe v. Pappenheim, Friedrich-Carl	Gen.Lt., Kdr. 97. Jäger-Div.	30.4.45
Radeck, Kurt	Hptm., Fhr. I./G. R. 176 + 30.3.44 on the Narva front (Russia)	23.2.44
Radel, Hans	Ofw., Zugf. in I./G. R. 4	23.2.44
Rademacher, Emil	Gefr., Gruppenf. in Fsch. Pi. Btl. 1 "HG"	23.2.45
Rademacher, Rudi	Lt., Flugzeugf. in I./J.G. 54	30.9.44
Radener, Waldemar	Oblt., Fhr. II./J.G. 26 "Schlageter"	12.3.45
Radermacher, Karl	Gefr., Granatwerfertruppf. in 6./G. R. 45	4.5.44
Radesinsky, Albert	Obgefr., s. MG-Schtz. in 4./Geb.Jäg. Rgt. 138 + 7.11.43 north of Melitopol in Russia of wounds	7.12.43
Radochla, Helmut	Lt., Zugf. in 2./Fest. Inf. Btl. XXIII./999	9.5.45
v. Radowitz, Joseph	Oberst, Fhr. 23. Pz.Div. 882nd Oak Leaves 9.5.45	17.9.44
Radowski, Eduard	Obstlt., Kdr. Pz.Jäg. Abt. 53	20.8.42
Radtke, Werner	Oblt., Chef I./Flak-Sturm-Rgt. 35 (mot.)	28.4.45
Radusch, Günther	Major, Kdr. II./NJ.G. 3 444th Oak Leaves 6.4.44	29.8.43
Radwan, Oskar	Obstlt., Kdr. II./I.R. 93 + 18.6.42 on Mius (Russia) as Oberst & Kdr. Schtz. Brig. 13	19.7.40
Radziej, Georg	Gen.Lt., Kdr. 169. I.D.	9.5.45
Raeder, Dr. phl. h. c. Erich	Großadmiral, Oberbefehlshaber der Kriegsmarine	30.9.39
Raeder, Kurt	Oblt. d.R., Fhr. I./G. R. "Feldherrnhalle" (mot.)	21.1.45

ELITE OF THE THIRD REICH

Raegener, Adolf	Obstlt., Kdr. I.R. 309 842nd Oak Leaves 17.4.45	25.6.40
Rämsch, Horst	Major, Kdr. II./Füs. Rgt. 27	24.12.44
Rätzel, Fritz	Hptm. d.R., Chef 7./Schtz. Rgt. 86 + 26.10.41 of wounds	11.10.41
Rafoth, Dr. Heinz	Lt., Fhr. 2./G. R. 48	20.4.45
Rahlenbeck, Robert	Gefr., Richtschtz. in 16./Jäg. Rgt. 38	23.8.43
Raht, Gerhard	Hptm., Staffelkpt. 1./N. J.G. 2 833rd Oak Leaves 15.4.45	24.6.44
Raithel, Heribert	Hptm., Kdr. II./Geb. A.R. 95	13.6.41
Raithel, Dipl.-Ing. Johann	Oberst, Kmdr. K.G. 77	17.10.41
v. Rakowitz, Andreas	Lt., St. Gesch. Fhr. in Feldersatz-Btl. 4 (L)	24.6.44
Rall, Carl	Oblt., Chef 11./Geb.Jäg. Rgt. 98	30.1.43
Rall, Günther	Oblt., Staffelkpt. 8./J.G. 52 134th Oak Leaves 26.10.42 34th Swords 12.9.43	3.9.42
Rall, Dr. -Ing. Victor	Korv. Kpt. d.R., Chef 15. Vorpostenflottille	10.6.44
Rambow, Günther	Hptm., Fhr. I./G. R. 1141	23.3.45
Rambow, Richard	Uffz., Geschützfhr. in 1./Pz.Jäg. Abt. 561 +26.10.43 in Russia, of wounds, as Feldw.	19.9.42
Ramcke, Hermann-Bernhard	Oberst, Kdr. Fallsch. Jäg. Sturm-Rgt. 145th Oak Leaves 13.11.42 99th Swords 19.9.44 20th Diamonds 19.9.44	21.8.41
v. Ramin, Hans-Georg	Hptm. d.R., Kdr. Pz.Jäg. Abt. 53	23.10.44
Rammelt, Karl	Major, Kdr. II./J.G. 51 "Mölders"	20.10.44
Rammelt, Siegfried	Lt., Pi. Zugf. Stabskp./Fsch. Jäg. Rgt. 3 + 21.3.44 at Monte Cassino (Italy); posthumously promoted to Oblt.	9.6.44
Rampel, Josef	Ofw., Halbzugf. in 11./Pz. Rgt. "GD" + 16.11.43 at Kriwoi Rog (Russia)	14.12.43
Rampf, Alois	Oblt. d.R., Fhr. 3./Pi. Btl. 88	4.10.44
Ramser, Günther	Obstlt., Kdr. G. R. 2	8.2.44
Ranck, Werner	Gen.Maj., Kdr. 121. I.D.	2.3.45
Rannersmann, Rolf	Hptm., Kdr. I./K.G. 4 "General Wever"	12.3.45
Graf zu Rantzau, Hans-Friedrich	Hptm., Fhr. II./Pz. A.R. "GD" + 28.9.44 in Kurland, as Btl. Kdr., died of wounds	9.6.44
v. Rantzau, Heino	Gen.Lt., Kdr. 2. Flak-Div. (mot.) + 2.11.46 in Camp Allendorf at Marburg (Lahn) in US captivity; final post General of Flak-Ausbildung in RLM	29.8.43
v. Rappard, Fritz-Georg	Gen.Lt., Kdr. 7. I.D. 751st Oak Leaves 24.2.45	20.10.44
Rappel, August	Oberfähnrich, Zugf. in 14./Geb.Jäg. Rgt. 100	29.11.44
Rappholz, Walter	Ofw., Zugf. in Pz.Jäg. Abt. 616 (Sf)	3.11.44

Rapräger, Dr. jur. Ernst-Wilhelm	Oblt., Kampfgr. Fhr. in Luftw. Rgt. "Barenthin"	10.5.43
Rasch, Herman	Kaptlt., Kdt. "U 106"	29.12.42
Rasp, Siegfried	Gen. Major, Kdr. 335. I.D.	15.4.44
Rass, Friedrich	Hptm., Kdr. i./Pz. G. R. 11	30.11.43
Rast, Johann	Oblt., Kp. Chef in Geb. Pi. Btl. 85 + 31.8.44 in Russia as Rgt. Fhr.; posthumously promoted to Oberstlt.	14.5.41
Ratajczak, Edmund	Ofw., Zugf. in 1./schw. Pz. Abt. 507	10.2.45
Ratcliffe, Alexander	Oberst, Kdr. I.R. 192	22.12.41
Rath, Ernst	Hptm., Kdr. II./G. R. 577	15.7.44
Rath, Hans-Joachim	Oberst, Kmdre. K.G. 4 "General Wever"	9.5.42
Ratzke, Wilhelm	Hptm., Kdr. I./G. R. 871	3.11.44
Rauch, Alfred	Fhj. -Ofw., Flugzeugf. in Stabsst./J.G. 51 "Mölders" simultaneously promoted to Lt.	28.4.45
Rauch, Erwin	Gen. Major, Kdr. 123. I.D.	22.12.41
Rauch, Hans	Oberst, Kdr. Flak-Sturm-Rgt. 41 (mot.)	6.12.44
Rauch, Josef	Oberst, Kdr. Pz. G. R. 192	8.8.44
Rauch, Karl-Heinz	Oblt., Schwadr. Chef/Div. Füs. Btl. 256 + 26.6.44 south of Witebsk (Russia) as Rittm.	15.3.44
Raucheisen, Franz-Xaver	Major, Kdr. I./I.R. 131 + 11.1.41 accidentally at Saintes (France)	5.8.40
Rauer, Karl	Major, Kdr. I./K.G. 53 "Legion Condor" + 1945 in Hameln shot by the British	29.2.44
Rauh, Paul-Hubert	Hptm., Kdr. II./N. J.G. 4	28.4.45
Raus, Erhard	Oberst, Kdr. 6. Schtz. Brigade 280th Oak Leaves 22.8.43	11.10.41
Rausch, Werner	Gefr., Geschützf. in 3./Pz.Jäg. Abt. 294	26.3.43
Rauschenbusch, Hermann	Major, Kdr. II./Jäger-Rgt. 83	26.3.43
v. Ravenstein, Johann	Oberst, Kdr. Schtz. Rgt. 4	3.6.40
Rebane, Alfons	Major Kdr. estn. Freiw. Btl. 658 875th Oak Leaves 9.5.45	23.2.41
Reber, Gustav-Peter (10)	SS-Obersturmführer, Kdt. Stabsquartier XI. SS-Pz. Korps & Fhr. of a Kampfgr. in Halbe pocket	28.4.45
Reber, Willy	Oblt. d.R., Adj. III./G. R. 30 (mot.) + 5.7.44 at Minsk (Russia)	4.5.44
Rebholz, Robert	Hptm., Fhr. Pz. Aufkl. Abt. "HG"	2.8.43
Rech, Erich	SS-Oberscharf., Zugf. in 2./SS-Pz. Aufkl. Abt. 10 "Frundsberg" + 4.10.44 at Bommel, north of Nymwegen (Holland) as SS-Untersturmfhr.	23.8.44
Reche, Reinhart	Kaptlt., Kdt. "U 255"	17.3.43

Rechel, Curt	Freg. Kpt. Kdt. Zerstörer "Z 29"	8.5.43
Recke, Heinrich	Gen.Lt., Kdr. 161. I.D. + 18.8.43 in Russia missing	4.9.43
Recknagel, Hermann	Oberst, Kdr. I.R. 54 319th Oak Leaves 6.11.43 104th Swords 23.10.44	5.8.40
Recktenwald, Wolf	Oblt. d.R., Chef Radf. Schwadron 255	24.5.43
v. Reden, Dr. phil. Edzard	Hptm. d.R., Kdr. Pz. Pi. Bl. 89	12.8.44
Reder, Engelhard	Uffz., Geschützf. in 1./Pz.Jäg. Abt. 173	9.6.44
Reder, Walter	SS-Hptsturmf., Kdr. I./SS-Pz. G. R. 1 "Totenkopf"	3.4.43
Redlich, Ernst	Hptm. d.R., Fhr. 2./Pi. Btl. 134	17.12.43
Redlich, Karl-Wolfgang	Oblt., Staffelkpt. 1./J.G. 27 + 29.5.44 at St. Pölten (Austria) in aerial combat as Major i.G. & Kdr. I./J.G. 27	9.7.41
Reeb, Adolf	SS-Untersturmf., Zugf. in 7./SS-Pz. Rgt. 2 "Das Reich" + 25.11.44 in the Ardennes at Manhay (Belgium)	23.8.44
Reeder, Deert	Major d.R., Kdr. II./G. R. 254 + early July 1944 as OTL d.R. & Rgt. Kdr.	30.11.43
Regeniter, Dr. med. Alfred	Lt. d.R., Fhr. 3./St. Gesch. Brig. 276	5.4.45
Rehbein, Max	Hptm. d.R., Kdr. Pi. Btl. 23	5.3.45
Rehle, Siegfried	Oblt., Beobachter in 2./K.G. 53 "Legion Condor" + 30.12.42 Welikije-Luki (Russia)	19.2.43
Rehm, Erich	Hptm. d.R., Fhr. Pz.Jäg. Kp. 1156	18.2.45
Rehm, Ernst	Major, Kdr. Pz. Aufkl. Abt. 14	16.11.43
Rehrn, Hans	Korv. Kpt., Chef 2. Minensuchflottille	31.12.41
Rehmer, Richard	Hptm., Kdr. Füs. Btl. 126 + 25.2.45	28.3.45
Rehnitz, Konrad	Lt. d.R., Fhr. 2./Pz.Jäg. Abt. 27	12.8.42
Reich, Johann	Uffz., Sturmzugfhr. in 6./G. R. 411	14.4. 45
Reich, Johann	Obstlt. d.R., Kdr. Pz. G. R. 10 + 1.3.45	29.11.44
Reich, Werner	Oblt., Chef 3./Pi. Btl. 5 (mot.)	18.4.43
Reich, Werner	Oberst, Kdr. G. R. 274 + 25.1.44 at Minturno (Italy)	29.2.44
Reichardt, Hans	Major, Kdr. III./I.R. 192 762nd Oak Leaves 5.3.45	24.7.41
Reiche, Werner	Hptm. d.R., Kdr. I./G. R. 434	14.1.45
Reichel, Erwin H.	SS-Sturmbannf., Fhr. SS-Pz. G. R. "Westland" + 28.2.43 in hospital, of wounds, at Dnjepropetrowsk (Russia)	28.2.43
Reichel, Helmut	Major, Kdr. II./Füs. Rgt. 26	6.4.44
Reichelt, Martin	Hptm. d.R., Kdr. I./G. R. 529	4.5.44

Reichelt, Paul	Gen. Major, Chef of Gen. St. Armee-Abt. Narwa	8.10.44
v. Reichenau, Walter	Gen. d. Art., OB 10. Arme simultaneously promoted to Gen. Oberst; + 18.1.42 in the southern sector of the Eastern Front as Gen. Feldm. & OB H.Gr. Süd	30.9.39
Reichert, Josef	Gen.Lt., Kdr. 711. I.D.	9.12.44
Reichert, Karl	Ofw., Zugf. in 1./Pz. Zerst. Abt. 156	13.11.44
Reichert, Rudolf	Gen. Major, Kdr. 292. I.D.	11.3.45
Reichhold, Otto	Ofw., Zugf. Stabskp./G. R. 448	23.12.43
Reichmann, Heinz	Obgefr., MG-Schtz. in 8./Jäg. Rgt. 459 (L) d. 6. Lw. -Feld-Div.	20.1.44
Reichwald, Gerhard	Lt., Zugf. in 3./Flak. Rgt. 12	1.8.42
Reifner, Egon	Oblt., Chef 3./Pz. Pi. Btl. 40	16.11.44
Reimann, Hans	Ofw., Fernsprechtruppf. in I./G. R. 358 + 31.1.45 of wounds	17.3.45
Reimann, Herbert	Feldw., Zugf. in 4. (MG)/G. R. 44	6.4.44
Reimann, Richard	Gen. Major, Kdr. 18. Flak-Div.	3.4.43
Reimann, Wilhelm	Hptm. d.R., Kdr. II./Jäger-Rgt. 724	26.12.44
Reimar, Gustav	Hptm., Chef 6./Pz. G. R. 4 582nd Oak Leaves 10.9.44	28.7.43
Reimling, Hans	SS-Oberscharf., Zugf. in 2./SS-Pz. Rgt. 1 "LSSAH" + 7.3.43 Walki (Russia)	28.2.43
Reimpell Gerhard	Obstlt. i.G., Ia of Kdt. v. Kowel	9.7.44
Rein, Siegfried	Gen.Lt., Kdr. 69. I.D. + 18.1.45 at Schloßberg (East Prussia)	24.2.45
Rein, Willi	Ofw., Flugzeugf. in Stabsst./K.G. 53 "Legion Condor" + 21.8.44	5.9.44
Reinardy, Josef	Lt., Flugzeugf. in (Fern-)Aufkl. Gr. 3 + 25.12.44 shot down over Krakow (Poland)	24.1.45
Reinbacher, Leander	Lt., Fhr. 1./G. R. 81	30.4.45
Reineck, Rudi	Oblt., Chef 8./Schtz. Rgt. 6 + 20.1.42 in Russia of wounds	20.3.42
Reinecke, Ewald	Uffz., Pz. Kdt. in St. Gesch. Abt. 1122	18.11.44
Reinecke, Gerhard	Lt., Flugzeugf. in 1. (F.)/Aufkl. Gr. 121	23.12.42
Reinefarth, Heinz	Feldw., Zugf. in 14. (Pz.Jäg.)/I.R. 337 608th Oak Leaves 30.9.44	25.6.40
Reineking, Paul	Oblt., Chef 3./Flak-Rgt. 36 (mot.) + 26.6.44 in Russia as Hptm. & Abt. Fhr.	26.3.44
Reinert, Ernst-Wilhelm	Uffz., Flugzeugf. in 4./J.G. 77 131st Oak Leaves 7.10.42 130th Swords 1.2.45	1.7.42
Reinhard, Hans-Wolfgang	Gen.D.Inf., Kom.Gen. LI. A.K.	22.9.41

Reinhardt, Alfred-Hermann	Obstlt., Kdr. I.R. 421 306th Oak Leaves 28.9.43 118th Swords 24.12.44	4.12.41
Reinhardt, Arnold	Gefr., Gruppenf. in 7./G. R. 166	24.9.43
Reinhardt, Georg-Hans	Gen.Lt., Kdr. 4. Pz.Div. 73rd Oak Leaves 17.2.42 68th Swords 26.5.44	27.10.39
Reinhardt, Hans	Major, Kdr. I./A.R. 241 + 4.9.41 in Russia	18.10.41
Reinhardt, Walter	Obstlt., Kdr. G. R. 1141	18.11.44
Reinhardt, Wilhelm	Ofw., Zugl. in 5./I.R. 518	22.2.42
Reinhart, Heinz	Oblt. d.R., Chef 6./G. R. 109 + 18.10.44	17.8.43
Reinhart, Karl	Lt. d.R., Fhr. 7./Sturm-Rgt. 215 + 10.3.44 at Nowoje-Seelo (Russia) as Fhr. d. Btl. Reserve II./Sturm-Rgt. 215	20.12.43
Reinhold, Leo-Hermann	SS-Sturmbannf., Kdr. II./SS-Pz. Rgt. 10 "Frundsberg"	16.10.44
Reinholds, Voldemars(19)	Waffen-Sturmbannf., Kdr. der SS Kdr. Waffen-Gren. Rgt. 43 d. SS	11.5.45
Reinicke, Gerhard	Feldw., Gruppenf. in 2./Pz. Rgt. 6	9.7.41
Reinicke, Hansjürgen	Kapt. z. See, Kdt. Schwerer Kreuzer "Prinz Eugen"	21.4.45
Reininghaus, Adolf	Ofw., Zugf. in 14./Fsch. Jäg. Rgt. 7	13.9.44
Reinke, Friedrich-Wilhelm	Major, Kdr. I./Flak-Rgt. 9 "Legion Condor"	9.10.43
Reinke, Heinrich	Ofw., Zugf. in 14. (Pz.Jäg.)/I.R. 89	9.1.42
Reinkober, Fritz	Oberst, Kdr. Festungs-Gren. Rgt. "Reinkober" in Festung Breslau	30.4.45
Reintjes, Heinz	Oblt. d.R., Fhr. Pz. Gren. Btl. 2102	18.11.44
Reinwald, Max	Obstlt. d.R., Kdr. G. R. 19 702nd Oak Leaves 18.1.45	29.2.44
Reinwald, Otto	Hptm., Kdr. Feldersatz-Btl. 212	9.4.44
Reiser, Sebastian	Gefr., Richtkan. in 1./A.R. 297	11.10.41
Reisig, Josef	Ofw., Zugf. in 11./I.R. 164	15.1.42
Reissinger, Dr. theol. Walter	Obstlt., Kdr. Gren. -Rgt. 215	17.12.42
Reißmann, Paul	SS-Oberscharf., stellv. Fhr. 4./SS-Kav. Rgt. 17 + 8.11.44 in Hungary of wounds	16.11.44
Reißmann, Werner	Hptm., Fhr. III./S. R. 104	28.7.42
Reiter, Hans	SS-Untersturmf., Fhr. Stabskp./SS-Pz. G. R. 21 "Frundsberg" + 15.8.44 at St. Clair (France)	23.8.44
Reittinger, Otto	Uffz., Gr. Fhr. in 4./Pz. Aufkl. Abt. 2 + 8.8.44	23.10.44
Frhr. v. Reitzenstein, Albin	SS-Oberstrumbannf., Kdr. SS-Pz. Rgt. 2 "Das Reich" + 30.11.43 (suicide) west of Kiew (Russia)	13.11.43
Remberg, Josef	Oblt., Flugzeugf. in 2. (F)/Aufkl. Gr. 11	25.2.44

Remer, Otto-Ernst	Major, Kdr. I./G. R. "GD" 325th Oak Leaves 12.11.43	18.5.43
Remlinger, Heinrich	Oberst, Kdt. v. Schneidemühl + Summer 1951 in Soviet captivity	30.1.45
Remmer, Hans	Hptm., Staffelkpt. 1./J.G. 27 + 2.4.44 at Graz (Steiermark) when bailing out	9.6.44
Remmert, Heinz	Hptm., stellv. Fhr. II./G. R. 464	10.9.44
Rendl, Otto	Uffz., Geschütz. in 14./I.R. 132	28.7.42
Rendulic, Dr. jur. Lothar	Gen.Lt., Kdr. 52. I.D. 271st Oak Leaves 15.8.43 122nd Swords 18.1.45	6.3.42
Renisch, Paul-Ernst (17)	Hptm., Kdr. III./Fsch. Jäg. Rgt. 1	31.10.44
Rennecke, Rudolf	Hptm., Fhr. II./Fsch. Jäg. Rgt. 3 664th Oak Leaves 25.11.44	9.6.44
Renner, Wilhelm	Oblt., Chef 8./Schtz. Rgt.	5.8.40
Rennhack, Günther	Hptm., Kdr. Pz.Jäg. Abt. 1818	30.12.44
Renoldner, Karl	Oblt. d.R., Fhr. 6./G. R. 462 + 17.8.43 south-west of Wjasma (Russia)	10.9.43
Renschler, Helmut	Oblt. d.R., Chef 1./A.R. 5 770th Oak Leaves 11.3.45	15.5.44
v. Renteln, Ewert	Obstlt. d.R., Kdr. Kosaken-Regiment 360	13.1.45
Rentrop, Fritz	SS-Obersturm., Chef 2./SS-Flak-Abt. 2 "Reich" + 2.2.45 in Hungary, of wounds, in Soviet captivity as SS-Sturmbannf. & Ia IV. SS-Pz. Korps	13.10.41
Rentschler, Emil	Hptm., Kdr. III./G. R. 537	18.10.43
Renz, Gerhard	Ofw., Flugzeugf. in II./K.G. 26	31.7.40
Renz, Gottlieb	SS-Hptsturmf., Kdr. SS-Schtz. Btl. (mot.) 6 + 3.1.45 at Bitsch (Lothringen) as SS-Sturrnbannfhr.	12.8.44
Renz, Joachirn	Hptm., Fhr. I./Fsch. Pz. Rgt. "HG" + 23.10.44 in Russia	6.12.44
Resch, Anton	Oblt., Staffelkpt. 3./J.G. 52	7.4.45
Resch, Rudolf	Hptm., Staffelkpt. 5./J.G. 52 + 11.7.43 at Orel (Russia) as Major & Kdr. IV./J.G. 51 "Mölders"	6.9.42
Reschke, Willi	Ofw., Flugzeugf. in Stab J.G. 301	20.4.45
v. Rettberg, Ralph	Hptm., Kdr. II./Z.G. 26 "Horst Wessel"	14.6.41
Rettberg, Rudolf (6)	SS-Sturmbannf., Kdr. II./SS-Pz. Rgt. 9 "Hohenstaufen"	6.5.45
Rettemeier, Josef	Hptm., Kdr. Pz. Abt. 5 425th Oak Leaves 13.3.44	5.12.43
Rettlinger, Karl	SS-Hptsturmf., Chef 3./SS-St. Gesch. Abt. 1 "LSSAH"	20.12.43
Retzlaff, Karl	Ofw., Fhr. 3./G. R. 4	30.9.44

Reusch, Ernst	Oblt., Staffelkpt. 5./Stuka-Geschw. 1 + 26.1.45 in hospital at Danzig of wounds as Major & Kdr. III./S.G. 1	3.11.42
Reuß, Franz	Gen. Major, Kdr. 4. Flieger-Div.	18.7.44
v. Reuß, Richard-Heinrich	Gen. Major, Kdr. 62. I.D. + 22.12.42 on the Don at Stalingrad (Russia)	24.1.43
Reußner, Rudi	Ofw., Flugzeugf. in 8./S.G. 2 "Immelmann"	29.2.44
Reuter, Alfred	Oblt. d.R., Fhr. 2./I.R. 418	21.2.43
Reuter, August	Lt., Zugf. in 2./Pz,Jäg. Abt. 219 + 9.2.45 at Hussehnen (East Prussia)	15.5.44
Reuter, Benno	Stabsfw., Fhr. 7./Jäger-Rgt. 49 633rd Oak Leaves 28.10.44	8.2.44
v. Reuter, Derfflinger	Obstl., Kdr. G. R. 45 + 13.4.45 at Fischhausen (East Prussia)	17.3.45
Reuter, Erich	Obstlt., Kdr. I.R. 122 710th Oak Leaves 21.1.45	17.8.42
Reuter, Erich	Hptm., Chef 3./schw. Pz.Jäg. Abt. 519	18.7.44
Reuter, Joachim	Oberst d.R., Kdr. G. R. 386	27.8.44
Reuter, Kurt	Obgefr., Gruppenf. in 6./G. R. 279	4.5.44
Reverchon, Heinz	Lt., Zugf. in I./Kradschtz. Btl. 43	16.9.42
Reymann, Hellmuth	Gen.Lt., Kdr. 13. Lw. Feld-Div. 672nd Oak Leaves 28.11.44	5.4.44
Rhein, Ernst-Martin	Oblt., Chef 5./I.R. 18	22.12.41
Rhein, Joseph	Hptm., Kdr. I./G. R. 530	23.2.44
Rhein, Karl	Oberst, Kdr. I.R. 439	6.3.42
v. Ribbentrop, Rudolf	SS-Obersturmf., Fhr. 6./SS-Pz. Rgt. 1 "LSSAH"	15.7.42
Richert, Johann-Georg	Gen. Lt-, Kdr. 35. I.D. 623rd Oak Leaves 18.10.44	17.3.44
Richter, Bruno	Rittm., Fhr. Div. Füs. Btl. 24 825th Oak Leaves 8.4.45	26.11.44
Richter, Emil	Uffz., Gruppenf. in 11 ./I.R. 401	25.8.42
Richter, Franz	Gefr., MG-Schtz. in 1./Pz. G. R. 114	14.5.44
Richter, Friedrich	Major, Kdr. III./G. R. 42 818th Oak Leaves 5.4.45	17.8.43
Richter, Friedrich(19)	SS-Sturmbannf., Kdr. III./SS-Pz. G. R. 21 "Frundsberg"	11.5.45
Richter, Gerhard	Oblt., Staffelkpt. 9. (K)/L.G. 1	24.11.40
Richter, Hans	Hptm., Fhr. I./G. R. 121 + 22.9.44 as Major & Kdr. Feldersatz-Btl. 121	29.1.44
Richter, Hans-Heinrich (17)	Hptm., Kdr. Fsch. Pz. AA 2	26.3.45
Richter, Heinz	Hptm., Kdr. III./K.G. 77 + 2.6.43 Silden (Mediterranean)	19.9.43
Richter, Heinz (17)	Lt., Fhr. 4./Fsch. Pi. Btl. 5	12.3.45

Richter, Joachim	SS-Obersturmbannf. d.R., Kdr. SS-Pz. A.R. 5 "Wiking"	23.2.44
Richter, Johannes	Lt., Fhr. 2./Pz. G. R. 304	30.9.44
Richter, Johannes	Ofw., Bordfunker in Stab NJ.G. 10	30.9.44
Richter, Kurt	Fhj. -Ofw., Ord.Offz. in Stab II./G. R. 31	28.3.45
Richter, Richard	Ofw., Zugf. in 7./Pz. Gren. Rgt. 33	7.1.44
Richter, Rudolf	Major d.R., Fhr. I.R. 97	7.8.42
Richter, Rudolf	Ofw., Flugzeugf. & Beob. in 3. (H)/Aufkl. Gr. 12	14.1.45
Richter, Walther	Ofw., Bordmechaniker in 5./K.G. 53 "Legion Condor"	28.2.45
Richter, Werner	Gen.Lt., Kdr. 263. I.D. + 3.6.44 in hospital at Riga (Latvia) of wounds	7.2.44
Richter, Wilfried	SS-Obersturmf., Fhr. SS-St. Gesch. Batt./ SS-Div. "Totenkopf"	21.4.42
Frhr. v. Richthofen, Dipl.-Ing. Dr. -Ing. Wolfram	Gen. Major, Kom.Gen. VIII. Fliegerkorps 26th Oak Leaves 17.7.41	17.5.40
Rick, Kurt	Hptm., Staffelkpt. 2./Stuka-Geschw. 77 + 5.2.43 at Stalingrad (Russia)	3.4.43
Rickert, Hans-Oskar	Hptm. Kdr. I./A.R. 320 + 13.4.44 in Russia as Major	30.12.43
Rickert, Josef	Obgefr., Gruppenf. in 1./Pz. G. R. 12	20.10.44
Rickmers, Boy	Obstlt., Fhr. G. R. 586	26.3.43
Riebicke, Klaus	Feldw., Flugzeugf. in 9./S.G. 10 + 6.6.44 at Lemberg (Poland)	6.10.44
Riechers, Karl	Ofw., Kp. Fhr. in I./Pz. G. R. 2 + 3.9.43 at Orel (Russia)	8.8.43
Riechert, Hans-Georg	Lt., Fhr. 5./I.R. 311 + 28.3.42 accidentally, as Oblt. & Kp. Chef	9.1.42
Rieckhoff, Herbert	Oberst, Kmdre., K.G. 2	5.7.41
Riedel, Franz	SS-Obersturmf., Chef 7./SS-Pz. Rgt. 10 "Frundsberg"	28.3.45
Riedel, Gerd	Oberst i.G., Fhr. Fsch. Jäg. Rgt. 7	8.5.45
Riedel, Walter	Lt. d.R., Fhr. 3./Pz. G. R. 73 + 24.9.43 in the bend of the Dnjepr (Russia) as Ord. -Offz. in Rgt. Stab	14.4. 43
Riedel, Willy	Hptm., Kdr. III/I.R. 524 186th Oak Leaves 25.1.43	8.10.42
Riedesel Frhr. zu Eisenbach, Volprecht	Hptm., Kdr. II./K.G. 76 696th Oak Leaves 14.1.45	7.10.42
Riedmüller, Adam	Feldw., Zugf. in 4./Jagd-Pz. Abt. II (Pz. Gr. -Div. Kurmark)	8.2.45

Name	Details	Date
Riefkogel, Waldemar	SS-Obersturmf., Fhr. 1/SS-Pz. Rgt. 3 "Totenkopf" + 30.7.44 in Siedlce (Russia) as SS-Hptsturmf. & Hptm. d. Schupo. of wounds	11.7.43
Rieflin, Fritz (6)	SS-Obersturmf., Chef 2./SS-Pz. Pi. Btl. 2 "Das Reich"	6.5.45
Riegel, Kurt	Hptm. Staffelkpt. 5./S.G. 3 + 1.7.44 at Dünaburg (Russia)	8.8.44
Rieger, Joachim	Oblt. Staffelkpt. 5./Stuka-Geschw. 1 + 2.12.41 at Forminsk (Russia); Posthumously promoted to Hauptm.	19.3.42
Rieger, Johann	Obgefr. Kp. Melder in 1./Pz. G. R. 59	26.3.44.
Rieger, Karl	Hptm. Kdr. I./G. R. 2 "Scharnhorst"	28.4.45.
Riekstins, Alfred	Waffen-Unterscharf., Zugf. in 1./Waffen SS-Füs. Btl. 19	5.4.45
Rienäcker, Herman	Lt., Fhr. 4./Heeres-Flak. -Art. -Abt. 272	17.3.45
Riepe, Julius	SS-Sturmbannf., Fhr. I./SS-Pz. G. R. 40 "Horst Wessel"	13.1.45
Riepold, Josef-Otto	Oblt., Chef 5./Pz. Rgt. 5 in DAK + 17.6.42 in North Africa; Posthumously promoted to Hptm.	29.7.42
Riesle, Karl	Objäg., Gewehrf. in 14./Geb.Jäg. Rgt. 85	29.2.44
Rieß, Karl	Hptm., Fhr. 7./G. R. 282	27.8.43
Rieß, Otto	Obgefr., Geschützf. in 14./G. R. 55	11.10.43
Rieth, Herbert-Albert	SS-Untersturmf. d.R., Fhr. 5./Freiw. SS-A.R. 54 "Nederland" + 29.4.45 at Halbe south of Berlin	11.12.44
Rietscher, Georg	Gefr., Richtschtz. in 14. (Pz.Jäg.)/I.R. 513 210th Oak Leaves 14.3.43	27.6.42
Rüpalu, Harald	Waffen-Obersturmbannf., Kdr. SS-Freiw. G. R. 45	23.8.44
Rindfleich, Bernhard	Ofw., Zugf. in 6./G. R. 575	12.8.44
Ring, Erich	Hptm., Kdr. II./I.R. 84 + 3.9.42 at Rshew (Russia) as Major	21.9.41
Ringel, Julius	Gen. Major, Kdr. 5. Geb. Div. 312th Oak Leaves 25.10.43	13.6.41
Ringhof, Jakob	Hptm., Kdr. Div. Füs. Btl. 215	23.12.43
Ringler, Helmut	Lt., s. MG-Halbzugf. in Sturmgruppe "Stahl" in Fsch. Sturmabt. "Koch" simultaneously promoted to Oblt.	15.5.40
Rinke, Adolf	Lt., Fhr. 2./schw. Pz. Abt. 502 +13.4.45 at Pillau (East Prussia)	17.4.45
Rinke, Karl-Eberhard	Oblt., Chef 8./G. R. 552	22.4.43
Rinkowski, Leo	Gefr., MG-Schtz. in 5./G. R. 670	21.9.44
Rintelen, Josef	Obstlt., Kdr. I./I.R. 478	5.8.40

KNIGHT'S CROSS OF THE IRON CROSS

Ripcke, Werner	Hptm. d.R., Kdr. I./G. R. 89 simultaneously promoted to Major d.R.	18.12.44
Risse, Eberhard	Hptm., Adj. Pz. G. R. 60	26.11.44
Risse, Walther	Oberst, Kdr. I.R. 474 704th Oak Leaves 18.1.45	22.9.41
Rittau, Stephan	Gen. Major, Kdr. 129. I.D. + 22.8.42 at Rshew (Russia) as Gen.Lt.	2.11.41
Graf von Rittberg, Georg	Gen. Major, Kdr. 88. I.D. 610th Oak Leaves 10.10.44	21.2.44
Rittel, Hans	Ofw., Zugf. in 13./G. R. 366	7.3.44
Ritter, Anton	Lt. d.R., Fhr. 3./G. R. 88	24.12.44
Ritter, Friedrich-Karl	Major d.R., Kdr. Inf. Btl. z.b.V. 560	20.10.44
Ritter, Georg	Major, Kdr. II./I.R. 62 + 17.10.41 near Moscow (Russia)	15.11.41
Ritter, Heinz	Hptm., Kdr. II./G. R. 44	20.4.45
Ritter, Hugo	Major, Kdr. II./G. R. 529	24.2.45
Ritter, Klaus	Hptm., Fhr. II./G. R. 67	28.10.44
Ritter, Willy	Hptm., Fhr. Pz. Pi. Btl. 13 + 1.4.44 in Russia as Major	15.1.44
Rittershausen, Walter	Hptm. d.R., Chef 3./I.R. 57 missing Febr. 1945 at Braunsberg (East Prussia) as Major d. Res. & Btl. Kdr. (2.10.60 declared dead by a court in Dillenburg)	25.2.42
Rittner, Arthur	Hptm. d.R., Fhr. III./I.R. 276	25.10.42
Ritz, Alfred	Hptm., Kdr. I./Pz. G. R. 1	11.12.44
Ritz, Otto	Feldw., Flugzeugf. in 10. (Pz.)/S.G. 9 + 12.2.45 at Jauer (Silesia)	30.9.44
Rixecker, Karl	Stabsobersteuermann, Kdt. "R 23" in 1. Räumbootsflottille	31.5.40
Rocholl, Rolf	Oblt. Fhr. 2./Pz. Rgt. 5 287th Oak Leaves 31.8.43	28.7.42
v. Rochow, Hans	Major d.R., Kdr. Radf. Abt. 176 + 2.5.45 in Mühlenbeek at Berlin as Kdr. of a Fest. Rgt.	20.1.43
v. Rochow, Hans-Joachim	Oberst, Kdr. G. R. 860	26.12.44
Rodamer, Johann	Ofw., Zugfhr. 7./G. R. 320	26.3.44
Rode, Werner	Oblt., Chef 2./Kradschtz. Btl. 34	17.9.41
Rodemich, Heinrich	Feldw., Zugf. in 7./G. R. 988	11.5.45
Rodenburg, Carl	Gen. Major, Kdr. 76. I.D. 189th Oak Leaves 31.1.43	8.10.42
Roderer, Georg	Feldw., Zugf. in 5./G. R. 545	9.12.44
Rodewald, Otto	Uffz., Gruppenf. in Nachr. Zug/G. R. 948	24.3.44
Rodt, Eberhard	Obstlt., Kdr. Aufkl. Abt. 25 847th Oak Leaves 28.4.45	25.6.40

Name	Details	Date
Roeckl, Heinrich	Major, Kdr. Radf. Btl. 402	8.9.41
Rödel, Gustav Siegfried	Oblt., Staffelkpt. 4./J.G. 27 255th Oak Leaves 20.6.43	22.6.41
Röder, Josef	Obgefr., Richtschtz. in 3./Pz.Jäg. Abt. 179 + 26.1.43 in Stalingrad (Russia)	19.1.43
Rödlich, Walter	Obstlt., Kdr. II./Pz. Rgt. 4 + 23.7.42 accidentally in Russia as Oberst & Kdr. Pz. Rgt. 4	5.8.40
Rögelein, (Fritz) Friedrich	Major, Kdr. I./G. R. 109 831st Oak Leaves 14.4. 45	7.1.44
Roeger, Hans	Uffz. Zugfhr. in 1./Pz. Füs. Rgt. "GD"	21.9.44
Röhder, Dr. Wolfgang	SS-Obersturmf., d.R., Chef 3./SS-St. Gesch. Abt. 2 "Das Reich" + 16.5.45 Prague (Czechoslovakia); final post SS-Sturmbannfhr. d.R. in SS-Hauptamt in Prague	1.12.43
Röhler, Herbert	Oberst d.R., Kdr. Flak-Sturm-Rgt. 4	24.10.44
Röhricht, Edgar	Gen.Lt., Kdr. 95. I.D.	15.5.44
Roehrig, Hans	Lt., Flugzeugf. in I./J.G. 53 + 7.7.43 posted missing at Catania following aerial combat as Staffelkpt. 9./J.G. 53; posthumously promoted to Hauptmann	2.10.42
Röhrig, Oskar	Oberfähnrich, Zugf. in 1./schw. Pz. Abt. 504	4.7.44
Rökker, Heinz	Oblt., Staffelkpt. 2./N. J.G. 2 781st Oak Leaves 12.3.45	27.7.44
Roell, Werner	Hptm., Staffelkpt. Stabsst./Stuka-G. 77	25.5.43
Röllecke, Josef	SS-Unterscharf., Meldestaffelf. in IR./SS-Pz. G. R. 5 "Totenkopf"	16.6.44
Röpke, Kurt	Gen. Major, Kdr. 46. I.D. 830th Oak Leaves 14.4. 45	17.11.43
Roesch, Rudolf	Oblt., Staffelkpt. 9./K.G. 51 + 28.11.44 over Nymwegen (Holland) as Hptm.	26.3.44
Röseke, Erich	Oblt. d.R., Fhr. 9./Jäger-Rgt. 1 "Brandenburg"	14.4. 45
Rösing, Hans Rudolf	Korv. Kpt., Chef 7. Unterseebootsflottille & Kdt. "U 48"	29.8.40
Roeske, Gerd	Hptm., Fhr. Btl. "Feldherrnhalle" + 19.2.45 at Reitwein/Oder	11.3.45
Roesler, Karl	Oberst, Kdr. G. R. 1056	20.10.44
Roesner, Rudolf	Hptm., Kdr. I./Jäg. Rgt. 38	18.4.43
Rössiger, Wilhelm-Richard	Oblt., Staffelkpt. 2./Erprobungs-Gruppe 210 + 27.9.40 shot down over the Channel	1.10.40
Roestel, Erwin Franz Rudolf (11)	SS-Obersturmbannf. d.R., Kdr. SS-Pz.Jäg. (St. Gesch.) Abt. 10 "Frundsberg" & Führer of a Kampfgruppe	3.5.45
Rötche, Hans	Fahnenjunker-Ofw., Flugzeugf. in 16./Transportgeschwader 1	18.11.44

Röthke, Siegfried	Oblt., Staffelkpt. 6./K.G. 4 "General Wever"	2.6.43
Roewer, Herbert	Ofw., Flugzeugf. in 9. (Eis.)/K.G. 3 "Lützow" + 5.3.43	3.7.43
Roewer, Peter	Major d.R., Fhr. G. R. 225	13.1.45
Rogalla v. Bieberstein, Konstantin	Major, Kdr. Pz. G. R. 114 + 14.7.43 in Bjelgorod; posthumously promoted to Oberstlt.	24.7.43
Rogalski, Franz	Ofw., Stoßtruppf. in Sturm-Btl. A.O.K. 8 775th Oak Leaves 11.3.45	17.3.44
Rogge, Alfred	SS-Obersturmführer, Fhr. 1./SS-Fest.-Rgt. 1, "Besslein" (Breslau) + 12.5.45 in Breslau-Lissa of wounds in a POW hospital	9.5.45
Rogge, Bernhard	Kapt. z. See, Kdt. Hilfskreuzer "Atlantis" (HSK 2) 45th Oak Leaves 31.12.41	7.12.40
Rogge, Rudolf	Hptm. d.R., Fhr. 1./A.R. 122 + 28.9.43 in northern Russia; posthumously promoted to Major d.R.	18.11.43
Roggenbau, Ulrich	Oblt. d.R., Chef 7./G. R. 254 + 7.7.44 west of Minsk (Russia) as Hptm. d.R. Kdr. FEB 110	30.11.43
Roggenland, Franz	Ofw., Zugf. in 10./Pz. G. R. 67	4.10.44
Rogner, Hans	Hptm., Fhr. Pi. Ers. & Ausb. Btl. 213	11.3.45
Rohde, Walter	Feldw., Zugf. in 6./Pz. G. R. 25 + 13.2.44 at Tschernaja-Retschka (Russia) as Ofw.	22.9.43
Rohlfs, Kurt	Hptm d.R., Kdr. Pi. Btl. 20	1.1.44
Rohr, Hans	Lt. d.R., Zugf. in 7./Geb.Jäg. Rgt. 139	20.6.40
von Rohr, Hans-Babo	Lt., Zugf. in 2./Pz. Rgt. 25 754th Oak Leaves 24.2.45	5.11.44
Rohrbacher, Josef	Owm., Zugf. in 3./St. Gesch. Brig. 245	4.5.44
Rohrbeck, Kurt	Oblt., stellv. Fhr. Aufkl. Lehr-Abt. 1	3.11.44
Rohweder, Hellmut	Kaptlt. (Ing.), L. I. "U 69" & "U 514"	14.11.43
Rohweder, Johannes	Hptm., Kdr. Pz.Jäg. Abt. 670(sfl)	23.8.41
Rohwer, Detlev	Lt., Flugzeugf. in I./J.G. 3 + 30.3.44 at Ibbenbüren of wounds; as Hptm. & Kdr. II./J.G. 3 "Udet"	5.10.41
Roka, Franz	Oblt., Staffelkpt. 6. Stuka-Geschw. 1 + 26.10.43 at Mohilew (Russia); posthumously promoted to Hptm.	9.10.43
Roland, Heinz	Hptm., Fhr. II./Pz. G. R. 73	9.12.44
Rollmann, Wilhelm	Kaptlt., Kdt. "U 34" + 6.11.43 in South Atlantic as Kdt. "U 848"; posthumously promoted to Freg. Kpt.	31.7.40
Rollwage, Herbert	Ofw., Flugzeugf. in 3./J.G. 53 713th Oak Leaves 24.1.45	6.4.44
Rolser, Otto	Uffz., Zugf. in 1./G. R. 727 + 1.5.43 as Feldw.	20.4.43

Frhr. von Roman, Rudolf	Gen. Major, Kdr. 35. I.D. 313th Oak Leaves 28.10.43	19.2.42
Romeike, Hans Georg	Oblt. d.R., Chef 6./G. R. 43 + 14.1.44 during an assault on Strutinka in southern Russia	3.9.43
Romm, Oskar	Ofw., Flugzeugf. in 1./J.G. 51 "Mölders"	29.2.44
Rommel, Erwin	Gen. Major, Kdr. 7. Pz.Div. 10th Oak Leaves 20.3.41 6th Swords 20.1.42 6th Diamonds 11.3.43	27.5.40
Romott, Hans	Ofw., Zugf. in 4. (MG)/G. R. 4 Groß-Born-Linde as Lt. & Zugfhr., accidentally; posthumously promoted to Oblt.	18.4.43
Rompzick, Johannes	Lt. d.R., Fhr. 6./G. R. 18	22.11.43
v. Roon, Arnold	Oblt., Chef 3./Fsch. Jäg. Rgt. 2	9.7.41
Roos, Ferdinand	Gefr., Kp. Tr. Fhr., in 3./Pi. Btl. 6	16.8.43
Roos, Fritz	Hptm., Fhr. II./Geb.Jäg. Rgt. 13 +29.1.45 died as Major i.G.	2.11.42
Roos, Hugo	Hptm., Chef 11./I.R. 119 (mot.)	13.9.42
Ropp, Max	Ofw., Zugf. in 11./Geb.Jäg. Rgt. 143	28.10.44
Rose, Willi	Ofw., Zugf. in 11./G. R. 96 + 4.12.43 Nevel (Russia) of wounds	22.1.44
Frhr. von Rosen, Kersten	Obstlt., Kdr. G. R. 88	26.12.44
Rosenbaum, Helmut	Kaptlt., Kdt. "U 73" + 10.5.44 at Konstanza (Rumania) during attack by enemy aircraft as Chef 30. U-Flottille; posthumously promoted to Korv. Kpt.	12.8.42
Rosenheinrich, Hans	Obgefr., Gruppenf. in 3./G. R. 173	5.11.44
Rosin, Willi	Oblt. d.R., Chef 6./G. R. 328	18.11.44
Roske, Dipl.-Ing. Fritz	Oberst, Kdr. I.R. 194	20.1.43
Roßbach, Heinrich	Hptm. d.R., Kdr. II./G. R. 89	12.12.42
Roßbach, Karl-Heinz	Feldw., Zugf. in 2./Pz. G. R. 7 + 25.2.44 at Luzk (Russia)	6.6.43
Roßfeld, Christian	Ofw., Zugf. in 10./I.R. 62	5.10.41
Roßhart, Emil	Obgefr., Gruppenf. in 2./Sturm-Rgt. 195	3.4.43
Rossiwall, Theodor	Hptm., Staffelkpt. 5./Z.G. 26 "Horst Wessel"	6.8.41
Rossler, Vincenz	Lt. d.R., Zugf. in Pz. Abt. 190	28.10.44
Roßmann, Edmund	Feldw., Flugzeugf. in 7./J.G. 52	19.3.42
Roßmann, Emil	Lt. d.R., Fhr. 2./Pz. Rgt. 26	23.10.44
Roßmann, Karl	Oblt., Chef 16./Flak-Rgt. "GG" (mot.) 725th Oak Leaves 1.2.45	12.11.41
Rossner, Erich	SS-Unterscharf., Geschützf. in 2./SS-Pz.Jäg. Abt. "Reich" + 12.9.41 Jelnja of wounds	25.8.41

KNIGHT'S CROSS OF THE IRON CROSS

Rost, Hans-Günther	Gen.Lt., Kdr. Reichsgren. Div. "Hoch- & Deutschmeister" + 23.3.45 at Stuhlweißenburg (Hungary)	21.3.45
Rostin, Erwin	Kaptlt., Kdt. "U 158" + 1.7.42 west of Bermuda in the Atlantic; posthumously promoted to Korv. Kpt.	28.6.42
Roth, Ernst August	Gen. Major, Fliegerführer Nord	6.11.43
Roth, Günther	Oblt., Flugzeugf. in IV. (K)/L.G. 1	26.3.44
Roth, Hans	Oberst, Kdr. Flak-Rgt. 38	9.1.45
Roth, Heinrich	Wachtm., Vorg. Beob. in 4./A.R. 235	18.1.45
Roth, Hermann	Oblt. d.R., Chef 1./F. E. B. 212 + 7.3.45 as Hptm. d.R. & Btl. Kdr.	27.7.44
Roth, Jakob	Uffz., Zugf. in 2./G. R. 208	4.6.44
Roth, Matthias	Oblt., Fhr. II./G. R. 105	21.2.44
Roth, Wilhelm	Owm., Zugf. in 1./Geb. Aufkl. Abt. 94	24.6.44
Rothardt, Heinz	Uffz., Zugf. in 2./Pz. Aufkl. Abt. 1 1	30.9.43
Rothe, Friedrich	Oblt., Fhr. 5./Pz. G. R. 93	17.3.45
Rothe, Gerhard	Feldw., Bordfunker in III./Stuka-G. 1	12.11.43
Rothenburg, Karl	Oberst, Kdr. Pz. Rgt. 25 + 28.6.41 south of Minsk of wounds; posthumously promoted to Gen. Major	3.6.40
Rothhaar, Willi	Lt., Fhr. 3. (MG)/G. R. 544	5.9.44
v. Rothkirch & Panthen, Friedrich-Wilhelm	Gen. Major, Kdr. 13. I.D. (mot.)	15.8.40
Graf v. Rothkirch & Trach, Hans-Siegfried	Hptm. d.R., Kdr. I./Pz. Rgt. 26	4.10.44
Rothmaier, Anton	Ofw., Zugf. in 6./G. R. 335	9.6.44
Frhr. v. Rotsmann, Dipl.-Ing. Fritz-Joachim	Major d.R., Kdr. I./A.R. 176 + 1943 in Stalingrad (Russia)	31.1.43
Rott, Rudolf	SS-Obersturmf., Chef 1./SS-Pz. Abt. 11 "Nordland" + 12.2.45 Klein-Silber (Pomerania); posthumously promoted to SS-Hauptsturmf.	28.2.45
Rott, Walter	Oblt., Chef 5./G. R. 1122	11.3.45
Rottensteiner, Johann	Obgefr., Gruppenf. in Stabskp./G. R. 353	18.2.45
Rotter, Josef	Ofw., Zugf. in 10./Jäger-Rgt. 204	9.8.43
Rowehl, Theodor	Obstlt., Kdr. Aufkl. Gr. OB d. Lw.	27.9.40
Rowohl, Willi	Ofw., Zugf. in 2./S. R. 115	12.7.42
Roy, Rudolf	SS-Oberscharf., Pz. Kdt. & Zugfhr. 1./SS-Pz.Jäg. Abt. 12 "Hitlerjugend" + 17.12.44 at Hollerath	16.10.44

Name	Description	Date
Rubarth, Walter	Feldw., Stoßtruppfhr. in 2./Pi. Btl. 49 (mot.) + 26.10.41 in Russia, of wounds, as Lt. & Offz. z.b.V.	3.6.40
Rubatscher, Karl	SS-Obersturmf. d.R., Adj. I./SS-G. R. 8 (mot.)	27.12.43
Rubensdörffer, Walter	Hptm., Kdr. Erprob. -Gr. 210 + 15.8.40 over Croydon (England) following aerial combat	19.8.40
Rubesch, Franz	Obstlt., Kdr. gern. Flak Abt. 303	30.9.44
Ruckau, Hans	Obstlt., Fhr. G. R. 1091	5.3.45
v. Ruckteschell, Hellmuth	Korv. Kpt. d.R., Kdt. Hilfskreuzer "Widder" (HSK 3) 158th Oak Leaves 23.12.42	31.10.40
Rudat, Erich	Rittm., Kdr. Div. -Füs. Btl. 227 (A.A.) + 29.3.44 in Wesenberg/Estonia of wounds; posthumously promoted to Major	29.2.44
Rudat, Horst	Oblt., Staffelkpt. 2./K.G. 55	24.3.43
Rudel, Hans-Ulrich	Oblt., Staffelkpt. 9./Stuka-Geschw. 2 "Immelmann" 229th Oak Leaves 14.4. 43 42nd Swords 25.11.43 10th Diamonds 29.3.44 1st Golden Oak Leaves 29.12.44	6.1.42
Rudler, Oskar	Gefr., Gr. Fhr. in 3./Jäger-Rgt. 229	5.4.45
Rudnik, Erich	Lt., Pi. Zugf. Stabskp./G. R. 45	18.2.45
Rudolf, Richard	SS-Oberscharf., Zugf. in SS-Pz.Jäg. Abt. 12 "Hitlerjugend"	18.11.44
Rudolph, Walter	Feldw., Zugf. in 6./G. R. 123 + 18.7.44 at Grodno (Russia) of wounds	2.6.43
Rudorffer, Erich	Lt., Flugzeugf. in 6./J.G. 2 "Richthofen" 447th Oak Leaves 11.4.44 126th Swords 26.1.45	1.5.41
Rübel, Karl	Gen.Lt., Kdr. 163. I.D. + 8.3.45 at Schievelbein (Pomerania)	13.1.45
Rübell, Günther	Lt., Flugzeugf. in 5./J.G. 51 "Mölders"	14.3.43
Rück, Julius	Uffz., Kp. Tr. Fhr. in 1./G. R. 438	12.8.44
Rüd, Adolf	SS-Ober-Scharf., Zugf. in Stabskp./SS-Pz. G. R. 3 "Deutschland" + 2.8.44 in Normandy at Marigny (France); posthumously promoted to SS-Hauptscharf.	23.8.44
v. Rüden, Wilhelm	Hptm. d.R., Adj. Div. Gruppe 330 + 11.7.44 as Hptm. d.R. & Fhr. Div. Füs. Btl. 342; posthumously promoted to Major	16.4.44
Ruederer, Ludwig	Obstlt., Kdr. Inf. Rgt. 332	23.10.41
Ruef, Karl	Major, Kdr. III./Geb.Jäg. Rgt. 143	28.10.44
Rüffler, Helmut	Ofw., Flugzeugf. in 4./J.G. 3 "Udet"	23.12.42
Rüger, Dr. jur. Josef	Hptm. d.R., Kdr. II./Pz. G. R. 63	7.3.44
Rühle v. Lilienstern, Dr. rer. pol Hans-Joachim	SS-Hptsturmf. d.R., Fhr. I./niederl. SS-Freiw. Pz. -G. R. 48 "General Seyffardt"	12.2.44
Rüngeler, Wilhelm	Hptm., Kdr. Sturm-Pi-Btl. 178	11.10.43

Frhr. v. Ruepprecht, Werner	Major, Fhr. Pz. G. R. 111 + 23.11.44 in France	12.12.44
Ruf, Hugo	SS-Oberscharf., Zugf. in 3./SS-Pz. Rgt. 5 "Wiking"	16.10.44
Ruffer, Rudolf-Heinz	Hptm., Staffelf. 10. (Pz.)/S.G. 9 + 16.7.44 at Lemberg (Poland)	9.6.44
Ruge, Friedrich	Kapt. z. See & Kommodore, Führer der Minensuchboote West	21.10.40
Ruge, Gerd	Hptm., Kdr. I./Pz. G. R. 128 648th Oak Leaves 16.11.44	7.9.43
Ruhl, Franz	Lt., Staffelf. 4./J.G. 3 "Udet" posted missing since 24.12.44 at Lüttich (Belgium); posthumously promoted to Oblt.	27.7.44
Ruhl, Heinrich	Major, Kdr. Div. Fus. Btl. (A.A.) 122 789th Oak Leaves 16.3.45	21.9.44
Ruhnke, Herbert	Uffz., Geschützf. in 3./PzJag. Abt. 294	8.2.43
Ruland, Karl	Uffz., Gr. Fhr. in 5./G. R. 306 + 26.2.44 south-east of Witebsk (Russia)	17.3.44
v. Rumohr, Detlev	Major, Kdr. G. R. 211	4.7.44
Rumohr, Joachim	SS-Obersturmbannf., Kdr. SS-A.R. 8 "Florian Geyer" 721st Oak Leaves 1.2.45	16.1.44
Rumpelhardt, Friedrich	Lt., Bordfunker in IV./NJ.G. 1	27.7.44
v. Rundstedt, Gerd	Gen. Oberst, OB H.Gr. Süd 519th Oak Leaves 1.7.44 133rd Swords 18.2.45	30.9.39
Runge, Fritz	Lt., stellv. Fhr. II./G. R. 532	2.11.43
Runge, Siegfried	Oberst, Kdr. I.R. 279 + 24.3.45 at Königstädten (Hessen) as Generalmajor & Stadtkdt. v. Mainz-Wiesbaden	20.12.41
Ruoff, Richard	Gen.D.Inf., Kom.Gen. V. A.K.	30.6.41
Rupp, Ernst	Gen.Lt., Kdr. 97. Jäg. Div. + 30.5.43 Kuban bridgehead (Russia)	7.3.43
Rupp, Friedrich	Lt., Flugzeugf. in 7./J.G. 54 + 15.5.43 shot down south-west of Helgoland; posthumously promoted to Oblt.	24.1.43
Ruppert, Hermann	Oblt., Staffelkpt. 6./Stuka-Geschw. 77 + 2.3.42 Stalino (Russia)	23.11.41
Ruppert, Hermann	Lt., Zugf. in 3./I.R. 15 (mot.) + 26.12.44 in Bastogne as Hptm.	12.1.42
Rupprecht, Siegfried	Oblt., Chef 6./Geb.Jäg. Rgt. 85 + 25.1.44 in Italy as Hptm. & Btl. Fhr.	10.9.43
Rust, Heinrich	Ofw., Zugf. in 9./G. R. 324	12.12.44
Rust, Dr. jur. Wolfgang	Hptm., Adj. G. R. 11 (mot.) 771st Oak Leaves 11.3.45	24.6.44
Rutkowski, Alfred	Hptm. d.R., Kdr. Fus. Btl. (A. A.) 126 + 16.9.44 at Lacisi (Modohn/Baltic)	15.4.44

Ryll, Wolfgang	Oblt., Fhr. 5./Pz. RgL. 7 + 21.1.41 as Hptm. & Kp. Chef	13.10.41

S

Saalbach, Rudolf	SS-Hptsturmf., Kdr. SS-Pz. Aufkl. Abt. 11 "Nordland" + 30.4.45 in Berlin as SS-Sturmbannfhr.	12.3.44
Saalwächter, Alfred	Gen. Admiral, Marine-Gruppenbefehlsh. West taken to Soviet Union on 6.12.45, + 1950 in Soviet captivity final post Gen. Admiral z. V.	9.5.40
Sabottki, Wilhelm	Stabsfeldw., Zugf. in 4./G. R. 1 +19.1.45	20.3.44
Sacha, Friedrich	Oblt., Chef 2./Pz.Jäg. Abt. 160	20.1.43
Sachenbacher, Hans-Hermann	Rittm., Chef Radf. Schwadr. 219 + 25.11.43 in Tscherkassy as Major & Kdr. II./Pz. Rgt. 11	14.12.41
Sacher, Otto	Obstlt., Kdr. G. R. 456 + in Soviet captivity	6.2.44
Sachs, Günther	Gen. Major, Kdr. 18. Flak-Div.	24.1.45
Sachs, Hans	Obgefr., Gr. Fhr. in 5./Pz. Füs. Rgt. "GD"	10.9.44
Sachsenberg, Heinz	Fhj. -Feldw., Flugzeugf. in 6./J.G. 52	9.6.44
Sachsenheimer, Max	Hptm., Kdr. II./Jäger-Rgt. 75 472nd Oak Leaves 14.5.44 132nd Swords 6.2.45	5.4.42
Sack, Emil	Ofw., Zugf. in 4. (MG)/I.R. 445 + 18.8.42 in Russia as Oblt. & Kp. Fhr.	29.9.41
Saenger, Friedrich	Oblt., Chef 10./A.R. 1352 + 15.4.45 at Hannberg at Höchstadt (Aisch)	28.3.45
Säumenicht, Rudolf	SS-Hptsturmf., Chef 2./SS-Pz. Rgt. 3 "Totenkopf' + 26.8.44 Czarnow on the Bug (Russia) as SS-Sturmbannf. & Kdr. I./SS-Pz. Rgt. 5 "Wiking"	13.10.43
Sahner, Günther	Uffz., VB in 3./G. R. 176 + 6.2.45 in East Prussia	5.3.45
Siler, Johann (6)	SS-Obersturmf., Fhr. 3./SS-Pz.Jäg. Abt. 9 "Hohenstaufen"	6.5.45
Salamon, Dr. med. Friedrich	Stabsarzt d.R., Btl. -Arzt II/Pz. G. R. 26	20.7.44
Salamon, Walter	Obstlt., Kdr. Flak-Sturm-Abt. 802 (v)	18.11.44
v. Saldern-Ballentin, Sylvester	Major, Kdr. II./G. R. 65	21.11.43
v. Saldern-Wilsnack, Burghardt	Hptm., Kdr. II./G. R. 51 (mot.)	4.5.44
de Salengre-Drabbe, Hans	Oberst, Kdr. I.R. 457 + 25.8.44 at Tiraspol (Bessarabia) as Gen.Lt. & Kdr. 384. I.D.	22.2.42
v. Salisch, Wilhelm	Hptm., Kdr. III./Jäger-Rgt. 49 533rd Oak Leaves 27.7.44	20.4.43

Prinz zu Salm-Horstmar, Karl-Walrad	Rittm., Kdr. Aufkl. Abt. 123	19.2.42
Salminger, Josef	Hptm., Kdr. III./Geb.Jäg. Rgt. 98 + 1.10.43 in Russia as Obstlt. & Rgt. Kdr.	31.8.41
v. Salmuth, Hans	Gen.Lt., Chef d. Gen. St. H.Gr.B	19.7.40
Saltzwedel, Martin	Korv. Kpt., Kdt. Zerstörer "Z 24"	15.6.43
Salwey, Benno	Oblt. d.R., Ord.Offz. in Stab I.R. 270	2.10.41
Salz, Wilhelm	Lt., Fhr. 6./G. R. 502	10.9.44
Salzmann, Walter	Oblt., Fhr. 6./I.R. 121	27.6.42
Sametreiter, Kurt	SS-Oberscharf., Zugf. in 3. (schw.)/SS-Pz.Jäg. Abt. 1 "LSSAH"	31.7.43
Sander, Ernst	Ofw., Zugf. in 7./S. R. 79 + 16.2.42 in Russia	13.10.41
Sander, Erwin	Gen. Major, Kdr. 170. I.D.	3.9.42
Sander, Joachim	Obstlt., Kdr. Pz. Rgt. 23 729th Oak Leaves 5.2.45	19.9.43
Sander, Walter	Lt. d.R., Fhr. 1./Fsch. Pi. Btl. 5	28.2.45
Sander, Wilhelm	Fhj. -Feldw., Zugf. in 1./Pz.Jäg. Abt. 370 + 24.10.43 south-west of Melitopol (Russia)	23.12.43
Sanders, Bernhard	Uffz., Gruppenf. in 7./G. R. 278	7.4.44
Sandig, Rudolf	SS-Sturmbannf., Kdr. II./SS-Pz. G. R. 2 "LSSAH"	5.5.43
Sandmann, Karlheinz	Uffz., Gruppenf. in 1./G. R. 102	8.2.44
Sandner, Johann	Objäg., Gruppenf. in 11./Geb.Jäg. Rgt. 100	13.6.41
Sandrock, Hans	Major, Kdr. III./Fsch. Pz. Rgt. "HG"	18.10.44
Sann, Fritz	Major, Fhr. Marine-Inf.Rgt. 8	14.4. 45
Sanne, Werner	Gen. Major, Kdr. 100. le. Inf. Div. + 26.9.52 in Camp Krasnopol (Russia) in Soviet. captivity; final post Gen.Lt.	22.2.42
Sardemann, Hermann	Oblt. (MA) d.R., Chef der Batterie "Lausitz" in Mar. Fla-Abt. 259 in Mar. Flak-Rgt. 9	20.4,45
Sartor, Bernhard	Oblt., Beobachter in Stab/K.G. 51	20.7.44
Frhr. v. Saß, Eduard	Obstlt., Kdr. G. R. 277 + 16.1.46 hanged by the Soviets at Welikije-Luki (Russia); final post Oberst	19.12.42
Sassen, Bruno	Feldw., Zugf. in 10./Fsch. Jäg. Rgt. 3	22.2.42
Sassenberg, Hans-Hermann	Lt., Zugf. in 2./Pz. Aufkl. Abt. 13 + 25.10.43 in southern Russia as Hptm. & Abt. Fhr.; posthumously promoted to Major	23.10.41
Sattig, Carl	Hptm., Staffelkpt. 6./J.G. 54 + 10.8.42 at Rshew (Russia) missing, probably died in Soviet captivity	19.9.42
Sattler, Georg	Lt., Flugzeugf. in 1. (K)/L.G. 1 675th Oak Leaves 6.12.44	5.2.44

Sattler, Günter	Hptm., Kdr. II./G. R. 520	15.5.44
Sattler, Hans-Karl	Oblt., Flugzeugf. in 8./Stuka-Geschw. 77 + 13.1.43 at Kertsch (Russia) as Staffelkpt.	16.2.42
Sattler, Karl	SS-Sturmbannf., Fhr. SS-Rgt. "Sattler"	16.1.45
v. Saucken, Dietrich	Gen. Major, Fhr. 4. Pz.Div. 281st Oak Leaves 22.8.43 46th Swords 31.1.44 27th Diamonds 8.5.45	6.1.42
Sauer, Hans	Lt., Flugzeugf. d. 4. (K)/L.G. 1 + August 1941 in Mediterranean area	5.7.41
Sauer, Hermann	Oberst, Kdr. Fest. Gren. Rgt. "Sauer" in Festung Breslau	30.4.45
Sauer, Johann	Hptm. d.R., Kdr. I./Pz. G. R. 93 + 19.5.44 of wounds in Russia as Major d.R.	15.5.44
Sauer, Konrad	Wachtm. d.R., Zugf. in 3./St. Gesch. Abt. 209 603rd Oak Leaves 30.9.44; posthumously promoted to Feldw.	26.9.42
Sauer, Walter	Major, Kdr. II./Füs. Rgt. 230	14.4. 45
Sauerbrei, Rudolf	Hptm., Kdr. II./G. R. 405	5.4.45
Sauerbruch, Peter	Hptm. i.G., Ib 14. Pz.Div. & Fhr. Kampfgr. "Sauerbruch"	4.1.43
Saul, Konrad	Uffz., Gruppenf. in 1./G. R. 337 + 27.2.43 in Russia of wounds	9.4.43
Sauter, Jordan (19)	Hptm. d.R., Kdr. II./Rgt. "Theodor Körner"	7.5.45
Sauvant, Bernhard	Major, Kdr. I./Pz. Rgt. 36 260th Oak Leaves 28.7.43	30.11.42
Sawatzki, Karl	Feldw., Zugf. in 14. (Pz.Jäg.)/G. R. 3	23.2.44
Sawatzki, Otto	Ofw., Zugf. in 14. (Pz.Jäg.)/I.R. 505 + 22.9.41	8.9.41
Sawatzki, Otto	Ofw., Zugf. in 3./Pi. Btl. 21 + 15.8.44	10.9.44
Prinz zu Sayn-Wittgenstein-Berleburg, Ludwig-Ferdinand	Obstlt., Kdr. Kav. Rgt. Süd + 21.11.43 at Zhitomir (Russia); posthumously promoted to Oberst	20.1.44
Prinz zu Sayn-Wittgenstein-Sayn, Heinrich	Hptm., Staffelkpt. 9./N. J.G. 2 290th Oak Leaves 31.8.43 44th Swords 23.1.44	2.10.42
Schaal, Ferdinand	Gen.Lt., Kdr. 10. Pz.Div.	13.7.40
Schaar, Gerhard	Oblt. z. See, Kdt. "U 957"	1.10.44
Schaarschmidt, Herbert	Uffz., in 3./Flak-Rgt. 40	9.2.45
Schaarschuh, Helmut	Hptm., Kdr. I./Füs. Rgt. 22	4.10.44
Schachner, Max	SS-Obersturmf. d.R., Fhr. 2./SS-Pz.Jäg. Abt. 8 "Florian Geyer" + 19.10.43 at Kriwoi Rog (Russia)	14.5.44
Schacht, Gerhard	Lt., Fhr. Sturmgruppe "Beton" in Fsch. Jäger-Sturmabt. "Koch" simultaneously promoted to Oblt.	12.5.40

KNIGHT'S CROSS OF THE IRON CROSS

Name	Details	Date
Schacht, Harro	Korv. Kpt., Kdt. "U 507" + 14.1.43 in mid-Atlantic off Brazil; posthumously promoted to Freg. Kpt.	9.1.43
Schacht, Heinz	Lt. d.R., Zugf. in 2./Pz.Jäg. Abt. 158	19.1.43
Schack, Friedrich-August	Oberst, Kdr. I.R. 392 597th Oak Leaves 21.9.44	24.7.41
Schack, Günther	Lt., Flugzeugf. in 9./J.G. 51 "Mölders" 460th Oak Leaves 20.4.44	29.10.43
v. Schack, Hans	Major, Fhr. SS-Kav. Rgt. 16 "Florian Geyer"	27.1.45
Schade, Karl-Heinz	Lt., Kp. Fhr. in Pz. Pi. Btl. 92	2.9.44
Schächter, Martin	Lt., Fhr. Sturmgruppe "Stahl" in Fsch. Jäger Sturmabt. "Koch" simultaneously promoted to Oblt.	12.5.40
Schädlich, Gottfried	Hptm., Kdr. I./G. R. 514	9.7.44
Schäfer, Albert	Obgefr., MG-Schtz. in 1./Pz. G. R. 33	12.9.44
Schäfer, Eberhard	Lt., Kommandofhr. d. Kgl. ungar. Kampfstaffel in III./K.G. 4 "General Wever" + 9.4.44 in hospital at Zamosc (Russia) of wounds; posthumously promoted to Oblt.	20.4.44
Schaefer, Eduard	Major, Kdr. I./G. R. 72	23.8.43
Schäfer, Eduard	Oblt., Fhr. II./G. R. 1115 + 6.2.45 of wounds	10.2.45
Schaefer, Elmar	Oblt., Flugzeugf. in 1./Stuka-Geschw. I	8.5.40
Schäfer, Erich	Hptm. d.R., Kdr. II./Ski-Jäger-Rgt. 2 + 26.1.45 at Jordanow (Russia)	31.1.45
Schäfer, Ernst	SS-Sturmbannf., Kdr. III./SS-I. R. 10 (mot.)	14.10.43
Schäfer, Friedrich	Oblt., Staffelf. 4./K.G. 200	24.10.44
Schäfer, Georg	Feldw., Zugf. in 2./Pz. Rgt. I + 13.10.44 in Nagy-Bajom (Hungary) as Ofw.	17.12.42
Schäfer, Günther	Lt. d.R., Fhr. of a Kampfgr. der Schule f. Fahnenjunker of Inf. VI.	3.11.44
Schäfer, Hans-Joachim	Major, Kdr. I./Flak-Rgt. 54 (mot.)	10.10.44
Schäfer, Heinrich	Ofw., Zugf. in 4./Jäg. Rgt. "HG"	8.8.44
Schäfer, Karl	Ofw., Flugzeugf. in 14. (Eis.)/K.G. 55	16.4.45
Schäfer, Kurt	Hptm., Btl. Kdr. in G. R. 516 + in Stalingrad (Russia)	29.1.43
Schäfer, Kurt	Hptm., Fhr. I./Pz. G. R. 33	12.8.44
Schäfer, Max	SS-Obersturmbannf., Kdr. SS-Pz. Pi. Btl. 5 "Wiking" 714th Oak Leaves 25.1.45	12.2.43
Schäfer, Oskar (8)	SS-Untersturmfhr., Fhr. 3./schw. SS-Pz. Abt. 503	29.4.45
Schäfer, Rudi	Gefr., Gruppenf. in II./G. R. 1082	11.3.45
Schägger, Peter	Major d.R., Kdr. Pz. Aufkl. Abt. 23 + 15.11.43 at Kriwoi Rog (Russia)	16.9.43
Schäzle, Bernd	Lt. d.R., Zugf. in 11./G. R. 380	3.1.44

Schaffner, Willi	Obergefr. in 9./G. R. 61 + 4.9.44 as Uffz.	26.10.43
Schairer, Hartmut	Oblt., Staffelkpt. 7./Stuka-Geschw. 1 + 19.7.42 at Staraja Russa (Russia) as Hptm.	30.8.41
Schalanda, Hans	Oblt., Flugzeugf. in 8./Stuka-Geschw. 1 630th Oak Leaves 24.10.44	3.4.43
Schaldach, Kurt	Obgefr., Geschützf. in 2./Pz.Jäg. Abt. 340 + 25.8.44 at Puhla 25 km west of Dorpat (Russia) as Lt. & Zugfhr.	9.8.42
Schalk, Johann	Obstlt., Kdr. III./Z.G. 26 "Horst Wessel"	5.9.40
Schall, Franz	Lt., Staffelfhr. in I./J.G. 52 + 10.4.45 Parchim (Mecklenburg) when making a forced landing as Staffelkpt. 10./J.G. 7; posthumously promoted to Hptm.	10.10.44
Schallenberg, Rudolf	Hptm., Fhr. I./G. R. 289	10.9.44
Schalles, Walter	Ofw., Flugzeugf. in 9./K.G. 27 "Boelcke"	12.4.42
Schaper, Siegfried	Major, stellv. Fhr. G. R. 3 + 20.9.44 at Walk (Latvia)	20.10.44
Schareina, Emil	Ofw., Zugfhr. in 8. (MG)/G. R. 24	10.5.43
Scharf, Heinz	Wachtm., Geschützfhr. in 3./Sturm. Gesch. Brig. 202	17.8.44
Scharf, Helmut	Gefr. in 3./Pz. G. R. 11 + 14.5.44 in NW Europe	20.7.44
Scharf, Konrad	Hptm., Kdr. I./G. R. 61	5.4.45
Scharff, Heinrich	Oblt., Chef I./G. R. 109	23.8.43
Scharnagel, Hermann	Hptm., Kdr. Pi. Btl. 173 602nd Oak Leaves 30.9.44	6.10.43
Scharpschneider, Hans	SS-Unterscharf., Mun. Staffelf. in 5./SS-Pz. A.R. 2 "Das Reich"	27.8.44
Schaßner, Kurt	Major, Fhr. Geb.Jäg. Rgt. 91	26.12.44
Schaten, Heinrich	Ofw., Zugf. in 6./G. R. 1	9.5.45
Schatz, Bruno	Oberst, Kdr. G. R. 977	9.12.44
Schaub, Oskar	Oblt., Chef I./Pz. G. R. 12	22.4.43
Schauer, Georg	Oblt. d.R., Schwadr. Fhr. in Div. Füs. Btl. (A.A.) 320 +13.1.44 in Russia as Rittm. d.R. of wounds	21.10.43
Schaumann, Horst	Lt. d.R., Fhr. 3./G. R. 2	17.4.45
Frhr. v. Schaumberg, Heinrich	Oblt., Chef Pz.Jäg. Kp. 1131 + 28.4.45 in East Prussia	14.4. 45
Schauwecker, Heinz-Eugen	Oblt. d.R., Chef 7./Pz. G. R. 115	31.12.44
Scheel, Günther	Lt., Staffelf. 3./J.G. 54 + 16.7.43 shot down over Orel (Russia)	5.12.43
Scheele, Alfons	Obgefr., MG-Schtz. & Melder in II./G. R. 405	30.9.44
v. Scheele, Hans-Karl	Oberst, Kdr. I.R. 191 217th Oak Leaves 2.4.43	4.7.40

KNIGHT'S CROSS OF THE IRON CROSS

Scheffel, Rudolf	Lt., Staffelf. 1./Z.G. 1	29.10.42
Scheffold, Konrad	Oblt., Fhr. 1./Pi. Btl. 24 + 9.7.44 at Cavigny (France) as Hptm. & Kdr. of the Armee-Pionier-Schule	18.4.43
Scheibe, Gerhard	Ofw., Bordfunker in I./N. J.G. 1 + 21.1.44 at Magdeburg in combat with a British bomber	10.12.43
Scheibe, Siegfried(19)	SS-Obersturmbannf., Kdr. SS-Frw. Pz. Gren. Rgt. 48 "General Seyffardt" + 17.4.45 at Baruth (Mark)	11.5.45
Scheibig, Erich	Ofvv., Zugf. in 14. (Pz.Jäg.)/G. R. 174	15.1.43
Scheid, Johannes	Ofw., Zugf. in 11./Gren. Rgt. 1 "HG"	21.6.43
Scheidies, Franz	Obstlt., Kdr. IR. 127 43rd Oak Leaves 31.12.41	5.8.40
Scheidig, Alben	Lt., Flugzeugf. in 1. (F)/Aufkl. Gruppe 122	16.4.42
Schelhorn, Fritz	Ofw., Zugf. in Stabskp./Schtz. Rgt. 66	4.9.42
Schell, Otto	Major, Kdr. III/I.R. 39 + 2.9.44 in Rumania as Fhr. 320. Inf. Div.; posthumously promoted to Gen. Major	19.11.41
Scheller, Walther	Gen.Lt., Kdr. 9. Pz.Div. + 21.7.44 at Brest-Litowsk (Russia) as Kdt. Festung Brest-Litowsk & Oberfeldkdt. 399	3.4.43
Schellhase, Walter	Lt. d.R., Battr. Ofiz. in 6./Werfer-Rgt. 52	30.10.43
Schellmann, Wolfgang	Major, Kmdr. J.G. 2 "Richthofen" + 22.6.41 at Grodno (Russia) as Kmdr. J.G. 27 (possibly captured and shot by the Soviets); posthumously promoted to Oberstlt.	18.9.40
Schellong, Conrad	SS-Obersturmbannf., Kdr. SS-Freiw. Sturmbrigade "Langemarck"	28.2.45
Schellong, Hans	Oblt., Staffelkpt. 3./K.G. 4 "General Wever" + 22.5.44 at Mariupol (Russia)	8.8.44
Schemm, Günther	Hptm., Fhr. I./Pz. Gr. Rgt. 11	6.10.44
Schemmel, Günther	Major, Kdr. I./Pz. G. R. 14	6.10.42
Schenck, Wolfgang	Oblt., Staffelkpt. 1./S. K.G. 210 139th Oak Leaves 30.10.42	14.8.41
Schenk, Rudi	Major, Kdr. II./G. R. 547 + 6.5.45 of wounds	8.8.44
Schentke, Georg	Ofw., Flugzeugf. in 9./J.G. 3 + 25.12.42 Pitomnik, Stalingrad (Russia) missing; posthumously promoted to Oblt.	4.9.41
Schepke, Joachim	Kaptlt., Kdt. "U 100" 7th Oak Leaves 1.12.40	24.9.40
Scherenberg, Rolf	Oberst, Kdr. Gren. Rgt. 532	26.3.43
Scherer, Fritz	hptm., Chef 2./St. Gesch. Abt. 236	14.12.43
Scherer, Theodor	Gen. Major, Kdr. 281. Sich. Div. 92nd Oak Leaves 5.5.42	20.2.42
Scherf, Fritz	Ofw., Zugf. in 2./Pz. Abt. 103 + 29.5.44 in Italy	30.9.44

ELITE OF THE THIRD REICH

Scherf, Walter	Oblt. d.R., Chef 3./schw. Pz. Abt. 503	23.2.44
Scherfling, Karl-Heinz	Ofw., Flugzeugf. in 12./NJ.G. 1 + 21.7.44 shot down over Moll (Belgium)	8.4.44
Scherg, Johannes	SS-Obersturmf., Chef 1./SS-Pol. Pz. Aufkl. Abt. 4	23.10.44
Scherling, Ewald	Obgefr., MG-Schtz. in 9./G. R. 15 (mot.) + 22.1.44 north of Castelforte (Italy)	26.1.44
Scherzer, Franz	SS-Obersturmf. d.R., Fhr. I./SS-Pz. Rgt. 10 "Frundsberg"	28.3.45
Scheuermann, Harald	Oblt. d.R., Fhr. 2./Div. Füs. Btl. 31	4.5.44
Scheuerpflug, Paul	Oberst, Kdr. Inf.Rgt. 116 791st Oak Leaves 16.3.45	6.9.42
Scheunemann, Kurt	Feldw., Pz. Kdt. & Zugf. in 2./Pz. Rgt. Führer-Begleit-Brigade	8.1.45
Scheunemann, Walter	Oblt., Chef 9./I.R. 272 202nd Oak Leaves 6.3.43	5.8.40
Schewe, Georg	Kaptlt., Kdt. "U 105"	23.5.41
Schewior, Fritz	Oblt. d.R., Fhr. Pz.Jäg. Kp. 1028	18.2.45
Schibau, Hans-Joachim	Oblt., Chef 8./Flak-Rgt. 36	4.11.41
Schiele, Wilhelm	Hptm., Kdr. II./G. R. 305 + 27.11.44	18.7.44
Schiemann, Alfred	Obgefr., Gruppenf. in I./G. R. 87 (mot.) + 13.7.43 during Op. "Zitadelle" (Russia)	28.4.43
Schiemann, Gustav	Hptm., Kdr. F. E. B. 346	9.5.45
Schier, Rudolf	Hptm. d.R., Kdr. III./Jäger-Rgt. 49	14.2.45
Sciciliolz, Hans-Georg	Ofw., Bordfunker in I./NJ.G. 3	29.10.44
Schieß, Franz	Oblt., Staffelkpt. 8./J.G. 53 + 2.9.43 south-west of Ischia (Mediterranean/Italy) as Hptm.	21.6.43
Schill, Gottlob	Obgefr., Pakschtz. in 14./G. R. 107	28.12.43
Schille, Kurt	Hptm., Chef 3. (mot.)/Pi. Btl. 24 544th Oak Leaves 8.8.44	25.8.42
Schiller, Friedrich	Lt., Fhr. 5./I.R. 131 + 21.8.42 on the Don (Russia) as Hptm. & Btl. Fhr.	16.1.42
Schiller, Horst	Major, Kdr. I./Stuka-Geschw. 3 + 2.6.43 at Sevastopol (Russia)	9.6.44
Schiller, Siegfried	Hptm., Kdr. Pz. Aufkl. Abt. 16	6.4.44
Schilling, Johannes	Lt. d.R., Zugf. in 1./Inf. Btl. z.b.V. 540	26.3.43
Schilling, Walter	Gen.Lt., Kdr. 17. Pz.Div. + 21.7.43 on the Kuban south of Isjum (Russia)	28.7.43
Schilling, Wilhelm	Ofw., Flugzeugf. in 9./J.G. 54	10.10.42
Schimanski, Johannes	Major, Kdr. I./G. R. 408	5.3.45
Schimmel, Hugo	Hptm., Kdr. III./I.R. 41 (mot.)	23.1.42
Schimmele, Josef	Obgefr., Richtschtz. in 14./Fds. Rgt. 34	8.8.44

Graf Schimmelmann v. Lindenburg, Theodor	Major, Kdr. II./Pz. Rgt. 15	14.5.41
Schimpf, Dipl.-Ing. Richard	Gen.Lt., Kdr. 3. FschJäg. Div.	6.10.44
Schimpff, Herbert	Oberst d.R., Kdr. G. R. 171 + in Soviet captivity	24.7.43
Schimpke, Horst	Lt., Zugf. in I./Fsch. Pz.Jäg. Abt. 1	5.9.44
Schindler, Walter	Hptm. d.R., Kdr. III./G. R. 106	4.5.44
Schirlitz, Ernst	Vizeadmiral, Kdt. Festung La Rochelle	11.3.45
Schirmer, Berthold	Major, Kdr. I./G. R. 32	27.8.44
Schirmer, Gerhart	Hptm., Fhr. II./Fsch. Jäger-Rgt. 2 657th Oak Leaves 18.11.44	14.6.41
Schirmer, Konrad	Lt. d.R., Zugf. in 3./Pi. Btl. 389 + 5.8.42 in great bend of the Don (Russia) as Kp. Fhr.; posthumously promoted to Oblt.	31.7.42
Schirner, Lothar	Gefr., Geschützkan. in 19./Flak-Rgt. "HG" + 19.3.45 in Heiligenbeil (East Prussia)	19.2.45
Schirp, Werner	Hptm., Chef 4./Pz. Rgt. 6	28.3.45
Schirrmacher, Fritz	Oblt., Chef 3./Pz. Pi. Btl. 13	14.5.41
Schitthelm, Karl	Obgefr., Melder in 6./Pz. G. R. 66	7.2.45
Schlagberger, Hans	Lt. d.R., Adj. I./G. R. 988 + 10.2.45 in the Eifel	31.1.45
Schlags-Koch, Walter	Major d.R., Kdr. 1./G. R. 365 876th Oak Leaves 9.5.45	5.9.44
Schlamelcher, Karl	SS-Sturmbannf., Fhr. III./SS-A.R. 5 "Wiking"	1.3.42
Schlang, Wilhelm	Feldw., Zugf. in 2./Pz.Jäg. Abt. z.b.V. 2	22.8.43
v. Schlebrügge, Hans	Major, Kdr. I./Geb.Jäg. Rgt. 139	20.6.40
Schlecht, Wilhelm	Ofw., Zugf. in 6./Sturm-Rgt. 195	23.7.43
Schlee, Joachim	Oberst, Kdr. G. R. 338	16.4.43
Schlee, Rudolf	Ofw., Zugf. in 6./Geb.Jäg. Rgt. 13 222nd Oak Leaves 6.4.43	23.10.41
Schleef, Hans	Feldw., Flugzeugf. in 7./J.G. 3 "Udet" + 31.12.44 at Bergzabern (Pfalz) as Oblt. & Staffelkpt. 16./J.G. 4	9.5.42
Schleef, Wilhelm	Obgefr., MG-Schtz. 1 in 7./Pz. G. R. 66	11.12.43
Schlegel, Heinz	Oberst, Kdr. G. R. 222	23.10.44
Schleinhege, Hermann	Lt., Flugzeugf. in 8./J.G. 54	28.1.45
Frhr. v. Schleinitz, Siegmund	Gen.Lt., Kdr. 9. I.D.	14.8.43
Schlemm, Alfred	Gen. d. Fsch. Tr., Kom.Gen. 1. Fsch. Korps	11.6.44
Schlemmer, Dipl.-Ing. Hans	Gen. Major, Kdr. 134. I.D. 369th Oak Leaves 18.1.44	21.4.42
Schlemminger, Erich	Major, Kdr. Div. Füs. Btl. 168	29.2.44

Schlepple, Eberhard	Oblt. d.R., Fhr. Pz. Aufkl. Abt. 26	27.7.44
Schlesiger, Otto	Major, Kdr. II./G. R. 1 + 26.4.44 at Dnjestr (Russia) of wounds	21.4.44
Prinz zu Schleswig-Holstein-Sonderburg-Glücksburg, Friedrich-Ferdinand	Major 1. G., Kdr. Pz. G. R. 40	22.2.45
Schlichting, Joachim	Hptm., Kdr. III./J.G. 27	14.12.40
v. Schlieben, Karl-Wilhelm	Oberst, Kdr. Brig. Stab z.b.V. 4 & Fhr. 208. I.D.	17.3.43
Schlieper, Franz	Oberst, Kdr. Gren. Brig. 1132 & Fhr. 73. I.D.	21.9.44
Schlieper, Fritz	Gen. Major, Kdr. 45. I.D.	27.12.41
Schliermann, Hermann (17)	Ofw., Flugzeugf. i. d. 5./T. G. 4 + April 1945 during a flight to Norway	31.10.44
Schließmann, Kurt	Hptm., Chef 1./St. Gesch. Brig 286	18.1.45
Schlingmann, Harry	Hptm., Kdr. Pi. Btl. 112	14.2.44
Frhr. v. Schlippenbach, Egon-Reiner	Kaptlt., Kdt. "U 453"	19.11.43
Schlömer, Helmuth	Oberst, Kdr. S. R. 5 161st Oak Leaves 23.12.42	2.10.41
Schlosser, Heinrich	Oblt. d.R., Flugzeugfhr. in 2./K.G. 50	18.9.41
Schlosser, Walter	Lt. d.R., Zugf. in 2./I.R. 456	16.9.42
Schlottmann, Carl	Major d.R., Kdr. Pi. Btl. 168 + in April 1944 in Kessel von Tarnopol (Russia) as Obstlt. D. R.	19.9.43
Schlüter, Adolf	Hptm., Kdr. II./G. R. 368	1.2.45
Schlüter, Wilhelm	SS-Sturmbannf. & Major d. Schupo, Fhr. SS-A.R. 54 "Nederland"	23.8.44
Schluifelder, Georg	SS-Standarten-Oberjunker, Fhr. 1./SS-Freiw. Pz. G. R. 49 "De Ruyter" + 24.1.45 Kaleti (Kurland) of wounds (suicide) as SS-Untersturmf. d.R.	26.11.44
Schlund, Franz	Ofw., Bordfunker in 4. (K)/L.G. 1	30.8.41
Schmahl, Adolf	Lt., Fhr. 10./I.R. 6	7.7.42
Schmalz, Alfons	Lt., Flugzeugf. in 8./Stuka-Geschw. 2 "Immelmann" + 21.7.42 at the main dressing station in Kalitwenskaja (Russia) of severe wounds	5.4.42
Schmalz, Eberhard	Lt., Zugf. in Pz.Jäg. Kp. 1102	11.3.45
Schmalz, Wilhelm	Major, Kdr. I./Schtz. Rgt. 11 358th Oak Leaves 23.12.43	28.11.40
Schmalzried, Otto	Oblt., Chef 12./I.R. 419	30.10.41
Schmekel, Heinz	Lt. d.R., Fhr. I./Pz. G. R. 108 + 6.6.44 north of Jassy (Rumania); posthumously promoted to Oblt. d.R.	27.7.44

Name	Details	Date
Schmeling, Jürgen	Hptm., Kampfgr. Fhr. in Div. Deneke	10.2.45
Schmelzer, Heinrich	SS-Obersturmf. d.R., Fhr. 16./SS-Pz. -G. R. "Das Reich" 756th Oak Leaves 28.2.45	12.3.44
Schmelzinger, Bruno	Uffz., Gewehr-Fhr. i. d. 4./G. R. 544	10.9.44
Schmetz, Heinrich	Hptm., Kdr. III./K.G. 100	29.10.44
Schmid, Alois	Ofw., Zugf. in 17./Geb.Jäg. Rgt. 91	9.1.45
Schmid, Anton	Oberst, Kgr. Fhr. 286. I.D.	10.2.45
Schmid, Franz	Lt., Fhr. 3./Schnelle Abt. 306	21.10.43
Schmid, Fritz-Wilhelm	Hptm., Kdr. II./Fsch. Pz. Gren. Rgt. 2 "HG"	6.10.44
Schmid, Georg	Lt. d.R., Adj. II./Jäg. Rgt. 229	2.6.43
Schmid, Günther	Lt., Staffelf. 5./Stuka-Geschw. 2 "Immelmann" + 14.7.43 at Bjelgorod (Russia) as Oblt. & Staffelkpt.	23.12.42
Schmid, Hans	Obstlt., Kdr. G. R. 850	13.4.44
Schmid, Johann	Hptm., Staffelkpt. 8./J.G. 26 "Schlageter" + 6.11.41 north of Calais (France) as Fhr. III./J.G. 26; posthumously promoted to Major	21.8.41
Schmid, Joseph	Gen. Major, Stab Pz.Div. "HG"	21.5.43
Schmid, Karl	Lt., Flugzeugf. in 14. (Eis.)/K.G. 27 "Boelcke"	19.8.43
Schmid, Walter	Lt. d.R., Adj. II./G. R. 390 + 22.9.44 at Bauske (Latvia) as Oblt. d.R.	15.5.44
Schmidhuber, Gerhard	Oberst, Kdr. Pz. G. R. 304 706th Oak Leaves 21.1.45	18.10.43
Schmidt, Arthur	Gen. Major, Chef d. Gen. St. 6 Armee	6.1.43
Schmidt, August	Oberst, Kdr. I.R. 20 371st Oak Leaves 23.1.44	27.10.39
Schmidt, August	Gen. d. Flakart., Kom.Gen. & Befehlsh. in Luftgau VI (Münster)	13.2.45
Schmidt, Burkhard	Major, Fhr. II./I.R. 411 + 28.2.43 at Jaswy (Demiansk/Russia) as Obstlt. & Kdr. Gr. Rgt. 410	6.11.42
Schmidt, Dietrich	Oblt., Staffelkpt. 8./N. J.G. 1	27.7.44
Schmidt, Erich	Lt., Flugzeugf. in III./J.G. 53 + 31.8.41 shot down by Soviet flak at Dubno (Russia) as Oblt.	23.7.41
Schmidt, Erich	Major, Kdr. schw. Pz. Abt. 507 877th Oak Leaves 9.5.45	9.6.44
Schmidt, Erich-Otto	Obstlt., Kdr. G. R. 679	4.8.43
Schmidt, Ernst	Lt. d.R., Fhr. Div. Sturmkp. 353	24.2.45
Schmidt, Franz	Oblt., Staffelkpt. in III./K.G. 55	19.8.43
Schmidt, Friedrich	Hptm., Fhr. III./I.R. 437	8.10.42
Schmidt, Fritz	Oblt., Adj. II./G. R. 15 (mot.) + 20.10.44 in Italy; posthumously promoted to Hptm.	9.12.44
Schmidt, Georg	Oblt., Chef 6./Jäger-Rgt. 56	9.12.44

Schmidt, Georg	Lt., Fhr. 7./G. R. 173 + 20.2.45 in Kurland	5.2.45
Schmidt, Gustav	Oberst, Kdr. I. R. 74 203rd Oak Leaves 6.3.43	4.9.40
Schmidt, Hans	Gen.Lt. z. V., Kdr. 260. I.D. 334th Oak Leaves 24.11.43	22.9.41
Schmidt, Hans	Gen.Lt., Kdr. 275. I.D.	16.10.44
Schmidt, Heinz	Lt., Flugzeugf. in 6./J.G. 52 124th Oak Leaves 16.9.42	23.8.42
Schmidt, Heinz	Oblt. d.R., Chef 1./G. R. 994	5.2.45
Schmidt, Hellmut	Hptm., Chef 1./Pz. Rgt. 10	16.9.43
Schmidt, Herbert	Oblt., Chef 1./Fsch. Jäger-Rgt. 1 + 16.6.44 Bretagne (France) as Major i.G. & Ia 2. Fsch. Jäg. Div. shot by partisans,	24.5.40
Schmidt, Herbert	Lt., Flugzeug. in I./S.G. 3 + 22.1.45 at Glienke (Mark) as Flugzeugf. in Stabsstaffel I./S.G. 77	9.6.44
Schmidt, Hermann	Hptm., Kdr. IV./A.R. 81	28.6.43
Schmidt, Hermann	Major, Kdr. I./K.G. 66	20.4.44
Schmidt, Hermann-Ludwig	Owm., Zugf. in 2./St. Gesch. Brig. 209	4.10.44
Schmidt, Hubert	Hptm. d.R., Fhr. I./G. R. 280	5.3.45
Schmidt, Johann	Hptm., Fhr. II./I.R. 62	18.1.42
Schmidt, Dipl.-Ing. Johannes	Obstlt., Kdr. I./Pz. Rgt. 27	15.10.42
Schmidt, Josef	Oberst, Kdr. G. R. 199 "List" + 28.1.43 at Woronesch (Russia); posthumously promoted to Gen. Major	31.1.43
Schmidt, Josef	Hptm. d.R., Fhr. I./G. R. 159	3.12.43
Schmidt, Jürgen	Obstlt. i.G., Ia 337. I.D. + 16.2.43 in Russia	I. 5.43
Schmidt, Karl-Heinz	Hptm., Fhr. Fest. Inf. Btl. XIV./999	11.6.44
Schmidt, Klaus-Degenhard	Oblt. z. See, Kdt. "S 54" in 10. Schnellbootsflottille + 22.12.44 off the Schelde as Kdt. "S 185"; posthumously promoted to Kaptlt.	22.12.43
Schmidt, Konrad	Oblt., Fhr. 12./G. R. 42 + 21.7.43 in Russia	23.8.43
Schmidt, Leonhard (5)	Hptm., Btl. Fhr. II./Fahsch. Jäg. Rgt. 4	30.4.45
Schmidt, Otto	Hptm., Staffelkpt. 7./Stuka-Geschw. 77	3.9.42
Schmidt, Paul	Lt., Beobacht. in Nahaufkl. Gr. 15	3.9.43
Schmidt, Richard	Obstlt., Kdr. I.R. 473	6.11.42
Schmidt, Rudolf	Gen.Lt., Kom.Gen. XXXIX. Pz. Korps 19th Oak Leaves 10.7.41	3.6.40
Schmidt, Rudolf	Feldw., Flugzeugf. in 5./J.G. 77	30.8.41
Schmidt, Rudolf	Hptm., Staffelkpt. 5./K.G. 76 + 5.9.42 Russia	2.10.42
Schmidt, Rudolf	Hptm., Kdr. II./K.G. 26	28.3.45

Name	Rank/Unit	Date
Schmidt, Walter	SS-Hptsturmf., Fhr. III./SS-Pz. G. R. 10 "Westland" 479th Oak Leaves 14.5.44	4.8.43
Schmidt, Werner	Major, Kdr. Fsch. MG-Btl. I	5.4.44
Schmidt, Werner	Hptm., Staffelkpt. 9./K.G. 55	19.8.44
Schmidt, Winfrid	Oblt., Staffelkpt. 8./J.G. 3	18.9.41
Schmidt-Falbe, Hans-Joachim	Hptm. d.R., Chef 10./G. R. 323	14.5.44
Schmidt-Hammer, Werner	Gen.Lt., Kdr. 168. I.D.	12.9.44
Schmidt-Hartung, Otto	Oberst, Kdr. I.R. 35	29.6.40
Schmidt-Ott, Gustav-Albrecht	Obstlt., Fhr. Pz. Rgt. 6	7.10.42
Ritter v. Schmidt, Hans	Major d.R., Fhr. Inf.Rgt. 546	24.8.42
Schmidtberg, Klaus	Fhj. -Ofw., Fluzeugf. in 1. (F)Nacht-Aufkl. Staffel	6.10.44
Schmidtmann, Fritz	Hptm., Staffelkpt. 4./K.G. 55	29.2.44
Schmidtmann, Hans-Albert	Obstlt., Kdr. Art.Rgt. 31	18.10.44
Schmied, Josef	Uffz., Gruppenf. in 3./Pi. Btl. 198	26.1.44
Schmied, Lorenz	Obgefr., Kp. Truppf. in 8./Geb.Jäg. Rgt. 100	29.11.44
Schmischke, Helmut	Hptm., Kdr. Pi. Btl. 36	22.7.43
Schmitt, Anton	Feldw., Zugf. in 2./G. R. 992	16.11.44
Schmitt, Artur	Gen. Major, Kdr. rückw. A. G. 556 & Fhr. a Kampfgr.	5.2.42
Schmitt, Erich	Ofw., Flugzeugf. in 2. (F)/Aufkl. Gr. 11	19.9.42
Schmitt, Erich	Obgefr., Gruppenf. in 3./G. R. 118	8.10.43
Schmitt, Jakob	Ofw., Zugfhr. in 13./G. R. 485	30.9.44
Schmitt, Norbert	Oblt., Staffelkpt. 3./S.G. 10 + 26.3.45 at Karmas (Hungary)	28.2.45
Schmitt, Stephan	Oblt., Staffelkpt. 5./S.G. 77 + 7.10.44 at Filyes-Gyaranaz (Hungary)	29.10.44
Schmitter, Wilhelm	Oblt., Flugzeugf. in II./K.G. 2 432nd Oak Leaves 24.3.44	19.9.42
Schmitz, Franz	San. Uffz., Gruppenf. in 3./G. R. 279	13.9.43
Schmitz, Günther	Fhj.-Ofw., Flugzeugf. in 10./T. G. 2 + 13.9.44 at Crete (Greece)	20.4.44
Schmitz, Wilfried	Oblt., Flugzeugf. in I./K.G. 4 "General Wever" + 4.2.45 at Frankfurt/Oder as Hptm.	21.8.42
Schmitzer, Franz	Obgefr., Richtschtz. in 4./A.R. 6	26.9.42
Schmölzer, Johann	Owm., Zugf. in 1./Radf. Abt. 68	24.9.42
Schmoll, Siegfried	Lt. d.R., Ord.Offz. in G. R. 217	9.6.44
Schmude, Ernst-Friedrich	Hptm., Kdr. II./G. R. 732	9.5.45

ELITE OF THE THIRD REICH

Schmückle, Willi	Fhj. -Ofw. in 6./Fhj. Rgt. 1241	15.3.45
Schmundt, Hubert	Konteradm., Befehlshaber der Aufklärungsstreit- kräfte & Fhr. d. Kampfgruppe Bergen	14.6.40
Schnabl, Ernst	Lt. d.R., Fhr. 9./Jäg. Rgt. 204	7.2.44
Schnappauf, Georg	Major, Kdr. Pz. Rgt. Führer-Begleit-Div.	9.5.45
Schnarr, Franz-Karl	Ofw., Zugf. in 13./G. R. 366	26.3.44
Schnatz, Helmut	Oblt., Fhr. 3./Flak-Rgt. 25 (mot.) + 19.9.42 south of Stalingrad (Russia)	17.10.42
Schnaubelt, Alois	SS-Unterscharf., Geschützf. in 3./SS-Flak-Abt. 5 "Wiking"	16.11.44
Schnaufer, Heinz-Wolfgang	Oblt., Staffelf. 12./N. J.G. 1 507th Oak Leaves 24.6.44 84th Swords 30.7.44 21st Diamonds 16.10.44	31.12.43
Schneck, Ernst	Hptm. d.R., Kdr. I./G. R. 698	16.11.44
Schneckenburger, Wilhelm	Gen.Lt., Kdr. 125. I.D. + 14.10.44 at Belgrade (Yugoslavia) of wounds as Gen.D.Inf. & Kom.Gen. Korpsgr. "Belgrad"	1.8.42
Schnee, Adalbert	Oblt. z. See, Kdt. "U 201" 105th Oak Leaves 15.7.42	30.8.41
Schneege, Rolf	Lt. d.R., Pi. Zugf. d. Stabskp./I.R. 120 (mot.) + 15.6.40 at Püttlingen, Maginot Line	14.5.41
Schneeweis, Wolfgang	Oblt., Flugzeugf. in Nachtjagdschwarm des Luftflottenkdo. 6 + 28.7.43 at Witebsk (Russia); posthumously promoted to Hptm.	15.11.43
Schneider, Adalbert	Korv. Kpt., I. Art. Offz. auf Schlachtschiff "Bismarck" + 27.5.41 in Atlantic off Iceland; posthumously promoted to Freg. Kpt.	27.5.41
Schneider, Albert	Hptm., Kdr. Feld-Ausb. Abt. 178	23.12.42
Schneider, Alfred	Lt. d.R., Fhr. 9./Geb.Jäg. Rgt. 206 + 3.6.42 south of Lake Ilmen (Russia) as Oblt. d.R. & Kp. Chef	7.6.42
Schneider, Eckhard	Oblt., Fhr. 6./Füs. Rgt. 202 + 4.10.43 in Russia of wounds	24.7.43
Schneider, Dipl.-Ing. Erich	Gen. Major, Kdr. 4. Pz.Div. 768th Oak Leaves 6.3.45	5.5.43
Schneider, Erich	Hptm., Fhr. II./Pz. Rgt. 9	10.2.44
Schneider, Friedrich	Hptm. d.R., Btl. Fhr. in G. R. 418	24.2.43
Schneider, Gerd-Dietrich	Oblt. z. See, Chef 8. Artillerie-Trägerflottille	3.10.44
Schneider, Heinrich	Ofw., Zugf. in Felders. -Btl. 211 + 27.6.44 at Styrzniec (Russia)	6.4.44
Schneider, Heinz	Oblt., Fhr. 3./Pz. Pi. Btl. 59	22.9.41
Schneider, Heinz	Hptm., Kdr. II./G. R. 669 + 3 1.7.44 on the Eastern Front; posthumously promoted to Major	20.10.44

KNIGHT'S CROSS OF THE IRON CROSS

Schneider, Herbert	Kaptlt., Kdt. "U 522" + 24.2.43 in Atlantic south of the Azores	16.1.43
Schneider, Herbert	Wachtm., Flakkampftruppf. in 6./Flak-Rgt. 49 (mot.)	5.2.44
Schneider, Josef	Ofw., Zugf. in 11./Jäger-Rgt. 207 389th Oak Leaves 10.2.44	27.6.42
Schneider, Josef	Ofw., Fhr. Sturmzug in 5./G. R. 521	18.1.44
Schneider, Kurt	Hptm. d.R., Chef 7./A.R. 129 + 10.10.43 in Russia of wounds	11.9.43
Schneider, Otto	SS-Obersturmf., Fhr. 7./SS-Pz. Rgt. 5 "Wiking" + posted missing early May 1945 in the Steiermark	4.5.44
Schneider, Otto	Lt., Fhr. Pi. Kp./Jäger-Rgt. 54 + 16.10.44 in Russia of wounds	28.10.44
Schneider, Paul	Hptm., Fhr. II./G. R. 959	18.11.44
Schneider, Rudolf	Oblt., Chef 1./Pz.Jäg. Abt. 342	4.10.42
Schneider, Walter-Erich	Kaptlt., Chef 25. Minensuchflottille	5.11.44
Schneider, Wilhelm	Wachtm., Stoßtruppf in Stabsschwdr. II./Reiter-Rgt. 32	30.4.45
Schneider-Kostalski, Ferdinand	Hptm., Kdr. III./Pz. Rgt. 6 + 7.8.44 at Dove (Normandy/France) as Major & Fhr. Pz. Rgt. 2; posthumously promoted to Oberstlt.	9.7.41
Schneidereit, Alfred	SS-Rottenf., Pz. Büchsentruppf. in 8./SS-Pz. Gr. Rgt. 1 "LSSAH"	20.12.43
Schneidermann, Willy	Feldw., Gruppenf. in Radf. Kp./G. R. 192	29.6.43
Schnell, Karl	Feldw., Kp. Truppf. in 1./G. R. 423	2.9.44
Schnell, Karl-Heinz	Oblt., Staffelkpt. 9./J.G. 51	1.8.41
Schnell, Siegfried	Lt., Flugzeugf. in II./J.G. 2 "Richthofen" 18th Oak Leaves 9.7.41	9.11.40
Schnepf, Wilhelm	Lt., Kp. Fhr. in schw. Heeres-Pz.Jäg. Abt. 654	31.1.45
Schniewind, Otto	Vize-admiral, Chef of Stabes der Seekriegsleitung in OKM	20.4.40
Schnitger, Albrecht	Ofw., Zugf. in 6./I.R. 18 + 13.3.43 at Rshew (Russia)	7.10.42
Schnocks, Herbert	Hptm., Btl. Kdr. G. R. 317	8.5.45
Schnörrer, Karl (17)	Lt. d.R., Staffelfhr. 11./J.G. 7	22.3.45
Schob, Herbert	Oblt., Flugzeugf. in 11./Z.G. 76	9.6.44
Ritter v. Schobert, Eugen	Gen.D.Inf., Kom.Gen. VII. A.K. + 12.9.41 Nikolajew (Russia) shot down, as Gen. Oberst & OB 11. Armee	29.6.40
Schöbitz, Ernst	Oblt., Staffelkpt. 11. (H)/Aufkl. Gr. 12	5.9.44
Schöck, Fritz	Hptm., Chef 2./schw. Pz. Abt. 507	5.9.44
Schoefbeck, Hans	Ofw., Flugzeugf. in 1./K. Gr. z.b.V. 9	14.3.43
Schölß, Josef	Hptm., Staffelkpt. 3./K.G. 51	25.5.43

ELITE OF THE THIRD REICH

Schoen, Helmut	Feldw., Zugf. in 5./Jäger-Rgt. 28	5.4.44
Schön, Rudolf	Lt. d.R., Fhr. 3./Pi. Btl. 8 (mot.)	12.12.44
Schönbeck, Viktor	Hptm., Chef 13./Geb.Jäg. Rgt. 139	20.6.40
Schönberg, Friedrich	Obstlt., Fhr. Div. Gr. 262	10.9.44
Schönberger, Georg	SS-Obersturmbannf., Kdr. SS-Pz. Rgt, 1 "LSSAH" + 20.11.43 at Brussilow (Russia)	20.12.43
Graf v. Schönborn-Wiesentheid, Clemens	Major, Kmdre. Stuka-Geschw. 77 + 30.8.44 at Sofia (Bulgaria) as Oberst & Luftattache in Bulgaria	21.7.40
Prinz v. Schönburg-Waldenburg, Wilhelm	Hptm., Chef 1./Pz. Rgt. 31 + 11.6.44 Tilly (Normandy/France) as Major & Kdr. II./Pz. Lehr-Rgt. 130; posthumously promoted to Obstlt.	18.5.41
Schönbusch, Heinrich	Feldw., Zugf. in 1./Pi. Btl. 1059	18.1.45
Schöne, Hans-Wolfgang	Oblt. d.R., Fhr. II./Fhj. G. R. 1242	23.3.45
Schönebeck, Hans	Hptm., Fhr. I./Pz. G. R. 64 + in April 1945	23.3.45
Schöneboom, Dietrich	Oblt. z. See, Kdt. "U 431" + 23.10.43 off Toulon (Mediterranean)	20.10.43
Schöneich, Hans	Obstlt. i.G., Ia 20. Pz.Div.	12.8.44
Schoenert, Rudolf	Oblt. d.R., Staffelkpt. 4./N. J.G. 2 450th Oak Leaves 11.4.44	25.7.42
v. Schönfeld, Carl-August	Oberst, Kdr. G. R. 949 + 16.4.44 in Tarnopol (Russia); posthumously promoted to Gen. Major	4.5.44
Schönfeld, Gerhard	Oblt., Fhr. 3./Pz. Pi. Btl. 40	25.8.42
Schönfeld, Henning	Obstlt., Kdr. Aufkl. Abt. 20 (mot.)	15.8.40
Schönfeld, Kurt	Ofw., Zugf. in 4./Pz. Rgt. 10	22.9.41
Schönfelder, Helmut	Ofw., Flugzeugf. in Stabsst./J.G. 51 "Mölders"	31.3.45
Schönfelder, Manfred	SS-Obersturmbannf., Ia 5. SS-Pz.Div. "Wiking"	23.2.44
Schöning, Wilhelm	Major d.R., Kdr. I./Füs. Rgt. "Feldherrnhalle" 707th Oak Leaves 21.1.45	7.2.44
Schönwald, Wolfram	Oblt. d.R., Fhr. II./G. R. 53	10.9.44
Schöpfel, Gerhard	Hptm., Kdr. III./J.G. 26 "Schlageter"	11.9.40
Schoepffer, Eberhard	Oberst, Kampf-Kdt. v. Elbing	9.2.45
Schörner, Ferdinand	Gen. Major, Kdr. 6. Geb. Div. 398th Oak Leaves 17.2.44 93rd Swords 28.8.44 23rd Diamonds 1.1.45	20.4.41
Schoknecht, Heinz	Lt. d.R., Zugfhr. in s. He. Pz.Jäg. Abt. 666 + 19.3.45 at Krumini (Estonia)	21.1.45
Schollen, Heinrich	Feldw., Zugf. in 2./Pz. G. R. 14	12.11.43
Scholtz, Klaus	Kaptlt., Kdt. "U 108" 123rd Oak Leaves 10.9.42	26.12.41
Scholz, Erich	Gen. Major, Kdr. Kampfgr. "Scholz"	26.12.44

KNIGHT'S CROSS OF THE IRON CROSS

v. Scholz Edler v. Rarancze, Fritz	SS-Oberführer, Kdr. SS-Rgt. "Nordland" 423rd Oak Leaves 12.3.44 85th Swords 8.8.44	18.1.42
Scholz, Fritz	Major, Kdr. I./G. R. 423	21.1.45
Scholz, Gerhard	Ofw., Fhr. 7./G. R. 317	21.9.44
Scholz, Helmut	SS-Untersturmf., Fhr. 7./SS-Freiw. Pz. G. R. 49 "De Ruyter" 591st Oak Leaves 21.9.44	4.6.44
Scholz, Karl	Lt. d.R., Fhr. 14./G. R. 4	9.5.45
Scholz, Siegfried	Hptm., Staffelkpt. I./K.G. 100 + 25.11.42 in Russia	24.3.43
Scholz, Dr. -Ing. Werner	Lt. d.R., Zugf. in 2./St. Gesch. Brig. 279 + 7.5.45 as Oblt. d.R.	5.3.45
Scholze, Georg	Oberst, Kdr. Inf. Lehr-Rgt. + 28.4.45 in Berlin-Potsdam as Gen. Major & Kdr. 20. Pz. Gren. Div.	17.2.43
Schomann, Karl-Heinz	Major, Kdr. I. (K)/L.G. 1	29.10.43
Schonder, Heinrich	Kaptlt., Kdt. "U 77" + 28.6.43 in the Atlantic south-west of Iceland as Kdt. "U 200"; posthumously promoted to Korv. Kpt.	19.8.42
Schopper, Erich	Gen.Lt., Kdr. 81. I.D.	30.4.43
Schormann, Wilhelm	Obergefr., Gruppenf. in 1./Pz. G. R. 74 + 16.10.44 in Russia	18.11.44
Schoßleitner, Reinhard	Lt., Staffelfhr. 8./K.G. 6 + 10.10.43 over Brussels; posthumously promoted to Oblt.	5.2.44
Schott, Albert	Uffz., Zugf. in I./G. R. 1077	10.9.44
Schrader, Hermann	Hptm., Fhr. Div. Füs. Btl. 49	9.12.44
Schrader, Hermann Albert	Oblt., Chef 11./I.R. 16 + 14.6.42 Sevastopol (Russia) as Hptm. & Fhr. III./I.R. 16	29, 5.40
Schrader, Dr. jur. Oskar	Obstlt., Kdr. Flak-Rgt. 104 + 12.9.42 at Stalingrad (Russia) of wounds; posthumously promoted to Oberst	8.9.42
v. Schrader, Otto	Admiral, Kom. Adm. Norwegische Westküste + 19.7.45 at Bergen (Norway) by suicide in captivity	19.8.43
Schrader, Werner	Lt., Fhr. 3./G. R. 17	24.12.44
Schramm, Herbert	Lt., Flugzeugf. in III./J.G. 53 736th Oak Leaves 11.2.45	6.8.41
Schramm, Richard	Owm., Zugf. in I./St. Gesch. Abt. 202 + 17.6.44 posted missing in Kurland	23.12.42
Schrank, Max-Günther	Obstlt., Kdr. I./Geb.Jäg. Rgt. 100	17.7.41
Schrauth, Werner	Oblt., Fhr. I./G. R. 80 + 14,9.43 north-west of Poltawa (Russia)	3.12.43
Schreckenbach, Fritz	Ofw., Zugf. in 4./Pz. Aufkl. Abt. 5	5.9.44
Schreiber, Alfred	Ofw., Zugf. in 6./G. R. 365	20.4.43
Schreiber, Franz	SS-Standartenf., Kdr. SS-Geb.Jäg. Rgt. 12 "Michael Gassmair"	26.12.44

Schreiber, Gustav	SS-Hptscharf., stellv. Fhr. 7./SS-Pz. G. R. 9 "Germania"	2.12.43
Schreiber, Hans-Jürgen	Oblt., Chef 4./Div. Aufkl. Abt. 22	3.1.43
Schreiber, Helmuth	SS-Hptsturmf., Chef 10./SS-Pz. G. R. "Deutschland"	30.7.43
Schreiber, Josef	Feldw., Zugf. in 4./Sturm-Rgt. 14 309th Oak Leaves 5.10.43	31.3.43
Schreiber, Kurt	Hptm., Kdr. II./G. R. 1 "HG"	21.6.43
Schreiber-Volkening, Dr. jur. Hellmuth	Oblt., Chef 9./I.R. 16 + 9.8.42 in Russia as Hptm. in Div. Stab a Pz.Div.	29.5.40
Schrems, Leopold	Obgefr., Gruppenf. in Stabskp./Geb.Jäg. Rgt. 85	27.7.44
Schrepfer, Karl	Oblt., Staffelkpt. 6./Stuka-Geschw. 1 850th Oak Leaves 28.4.45	19.6.42
Schriefer, Martin	Obstlt., Kdr. G. R. 168	24.6.44
Schrijnen, Richard (Remi)	SS-Sturmmann, Richtschtz. in 2./SS-Freiw. Sturmbrigade 6 "Langemarck"	21.9.44
Schroeder, Albert	Hptm., Chef 3./Heeres-Flak-Art. Abt. 287	9.12.44
Schroeder, Ferdinand	Oblt., Chef 5./G. R. 1124	17.3.45
Schröder, Hans-Erwin	Uffz., Geschützf. in 1./Pz.Jäg. Abt. 20 + 10.8.43 in Russia as Feldw.	4.12.41
Schröder, Heinz	Oblt., Chef 4./A.R. 260	4.11.43
Schröder, Dr.-Ing. Kurt	Obstlt., Kdr. Pi. Btl. 74	19.2.42
Schröder, Wilhelm	Obstlt., Kdr. G. R. 580 779th Oak Leaves 13.3.45	26.3.44
Schroedter, Erich	Rittm., Kdr. Pz. Aufkl. Abt. "GD" 808th Oak Leaves 28.3.45	23.10.44
Schroepfer, Michael	Obgefr., Richtschtz. in 14./I.R. 111	27.12.41
Schroer, Werner	Lt., Staffelf. 8./J.G. 27 268th Oak Leaves 2.8.43 144th Swords 19.4.45	20.10.42
Schroeteler, Heinrich	Kaptlt., Kdt. "U 1023"	2.5.45
Schroeter, Anton	Oblt., Fhr. Div. Füs. Btl. 126 + 31.1.45	26.3.44
Schröter, Erich	Hptm., Kdr. I./I.R. 120 (mot.) + 26.5.42 in Russia as Major	8.9.41
Schröter, Fritz	Oblt., Staffelkpt. 10./J.G. 2 "Richthofen"	24.9.42
v. Schroeter, Horst	Oblt. z. See, Kdt. "U 123"	1.6.44
Schroth, Walther	Gen.D.Inf., Kom.Gen. XII. A.K. + 6.10.44 accidentally at Wiesbaden as Befehlsh. in Wehrkreis II (Wiesbaden)	9.7.41
Schrupp, Ernst	Hptm., Fhr. 3./A.R. 1176	28.3.45
Schubach, Joachim	SS-Sturmbannf., Kdr. II./SS-Pz. -G. R. "Totenkopf "	3.4.43
Schubert,	Gefr. in Festung Glogau (Lower Silesia)	9.5.45
Schubert, Albrecht	Gen.D.Inf., Kom.Gen. XXIII. A.K.	17.9.41

KNIGHT'S CROSS OF THE IRON CROSS

Schubert, Carl-Heinz	Lt., Fhr. 9./Pz. A.R. 2	18.4.43
Schubert, Günther	Obstlt., Kdr. I./I.R. 49 + 30.8.41 in Russia as Oberst & Rgt. Kdr.	5.6.40
Schubert, Gustav	Ofw., Flugzeugf. in 8./Stuka-Geschw. 1 629th Oak Leaves 24.10.44	22.5.43
Schubert, Paul-Georg	Ofw., Zugf. in 3./Pi. Btl. 3 (mot.)	2.3.44
Schuck, Josef	Oblt. d.R., Fhr. 3./G. R. 351 + 19.7.44 in Russia as Hptm. d.R.	4.6.44
Schuck, Walter	Ofw., Flugzeugf. in 7./J.G. 5 616th Oak Leaves 30.9.44	8.4.44
Schübel, Helmut	Oblt., Staffelkpt. 10. (Pz.)/S.G. 2 "Immelmann" + 25.8.44 in hospital at Buzau (Rumania) of wounds; posthumously promoted to Hptm.	18.11.44
Schüler, Hans	Major, Kdr. I.R. 633 + 10.12.44 as Oberst	5.8.40
Schüler, Heinrich	Hptm. d.R., Fhr. II./I.R. 525 218th Oak Leaves 2.4.43	18.9.42
Schüler, Herbert	Ofw., Zugf. in 9./G. R. 697	12.8.44
Schülke, Willi	Oblt., Fhr. III./Ski-Jäg. Rgt. 1 740th Oak Leaves 16.2.45	28.10.44
Schümers, Karl	SS-Sturmbannfhr. & Major der Schupo, Kdr. II./SS-Pol. Schtz. Rgt. 1 + 18.8.44 Arta (Greece) as SS-Standartenf. & Oberst der Schupo & stellv. Fhr. 4. SS-Pol. Pz. Gr. Div.	30.9.42
Schünemann, Otto	Oberst, Kdr. I. R. 184 339th Oak Leaves 28.11.43	20.12.41
Schürmann, Dipl.-Ing. Paul	Gen. Major, Kdr. 25. Pz. Gren. Div.	2.9.44
Schürmeyer, Fritz	Oblt., Staffelkpt. 3. (F)/Aufkl. Gr. Ob. d. Lw.	1.10.40
Schüßler, Josef	Feldw., Zugf. in 5./G. R. 106	14.6.43
Schuett, Christian	Ofw., Flugzeugf. in 1./S.G. 77 + April 1945 at Ingolstadt	18.11.44
Schütt, Fritz	Hptm. d.R., Fhr. II./G. R. 502	26.3.43
Schütt, Kurt	Major, Kdr. Feld-Ers. Btl. 299	14.2.45
Schütte, Ludwig	Major, Kdr. Div. Füs. Btl. 131	23.2.44
Schütten, Wilhelm	Ofw., Zugf. in 3./Pz. G. R. 4	4.6.44
Schütz, Erwin	Hptm., Kdr. II./G. R. 1127	11.5.45
v. Schütz, Harald	Major, Kdr. Pz. Aufkl. Abt. 7 + 9.5.45 in Russia	5.4.45
Schütz, Hermann	Hptm. d.R., Fhr. I./G. R. 273	21.4.44
Schütze, Rudolf	Lt., Flugzeugf. in Wettererkundungsstaffel 5 + 26.8.43 Banak (Arctic Sea) as Oblt.	14.3.43
Schütze, Viktor	Korv. Kpt., Kdt. "U 103" 23rd Oak Leaves 14.7.41	11.12.40

ELITE OF THE THIRD REICH

Schug, Otto	Uffz., Gruppenfhr. in 2./Pi. Btl. 235	3.11.44
Schuhart, Otto	Kaptlt., Kdt. "U 29"	16.5.40
Schuhmacher, Leo (17)	Lt., Flugzeugf. in II./J.G. 1	1.3.45
Schuldt, Hinrich	SS-Obersturmbannf., Kdr. SS-Totenkopf-Rgt. 4 220th Oak Leaves 2.4.43 56th Swords 25.3.44	5.4.42
Graf v. d. Schulenburg, Wolf-Werner	Major z. V., Kdr. I./Fsch. Jäg. Rgt. 1 + 15.7.44 at St. Lo (Normandy/France) as Kdr. Fsch. Jäg. Rgt. 13; posthumously promoted Obstlt.	20.6.43
Schuler, Emil	Oberst, Kdr. Geb.Jäg. Rgt. 218	9.12.44
Schuller, Sebastian	Uffz., Geschützf. in 1./Pz.Jäg. Abt. 10 (mot.)	31.7.43
Schulte, Ernst	Obgefr., Geschützf. in 1./Flak-Rgt. 14 (mot.) + 17.4.42 in Russia of wounds	23.6.42
Schulte, Franz	Feldw., Flugzeugf. in 6./J.G. 77 + 12.8.42 at Woronesh (Russia)	24.9.42
Schulte, Helmuth	Hptm., Kdr. II./N. J.G. 6	17.4.45
Schulte, Hubert	Hptm. d.R., Fhr. I./Pz. G. R. 1 Führer-Begleit-Div.	30.4.45
Schulte-Heuthaus, Hermann	Obstlt., Kdr. Kradschtz. Btl. 25	23.1.42
Schultz, Erich	Hptm., Fhr. I./G. R. 94	22.1.44
Schultz, Fritz-Rudolf	Hptm. d.R., Kdr. I./Pz. Rgt. 35 636th Oak Leaves 28.10.44	21.4.44
Schultz, Harald	Gen. Major, Kdr. 24. I.D.	5.4.45
Schultz, Otto	Ofw., Flugzeugf. in 4./J.G. 51 "Mölders"	14.3.43
Schultz, Paul	Oberst, Kdr. I.R. 308 284th Oak Leaves 26.8.43	3.9.42
Schultz, Willi	Feldw., Flugzeugf. in 6./K.G. 30	19.6.40
Schultze, Heinz-Otto	Kaptlt., Kdt. "U 432" + 25.11.43 in south Atlantic as Kdt. "U 849"; posthumously promoted to Korv. Kpt.	9.7.42
Schultze, Herbert-Emil	Kaptlt., Kdt. "U 48" 15th Oak Leaves 12.6.41	1.3.40
Schulz, Adalbert	Hptm., Chef I./Pz. Rgt. 25 47th Oak Leaves 31.12.41 33rd Swords 6.8.43 9th Diamonds 14.12.43	29.9.40
Schulz, Artur	Major, Kdr. I./I.R. 233	7.8.42
Schulz, Bruno-Richard	Ofw., Flugzeugf. in 4./S.G. 77 + 25.8.44 at Brünn (Czechoslovakia) as Flugzeugfhr. in I./S.G. 152	29.10.44
Schulz, Dr. Erich	Major d.R., Kdr. I./G. R. 6	10.9.44
Schulz, Friedrich	Oberst i.G., Chef d. Gen. St. XXXXIII. A.K. 428th Oak Leaves 20.3.44 135th Swords 26.2.45	29.3.42
Schulz, Friedrich	Ofw., Zugf. in Feldersatz-Btl. 361	9.6.44

KNIGHT'S CROSS OF THE IRON CROSS

Schulz, Hans-Otto	Oblt., Chef 4./le. Flak-Abt. 753	9.1.45
Schulz, Heinrich	Gefr., Flammenwerferschtz. in 3./Pi. Btl. 161	18.10.41
Schulz, Helmut	Lt., Fhr. 5./G. R. 96	20.10.44
Schulz, Johannes	Major, Kdr. I./I.R. 49	6.10.41
Schulz, Dr. phil. Johannes	Oberst, Kdr. Pz. G. R. 10 + 27.11.43 at Kriwoi Rog (Russia) as Fhr. 9. Pz.Div.; posthumously promoted to Gen. Major	19.9.43
Schulz, Karl	Major d.R., Kdr. I./I.R. 699	18.9.42
Schulz, Karl	Oblt. z. See d.R., Gruppenf. & Kdt. "VP 1509" in 15. Vorpostenflottille	26.8.44
Schulz, Karl-Heinrich	Gen. Major, Chef d. Gen. St. Luftflotte 4	9.6.44
Schutz, Karl-Heinz-Lepel	Oblt. d.R., Chef 6./G. R. 552	13.9.43
Schulz, Karl-Lothar	Hptm., Kdr. III./Fsch. Jäg. Rgt. 1 459th Oak Leaves 20.4.44 112th Swords 18.11.44	24.5.40
Schulz, Ludwig	Major, Kdr. I./K.G. 76 747th Oak Leaves 19.2.45	16.8.40
Schulz, Manfred	Hptm., Kdr. I./G. R. 23	10.9.44
Schulz, Otto	Oblt., Chef 3./I.R. 125 + 6.4.41	19.6.40
Schulz, Otto	Ofw., Flugzeugf. in II./J.G. 27 + 7.6.42 at Sidi Rezegh (North Africa) as Oblt. posted missing	22.2.42
Schulz, Otto	Konteradrniral, Seekommandant Crimea	17.5.44
Schulz, Wilhelm	Kaptlt., Kdt. "U 124"	4.4. 41
Schulz-Merkel, Dr. med. Hans-Joachim	Stabsarzt, Truppenarzt I./Pz. Rgt. 35	23.12.43
Schulz-Streeck, Karlheinz	SS-Sturmbannf. d.R., Kdr. SS-St. Gesch. Abt. 11 "Nordland"	9.5.45
Schulze, Franz-Joseph	Oblt., Chef 3./Flak-Sturm-Rgt. 241	30.11.44
Schulze, Hans-Christian	SS-Standartenf. & Oberst d. Schupo, Kdr. SS-Pol. Schützen-Rgt. 2 + 13.9.41 at Luga in a field hospital at Nikolajewska (Russia) of wounds; posthumously promoted to SS-Brigadef. & Gen. Major d. Pol.	11.9.41
Schulze, Heinrich	Stabsfeldw., Zugf. in 2./Pz. Abt. 116 + 25.3.45 as Oblt.	14.8.43
Schulze, Herbert	SS-Sturmbannf, Kdr. II./SS-Pz. G. K. 4 "Der Führer"	16.12.43
Schulze, Johannes	Hptm. d.R., Kdr. I./G. R. 191	14.1.45
Schulze, Kurt	Major, Kdr. I./Pz. G. R. 3	14.4. 45
Schulze, Otto	Lt. d.R., Fhr. 8./I.R. 386	19.6.42
Schulze, Paul	Hptm., Kdr. II./Pz. Rgt. 21 538th Oak Leaves 28.7.44	30.12.43
Schulze, Walter	Feldw., Zugf. in 6./G. R. 9	5.4.44

Schulze, Werner	Major d.R., Kdr. II./I.R. 510 557th Oak Leaves 23.8.44	1.3.42
Schulze, Dr. Wolfgang	Oblt., Flugzeugf. in 1. (H)/Aufkl. Gr. 5	17.3.45
Schulze-Dickow, Fritz	Oblt., Staffelkpt. 8./Z.G. 26 "Horst Wessel"	7.3.42
Schulze-Hinrichs, Alfred	Kapt. z. See, Chef 6. Zerstörerflottille	15.6.43
Schumacher, Carl-Alfred	Obstlt., Kmdre. J.G. 1	21.7.40
Schumacher, Gerd	Lt. d.R., Fhr. 5./G. R. 337 + 10.12.43 at Schitomir (Russia)	15.1.44
Schumacher, Kurt	SS-Untersturmf., Fhr. 3./SS-Pz. Rgt. 5 "Wiking" + 20.3.45 in Stuhlweißenburg (Hungary), in an accident, as SS-Obersturmf.	4.5.44
Schumacher, Paul	Oblt. d.R., Chef 2./Gr. Rgt. 427	11.12.43
Schumann, Heinz	Hptm., Staffelkpt. 10./J.G. 2 "Richthofen" + 8.11.43 at Bastogne (Belgium) as Major & Kmdr. S. K.G. 10 in aerial combat	18.3.43
Schunck, Karl	Hptm., Fhr. II./G. R. 157	9.6.44
Schuncke, Wilhelm	Oblt. d.R., Fhr. II./Sturm-Rgt. AOK 4	28.3.45
Schurig, Hans	Obstlt., Kdr. G. R. 260 missing at Stalingrad (Russia) as Oberst.	28.1.43
Schurreit, Gerhard	Ofw., Zugf. in 4./G. R. 44	26.11.44
Schury, Otto	Major, Kdr. II./Geb.Jäg. Rgt. 100 592nd Oak Leaves 21.9.44	17.7.41
Schuss, Joseph	Obgefr., MG-Schütze in 3./I.R. 520	4.9.42
Schuster, Erich	Feldw., Gruppenf. in 3./Fsch. Jäg. Sturm-Rgt. + 11.1.43 Tunisia (North Africa) as Chef 1./Fsch. Jäg. Rgt. 5; posthumously promoted to Oblt.	21.8.41
Schuster, Karl	Obgefr., Richtschtz. in 8./Pz. G. R. 126	5.2.45
Schwabach, Theo	Oblt., Bttr. Chef in I./Flak-Rgt. 33	30.6.41
Schwabenberger, Josef	Feldw., Zugf. in 2./G. R. 467 + 30.3.44 at Krasniza(Russia) as Ofw. & stellv. Kp. Fhr.	10.9.43
Schwärzel, Günther	Hptm., Staffelkpt. 9./Stuka-Geschw. 2 "Immelmann" + 26.9.42 in a field hospital at Kursk (Russia) of wounds as stellv. Kdr. III./Stuka-Geschw. 2	22.6.41
Schwaiger, Franz	Uffz., Flugzeugf. in 6./J.G. 3 "Udet" + 24.4.44 at Rain on Lech during a forced landing as Lt. & Staffelfhr. 1./J.G. 3 "Udet"	29.10.42
Schwalb, Helmut	Hptm., Chef 1./St. Gesch. Brig. 190	23.8.44
Schwalbe, Eugen-Felix	Oberst, Kdr. I.R. 461	13.7.40
Schwamberger, Richard	Hptm., Kdr. III./G. R. 117	20.4.43
Schwanbeck, Walter	Uffz., Gruppenf. in 2./Reiter-Rgt. 31	5.10.44
Schwaneberg, Edgar	Hptm., Staffelkpt. 2./Transp. Geschw. 3	26.3.44
Schwanitz, Joachim	Hptm., Fhr. II11./G. R. 3	9.5.45

Name	Details	Date
Schwappacher, Oskar	SS-Hptsturmf., Kdr. V./SS-Art. Ausb. & Ers. Rgt. & Fhr. of a Kampfgruppe + 2.5.45 near the Reichskanzlei Berlin of wounds as SS-Sturmbannf.	26.12.44
Schwark, Hugo	Oblt. d.R., Fhr. I./Gren. Rgt. 911	23.10.44
Schwarm, Kurt	Obgefr., Kradmelder in Stab/Pz. Gren. Rgt. 98	11.1.45
Schwarting, Heinrich	Hptm. d.R., Chef 6./I.R. 154 + 26.8.41 at Georgijewski in north Russia as Major d.R. & Kdr. III./I.R. 154	15.8.40
Schwartzkopff, Günter	Oberst, Kmdr. Stuka-Geschw. 77 + 14.5.40 at Le Chesne-Sedan (France); posthumously promoted to Gen. Major	24.11.40
Schwarz, Friedrich	Oblt. d.R., Fhr. 3./Pz. G. R. 35 + 4.3.45 of wounds	21.1.45
Schwarz, Heinrich	Obgefr., Richtkan. in 10./A.R. 3 (mot.)	15.1.43
Schwarz, Manfred	Lt. d.R., Chef 1./Pz.Jäg. Abt. 10 (mot.)	25.8.41
Schwarzenbacher, Josef	Uffz. d.R., Geschützf. in 1./St. Gesch. Brig. 912 + 16.8.44 at Birsen (Riga/Latvia) as Wm. d.R.	27.8.44
Schwarzer, Enül-Gerhard	Oblt. d.R., Adj. II./A.R. 158	23.2.44
Schwarzer, Otto	Hptm., Kdr. I./I.R. 187	6.10.42
Schwarzgruber, Rudolf	Objäg., s. MG-Fhr. in 10./Geb.Jäg. Rgt. 13	30.4.45
Schwarzmann, Alfred	Oblt., Zugf. in 8./Fsch. Jäg. Rgt. 1	24.5.40
Schwarzrock, Rudolf (Udo)	Major, Kdr. 1./Pz. G. R. "GD"	19.8.44
Schwede, Hugo	Lt., Fhr. Nachr. Zug/G. R. 82 + 10.11.43 north-west of Tschernigow (Russia)	5.1.44
v. Schwedler, Viktor	Gen. d. Inf, Kom.Gen. IV. A.K.	29.6.40
Schwegler, Matthias	Oblt., Staffelkpt. in I./K.G. 51 + 18.4.45 at Neuses (Ansbach) as Major	18.12.41
Schweickhardt, Heinrich	Oblt., Staffelkpt. in 8./K.G. 76 138th Oak Leaves 30.10.42	4.2.42
Schweiger, Franz	Oblt., Chef 8./Flak-Rgt. 25 + 26.10.43 in Italy as Hptm. & Abt.Kdr.	14.2.42
Schweim, Heinz-Herbert	Major i.G., Ia Fsch. Pz. Gren. Div. 2 "HG"	28.2.45
Schweitzer, Heinz	Gefr., MG-Schtz. 1 i. d. 13./Pz. G. R. 103	9.7.44
Schweitzer, Willi (7)	SS-Sturmbannfhr., Kdr. SS-Pz. Gr. Ausb. Btl. 11 Fhr. at Kampfgruppe	24.4. 45
Schweizer, Heinz	Hptm. (W), Fhr. Sprengkdo. 1/IV Ratingen-Düsseldorf	28.6.43
Schweizer, Ignatz	Feldw., Flugzeugf. in 8./S.G. 10 + 26.10.44 at Budapest (Hungary)	30.9.44
Schwender, Herbert	Major, Fhr. G. R. 3 442nd Oak Leaves 6.4.44	11.3.43

Name	Details	Date
Schwerdfeger, Johann	Feldw., Zugf. in 1./Jäger-Rgt. 228 474th Oak Leaves 14.5.44	17.5.43
v. Schwerin, Albert	Lt. d.R., Flugzeugf. in I./K.G. 26 + 19.11.40 over England	31.7.40
Graf v. Schwerin, Gerhard	Oberst, Kdr. I.R. 76 (mot.) 240th Oak Leaves 17.5.43 41st Swords 4.11.43	17.1.42
Schwerin, Werner	Feldw., Zugf. in 9./Füs. Rgt. 27	21.12.44
Schwerk, Otto	Hptm., Kdr. I./G. R. 96 + 2.5.45 at Wittstock (Krs. Glienicke)	15.7.44
Schwermann, Paul	Hptm., Fhr. He. Fla. Abt. 315 + 3.4.45 at Emsbüren (Krs. Rheine)	11.3.45
Schwertherr, Josef	Uffz., Gruppenf. i. I./I.R. 77 + 21.1.43 on the middle Don (Russia) as Feldw. & Zugfhr.	6.10.42
Schwieger, Hans-Gunnar	Major, Kdr. Div. Füs. Btl. 72	23.9.43
Schwill, Helmut	Hptm., Fhr. I./G. R. 45	17.3,44
Schwing, Hellmuth	Major, Kdr. Pz. Pi. Btl. 39	30.12.43
Schwirblat, Hans	Lt., Flugzeugf. in 1./S.G. 2 "Immelmann"	20.7.44
Schwöppe, Heinz	Hptm., Kdr. Feld-Ers. Btl. 21 (L)	26.3.45
v. Scotti, Friedrich	Gen.Lt., Kdr. 227. I.D.	8.6.43
Frhr. v. Seckendorff, Erich	Obstlt., Kdr. Kradschtz. Btl. 6 + 23.9.44 at Lagarde (France) as Kdr. 113. Pz. Brig.; posthumously promoted to Gen. Major	4.9.40
Seckler, Karl	Hptm., Kdr. 11./Pz. G. R. 13 + 17.7.44 in Russia; posthumously promoted to Major	23.8,44
Seebach, Walter	SS-Obersturmf., Fhr. 5./SS-Freiw. Pz. G. R. 24 "Danmark"	12.3.44
v. Seebeck, Bernhard-Georg	Hptm., Fhr. I./G. R. 361 (mot.)	14.10.44
Seeber, Helmut	Hptm., Kdr. II./Jäger-Rgt. 229	5.4.45
Seeber, Werner	Obgefr., Richtschtz. i. d. 14./G. R. 952	16.4.44
Seeger, Günther	Lt., Flugzeugf. in 7./J.G. 53	26.3.44
Seela, Max	SS-Hptsturmf., Chef 3./SS-Pi. Btl. "Totenkopf"	3.5.42
Seelrnann, Georg	Lt., Staffelkpt. II./J.G. 51	6.10.41
Sehringer, Hans	Oblt., Flugzeugf. in 2. (F)/Aufkl. Gr. 123	9.12.42
Seib, Robert	Oblt., Staffelkpt. 6./K.G. 55	9.10.43
Seibel, Josef	Lt. d.R., Fhr. I./G. R. 332	4.5.44
Seibicke, Günther	Kaptlt., Kdt. "U 436" + 3.6.43 in Atlantik; posthumously promoted to Korv. Kpt.	27.3.43
Seibold, Emil (6)	SS-Hptscharf., Zugfhr. in 8./SS-Pz. Rgt. 2 "Das Reich"	6.5.45
Seidel, Erich	Oberst, Kdr. G. R. 236 + 11.4.45 at Dobel-Wildbach (Schwarzwald) as Gen. -Major and Kdr. 257. Volks. Gr. Div.	10.9.44
Seidel, Dr. jur. Heinrich	Oblt., Fhr. II./I.R. 422	14.12.41

KNIGHT'S CROSS OF THE IRON CROSS

Seidemann, Hans	Oberst i.G., Chef d. Gen. St. Luftflotte 2 658th Oak Leaves 18.11.44	20.3.42
Seidensticker, August	Major, Fhr. schw. Pz. Abt. 504	17.7.43
Seidenstücker, Dr. jur. Herbert	Hptm. d.R., Kdr. II./G. R. 428	18.11.43
Seidl, Josef	Ofw., Zugf. in G. R. 520	15.5.44
Seifert, Ernst	Major, Kdr. II./schw. A.R. 48	29.9.40
Seifert, Hans	Lt., Zugf. in 13./G. R. 952 + 26.3.44 east of Brody (Russia); posthumously promoted to Oblt.	9.6.44
Seifert, Johannes	Hptm., Kdr. I./J.G. 26 "Schlageter" + 25.11.43 shot down over Bethune (France) as Kdr. II./J.G. 26; posthumously promoted to Obstlt.	7.6.42
Seifert, Werner	Hptm. d.R., Kdr. I./G. R. 95	2.9.44
Seiffert, Heinz	Oblt., Staffelkpt. 3./K.G. 3 + 13.1.45 over the Rhine when bailing out as Oblt. & Staffelkpt. 12./J.G. 54	31.12.43
Seiler, Alfred	Lt., Fhr. Div. Stabskp. 389. I.D.	5.4.45
Seiler, Herbert	Lt. d.R., Fhr. II./G. R. 445	7.9.43
Seiler, Reinhard	Hptm., Kdr. III./J.G. 54 419th Oak Leaves 2.3.44	20.12.41
Seitz, Adolf	Major, Kdr. II./Geb.Jäg. Rgt. 99	5.8.40
Seitz, Hermann	Obstlt., Kdr. Aufkl. Abt. 20 (mot.) 140th Oak Leaves 31.10.42	12.4.42
Seitz, Rudolf	SS-Unterscharfhr. & Wachtm. d. Schupo, Geschützf. in I./SS-Pol. Pz.Jäg. Abt.	21.10.42
Sekund, Alfred	Wachtm., Vorgesch. Beob. in 6./A.R. 11	10.9.44
Selhorst, Eugen	Oblt., Fhr. I./I.R. 186	6.10.42
Selinger, Karl	Feldw., Zugf. in Stabskp. II./. Geb.Jäg. Rgt. 144	12.12.44
Sell, Hans-Joachim	Hptm., Kdr. Pz. Aufkl. Abt. 8	14.4. 45
Sell, Hermann	Major, Fhr. Flak-Rgt. 48 (mot.) + 11.5.1945 killed by Czech insurgents	9.6.44
Sell, Wilhelm	Major, Kdr. Nahaufkl. Gruppe 5	5.9.44
Selle, Erich	Hptm. d.R., Chef 12./I.R. 410 + 1.2.45 as Btl. Kdr.	9.12.42
Semelka, Waldemar	Lt., Flugzeugf. in 4./J.G. 52 + 21.8.42 at Stalingrad (Russia)	4.9.42
Semmer, Wolfgang	Lt., Chef 5./I.R. 85	24.6.40
Sempert, Günther	Hptm., Chef 5./Fsch. Pz.Jäg. Abt. 1	30.9.44
Semrau, Norbert	Lt. d.R., Zugf. in I./G. R. 29 (mot.)	6.4.44
Semrau, Paul	Hptm., Staffelkpt. 3./NJ.G. 2 841st Oak Leaves 17.4.45	7.10.42

Semrau, Paul	Lt., Fhr. 7./Pz. G. R. 25	30.9.44
Senft v. Pilsach, Ott-Friedrich	Oblt., Chef 4./Pz. Rgt. 5	27.6.41
Senft, Josef	Lt., Fhr. 6./G. R. 1122	11.3.45
v. Senger u. Etterlin, Fridolin	Gen. Major, Kdr. 17. Pz.Div. 439th Oak Leaves 5.4.44	8.2.43
Senghas, Paul	SS-Obersturmf., Fhr. I./SS-Pz. Rgt. 5 "Wiking"	11.12.44
Sengschmidt, Fritz	Oblt., Flugzeugf. in 1./K.G. 2 + 11.1.44 at Elbingerode (Harz) as Oblt. & Staffelkpt, 2./Z.G. 76	24.9.42
Sensbergs, Karlis (19)	Waffen-Unterscharführer, Gruppenfhr. of the Alarm-Einheit of 19. SS-Waffen-Gren. Div. + 1945 in Berlin	11.5.45
Sensfuß, Franz	Gen.Lt., Kdr. 212. I.D. 881st Oak Leaves 9.5.45	22.8.44
Serck, Julius	Owm., Zugf. in 3./St. Gesch. Brig. 300	23.3.45
Settner, Kurt	Hptm., Fhr. II./G. R. 1076	18.11.44
Setz, Heinrich	Oblt., Staffelkpt. 4./J.G. 77 102nd Oak Leaves 23.6.42	31.12.41
Seuss, Richard	Oblt. (MA) d.R., Chef Marine-Küsten-Bttr. "Ile de Cezembre" in Mar. Art. Abt. 608 577th Oak Leaves 2.9.44	15.8.44
Severloh, Rudolf	Lt., Fhr. 11./G. R. 17	25.1.45
Seyd, Otto	Hptm., Fhr. 1./G. R. 407 + 21.2.45	5.3.45
v. Seydlitz-Kurzbach, Walther	Gen. Major, Kdr. 12. I.D. 54th Oak Leaves 31.12.41	15.8.40
Seyfahrt, Kurt	Hptm., Staffelkpt. Stabsstaffel/K.G. 2	5.9.44
Seyffardt, Fritz	Lt., Flugzeugf. in 5./S.G. 2 "Immelmann"	8.8.44
Seyffardt, Paul	Oberst, Kdr. I.R. 111	17.1.42
Seyrl, Rudolf	Hptm., Fhr. I./Pz. G. R. 73	14.5.44
Sibbel, Emil	Ofw., Zugf. in 5./G. R. 151	28.3.45
Sichart v. Sichartshofen, Wolfg.	Major, Fhr. G. R. 43 + 13.2.45 in East Prussia as Obstlt.	4.5.44
Sichelschmidt, Herbert	Major, Kdr. St. Gesch. Brig. 210 + 17.7.44 at a main dressing station, Sokal (Russia) of wounds	4.5.44
Siebenthaler, Richard	Ofw., Zugf. in 6./Pz. Rgt. 2	14.4. 45
Sieber, Bernhard	Oberst, Kdr. Jäger-Rgt. 228 + 21.9.44 at Medzilaberge (Russia)	24.6.44
Sieber, Horst	Lt., Fhr. Jagdpz. Kp. 1257	9.5.45
Sieberg, Friedrich	Obstlt., Kdr. Pz. Rgt. 10 + 3.11,43 in hospital at Kirowograd (Russia) as Kdr. 14. Pz.Div. of wounds; posthumously promoted to Gen.Lt.	16.6.40

Name	Details	Date
Siebert, Franz	Ofw., Zugf. in 3./Pz.Jäg. Abt. 306	9.7.44
Siebert, Friedrich	Gen.Lt., Kdr. 44 in	18.1.41
Siebken, Bernhard	SS-Obersturmbannf., Kdr. SS-Pz. G. R. 2 "LSSAH" + 20.1.1949 hanged by a British court in Hameln	17.4.45
Sieckenius, Rudolf	Obstlt., Kdr. Pz. Rgt. 2 + 28.4.45 Berlin (Märkisch-Buchholz) (suicide) as Gen. Major & Kdr. 391. Inf. Div.	17.9.41
Sieder, Heinz	Oblt. z. See, Kdt. "U 984" + 26.8.44 Bay of Biscay west of Brest	8.7.44
Siegel, Hans	SS-Hauptsturmf., Chef 8./SS-Pz. Rgt. 12 "Hitlerjugend"	23.8.44
Siegel, Rudolf	Obstlt. d.R., Kdr. G. R. 1084 Feldw., Zugf. in 3./I.R. 133	14.2.45
Sieger, Robert	+1.4.45 at Hünfeld as Lt.	14.12.41
Siegert, Wilhelm	Ofw., Zugf. in Stabskp./G. R. 1410	11.4.44
Siegler, Hans	Jäger, MG-Schtz. 1 in 5./Jäger-Rgt. 49	12.8.44
Siegler, Peter	Feldw., Flugzeugf. in 3./J.G. 54 + 24.9.42 over Leningrad (Russia)	3.11.42
Siegling, Alfred	SS-Oberscharf., Spähtruppf. in I./SS-Pz. Aufkl. Abt. "Das Reich"	2.12.43
Siegmund, Bernhard	Oblt., Chef I./G. R. 7	14.4. 45
v. Siegroth, Joachim	Oberst, Kdr. of a Kampfgruppe of Fhj. -Schule VI der Inf. Metz 878th Oak Leaves 9.5.45	18.10.44
Sielemann, Kurt	Uffz. in 2./G. R. 1129	14.4. 45
Sieler, Ernst	Oberst, Kdr. I.R. 46 502nd Oak Leaves 24.6.44	12.9.41
Sieling, Bruno	Oblt. d.R., Fhr. I./G. R. 401	5.3.45
Sierts, Friedrich	Oberst d.R., Kdr. G. R. 438	23.10.44
Sievers, Karl	Gen. Major, Kdr. 719. I.D.	18.11.44
Sievers, Walther	Hptm. d.R., Kdr. III./I.R. 415 379th Oak Leaves 29.1.44	19.12.42
Sievert, Hans-Carl	Oblt., Staffelkpt. in 2./K.G. 4 "General Wever"	30.12.42
Siewert, Curt	Gen. Major, Kdr. 58. I.D.	29.2.44
Sigel, Walter	Hptm., Kdr. I/Stuka-Geschw. 3 116th Oak Leaves 2.9.42	21.7.40
Siggel, Hermann	Obstlt., Kdr. G. R. 172 552nd Oak Leaves 16.8.44	9.6.44
Sigmund, Hans	SS-Oberscharf., Zugf. in 11./SS-Pz. G. R. 9 "Germania"	5.4.45
Sigmund, Rudolf	Hptm., Staffelkpt. 11./N. J.G. 1 + 3.10.43 over Kassel by German flak as Kdr. III./N. J.G. 3	2.8.43
Silzner, Franz	Oblt. d.R., Chef 11./I.R. 501	21.10.42

Name	Details	Date
Simke, Willy	SS-Hauptscharf., Zugf. in 5./SS-Pz. Rgt. "Das Reich"	16.12.43
Simm, Alfred	Stabsfw., Zugf. in 2./I.R. 31 832nd Oak Leaves 14.4. 45	27.7.41
Simon, Herbert	Obstlt., Kdr. Schtz. Rgt. 112	24.7.41
Simon, Klaus	Hptm. z. V., Kdr. I./G. R. 89	23.2.44
Simon, Ludwig	Lt. d.R., Fhr. 2./Pz. G. R. 35	5.3.45
Simon, Max	SS-Oberf., Kdr. SS-Totenkopf-Inf.Rgt. I 639th Oak Leaves 28.10.44	20.10.41
Simoneit, Dr. phil. habil. Max	Hptm. d.R., Chef Stabskp./G. R. 919	23.6.44
Simons, Arnold	Major, Fbr. Inf.Rgt. 190 + 1943 in Stalingrad (Russia)	4.3.42
Simons, Gerhard	Oblt. d.R., Zugf. Rgt. Nachr. Zug/A.R. 240 547th Oak Leaves 11.8.44	29.2.44
Simsch, Siegfried	Oblt., Staffelkpt. 5./J.G. 52 + 8.6.44 shot down over Rennes (France) as Hptm. & Kdr. I./J.G. 11	1.7.42
Singer, Herbert (19)	Hptm., Kdr. II./Füs. Rgt. 22	5.5.45
Sinn, Helmut	Oblt., Beobachter in 2. (F)/Aufkl. Gr. 22	31.12.43
Sinnhuber, Johann	Gen.Lt., Kdr. 28. I.D.	5.7.41
Sinning, Helmut	Feldw., Zugf. in 6./G. R. 181	15.3.44
Sinram, Klaus	Major, Fhr. G. R. 309	23.10.44
Sintzenich, Rudolf	Gen. Major, Kdr. 33. I.D.	15.8.40
Sinzinger, Adolf	Oberst, Kdr. I. R. 257	9.2.42
Siry, Maximilian	Gen. Major, Kdr. 246. I.D.	13.6.42
Sitt, Wilhelm (1)	Btl. Fhr. 1. Volkssturm Köln, Sprengmeister der Polizei + 7.3.45 in Köln/Rhein	7.2.45
Sitter, Günther	SS-Hauptsturmf., Fhr. II./SS-Pz. G. R. 10 "Westland" + 25.7.44 in Russia accidentally as SS-Sturmbannfhr.	12.9.43
v. Sivers, Karl	Major, Kdr. I./Pz. Rgt. 15 + 10.4.44 at Proskuroff (Russia) as Kdr. Pz. Rgt. 15; posthumously promoted to Obstlt.	6.3.44
Six, Walter	Feldw., Zugf. in 4. (MG)/Pz. G. R. 12 +20.12.43 at Retschiza (Russia)	5.4.44
Sixt, Friedrich	Gen.Lt., Kdr. 50 I.D. 772nd Oak Leaves 11.3.45	17.12.43
Sixt v. Armin, Hans-Heinrich	Gen.Lt., Kdr. 95. I.D. + 1.4.52 in Soviet captivity; final post Kdr. 113 Inf. Div.	22.9.41
Skorczewski, Wolfgang	Oblt., Staffeikpt. in I./K.G. 27 "Boelcke"	17.9.41

Name	Rank/Unit	Date
Skorzeny, Dipl.-Ing. Otto	SS-Hauptsturmf. d.R., Kdr. des Sonderverbandes z.b.V. Friedenthal 826th Oak Leaves 9.4.45	13.9.43
Skrzipek, Eduard	Oblt., Flugzeugf. in 5./K.G. 27 "Boelcke" 509th Oak Leaves 24.6.44	16.4.43
Smidt, Alfred-Karl	Kapt. z. See, Kdt. Zerstörer "Z 27"	15.6.43
Smola, Rudolf	Oblt., Staffelfhr. 5./S.G. 2 "Immelmann" + 27.3.45 at Zinten (East Prussia) as Hptm. & Kdr. I./S.G. 3	27.7.44
Smollich, Rudolf	Oblt., Fhr. Div. Füs. Btl. 168	16.11.44
Sniers, Hubert	Lt., Fhr. 9./Fsch. Jäg. Rgt. 15	24.10.44
Snoek, August	Oblt. d.R., stellv. Fhr. Pz. Pi. Btl. 209 + 6.10.44 at Coincourt (Lothringen)	5.11.44
Sobotta, Paul	Lt. d.R., Fhr. 9./G. R. 110	26.6.44
Sochatzy, Kurt	Oblt., Staffelkpt. 7./J.G. 3	12.8.41
Socke, Erich	Ofw., Zugf. in 2./Pz. Rgt. 36	5.11.44
Sodan, Ralf	Oberst, Kdr. I.R. 338 + 2.3. April 1945 (suicide) in Cottbus as Gen.Lt. & Kdt. v. Cottbus	16.6.40
v. Sodenstern, Georg	Gen.Lt., Chef d. Gen. St. H.Gr.A	19.7.40
Söchting, Fritz	Gefr., Richtschtz. in 3./Schn. Abt. 329 + 19.3.45 at Frauenburg (East Prussia)	16.4.43
Söhlke, August	Oberfeldw., Fhr. 3./G. R. 211	14.4. 45
Sölter, Willi,	Hptm., Kdr. I./K.G. 77	9.8.44
Söth, Wilhelm	Hptm., Kdr. II./A.R. 56	28.11.40
Soldner, Gustav	Oblt. d.R., Chef 1./Pz. Gr. Rgt. 66	18.7.44
Sommer, Clemens	Major, Kdr. II./Pz. G. R, "GD"	18.1.45
Sommer, Gerhard	Hptm., Staffelkpt. 4./J.G. 11 + 12.5.44 at Lippstadt (Westf.)	27.7.44
Sommer, Joachim	Hptm., Staffelkpt. 4. (H)/Aufkl. Gr. 31	25.11.44
Sommer, Ruprecht	Major, Kdr. 1./Pz. G. R. Führer-Gren. Div.	5.4.45
Sonne, Heinrich	SS-Obersturmf. d.R., Chef Kradschtz. Kp./1. SS-Inf. Brigade (mot.)	10.12.43
Sonntag, Christian	Major, Fhr. a Kampfgr. Fhr. Div. Gruppe 255 573rd Oak Leaves 5.9.44	12.2.44
Sonntag, Ernst	Oberst, Kdr. Jäger-Rgt. 749	17.4.45
Sonntag, Eugen	Hptm., Kdr. I./Gren. Rgt. 117	9.12.44
Sonntag, Karl-Heinrich	Oblt. d.R., Fhr. 1./schw. Kav. Abt. 4 (mot.)	4.10.44
Sonntag, Paul	Lt. d.R., Zugf. in Pz. Rgt. 27	19.1.43
Sorge, Ernst	Hptm., Flugzeugf. in 1. (F)/Aufkl. Gr. 124 (Kette Lappland)	26.3.44
Sorge, Karl-Heinz	Oblt., Chef 5./Pz. Rgt. 6	7.2.44

ELITE OF THE THIRD REICH

Sorko, August	Obstlt., Kdr. II./Geb.Jäg. Rgt. 137 + 19.7.41 at Winniza (Russia) as Oberst & Kdr. Geb.Jäg. Rgt. 13	20.6.40
Sowada, Bernhard	Lt. d.R., Zugf. in 1./St. Gesch. Brig. 237 + 25.12.44 at Kapolnasnyek (Hungary); posthumously promoted to Oblt. d.R.	12.10.43
Soyka, Heinz	Oblt., Chef 2./G. R. 96	13.1.44
Spadiut, Hubert	Oblt., Staffelkpt. 5./K.G. 76	26.3.44
Späte, Wolfgang	Oblt., Flugzeugf. in 5./J.G. 54 90th Oak Leaves 23.4.42	5.10.41
Spaeter, Helmuth	Rittm., Chef 2./Pz. Aufkl. Abt. "GD"	28.7.43
Späthe, Heinz	Lt. d.R., Fhr. 8./Pz. Rgt. 26	20.10.44
Spandau, Hermann	Hptm. d.R., Kdr. I./I.R. 396	9.9.42
v. Spangenberg, Hans-Christoph	Obstlt. d.R., Kdr. G. R. 203	22.1.43
Sparbier, Heinz	Oblt. d.R., Fhr. 9./I.R. 6 + Okt. 1944 in Kurland	17.10.42
Spari, Julius	Stabsfw., Zugf. in 7./Geb.Jäg. Rgt. 138 + 12.12.44 in Hungary	10.9.44
Specht, Günther	Major, Kdr. II./J.G. 11 1.1.44 missing over Brussels (Belgium) as Kommodore; posthumously promoted to Oberstlt.	8.4.44
Specht, Karl-Wilhelm	Oberst, Kdr. I.R. 55 60th Oak Leaves 16.1.42	8.9.41
Specht, Wilhelm	Oblt., Chef 7./I.R. 62	27.7.41
Ritter v. Speck, Hermann	Gen.Lt., Kom.Gen. XVIII. A.K. + 15.6.40 in France; posthumously promoted to Gen. d. Art.	17.10.40
Speckenheier, Helmut	Oblt., Fhr. 3./Heeres-Fla-Abt. 312 + 10.12.42 north of Stalingrad (Russia)	7.10.42
Speckter, Hans	Oblt., Chef 4./schw. Pz.Jäg. Abt. 563 + 31.3.44 south-west of Luga (Russia); posthumously promoted to Hptm.	9.4.44
Speich, Paul	Uffz., Gruppenf. in 1./Pi. Btl. 162	18.11.41
Speidel, Dr. phil. Hans	Gen.Lt., Chef d. Gen. St. 8. Armee	1.4.44
Speidel, Kurt	Oblt., Fhr. 2./Pz. Pi. Btl. 86	22.9.41
Spengler, Fritz	Hptm., Kdr. I./G. R. 289 + 30.4.45 at Cornuda on the Piave (Italy)	6.5.45
Sperl, Rudolf	Gen.Lt., Kdr. 61. I.D.	10.2.45
Sperling, Max	Obstlt., Kdr. Pz. G. R. 11	6.4.44
Sperrle, Hugo	Gen. d. Flieger, Chef Luftflotte 3	17.5.40
Speth, Hans	Gen.Lt., Kdr. 28. Jäger-Div.	23.2.44
Spiegel, Edmund	Major, Kdr. I./G. R. 544 + 10.8.44 in Russia	8.8.44
Spiegel, Joachim	Hptm., Kdr. I./G. R. 4 + 17.3.43 in Russia as Major	19.1.43

KNIGHT'S CROSS OF THE IRON CROSS

Name	Details	Date
Spiegel, Wendelin	Hptm. d.R., Kdr. 1./G. R. 279	28.2.45
Spielmann, Johann	Oblt., Zugf. in 1./St. Gesch. Abt 197 804th Oak Leaves 28.3.,45	27.3.42
Spier, Paul	Major, Kdr. Pz.Jäg. Abt. 299	10.9.44
Spies, Wilhelm	Hptm., Staffelkpt. 1./Z.G. 26 "Horst Wessel" 85th Oak Leaves 5.4.42	14.6.41
Spieß, Jakob	Lt. d.R., Schwdr. Fhr. In Kav. Rgt. 5 "Gen. Feldm. v. Mackensen" + 8.8.44 on Narev (Russia) of wounds	15.8.44
Spieth, Albert	Ofw., Flugzeugf. in 3./K.G. 51 +4.10.43 Bobruisk (Russia)	24.3.43
Spiethoff, Armin	Oberst, Kdr. G. R. 442	5.3.45
Spindler, Ludwig	SS-Sturmbannf, Kdr. I./SS-Pz. A.R. 9 "Hohenstaufen" + 27.12.44 in den Ardennes as SS-Obersturmbannf. & Rgt. Kdr.	27.9.44
Spindler, Werner	Ofw., Beobachter in 2. (H)/Aufkl. Gr. 3	30.9.44
Spindler, Wilhelm	Lt., Zugf. in 13./Geb.Jäg. Rgt. 98 718th Oak Leaves 31.1.45	21.12.40
Spitäller, Friedrich	Major d.R. z. V., Kdr. Jäg. Btl. 8 + 10.10.44 as Oberstlt. d.R. z. V. in a flying accident	25.7.43
Spitzer, Robert	Oblt., Chef 2./Pz.Jäg. Abt. 1541	5.4.45
Spörle, Richard	SS-Hptsturmf. d.R., Fhr. II./SS-Freiw. Pz. G. R. "Norge" + early April 1945 at Ihlow east of Berlin	16.11.44
Graf v. Sponeck, Hans	Gen.Lt., Kdr. 22. I.D. + 23.7.44 (hanged) Wehrmachtsgefängnis Germersheim (20.7.44); final post m.F.b. XXXXII. A.K.	14.5.40
Graf v. Sponeck, Theodor	Oberst, Kdr. Schtz. Rgt. 11	12.9.41
Sponheimer, Otto	Gen.Lt., Kdr. 21. I.D.	8.8.41
Sporck, Kaspar	SS-Unterscharf., Geschützfhr. in 5./SS-Freiw. Pz. Aufkl. Abt. 11 "Nordland" + 8.4.45 in a base hospital at Bayreuth of wounds	23.10.44
Spott, Alfred	Oblt., Chef 8. (MG)/G. R. 1124 + 14.2.45 in East Prussia	5.3.45
Sprang, Max	Major, Kdr. Div. Kampfschule 349	9.12.44
Spranz, Bodo	Oblt., Chef 1./St. Gesch. Abt. 237 308th Oak Leaves 3.10.43	3.10.43
Spreitzer, Karl	Lt., Flugzeugf. in 10. (Pz.)/S.G. 2 "Immelmann"	1.4.45
Sprengel, Alfred	Ofw., Zugf. in 5./G. R. 405	26.3.44
Spreu, Willy	Major d.R., Fhr. Pz. G. R. 192	24.2.45
Sprick, Gustav	Lt., Flugzeugf. in 8./J.G. 26 "Schlageter" + 28.6.41 shot down at Holgue (France) as Oblt. & Staffelkpt.	1.10.40

Springer, Gustav	Feldw., Zugf. in 2./Pz.Jäg. Abt. 253	30.4.45
Spnnger, Heinrich	SS-Hptsturmf., Fhr. 3./SS-Inf.Rgt. (mot.) "LSSAH"	12.1.42
Springmann, Josef	Objäg., Gr. Fhr. in 11./Jäg. Rgt. 229	5.4.45
Sprung, Helmuth	Lt., Flugzeugf. in 7./K.G. 1 "Hindenburg"	12.11.43
Staar, August	Lt., Fhr. 4. (MG)/G. R. 112 + 17.4.45 in Nierenhofen	22.8.43
Staats, Georg	Kaptlt., Kdt. "U 508" + 12.11.43 in the Bay of Biscay	14.7.43
Staba, Erich	Lt., Fhr. 1./Feldersatz-Abt. 89	21.9.44
Stach, Erich	Oblt. d.R., Fhr. I./G. R. 149	9.1.45
Stachelhaus, Hermann	Oblt., Kp. Fhr. in 1./Pz. G. R. 103 + 20.8.44	4.5.44
Stadermann, Waldemar	Lt., Flugzeugf. in 6./K.G. 77 + 15.2.42 over Malta	12.11.41
Stadler, Sylvester	SS-Sturmbannf., Kdr. II./SS-Pz. G. R. "Der Führer" 303rd Oak Leaves 16.9.43 152nd Swords 6.5.45	6.4.43
Staedke, Helmut	Oberst i.G., Chef d. Gen. St. XXXV. A.K.	14.8.43
Stähler, Wilhelm	Lt., Staffelf. 7./S.G. 2 "Immelmann" 812th Oak Leaves 28.3.45	20.7.44
Stäudle, Ernst	SS-Oberscharf. d.R., V. B. in 8./SS-Art.Rgt. "Totenkopf" + 11.7.46 in Soviet captivity in Camp Jaworznow at Kattowitz; final post SS-Obersturmf. d.R	10.4.42
Stahel, Rainer	Obstlt., Kdr. Flak-Rgt. 99 (mot.) 169th Oak Leaves 4.1.43 79th Swords 18.7.44	18.1.42
Stahl, Erhard	Ofw., Flugzeugf. in 3. (K)/L.G. 1 + 13.9.42 in Mediterranean as Staffelkpt.; posthumously promoted to Oblt.	16.4.42
Stahl, Hendrik	Lt., Flugzeugf. in 8./Stuka-Geschw. 2 "Immelmann" 506th Oak Leaves 24.6.44	23.12.42
Stahl, Dr. jur. Paul	Major d.R., Fhr. Pz. G. R. 114 879th Oak Leaves 9.5.45	4.5.44
Stahlann, Wilhelm	Feldw., Zugfhr. in 8./G. R. 497 + 29.2.44 north of Rogschew (Russia)	16.3.44
Stahlschmidt, Hans-Arnold	Lt., Staffelf. 2./J.G. 27 365th Oak Leaves 3.1.44	20.8.42
Stahnke, Karl-Heinz	Oblt., Staffelkpt. 3./K.G. 40	20.10.44
Staiger, Friedrich	Major, Kdr. I./G. R. 185	23.8.44
Staiger, Hermann	Oblt., Staffelkpt. 7./J.G. 51	16.7.41
Stamer, Dr. phil. Heinz	Korv. Kpt. z. V., Chef 8. Vorpostenflottille	20.4.45
Stammerjohann, Reinhold	Oberst, Kdr. Pz. Gren. Rgt. 76 + 17.4.45 at Frankfurt a. d. Oder	14.4. 45
Stamp, Gerhard	Oblt., Flugzeugf. in 1. (K)/L.G. 1	24.3.43

KNIGHT'S CROSS OF THE IRON CROSS

Stampfer, Otto	Hptm., stv. Fhr. III./Geb.Jäg. Rgt. 136	23.7.42
Stams, Otto	Hptm., Kdr. II./K.G. 1 "Hindenburg"	1.8.41
Stannek, Friedrich	Fhj. -Ofw., Beobachter in 4. (H)/Aufkl. G. R. 12 + 25.10.44	12.11.43
Stapf, Otto	Gen.Lt., Kdr. 111. I.D. Ritterkreuz des Kriegsverdienstkreuzes w/Swords as Gen.D.Inf. & Chef Wehrmachtwirtschaftstab Ost 10.9.44	31.8.41
v. Starck, Wilhelm	Hptm. d.R., Fhr. I./A.R. 1553	23.10.44
Starke, Heinrich	Lt., Flugzeugf. in 6./S.G. 10	28.1.45
Starl, Matthias (14)	Hptm., Kdr. I./Geb.Jäg. Rgt. 98	1.6.45
Starosta, Otto	Ofw., Zugf. in 1./G. R. 686	8.5.43
Stather, Heribert	Major, Fhr. G. R. 482	8.8.43
Staubach, Alfred	Uffz., Gruppenf. in 7./G. R. 697	27.8.43
Staudegger, Franz	SS-Unterscharf., Pz. Kdt. in 13./SS-Pz. Rgt. "LSSAH"	10.7.43
Staufenbiehl, Paul	Oblt., Chef Stabskp./Jäger-Rgt. 49	17.4.45
v. Stauss, Sven	Hptm. d.R., Kdr. II./Pz. G. R. 98 + in April 1945 at Raum Brünn (Böhmen-Mähren)	30.4.45
Stautner, Ludwig	Major, Kdr. I/Geb.Jäg. Rgt. 139	20.6.40
Stechmann, Hans	Ofw., Flugzeugf. in 9./J.G. 3	4.9.41
Stecken, Albert	Major i.G., Ia 8. Fallsch. Jäg. Div.	28.4.45
Steckmeier, Jakob	Lt., Fhr. 3./G. R. 485	9.4.44
Steen, Ernst-Siegfried	Hptm., Kdr. III./Stuka-Geschw. 2 "Immelmann" + 23.9.41 Kronstadt (Russia)	17.10.41
Steenbock, Kurt	Obgefr., Meldestaffelfhr. in III./G. R. 53	14.5.44
Steets, Konrad	Gefr., Btl. Melder in II./Fsch. Pz. G. R. 2 "HG"	30.11.44
Steffani, Wilhelm	Gefr., Richtschtz. in 13. (I. G.)/G. R. 948	4.5.44
Steffen, Helmut	Ofw., Flugzeugf. in 5. (F)/Aufkl. Gr. 122	5.12.43
Steffen, Karl	Feldw., Flugzeugf. in 9./J.G. 52 8.8.43 posted missing following forced landing near Bjelgorod (Russia) as Ofw.	1.7.42
Steffen, Walter	Hptm., Kdr. Rgts. -Gruppe 510 posted missing 28.8.44 as Major	4.7.44
Steger, Fritz	Lt. d.R., Zugf. in I.R. 20 (mot.)	15.8.40
Steger, Wilhelm	Feldw., Zugf. in 6./Pz. G. R. 10	20.4.43
Steglich, Martin	Hptm., Fhr. II./Füs. Rgt. 27 816th Oak Leaves 5.4.45	25.1.43
Stegmann, Karl	Uffz., Hilfsbeobachter in 7./A.R. 198 + 6.11.43 Kertsch (Russia); posthumously promoted to Wachtm.	20.1.44
Stegmann, Rudolf	Gen. Major, Kdr. 36. I.D.; + 18.6.44 at Briequebec (France) as Kdr. 77. I.D.; posthumously promoted to Gen.Lt.	20.1.44

Stehle, Werner	Lt., Zugf. in 3./Fsch. St. Gesch. Brig. 12	28.4.45
Steidl, Konrad	Hptm. d.R., stv. Fhr. I./2. jäg. Rgt. "Brandenburg"	26.1.44
Steidle, Luitpold	Obstlt., Kdr. G. R. 767	22.1.43
Stelgelmann, Eugen	Feldw., Zugf. j. d. 8./G. R. 80	9.6.44
Stein, Erich	Oblt. d.R., Fhr. II./G. R. 105	3.1.44
Stein, Gerhard	Hptm., Fhr. Div. Füs. Btl. 30 + 5.2.45 in Russia	26.11.44
Stein, Günther (18)	Feldw., Bordfunker in 6./K.G. 2	26.3.44
Stein, Walter	Major, Kdr. III./G. R. 485	28.11.43
Stein, Werner	Feldw., Bordschtz. in i./Stuka- Geschw. 2 "Immelmann"	19.8.43
Frhr. v. Steinaecker, Heinz-Eberhard	Lt., Fhr. 2./Flak-Rgt. 61 (mot.)	26.3.44
Steinbach, Dr. phil. Heinz	Lt. d.R., Zugf. in 3./Pz. Pi. Btl. 19 + 22.8.43 nordwest of Charkow (Russia) of wounds	27.9.43
Steinbacher, Fritz	Hptm., Fhr. I./A.R. 172	21.2.44
Steinbatz, Leopold	Feldw., Flugzeugf. in 9./J.G. 52 96th Oak Leaves 2.6.42 14th Swords 23–6.42	14.2.42
Steinborn, Eberhard	Hptm. d.R., Fhr. Pz. Zerst. Abt. Kampfgr. D (Pz.Jäg. Abt. 156)	11.7.44
Steinbrenner, Walter	Hptm. d.R., Chef 7./G. R. 211	9.7.44
Steiner, Felix	SS-Oberführer, Kdr. SS-Inf.Rgt. (mot.)"Deutschland" 159th Oak Leaves 23.12.42 86th Swords 10.8.44	15.8.40
Steinert, Gerhard	Oblt., Chef 9./G. R 532	21.4.44
Steinführer, Gerhard	Ofw., Zugf. in 2./Pz. G. R. 394 + 4.7.43 Kursk-Orel at Garzowka (Russia) as Oberfähnrich	8.5.43
Steinhardt, Dietrich	Oblt., Chef 2./I.R. 51 (mot.) + 15.4.42 Lowat south of Lake Ilmen (Russia) as Hptm. & Kdr. III./I.R. 51	27.10.39
Steinhausen, Günter	Feldw., Flugzeugf. in I./J.G. 27 + 6.9.42 shot down over El Alamein (North Africa); posthumously promoted to Lt.	3.11.42
Steinhauser, Georg	Uffz., Gruppenf. in 5./G. R. 316	31.1.45
Steinhoff, Georg	Ofw., stellv. Zugf. Pi. -Zug/Stabskp. I./G. R. 431 + March 1945 at Zinthen (East Prussia)	29.11.44
Steinhoff, Johannes	Oblt., Staffelkpt. 4./J.G. 52 115th Oak Leaves 2.9.42 82nd Swords 28.7.44	30.8.41
Steinhorst, Paul	Oblt., Chef 6./G. R. 410 + 19.10.44 as Hptm.	20.10.44
Steinkamp, Hans-Hermann	Oblt., Staffelkpt. 14. (Pz.)/S.G. 9	24.10.44
Steinke, Erhard (8)	Hptm., Btl. Fhr. in der 129. Inf. Div.	20.4.45

Name	Rank/Unit	Date
v. Steinkeller, Friedrich-Carl	Obstlt., Kdr. Pz. G. R. 7	31.3.43
Steinkopf, Herbert	Oblt. d.R., Chef 3./G. R. 467	15.5.44
Steinmann, Wilhelm (17)	Major d.R., Kdr. I./J.G. 4	22.3.45
Steinwachs, Hans	Hptm., Staffelkpt. 4./Stuka-Geschw. 1 + 14.2.45 at Naumburg/Bober as Kdr. II./S.G. 151	5.2.44
Steinwachs, Heinrich	Obstlt. z,. V., Kdr. Pz. A.R. 116	15.4.44
Steinwachs, Walter	Oblt., Adj. G. R. 432 + 23.3.45 at Heiligenbeil (East Prussia)	30.4.45
Steiof, Josef	Major, Fhr. G. R. 1096 + 23.1.45 at Tapiau (Lithuania) as Oberstlt.	22.10.44
Stellmann, Wilhelm	Obgefr., Richtkan. in 5./Res. Flak-Abt. 115 + 1945 as Wachtm.	16.11.42
Stellwagen, Friedrich	Hptm., Kdr. II./G. R. 106	17.3.45
Stemmermann, Wilhelm	Gen. d. Art., Kom.Gen. XI. A.K. 399th Oak Leaves 18.2.44	7.2.44
Stemmler, Wilhelm	Major, Kmdre. K.G. 77	6.10.44
Stentzler, Edgar	Major, Kdr. II./Fsch. Jäg. Sturm-Rgt. + 20.10.41 in hospital at Tilsit (East Prussia) of wounds	9.7.41
Stenwedel, Albert (15)	SS-Sturmbannf., Kdr. II./Waffen-Geb.Jäg. Rgt. 27 der SS	3.5.45
Stenzel, Heinrich	Oblt., Chef 2. (Radf.)/Div. Aufkl. Abt. 12 + 19.1.42 as Abt.Kdr. at Demjansk (Russia); posthumously promoted to Rittm.	92.12.41
Stenzel, Herbert	Hptm., Fhr. I./Pz. G. R. 108	5.3.45
Stephan, Alois	Lt. d.R., Fhr. 1./G. R. 1084	10.2.45
Stephan, Eberhard	Major, Kdr. Pz. Aufkl. Abt. 116	12.1.45
Stephani, Kurt	Major d.R., Fhr. Fsch. Jäg. Rgt. 9 + 20.8.44 in Ecorches (Normandy/France) of wounds in a British hospital	30.9.44
Stepp, Hans-Karl	Oblt., Staffelkpt. 7./Stuka-Geschw. 2 "Immelmann" 462nd Oak Leaves 27.4.44	4.2.42
Steputat, Jürgen	Lt., Flugzeugf. in Erprob. St. I./K.G. 30 + 8.9.41	20.12.41
Stern, Hans	Hptm., Chef 3./Pz. Regt. 11	15.7.41
Reichsfrhr. v. Sternbach, Franz	Hptm., Kdr. III./G. R. 688 + 21.11.43 at Krapiwna (Smolensk/Russia) of wounds	12.11.43
Sterr, Heinrich	Ofw., Flugzeugf. in 6./J.G. 54 + 26.11.44 shot down over the airfield at Vörden, Osnabrück, as Oblt. & Staffelkpt. 16./J.G. 54	5.12.43
Stettin, Günter	Major, Kdr. Pz. Pi. Btl. 92	24.1.44

ELITE OF THE THIRD REICH

Stettner Ritter v. Grabenhofen, Walter	Oberst, Kdr. 1. Geb. Div. + 18.10.44 at Belgrade (Yugoslavia) as Gen.Lt.	23.4.43
Steudel, Fritz	Ofw., Bordfunker in Stab II./K.G. 53 "Legion Condor"	28.2.45
Steudel, Josef	Hptm., Staffelkpt. 8./K.G. 2	29.10.44
Steuer, Dr. jur. Friedrich-Wilhelm	Major, Kdr. III./Pz. G. R. 129	26.8.43
Stichtenoth, Friedrich	Obstlt., Kdr. Pz. G. R. 128	5.9.44
Stiefelmayer, Otto	Oblt., Chef 1./Pz. Rgt. 8 + 3.11.42 as Hptm. & Kdr. I./Pz. Rgt. 8 in North Africa	12.7.42
Stiefvater, Hermann	Major, Kdr. Pz.Jäg. Abt. 173	18.5.41
Stiegert, Rolf	Hptm. d.R., Fhr. II./G. R. 316	16.1.45
Stiegler, Johann	Ofw., Zugf. in Pz.Jäg. Abt. "Feldherrnhalle"	1.2.45
Stier, Gottwald	Uffz. d.R., Geschützf. in 1./St. Gesch. Abt. 667	13.8.43
Stier, Dipl.-Ing. Paul	Oblt. d.R., Fhr. 2./Pi. Btl. 741 + 21.9.42 at Leningrad (Russia)	8.10.42
Stifter, Kurt	Lt., Flugzeugf. in 9./Stuka-Geschw. 77 + 21.12.42 at Fissenkowo (Russia) as Adjutant III./Stuka-Geschw. 77	22.1.43
Stigler, Josef	Oblt. d.R., Fhr. II./I.R. 42	10.7.42
Stillger, Fritz	Lt., Fhr. 7./G. R. 1	14.6.43
Stimmer, Albert	Oberfähnrich, V. B. in A.R. 342	6.10.44
Stimpel, Walter	Oblt., Staffelkpt. 6./Stuka-Geschw. 77	7.6.42
Stock, Ernst	Major, Fhr. G. R. 849	12.11.43
Stock, Hans-Christian	Lt., Zugf. in 2./St. Gesch. Abt. 270 628th Oak Leaves 23.10.44	22.8.43
Stocker, Wolfgang	Feldw., Zugf. in 6./G. R. 97	4.5.44
v. Stockhausen, Hans-Gerrit	Korv. Kpt., Kdt. "U 65" + 15.1.43 in Berlin as Chef 26. U-Bootsflottille in an accident	14.1.41
Stodieck, Otto	Oblt., Chef 5./Pz. Rgt. 1 + 24.12.43 east of Korosten (Russia); posthumously promoted to Hptm.	31.1.44
Stöckert, Herbert	Gefr., MG-Fhr. in 9./I.R. 156 (mot.) + 4.10.41 near Moscow (Russia) of wounds; posthumously promoted to Uffz.	10.10.41
Stoeckl, Alois	Oberst, Kmdre. K.G. 55 + 14.8.40 shot down over England	4.7.40
Stoecks, Helmut	Uffz. beim Kdt. Fester Platz Wilna (missing)	20.7.44
Störchel, Helmut	Major, Kdr. III./K.G. 30	22.11.43
Störck, Georg	Lt. d.R., Fhr. Pi. Zug Stabskp./Schtz. Rgt. 394 880th Oak Leaves 9.5.45	22.9.41
Störl, Johannes	Hptm. d.R., Chef 2./A.R. 156	10.9.43
Stoessel v. d. Heyde, Arno	Obstlt., Kdr. 1./I.R. 78	30.8.42

Name	Rank/Unit	Date
Stoewaß, Karl-Friedrich	Hptm. d.R., Chef 2./Pz. Aufkl. Abt. 14	14.4.45
Stoffers, Arnold	SS-Obersturmbannf., Kdr. SS-Freiw. - Pz. G. R. 23 "Norge" + 25.2.44 at Narva (Russia)	12.3.44
Stoffleth, Horst	Oblt., Kp. Fhr. in gem. Aufkl. Abt. 178 + in Russia as Rittm. & IIa 78. Sturm-Div.	20.8.42
Stoffregen, Erich	Hptm., Kdr. II./K.G. 30 + 14.1.43 at Comiso (Italy)	13.8.42
Stohwasser, Hans	Konteradm., Befehlshaber der Sicherung d. Ostsee	30.11.40
Stoll, Hermann	HPtm., Kdr. II./G. R. 521 + 19.2.44 Rogatschew (Russia); posthumously promoted to Major	9.6.44
Stoll, Paul	Uffz., Truppf. in 7./Pz. G. R. 128	2.9.44
Stoll-Berberich, Egon	Hptm. d.R., Staffelkpt. 7./Stuka-Geschw. 1	29.2.44
Stolle, Bruno	Hptm., Staffelkpt. 8.,/J.G. 2 "Richthofen"	17.3.43
Stollnberger, Hans	Lt., Staffel. 8./S.G. 1	14.10.42
Stolte, Anton	Ofw., Zugf. in Statbskp./G. R. 943 20.8.44 posted missing	19.8.44
Stoltenburg, Johannes	Oberst, Kdr. A.R. 177	11.8.44
Stolz, Edwin	Feldw., Zugf. in 14. (Pz.Jäg.)/G. R. 353 498th Oak Leaves 12.6.44	8.2.43
Stolz, Dipl.-Ing. Harald	Obstlt., Kdr. Kradsch. Btl. 43	28.8.42
Stolz, Josef	Lt., Zugf. in 10./I.R. 51 (mot.) + 24.6.41 Bjeloy (Russia) as Oblt. & Chef 2./Kradschtz. Btl. 38; posthumously promoted to Hptm.	27.10.39
v. Stolzmann, Joachim	Obstlt., Kdr. III./I.R. 17	29.9.40
Storek, Erich	Lt., Fhr. 8./Pz. G. R. 108	5.4.44
Storp, Walter	Hptm., Kdr. 19./K.G. 76 22nd Oak Leaves 14.7.41	21.10.40
Stotten, Hans-Günther	Lt., Fhr. 1./Pz. Rgt. 3 236th Oak Leaves 10.5.43	4.7.40
Stotz, Max	Ofw., Flugzeugf. in 5./J.G. 54 137th Oak Leaves 30.10.42	19.6.42
Stoy, Otto	Lt., Fhr. 3./A.R. 171	5.11.44
Graf Strachwitz v. Groß-Zauche & Camminetz, Ernst	Hptm., Fhr. II./Geb.Jäg. Rgt. 137	26.11.44
Graf Strachwitz v. Groß-Zauche & Camminetz, Hyazinth	Major d.R., Kdr. 1./Pz. Rgt. 2 144th Oak Leaves 13.11.42 27th Swords 28.3.43 11th Diamonds 15.4.44	25.8.41
Frhr. v. Strachwitz, Mauritz	Gen.Lt., Kdr. 87. I.D. + 23.10.53 in Soviet captivity in Camp Asbest at Swerdlowsk (Russia)	9.1.45
Stracke, Walter	Oblt. d.R., Chef 2./Kradschtz. Btl. 53	21.11.42
Straehler-Pohl, Günther	Hptm., Kdr. II./Fsch. Jäg. Rgt. 3	10.5.43

Strahammer, Martin	Obstlt., Kdr. Pz.Jäg. Abt. 240 545th Oak Leaves 11.8.44	30.1.42
Strakeljahn, Friedrich-Wilhelm	Hptm., Staffelkpt. 14. (Jabo)/J.G. 5 + 6.7.44 Dünaburg (Russia) as Hptm. & Kdr. II./S.G. 4	19.8.43
Strapatin, Stefan	SS-Rottenf., Fernsprecher, in II./(niederl.) SS-Freiw. Pz. G. R. 49 "De Ruyter"	16.11.44
Strasser, Erwin	Oblt., Fhr. 5./Pz. Rgt. 33	5.3.45
Straßl, Hubert	Ofw., Flugzeugf. in 8./J.G. 51 "Mölders" + 8.7.43 shot down over Ponyri (Russia)	12.11.43
Straßmair, Hannes	Lt., Flugzeugf. in 2. (F)/Aufkl. Gr. 122	3.4.43
Stratemann, Hinrich	Hptm. d.R., Chef 8./G. R. 76 (mot.)	2.10.43
Straub, Johann	Lt., Zugf. in Pz.Jäg. Abt. 7	12.8.44
Straube, Erich	Gen. Major, Kdr. 268. I.D. 609th Oak Leaves 30.9.44	19.7.40
Straube, Georg	Ofw., Zugf. in 2./Pz.Jäg. Abt. 18 (mot.)	2.6.43
Strauß, Adolf	Gen.D.Inf., Kom.Gen. II. A.K.	27.10.39
Strauß, Gustav	Ofw., Zugf. in 10./I.R. 267	25.10.42
Strauß, Hubert	Oblt. d.R., Fhr. 9./G. R. 361 (mot.) + 20.10.44 Castel S. Pietro (Italy); posthumously promoted to Hptm. d.R.	4.10.44
Streck, Werner	Hptm. d.R., Fhr. Feldersatz-Btl. 81	28.12.43
Streckenbach, Bruno	SS-Brigadef. & Gen. Major d. W-SS, Kdr. 19. Waffen-Gren. Div. d. SS 701st Oak Leaves 16.1.45	27.8.44
Strecker, Karl	Gen.Lt., Kdr. 79. I.D.	26.10.41
Strecker, Wolfgang	Obstlt., Fhr. G. R. 545	5.4.45
Strehlau, Erwin	Gefr., Gruppenf. in 2./Pz. G. R. 5	9.6.44
Streib, Werner	Oblt., Staffelkpt. 2./N. J.G. 1 197th Oak Leaves 26.2.43 54th Swords 11.3.44	6.10.40
Streich, Johannes	Oberst Kdr. Pz. Rgt. 15	31.1.41
Streich, Otto	Uffz., Gruppenf. in 1./G. R. 187 + April 1945 in Berlin simultaneously promoted to Feldw.	28.3.45
Streil, Ludwig	Obstlt., Kdr. I.R. 61 + 17.5.40 on the Charleroi-Canal (Belgium)	30.6.41
Streit, Dipl.-Ing. Gerhard	Major d.R., Kdr. Pi. Brückenbau-Btl. 646 (mot.)	9.6.44
Streit, Karl	Feldw., Zugf. in 11./G. R. 461 + 9.11.43 at Gorodok (Russia)	26.8.43
Streit, Ludwig	Oblt. d.R., Fhr. 5./A.R. 114	10.9.43
Streit, Werner	Hptm., Chef 5./G. R. 51 (mot.)	14.4. 43
Strelow, Hans	Lt., Staffelf. 5./J.G. 51 "Mölders" 84th Oak Leaves 24.3.42	18.3.42

KNIGHT'S CROSS OF THE IRON CROSS

Strelow, Siegfried	Kaptlt., Kdt. "U 435" + 15.7.43 in the Atlantic west of Spain; posthumously promoted to Korv. Kpt.	27.10.42
Strich, Waldemar	Hptm. d.R., Kdr. G. R. 1114 + 27.1.45	23.3.45
Stricker, Karl-Heinz	Hptm., Kdr. I./S. K.G. 210 + 13.9.41 shot down over Akulitschi (Russia)	2.10.42
Strippel, Hans	Ofw., Zugf. in 2./Pz. Rgt. 1 485th Oak Leaves 4.6.44	22.1.43
Strobel, Anton	Major d.R., Kdr. II./A.R. 219	13.4.44
Strobel, Paul	Hptm., Staffelkpt. 7./K.G. 4 "General Wever" + 19.9.43 at Orscha (Russia) m. d. W. d. G. beauftr. III./K.G. 4	26.3.44
Strobl, Heinrich	Lt., FAK 202 Einheit "Schill"	9.5.45
Strohm, Friedrich	Major, Kdr. 1./G. R. 480 613th Oak Leaves 18.10.44	18.1.44
Strohmaier, Paul	Oblt., Chef 3./Flak-Rgt. 297 (mot.)	8.8.44
Strojek, Helmut	Feldw., Zugf. in 4./G. R. 986	17.3.45
Stronk, Wolfram	Hptm., Chef 6./Fsch. Pz. Rgt. "HG"	18.10.44
Strotmann, Heinrich	Feldw., Zugf. in 12./G. R. 371 +27.4.44 north of Calfa on the Dnjestr (Russia)	18.11.43
Struckmann, Rudolf	Oblt., Adj. Stab/Schtz. Rgt. 115 + 19.2.44 at Cassino (Italy) as Hptm. & Kdr. II./Pz. G. R. 104	21.1.42
Strüning, Heinz	Lt. d.R., Flugzeugf. in 3./N. J.G. 1 528th Oak Leaves 20.7.44	29.10.42
Stry, Herbert	Oblt., Flugzeugf. in 5./Stuka-Geschw. 3 + 21.9.43 as Staffelkpt. at Kepfalonia (Greece); posthumously promoted to Hptm.	24.9.42
Stubenrauch, Karl	Hptm. d.R., Chef 4./G. R. 282 missing May 1945 in Berlin as Major d.R. & Adj.	22.4.43
Stuchlick, Werner	Hptm., Fhr. II./Fsch. Pz. Gren. Rgt. 2 "HG"	30.11.44
Stuckmann, Hermann	Oblt. z. See, Kdt. "U 621" + 23.8.44 in the Bay of Biscay	11.8.44
Student, Kurt	Gen.Lt., Kdr. 7. Flieger-Div. 305th Oak Leaves 27.9.43	12.5.40
Studte, Otto	Oblt. d.R., Chef 8./A.R. 389 + 9.10.44 in Russia of wounds	16.10.44
Stück, Adolf	Wachtm. d.R. Vorgesch. Beob. in 1./A.R. 251	26.10.43
Stüdemann, Gerhard	Oblt., Staffelkpt. 9./Stuka-Geschw. 77 813th Oak Leaves 28.3.45	26.3.44
Stühmer, Gustav	Feldw., Zugf. in 11./G. R. 399 simultaneously promoted to Ofw. 422nd Oak Leaves 6.3.44	29.12.42
v. Stülpnagel, Carl-Heinrich	Gen.D.Inf., OB 17. Armee + 30.8.44 hanged in Berlin-Plötzensee (20.7.44); final post Militärtbefehlshaber France	21.8.41

Name	Details	Date
v. Stünzner, Ewald	Hptm., Chef 3./Pz. Abt. 103	10.9.42
v. Stünzner, Georg	Obstlt. 1. G., Ia 29. Pz. Gren. Div. + 3.9.43 in field hospital at Laureana (South Italy) of wounds; posthumously promoted to Oberst i.G.	17.9.43
Stürber, Vitus	Obstlt., Fhr. G. R. 71 (mot.) + 1943 in Stalingrad (Russia)	29.12.42
Stürtz, Fritz	Major d.R., Kdr. Pi. Btl. 161 + 29.2.44 on the Narva front (Russia); posthumously promoted to Oberstlt. d.R.	29.2.44
Stützle, Nepomuk	Obgefr. in Pz.Jäg. Abt. "GD"	8.5.45
Stüwe, Eberhard	Hptm., b. m. d. W. d. G. III./K.G. 77 + 7.6.44; posthumously promoted to Major	5.9.44
Stuhlberger, Wilhelm	Hptm., Chef 5./Flak-Rgt. 29 (mot.)	9.6.44
Stumme, Georg	Gen. d. Kav., Kom.Gen. XXXX. A.K. + 24.10.42 at El Alamein (North Africa) as Gen. d. Pz. Tr, & m.F.b. Pz. Armee Afrika	19.7.40
Stumpe, Erich	Oblt., Flugzeugf. in 1. (F)/Aufkl. Gr. 121	17.3.43
Stumpf, Werner	Ofw., Flugzeugf. in III./J.G. 53 + 13.10.42 shot down by flak in North Africa	13.8.42
Stumpf, Wolfgang	Hptm. d.R., Chef 2./s. Art. Abt. 834 + 3.10.43 in Russia	7.2.44
Stumpff, Hans-Jürgen	Gen. Oberst, Chef Luftflotte 5 & Befehlshaber Nord	18, 9.41
Stumpff, Horst	Gen.Lt., Kdr. 20. Pz.Div.	29.9.41
Stuppi, Joseph	Major, Kdr. II./I.R. 94	2.2.42
Sturm, Alfred	Oberst, Kdr. Fsch. Jäg. Rgt. 2	9.7.41
Sturm, Hans	Gefr., Melder in 6./I.R. 473	26.9.42
Sturm, Hans-Hermann	Oblt., Chef 3./St. Gesch. Brig "GD"	9.6.44
Sturm, Heinrich	Lt., Staffelf. 4./J.G. 52 + 23.12.44 in an accident at Czor (Hungary) as Hptm. & Staffelkpt. 4./J.G. 52	26.3.44
Sturm, Simon	Feldw., Zugf. in 6./G. R. 82 simultaneously promoted to Ofw.	30.4.43
v. Stutterheim, Wolfgang	Gen. Major, Kmdre. K.G. 77 + 3.12.40 in Berlin of wounds	4.7.40
Styr, Josef	SS-Hauptscharf., Zugf. in 10./SS-Pz. G. R. 9 "Germania"	5.4.45
Südel, Heinrich	Oblt., Beobachter & Ia I./K.G. 55	7.4.45
Sürig, Rudolf	Oblt. d.R., Chef 2./Jäger-Btl. 13 + 28.11.42 south-east of Toropez (Russia)	8.2.43
Suermann, Burghard	Oblt. d.R., Chef 7./G. R. 324	24.12.44

KNIGHT'S CROSS OF THE IRON CROSS

Süß, Ernst	Ofw., Flugzeugf. in 9./J.G. 52 + 20.12.43 at Wardenburg (Oldenburg) shot following bail-out as Staffelf. 9./J.G. 11; posthumously promoted to Oblt.	4.9.42
Süß, Walter	Feldw., Zugf. in Stabskp./G. R. 273 717th Oak Leaves 25.1.45	9.6.44
Suhr, Friedrich	SS-Obersturmbannf., Fhr. of a Kampfgr. (Bfth. Sipo France)	11.12.44
Suhr, Rudolf	Hptm., Kdr. Pz.Jäg. Abt. 150	18.2.45 + 20.1.45
Suhren, Gerd	Oblt. (Ing.), Leit. Ing. auf "U 37"	21.10.40
Suhren, Reinhard	Oblt. z. See, I. Wach-Offz. auf "U 48" 56th Oak Leaves 31.12.41 18th Swords 1.9.42	3.11.40
v. Le Suire, Karl	Gen. d. Geb. Tr., Kom.Gen. XXXXIX. Geb. Korps + 1955 in Soviet captivity at Stalingrad (Russia)	26.11.44
Sulzer, Rudolf	Hptm. d.R., Kdr. II./G. R. 161	11.1.44
Sumpf, Hans	Oblt., Staffelkpt. 5./K.G. I "Hindenburg" + 26.3.42 in Russia; posthumously promoted to Hptm.	20.8.42
Sumpf, Walter (17)	Feldw., Flugzeugf. in 1./K.G. 100	12.3.45
Sundmacher, Heinz	Major d.R., Kdr. 1./G. R. 431	28.2.45
Sunkel, Kurt	Oblt., Chef 3./G. R. 107	14.5.44
v. Svoboda Edler v. Asticotal, Hubert	Obstlt., Kdr. Flak-Rgt. 46 (mot.)	14.1.45
Swientek, Josef	SS-Obersturmbannf., Kdr. SS-Pz. A.R. 3 "Totenkopf"	16.6.44
Swierzinski, Lothar	SS-Rottenf., Gruppenf. in 10./SS-Pz. G. R. "Totenkopf " + 29.10.44 west of Legionowo at Warsaw (Poland) of wounds as SS-Unterscharf.	16.12.43
Sy, Erwin	Oblt., Staffelkpt. 4. (K)/L.G. 1 + 2.12.42 at Tobruk (North Africa); posthumously promoted to Major	22.5.42
Sydow, Otto	Gen. Major, Kdr. 1. Flak-Div. Berhn	28.2.45
Syrowy, Jan	Uffz., Zugf. in 3./Reiter-Rgt. 32	30.4.45
Szameitat, Paul	Hptm., Kdr. I./N. J.G. 3 + 2.1.44 Bückeburg during forced landing	6.4.44
Szelinski, Arnold	Oberst, Kdr. I.R. 525 + 9.12.43 at Krementschug (Russia) as Gen.Lt. & Kdr. 376. I.D.	18.11.41
Szyskowitz, Joachim	Freg. Kpt., Hafenkommandant Antwerp (Belgium) + 10.9.44 in Antwerp (Belgium), posthumously promoted to Kapt. z. See	13.10.44

T

Name	Rank/Unit	Date
Tabel, Franz	Feldw., Zugf. in 3./Pi. Btl. 246	25.1.45
Tadje, Fritz	Lt., Fhr. 2./St. Gesch. Abt. 190	21.10.42
Taeger, Ench	Oblt., Staffelkpt. 7./K.G. 1 "Hndenburg"	2.10.42
Tanczos, Hermann	Uffz. in 4./A.R. 157	21.2.44
Tange, Otto	4./J.G. 51 "Mölders" Ofw., Flugzeugf. i. d. 4./J.G. 51 "Mölders" + 30.7.43 direct hit by flak south west of Bolchow (Russia) as Flugzeugf. in Stabsstaffel/J.G. 51 "Mölders"; posthumously promoted to Oblt.	19.3.42
Tank, Walter	Oblt. d.R., Chef 6./Pz. G. R. 3	24.9.42
Tanneberger, Willi	Ofw., Kp. Trf. in 3./G. R. 156 (rnot.)	10.2.44
Tannert, Karl	Hptm., Kdr. III./Fsch. Jäg. Rgt. 2	5.4.44
Tanzer, Kurt	Ofw., Flugzeugf. in 12./J.G. 51 "Mölders"	5.12.43
Tappe, Martin	SS-Obersturmbannf., Kdr. II./SS-Pol. Pz. G. R. 8	28.3.45
Tarin, Walter	Major, Fhr. A.R. 121	20.10.44
Taubert, Richard	Hptm., Staffelkpt. 5. (F)/Aufkl. Gr. 122	16.11.42
Taulien, Arno	Oblt., Chef 7./Pz. Rgt. 6	18.10.43
Tech, Harry	Hptm. d.R., Kdr. He. Art. Abt. 934 (mot.)	3.3.43
Tegtmeier, Fritz	Ofw., Flugzeugf. in 2./J.G. 54	28.3.44
Teichert, Max-Martin	Kaptlt., Kdt. "U 456" + 12.5.43 in north Atlantic	19.12.43
Teichmann, Friedrich	Lt., Zugf. Rgts. Nachr. Zug/G. R. 712 + 20.1.45	24.2.45
Teige, Waldemar	Ofw., Flugzeugf. in 6./K.G. 53 + 3.10.42 at Leningrad (Russia) as Flugzeugfhr. in a Nachtjagdschwarm/KG 53	7.6.42
Telkamp, Eberhard	SS-Sturmbannf., Kdr. II/SS-Pz. Rgt. 9 "Hohenstaufen"	23.8.44
Telkemeyer, Heinrich	Hptm. d.R., Kdr. IV./A.R. 172 + Nov. 1948 by accident in Soviet captivity	28.10.44
Tellgmann, Eugen	Oblt. z. See d.R., Kdt. Vorpostenboot "VP 1313" 13. Vorpostenflottille	5.10.44
Telschig, Ernst	Major d.R., Kdr. Pi. Btl. 187	8.8.44
Temming, Hans	Kaptlt., Kdt. Torpedoboot "T 28"	6.5.45
de Temple, Carl	Obstlt., Kdr. Füs. Rgt. 230 + 16.11.44 in Hungary as Oberst	26.6.44
Tenner, Hans	Hptm., Chef 1./G. R. 487 + 29.3.43	24.4. 43
Tennhardt, Werner	Oblt., Adj. l. R. 446 + 11.10.41	13.10.41
Tenschert, Günther (18)	Major, Kdr. II./Festgs. Rgt. Mohr (Festung Breslau)	28.4.45
Terharen, Heinrich	Lt. d.R., Fhr. 5./G. R. 956	9.12.44

Name	Details	Date
Teriete, Heinrich	Lt., Zugf. in schw. Pz.Jäg. Abt. 635	22.7.43
Tesch, Hermann	Lt. d.R., Fhr. 11./G. R. 67 + 12.6.44 at Norkino south-east of Ostrowo (Russia) of wounds; posthumously promoted to Oblt. d. R	11.5.45
Tesch, Karl-Heinz	Stabsgefr., stellv. Gruppenf. in 7./Pz. G. R. 26	27.7.44
Teske, Georg (17)	Major, Kdr. I./K.G. 26	31.10.44
Tessenow, Rudi (19)	Wachtm. in 11./Pz. Rgt. 24	9.5.45
Tetsch, Ernst	SS-Sturmbanrif., Kdr. I./SS-Pz. Rgt. 10 "Frundsberg"	28.3.45
v. Tettau, Hans	Gen.Lt., Kdr. 24. I.D. 821st Oak Leaves 5.4.45	3.9.42
Teubel, Heinz	Lt. d.R., Fhr. 2./G. R. 546	30.9.44
Teumer, Alfred	Oblt., Staffelkpt. 7./J.G. 54 + 4.10.44 shot down at Hesepe airfield, Osnabrück as Oblt. in Erprobungskdo. Nowotny (Me 262); posthumously promoted to Hptm.	19.8.44
Teusen, Hans	Lt., Zugf. in 6./Fsch. Jäg. Rgt. 2	14.6.41
Teuwsen, Adolf	Obgefr., MG-Schtz. 1 in 3./Jäg. Rgt. 25(L)	14.5.44
Thaler, Andreas	Hptm., Fhr. II./Pz. Rgt. 25	13.1.44
Thaler, Johann	SS-Unterscharf., Pz. Fahrer in 6./SS-Pz. Rgt. 2 "Das Reich" + 7.4.45 Wien as SS-Oberscharf. & Pz. Kdt.	14.8.43
Thaler, Rudolf	Objäg., Gr. Fhr. in 13./Geb.Jäg. Rgt. 13	9.12.44
Theilen, Hans	Lt. in 2./Heeres-Küsten-Art. Abt. 289 + 1.2.44 in Russia as Oblt. & Bttr. Chef	22.4.43
Theilen, Heinrich	Obgefr., Gruppenfhr. in 6./Pz. G. R. 2	4.8.43
Theissig, Franz	Uffz., Gr. Fhr. in 13./G. R. 32	14.4. 45
Thelen, Johann	Owm., Bttr. Offz. in 5./A.R. 253	3.11.44
Thiede, Armin	Lt., Flugzeügf. in 7./Stuka-Geschw. 2 "Immelmann" + 9.7.43 at Varasdin (Croatia) as Hptm. & Kdr. II./Stuka-Geschw. 151 accidentally	14.6.41
Thiel, Edwin	Oblt., Staffel 2./J.G. 51 "Mölders" + 14.7.44 shot down at Kobryn (East Prussia) by Soviet flak as Hptm. & Fhr. Stabsstaffel/J.G. 51 "Mölders"	16.4.43
Thiel, Erich	Oblt., Staffelkpt. 7./K.G. 27 "Boelcke" + 22.4.43 as Major u. Kdr. III./K.G. 27	23.7.4
Thiel, Franz	Ofw., Zugf. in 7./Füs. Rgt. 22 + 14.1.45 in Schloßberg (East Prussia)	11.3.45
Thiel, Gerhard	Rittm., Fhr. III./Pz. Rgt. 24 + 10.4.43 in Soviet captivity	20.1.43
Thiel, Karl	Uffz., Geschützf. in 1./A.R. 217	8.8.44

ELITE OF THE THIRD REICH

Thiele, Arno	Oblt., Zugf. in 4./Pz. Rgt. 29 + 3.8.42 at Leningrad (Russia) of wounds	24.9.42
Thiele, August	Kapt. z. See, Kdt. Schwerer Kreuzer "Lützow" 824th Oak Leaves 8.4.45	18.1.41
Thiem, Egon	Hptm., Staffelkpt. 5./(S) L.G. 2	21.7.40
Thiem, Ernst	Owm., Zugf. in 1./Aufkl. Abt. 298 + 19.9.43 as Stabswachtm.	17.9.41
Thieme, Carl	Hptm., Kdr. I./Pz. G. R. 110 627th Oak Leaves 23.10.44 156th Swords 9.5.45	30.10.43
Thieme, Heinz	Obgefr., Richtschtz. in 14. (Pz.Jäg.)/G. R. 446 + 17.12.43 in Russia of wounds	20.1.44
Thierfelder, Helmut	Ofw., Zugf. in 6./Pz. G. R. 33	2.9.44
Thierfelder, Werner	Oblt., Staffelkpt. in II./Z.G. 26 "Horst Wessel" + 18.7.44 shot down in a Me 262 at Landsberg/Lech as Hptm. & Fhr. Erprobungskdo. Lechfeld	10.10.41
Thiessen, Hans	Lt., Fhr. 2./He. Fla-Abt. "GD" + February 1945 at Bartenstein (East Prussia)	9.5.45
Thörner, Johannnes	Hptm., stv. Fhr. III./Jäg. Rgt. 738	11.7.44
Thofern, Werner	Lt., Zugf. in 1./I.R. 5 (mot.)	25.8.41
Thom, Walter	Obgefr., Gesch. Führer in 14. (Pz.Jäg.)/G. R. 7 + 22.10.44 in Lithuania as Feldw.	23.10.44
Thoma, Heinrich	Gen. Major, Kdr. I.R. 519 + 29./30. Oct. 1948 in Soviet captivity; final post Gen.Lt. & Kdr. Div. Nr. 432 as well as Befh. in W. K. VIII (Rest)	27.10.41
Thoma, Helmut	Oblt., Chef 9./A.R. 119	3.5.42
Thoma, Kurt	Korv. Kpt., Chef 2. Minensuchflottille	6.10.40
Ritter v. Thoma, Wilhelm	Gen. Major, Kdr. 20. Pz.Div.	31.12.41
Thomae, Dr. rer. pol. Adolf	Hptm. d.R., Kdr. II./G. R. 980	24.2.45
Thomale, Wolfgang	Obstlt., Kdr. Pz. Rgt. 27	10.2.42
Thomas, Karl-Anton (17)	Oberfeuerwerker in einem Sprengkdo. der Luftwaffe in Münster (Westf.)	21.4.45
Thomas, Wilhelm	Oberst, Kdr. I.R. 71 (mot.)	13.10.41
Thomaschki, Siegfried	Gen. Major, Kdr. 11. I.D. 299th Oak Leaves 11.9.43	1.11.42
Thomsen, Ernst-Heinrich	Major, Kdr. III./K.G. 26	24.10.44
Thomsen, Rolf	Kaptlt., Kdt. "U 1202" 852nd Oak Leaves 29.4.45	4.1.45
Thor, Hans	Hptm., Kdr. I./Fsch. Pz. G. R. 2 "HG" + 26.6.44 in Italy	30.9.44
Thorey, Andreas	Oblt., Schwadr. Fhr. in Aufkl. Abt. 94 349th Oak Leaves 7.12.43	14.9.42

Thormählen, Viktor	Oblt., Chef 2./Kav. Rgt. "Nord" + 16.1.44 south west of Nowgorod (Russia)	12.3.44
Thorwest, Friedrich-Wilhelm	Korv. Kpt. d.R., Chef 2. Geleitflottille "Adria" + 1.11.44 in combat in the Adriatic; posthumously promoted to Freg. Kpt. d.R. Freg. Kpt.	5.11.44
Thoß, Werner	Oblt., Staffelkpt. 4./K.G. 55	29.10.44
Thünemann, Heinrich	Major, Kdr. Pz. Pi. Btl. 79	14.5.44
Frhr. v. Thüngen, Karl	Gen.Lt., Kdr. 18. Pz.Div. + 24.10.44 hanged in Zuchthaus Brandenburg at Havel (20.7.44); final post Inspekteur der Wehrsatz-Inspektion III (Berlin)	6.4.43
Thulke, Willi	Oblt. d.R., Chef 6./G. R. 501 424th Oak Leaves 13.3.44	7.1.43
Thumann, Jakob	Hptm., Fhr. II./G. R. 351 + 8.9.43 Orel (Russia)	29.8.43
Thumbeck, Georg	Obgefr., Gruppenf. in 10./G. R. 60 (mot.)	12.11.43
Thumm, Helmuth	Obstlt., Kdr. I. R 56 166th Oak Leaves 23.12.42	30.6.41
Thunert, Eberhard	Gen. Major, Kdr. 1. Pz.Div.	1.2.45
Thurmann, Karl	Korv. Kpt., Kdt. "U 553" + 28.1.43 in the Atlantic	24.8.42
Thurner, Hans	Lt., Flugzeugf. in III./K.G. 55 587th Oak Leaves 17.9.44	6.8.41
Thurnhuber, Josef (17)	Lt., Flugzeugf. in I./K.G. 200	12.3.45
Thyben, Gerhard	Oblt., Staffelkpt. 7.,/J.G. 54 822nd Oak Leaves 8.4.45	6.12.44
Thylmann, Hans	Major, Kdr. I./Pz. G. R. 26	18.2.45
Tiburzy, Ernst	Volkssturm-Btl. Fhr. im Volkssturm-Btl. 25/82 in der Festung Königsberg	10.2.45
Tichy, Ekkehard	Oblt., Staffelkpt. 9. (Sturm-)/J.G. 3 "Udet" + 16.8.44 at Hannoversch-Münden when ramming a bomber; posthumously promoted to Hptm.	14.1.45
Tiedtke, Werner	Lt., Fhr. 2./A.R. 349	5.4.45
Tiefensee, Arthur	Lt., Fhr. 7./G. R. 43	3.8.44
Tiemann, Otto	Gen.Lt., Kdr. 93. I.D.	28.4.43
Tiesler, Kurt	Obstlt. d.R., Kdr. Jäg. Rgt. 38 + 1951/52 in Soviet. captivity; final post Oberst d.R. & stellv. Kdt. Fest. Breslau	16.4.44
Frhr. v. Tiesenhausen, Hans-Diedrich	Kaptlt., Kdt. "U 331"	27.1.42
Tietjen, Cord	Lt., Zugf. in 5./Fsch. Jäg. Rgt. 1	24.5.40
Tietz, Hermann	Hptm., Kdr. II./A.R. 240	27.7.44

Tietzen, Horst	Hptm., Staffelkpt. 5./J.G. 51 + 18.8.40 shot down over the Channel	20.8.40
Tilebein, Bruno	Oblt., Beob. & Staffeloffz. in 8./K.G. 4 "General Wever"	9.10.43
Tilgner, Herbert	Oblt. d.R., Chef 2./Pz.Jäg. Abt. 61	18.12.44
Tilgner, Walter	Major d.R., Btl. Kdr. in Rgt. "Mohr" in Festg. Breslau (Kdr. Jäg. Ers. & Ausb. Btl. 49)	9.4.45
Tillmann, Johannes	Lt. d.R., Fhr. 10./G. R. 183 + 9.1.43 in the great bend of the Don (Russia) of wounds	2.1.43
Tilmann, Wido	Lt., Zugf. in 2./Pi. Btl. 297	22.12.41
Timm, Erich	Major, Kdr. Fsch. Jäg. Rgt. 12	3.10.44
Timm, Heinrich	Korv. Kpt., Kdt. "U 862"	17.9.44
Timpe, Heinz (12)	Lt., Chef 1./St. Gesch. Brig. 300 (F)	7.5.45
v. Tippelskirch, Adolf-Hilmar	Oblt., Chef 1./A.R. 3 (mot.) + 28.6.44 Mogilew (Russia) as Major i.G.	29.9.41
v. Tippelskirch, Kurt	Gen.Lt., Kdr. 30. I.D. 539th Oak Leaves 30.7.44	23.11.41
Tischendorf, Herbert	Hptm., Kp. Chef i. d. s. Pz. Abt. 509	11.3.45
Tischer, Kurt	Gefr., MG-Schtz. in Div. Füs. Btl. 320 + 16.4.44 in Russia	15.6.44
Titel, Georg	Ofw., Tr. Fhr. in 2./G. R. 757	31.1.45
Titschkus, Alfred	SS-Unterscharf., Gruppenf. in 3./SS-Pz. Aufkl. Abt. 3 "Totenkopf' + 5.4.45 in Soviet captivity of wounds	11.12.44
Tittel, Rolf	Feldw., Zugf. in 3./G. R. 31	23.8.44
Tödt, Heinz-Eduard	Oblt. d.R., Chef 1./A.R. 66	2.9.44
Töniges, Werner	Oblt. z. See, Kdt. "S 102" in 1. Schnellbootsflottille 143rd Oak Leaves 13.11.42	25.2.41
Tönnjes, Hermann	Oberfähnrich, Ord.Offz. inl./G. R. 255	20.4.44
Töpfer, Hans	Oblt., Staffelkpt. 1./S.G. 3	20.7.44
Toll, Otto	Lt. d.R., Zugf. in Pi. Btl. 200 + 10.6.44 at Caen (France) as Hptm. d.R. zur 12. SS Pz.Div. "Hitlerjugend" (Kp. Fhr. in SS-Pz. Pi. Btl. 12) kdrt.	10.6.41
Tolsdorff, Theodor	Oblt., Chef 14./I.R. 22 302nd Oak Leaves 15.9.43 80th Swords 18.7.44 25th Diamonds 18.3.45	4.12.41
Tonne, Günther	Oblt., Flugzeugf. in I./S. K.G. 210 632nd Oak Leaves 24.10.44	5.10.41
Tonne, Wolfgang	Oblt., Staffelkpt. 3./J.G. 53 128th Oak Leaves 24.9.42	6.9.42
Topp, Erich	Oblt. z. See, Kdt. "U 552" 87th Oak Leaves 11.4.42 17th Swords 17.8.42	20.6.41

Torley, Karl	Oblt., Chef 2./I.R. 60 (mot.) 132nd Oak Leaves 11.10.42	23.11.41
Tornau, Gottfried	Hptm., Fhr. Sturmart. Brig. der Führer-Gren. Div. "GD"	5 3.45
Toschka, Rudolf	Oblt., Zugf. in 1./Fsch. Jäg. Sturm-Rgt. 1 + 21.2.44 at Monte Cassino (Italy) as Hptm. & Btl. Kdr.	14.6.41
Tost, Ewald	Ofw., Zugf. in 1./G. R. 507	27.8.44
Trabandt, Paul	SS-Hauptscharf., Zugf. in 2./SS-Pz.Jäg. Abt. 5 "Wiking"	14.10.43
Trabandt, Wilhelm	SS-Standartenf., Fhr. 1. SS-Inf. Brig. (mot.)	6.1.44
Traber, Willy	Oblt., Fhr. 1./G. R. 309	23.3.45
Trägner, Josef	Wachtm., Geschützf. in 1./St. -Gesch. Abt. 667	23.8.43
Tratt, Eduard	Oblt., Flugzeugf. in I./Z.G. 1 437th Oak Leaves 26.3.44	12.4.42
Traupe, Hans	SS-Sturmbannf. & Major d. Schutzpolizei, Kdr. I./SS-Pol. G. R. 3	23.2.44
Trausnitz, Josef	Ofw. in 3./Ski-Pi. Btl. 85	3.11.44
Traut, Hans	Obstlt., Kdr. I./I.R. 90 67th Oak Leaves 23.1.42	5.8.40
Trautloft, Hannes	Major, Kmdre. J.G. 54	27.7.41
Trautmann, Karl	Oberst, Kdr. Fäs. Rgt. 22 + 21.4.45 of wounds	17.3.45
Trautwein, Heinz	Oblt. z. See d.R. Kdt. "U-jäger 202" + 1.11.44 in combat in the Adriatic	5.11.44
Trebes, Horst	Oblt., Fhr. III./Fsch. Jäg. Sturm-Rgt. + 29.7.44 in Normandy (France) as Hptm. & Kdr. III./Fsch. Jäg. Rgt. 6	9.7.41
Treckmann, Wilhelm	Hptm., Kdr. II./G. R. 53 + 13.7.44	4.5.44
Treeck, Dr. Egon	Major, Kdr. II./Geb.Jäg. Rgt. 85	8.8.41
Treffer, Franz	Oblt. d.R., Chef 5./I.R. 20 (mot.) + 10.8.41 in central Russia	23.8.41
Trenke, Hannes(Johann)	Fhj. -Fw., Flugzeugf. in 6./K.G. 1 "Hindenburg"	5.9.44
Trenkel, Rudolf	Ofw., Flugzeugf. in 2./J.G. 52	19.8.43
Trenkmann, Friedhelm	Uffz., Zugf. in 7./G. R. 365 + 17.9.44	21.9.44
Trenn, Rudolf	Oblt., Staffelkpt. 8./S.G. 77 + 16.4.43 Poix airfield (North France) as Staffelkpt. 3./S. K.G. 10 accidentally; Posthumously promoted to Hptm.	25.5.43
Treptau, Max	Gefr., Pion. in 3./Pz. Pi. Btl. 86	11.3.45
v. Tresckow, Joachim	Gen.Lt., Kdr. 18. Luftw. Feld-Div.	19.9.44
Trettner, Heinrich	Major i.G., Ia 7. Flieger-Div. 586th Oak Leaves 17.9.44	24.5.40

ELITE OF THE THIRD REICH

Trey, Werner	Hptm., Kdr. 1./G. R. 1058	12.12.44
Tribukait, Günther	Major, Kdr. Jäger-Btl. 5 + 26.2.1947 hanged at Belgrade (Yugoslavia) as Oberst	8.2.43
Triebe, Theodor	Hptm., Chef 1./Flak-Rgt. 7 (mot.) + 28.3.45 in Küstrin as Major & Kdr. a Flak-Rgt.	18.12.41
Trierenberg, Wolf-Günther	Gen.Lt., Kdr. 167. I.D.	10.5.43
Trinko, Otto	Feldw. in 4. (MG)/G. R. 577	30.4.45
Trippensee, Kurt	Ofw., Zugf. in 7./Geb.Jäg. Rgt. 144 + 16.2.43 at Oroschilowgrad (Russia)	2.4.43
Tritsch, Willy	Feldw., Flugzeugf. in 1./S.G. 1	23.12.42
Trittel, Rudolf	Major, Kdr. III./G. R. 479 799th Oak Leaves 23.3.45	14.8.43
Tröger, Hans	Gen. Major, Fhr. 17. Pz.Div.	4.5.44
Tröger, Rudolf	Ofw., Ord.Offz. in II./G. R. 102	17.4.45
Trojer, Hanns-Hartwig	Oblt. z. See, Kdt. "U 221" + 2.10.43 in Atlantic, south of Ireland as Kaptlt.	24.3.43
Tromm, Heinrich	Obstlt., Kdr. I.R. 411 + 19.6.42 at Cholm, south-east of Lake Ilmen (Russia); posthumously promoted to Oberst	15.11.41
Trompeter, Friedrich	Oberst, stv. Fhr. 305. I.D.	21.1.45
Tronnier, Louis	Oberst, Kdr. G. R. 70 + 27.1.52 in Camp Woikowo (Russia) in Soviet captivity; final post Gen. Major & Kdr. 62. Inf. Div.	28.11.42
Trost, Ewald-Günther	Hptm. Staffelkpt. 12./K.G. 26	12.11.43
Trotz, Herbert	Hptm., Kdr. Fest. Gren. Btl. "Trotz" in Festung Breslau (Kdr. II./Fsch. Jäg. Rgt. 26)	30.4.45
Trowitz, Adolf	Gen. Major, Kdr. 57. I.D.	21.2.44
Trummer, Hans	Feldw., Bordfunker in 1./S.G. 5	4.5.44
Truxa, Rolf	Oblt., Fhr. 2./St. Gesch. Abt. 190	17.12.43
Tscherning, Willy	Ofw., Bordfunker 1. d. 9./K.G. I "Hindenburg"	18.11.44
Tschierschwitz, Gerhard	Oblt., Chef 2./Fsch. Pz. Rgt. "HG"	6.12.44
Tschoerner, Philipp-Karl	Oblt., Beob. & Flugzeugkdt. in 5. (H)/Aufkl. Gr. 41 + 11.6.44	20.7.44
Trüke, Gerhard	Oblt. d.R., Chef 3./I.R. 29 (mot.)	17.12.42
Tulodetzki, Herbert	Ofw., Fhr. 2./G. R. 407	5.11.44
Tummer, Heinrich	Obgefr., Schütze 1 i. d. 13./G. R. 19 "List"	18.11.44
Twillemeyer, Alois	Gefr., Krad-Melder in Stab Füs. Btl. (A.A.) 81	15.3.44
Tychsen, Christian	SS-Sturmbannf., Kdr. II./SS-Pz. Rgt. 2 "Das Reich" 353rd Oak Leaves 10.12.43	31.3.43
v. Tycowicz, Rudolf (Thiegs v. Tycowicz)	Oberst, Kdr. G. R. 407	2.9.44
Tykiel, Alfred	Ofw., Zugf. in 6./Schtz. Rgt. 10	6.8.41

KNIGHT'S CROSS OF THE IRON CROSS

Tyroller, Georg	Obstlt., Kdr. le. Flak-Abt. 84 (mot.) & Fhr. a Kampfgruppe	23.12.42

U

Ubben, Kurt	Oblt., Staffelkpt. 8./J.G. 77 80th Oak Leaves 12.3.42	4.9.41
Ude, Otto	Owm., Zugf. in 1./Radf. Abt. 30	15.1.43
Udet, Dr.-Ing. h. c. Ernst	Gen. d. Flieger, Generalluftzeugmeister in OKL + 17.11.41 in Berlin (suicide) as Gen. Oberst	4.7.40
Uebe, Klaus	Gen. Major, Chef d. Genst. St. Luftflotte 2	9.6.44
Überschaar, Friedrich	Hptm., Fhr. III./Geb.Jäg. Rgt. 91	9.12.44
Ueltzhöfer, Eugen	Gefr. in Festg. Schneidemühl Kraftf. in 3./Art. Lehr-Rgt. 5 (mot)	12.2.45
Uhde, Hans	Oblt. d.R., Fhr. 11./G. R. 424	15.1.43
Uhl, Hans	Hptm., Fhr. II./G. R. 430	22.1.43
Uhl, Rudolf	Lt. Adj. II./Geb.Jäg. Rgt. 141	5.11.44
Uhlig, Alexander	Ofw. d.R., Zugf. in 16./Fsch. Jäg. Rgt. 6	29.10.44
Uhlig, Gottfried	Hptm., Kdr. II./G. R. 43	26.11.44
Uhlig, Martin	Hptm., Kdr. schw. Pz.Jäg. Abt. 88	11.3.45
Uhren, Franz	Feldw., Zugf. in 13. (I. G.)/G. R. 366	28.10.44
Ulich, Max	Oberst, Kdr. G. R. 15 (mot.)	2.11.43
Ullrich, Karl	SS-Sturmbannf., Kdr. SS-Pi. Btl. "Totenkopf" 480th Oak Leaves 14.5.44	19.2.42
Ulms, Ulrich	Oberstlt. i.G., Chef of Stabes of Korpsgruppe "v. Gottberg" (XII. SS-A.K.)	12.8.44
Ulrich, Emil	Uffz., Gr. Fhr. in 5./Gren. Rgt- "Feldherrnhalle"	7.2.45
Unfried, Willibald	Gefr., MG-Schütze 1 i. d. 9./I.R. 213	4.3.42
Unger, Heinz	Hptm., Chef 1./Schtz. Rgt. 10	4.9.41
Unger, Willy	Fhj. -Fw., Flugzeugf. in IV. (Sturm-)/J.G. 3 "Udet"	23.10.44
v. Unold, Georg	Oberst i.G., stellv. Fhr. 227. in + 1953 in Soviet captivity; final post Fhr. 252. Inf. Div.	20.3.45
Unrau, Heinz (17)	Major, Kdr. I./K.G. 51	1.5.45
Unrein, Martin	Oberst, Kdr. Pz. G. R. 4 515th Oak Leaves 26.6.44	10.9.43
Unruh, Kurt	Oblt., Flugzeugf. in 2./K.G. 53 "Legion Condor"	29.2.44
Unruhe, Johannes	Ofw., Zugf. in 2./Pz. Aufkl. Abt. 12	28.3.45
v. Usedom, Horst	Major, Kdr. Kradschtz. Btl. 61 809th Oak Leaves 28.3.45	31.12.41

Usinger, Christian	Gen. Major, Fhr. 81. I.D. + 1949 in Soviet captivity; final post Gen.Lt. & Fhr. I. A.K.	15.9.44
Frhr. v. Uslar-Gleichen, Horst	Major, Kdr. Pz. Abt. 190 + 23.10.44 at Großwaltersdorf (East Prussia) as Kdr. Pz. Abt. Führer-Begleit-Brigade "GD"; posthumously promoted to Oberstlt	11.7.44
Utgenannt, Richard	SS-Hauptsturmf, Chef 3./SS-Pz. Abt. 4	16.11.44
Uthe, Konrad	Major, Kdr. Pz. Gren. -Lehr. Rgt. 901 + 25.6.44 at Caen (Invasion front/France); posthumously promoted to Obstlt.	12.8.44
Utta, Ewald	Lt. d.R., Fhr. 5./G. R. 944 + 27.10.44 at Nizni Pisana (Russia)	23.10.44
Utz, Willibald	Oberst, Kdr. Geb.Jäg. Rgt. 100	21.6.41

V

v. Vaerst, Gustav	Oberst, Kdr. 2. Schtz. Bngade	30.7.40
Vahl, Herbert-Ernst	SS-Oberführer, Fhr. SS-Pz. Gren. Div. "Reich" + 22.7.44 in Greece accidentally as SS-Brigadef. & Gen. Major d. W-SS & Kdr. der 4. SS-Pol. Pz. Gren. Div.	31.3.43
Valet, Hans-Joachim	Lt., Flugzeugf. in 3./Transp. Geschw. 2 + 3.12.44 in Russia as Oblt. in 1./K.G. 51	20.4.44
Valle, Hermann	Oblt. d.R., Chef 4./Schtz. Rgt. 112 + 13.2.43 north of Kursk (Russia) as Major d.R. & Btl. Kdr.	31.12.41
Valtiner, Helmuth	Gefr., Spähtruppf. in 1./Gebjäg. Rgt. 143	13.6.41
Vandieken, Anton	SS-Hptsturmf. d.R., Kampfgfhr. SS-Kav. Rgt. 15 "Florian Geyer"	26.12.44
Vaulot, Eugene (7)	Waffen-Unterscharf., Gruppenf. in 33. (franz.) SS-Freiw. Div. "Charlemagne" in Berlin area + 2.5.45 in Berlin on R. L. M.	29.4.45
Vechtel, Bernhard	Fhj. -Ofw., Flugzeugf. in 10./J.G. 51 "Mölders"	27.7.44
Veeser, Peter	Ofw., Stoßtruppf. in 7./I.R. 125	14.5.41
Vehse, Fritz	Gefr., stellv. Gruppenf. in 3./Pi. Btl. 342	4.10.44
Veiel, Rudolf	Geri. Lt., Kdr. 2. Pz.Div.	3.6.40
Veiss, Voldemars	Waffen-Standartenf., Kdr. (lett.) SS-Freiw. Rgt. 48 + 16.4.44 at Nowovskew (Russia) as Waffen-Oberfuhrer	9.2.44
Veith, Alfred	Oblt., Beob. in 5./K.G. 55	24.10.44
Veith, Johann	SS-Obersturmf., Fhr. 3./SS-Pz. Rgt. 2 "Das Reich" + Jan. 1945 in the Ardennes	14.2.45
Veldkamp, Martin	Uffz., Gruppenf. in 6./G. R. 76 (mot.)	28.11.43

KNIGHT'S CROSS OF THE IRON CROSS

Velke, Paul	Obstlt., Kdr. Pi. Btl. 45 + 28.7.42 on the bend of the Don as Oberst & Kdr. a Pi. Rgt. Stab	15.8.40
Velten, Otto	Feldw., Fhr. Inf. Pi. Zug/G. R. 436	5.4.45
Velten, Theodor	Lt., Fhr. 3./Pz. Aufkl. Abt. 14 + 1945 in Kurland	4.10.44
Verhein, Siegfried	Gen. Major, Fhr. Kampfgr. 551 V.G.D.	28.2.45
Vernhold, Josef	Uffz., in 8./I.R. 60 (mot.)	22.2.42
Versock, Kurt	Oberst, Kdr. I.R. 31	25.8.42
Vesenmayer, Dr. agrar. Hans	Oblt., Chef 2./le. Flak-Abt. 77 (mot. s.)	18.11.44
Veth, Kurt	Hptm., Kdr. II./Fsch. Jäg. Rgt. 3	30.9.44
Vetter, Alfred	Lt. (V.), Gruppenf. in Marine-Kleinkampf-flottille 211 (simultaneously awarded EK II. & I. Klasse)	12.8.44
Vetter, Johann	Gefr., Pak-Schütze in 14. (Pz.Jäg.)/G. R. 147 + 4.6.44 south of the Albaner mountains (Italy); posthumously promoted to Obergefr.	15.6.44
Vetter, Martin	Major, Kdr. II./K.G. 26	16.5.40
Vetter, Max	Uffz., Zugf. in I./G. R. 380	7.2.44
Vial, Alexander	Oberst, Kdr. G. R. 60 (mot.)	18.12.42
Vicinius, Hermann	Hptm. d.R., Kdr. I./G. R. 866	16.9.43
Vickendey, Willi	Obgefr., Gruppenf. in 7./Ski-Jäger-Rgt. 1	17.9.44
Viebig, Hans	Oberst, Kdr. G. R. 258	21.2.44
Viechter, Korbinian	Lt. d.R., Fhr. 4./G. R. 42	20.10.44
Viedebantt, Helmut	Oblt., Staffelkpt. in II./Z.G. I + 1.5.45 shot down over Wusterhausen whilst on a flight to Berlin as Major	30.12.42
Viehmann, Wilhelm	Obstlt., Kdr. G. R. 453	17.4.45
Viehweg, Gottfried	Oblt. d.R., Chef 3./G. R. 456	13.1.44
Vielhauer, Ernst	Major, Kdr. II./G. R. 461 + 30.9.43 in hospital at Breslau (Silesia) of wounds	21.5.43
Vielwerth, Wilhelm-August genannt: Erich	Ofw., Zugf. i d. 1./I.R. 87 (mot.)	18.10.41
Vierecker, Fritz (8)	Hptm., Fhr. a Alarmeinheit in Oder sector	28.4.45
Vierow, Erwin	Gen.D.Inf., Kom.Gen. IV. A.K.	15.11.41
Viertel, Willi	Oblt., Staffelkpt. 7./Stuka-Geschw. 1 + 31.8.43 at Gluchow (Russia); posthumously promoted to Hptm.	5.2.44
v. Vietinghoff gen. v. Scheeli Heinrich-Gottfried	Gen. d. Pz.Tr., Kom.Gen. XIII. A.K. 456th Oak Leaves 16.4.44	24.6.40
Viezenz, Günther	Oblt., Chef 10./G. R. 7	7.1.44

Villinger, Heinrich	Lt., Fhr. 6./Geb.Jäg. Rgt. 99 + 12.12.44 on the Eastern Front	1.2.45
Vincon, Otto	Hptm. d.R., stellv. Fhr. I./G. R. 460 728th Oak Leaves 5.2.45	3.12.43
Vinke, Heinz	Feldw., Flugzeugf. in 11./N. J.G. 1 465th Oak Leaves 25.4.44	19.9.43
Virkus, Gerhard	Ofw., Kp. Tr. Fhr. in 2./Pz. G. R. 25	7.9.43
Vischer, Kurt	Obgefr., Gruppenf. in 6./Jäger-Rgt. 40(L)	18.12.44
Vitali, Viktor (5)	Lt., Zugf. in 5./Fsch. Jäg. Rgt. 4	30.4.45
Vocke, Helmut	Hptm., Kdr. II./Pz. G. R. 40 + 28.10.43 Nish-Ssevogosy (Russia) as Major & Kdr. Pz. Aufkl. Abt. 17	26.3.43
Vögerl, Georg (17)	Lt. in Fallsch. Jäg. Rgt. 26	28.3.45
Vögtle, Helmut (14)	Hptm. d.R., Kdr. II./Geb.Jäger-Rgt. 99	1.6.45
Völckers, Paul	Gen.Lt., Kdr. 78. Inf. Div. + 25.1.46 in Soviet captivity; final post Gen.D.Inf. & Kom.Gen. XXVII. A.K.	11.12.42
Völk, Hermann	Hptm., Kdr. Pz.Jäger-Abt. 92	26.3.44
Völkel, Helmut	Feldw., Zugf. in 6./Geb.Jäg. -Rgt. 91 + 26.10.42 in southern Russia (Caucasus) of wounds	13.11.42
Völker, Dr. jur. Gerhard	Oblt. d.R., Fhr. II./Pz. G. R. 25	26.11.44
Vogel, Emil	Gen.Lt., Kdr. 101. Jäger-Div. 475th Oak Leaves 14.5.44	7.8.43
Vogel, Robert	Feldw., Zugf. in 7./G. R. 119 (mot.)	26.8.43
Vogel, Walter	Major, Kdr. I/G. R. 6	29.8.43
Vogelsang, Friedrich	Ofw., Zugf. in 12./I.R. 78	4.9.42
Vogelsang, Dr. med. dent. Friedrich	Obstlt., Kdr. G. R. 505	14.12.43
Vogelsang, Karl	Major d.R., Kdr. II./A.R. 157	14.1.45
Vogler, Emil	Uffz., Kradmeldestaffelf. in Stab I./Pz. G. R. 93	24.1.44
Vogt, Adolf	Oblt., Chef 12./G. R. 1054	16.10.44
Vogt, Emil	Oberschirrmeister (Pi.) in Stabskp./Pz. G. R. 101	26.3.43
Vogt, Fritz	SS-Obersturmf., Zugf. in the 2./SS-Aufkl. Abt./SS-Verf. Div. 785th Oak Leaves 16.3.45	4.9.40
Vogt, Gerhard	Lt., Staffelf. 5./J.G. 26 "Schlageter" + 14.1.45 at Wittingen (Hannover) as Oblt.	25.11.44
Vogt, Ludwig	Lt. d.R., Fhr. 4. (MG)/G. R. 915	17.2.45
Vohburger, Hans	Oblt., Chef 7./I.R. 19 + 18.8.42 in Russia as Hptm.	14.12.41
Voigt, Gerhard	Oblt., Chef 2./Pi. Btl. 18	25.6.40
Voigt, Hans (8)	Gen. Major, Kdt. Festg. Arnswalde (Pomerania)	28.4.45

Voigt, Hans-Günther	Oblt., Chef 5./G. R. 154 + 12.1.44 north-west of Nevel (Russia)	29.2.44
Voigt, Walter	Ofw., Zugf. in 14. (Pz.Jäg.)/G. R. 31	16.10.44
Voigtsberger, Heinrich	Major, Kdr. MG-Btl. 2 351st Oak Leaves 9.12.43	9.7.41
Volckamer v. Kirchensittenbach, Friedrich-Jobst	Gen.Lt., Kdr. 8. Jäger-Div.	26.3.44
Volckens, Hennecke	Hptm., Chef 7./Pz. Rgt. 6 + 16.12.42 north of Terek (Russia)	17.12.42
Volk, Kurt	Uffz., Geschtzf. in 2./Pz.Jäg. Abt. 9	10.5.43
Volke, Herbert	Owm., Zugf. in I./Pz. Aufkl. Abt. 5	16.11.44
Volker, Heinrich	Hptm., Chef Stabskp./Pz. G. R. 73	19.1.43
Volkmann, Heinz	Lt. d.R., Battr. -Offz. in 2./A.R. 240 + 15.3.42 at Bladian (East Prussia)	8.2.43
Vollbracht, Friedrich	Obstlt., Kmdre. Z.G. 2	13.10.40
Vollmer, Götzpeter	Oblt., Staffelkpt. 1./Stuka-Geschw. 2 "Immelmann" + 19.12.44 as Major & Lehrer in Verbandsführerschule Königsberg (Neumark) accidentally	22.6.41
Vollmer, Günter	Oblt. d.R., Fhr. 3./G. R. 411	20.4.43
Vonhoff, Heinrich	Oblt. d.R., Chef 12./I.R. 408 + 1.10.42 south of Lake Ladoga (Russia) of wounds	25.9.42
Voormann, Klaus	Oblt., Chef 10./I.R. 134 + 30.11.42 Stalingrad	10.9.42
Vorbrugg, Oskar	Oberst, Kdr. Flak-Rgt. 21 (mot.) + 21.5.46 in British captivity at Rimini (Italy) accidentally; final post Gen. Major & Kdr. 25. Flak-Div.	3.6.44
v. Vormann, Nikolaus	Gen.Lt., Kdr. 23. Pz.Div.	22.8.43
Voshage, Werner (19)	Major, Kdr. Heeres-Fla-Abt. "Brandenburg"	8.5.45
Voß, Ernst	Obstlt., Kdr. G. R. 585 314th Oak Leaves 28.10.43	18.4.43
Voß, Herbert	Major, Kdr. II./K.G. 51	5.2.44
Voß, Johann-Joachim	Oblt. d.R., Fhr. 5./Schtz. Rgt. 93	27.5.42
Voß, Reimer	Oblt., Staffelkpt. 4./K.G. 26	12.3.45
Voutta, Heinrich	Hptm., Fhr. Pz. Aufkl. Abt. 9 + 1.4.45 at Niederlaasphe (Dillenburg)	23.3.45

W

Wabro, Franz	Uffz., Gruppenf. in Stabskp./G. R. 534	4.7.44
Wachowiak, Friedrich	Uffz., Flugzeugf. in III./J.G. 52 + 16.7.44 in Normandy (France) as Lt. & Flugzeugf. in III./J.G. 3 "Udet"	5.4.42

ELITE OF THE THIRD REICH

Wack, Hans	Hptm., Kdr. II./Inf.Rgt. 485 + 30.6.44 in Russia as Fhr. Gr. Rgt. 51 (mot.); posthumously promoted to Oberst	23.10.41
Wätjen, Rudolf	Major, Kdr. Pz. Aufkl. Abt. "GD"	14.4. 43
Wagener, Carl	Oberst i.G., Chef d. Gen. St. 1. Pz. Armee	14.5.44
Wagener, Dr. Otto (3)	Gen. -Major, Kdr. Div. "Insel Rhodos"	5.5.45
Wagenfeld, Ludwig	Hptm., Staffelkpt. 3. (F)/Aufkl. Gr. 122	24.3.43
Wagner, Edmund	Ofw., Flugzeugf. in 9./J.G. 51 + 13.11.41 Pafmutowka (Russia)	17.11.41
Wagner, Erich	Obgefr., Geschützf. in 16./Jäger-Rgt. 38	23.8.43
Wagner, Ferdinand	Uffz., Gewehr-Fhr. in 4./G. R. 32	12.12.44
Wagner, Gustav	Oberst, Kdr. I.R. 44	14.12.41
Wagner, Hans	Oberst, Kdr. A.R. 5	18.4.43
Wagner, Hans-Joachim	Hptm. d.R., Chef Stabsbattr./St. Gesch. Brig. 286	25.1.45
Wagner, Heinz	Lt. d.R., Zugf. in Kradschtz. Btl. 6 + 16.8.44	24.1.43
Wagner, Helmut	Lt., Zugf. in 6./Fsch. Jäger. Rgt. 1 + 7.6.44 in Normandy (France) as Oblt. & Kp. Fhr.; posthumously promoted to Hptm.	24.1.42
Wagner, Helmut	Hptm. d. R, Kdr. I./G. R. 431 + Oct. 1944 in Rominter Heide (East Prussia)	9.12.44
Wagner, Herbert	Gen.Lt., Kdr. 132. I.D.	23.10.44
Wagner, Josef	Oblt., Chef 1./Jäger-Rgt. 227	18.2.45
Wagner, Jürgen	SS-Oberf., Kdr. SS-Pz. G. R. 9 "Germania" 680th Oak Leaves 11.12.44	24.7.43
Wagner, Klaus	Oblt., Fhr. 3./St. Gesch. Abt. 667	4.9.42
Wagner, Rudolf	Lt., Flugzeugf. in 12./J.G. 51 "Mölders" + posted missing 11.12.43 at Zhitomir (Russia) as Staffelfhr. following aerial combat	26.3.44
Wagner, Werner	Oblt., Chef 3./Pz.Jäg. Lehr-Abt. 130	14.4. 45
Wagner, Wilhelm	Major, Kdr. II./A.R. 158	11.4.44
Wagner, Willi	Owm., Zugf. in 3./He. Küst. Art. Abt. 789	17.5.43
Wahl, Dietmar	Major, Kdr. 1./G. R. 282 + 13.8.43 in Simferopol (Crimea/Russia) of wounds	29.8.43
Wahl, Ernst	Uffz., Zügf. in 2./Pi. Btl. 389	17.9.44
Wahl, Hans	Oblt. d.R., Fhr. 3./G. R. 23	26.3.44
Wahl, Kurt	SS-Hptsturmf., Fhr. of a Kampfgr. in SS-Pz. G. R. 38 "Götz v. Berlichingen" 720th Oak Leaves 1.2.45	23.8.44
Wahl, Wolfgang	Hptm., Kdr. II./Pz. Rgt. 8	6.1.42
Waldecker, Helmut	Hptm., Staffelkpt. i. d. I./K.G. 6	22.11.43
Walden, Bruno	Major d. Schupo, Kdr. III/SS-Pol. -Rgt. 2	18.1.45

KNIGHT'S CROSS OF THE IRON CROSS

v. Waldenburg, Siegfried	Oberst, Fhr. 116. Pz.Div.	9.12.44
Frhr. v. Waldenfels, Rudolf	Oberst, Kdr. Schtz. Rgt. 4 476th Oak Leaves 14.5.44	11.10.41
Waldhauser, Johann	Oblt., Staffelkpt. 9./Stuka-Geschw. 77 + 13.5.42 Kertsch (Russia)	24.1.42
Waldmann, Hans	Feldw., Flugzeugf. in 6./J.G. 52 + 18.3.45 at Kaltenkirchen (Holstein) as Oblt. & Staffelkpt. 3./J.G. 7	5.2.44
Waldmüller, Hans	SS-Sturmbannf., Kdr. I./SS-Pz. G. R. 25 "Hitlerjugend" + 8.9.44 at Basse-Bodeux (Belgium), as SS-Obersturmbannfhr., killed by Belgian partisans	27.8.44
Waldner, Franz	Obgefr., Richtschtz. in 2./schw. Pz.Jäg. Abt. 655	12.8.44
Waldow, Hermann	Oblt., Chef Pz. Späh-Kp. 700	30.1.43
Walle, Gustav	Major, Kdr. Pz.Jäg. Abt. "GD"	8.5.45
Wallhäuser, Heinz	Oblt. d.R., Fhr. 1./Fsch. Pz.Jäger-Abt. "HG"'	30.11.44
Wallowitz, Walther	Lt., Fhr. 5./G. R. 82 + 20.10.43 in Russia; posthumously promoted to Oblt.	14.11.43
Walter, Domenikus	Ofw., Flugzeugf. in IV./K.G. z.b.V. 1	24.12.42
Walter, Gerhard	Ofw., Zugf. in 5. (MG)/G. R. 29 (mot.) + 30.1.44 in Italy	1.1.44
Walter, Helmut	Hptm., Btl. Fhr. in Feld-Uffz. -Schule Dahlhausen (2. Pz.Div.)	9.5.45
Walter, Karl	Obstlt., Kdr. G. R. 131	22.1.43
Walter, Kurt	Major, Kdr. II./I.R. 32 345th Oak Leaves 5.12.43	25.9.42
Walter, Kurt	Hptm., Kdr. III./Stuka-Geschw. 3 + 26.10.42 at El Alamein (North Africa)	26.3.43
Walterbach, Bernhard	Uffz., Zugf. in 2./Pi. Btl. 253	22.9.43
Walther, Erich	Major, Kdr. I./Fsch. Jäg. Rgt. 1 411th Oak Leaves 2.3.44 131st Swords 1.2.45	24.5.40
Walther, Gerhard	Hptm., Kdr. II./S.G. 4 + 18.5.44 at Rieti (Italy)	26.3.44
Walther, Wilhelm	Oblt., Stoßtruppf in 4./Bau-Lehr-Btl. z. b. V 800 "Brandenburg"	24.6.40
Walz, Hans	Oblt., Chef 1./Pz. Abt. 103	14.4.45
Wandel, Friedrich-Wilhelm	Hptm., Kdr. I./G. R. 347 + 26.10.43 in Russia of wounds; posthumously promoted to Major	27.10.43
Wandel, Joachim	Hptm., Staffelkpt. 5./J.G. 54 + 7.10.42 shot down over Ostaschkow (Russia) south of Lake Ilmen	21.8.42
Wandel, Martin	Gen. Major, Kdr. 121. I.D. + 14.1.43 at Chilino (Russia) as Gen. d. Art. & Kom.Gen. XXIV. Pz. Korps	23.11.41

Wandersleb, Martin	Hptm. d.R., Chef 10./G. R. 12 + 28.8.43 at Borissowa (Russia)	31.7.43
Wandmaker, Helmut	Major d.R., Kdr. II./Pz. G. R. 76	5.4.45
Wandrey, Max	Oblt. d.R., Chef 11./Jäger-Rgt. 1 "Brandenburg" 787th Oak Leavea 16.3.45	9.1.44
v. Wangelin, Hans-Joachim	see Jacobi v. Wangehn	
Wangerin, Friedrich-Wilhelm	Hptm., Kdr. III./Fsch. Jäg. Rgt. 16. Ost.	24.10.44
Wanhöfer, Günter	SS-Hptsturmf., Kdr. SS-Pi. Btl. 54 "Nederland"	27.8.44
Wanka, Karl	Oblt. d.R., Fhr. I./G. R. 446 800th Oak Leaves 23.3.45	23.2.44
Wanke, Artur	Obstlt., Kdr. G. R. 680	25.10.43
Wapnitz, Erich	Uffz., Gr. Fhr. in Stabskp. (Radf. Zug)/G. R. 671	17.3.45
Warnecke, Fritz	Major, Kdr. III./G. R. 517	22.1.43
Warnhoff, Karl	Major, Fhr. G. R. 587 + 2.9.43 at Charkow (Russia); posthumously promoted to Obstlt.	30.9.43
Warnkross, Wolfgang	Lt. d.R., Fähnnchsvater in Lehrkp. Gren. Feldausb. Rgt. 640	12.8.44
Warrelmann, Hinrich	Oberst, Kdr. G. R. 502 555th Oak Leaves 19.8.44	16.4.44
Warrelmann, Wilhelm	Uffz., Zugf. in 6./G. R. 328 + 13.2.44 south of Leningrad (Russia); posthumously promoted to Feldw.	15.3.44
Warschnauer, Horst	Oblt. d.R., Chef 2./Pi. Btl. "GD" (mot.) 753rd Oak Leaves 24.2.45	12.12.42
v. Wartenberg, Guido	Major, Fhr. Pz. G. R. 111 + 16.9.44 as Obstlt. & Brig. Kdr. (P7); posthumously promoted to Oberst	6.10.43
Warwel, Friedrich-Karl	Stabsfw., Zugf. in 14./G. R. 477	13.9.43
Waßmann, Adolf	Obgefr., MG-Schtz. in 6./G. R. 255	16.3.44
Wawrok, Ernst	Ofw., Zugf. in 13./Jäger-Rgt. 28	9.2.43
Weber, Alfons	Hptm., Fhr. II./Geb.Jäg. Rgt. 91	9.6.44
Weber, Alois	Major, Kdr. 1./I.R. 19 579th Oak Leaves 10.9.44	26.11.41
Weber, Alois	SS-Hptscharf., Zugf. in 16. (Pi.)/SS-Pz. G. R. "Deutschland"	30.7.43
Weber, Benno	Uffz., Gruppenf. in 2./G. R. 467 + 8.8.44 east of Augustowo (Russia) as Ofw. & Zugf.	23.12.43
Weber, Franz	Obgefr. in 8./Jäger-Rgt. 28	28.10.44
Weber, Friedrich	Obstlt., Kdr. I.R. 481	8.6.40
Weber, Gerhard	Oberst, Kdr. G. R. 41 (mot.) + 13.1.44 at Kulpanka (Russia); posthumously promoted to Gen. Major	26.10.43

KNIGHT'S CROSS OF THE IRON CROSS

Weber, Gottfried	Major, Kdr. I./I.R. 162 490th Oak Leaves 9.6.44	13.10.41
Weber, Hans-Joachim	Hptm., Kdr. III./Füs. Rgt. 27	27.12.44
Weber, Horst	Oblt. z. See d.R., Kdt. "S 55" in 3. Schnellbootsflottille	5.7.43
Weber, Jakob	Feldw., Halbzugf. in 2./Pz. Abt. 21	16.8.43
Weber, Karl-Heinz	Oblt., Staffel£ 7.1J.G. 51 "Mölders" 529th Oak Leaves 20.7.44	12.11.43
Weber, Otto	Major d.R., Kdr. G. R. 933 + 14.9.44. of wounds	31.10.44
Weber, Paul	Lt. d.R., Fhr. 9./G. R. 508	25.7.43
Weber, Paul-Friedel	Oblt., Chef 2./schw. He. Fla-Abt. 303	10.10.42
Weber, Rudolf	Feldw., Zugf. in 9./Pz. Rgt. 4	14.2.45
Weber, Siegfried	Oblt., Fhr. III./Jäg. Rgt. 49	30.10.42
Weber, Walter	Uffz., Kp. Truppf. in 7./Inf.Rgt. 211	13.10.41
Weber, Wilhelm (7)	SS-Obersturmf., Fhr. d. Div. -Kampfschule der 33. (französ.) SS-Freiw. -Gren. Div. "Charlemagne"	29.4.45
Frhr. v. Wechmar, Irnfried	Obstlt., Kdr. Aufkl. Abt. 3	13.4.41
Wechsung, Willi	Oblt., Chef I./G. R. 426	1.10.43
Weck, Hans-Joachim (5)	Lt., Fhr. 3./Fsch. Jäg. Rgt. 4	30.4.45
Wecker, Franz	Obstlt., Kdr. Jäg. Rgt. 734	9.5.45
Weddig, Ernst	Lt., Fhr. 4./Pz. G. R. 101 + 8.3.43; posthumously promoted to Oblt.	20.4.43
v. Wedel, Busso	Oberst, Kdr. G. R. 89	18.5.43
v. Wedel, Hermann	Oberst, Kdr. G. R. 590' + 5.2.44 of wounds in hospital at Dorpat (Estonia) as Gen. Major & Kdr. 10. Luftw. Feld-Div.	8.6.43
Wegener, Paul	Wachtm., Gechützf. in I./St. Gesch. Abt. 237	18.10.43
Wegener, Werner	Major d.R., Kdr. Pi. Btl. 3 (mot.)	24.12.44
Wegener, Wilhelm	Oberst, Kdr. I.R. 94 66th Oak Leaves 19.1.42 97th Swords 17.9.44	27.10.41
Weger, Alois	Oblt. d.R., Chef 3./Pz. G. R. 33	9.12.44
Wegerer, Ferdinand	Uffz., Zugf. in I./Pz. G. R. 10 483rd Oak Leaves 4.6.44	8.10.43
Weglehner, Friedrich	Major d.R., Kdr. II./G. R. 390	12.8.44
Wegner, Wilhelm	Owm., Zugf. in 1./St. Gesch. Abt. "GD"	13.6.43
Wehinger, Anton	Oblt. d.R., Chef I./G. R. 578	9.1.45
Wehking, Hermann	Owm., V. B. in I./A.R. 146 (mot.)	15.1.44
Wehlitz, Lothar	Hptm. d.R., Chef 1./schw. Art. Abt. 845	6.2.44

Wehmeyer, Alfred	Oblt., Staffelkpt. 7./Z.G. 26 "Horst Wessel" + 1.6.42 west of Tobruk (North Africa) by a direct hit from flak	4.9.42
Wehrmann, Gerhard	Hptm., Fhr. Pz. Gr. Feldersatz-Btl. 3	3.11.44
Weible, Ernst	Ofw., Flugzeugf. in 3./K.G. 54 + 25.3.44	6.4.44
Frhr. v. & zu Weichs an der Glon, Maximilian	Gen. d. Kav., OB 2. Armee 731st Oak Leaves 5.2.45	29.6.40
Weichsel, August	Uffz., Gr. Fhr. in 6./G. R. 948	30.4.45
Weichsel, Ernst	Major, Kdr. II./Pz. G. R. 115	5.5.45
Weidenbrück, Wilhelm	Oblt., Chef 5./Pz. Rgt. 3 649th Oak Leaves 16.11.44	16.9.42
Weldhofer, Otto	Ofw., Zugf. in 8./G. R. 162 + 1944	15.5.44
Weidinger, Otto	SS-Sturmbannf., Kdr. SS-Pz. Aufkl. Abt. 2 "Das Reich" 688th Oak Leaves 26.12.44 150th Swords 6.5.45	21.4.44
Weidling, Helmuth	Gen. Major, Kdr. 86. I.D. 408th Oak Leaves 22.2.44 115th Swords 28.11.44	15.1.43
Weigel, Hermann	Major, Fhr. G. R. 328	19.2.45
Weigel, Rudolf	Stabsfw., Flugzeugf. in 7./Stuka-Geschw. 77 + 18.4.45 in Wriezen, Berlin as Hptm. & Staffelkpt. i. Pz. S.G. 9	27.4.42
Weihrauch, Werner	Ofw., Flugzeugf. in 2./Stuka-Geschw. 77	19.2.43
Weik, Hans	Lt., Staffelf. 10./J.G. 3 "Udet"	27.7.44
Weiler, August	Hptm., Btl. Fhr. in Rgt. "v. Stössel"	16.11.44
Weiler, Bruno	Oberst, Kdr. Ski-Jäg. Rgt. 1 + 8.5.45 by suicide at Landskron, before the surrender, as Fhr. 1. Ski-Jäger-Div.	9.5.45
Weimer, Kilian	Hptm., Kdr. I./I.R. 109 478th Oak Leaves 14.5.44	31.8.41
Weimer, Otto	Lt. d.R., Fhr. 2./G. R. 957 + 5.5.45 at Wissen/Sieg	24.12.44
Weinbuch, Georg	Owm., Zugf. in 6./schw. Art.Rgt. 46 + 24.5.42 Charkow (Russia) of wounds	28.7.42
Weineck, Johannes	Oblt., Beob. in 5. (F)/Aufkl. Gr. 122	29.2.44
Weinelt, Rudolf	Lt. d.R., Fhr. 2./Pz. Pi. Btl. 19	12.11.43
Weinknecht, Friedrich-August	Gen. Major, Kdr. 79. I.D.	15.7.44
Weinlig, Werner	Kaptlt., Kdt. Torpedoboot "T 23"	6.5.45
Weinreich, Fritz	Uffz., Zugf. in 4./Reiter-Rgt. 41	17.3.45
Weinreich, Helmut	Oblt., Staffelkpt. in III./K.G. 30 + 18.11.43 shot down over Frankfurt a. M. (Rhein-Main) as Kmdre J.G. 301; posthumously promoted to Obstlt.	21.1.43
Weippert, Gustav	Ofw., Flugzeugf. & Beob. in 2. (H)/Aufkl. Gr. 4	30.9.44

KNIGHT'S CROSS OF THE IRON CROSS

Weise, Hubert	Gen. d. Flakart., Kom.Gen. I. Flak-Korps	24.6.40
Weisenberger, Karl	Gen.Lt., Kdr. 71. I.D.	29.6.40
Weiser, Hermann	SS-Obsturmf. d.R., Fhr. 2. Kradschtz. Kp./Aufkl. Abt./"LSSAH"	28.3.43
Weisleder, Hans-Georg	Hptm. d.R., Kdr. III./G. R. 453	21.9.44
Weismann, Ernst	Lt., Flugzeugf. in 12./J.G. 51 "Mölders" + 13.8.42 posted missing north of Rshew (Russia) after bailing out; posthumously promoted to Oblt.	21.8.42
Weiß, Adolf	Ofw., Flugzeugf. in 4./Stuka-Geschw. 77	29.2.44
Weiß, Christian	Hptm., Kdr. II./I.R. 26	10.4.42
Weiß, Ernst	Oberst, Kdr. G. R. 572 + 23.8.44 in Rumania	24.6.44
Weiß, Franz	Major d.R., Kdr. III./Pz. Rgt. 2	11.3.45
Weiß, Friedrich	Uffz., Geschützf. in 1./Flak-Rgt. 36 (mot.)	21.12.42
Weiß, Georg	Uffz., Gruppenf. in 6./G. R. 521	12.11.43
Weiß, Hans	SS-Hptsturmf., Kdr. SS-Pz. Aufkl. Abt. 2 "Das Reich"	6.4.43
Weiß, Herbert	Hptm. d.R., Kdr. II./G. R. 418 + 20.2.45 as Major in Fhj. -Schule IV. der Inf.	7.1.43
Weiß, Josef	Obgefr., Kp. Trupp-Melder in 1./G. R. 24	23.3.45
Weiß, Otto	Hptm., Kdr. II. (S.)/L.G. 2 52nd Oak Leaves 31.12.41	18.5.40
Weiß, Paul	Obgefr., Gruppenf. in 6./G. R. 481	16.9.43
Weiß, Richard	Major d.R., Kdr. Pz. Abt. 8	30.4.45
Weiß, Robert	Oblt., Staffelkpt. 3./J.G. 54 782nd Oak Leaves 12.3.45	26.3.44
Weiß, Walter	Gen. Major, Kdr. 26. I. D 646th Oak Leaves 5.11.44	12.9.41
Weißberg, Wilhelm	Hptm., Kdr. I./Flak-Rgt. 25 (mot.)	24.10.44
Weisse, Bruno	Hptm. d.R., Fhr. II./G. R. 430	28.10.44
Weissenberg, Horst	Major, Kdr. G. R. 1	23.3.45
Weissenberger, Theodor	Lt., Flugzeugf. in 6./J.G. 5 266th Oak Leaves 2.8.43	13.11.42
Weißflog, Erich	Oblt., Nachr. Offz. & Bordfunker des N. J.G. 1	24.6.44
Weißflog, Hans-Joachim	Lt., Fhr. 2./Pz. Rgt. 16	5.3.45
Weißmann, Eginhard	Lt., Flugzeugf. in I./S.G. 2 "Immelmann"	5.9.44
Weißmüller, Ludwig	Hptm., Kdr. II./G. R. 462 + 18.8.43 Orel (Russia)	11.10.43
Weiter, Josef	Feldw., Zugf. in I./G. R. 697 + 30.7.44	24.6.44
Weitkunat, Adolf	Rittm. d.R., Chef Aufkl. Schwadr. 206 346th Oak Leaves 5.12.43	4.11.41
Weitkus, Paul	Obstlt., Kmdr. K.G. 53 "Legion Condor"	18.9.41

Name	Details	Date
Weitzel, Adalbert	Obstlt., Kdr. Pz. G. R. 6 + 17.8.44 at Kelme (Lithuania); posthumously promoted to Oberst	23.8.44
Wekenmann, Martin	Oblt. d.R., Fhr. I./Pz. G. R. 35	5.2.45
Welken, Heinrich	Oblt., Chef 2./Flak-Rgt. 231 (mot.)	5.9.44
Weller, Franz	Major, Fhr. I.R. 54 626th Oak Leaves 23.10.44	4.9.41
Wellmann, Ernst	Obstlt., Kdr. I./Pz. G. R. 3 342nd Oak Leaves 30.11.43	2.9.42
Welsch, Willi	Hptm., Chef 2./Schtz. Rgt. 110 + 27.7.44 at St. Lo (Normandy/France) as Kdr. Pz. Gren. Lehr-Rgt. 902; posthumously promoted to Obstlt.	29.9.41
Welskop, Heinrich	Ofw., Zugf. in II./Fsch. Jäg. Rgt. 3	21.8.41
Welter, Kurt	Lt., Flugzeugf. in 2./N. J.G. 11 769th Oak Leaves 11.3.45	18.10.44
Welzel, Franz-Josef	Major, Kdr. I./I. R. 461	19.7.40
Welzel, Karl-Heinrich	Feldw., Flugzeugf. in 7./S.G. 10	5.9.44
Wenck, Walther	Oberst i.G., Deutscher Chef d. Gen. St. d. 3. rumän. Armee	28.12.42
Wendenburg, Gerhard	Major, Kdr. Pz. Abt. 67	15.8.40
Wendland, Heinrich	Oblt. d.R., Chef 5./Pz. G. R. 304 + 18.6.44 in Normandy (France); posthumously promoted to Hptm.	20.7.44
Wendlandt, Siegfried	Hptm. d.R., Kdr. I./G. R. 320	16.1.45
Wendorff, Helmut	SS-Untersturmf., Zugf. in 13. (schw.)/SS-Pz. Rgt. 1 "LSSAH" + 6.8.44 at Merzieres south-east of Caen (France) as SS-Obersturmf.	12.2.44
Wendrinsky, Gustav	SS-Oberscharf., Zugf. in 1./SS-Pz.Jäg. Abt. 8 "Florian Geyer" + early February 1945 in Budapest missing; posthumously promoted to SS-Hauptscharf.	27.1.45
Wendt, Karl	Ofw., Zugf. in 2./G. R. 412 + 17.9.44 in Russia	21.9.44
Wendt, Manfred	Hptm., m.F.b. I./Pz. G. R. 66	9.7.44
Wendt, Rudi	Ofw., Flugzeugf. Stab/S.G. 2 "Immelmann" + 8.5.45 in Czechoslovakia by partisans	17.4.45
Wendt, Wilhelm	Hptfeldw., Kp. Feldw. 5./Pz. Rgt. 5	30.6.41
Wendt, Wolf	Hptm., Adj. G. R. 88	12.8.44
Wenger, Leopold	Oblt., Staffelkpt. 4./S.G. 10 + 10.4.45 at Deutsch-Wagram (Austria) as Staffelkpt. 6./S.G. 103	14.1.45
Wengler, Maximilian	Obstlt. d.R., Kdr. I.R. 366 404th Oak Leaves 22.2.44 123rd Swords 21.1.45	6.10.42
Weniger, Karl	Kapt. z. See, Fhr. 2. Sich. Div. + 1.10.41 by enemy aircraft at Dieppe (France)	15.11.41

Name	Details	Date
Wenigmann, Josef	Ofw., Flugzeugf. in 3./Stuka-Geschw. 3 + 3.7.42 El Alamein (North Africa); posthumously promoted to Oblt.	5.7.41
Wenke, Klaus	Oblt. z. See d.R., Kdt. "U-Jäger 208" + 1.11.44 during combat in the Adriatic	5.11.44
Wensauer, Matthias	Major, Fhr. G. R. 442	30.4.45
Wentzell, Fritz	Gen. Major, Chef d. Gen. St. 10. Armee	23.10.44
Wenz, Alfred	Oblt., Chef 7./G. R. 435 + 19.9.44 in Russia as Btl. Fhr.	21.9.44
Wenzel, Bernhard	Oblt., Chef 12./Pz. Rgt. 24 + 22.9.44 Dukla Pass (Poland) as Rittm. & Kdr. III./Pz. Rgt. 24; posthumously promoted to Major	12.8.44
Wenzelburger, Georg	Hptm., Fhr. II./G. R. 1098	26.12.44
v. Werder, Richard	Obstlt., Kdr. II./I.R. 102	4.9.40
Werfft, Dr. chem. Peter	Hptm., Kdr. III./J.G. 27	28.1.45
Welin, Wilhelm	Hptm., Staffelkpt. in 1./K.G. 27 "Boelcke"	30.12.42
Wermter, Rudolf	Hptm., Fhr. 1./G. R. 415	13.12.42
Werner, Ernst	Hptm., Fhr. III./I.R. 516 + 23.9.44 in Russia as Major & Rgt. Fhr.	10.9.42
Werner, Ernst-August	Hptm. d.R., Kdr. II./G. R. 980 +4.2.45 as Major d.R. & Fhr. Gren. Rgt. 1083	19.8.44
Werner, Gerhard	Oblt., Chef 5./Jagd-Kdo. 8 793rd Oak Leaves 23.3.45	23.2.42
Werner, Heinz	Major, Kdr. 1./A.R. 240 + 26.1.44 at Wosskresssenskoje south of Leningrad (Russia)	6.3.44
Werner, Heinz	SS-Hptsturmf., Fhr. III. (gep.)/SS-Pz. G. R. 4 "Der Führer" 864th Oak Leaves 6.5.45	23.8.44
Werner, Otto	Ofw., Zugf. in 3./schw. Pz.Jäger-Abt. 666 + 18.12.43 north-west of Newel (Russia)	22.1.44
Werner, Paul-Hermann	Oberst, Kdr. Pz. Rgt. 31 + 30.6.40 in France	3.6.40
Werner, Walter	Feldw., Gruppenf. in 1./Fsch. Pi. Btl. 1	9.6.44
Wernicke, Heinz	Lt., Flugzeugf. in 1./J.G. 54 + 27.12.44 at Doblen (Kurland) tödl. abgestürzt as Staffelfhr.	30.9.44
Wernig, Emil	Feldw., Zugf. in 4./G. R. 105 + 20.11.43 Tscherkassy (Russia) as Lt. d.R. & Kp. Fhr.	25.6.43
Wernitz, Ulrich	Feldw., Flugzeugf. in 4./J.G. 54	29.10.44
Baron v. Werra, Franz	Oblt., Adj. II./J.G. 3 + 25.10.41 shot down over Vlissingen (over the North Sea) as Hptm. & Kdr. 1./J.G. 53	14.12.40
Werther, Hellmuth	Oblt. z. See d.R., Kdt. & Gruppenf. in Küstenschutzflottille the "Attika"	8.11.44
Frhr. v. Werthern, Thilo	Oblt., Chef 3./Schtz. Rgt. 394	8.9.41

Frhr. & Herr v. Werthern-Beichlingen, Thilo	Oblt., Chef I./Pz. Rgt. 27	18.11.41
Wesche, Willy	Major, Kdr. G. R. 430 541st Oak Leaves 6.8.44	9.4.43
Wessel, Rudolf	Uffz., Gruppenf. in I./G. R. 1076	26.12.44
Wessel, Walter	Oberst, Kdr. I.R. 15 (mot.) 76th Oak Leaves 17.2.42	15.8.40
Wessels, Johann-Friedrich	Kaptlt. (Ing.), Leit. Ing. auf "U 198"	9.3.44
Weßlng, Otto	Ofw., Flugzeugf. in 9./J.G. 3 "Udet" 530th Oak Leaves 20.7.44	3.9.42
Westberg, Günter	Lt., Fhr. 1./Aufkl. Abt. 8 + 16.12.44	31.1.45
Westenberger, Walter	Hptm., Kdr. I./G. R. 255	12.11.43
Westermann, Wilhelm	Lt., Fhr. I./Kradschtz. Btl. 25	15.9.41
Westhofen, Heinrich	Oblt., Chef 3./Schtz. Rgt. 73	1.3.42
Westhoven, Franz	Gen.Lt., Kdr. 3. Pz.Div.	25.10.43
Westphal, Siegfried	Oberst i.G., Ia Dtsch. -ital. Pz. Armee	29.11.42
Westphalen, Otto	Oblt. z. See, Kdt. "U 968"	23.3.45
Wetjen, Heinrich	Hptm. d.R., Kdr. I./Jäg. Rgt. 49	28.3.45
Wettengel, Alfred	Oblt. d.R., Chef Stabsbatt. I./A.R. 60	21.9.44
Wettengel, Karl	Hptm. d.R., Adj. G. R. 559	24.1.44
Wetzel, Friedrich	Uffz., Gruppenf. in 7./G. R. 438	19.8.44
Wetzel, Wilhelm	Gen.D.Inf., Kom.Gen. V. A.K.	7.8.42
Wevelsiep, Kurt	Oblt. d.R., Chef 2./Pi. Btl. 327 + 12.10.44 at Jurmalciems (France)	30.9.44
Wever, Walter	Lt., Flugzeugf. in 3./J.G. 51 "Mölders" + 10.4.45 shot down at Neuruppin as Oblt. & Flugzeugf. in J.G. 7 (Me 262)	28.1.45
Weyel, Erich	Oblt., Fhr. 14. (Pz.Jäg.)/I.R. 506	20.12.41
Weyher, Kurt	Freg. Kpt., Kdt. Hilfskreuzer HSK 1 "Orion"	21.8.41
Weymann, Martin	Obstlt., Kdr. Pz. G. R. 3 died later of wounds in hospital, as Oberst.	10.2.45
v. Weyrauch, Ernst	Hptm., Staffelkpt. 2. (H)/Aufkl. Gr. 14 + 17.3.44 shot down over Tours (France) as Hptm. in 1./SKG. 10	31.12.43
Weyrauch, Helmut	Lt., Fhr. 4. (MG)/G. R. 81	7.12.43
Wichert, Willy	Hptm. d.R., Chef 3./Div. Füs. Btl. 291 + 10.3.44 at Buczacz south of Tarnopol (Russia) as Kdr. 1./Gr. Rgt. 505 of wounds	6.11.43
Wick, Helmut	Oblt., Staffelkpt. 3./J.G. 2 "Richthofen" 4th Oak Leaves 6.10.40	27.8.40
Wicke, Wolfhart	Oblt. d.R., Chef 5./Geb.Jäg. Rgt. 144	8.2.43

Name	Details	Date
v. Wickede, Thomas-Emil	Obstlt., Kdr. I.R. 4 + 23.6.44 at Hartberg/Nähe Graz (Steiermark) as Gen.D.Inf. & Kom.Gen. X. A.K., when his aircraft crashed	15.8.40
Wickel, Paul	Hptm. d.R., Fhr. 1./G. R. 57	4.6.44
Wickmann, Theo	Hptm., Fhr. G. R. 248 + 6.5.45 at Rosenhain O./L. as Fhr. G. R. 95	23.3.45
Widmayer, Erwin	Feldw., Zugf. in 11./G. R. 358	12.8.44
Wiebe, Karl-Heinz	Kaptlt. (Ing.), Leit. Ing. auf "U 178"	22.5.44
Wiechec, Franz-Josef	Major, Fhr. Fähnrichs-Rgt. 3 (Div. "Märk.-Friedland")	5.4.45
Wiechoczek, Josef	Lt. d.R., Fhr. 5./Jäger-Rgt. 28	9.12.44
Wiede, Friedrich-Wilhelm	Hptm. d.R., Chef 9./A.R. 238 + 12.7.44 in Russia of wounds as Abt.Kdr.; posthumously promoted to Major d.R.	7.2.44
Wiedemann, Wolfgang	Hptm., Kdr. Pz. Aufkl. Abt. 125 + 6.9.43 west of Wjasma (Russia)	10.9.43
Wiegand, Karl	Oblt., Chef 2./Flak-Rgt. 18 (mot.)	9.5.42
Wiegand, Kurt	Obgefr., Richtschtz. in Pz.Jäg. Abt. 32	5.1.44
Wieland, Friedrich	Rittrn. d.R., Kdr. Aufkl. Abt. 94	16.10.44
Wieland, Willy	Uffz., Zugf. in 11./Pz. G. R. 35	25.1.45
Wienke, Hans	Hptm. d.R., Kdr. 1./G. R. 196 + 13.8.43 nordwest of Charkow (Russia)	13.10.43
Wienke, Walter	Hptm., Fhr. II./I.R. 426	20.8.42
Wienrich, Arno	Stabsgefr., VB-Funker in 2./A.R. 11	5.5.45
Wierschin, Helmuth	Stabsfw., Zugf. in 2./Pz. Rgt. 18 + 10.4.44 of wounds	12.1.42
Wiese, Erich	Hptm., Beobachter in 1. (F)Nacht-Aufkl.-Staffel + 31.12.43 at Perwomaisk (Russia)	26.3.44
Wiese, Friedrich	Oberst, Kdr. I.R. 39 372nd Oak Leaves 24.1.44	14.2.42
Wiese, Heinrich	Hptm., Kdr. III./G. R. 361 (mot.)	4.10.44
Wiese, Hubert	Oberst, Kdr. GR. 552	5.5.45
Wiese, Johannes	Hptm., Staffelkpt. 2./J.G. 52 418th Oak Leaves 2.3.44	5.1.43
Wieselhuber, Helmut	Lt., Zugf. in I./s. Werfer-Rgt. 1	14.5.44
Wiesemann, Emil	SS-Hptsturmfhr. d.R., Chef 2./SS-St. Gesch. Abt. 1 "LSSAH" + 14.11.43 east of Zhitomir (Russia)	20.12.43
Wiesemann, Otto	Feldw., Zugf. in 1./Pz. Rgt. 1 + 1944	11.12.44
Wiesmann, Hugo	Uffz., Richtschtz. in 1./Pz. Rgt. 11	21.9.44
Wiesner, Herbert	Oblt., Fhr. 3./He. Pi. Btl. 42	21.9.44
Wiesner, Willi	Major, Kdr. 1./A.R. 257	29.9.41
Wiest, Xaver	Objäg., Gruppenfhr. in 3./Ski-Jäg. Rgt. 1	26.11.44

v. Wietersheim, Gustav	Gen. d. Inf, Kom.Gen. XIV. A.K.	20.4.41
v. Wietersheim, Walter	Hptm., Kdr. II./Pz. Rgt. "GD"	15.5.44
v. Wietersheim, Wend	Obstlt., Kdr. Schtz. Rgt. 113 176th Oak Leaves 12.1.43 58th Swords 26.3.44	10.2.42
Wieting, Franz	Oblt., Staffelkpt. 6./K.G. 30 + 29.6.41 over Bulgaria as Hptm. in Stabe X. Fliegerkorps	14.6.40
Wiktorin, Mauritz	Gen.Lt., Kdr. 20. ID (mot.)	15.8.40
Wilborn, Karl-Heinz	Uffz. d.R., Gr. Fhr. in 9./Pz. Gren. Rgt. 25	6.5.45
Wilcke, Dr. med. Horst	Oberarzt d.R., Truppenarzt III./I.R. 120 (mot.)	25.7.42
Wilcke, Wolf-Dietrich	Hptm., Kdr. III./J.G. 53 122nd Oak Leaves 9.9.42 23rd Swords 23.12.42	6.8.41
Wild, Philipp	SS-Oberscharf., Pz. Kdt. in I./SS. -Pz. Abt. 11	21.3.44
Wilde, Heinz	Stabsintendant, Div. Int. 353. I.D. & Fhr. e, Kampfgruppe	21.9.44
Wildermuth, Dr. jur. Hermann-Eberhard	Major d.R., Kdr. II./I.R. 272	15.8.40
Wildner, Anton	Obgefr., Gruppenfhr. in I./Rgt. Gruppe 482	10.9.44
Wildschütz, Waldemar	Hptm., Fhr. I./I.R. 419	2.10.42
Wilfling, Günther	Lt. d.R., Fhr. II./G. R. 501	5.5.43
Wilhelm, Hans-Joachim	Oblt., Flugzeugf. in 9./K.G. 1 "Hindenburg" + 13.4.45	29.10.44
Wilhelm, Karl-Heinz	Oblt. d.R., Chef 3./G. R. 46 + 14.8.43 in Russia	31.3.43
Wilhelm, Paul (12)	Hptfeldw., Fhr. a Alarmkp. in Marsch-Btl. 469	5.5.45
Wilke, Giselher	Lt. d.R., Zugf. in 1. (Jägdpz.)/Pz.Jäg. Abt. 19	14.4. 45
Wilke, Gustav	Obstlt., Kdr. Kampfgr. z.b.V. 11	24.5.40
Wilke, Heinrich	Feldw., Bordfunker in II./N. J.G. 100	6.12.44
Wilke, Karl-Heinz	Lt., Flugzeugf. & Beob. in 2. (H)/Aufkl. Gr. 4	25.11.44
Will, Fritz	Feldw., Flugzeugf. in 6./K.G. 53 "Legion Condor" + 28.8.44 in Hunsrück at Hahn as Lt.	22.5.43
Willig, Karl	Hptm., Fhr. II./I.R. 120 (mot.) 179th Oak Leaves 18.1.43	25.7.42
Willing, Gerhard	Major, Kdr. III./Pz. Rgt. 33 + 29.10.43 at Kriwoj Rog as Kdr. schw. Pz. Abt. 506	7.3.43
Willius, Karl	Lt., Staffelf. 2./J.G. 26 "Schlageter" + 8.4.44 shot down over the Zuider-See (Holland) as Staffelkpt.; posthumouslypromoted to Oblt.	9.6.44
Willms, Kurt	Lt., Zugf. in I./Pi. Btl. 36 + 13.2.45 Schlagenthin (West Prussia)	23.2.44
Wimmer, Alfred	Oblt., Fhr. III./G. R. "Oberrhein" + 9.1.45 at Straßburg-Herrlisheim (Alsace)	16.1.45
Wimmer, Friedrich	Ofw., Zugf. in 8./G. R. 412	30.9.44

KNIGHT'S CROSS OF THE IRON CROSS

Wimmer, Johann	Hptm., Kdr. 1./Fsch. Pz. Ausb. & Ers. Rgt. "HG"	28.1.45
Winckler, Rainer	Hptm, Fhr. III./G. R. 57 + 1.11.43 at Bobriza (S. Ukraine/Russia); posthumously promoted to Major	21.10.43
Windbiel, Anton	Hptni., Kdr. III./Jäger-Rgt. 56	21.11.42
Windisch, Alois	Oberst, Kdr. Geb.Jäg. Rgt. 139	20.6.40
Windisch, Johann	Obgefr., Gruppenf. in 5./G. R. 519	18.11.43
Windmann, Erich	Oberst, Art. Kdr. 35	6.11.44
Windschügl, Harald	Major, Div. Adj. 227. I.D. + 21.3.45 in East Prussia	14.4.45
Windschüttl, Peter	Uffz,. d.R., Geschützf. in 14. (Pz.Jäg.)/G. R. 72	22.7.43
Winkler, Kurt	Obstlt., Kdr. G. R. 101	17.3.45
Winnerl, Rudolf	Ofw., Flugzeugf. in 4./K.G. 1 "Hindenburg"	18.4.43
Winter, Friedrich	Feldw., Flugzeugf. in 2. (H)/Aufkl. Gr. 16	6.12.44
Winter, Kurt	Major, Kdr. III./Jäger-Rgt. 83	2.9.44
Winter, Michael	Uffz., Geschützf. in 14. (Pz.Jäg.)/G. R. 168	9.6.44
Winter, Werner	Kaptlt., Kdt. "U 103"	5.6.42
v. Winterfeld, Hild-Wilfried	Obstlt., Kdr. I./Pz. Rgt. 24 + in March 1943 in Soviet captivity in Camp Begetowka at Stalingrad (Russia)	22.1.43
v. Winterfeldt, Alexander	Major d.R., Kdr. III./J.G. 77 + 16.5.42 shot down at Wien-Schwechat as Kdr. Jagdflieger-Vorschule 4; posthumously promoted to Oberstlt. d.R.	5.7.41
Winterhoff, Karl	Lt. d.R., Zugf. in 3./Pz. G. R. 115	18.12.44
Wintershoff, Eduard	Uffz., Geschützf. in 2./Pz.Jäg. Abt. 8 + 18.1.44 in Russia as Feldw.	25.8.42
Winzen, Karl	Obstlt., Kdr. G. R. 289 + 1944 in Italy	20.10.44
Winzer, Willy	Oberst, Kdr. I.R. 578 + 17.10.42 Stalingrad (Russia)	3.11.42
Wipfler, Franz	Feldw., Zugf. in 11./Jäger-Rgt. 56	15.5.42
Wippermann, Max	Oblt., Zugf. in 7./Flak-Rgt. 4 (mot.) + 24.4.45 as Hptm.	16.11.42
Wirsching, Maximilian	Oblt., Chef 2./schw. Pz. Abt. 507	7.2.45
Wirth, Georg	Feldw., Zugf. in 14. (Pz.Jäg.)/G. R. 21	22.10.43
Wisch, Theodor	SS-Sturmbannf., Kdr. II./"LSSAH" 393rd Oak Leaves 12.2.44 94th Swords 30.8.44	15.9.41
Wischhusen, Dr. med. Werner	Oberfeldarzt, Div. Arzt 22. I.D. & Kdr. San. Abt. 22	26.5.40
Wischnewski, Hermann	Fhj. -Ofw., Flugzeugf. in 2./J.G. 300	16.12.44
Wisliceny, Günther	SS-Sturmbannf., Kdr. III./SS-Pz. G. R. "Deutschland" 687th Oak Leaves 26.12.44 151st Swords 6.5.45	30.7.43

Wissemann, Hans-Joachim	Hptm., Chef 2./Kradschtz. Btl. 6 + 30.12.42 Stalingrad (Russia)	8.2.43
Witsch, Rudolf	Lt. d.R., Zugf. in 7./I.R. 308 + 2.9.43 in Russia as Oblt. d.R. & Kp. Fhr.	3.9.42
Witschel, Kurt	Ofw., Fhr. 2./Jäger-Rgt. 28 773rd Oak Leaves 11.3.45	4.1.43
Witt, Fritz	SS-Sturmbannf., Kdr. I./SS-I.R. "Deutschland" 200th Oak Leaves 1.3.43	4.9.40
Witt, Hans	Kaptlt., Kdt. "U 129"	17.12.42
Witt, Heinrich	Oblt. (MA) d.R., Chef Battr. "Sagorsch" in M.-Fla-Abt. 259 (M. Flak-Rgt. 9)	20.4.45
Witt, Heinz	Feldw., Zugf. in 2./G. R. 4	5.9.44
Witt, Hellmuth	Oberst, Kdr. A.R. 134	27.7.44
Witt, Hermann	Freg. Kpt., Hafenkdt. Cherbourg (France)	24.9.44
Witt, Otto	Feldw., Zugf. in 8./G. R. 43	21.9.44
Wittchow v. Brese-Winiary, Heinz	Hptm., Kdr. I./Pz. G. R. 108 441st Oak Leaves 6.4.44	15.5.43
Witte, Albert	Owm., Zugf. in I./St. Gesch. Brig. 394	11.3.45
Witte, Gerhard	Major, Kdr. II./Pz. G. R. 25	23.8.44
Witte, Heinrich	Obgefr., Richtkan. in 7./Flak-Rgt. "HG"	18.5.43
Witte, Helmut	Kaptlt., Kdt. "U 159"	22.10.42
Wittenstein, Heinz-Willi	Hptm., Kdr. II./Pz. G. R. 146	14.2.45
Wittenzellner, Hans	Ofvv., Zugf. in 1./Geb.Jäg. Rgt. 144	9.6.44
Frhr. v. Wittgenstein Leo-Volkhard	Hptm., Kdr. III./G. R. 410 + 22.2.45 at Bonn/Rhein as Major i.G. accidentally	6.4.43
Witthöft, Joachim	Gen.Lt., Kdr. 86. I.D.	14.12.41
Wittholz, Karl-Friedrich	Lt. d.R., Zugf. in 6./Pz. Rgt. 36 + spring 1943 in Camp Jelabuga (Russia) in Soviet captivity, of spotted fever	7.12.42
Wittig, Hans-Karl	Feldw., Fhr. 11./Fsch. Jäger-Rgt. 1	5.2.44
Wittkamp, Kaspar	Feldw. in 4. (MG)/G. R. 77	18.10.43
Wittkopf, Heinrich	Oberst, Kdr. I.R. 530 + 12.2.46 in Russiade (Belgium) in British captivity; final post Gen. Major & Kdt. Greifswald (Pomerania)	29.9.41
Wittmann, Alfred	Obstlt., Kdr. G. R. 546	15.5.44
Wittmann, August	Obstlt., Kdr. Geb. Art.Rgt. 95	21.6.41
Wittmann, Herbert	Hptm., Staffel. kpt. Stabsst./K.G. 53 "Legion Condor" 735th Oak Leaves 11.2.45	23.11.41
Wittmann, Michael	SS-Untersturmf., Zugf. in 13. (schw.)/SS-Pz. Rgt. 1 "LSSAH" 380th Oak Leaves 30.1.44 71st Swords 22.6.44	14.1.44

KNIGHT'S CROSS OF THE IRON CROSS

Name	Rank/Unit	Date
Wittmer, Heinrich	Hptm., Kdr. III./K.G. 55	12.11.41
Wittrock, Josef	Lt. d.R., Fhr. 1./G. R. 453	10.9.44
v. Witzendorff, Kurt	Oblt., Chef 13./I.R. 178	30.8.41
Witzig, Rudolf	Oblt., Fhr. Sturmgruppe "Granit" in Fsch. Jäg. Sturmabt. "Koch" 662nd Oak Leaves 25.11.44 Simultaneously promoted to Hptm.	10.5.40
v. Witzleben, Erwin	Gen. Oberst, OB 1. Armee + 8.8.44 hanged (20.7.44) in Berlin-Plötzensee; final post Gen. Feldm. & OB West (until 15.3.42)	24.6.40
v. Witzleben, Henning	Major, Kdr. Pz. Aufkl. Abt. 16	6.2.42
Wodrig, Albert	Gen. d. Art., Kom.Gen. XXVI. A.K.	19.7.40
Woehl, Edmund (19)	Oberstlt., Kdr. Pz. Gr. Rgt. 30 + 3.5.45 during attempted breakout from Berlin at Staaken	28 4.45
Wöhler, Otto	Gen.D.Inf., Kom.Gen. I. A.K. 671st Oak Leaves 28.11.44	14.8.43
Wöhnert, Ulrich	Lt., Flugzeugf. in 5./J.G. 54	6.12.44
Woelfel, Erich	Obstlt., Kdr. I.R. 534	28.1.43
Wohlers, Heinrich	Hptm., Kdr. I./Nacht-Jagd-Geschw. 6 + 15.3.44 shot down over Echterdingen; as Major & Kmdr. N. J.G. 6	31.12.43
Wohlfahrt, Helmut	Oberst, Kdr. G. R. 110	29.8.43
Wohlfahrt, Herbert	Kaptlt., Kdt. "U 556"	15.5.41
Wohlfeil, Otto	Hptm., Kdr. I./G. R. 371	5.9.43
Wohlgemuth, Karl	Major, Kdr. Div. Füs. Btl. 1	30.9.44
Woidich, Franz	Lt. d.R., Flugzeugf. in 3./J.G. 52 simultaneously promoted to Oblt. d.R.	11.6.44
Wojak, Alfred	Oblt., Chef 11./Pz. A.R. 73 + 4.11.44 as Hptm.	9.6.44
Woldenga, Bernhard	Major, Kmdre. J.G. 77	5.7.41
Wolf, Adolf	Obstlt., Kdr. I./Flak. -Rgt. 64 (mot.)	20.6.40
Wolf, Adolf	Hptm., Kdr. I./I.R. 431 + 25.12.44 as Oberstlt. & Rgt. Kdr.	11.10.41
Wolf, Albin	Ofw., Flugzeugf. in 6./J.G. 54 464th Oak Leaves 27.4.44	22.11.43
Wolf, Alfred	Major, Kdr. I./Pz. Rgt. 23	15.4.44
Wolf, Alois	Hptm., Chef 3./Pi. Btl. 161	14.2.45
Wolf, Cosmas	Ofw., Kp. Tr. Fhr. in 3./G. R. 279	25.1.45
Wolf, Eberhard	Hptm., Kdr. He. Pi. Btl. 505	20.7.44
Wolf, Hermann (17)	Lt., Flugzeugf. in 9./J.G. 11	24.4.45
Wolf, Karl	Uffz., Gruppenf. in II./G. R. 432	28.2.45
Wolf, Richard	Obstlt., Kdr. G. R. 208	20.1.43
Wog, Richard	Lt. Kampfgr. "Tenschert" in Festung Breslau	4.3.45

ELITE OF THE THIRD REICH

Wolf, Walter	Ofw., Zugf. in 4./Pz. Rgt. 35 + 18.9.44 at Durben (Kurland)	16.10.44
Wolf, Werner	Hptm. d.R., Fhr. MG-Btl. 420	18.2.45
Wolf, Wilhelm	Stabsfw., Zugf. in 2./Pz. Abt. 103 + 1943 at Stalingrad (Russia) of wounds	7.8.42
Wolff, Dr. Gottlieb	Oberst, Kmdr. K.G. 4 "General Wever"	5.1.43
Frhr. v. Wolff, Hans	Hptm., Kdr. I./Schtz. Rgt. 8 61st Oak Leaves 16.1.42	13.7.40
Wolff, Hans	Hptm., Staffelkpt. 1. (F)/Aufkl. Gr. 124	12.1.42
Wolff, Hans	Oblt., Fhr. 3./Inf. Btl. z.b.V. 540	8.2.43
Wolff, Heinz	Hptm. d.R., Fhr. I./Pz. G. R. 110 + 22.2.45	12.12.44
v. Wolff, Horst	Oberst, Kdr. I.R. 478 + 10.10.41 at Woroniski/near Wjasma (Russia); posthumously promoted to Gen. Major	10.10.41
Wolff, Joachim-Helmut	Obstlt., Kdr. Gren. Rgt. "Feldherrnhalle"	21.1.45
Wolff, Kurt	Hptm., Kdr. I./G. R. 415 + 12.10.43 at Saporoshje (Russia)	30.11.43
Wolff, Ludwig	Oberst, Kdr. I.R. 192 100th Oak Leaves 22.6.42	26.5.40
Wolff, Max-Eckart	Korv. Kpt., Kdt. Zerstörer "Georg Thiele"	4.8.40
Wolff, Otto	Oblt. d.R., Chef 3./Div. Füs. Btl. 263 + 9.7.44 in Russia; posthumously promoted to Major d.R.	29.2.44
Wolff, Richard	Feldw., Zugf. in I./Füs. Rgt. 202	12.3.44
Wolff, Werner	SS-Untersturmf., Adj. III./(gep.)/SS-Pz. G. R. "LSSAH" + in March 1945 at Innota in Hungary as SS-Obersturmf. & Chef 7./SS-Pz. Rgt. 1 "LSSAH"	7.8.43
Wolff, Wilhelm	Oberst, Kdr. Flak-Rgt. 37 (mot.)	24.1.43
Wolff, Wilhelm	Oblt. d.R., Chef 10./Pz. Rgt. 36 + 31.10.43 Kriwoij Rog (Russia); posthumously promoted to Hptm.	9.12.43
Wolfram, Eberhard	Konteradm., Befehlshaber der Sicherg. d. Nordsee	25.5.41
Wolfram, Eberhard	Hptm., Chef 4./I.R. 82	13.11.42
Wolfrum, Walter	Lt., Flugzeugf. in 5./J.G. 52	27.7.44
Wolkewitz, Erich	Oberst, Kdr. G. R. 478	30.4.43
Woll, Balthasar	SS-Rottenf., Richtschtz. in 13. (schw.)/SS-Pz. Rgt. 1 "LSSAH"	16.1.44
Wollschläger, Artur	Oblt., Chef 2./Pz. Rgt. 35	12.1.42
Wollschlaeger, Herbert	Lt. d.R., Batt. Offz. in A.R. 32	22.10.43
Wolz, Alwin	Oberst, Kdr. Flak-Rgt. 135 (mot.)	4.6.43
Wonde, Hermann	Lt., Fhr. 6./Reiter-Rgt. 41	23.3.45

KNIGHT'S CROSS OF THE IRON CROSS

Wontorra, Kurt	Hptm. d.R., Fhr. II./G. R. 239 + 16.7.43 south-east of Bielgorod on the Donets (Russia)	21.7.43
Woock, Heinz	Hptm., Kdr. III./G. R. 274	18.7.44
Worthmann, Karl-Heinz	SS-Hptscharf., Zugf. in 6./SS-Pz. Rgt. 2 "Das Reich" + 6.7.43 Charkow/north of Bjelgorod (Russia); as SS-Untersturmf. & Kp. Fhr.	31.3.43
Wosnitza, Alois	Ofw., Flugzeugf. in 6./S.G. 77	26.3.44
Woszella, Gustav	Lt., Fhr. 8. (MG)/G. R. 208	4.7.44
Wrangel, Werner	Gefr., Richtschtz. in 1./Pz.Jg. Abt. 183 + 24.3.45 at Trebur	8.2.43
Frhr. v. Wrede, Theodor	Gen.Lt., Kdr. 290 in	22.2.42
Wriedt, Walter	Ofw., Zugf. in 13./Geb.Jäg. Rgt. 138	25.10.43
Wrona, Günther	Hptm. d.R., Kdr. Div. Füs. Btl. 176	4.5.44
Wünnenberg, Alfred	SS-Standartenfhr. & Oberst d. Schupo, Kdr. SS-Pol. Schtz. Rgt. 3 91st Oak Leaves 23.4.42	15.11.41
Wünning, Joachim	Korv. Kpt. d.R., Kdt. Minenschiff "Drache" + 22.9.44 in der Aegean following attack by enemy aircraft	22.10.44
Wünsche, Max	SS-Sturmbannf., Kdr. I./SS-Pz. Rgt. 1 "LSSAH" 548th Oak Leaves 11.8.44	28.2.43
Würdemann, Erich	Kaptlt., Kdt. "U 506" + 14.7.43 in the Bay of Biscay	14.3.43
Würfel, Otto	Ofw., Flugzeugf. in 9./J.G. 51 "Mölders" 23.2.44 collided over Rogatschew (Russia) with a comrade + 22.12.44 in Camp 280/5 in Stalino (Russia) in Soviet captivity; posthumously promoted to Lt.	4.5.44
Wüstenhagen, Albrecht	Oberst, Kdr. A.R. 129;Fhr. e. s. l. G. Kp./Festung/Kustrin + 26.4.44 south-west of Witebsk (Russia) as Gen.Lt. & Kdr. 256. I.D.	2.12.42
Wüstenhagen, Albrecht	Hptm., Fhr. s. l. G. Kp. Festung Küstrin	14.4. 45
Wulf, Hermann	Oblt., Chef 9./I.R. 76 (mot.) 520th Oak Leaves 3.7.44	13.10.41
Wulf, Rudolf	Major, Fhr. I.R. 422 556th Oak Leaves 19.8.44	13.11.42
Wulff, Erich	Oblt. z. See, Kdt. in 18. Vorpostenflottille	24.4. 44
Wulff, Erich	SS-Sturmbannf., la der 15. SS-Waffen-Gren. Div. + 3.2.45 during breakout from the Flederborn pocket at Landeck (Pomerania)	9.5.45
Wulff, Hermann	Lt. d.R., Zugf. in 2./G. Rgt. 333	19.10.44
Wulff, Karl	Oblt., Flugzeugf. & Beob. in 12. (H)/Aufkl. Gr. 13	29.10.44
Wunberger, Karl-Heinz	Hptm., Fhr. I./G. R. 96 + 16.3.44 north-west of Nevel (Russia) of wounds; posthumously promoted to Major	17.3.44

Wunderlich, Achim	Major, Kdr. Div. Füs. Btl. 205	31.12.44
Wunderlich, Friedrich	Korv. Kpt. z. V., Chef 14. U-Jagdflottille	3.12.42
Wunn, Heinrich	Lt. d.R., Fhr. 7./G. R. 147 + 28.11.44 at main dressing station at Bologna (Italy) as Oblt. d.R. & Kp. Chef, of wounds	11.6.44
Wunram, Heinz	Ofw., Kp. Truppf. in 2./G. R. 220 + 3.4.45 Samland	5.1.44
Wuppermann, Siegfried	Oblt. z. See, Kdt. "S 60" in 3. Schnellbootsflottille 226th Oak Leaves 14.4.43	3.8.41
Wurdak, Franz	Feldw. d.R., Zugf. in 4./Pi. Btl. 137	13.9.43
Wurl, Walter	Ofw., Zugf. in 2./G. R. 509 + 7.2.45	18.2.45
Wurmheller, Josef	Ofw., Flugzeugf. in 9./J.G. 2 "Richthofen" 146th Oak Leaves 13.11.42 108th Swords 24.10.44	4.9.41
Wuthmann, Rolf	Gen. d. Art., Kom.Gen. IX. A.K.	22.8.44
Wutka, Bernhard	Oblt., Staffelkpt. 8./Stuka-Geschw. 2 "Immelmann" + 8.7.43 at Werchnopenje (Russia) as Hptm.	16.11.42
Wutzel, Otto	Hptm., Fhr. I./G. R. 81	14.4.45
Wyczisk, Georg	Obgefr., Geschützf. in 1./Pz.Jäg. Abt. 53 + 1.9.43; posthumously promoted to Uffz.	2.9.42

X

Ritter & Edler v. Xylander, Wolf-Dietrich	Gen.Lt., Chef d. Gen. St. H.Gr. Mitte + 15.2.45 at Struppin (near Pirna/Saxony) when his aircraft was shot down	20.2.45

Z

Zachariae-Lingenthal, Edel-Heinrich	Hptm., Kdr. II./Pz. Rgt. 15	18.9.43
Zähr, Erich	Major, Kdr. K. Gr. z.b.V. 172	23.12.42
Zahn, Alfred	Hptm. d.R., Fhr. III./G. R. 96 + 4.4. 43 in Russia of wounds	17.3.43
Zahn, Dr. rer-pol. Eberhard	Lt. d.R., Zugf. in 2./Pz.Jäg. Abt. 33204th Oak Leaves 6.3.43	30.6.41
Zahn, Hilmar	Oblt., Chef 5./Fsch. Jäg. Rgt. 1	9.6.44
Zahn, Lothar	Major, Kdr. III./G. R. 30 (mot.)	2.10.43
Zahn, Willi	Ofw., Zugf. in 14. (Pz.Jäg.)/G. R. 507 + 16.7.43 south of Orel (Russia)	18.7.43
Zander, Helmut	Obstlt., Kdr. Pz. G. R. 60	5.4.45
v. Zangen, Gustav-Adolf	Oberst, Fhr. 17. Inf. Div. 647th Oak Leaves 5.11.44	15.1.42

KNIGHT'S CROSS OF THE IRON CROSS

Zapf, Albert	Oblt., Fhr. III./Pz. G. R. 129 + 28.1.45 in hospital in Italy as Hptm. & Btl. Kdr.	23.2.44
Zapp, Robert-Richard	Korv. Kpt., Kdt. "U 66"	23.4.42
Zastrow, Max	Gefr., MG-Schtz, in 2./Pi. Btl. 81	6.3.44
Zauner, Franz	Major, Kdr. III./K.G. 54	5.2.44
Zebhauser, Paul	Ofw., Flugzeugf. in 16./T. G. 1	18.11.44
Zecherle, Konrad	Lt. d.R., Zugfhr. in 1./Pz. Aufkl. Abt. 90' (Afrika)	10.5.43
Zehender, August	SS-Ob. Sturmbannf., Kdr. SS-Kav. Rgt. 1 "Florian Geyer" 722nd Oak Leaves 1.2.45	10.3.43
Zehnder, Eugen	Objäg., Gruppenf. in 1./Geb.Jäg. Rgt. 13	7.3.43
Zeidler, Markus	Major, Kdr. K. Gr. z.b.V. 600	9.5.42
Zeiher, Robert	Hptm. d.R., Fhr. I./SS-Gren. Rgt. "Radolfzell"	16.1.45
Zeitzler, Kurt	Oberst i.G., Chef d. Gen. St. d. Pz. Gruppe 1	18.5.41
Zejdlik, Franz	Major, Kdr. Pz. Pi. Btl. 51	4.10.42
Zeller, Conrad	Hptm. d.R., Kdr. I./G. R. 380 495th Oak Leaves 9.6.44	5.1.44
Zeller, Ernst	Oblt. d.R., Fhr. 3./A.R. 114 + 12.8.44	16.11.43
Zeller, Willy	Lt., Fhr. 9./G. R. 380	7.2.44
Zellner, Johann	Feldw., Flugzeugf. in 3./Stuka-Geschw. 77 + 27.2.45 shot down at Hof/Saale at Überführungsflug as Ofw.	20.7.44
Zellner, Karl	Feldw., Flugzeugf. in 1./Stuka-Geschw. 77 + 13.9.43 at Poltawa (Russia)	29.2.44
Zellot, Walter	Lt., Flugzeugf. in I./J.G. 53 + 10.9.42 shot down at Stalingrad (Russia)	3.9.42
Zempel, Friedrich	Lt. d.R., Fhr. 3./Div. Füs. Btl. 112 + 27.7.44 at Stock/35 km west of Grodew (Russia); as Oblt. d.R.	4.5.44
Zemsky, Johann	Hptm., Kdr. II./Stuka-Geschw. 1 117th Oak Leaves 3.9.42	4.2.42
Zenker, Franz	Hptm., Kdr. Pz.Jäg. Abt. 12	10.9.44
Zepf, Gottfried	Ofw., Zugf. in 3./Pz. Rgt. 36	26.11.44
Zepner, Alois	Hptm., Fhr. III./Jäger-Rgt. 38 + 14.11.44 at Vatta (Hungary)	10.9.44
Zepper, Erich	SS-Hptscharf., stellv. Fhr. 2./SS-Pz. G. R. 10 "Westland" + 8.10.44 at Benacourt (France) as SS-Untersturmf.	2.12.43
Zernin, Erich	Oblt., Fhr. 5./Pz. Rgt. 11 + 13.8.43 Charkow (Russia); posthumously promoted to Hptm.	13.9.43
Zerth, Jakob	Gefr., stellv. Gruppenf. in 3./G. R. 467 + 15.8.44 as Uffz. in a base hospital, of wounds	21.4.44

Name	Details	Date
Zettler, Rudolf	Hptm., Kdr. St. Gesch. Abt. 667 + 27.6.44 east of Minsk (Russia) as Major	18.10.43
Zickwolff, Friedrich	Gen.Lt., Kdr. 113 I.D. + 17.9.44 of wounds (received 25.8.43) as Kdr. 343. I.D.	2.6.42
Zieger, Günter	Oblt., Chef 2./St. Gesch. Abt. 600	8.2.44
Ziegler, Arthur	Oblt.,Rgt. Adj. G. R. 974	23.8.44
Ziegler, Gerhard-Georg	Obstlt. d.R., Fhr. G. R. 353	12.2.44
Ziegler, Heinz	Gen.Lt., Fhr. of a Kampfgruppe i. Stab H.Gr. Afrika stellv. Fhr. 5. Pz. Arrnee & d. Deutschen-Afrika-Korps	16.4.43
Ziegler, Joachim	SS-Brigadef. & Gen.Maj. d. W-SS, Kdr. 11. SS-Freiw. Pz. Gr. Div. "Nordland" 848th Oak Leaves 28.4.45	5.9.44
Ziegler, Karl	Major, Kdr. III./Jäger-Rgt. 207	8.4.43
Ziegler, Werner	Lt., Fhr. 2./I.R. 186 121st Oak Leaves 8.9.42 102nd Swords 23.10.44	31.12.41
Ziehr, Leonhard	Ofw., Flugzeugf. in 13./T. G. 1	16.12.44
Ziemann, Alfred	Oblt., Chef 1./schw. Pz.Jäg. Abt. 93	9.1.44
Ziemer, Ernst	Ofw., Radf. Zugf. in 15./I.R. 94 317th Oak Leaves 2.11.43	14.12.41
Zierach, Otto	Oblt., Lastenseglerpilot in Fsch. Jäg. Sturm-Abt. "Koch" simultaneously promoted to Hptm.	15.5.40
Zierhofer, Karl	Gefr., MG-Schtz. in 1./Pz. G. R. 126	4.10.44
Zilger, Erwin	Hptm., Chef 1./Pz.Jäg. Abt. 186	4.8.43
Zillich, Karl	Oblt., Beob. in Stab II./K.G. 27 "Boelcke" + 14.4. 44 in Russia of wounds	20.7.44
Zillies, Karl-Hemz	Lt. d.R., Fhr. 10./G. R. 8 (mot.)	11.12.44
Zillmann, Erich	Stabswm., Zugf. in 3./St. Gesch. Brig. 245	8.8.44
Zimmer, Karl	Oblt., stellv. Fhr. II./G. R. 105	18.2.45
Zimmer, Richard	Gen.Lt., Kdr. 17. I.D.	16.10.44
Zimmermann, Ernst	Hptm., Kdr. 1./G. R. 105 + 1.7.43 as Major	21.5.43
Zimmermann, Fritz	Hptm., Kdr. I./Flaksturm-Rgt. 241 (mot.) + 7.6.44 in Italy of wounds	8.8.44
Zimmermann, Hans	Hptm., Chef 8./Pz. G. R. 26	22.1.43
Zimmermann, Herbert	Hptm., Fhr. II./G. R. 225 + 29.10.44 in the Vosges	12.1.45
Zimmermann, Herbert	Hptm., Chef 1./Pz. Rgt. 36	5.4.45
Zimmermann, Hermann	Major, Kdr. II./Schtz. Rgt. 3	4.9.40
Zimmermann, Jacob	Major, Fhr. G. R. 509	1.2.45
Zimmermann, Jakob	Hptm., Kdr. I./Pz. G. R. 10 + 8.10.43 Orel (Russia) of wounds; posthumously promoted to Major	31.7.43
Zimmermann, Manfred	Hptm. d.R., Fhr. I./G. R. 199 "List"	14.5.44

KNIGHT'S CROSS OF THE IRON CROSS

Zimmermann, Oskar	Lt., Flugzeugf. in 9./J.G. 3 "Udet"	29.10.44
Zimmermann, Otto	Feldw., Zugf. in 4. (MG)/G. R. 504	26.3.44
Zimmermann, Robert(17)	Hptm., Kdr. I./Flak-Rgt. 29 (mot.) + 16.4.45 in Fischhausen (East Prussia)	1.4.45
Zimmermann, Walter	Owm., V. B. in 12./A.R. 205	10.2.45
Zimmermann, Willy	Feldw., Zugf. in 6./G. R. 80	23.10.44
Zingel, August	SS-Unterscharf., Stoßtruppf. in Kampfgr. "Krauth" in 15./Totenkopf-Inf.Rgt. 1	4.10.42
Zinsser, Ludwig	Oblt. d.R., Fhr. 8./A.R. 148	16.11.44
Zintl, Franz	Oblt., Fhr. I./Geb.Jäg. Rgt. 206	6.7.42
Zipfel, Kuno	Feldw., Zugf. in 1./Jäg. Rgt. 56	10.9.44
Zipfel, Willibald	Feldw., Bordfunker in 3./S.G. 2 "Immelmann"	6.12.44
Ziran, Carl	Uffz., Zugfhr. in 3./G. R. 461	29.11.44
Zischka, Wilhelm	Wachtm., V. B. in 6./A.R. 41 (mot.)	23.10.44
Zitzen, Kurt	Oblt. d.R., Chef 2./St. Gesch. Abt. 177	4.8.43
Zmugg, Alois	Uffz. in 3./Schtz. Rgt. 114	18.10.41
Zobel, Horst	Hptm., Kdr. Pz. Abt. in Pz.Div. "Müncheberg"	14.4. 45
Zöllner, Heinz	Hptm., Staffelkpt. 6./K.G. 53 "Legion Condor" + 5.11.44 over the North Sea	5.4.44
Zoll, Erhard	Hptm. d.R., Chef 14. (Pz.Jäg.)/G. R. 437	18.1.45
Zonewitz, Gerhard	Oblt., Chef 2./I.R. 151	4.12.41
Zoppoth, Gerhard	Lt., Fhr. 6./G. R. 732	9.5.45
Zorn, Eduard	Oberst i.G., Fhr. 189. I.D.25.12.44 739th Oak Leaves	16.2.45
Zorn, Gerhard	Major, Kdr. Pz.Jäg. Abt. 159	28.3.45
Zorn, Hans	Gen. Major, Kdr. 20. I.D. (mot.) 291st Oak Leaves 3.9.43	27.7.41
Zorner, Paul	Hptm., Staffelkpt. 8./N. J.G. 3 588th Oak Leaves 17.9.44	9.6.44
Zubrod, Heinrich	Lt. d.R., Kp. Fhr. in G. R. 1213 + 27.1.45	18.1.45
Zühlsdorff, Hermann	Ofw., Zugf. in 1./I.R. 94 + 26.6.44 in Russia as Kp. Chef; Posthumously promoted to Hptm.	9.1.42
Zürn, Erich	Oblt. (Ing.), Leit. Ing. auf "U 48"	23.4.41
Zürn, Rudolf	Major, Kdr. II./I.R. 65 + 15.10.41 in Bucharest (Rumania) of wounds	16.6.40
Zürner, Hermann	Oblt. d.R., Fhr. II./Pz. G. R. 10	28.12.44
Zugehör, Günter	Hptm., Kdr. II./A.R. 19 (mot.)	12.9.41
Zumfelde, Hugo	Hptm. d.R., Kdr. II./G. R. 546	9.12.44
Zurin, Alfred	Lt., Fhr. 3./G. R. 189	9.5.45
Zurmöhle, Walter	Oblt. d.R., Chef 1./Pi. Btl. 6 (L)	5.4.44

Zweigart, Eugen-Ludwig	Ofw., Flugzeugf. in 5./J.G. 54 + 8.6.44 in Normandy as Oblt. & Staffelkpt. in III./J.G. 54	22.1.43
Zwer, Franz	Ofw., Zugf. in 6./G. R. 530	6.4.44
Zwernemann, Josef	Ofw., Flugzeugf. in 7./J.G. 52 141st Oak Leaves 31.10.42	23.6.42
Zwesken, Rudi (17)	Ofw., Flugzeugf. in 6./J.G. 300	21.3.45
Zwickenpflug, Hans	Major, Kdr. II./Geb.Jäg. Rgt. 100	5.4.45
Zwipf, Heinrich	Hptm., Staffelkpt. 3./Stuka-Geschw. 77 + 7.4.44 over Rieti airfield (Italy) as Kdr. I./Schlacht. Geschw. 4	31.12.43
Zymalkowski, Felix	Korv. Kpt., Chef 8. Schnellbootsflottille	10.4.45

Appendix I

Ordinance Concerning the Re-formation of the Order of the Iron Cross, 1 September 1939 with additions

The Iron Cross, in four classes of merit, is to be awarded exclusively for exceptional gallantry in the face of the enemy and for outstanding merit in command. The medals will not be awarded for other kind of meritorious service or under the conditions of the earlier Iron Cross on the white and black ribbon.

In addition to the Iron Cross First and Second Class and the Great Cross, the decision to award which the Führer and Supreme Commander has reserved to himself, a new award, the Knight's Cross of the Iron Cross, has been created. It is to be worn as a medal around the neck and is broadly comparable to the earlier Pour le Mérite medal. The ribbon of the Iron Cross will show the colours black, white and red.

In keeping with the National Socialist spirit of the new Wehrmacht, all classes of the medal can be awarded without any distinction relating to rank. Even a simple private can be awarded the Knight's Cross, that is, the medal to be worn around the neck.

If the recipient already holds one or both classes of the Iron Cross from the Great War, in place of a second cross he will receive a silver clasp.

The order concerning the re-formation of the Order of the Iron Cross reads as follows:

Article 1

The Iron Cross shall be awarded in the following sequence of merit classes:

Iron Cross 2nd Class
Iron Cross 1st Class
Knight's Cross of the Iron Cross
Great Cross of the Iron Cross

Article 2

The Iron Cross will be awarded exclusively for exceptional gallantry in the face of the enemy and for outstanding merit in command. The award of a higher class of the medal is subject to the condition that the recipient already holds the previous class of medal.

Article 3

I reserve to myself the decision to award the Great Cross for particularly outstanding deeds which decisively influence the course of combat actions.

Article 4

The Second Class and the First Class of the Iron Cross resemble the previous Iron Cross in size and design except for the fact that on the front of the new medal are shown the swastika and the year 1939.

The Iron Cross Second Class shall be worn on a black, white and red ribbon in the buttonhole or on the ribbon, and the Iron Cross First Class shall be worn without a ribbon on the left breast.

The Knight's Cross is larger than the Iron Cross First Class and is worn around the neck on a black white and red ribbon.

The Great Cross is about twice as large as the Iron Cross First Class, is edged in gold or instead of silver and is worn around the neck on a broader black white and red ribbon.

THE RE-FORMATION OF THE ORDER OF THE IRON CROSS

Article 5

If the recipient already holds one or both classes of the Iron Cross from the Great War, in place of a second Cross he will receive a silver clasp to his Iron Cross from the Great War, marked with the imperial insignia and the year 1939; in the case of the Iron Cross Second Class the clasp will be worn on the ribbon, in the case of the Iron Cross first Class it will be fixed over the cross.

Article 6

The recipient shall receive a deed of ownership.

Article 7

After the demise of the recipient, the Iron Cross will remain as a memorial for those he has left behind.

Article 8

Implementation of these conditions is ordered by the Chief of the Wehrmacht High Command in agreement with the Minister of State and the Head of the Presidial Chancellery.

Berlin, 2 September 1939 (RGBl. I. page 1573)

The Führer
Adolf Hitler

The Chief of the Wehrmacht High Command
Keitel

The Reich Minister of the Interior
Dr. Frick

The Minister of State and Head of the Presidial Chancellery of the Führer and Reich Chancellor
Dr. Meissner

Orders for amendment of the Ordinance concerning the Re-formation of the Order of the Iron Cross of 3.6.1940 (RGBl. I page 849)

Knight's Cross of the Iron Cross with Oak Leaves
2. Amendment Order of 29.12.1944 (RGBl. 1945 I page 11)

Knight's Cross of the Iron Cross with Oak Leaves in Gold with Swords and Diamonds

This decoration is only to be awarded to 12 men who have proved themselves in hand-to-hand combat.

Appendix II

Guidelines for the award of the Knight's Cross of the Iron Cross (OKH/PA), 3 June 1941

I. Conditions for the award of the Knight's Cross

a) The Knight's Cross of the Iron Cross can be awarded for

exceptional acts of gallantry which decisively affect combat actions

The conditions for this are:

"Individual decision to act on own initiative, outstanding personal bravery

and

"decisive success in the context of the overall conduct of the action

In the case of soldiers from the rank of private up to and including company etc. commander, the service rank and the service post held by the man in question is to be taken into account insofar as individual achievements with significant local success which have proved advantageous for the overall action can be evaluated and considered for possible recommendation for the award of the Knight's Cross.

If the Iron Cross Second Class or First Class has not yet been awarded or was awarded for the same action for which the Knight's Cross is being recommended, particular reasons should be given to justify the higher award of the Knight's Cross.

b) Apart from the Knight's Cross, in the case of particular

exceptional cases of outstanding personal bravery, the following other awards can be considered (even for soldiers who have already been awarded the Knight's Cross and have particularly distinguished themselves for a second time):

1. Mentioned in dispatches,
2. Special written recognition by the Armed Forces Supreme Commander,
3. Recommendations for enhancement of seniority or promotion to the next service rank. Promotion in the first instance for officers in the rank of Leutnant up to and including Hauptmann, for NCOs and other ranks up to the highest NCO service rank (Oberfeldwebel), in exceptional cases even to Leutnant.

II. The award of the Oak Leaves to the Knight's Cross of the Iron Cross

Has been reserved by the Führer as a matter for his own personal decision. Recommendations for the award of the Oak Leaves are therefore not to be made.

If, in the course of combat actions, units commanded by recipients of the Knight's Cross carry out decisive actions, details of these exceptional achievements, together with details of the unit and the holder of the Knight's Cross are to be immediately reported through official channels via OKH/PA 1 Staffel for recommendation to the Führer.

III. Recommendations for the award of the Knight's Cross to soldiers who have already been recommended on an earlier occasion for the award of the Knight's Cross, but to whom the award has not yet been made

If a soldier who, after being recommended by his unit for the award of the Knight's Cross, has not yet received the decoration, is recommended for the award of the Knight's Cross for further acts of exceptional gallantry, the second report recommending the award should, in addition to mentioning the most recent acts of gallantry, also include details of the circumstances leading to the first recommendation.

If these circumstances are not known to the reporting authority, OKH will itself consider the events described in its own personnel records in coming to a decision regarding recommendation to the Führer and Supreme Commander of the Wehrmacht.

IV. Procedure for recommendation of awards

a) Recommendations for the award of the Knight's Cross of the Iron Cross are to be made via the service authorities responsible for command at the time of the combat actions in question, to OKH/PA 1. Staffel, which is to comment on the recommendation.

The grounds for recommendation are to be stated briefly, clearly and objectively. If possible a combat report with an explanatory sketch is to be attached to the recommendation.

b) In particular cases a recommendation can, after the agreement of the relevant Armeeoberkommando and Heeresgruppekommando has been obtained, be made by telegram to OKH/PA 1. Staffel, for example if the candidate is in danger of his life or is severely wounded, or if the distance is so great that the process for making the recommandation is likely to be subject to unacceptable delays.

c) The following can be taken as a guide to making a written recommendation of for an award: a short appreciation of the man's service to date and any outstanding achievements, a short description of the particular mission with precise details of unit, location and time. Description of the action, which must clearly indicate that the decision was made by the individual on his own initiative. The decisive factor which contributed to to the success of the overall large-scale action must be clearly shown to be a result of the particular action in question.

The first condition for the award of the Knight's Cross is the outstanding personal bravery of the candidate, not the bravery of the unit.

Recommendations for outstanding merit in command are only to be made for the responsible unit commander himself. Recommendations for the award to assistant commanders can only be considered if, in the absence of the responsible commander, the officer in question made a decision on his own initiative which had a decisive effect on the overall action.

d) The lists of recommendations are to be completed in duplicate with the greatest care and must contain the following fundamental information:

1. the name of the candidate
2. his Christian name (nickname)
3. his place and date of birth
4. service rank and unit at the time of the act of gallantry
5. brief grounds for the recommendation and observations by the man's immediate superior

In addition to these basic details, the following information is also to be included in the report:

1. In what branch of the service the candidate is serving (Truppen-Offizier, Ersatz-Offizier der Reserve, der Landwehr, etc.)
2. in the case of regular soldiers, the candidate's peacetime unit,
3. in the case of soldiers on home or administrative service, the responsible Defence Area Command,
4. the candidate's seniority,
5. whether the candidate has been awarded any decorations in the present war and , if so, which decorations were awarded,
6. home address of the candidate and nearest relatives (wife, parents or brothers and sisters),
7. in the case of NCOs and other ranks, a curriculum vitae (to be attached or sent on afterwards).

e) If available, 4 photographs of the candidate are to be attached to the recommendation. If there are no available photographs of the

GUIDELINES FOR THE AWARD OF THE KNIGHT'S CROSS

candidate, these are to be sent directly to OKH/PA 1. Staffel immediately after notification of the award of the Knight's Cross.

f) On the citation for the award of the Knight's Cross of the Iron Cross should be entered the service rank of the holder on the day on which the act took place for which the decoration is being awarded.

If this rank is not the same as the rank held by the candidate at the time the recommendation was made, in the section 'service rank' on the recommendation list should be added the note: 'service rank for the citation'.

g) For the format of the recommendation list see Appendix 5.

V. General observations

1. For inclusion on a list of all recipients of the Knight's Cross which is to be prepared for the Führer and Supreme Commander of the Wehrmacht, an ongoing process of notification to OKH/PA of all amendments to the details of recipients of the Knight's Cross under their command, giving details of their position and unit, is to be maintained by the Div. Gen. Kdo, AOKs (the AOK should collate the information) and the H.Gr. Kdo. (who should sent the report directly to OKH/PA.).

2. The recipients of the Knight's Cross of the Iron Cross are not to be referred to as Ritter, but as Inhaber.

3. After the award of the Knight's Cross the citation is to be sent to the holder at the home address detailed on the recommendation.

   The citation measures 45 x 37cm and is not suitable for being sent by Feldpost.

5. The death of a holder of the Knight's Cross is to be immediately notified by telegram to OKH/PA.

OKH, 3.6.41
29a – P2 Gr. V/Va

Appendix III

Promotions and awards made on the autonomous authority of Army Groups and Armies 1945

During the last days of the war and also after 8 May 1945, many promotions and awards of decorations were announced on the autonomous authority of Heeresgruppen and other command authorities. For a long time there was no kind of documentary evidence which could substantiate the legal basis for these promotions. In the *Rangliste des deutschen Heeres 1944/45*, published in 1955 by W. Keilig, it was already possible to adduce the evidence of authority issued by the Führer in April 1945 which provided such substantiating evidence, at least for promotions up to the rank of Hauptmann.

In the meantime, the discovery of further original documentation from the HPA has made it possible finally to clarify these questions. In summarising the telegrams from the OKH/P A, the text of which is reproduced on the following pages, the following points still require confirmation:

1. The authority granted only applied to preferential, not to planned promotions.
2. Authority was not also given to announce promotions to general service rank.
3. Autonomous armies in the sense of the authority granted by the Fuhrer were at this time only Geb. AOK 20 in Norway and AOK East Prussia. While, in accordance with telegrams of 22 April 1945, it was possible, because of the situation at the time (e. g. the failure of signals communications), to extend this authority wholly or

partly to non-autonomous Heeresgruppen and commandants of Festungen, the extended authority of 3 May 1945 was reserved exclusively for the commanders of Heeregruppen and the two autonomous Armies mentioned above, and it was not permissible to extend this authority further.

The empowering orders to not mention any possibility of extending this authority to Corps or Divisional level.

4. The radio message of 12 May 1945 proves that, with effect from 11 May 1945, authority for all promotions and decorations was suspended.

5. Thus it is clear that all promotions, etc. authorised in contravention of these conditions were inadmissible and invalid.

Power of Authority Order of 22.4.1945

(issued by telegram or by radio)

To:	Copies to:
1. OB Aussenstelle A	1. Head, OKW
2. OB Aussenstelle B	2. Reichsführer-SS
3. OB Northwest (H.Gr.H.)	3. Head, WFST
4. OB Northwest	4. Head, General Staff, Heer
5. OB H.Gr.G.	5. OB Ersatz
6. OB Southwest (H.Gr.C.)	6. Head, NS-Führungsstab, OKW
7. OB Southeast (H.Gr.E.)	7. Head, NS-Führungsstab des Heeres
8. OB H.Gr. Süd	8. A.W.A.
9. OB H.Gr. Mitte	9. W.Z.A.
10. OB H.Gr. Weichsel	10. MPA /Ag P 1 for notification to MPA.
11. OB H.Gr. Kurland (by radio)	
12. OB AOK East Prussia (by radio)	
13. OB (Geb.) AOK 20	
14. OB Denmark	

AWARDS MADE ON THE AUTONOMOUS AUTHORITY

The Führer has extended to the Supreme Commanders of Heeresgruppen and autonomous Armies authority for the following:

1. Promotion to Oberfähnrich of soldiers nominated as Fahnenjunker, after interim promotion to Fahnenjunker-Feldwebel.

    Promotions of Oberfähnriche to Leutnant after a four-week period of probation. Preferential promotions from Leutnant to Oberleutnant and from Oberleutnant to Hauptmann within the framework of the conditions established for preferential promotions. Promotions to Leutnant to be reported to H PA/P 4, giving details of Christian name and surname, date and place of birth, military service status, WBK and field unit.

    Promotions to Oberleutnant and Hauptmann are to be reported to H PA/Ag P 1, and in the case of special career and TSD officers to H PA/Ag P 6, giving details of Christian name and surname, date and place of birth, military service status, WBK and field unit.

2. Appointments up to and including Brigadekommandeur.

    All changes to appointments which are subject to the decision of the HPA are to be reported to HPA/Ag P1/P 3 or Ag P 6.

    The final authority for appointments from Divisional commanders upwards from now on shall rest with the commander.

    Appointments from Divisional commanders upwards which are required to meet the demands of the immediate situation are therefore only to be regarded as temporary deputising posts; application details are to be submitted to HPA/1. Staffel at the same time as the appointment is made.

3. Demotions of officers to the rank of Leutnant, and of NCOs and other ranks to the lowest service rank.

    Demotions of demotions of officers are to be reported to HPA/Ag P 2, giving details of Christian name and surname, date and place of birth, military service status, WBK and field unit.

4. Authority for awarding the German Cross in Gold, the Ehrenblattspange and the Iron Cross First and Second Class to members of Staffs.

    Authority for the decisions outlined above can, if the situation

385

requires (e. g. in the event of signals communications being severed), be extended entirely or in part to Armeen and the commandants of Festungen.

The Head of the Army Personnel Office (HPA): Burgdorf, General der Infanterie.

Copies after dispatch to: Adjutant to head of PA – Deputy Head of PA – Aussenstelle PA/A.

Order of 3.5.1945, further extending power of authority
(issued by telegram or by radio)

This order extends to OBs of Heeresgruppen and autonomous Armies authority for the following, thereby further extending the authority granted in the order of 22 April:

1. Promotions of officers of all ranks up to and including the rank of Oberst, subject to the strictest adherence to the conditions already established for preferential promotions.
2. Demotions of officers down to the lowest service rank.

    Decisions concerning reinstatement and re-promotion of former officers in accordance with AHM paragraph 515 (recently re-stated in AHM 44, para. 210) are until further notice to be made by the OBs of Heeresgruppen and OBs with the same level of authority.

    Such decisions, including brief reasons for the decision, are to be reported by telegram or by radio to OKH/HPA/Ag P 2. If at all possible, this should be followed up as quickly as possible by a detailed report.
3. Authority for awarding the Knight's Cross.

    The authority for the decisions set out above cannot be extended to subordinate commanders etc.

    The Head of the Army Personnel Office (HPA): Burgdorf, General der Infanterie.

Order of 12.5.1945 suspending promotions and decorations
(issued by telegram or by radio)

To:

1. OB West
2. OB Southwest (H.Gr.C)
3. OB Southeast (H.Gr.E)
4. Heeresgruppe Ostmark
5. H. Gruppe Mitte
6. W. Kdo. röm. 18
7. For announcement to HPA/Aussenstelle via Führungsstab A. Grossadmiral has ordered the suspension of all decorations and promotions with effect from 11.5.45. Backdating is inadmissible and therefore invalid.

OKH/HPA/1. Staffel, I. A.: Maisel, Generalleutnant and Deputy Head, PA

Copies after dispatch to:
Head, Führungsstab B – Führungsstab B – HPA/1. Staffel – HPA/2. Staffel – P 5

Source: Transcriptions from original text of orders issued by OKH/PA/P 5.

Appendix IV

Copy of the Award sheet OKH/PA/P5, Northern zone (Flensburg)

Knight's Cross

Walle	Sprute
Rieger	Rau
Meyer, Walther	Stecken
Niegsch	Methner
Jensen*	Reinbacher
Lindner	Riedel
Weichsel	Fiebig
Jürgens	Stehle
Schnocks	Becher*
Knaust	Brandt*
Göbel	Muster
Fischer	Turnwald
Müller, Rudi	Stützle
Kliemann	Schürmann
Wienrich*	Hofmann, Gren.
Jochimsen	Hollmann
Niedzwitzki	Lotze
Linde*	Anding
Belz	Riedel
Otte	Berzen
Freimanis*	Gaigals
Wiese*	v. Amsberg
Wilborn*	Hengstler
v. Leipzig	Gersteuer

Oak Leaves

Matzky
Ziegler
v. Bostell
Laebe
Mokros

v. Obstfelder
Rodt
Plocher
Jodl

Swords

Blaskowitz

Appendix V

Post-War Name Changes

Barkmann, Ernst	Name change:	Schmuck-Barkmann, Ernst
Becker, Artur	Name change:	Becker-Neetz, Artur
v. Born-Fallois, Gerd	see under:	v. Fallois, Gerd
v. Brese, Heinz	see under:	Wittchow v. Brese-Winiary, Heinz
Briel, Jakob	see under:	Fick, Jakob
Bukatschek, Otto	Name change:	Wünsche, Otto
Carsten, Günter	see under:	Chrzonsz, Günter
Chrzonsz, Günter	Name change:	Carsten, Günter
Cierpka, Walter	Name change:	Moll, Walter
v. Fallois, Gerd	see under:	v. Born-Fallois, Gerd
Fick, Jakob	see under:	Briel, Jakob
Kiefer, Eduard	Name change:	Kiwe, Tilman
Kirn, Dietrich	Name change:	Witzel-Kirn, Dietrich
Kiwe, Tilman	see under:	Kiefer, Eduard
Leitzmann, Wilhelm	see under:	Schulze-Ostwald, Wilhelm
Lingenthal, Edel	see under:	Zachariae v. Lingenthal, Edel- Heinrich
v. Manstein, Erich	see under:	v. Lewinski, gen. v. Manstein, Erich
Meyer, Friedrich-August	Name change:	Meyer-Schewe, Friedrich-August
Meyer-Schewe, Friedrich-August	see under:	Meyer, Friedrich-August
Moll, Walter	see under:	Cierpka, Walter
Graf v. Plettenberg, Georg	Name change:	v. Dücker Graf v. Plettenberg, Georg
Plöger, Karl-Heinrich	Name change:	Schneekloth-Plögar, Karl-Heinz
Rittmeyer, Konrad	see under:	Zecherle, Konrad
Schmuck-Barkmann, Heinz	see under:	Barkmann, Ernst
Schneekloth-Plögar, Karl-Heinz	see under:	Plöger, Karl-Heinrich

Schulze-Ostwald, Wilhelm	Name change:	*Leitzmann, Wilhelm*
Wittchow v. Brese-Winiary, Heinz	Name change:	*v. Brese, Heinz*
Witzel-Kirn, Dietrich	see under:	*Kirn, Dietrich*
Wünsche, Otto	see under:	*Bukatschek, Otto*
Zachariae v. Lingenthal Edel-Heinrich	Name change:	*Lingenthal, Edel*
Zecherle, Konrad	Name change:	*Rittmeyer, Konrad*

Appendix VI

Letter From Grand Admiral Dönitz, 20 September 1970

DÖNITZ
Grossadmiral (ret.)

2055 Aumühle (Holstein)
Pfingstholzallee 4
Telephone 3069
20.9.70

To the
Ordensgemeinschaft der Ritterkreuzträger
Awards Commission
by hand to Herr Oberst d Res. Martin Steglich
5224 Ruppichteroth
Haus Maro

Shortly before the Act of Surrender came into force, probably on 7 May 1945, I issued the following verbal order:

"All recommendations for the award of the Knight's Cross of the Iron Cross and the higher classes of these awards which had arrived at the Oberkommando der Wehrmacht – Wehrmachtsführungsstab before the Act of Surrender came into force are approved by me, subject to the provision that the recommendations were supported in proper form, up to the level of Armee and Heeresgruppe commanders, by the officers authorised to make recommendations in the Wehrmacht units, Heer (including the Waffen-SS), Navy and Luftwaffe."

With comradely greetings
    Dönitz

Appendix VII

Comparative Table of Ranks

	Heer & Luftwaffe	Kriegsmarine	Waffen-SS
1.	Schütze, Grenadier, Flieger, Kanonier, Pionier, etc.	Matrose	SS-Schütze, SS-Grenadier etc.
2.	Oberschütze	—	SS-Oberschütze
3.	Gefreiter	Matrosengefreiter	SS-Sturmmann
4.	Obergefreiter	Matrosengefreiter	SS-Rottenführer
5.	Stabsgefreiter	Matr. -Haupt-, Stabs- & Oberstabsgefreiter	—
6.	Unteroffizier, Oberjäger	Maat	SS-Unterscharführer
7.	Unterfeldwebel, Unterwachtmeister	Obermaat	SS-Scharführer
8.	Fähnrich	Fähnrich z. See	SS-Standartenjunker
9.	Feldwebel, Wachtmeister	Feldwebel, Stabsfeldwebel (F)	SS-Oberscharführer
10.	Oberfeldwebel, Oberwachtmeister (Hauptfeldwebel), Oberfähnrich	Oberfeldwebel, Oberfähnrich z. See	SS-Hauptscharf., SS-Standartenoberjunker (SS-Stabsscharführer)
11.	Stabsfeldwebel, Stabswachtmeister	Stabsoberfeldwebel	SS-Sturmscharführer
12.	Leutnant	Leutnant z. See	SS-Untersturmführer
13.	Oberleutnant	Oberleutnant z. See	SS-Obersturmführer
14.	Hauptmann, Rittmeister	Kapitänleutnant	SS-Hauptsturmführer
15.	Major	Korvettenkäpitan	SS-Sturmbannführer
16.	Oberstleutnant	Fregattenkapitän	SS-Obersturmbannführer

Heer & Luftwaffe	Kriegsmarine	Waffen-SS
17. Oberst	Kapitän z. See, Kapitän z. See & Kommodore	SS-Standartenführer, SS-Oberführer
18. Generalmajor	Konteadmiral	SS-Brigadeführer und Gen. -Maj. d. W-SS
19. Generalleutnant	Vizeadmiral	SS-Gruppenführer u. Gen.Lt. d. W-SS
20. General d. Inf., Kav., Art., Flieger etc.	Admiral	SS-Obergruppenf. u. Gen. d. W-SS
21. Generaloberst	Generaladmiral	SS-Oberstgruppenf. u. Gen. Ob. d. W-SS
22. Generalfeldmarschall	Großadmiral	—

Non-commissioned officer ranks of the Kriegsmarine linked their designation with their service grade, for example Botsmannsmaat. The officers — save those serving aboard ships — carried their career designation in paranthesis after their rank, for example Leutnant (Ing.). From about 1943 Waffen-SS officers could also display their police rank, for example SS-Hauptsturmführer Hauptmann der Schup.

* H.Gr. Kurland, awarded by the commanding officer on the basis of supplemental decrees dated 22.4 and 3.5.45.

Images of the Knight's Cross

Great Cross of the Iron Cross

Knight's Cross of the Iron Cross with Golden Oak
Leaves, Swords and Diamonds

IMAGES OF THE KNIGHT'S CROSS

Knight's Cross of the Iron Cross with Oak Leaves, Swords and Diamonds

ELITE OF THE THIRD REICH

Knight's Cross of the Iron Cross with Oak Leaves and Swords

IMAGES OF THE KNIGHT'S CROSS

Knight's Cross of the Iron Cross with Oak Leaves

Knight's Cross of the Iron Cross

Also available from Helion & Company Limited

Adventures in my Youth:
A German Soldier on the Eastern Front 1941–45

Armin Scheiderbauer – 224pp – Hardback – ISBN 1-874622-06-X

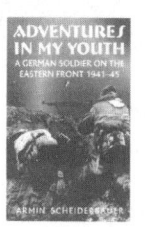

Hitler's Miracle Weapons.
Secret Nuclear Weapons of the Third Reich and their Carrier Systems.
Volume 1: Luftwaffe and Kriegsmarine

Friedrich Georg – 136pp, 16pp colour plates, 30 b/w photos, maps. – Hardback – ISBN 1-874622-91-4

A selection of forthcoming titles:

Twilight of the Gods. A Swedish Waffen-SS Volunteer's Experiences with the 11th SS-Panzergrenadier Division 'Nordland', Eastern Front 1944–45
Thorolf Hillblad (ed.)   ISBN 1-874622-16-7

For Rex and For Belgium. Léon Degrelle and Walloon Political & Military Collaboration 1940–45
Eddy de Bruyne & Marc Rikmenspoel   ISBN 1-874622-32-9

Some Additional Services From Helion & Company

BOOKSELLERS
- over 20,000 military books available
- four 100-page catalogues issued every year

BOOKSEARCH
- Free professional booksearch service. No search fees, no obligation to buy

Want to find out more?
Visit our website – www.helion.co.uk

Our website is the best place to learn more about Helion & Co. It features online book catalogues, special offers, complete information about our own books (including features on in-print and forthcoming titles, sample extracts and reviews), a shopping cart system and a secure server for credit card transactions, plus much more besides!

HELION & COMPANY
26 Willow Road, Solihull, West Midlands, B91 1UE, England
Tel: 0121 705 3393   Fax: 0121 711 4075
Email: publishing@helion.co.uk   Website: http://www.helion.co.uk